KU-510-197

# Aging and Everyday Life

*Edited by*

Jaber F. Gubrium
*and*
James A. Holstein

Copyright © Blackwell Publishers Ltd 2000; editorial introductions and arrangement copyright © Jaber F. Gubrium and James A. Holstein 2000

First published 2000

2 4 6 8 10 9 7 5 3 1

Blackwell Publishers Inc.
350 Main Street
Malden, Massachusetts 02148
USA

Blackwell Publishers Ltd
108 Cowley Road
Oxford OX4 1JF
UK

All rights reserved. Except for the quotation of short passages for the purposes of criticism and review, no part of this publication may be reproduced, stored in a retrieval system, or transmitted, in any form or by any means, electronic, mechanical, photocopying recording or otherwise, without the prior permission of the publisher.

Except in the United States of America, this book is sold subject to the condition that it shall not, by way of trade or otherwise, be lent, resold, hired out, or otherwise circulated without the publisher's prior consent in any form of binding or cover other than that in which it is published and without a similar condition including this condition being imposed on the subsequent purchaser.

*Library of Congress Cataloging-in-Publication Data* .

Aging and everyday life / edited by Jaber F. Gubrium and James A. Holstein.
        p.     cm. — (Blackwell readers in sociology)
    Includes bibliographical references and index.
    ISBN 0-631-21707-X (hb : alk. paper) — ISBN 0-631-21708-8 (pb : alk. paper)
    1. Aged—Social conditions.  2. Aging.  I. Gubrium, Jaber F.  II. Holstein, James A.  III. Series.

    HQ1061 .A4248 2000
    305.26—dc21

                                                                99-086006


*British Library Cataloguing in Publication Data*
A CIP catalogue record for this book is available from the British Library.

Typeset in 10 on 12 pt Sabon
by Ace Filmsetting Ltd, Frome, Somerset
Printed in Great Britain by T. J. International, Padstow, Cornwall

This book is printed on acid-free paper.

# Contents

# List of Contributors

## The Editors

**Jaber F. Gubrium** is Professor of Sociology at the University of Florida. His research focuses on the descriptive organization of personal identity, family, the life course, aging, and adaptations to illness. He is the editor of the *Journal of Aging Studies* and the author or editor of twenty books, including *Living and Dying at Murray Manor*, *Oldtimers and Alzheimer's*, *Out of Control*, and *Speaking of Life*.

**James A. Holstein** is Professor of Sociology at Marquette University. He has studied diverse people processing and social control settings, including courts, schools, and mental health agencies. He is the author or editor of numerous books, including *Court-Ordered Insanity*, *Dispute Domains and Welfare Claims*, *Reconsidering Social Constructionism*, and *Social Problems in Everyday Life*. He also is co-editor of the research annual *Perspectives on Social Problems*.

Collaborating for over a decade, Gubrium and Holstein have developed their distinctive constructionist approach to everyday life in a variety of texts, including *What is Family?*, *Constructing the Life Course*, *The Active Interview*, and *The New Language of Qualitative Method*. They continue to explore the theoretical and methodological implications of interpretive practice as it unfolds at the intersection of narrative, culture, and social interaction. Their most recent work – companion volumes *The Self We Live By: Narrative Identity in a Postmodern World* and *Institutional Selves: Troubled Identities in a Postmodern World* – considers the impact on self construction of a postmodern world of increasingly varied institutional identities.

## The Authors

**Emily K. Abel** is Professor of Public Health at the University of California, Los Angeles.

**Steven M. Albert** is affiliated with the G. H. Sergievsky Center, Columbia University.

**Robert C. Atchley** was, before his retirement, Professor of Sociology at Miami University in Ohio.

**Judith C. Barker** is affiliated with the Medical Anthropology Program at the University of California, San Francisco.

**Elaine Cumming** is a sociologist and was, before her retirement, affiliated with Mental Health Research Units at Syracuse University and the State University of New York, Albany.

**Timothy Diamond** is Professor of Sociology at California State University, Los Angeles.

**Janet Finch** is Vice Chancellor of the University of Keele, United Kingdom.

**Doris Francis** was, for many years, affiliated with the Graduate School of Management and Social Policy at the New School for Social Research, New York.

**Kenneth J. Gergen** is Professor of Psychology at Swarthmore College.

**Mary M. Gergen** is Associate Professor of Psychology and Women's Studies at Pennsylvania State University.

**Judith Globerman** is Professor of Social Work at the University of Toronto, Canada.

**Hava Golander** is Professor of Nursing in the Sackler Faculty of Medicine at Tel Aviv University, Israel.

**James S. Goodwin** is Professor of Internal Medicine and Geriatrics at the University of Texas Medical Branch in Galveston.

**Betty Risteen Hasselkus** is Professor of Occupational Therapy at the University of Wisconsin.

**Haim Hazan** is Professor of Anthropology at Tel Aviv University, Israel.

**Arlie Russell Hochschild** is Professor of Sociology at the University of California, Berkeley.

**David A. Karp** is Professor of Sociology at Boston College.

**Sharon R. Kaufman** is Research Anthropologist at the Institute for Health and Aging at the University of California, San Francisco.

**Jennifer Klapper** is affiliated with the Polisher Research Institute at the Philadelphia Geriatric Center.

**Pia C. Kontos** is affiliated with the Department of Behavioral Science in the Faculty of Medicine at the University of Toronto, Canada.

**Karen A. Lyman** is Professor of Sociology at Chaffey College, California.

**Jennifer Mason** is on the faculty of the University of Leeds, United Kingdom.

**Sarah H. Matthews** is Professor of Sociology at Cleveland State University.

**Linda S. Mitteness** is Professor of Medical Anthropology at the University of California, San Francisco.

**Miriam Moss** is affiliated with the Polisher Research Institute at the Philadelphia Geriatric Center.

**Sidney Moss** is affiliated with the Polisher Research Institute at the Philadelphia Geriatric Center.

**Barbara Myerhoff** was, before her death, Professor of Anthropology at the University of Southern California.

**Aviad E. Raz** is affiliated with the Department of Sociology and Anthropology at Tel Aviv University, Israel.

**Carol Rambo Ronai** is Associate Professor of Sociology at the University of Memphis.

**Arnold M. Rose** was, before his death, Professor of Sociology at the University of Minnesota.

**Robert L. Rubinstein** is Professor of Anthropology at the University of Maryland, Baltimore County.

**Joel Savishinsky** is Professor of Anthropology at Ithaca College, New York.

**Joyce Stephens** is Professor of Sociology at the State University of New York, Fredonia.

**Deborah Kestin Van Den Hoonard** is Assistant Professor of Gerontology and Sociology at St. Thomas University, Canada.

# Acknowledgments

The authors and publishers gratefully acknowledge the following for permission to reproduce copyright material:

Abel, Emily K., "Parental Dependence and Filial Responsibility in the Nineteenth Century: Hial Hawley and Emily Hawley Gillespie, 1884–1885," from *The Gerontologist*, republished with permission of the Gerontological Society of America, 1030 15th Street, NW, Suite 250, Washington, D.C. 20005. *Parental Dependence and Filial Responsibility in the Nineteenth Century*, E. K. Abel, *The Gerontologist*, 1992, vol. 32. Reproduced by permission of the publisher via Copyright Clearance Center, Inc.;

Albert, Steven M., "The Dependent Elderly, Home Health Care, and Strategies of Household Adaptation," from (ed. Jaber F. Gubrium and Andrea Sankar) *The Home Care Experience: Ethnography and Policy* (Sage Publications Inc., Newbury Park, CA, 1990);

Atchley, Robert C., "A Continuity Theory of Normal Aging," from *The Gerontologist*, republished with permission of the Gerontological Society of America, 1030 15th Street, NW, Suite 250, Washington, D.C. 20005. *A Continuity Theory of Normal Aging*, Robert C. Atchley, *The Gerontologist*, 1989, vol. 29. Reproduced by permission of the publisher via Copyright Clearance Center, Inc.;

Atchley, Robert C., "Retirement as a Social Role," from *The Sociology of Retirement* (Schenkman Publishers, New York, 1976);

Cumming, Elaine, "Further Thoughts on the Theory of Disengagement," from *International Social Science Journal*, 1963, vol. 15, copyright © UNESCO;

Diamond, Timothy, "Nursing Homes as Trouble," from (ed. Emily K. Abel and Margaret Nelson) *Circles of Care: Work and Identity in Women's Lives* (State University of New York Press, Albany, 1990, courtesy Sage Publications Inc.);

Finch, Janet and Jennifer Mason, "Filial Obligations and Kin Support for Elderly People," from *Ageing and Society*, 1990, vol. 10, no. 2 (Cambridge University Press, Cambridge, 1990);

Francis, Doris, "The Significance of Work Friends in Late Life," from *Journal of Aging Studies*, 1990, vol. 4 (reprinted with permission from Elsevier Science);

Gergen, Mary M. and Kenneth J. Gergen, "Narratives of the Gendered Body in Popular Autobiography," from (ed. Ruthellen Josselson and Amia Leiblich) *The Narrative Study of Lives*, vol. 1 (Sage Publications Inc., Newbury Park, CA, 1993);

Globerman, Judith, "The Unencumbered Child: Family Reputations and Responsibilities in the Care of Relatives with Alzheimer's Disease," from *Family Process*, 1995, vol. 34. Reproduced by permission of the publisher via Copyright Clearance Center, Inc.;

Golander, Hava and Aviad E. Raz, "The Mask of Dementia: Images of 'Demented Residents' in a Nursing Ward," from *Ageing and Society*, 1996, vol. 16, no. 3 (Cambridge University Press, Cambridge, 1996);

Goodwin, James S., "Geriatric Ideology: The Myth of the Myth of Senility," from

*Journal of the American Geriatric Society*, 1991, vol. 39;

Hasselkus, Betty Risteen, "Death in Very Old Age: A Personal Journey of Caregiving," from *American Journal of Occupational Therapy*, 1993, vol. 47;

Hazan, Haim, "The Cultural Trap: The Language of Images," from *Old Age: Constructions and Deconstructions* (Cambridge University Press, Cambridge, 1994);

Hazan, Haim, "The Personal Trap: The Language of Self-Presentation," from *Old Age: Constructions and Deconstructions* (Cambridge University Press, Cambridge, 1994);

Hochschild, Arlie Russell, "An Old Age Community," from *The Unexpected Community* (University of California Press, Berkeley, 1973);

Karp, David A., "A Decade of Reminders: Changing Age Consciousness between Fifty and Sixty Years Old," *The Gerontologist*, republished with permission of the Gerontological Society of America, 1030 15th Street, NW, Suite 250, Washington D.C., 20005. *A Decade of Reminders: Changing Age Consciousness Between Fifty and Sixty Years Old*, David A. Karp, from *The Gerontologist*, 1988, vol. 6. Reproduced by permission of the publisher via Copyright Clearance Center, Inc.;

Kaufman, Sharon R., "The Ageless Self," from *The Ageless Self: Sources of Meaning in Late Life* (University of Wisconsin Press, Madison, 1986). © 1986. Reprinted by permission of The University of Wisconsin Press;

Klapper, Jennifer, Sidney Moss, Miriam Moss, and Robert L. Rubinstein, "The Social Context of Grief Among Adult Daughters Who Have Lost a Parent," from *Journal of Aging Studies*, 1994, vol. 8 (reprinted with permission from Elsevier Science);

Kontos, Pia C., "Resisting Institutionalization: Constructing Old Age and Negotiating Home," from *Journal of Aging Studies*, 1998, vol. 12 (reprinted with permission from Elsevier Science);

Lyman, Karen A., "Bringing the Social Back In: A Critique of the Biomedicalization of Dementia," from *The Gerontologist*, republished with permission of the Gerontological Society of America, 1030 15th Street, NW, Suite 250, Washington, D.C. 20005. *Bringing the Social Back In: A Critique of the Biomedicalization of Dementia*, K. A. Lyman, *The Gerontologist*, 1989, vol. 29. Reproduced by permission of the publisher via Copyright Clearance Center, Inc.;

Matthews, Sarah H., "Friendship Styles," from *Friendships Through the Life Course: Oral Biographies in Old Age* (reprinted by permission of Sage Publications Inc., 1986);

Mitteness, Linda S. and Judith C. Barker, "Stigmatizing a 'Normal' Condition: Urinary Incontinence in Late Life," from *Medical Anthropology Quarterly*, vol. 9, no. 1, June 1995, reproduced by permission of the American Anthropological Association from *Medical Anthropology Quarterly*, June 1995, vol. 1, no. 1. Not for further reproduction;

Myerhoff, Barbara, "A Death in Due Time: Conviction, Order, and Continuity in Ritual Drama," from (ed. Marc Kaminsky) *Remembered Lives: The Work of Ritual, Storytelling, and Growing Older* (University of Michigan Press, Ann Arbor, 1992);

Ronai, Carol Rambo, "Managing Aging in Young Adulthood: The 'Aging' Table Dancer," *Journal of Aging Studies*, 1992, vol. 6 (reprinted with permission from Elsevier Science);

Rose, Arnold M., "A Current Theoretical Issue in Social Gerontology," from *The*

*Gerontologist*, republished with permission of the Gerontological Society of America, 1030 15th Street, NW, Suite 250, Washington, D.C. 20005. *A Current Theoretical Issue in Social Gerontology*, Arnold M. Rose *The Gerontologist*, 1964, vol. 4. Reproduced by permission of the publisher via Copyright Clearance Center, Inc.;

Savishinsky, Joel, "The Unbearable Lightness of Retirement: Ritual and Support in Modern Life Passage," from *Research on Aging*, 1995, vol. 17;

Stephens, Joyce, " 'One of Your Better Low-Class Hotels'," from *Loners, Losers, and Lovers: Elderly Tenants in a Slum Hotel* (University of Washington Press, Seattle, 1976);

Stephens, Joyce, " 'Making It'," from *Loners, Losers, and Lovers: Elderly Tenants in a Slum Hotel* (University of Washington Press, Seattle, 1976);

Van Den Hoonard, Deborah Kestin, "Identity Foreclosure: Women's Experiences of Widowhood as Expressed in Autobiographical Accounts," from *Ageing and Society*, 1997, vol. 17 (Cambridge University Press, Cambridge, 1997).

The publishers apologize for any errors or omissions in the above list and would be grateful to be notified of any corrections that should be incorporated in the next edition or reprint of this book.

# Introduction

## Jaber F. Gubrium and James A. Holstein

Social gerontology is the study of the social lives of older people. This covers a large territory, ranging from interpersonal relationships, living arrangements, and retirement, to social inequality, the politics of age, health, caregiving, death, and bereavement. Because of its wide scope, the field is informed by research from several disciplines, including anthropology, economics, history, nursing, political science, social psychology, social work, and sociology. Researchers employ distinctive ways of looking at the world to help understand the varied dimensions of what it means to be older in contemporary society. They reach back to compare today's experience to what it was like to be old in the past, as well as look ahead to what the future holds for later life.

There is a negative stereotype that social gerontology is all about inflexibility, cognitive decline, sickness, and death. There also is an exaggeratedly positive view that the aged are uncommonly wise or indulge themselves in leisure and recreation. But these stereotypes are far from being the true picture, as anthropologist Haim Hazan cautions in chapter 1. If we don't listen carefully to older people or fail to encourage them to speak for themselves, our own stereotypic views can easily color their lives so that they appear to be "different." Their lives can be seen much more negatively or positively than they actually are. According to Hazan, this is magnified when younger people communicate more with themselves about the later years than they do with those who are living through them. As Hazan (1994, p. 3) explains, "Communication about aging does not necessarily rely on communication with the aging, much less communication amongst the aged."

This Reader offers a contrasting perspective. We believe that much, if not most, of the research that might apply at any point of life can be applied to the later years. Whatever happens to most of us can occur in old age as well. Given similar circumstances, the later years comprise lives much like our own. For example, while the issue of personal identity is a common topic of research on adolescence, it also confronts older people, especially as changes in roles such as becoming a grandparent or moving into a retirement community affect how they view themselves. Just like younger persons, older people experience both change and stability, enter into new roles, and depart from old ones. This takes place in varied spheres of life – the worlds of home and family, work, and friendship, among the many social contexts in which older people live their lives. *Similarity*, in this regard, rather than difference is the watchword.

### The Field of Social Gerontology

As a field of research, social gerontology developed rapidly in the years following World War II and has expanded by leaps and bounds ever since. This is a response to a rapidly growing population of older people, as well as to newly emerging views of social life (Bengtson and Schaie 1999). During the early twentieth century, the proportion of the US population who were aged 65 or older was relatively small and fairly steady, remaining at 4 to 5 percent of the total. This proportion began to grow from the 1940s to what it is today (1999), nearly 13 percent of the total. Projections for the future growth of the population aged 65 or older rise dramatically. By the year 2030, it is estimated that fully 20 percent of the US population, one out of every five persons, will be elderly (U.S. Bureau of the Census 1993). The huge generation of babies born just after World War II – known as "baby boomers" because there was a marked boom in births after the war – will be elderly in the early decades of the twenty-first century, adding significantly to the share of older people in the population.

At the same time, there has been an increased research interest in experience across the life course. Decades ago, researchers focused on the earlier years of life – childhood, youth, and early adulthood. Psychologists, in particular, paid a great deal of attention to the formative years and produced varied perspectives on childhood development, some of which became popularized into stage models of growth and maturation. Sociologists conceptualized early life as the process of becoming a member of society and formulated theories of socialization. The rapid expansion of the American high school following World War II propelled interest in adolescence. Indeed, being a "teenager" gradually became viewed as a distinct stage of the life course, located between the dependence of childhood and the independence of the adult years.

As the population significantly aged in the second half of the twentieth century, the purview of life course research expanded to the later years. Prominent psychologist Erik Erikson (1959), for example, extended Sigmund Freud's stage model, which had been limited to childhood and adolescence, so that it also applied to adult life and aging. Erikson's now famous model of psychosocial development has eight stages, the last two of which pertain to middle adulthood and old age. Anthropologists also increasingly turned to the later years to inform us not only of what it was like to be a child in different cultures, but they also presented the great variety of ways there were to be old from one society to another (Fry 1981; Keith 1982; Kertzer and Keith 1984; Sokolovsky 1997). Historians, too, seemed to discover the later years and engaged in a lively debate about the shifting character of aging as societies moved from being predominantly agricultural to extensively industrial. The discussion centered on the questions of how and when the social status of older people changed over time (Achenbaum 1978; Fischer 1977; Haber 1983). One of the most poignant debates in the 1980s and 1990s dealt with the issue of the continuing viability of our system of social security. The rapidly expanding retirement population, which was described alarmingly by some as a devastating burden on working adults because the latter's social security payments could no longer support the growing proportion of retirees, became a major issue in the political economy of aging (Pampel 1998).

All of this has developed to the point where we now have full-blown research endeavors as well as theoretical perspectives across the disciplines focused on the later years. The life course overall, from birth all the way to death, is being given fuller and more complex shape as social gerontologists learn how events in the early years influence the ways we experience life in old age. The field of social gerontology has come a long way from the early days, when conceptualizations of the aging experience were limited to the activity and disengagement perspectives, which are discussed here in chapters written by sociologists Elaine Cumming and Arnold Rose. These perspectives focused exclusively on old age, but many researchers are currently arguing that the older years cannot be properly understood unless we know what preceded them. The field of social gerontology now presents aging and the life course to us more comprehensively, extending our knowledge of experience through time well beyond what a focus on the early years could have ever produced.

## Everyday Life in Old Age

Important as these developments have been, something is missing from the picture. Yes, there has been an extension of interest across the life course and, undoubtedly, we now know more about growing up and growing older than we ever had. Our data bases in areas such as health and aging, work and retirement, nursing and social services, and the older family, have grown in astronomical proportions. Not only can we compare experiences across lifetimes, but cross-cultural and historical research has extended comparison across societies and across historical time. What is missing is a distinct view of the *everyday life of older people.*

This perspective focuses on the ordinary ways the elderly experience daily living, how they manage both successes and failures, and on the manner they construct their pasts and futures in relation to present events and developments. This comprises a field of meanings centered on how people *themselves* interpret and discern what it's like to grow older and be old in today's world. The field, indeed, has its own organization and shouldn't be subsumed under other perspectives such as the political economy of aging or the psychology of later life.

This absence is perhaps an occupational hazard; it's easy for researchers to overlook everyday life when massive research accomplishments are leading the way. Across the various disciplines that contribute to social gerontology, there are new methods being developed to measure and assess variables of interest, well articulated conceptual frameworks, and huge amounts of empirical findings. It's all very heady, but it also ignores the ordinary rhythms of daily living. These are the working thoughts, feelings, and actions that make up the aging experience in the first place. They include the mundane inner worlds of personal meaning as well as the social worlds that interpersonally form around the many and varied "good days" and "bad days" that comprise old age.

Everyday life centers on meaning-making, which in the later years is undertaken by the aged *on their own terms.* Studying everyday life turns us to older people as older people (see Keith 1982). These are not the subjects of psychological experiments; they are not the aged who respond to social surveys. Nor are they the older people presented in statistical profiles. Of course, all of these produce insights into the aging experience, but they are far from being the whole story. While everyday life may receive passing attention in these endeavors, they neglect the body of knowledge formed around the stories told by older people in their own right. Aging and everyday life features what older people themselves make of who and what they are, as well as how they view their worlds.

This Reader in social gerontology focuses on everyday life in old age, contributing to its development as a field of its own. It takes us to personal experiences and social worlds often lost in the shuffle of gerontological research. In some sense, it actually returns the gerontologist to his or her stock-in-trade, to the experiential grounds of the later years. The Reader features ordinary questions of daily living. What am I now that I'm a widow? Who am I behind my aging body? How will I make do now that I've retired? What new worlds will there be to conquer as I grow older? These are the sorts of questions older people regularly ask themselves, whose answers the chapters present in older people's own terms.

## A World of Meanings

This perspective opens to view a world of meanings. It is a world made up of particular kinds of fact – not numbers especially, not frequency tables, not statistical tests – but facts according to those whose lives are under consideration. These are facts of life constructed by those whose lives are in question. In a research environment dizzy with numerical facts, it might seem odd to say that meanings are factual, but meanings are indeed real features of everyday living. Perhaps more than any other kind of fact, meanings inform us of how lives are organized according to those who live by them. These meaningful facts are composed of older individuals' own feelings, their own thoughts, their own ways of knowing and figuring the world they inhabit. If social gerontologists themselves didn't have a corner on the theory market in the field of aging, we might add that these facts extend to older people's own "theories" of aging, to their own ideas about and explanations for what it means to grow older and be aged in today's world (Gubrium and Wallace 1990).

### A complex world

What are the characteristics of a world of meanings? First of all, such a world exists in complex relationship to what those meanings are about. Take the ostensible fact of age in this regard. On the basis of chronological age, which is the age we are in numbers, we can be placed in a particular age category. If we turn to those in their eighties, for example, on the basis of years alone, we could categorize such individuals as elderly. But does such an assignment have any meaning for those categorized? Does the chronological fact of being in one's eighties translate into specific understandings for these individuals? Do those in their eighties see themselves and their worlds from the point of view of the category in which they have been placed?

Several of the chapters in this Reader suggest that for those in their eighties, or even in their sixties, seventies, and nineties, everyday life is not necessarily viewed in terms of specific age categories. Indeed, for some, old age hardly comes up at all as a significant framework for perceiving themselves, orienting to their pasts and futures, or for guiding interaction with others. Rather, a much more complex set of categories organizes their worlds, such as being lifelong friends, caring for loved ones, making a living, and resisting moving into a new environment, among other things – just like the rest of us. As anthropologist Sharon Kaufman (1986, p. 6) notes, "The old Americans I studied do not perceive meaning in aging itself; rather, they perceive meaning in being themselves in old age." Thus we learn as we hear their stories that except for their age category, eighty-year-olds could be men and women of any age, as they sometimes view themselves as being.

The complexity stems from the fact that in everyday life there is no simple one-to-one relationship between chronological age on the one hand, and our sense of where we are in the course of life on the other. Chronological age (objective age) is not necessarily related to what age means to us (subjective age). In everyday life, feeling old or being, say, eighty, may be episodic, not continuous. We might feel as old as our eighty years when we are with particular people who make us feel old, but otherwise not think or feel anything at all about age. Of course, the same could apply earlier in life. Where a child might feel quite "like a child" when she's with her parents, with her friends she could very well not think or feel about it at all, just like an eighty-year-old's experience of age. For both the child and the older person, the experience of age is something organized in relation to others, not in relation to years alone.

We learn from such examples taken from everyday life that meaning as it applies to age is not fixed chronologically. Rather, the meaning of age is *socially* constructed. The chapters in this Reader take this seriously, presenting their subjects in relation to the complex constructed details of their everyday lives. The chapters instruct us that where we are, who we're with, and what's going on at the moment can have significant bearing on the meaning of age, whatever age we are. As sociologist Carol Rambo Ronai shows in her chapter on the "aging" table dancers who work in drinking and entertainment establishments, dancers can be made to feel quite elderly and actually be forced to retire because their bodies are "too old" when they reach their thirties.

### Socially formulated meaning

A second characteristic of a world of meanings is that it is socially formulated. The meaning of things doesn't just drop down from the sky in pristine form or come to us automatically from the inner reaches of our being. While we might feel deeply about the retirement years, for example, those feelings relate to understandings we share with others about how one could possibly feel about them. We come to understand our experiences, including the meaning of being retired, from what others say, from what's presented at work, from things learned in the newspaper and other mass media, among other social contexts. There are endless ways meaning is conveyed to us, all of which supply us with options for thinking, feeling, and taking action in relation to events in our lives.

Consider how a new social understanding can cast a distinctive shadow on the personal meaning of leaving work in the later years. In one of the chapters on work and retirement, Robert Atchley presents us with a sociologist's take on the popular view that the retirement role unfolds in stages, from pre-retirement anticipation to phases of post-retirement adjustment. It's a familiar way of thinking about any social process, the idea being that experiences which progress through time occur in distinct segments and in a particular sequence, not all at once or chaotically. The chapter and the popular view of the retirement role provide those about to retire with a way of orienting to their experience. It presents them with a framework for understanding what they are going through as well as how to feel about it. In a way, such frameworks operate like experiential recipes in that they can be used to organize our sense of who and what we are through time. We wouldn't know what to make of work, the retirement process, and the retirement years, if such frameworks weren't available to us.

Before frameworks of understanding such as Atchley's became popular, we might guess that the process of leaving work was personally pretty murky. One could very well have been in a continuous quandary about what he or she was going through or where one would arrive. While there were likely to have been simmering thoughts and feelings accompanying the process of retirement, what the overall meaning of those thoughts and feelings was, wasn't readily fathomed. But the popularization of a stage model of the retirement process, for one, changes that, offering a way to broadly understand what we're going through.

A world of meanings also offers a basis for understanding our relations with others. If we accept the view that the retirement experience is organized in stages, we have a framework for comparing our own place in the process in relation to others who may be our work associates, friends, or even strangers who soon, too, may be retiring. Comparison may prompt us to feel good or bad about ourselves or, in turn, to feel good or badly for others who are experiencing the same process.

### Local applicability

If an everyday world of meanings is socially formulated, it is not necessarily shared in the same way by all. Some meanings appear to virtually belong to the way of life of a particular set of individuals. Let's return to the meaning of retirement for a moment. Does a popular model of the retirement process, which portrays it as unfolding in stages, describe departure from work life in the later years for everyone? Does every worker look forward to what's ahead in the same way?

The chapters from Joyce Stephens's (1976) book *Loners, Losers, and Lovers*, which are reprinted here in Part III, on work and retirement, are instructive in suggesting that this popular way of thinking about retirement doesn't apply to some workers. She reports on her study of what is called an "SRO," a single-room occupancy hotel. Stephens names the particular hotel she studied the "Guinevere." Like most SROs, this is a comparatively small building, whose rooms are limited to one occupant each. Most SROs are actually residential hotels and the tenants usually stay there for more than a few days. Again, as in most of SROs, the Guinevere's residents are poor, some destitute. At one time, SROs were a familiar sight surrounding the central downtown area of American cities. Derisive terms were applied to the most dilapidated, which were commonly known as "flop houses" and "flea bags." Being "one of your better low-class hotels," the Guinevere seemingly rises above the worst of these residences.

The chapter entitled "Making It" presents the work lives of the Guinevere's elderly tenants. Most are engaged in nontraditional kinds of work in order to survive or "make it." The men pursue a variety of "hustles," including "hawking" balloons on the street, begging or panhandling, and scavenging for discarded goods to be resold at "we buy anything" stores. The elderly women are more likely to engage in prostitution, selling sexual favors to the elderly men in the hotel, or involve themselves in other less personally risky hustles in association with male residents. None of these residents shows any indication of "retiring" from work; indeed, retirement from these activities portends even greater impoverishment. Many have been without regular employment their entire adult lives, supporting themselves instead by hustling.

As we read these chapters from Stephens's book, we come away with a strikingly different impression of "retirement," if we can even use the term to convey the meaning of work experience in these later years. We quickly learn that Atchley's stage model of the retirement process doesn't at all pertain to these people. In these elderly tenants' local understanding, work is definitely not something one leaves to enjoy life. We can imagine that if the idea of retirement were to come up for consideration in interviews with tenants or for discussion among them, it would likely be laughed off as wishful thinking or sarcastically dismissed.

The lesson here is clear. The world of meanings does not apply the same way to everyone, but is locally applicable. While Atchley's stage model is a popular way of figuring the retirement process, not all understand their work lives in those terms. Many indeed cannot, even while they might mockingly imagine themselves in those terms if they were "well to do." At the Guinevere Hotel, elderly tenants draw in a very limited way from this world of meanings that popularly presents the retirement experience.

As far as retirement is concerned, Stephens teaches us that one of the characteristics of this world of meanings is that retirement cannot be understood separate from the nature of work life. For the elderly residents of the Guinevere Hotel and similar SROs, the term "retirement" is not very meaningful, at least not meaningful in the terms assigned to it by adherents to models of the retirement process. That particular set of meanings belongs to those who have had orderly careers, from which retirement can be "staged," whose retirement role unfolds in a relatively scripted fashion.

## The meaningful body

A fourth characteristic of a world of meanings is that it is materially mediated. It doesn't float above us, symbolically distinct from our material lives, but rather is part and parcel of those lives. In particular, the world of meanings for older people extends to the material body. This might seem curious because the body appears to be a relatively objective entity, something not as subject to meaningful interpretation as, say, intentions, values, social interaction, or work and retirement. The body is commonly figured in terms of size, physical appearance, growth, health, sickness, and degeneration. When it is well, it is described in relation to functioning systems; when it's sick, disease categories apply. This is the language of the objective body, of an entity viewed as separate and distinct from the world of meaning.

The objective body has a constant meaning as long as its physical status remains the same. Objectively, a youthful body should be pretty much the same category of body whether it is the body of an immigrant or someone who is native born. Objectively, the lithe, athletic body of a migrant laborer should be as functional as the similar body of a heavy equipment operator. The body in chronic pain or one that is stigmatized by urinary incontinence is a source of agony and embarrassment regardless of whether its possessor is prominent or undistinguished.

When we turn to everyday life, however, it is evident that the body is assigned an enormous range of meanings despite its objective condition. And it makes a great deal of difference what those meanings are. While the language of the meaningful body may not be as scientific or professional-sounding as the terms of reference used to describe the objective body, the language nonetheless can be of great significance to those concerned. To have one's body casually described as youthful, aged, or death-like can be uplifting or devastating. To look in the mirror and view oneself as "pretty good for my age" can be as different as night and day in its consequences for self-esteem as the aftermath of peering into the mirror and figuring that an "old man" or "old woman" looks back. Or indeed, in a person's imagination, what looks back may have little bearing on how one feels behind the "mask of aging" (Featherstone and Hepworth 1991).

This is the subjective body. It is the body discerned from a particular perspective, not the body that stands separate and distinct from the world of everyday life. The subjective body is addressed in several chapters of this book. Its meaning depends on who is around and on where one is. And meaning can vary considerably because of whose body it is. In this regard, consider how much difference one's gender makes in assigning meaning to the body. The chapter by social psychologists Mary and Kenneth Gergen casts an interesting cultural light on this. Analyzing bodily descriptions presented in the autobiographies of celebrities such as tennis champion Martina Navratilova and long-term boss of IBM Thomas J. Watson, the Gergens find that the subjective body draws meaning from the cultural imperatives of description. While we all undoubtedly have extensive casual knowledge that the body varies considerably in meaning depending upon whether one is male or female, the Gergens show us that this even affects how the body is publicly communicated in writing.

In their autobiographies, the female celebrities present themselves across the life course as more emotionally involved with their bodies. Their bodies seem to provide a more extensive base for conveying their identities than it does for the males. The women's autobiographies indicate that self-worth – one's value to oneself as a person – very much relates to how one views the body. Males, in contrast, mostly take their bodies for granted. If anything, they present their bodies instrumentally, as a kind of tool they used to accomplish what they did. Otherwise, males' bodies play a comparatively minor role in conveying their identities.

In accounts of childhood and puberty, the women present themselves as worried about how attractive they are physically, anxious that the slightest gain in weight will have devastating effects on their public personas. This is relatively absent in male accounts of the early years. These differences persist through adulthood, extending to the later years of life, although, as the Gergens note, complications arise in relation to the physical status of the aging body. The males especially account for what they didn't achieve because deteriorating bodies didn't permit it. The instrumental theme continues, but the body now is used to explain how a career slowed down because of aging.

This brings us to the topic of death and bereavement and its relation to the aging body. Here, the body seems to explode with meaning, perhaps more so than at any other time of life. Dying, the body enters what anthropologists call a "liminal" period, a twilight time located somewhere between life and death. Rent with the unknown, it is a gray area of meaning that isn't as clear as at other times of life. Periods of uncertainty present us with feelings of uneasiness and, as we might expect, anything that serves to reduce the uneasiness and provide direction is welcomed. As a result, at this time of life, the body is surrounded by ritual – patterns of conduct that work against uncertainty because they are routinized, repetitive, and filled with recognition. As anthropologist Barbara Myerhoff illustrates in her chapter, the work of ritual can begin well ahead of time, in anticipation of the social need for meaning and order that impending bodily death takes away from us.

## A Qualitative Approach

Everyday life and its world of meanings are too complex, socially mediated, and locally differentiated to be adequately captured by a quantitative approach, such as laboratory experiments and social surveys. These orient to their subject matter as if it were simply "out there" and available for data collection. In contrast, as the chapters of this Reader show, what is out there – such as work, retirement, and the body – engenders a great deal of meaning-making, and it is for this reason that a qualitative approach is preferred, one whose stock-in-trade is precisely everyday life and its world of meanings.

At the same time, the distinction between quantitative and qualitative approaches should not be invidious. In general, we should not compare them for whether one is better or worse than the other. They do different things as methods of procedure. A qualitative approach is better at portraying a world of social processes and emergent meanings. A quantitative approach is more suitable when the subject matter is fixed in meaning and straightforward in variation.

A qualitative approach can take a number of research directions (see Gubrium and Sankar 1994). One is open-ended interviewing. The term "open-ended" refers to interviews whose structure is open to the interviewer and the interviewee participating in the development of responses, encouraging them to explore the complexity of the topics under consideration. This is sometimes referred to as "qualitative interviewing," because it centers on the documentation of the qualities – or meanings – that various aspects of experience have for those whose lives are being studied. Some researchers, especially anthropologists, also may refer to this form of interviewing as "ethnographic interviewing," since it is often applied alongside observational methods, usually within a specific field setting such as a retirement community, nursing home, or a support group.

Several chapters of this book explore their subject matter with this form of interviewing. Sociologist David Karp, for example, examines the meaning of a career for those in their fifties, when many have "made it" and are looking forward to making good on what they have accomplished. His concern is with the meaning of this mid-life location in a career trajectory for one's sense of aging. Social worker Judith Globerman also uses open-ended interviews, some of which last three hours, to analyze differences in the meaning of family responsibility among relatives of Alzheimer's disease sufferers. Globerman finds the method especially helpful for revealing the complex differences in the assigned meaning of responsibility that come with reputations held earlier in life for being or not being a responsible person.

Some of the chapters rely upon participant observation to gather their empirical data. This places the researcher within the actual scene of life that is the topic of the research. When the focus is the social organization of care in the nursing home, for example, the researcher becomes an active participant in the life of such a facility and systematically observes social interaction on the premises. Nurse anthropologist Hava

Golander and her associate Aviad Raz, in their chapter on the "mask of dementia," conducted months of participant observation in an Israeli geriatric center in order to discern the social processes by which a demented status was assigned to particular residents. Sociologist Timothy Diamond conducted participant observation in an American nursing home, considering the everyday "bed-and-body" work of the front-line staff to illustrate how the meaning of nursing home work was mediated by a medical model of care that continually clashed with the everyday needs of the residents.

Other chapters apply narrative analysis in approaching their subject matter. Narrative analysis refers broadly to the analysis of stories conveyed by respondents. These differ from traditional interview responses in that interviewees are encouraged to elaborate on their experiences in extended accounts rather than to just briefly respond to questions about them. The usefulness of this approach lies in the capacity of the story to convey the complex and varied ways that respondents link together their experiences, which tend to be separated from each other in traditional interviews. Anthropologist Sharon Kaufman, for example, applies methods of narrative analysis to display the way respondents link together events in their past in relation to their present lives.

Other qualitative researchers combine methods. Sociologist Arlie Hochschild's fieldwork, in a residence she calls "Merrill Court," combines open-ended interviewing and participant observation to reveal the variegated set of social relationships and statuses organized on the premises. Still others use historical materials to illuminate everyday meanings in the past. Historian Emily Abel, for example, analyzes diaries written by an Iowa farm woman and her daughter to reconstruct the sentiments surrounding intergenerational residential arrangements in nineteenth-century America.

Taken together, these methods cover the procedural waterfront of qualitative research. As a result, in the following chapters the lives of older people are presented in some of their richest detail, the purview extending from the aging mind to the aging body, from images of normal aging to responses to death, and from the emotional contours of interpersonal relationships to the care of frail loved ones. To supplement this, we have added further readings at the end of each part. All contribute to the endless variety of meanings that aging can bring to everyday life.

## References

Achenbaum, W. Andrew. 1978. *Old Age in the New Land: The American Experience Since 1790*. Baltimore: Johns Hopkins University Press.

Bengtson, Vern L. and K. Warner Schaie (eds.). 1999. *Handbook of Theories of Aging*. New York: Springer.

Erikson, Erik. 1959. "Identity and the Life Cycle: Selected Papers," *Psychological Issues* 1. Monograph No. 1.

Featherstone, Mike and Mike Hepworth. 1991. "The Mask of Aging and the Postmodern Life Course." Pp. 371–89 in *The Body*, edited by Mike Featherstone, Mike Hepworth, and Bryan S. Turner. London: Sage.

Fischer, David Hackett. 1977. *Growing Old in America*. New York: Oxford University Press.

Fry, Christine L. (ed.). 1981. *Dimensions: Aging, Culture, and Health*. New York: Praeger.

Gubrium, Jaber F. and Andrea Sankar (eds.). 1994. *Qualitative Methods in Aging Research*.

Thousand Oaks, CA: Sage.

Gubrium, Jaber F. and W. Brandon Wallace. 1990. "Who Theorizes Age?" *Ageing and Society* 10: 131–49.

Haber, Carole. 1983. *Beyond Sixty-Five: The Dilemma of Old Age in America's Past.* New York: Cambridge University Press.

Hazan, Haim. 1994. *Old Age: Constructions and Deconstructions.* Cambridge: Cambridge University Press.

Kaufman, Sharon. 1986. *The Ageless Self: Sources of Meaning in Late Life.* Madison, WI: University of Wisconsin Press.

Keith, Jennie. 1982. *Old People As People: Social and Cultural Influences on Aging and Old Age.* Boston: Little, Brown and Co.

Kertzer, David I. and Jennie Keith. 1984. *Age and Anthropological Theory.* Ithaca, NY: Cornell University Press.

Pampel, Fred C. 1998. *Aging, Social Inequality, and Public Policy.* Thousand Oaks, CA: Pine Forge Press.

Sokolovsky, Jay (ed.). 1997. *The Cultural Context of Aging: Worldwide Perspectives.* Westport, CT: Bergin & Garvey.

Stephens, Joyce. 1976. *Loners, Losers, and Lovers: Elderly Tenants in a Slum Hotel.* Seattle: University of Washington Press.

U.S Bureau of the Census. 1993. *Historical Statistics of the United States.* Washington, D.C.: U.S. Government Printing Office.

# Part I

## Conceptualizing the Aging Experience

# 1 The Cultural Trap: The Language of Images

## Haim Hazan

The viability of stereotypes is often held to be inversely related to the amount of concrete evidence available about their objects: the more informed we are, the less valid is the stereotype. There is, however, considerable evidence that concrete information does not necessarily invalidate a stereotype but, on the contrary, may serve to reinforce it (Allport 1959). The information received about old people is often ambiguous, and because of this the stereotype overrides our perception of them even in face-to-face interaction. Stereotypes govern our behaviour by obscuring characteristics which, to an unbiased observer, would be clearly visible. A stereotype is presumed universally applicable, without regard to interpersonal differences. It is enormously flexible and therefore useful in handling variegated and changing situations; where it seems appropriate to shift attention to the concrete information at hand, a stereotype may be temporarily set aside. Stereotypes may display contradictions both internally and among themselves. All these characteristics of stereotypes are apparent in the attribution of cultural constructs to the aged.[1]

One of the most deeply rooted stereotypes of the aged is that they are conservative, inflexible, and resistant to change. The aged are perceived as incapable of creativity, of making progress, of starting afresh. Only in art and the domain of the spirit are they licensed to continue to be creative. 'Ordinary' old people are seen to have entered a state of intellectual sterility and emotional impotence.

Perhaps the most common manifestation of this general image of infertility and inertia is the perception of the aged as devoid of sexuality. Contrary to this popular perception, all the research evidence available categorically disproves the image of the elderly as asexual (Hendricks and Hendricks 1977). A further manifestation of this attitude is the imputation to the aged of inability to learn – to store and process information. Studies examining this hypothesis invariably demonstrate that, notwithstanding motoric and sensory deficiencies associated with the ageing process, there are no significant differences between older and younger people in their capacity to learn (Baltes and Schaie 1977). Indeed, when equal opportunities are granted to elderly students and personal motivation meets with social approval, they are capable of pursuing any course of study (Midwinter 1982, 1984). One of the arguments suggested by this line of research is that the apparent differences derive not so much from discrepancies in perception or in the ability to absorb and process new information as from different levels of technical skill, such as difficulties in hearing, sight, and coordination. Marked differences in modes of perception may also be attributed to gaps in formative life experiences having nothing to do with old age itself. Moreover,

Original publication: Hazan, Haim, "The Cultural Trap: The Language of Images," from *Old Age: Constructions and Deconstructions* (Cambridge University Press, Cambridge, 1994), pp. 28–32.

the social creativity of certain groups of older persons is often comparable with that of youth. The development of communities of the aged requires the organization of novel lifestyles and renewal of identity that would do justice to any young people's 'commune'. In terms of the cultural opportunities available for self-realization, life in these communities is often richer and more varied than that hitherto experienced by their inhabitants.

Another stereotype of old people is that they are 'senile'. Here there is an important difference between the formal medical definition and the image evoked by popular use of the term (Gubrium 1986). For the physician, senile dementia is a condition in which the blood vessels in the brain become clogged, reducing the supply of blood to the brain cells and leading to the death of those cells and the consequent loss of certain emotional and cognitive capacities. Another common form of brain pathology in the elderly, affecting approximately 10 percent of old people, is the condition known as 'Alzheimer's disease', which causes changes in the brain tissue resulting in gradual loss of mental abilities such as memory, orientation, and verbal communication. Among lay people, there is a tendency to consider certain behaviour as evidence of senility, disregarding alternative explanations for that behaviour. The concept of senility, supported by the image of ageing as an illness, serves as an umbrella interpretation so wide that few old people can escape its range. Furthermore, since one of the presumed consequences of senility is inability to make decisions, it is often used to justify the assumption of responsibility by others for older people's lives. Thus the aged may be committed to institutional custody against their will on the grounds that they are incapable of handling their own affairs. This move often entails the exertion of socio-psychological pressure on older persons to act in accordance with the objects of those who take charge of their interests. The attribution of 'senility' to the aged may serve as a powerful weapon in the hands of those who seek to deprive them of control of and sometimes to appropriate their property, capital, and other material assets. The fact that few offenders are charged with criminal activity in cases of this kind suggests a conspiracy of silence that benefits from the fear and dependency of the elderly victims.

Failure to distinguish genuine physiological senility from imputed social senility reinforces the notion that gradual biological deterioration (resulting in mental erosion) is inevitable, uncontrollable, and irreversible. Observations conducted in day centres for the elderly have revealed, in contrast, that some who had been regarded as senile prior to their admission showed signs of resumed mental alertness (Hazan 1980a). These elderly persons may not have been physiologically senile; rather, their behaviour may have been a response to their socio-cultural situation.

The mirror image of this stereotype is the idea that old people are supernaturally wise, that is to say, possessed of a perspective on reality of an entirely different order to that of ordinary persons. On occasion we ask their advice, attempting to draw on their life experiences for answers to our most fundamental existential questions. In some societies, such reverence is traditionally bestowed on the seer and the wise man; in others, a parallel may be found with the madman and the court jester, ambiguous symbolic types[2] of a similar stereotypical configuration. Clearly, persons who are supposed to be incapable of making decisions in day-to-day life cannot be expected to offer reliable guidance. The attribution of the latter capacity to the elderly is made possible by the image of them as preoccupied with matters of the spirit. In fact, however, research demonstrates that old people just as often abandon the path of religion, reject life-long metaphysical world views, and adopt cynical and secular viewpoints (Myerhoff 1978a, ch. 2). This process of disenchantment is often construed as 'withdrawal', 'regression', or 'stubbornness' – all terms indicating non-compliance and resistance to social expectations.

Since the elderly are conceived of as incapable of initiative and sound judgement as to their own needs, frameworks for their management are designed by others that impel them into dependence. Old people who enter old-age homes as independent individuals are immediately denied their freedom, and it may come as no surprise that they soon demonstrate signs of withdrawal and indifference.

Alongside and contradictory to this image of powerlessness and dependence, older people are often seen as disturbing and threatening. It is much more difficult, for example, to recruit staff for services relating to the aged, in particular services entailing physical contact, than for work of a similar nature with children or the handicapped. Similarly, geriatrics suffer from a severe shortage of qualified manpower. While there are no doubt a number of reasons for this shortage, one of them is fear of, and resistance to becoming professionally and emotionally involved with old people (Hochschild 1983). This revulsion arises from the connection between the old and death (which, with increasing life expectancy, has gained empirical validity in the course of the past century), the image of infertility and asexuality associated with them and our disgust with human excrement and other bodily discharges. Incontinence, from drooling to involuntary defecation, is a reminder of the association between old age and corporeal disintegration.[3] Thus the aged are conceived of as at once dependent, incapable of influencing or controlling their environments, and threatening. In traditional societies, older people are often victims of witchcraft accusations. This indictment, the cultural manifestation of marginality and powerlessness, may lead to trial by poison ordeal, excommunication, banishment, and death (Turnbull 1984: 231–8).

Another stereotype is that the aged dwell on and draw their life meaning from the past. The present is deemed to hold no real interest for them, and we are often told that in order to understand and communicate with them it is imperative to appeal to their nostalgic recollections. In diametric opposition to this, it is often held that little interests them but the immediate gratification of their most basic day-to-day needs. When we wish to ignore those needs, it is convenient to say that the aged live in the past. When we want to dismiss their past status, it is convenient to argue that they live for the present.

This flexibility in stereotypic thinking is pertinent to yet another stereotype of old people – that they seek the company of their peers for reasons of pure sociability rather than from any desire for practical, instrumental gain or as part of a quest for meaning, identity and knowledge. According to this stereotype, the elderly are presumed to socialize with other persons as a panacea for all psychological and social maladies. The practical implementation of this stereotype is the allocation of significant amounts of social and economic resources to the establishment of old-age clubs and day centres in order that the aged may huddle together to enjoy the remedial benefit of each other's company. In contradiction to this imputed desire for company for company's sake, aged people may also be viewed as willingly detaching themselves from society, content with their own company or that of their nearest and dearest. In this view, elderly persons have strong ties to their immediate social milieux, and it is necessary to develop community services to enable them to maintain their familiar networks. Yet another contradictory stereotype is that the aged are prisoners of space and time, existential loners doomed to solitude and withdrawal. This view provides tacit justification for removing them from their social settings and relocating them in care facilities.

Finally, perhaps the most extreme and omnipresent stereotype of the aged is that they are depressed, unhappy, and pervaded with a sense of failure, disintegration, and pointlessness. It would be easy to refute the alleged universality of this and all other stereotypes, but the point here is that stereotypes are useful for camouflaging the social arrangements which we impose upon the aged members of our society. As the unspoken assumptions upon which 'scientific' theories of ageing are constructed, they become doubly dangerous, being mindfully or inadvertently employed to determine the fate of fellow human beings.

*See end of chapter 2, pp. 22–4, for Notes and References.*

# 2 The Personal Trap: The Language of Self-Presentation

## Haim Hazan

If we accept that aged people are surrounded by a society that assigns them false images and that they are therefore trapped in a labyrinth of distorting mirrors, then the question arises of what self-conception they can possibly project.[1] According to the concept of the 'looking glass self' (Mead 1934; Cooley 1972) we see ourselves as we imagine others see us, and therefore the behaviour of older people and their attitudes towards themselves are shaped and reinforced by society's prevailing images of them. By adopting these images, the elderly in turn confirm and strengthen them.

Old people, for example, are thought to dress in drab, uniform clothing appropriate to the dull world in which they are considered to live. Many elderly people, upon accepting the label of 'aged', do indeed change their style of dress. Those who are reluctant to alter their appearance or prefer the fashionable arouse derision or surprise. A more extreme example is the physical limitations which older people adopt once they accept their definition as aged. Some may begin to stoop and shuffle, others may develop hearing deficiencies that have no apparent physiological basis (a kind of 'social deafness' that develops when people consciously or unconsciously choose not to hear). Some complain of deteriorating vision, others adopt movements characteristic of the physically handicapped in the absence of any such serious limitations (Esberger 1978; Levy 1979). Many older persons seek what they now regard as appropriate forms of social activity; they join old-age clubs and day centres or the 'club house of the park benches', where they engage in seemingly aimless conversations. All these types of behaviour bolster the image of the aged as needy, hopeless, sick, and incapable of social involvement – in short, people whose lives are no longer worth living.

In order to be acceptable to others, the elderly may make an effort to appear harmless, inoffensive, and easy-going. Some may go farther, attempting to efface their sexual identities. Fully capable of engaging in sexual activity from a biological point of view, they behave as if they had lost all erotic desire. Again, older people are often resistant to learning, adopting society's assumption that they are incapable of absorbing and acquiring new knowledge.

What we have here is apparently a vicious circle wherein the behaviour adopted by the elderly reinforces the negative images attached to them. However, a closer look at this psychological model of internalization reveals that it may be challenged on three counts. First, in line with the sociological concept of anomie – the absence of social

Original publication: Hazan, Haim, "The Personal Trap: The Language of Self-Presentation," from *Old Age: Constructions and Deconstructions* (Cambridge University Press, Cambridge, 1994), pp. 33–8.

values and norms – it may be argued that the sense of alienation experienced by old people is so strong that conventional social pressures operate to a far lesser degree than they do under ordinary circumstances. According to this view, the aged enjoy relative freedom. Because of the relaxation of social control and the disarray and lack of coordination of the various elements making up their social milieux, the aged are relatively free to manoeuvre and recognize the scant resources at their disposal to suit their needs. Second, the aged have personal histories and present commitments, involvements, and social networks that cannot be dismissed out of hand. Finally, the situations of elderly persons undergo transformations which offer them the opportunity to exercise a certain degree of freedom of choice. In sum, the impression that older people are trapped by the social images applied to them is often incorrect. In fact they employ a variety of behavioural strategies to counter those images.

One such strategy, rooted in a discrepancy between behaviour and conviction, is a mechanical and ritualized conformity to social expectations in selected settings – for example, in the presence of strangers. Among their peers, in contrast, these individuals may be able to explore newly acquired rewarding self-images and social identities in the company of others subject to similar pressures (Keith 1980a).

Another behavioural response is withdrawal – rejection of society's expectations through dissociation from them. Detachment from the surrounding society is achieved through immersion in recollections and reminiscences. This behaviour is prevalent among significant numbers of the elderly, especially in old age homes or other environments which exert strong and ongoing pressures on the aged (Vesperi 1980).

Yet another reaction may be described as rebellion – the dismissal of the basic cultural assumptions upon which the stereotypes of the aged are constructed – and may take two different forms. The first is defiance, and elderly persons adopting this approach may be characterized as 'stubborn' or 'contrary'. Examples of such acts of rebellion include appearing in public places or in institutional settings dressed in a sloppy or indecent fashion, stockpiling food, or engaging in petty theft. By perpetrating minor offenses they declare their independence and force others to pay attention. In effect, this behaviour is a plea for social recognition of selfhood, dignity, and the right to free expression. Actions with no apparent rational explanation that are commonly ascribed to senility are made explicable in this light. A constructive form of rebellion involves intentional separation from the oppressive milieu of everyday life in order to construct an alternative reality. On occasion this phenomenon is accompanied by the development of an ideology, sometimes to the point of constituting a 'counter-culture' of the aged. Provided that the separation is well defined and the barriers and boundaries firm, aged persons may thus create amongst themselves an alternative social world.

A further response on the part of the aged may be described as 'walking a tight-rope'. This strategy implies taking a great deal of care not to stumble into the social traps laid for the elderly by selecting the symbols, situations, and the people over which they have control and rejecting the rest. The aged may move, for example, to settings inhabited primarily by old people and detached from family frameworks, discard the symbols and insignia of their former social status, and cease to speak in terms of change or future social rewards.

Sometimes symbols of weakness, dependency, and impotence may be transformed into signs of strength, activity, and integrity. For example, the political movement in the United States called the Grey Panthers (a label adopted from the Black Panthers, a group which converted the social stigma of colour into a source of pride) seeks to transform the position of the elderly from feebleness to power sharing in the making of policy. The movement, has in fact succeeded far beyond expectations – it has been instrumental in changing a number of age-discriminating laws and altering the attitude towards the aged in a variety of sectors of American society. This success is due not only to its effective mobilization of sympathy but, in large part, to the focused and efficient recruitment of political and economic resources at the disposal of a substantial portion of elderly American citizens.

An alternative response on the part of old people consists of deciding for themselves to retire from their earlier occupations and pursue new directions. Such a change relatively late in life is possible in our society because life expectancy continues to rise and physical afflictions are on the decline. In some cases, retirement may take place as early as fifty-five, leaving a significant number of active years between retirement and death. This gap may often be as much as twenty or thirty years – enough time to start afresh. Such phenomena, however, remain rare though there is some evidence for late career changes, particularly in business and the arts.

Given sufficient means, the elderly person can travel and explore new horizons. Many older people feel suddenly free to engage in often harsh social criticism, daring to say what others cannot because they are no longer subject to the normal social pressures. In essence, the social vacuum in which they find themselves gives them license to act as if they had nothing to lose, an attitude reinforced by the tendency to humour the aged. In this they may be compared to the court jester who can say anything that occurs to him without fear of penalty (see Handelman 1981). Only marginal social types can afford to indulge in social behaviour otherwise illegitimate. (Perhaps, indeed, it is their marginality that is the source of the wisdom sometimes attributed to the elderly.)

Finally, perhaps the most extreme reaction to the identity crisis of the aged is self-inflicted death, whether by suicide or euthanasia. The will to die, be it conscious or unconscious, is a significant factor in determining 'the hour of our death' (Ariès 1983); conversely, the anticipation of an important occasion such as a birthday or the arrival of a loved one may prolong life (Zarit 1977: 282). Anthropologists are familiar with ritualistically inflicted forms of voodoo death, whereby the community declares a person socially dead and that person often dies without any trace of a biological cause. It may be that forces of a similar biopsychocultural nature are at work in our own society.[2]

## Ethnographic Reflection: Practices of Separation

The transition from a multidimensional existence to membership in a one-dimensional category may be understood in empirical terms of symbolic labelling and social relocation. The following case study, based on anthropological research in an old-age home, illustrates these two interwoven processes.

The old-age home in question was administered by Mishaan, a welfare organization affiliated with the largest trade union federation in Israel, the Histadrut. Eligibility for Mishaan services was dependent upon being a member (or the parent of a member) of the Histadrut. Such membership, however, was by no means a sufficient condition for admission. The imbalance between the limited number of vacancies in the old-age home and the growing demand for them made selection in favour of the able-bodied inevitable. In addition to being able-bodied and mentally alert, to enter the home and stay there required the aged to use personal contacts and wield political power within the organization.

Once admitted, inmates themselves were primarily responsible for whether they were judged fit to remain. In the terminology of the home they were under threat of removal should they become incapable of 'proper functioning', that is looking after themselves. Although certain vague criteria guided this assessment, it was open to various interpretations, and lack of functioning might range from mobility difficulties to incontinence and mental disturbance. 'Functioning' also included participation in the social life of the home. Active involvement in group activities and public meetings was highly praised by the director, who lost no opportunity to stress the direct link between social involvement and 'proper functioning'.

Removal from the home was perceived as the start of an inevitable process of deterioration ending in death. For most inmates, death seemed close both cognitively and physically. Transfer to the sickrooms served as a kind of preparation for the onset of death, since in many instances inmates never returned to their rooms. Other inmates tended to avoid the sick wing. It was customary not to talk about the death of an inmate; in the event that a death was mentioned, it was emphasized that life goes on despite it. This denial of death was even more striking in the inmates' perception of the structure of the old-age home. At the top of the ladder were the active and healthy in mind and body, while at the bottom were the physically and mentally frail. Ironically, it was the latter category that constituted the physical and cognitive barrier between the former and death. The perceived gulf between them was expressed in the derogatory labels attached to the frailer inmates (the 'exhibition', 'vegetables', 'animals'), which served to exclude those so designated from any human frame of reference. Since the frailer inmates were the most likely candidates for transfer and for death, the creation of this non-human category served as a barrier both against death and against the possibility of removal from the home. Thus, a sort of social death sentence had been imposed upon them.

## Notes to chapters 1 and 2

*Chapter 1   The cultural trap: the language of images*

1   On stereotypes of the aged, see Bateson (1950), Stennett and Thurlow (1958), Lehr (1983), and Gruman (1978). For reflection on stereotype-riddled studies in gerontology, see Maddox (1969), Thomas (1981), and Manheimer (1990).

2   The concept of 'symbolic type' is an outgrowth of anthropological discussion of the splitting of the 'me' (the negotiated persona) from the 'I' (inner self), presenting inner as outer but still as non-negotiable and socially independent of context (see Grathoff 1970; Handelman and Kapferer 1980; Handelman 1991). A symbolic type is a reified cultural paradigm which, though itself independent of context, can shape it and, though itself closed to social negotiation and role interplay, has an impact on these processes. Symbolic types emerge when social order collapses, boundaries become blurred and elusive, and social

action is no longer informed by corresponding cultural meaning.

3   This triple taboo – death, sex, and excrement – may be the core image in our attitude towards AIDS.

## Chapter 2   *The personal trap: the language of self-presentation*

1   Since I do not presume to delve into the inner selves of the aged, the only information at my disposal is that of observable behaviour. On the one hand, behaviour may be seen as a means by which feelings and cognitions may be deduced. On the other, self-presentation can be seen as a form of impression management and worthy of explanation in and of itself (Goffman 1959).

2   For an exposition of various dimensions of the holistic bio-psychosocial model in medicine, see Reiser and Rosen (1984).

## References to chapters 1 and 2

Allport, G. W. 1959. *The Nature of Prejudice*. Cambridge, MA: Addison-Wesley.

Ariés, P. 1983. *The Hour of Our Death*. London: Penguin.

Baltes, P. B. and K. W. Schaie. 1977. 'Aging and I.Q.: The Myth of the Twilight Years'. Pp. 67–71 in *Readings in Aging and Death: Contemporary Perspectives*, edited by S. H. Zarit. New York: Harper & Row.

Bateson, G. 1950. 'Cultural Ideas About Aging'. In *Proceedings of a Conference Held on August 7–10, 1950 at the University of California, Berkeley*, edited by H. E. Jones. New York: Pacific Coast Committee on Old Age Research, Social Science Research Council.

Cooley, C. H. 1972. 'The Looking Glass Self'. Pp. 231–3 in *Symbolic Interaction*, edited by J. Manis and A. Meltzer. Boston: Allyn & Bacon.

Esberger, K. 1978. 'Body Image', *Journal of Gerontological Nursing* 4: 35–8.

Goffman, E. 1959. *The Presentation of Self in Everyday Life*. New York: Doubleday.

Grathoff, R. 1970. *The Structure of Social Inconsistencies*. The Hague: Nijhoff.

Gruman, G. J. 1978. 'Cultural Origins of Present-Day "Agism": The Modernization of the Life-Cycle.' In *Aging and the Elderly: Humanistic Perspectives in Geronotology*, edited by K. Woodward, M. Kathleen Van Tassell, and D. Van Tassell. Atlantic Highlands, NJ: Humanities Press.

Gubrium, J. F. 1986. *Oldtimers and Alzheimer's: The Descriptive Organization of Senility*. Greenwich, CT: JAI Press.

Handelman, D. 1981. 'The Ritual Clown: Attributes and Affinities', *Anthropos* 76: 321–70.

Handelman, D. 1991. 'Symbolic Types, the Body, and Circus', *Semiotica* 85: 205–27.

Handelman, D. and B. Kapferer. 1980. 'Symbolic Types, Mediation, and the Transformation of Ritual Context: Sinhalese Demons and Tewa Clowns', *Semiotica* 30: 41–71.

Hazan, H. 1980a. *The Limbo People: A Study of the Constitution of the Time Universe Among the Aged*. London: Routledge & Kegan Paul.

Hendricks, J. and C. D. Hendricks. 1977. 'Sexuality in Later Life'. Pp. 304–11 in *Aging in Mass Society*. Cambridge, MA: Winthrop.

Hochschild, A. 1983. *The Managed Heart*. Berkeley, CA: University of California Press.

Keith, J. 1980a. 'Old Age and Community Creation'. Pp. 170–97 in *Aging in Culture and Society*. New York: J. F. Bergin.

Lehr, U. 1983. 'Stereotypes of Aging and Age Norms'. Pp. 101–12 in *Aging: Challenge to Science and Society, vol. III, Behavioral Sciences and Conclusions*, edited by J. A. Birren, M. A. Munnichs, H. Thomae, and M. Marvis. Oxford: Oxford University Press.

Levy, S. 1979. 'Temporal Experience in the Aged: Body Integrity and the Social Milieu', *Inter-*

*national Journal of Aging and Human Development* 9: 316–44.

Maddox, G. 1969. 'Growing Old: Getting Beyond the Stereotypes'. Pp. 5–16 in *Foundations of Practical Gerontology*, edited by Boyd and Oakes. Columbia, SC: University of South Carolina Press.

Manheimer, R. 1990. 'The Narrative Quest in Qualitative Gerontology', *Journal of Aging Studies*, 3: 253–62.

Mead, G. H. 1934. *Mind, Self, and Society*. Chicago: University of Chicago Press.

Midwinter, E. 1982. *Age Is Opportunity: Education and Older People*. London: Centre for Policy on Ageing.

Midwinter, E. (ed.). 1984. *Mutual Aid Universities*. London: Croom Helm.

Myerhoff, B. 1978a. *Number Our Days*. New York: Dutton.

Reiser, D. and D. H. Rosen (eds.). 1984. *Medicine as a Human Experience*. Baltimore: University Park Press.

Stennett, R. and M. Thurlow. 1958. 'Cultural Symbolism: The Age Variable', *Journal of Consulting Psychology* 22: 496.

Thomas, W. C. 1981. 'The Expectation Gap and the Stereotype of the Stereotype: Images of Old People', *The Gerontologist* 21: 402–7.

Turnbull, C. 1984. *The Human Cycle*. London: Jonathan Cape.

Vesperi, M. 1980. 'The Reluctant Consumer: Nursing Home Residents in the Post-Bergman Era', *Practicing Anthropology* 3: 23–4 and 70–80.

Zarit, S. (ed.). 1977. *Readings in Aging and Death: Contemporary Perspectives*. New York: Harper & Row.

# 3 Further Thoughts on the Theory of Disengagement

## Elaine Cumming

The usefulness of a theory depends upon its ability to explain the present and predict the future. In this essay, I shall amplify and elaborate the 'disengagement' theory of ageing that W.E. Henry and I developed with our colleagues between 1957 and 1960.[1] I hope in this way to make that theory better able to describe and predict both the range and the limits of the ageing process. In its original form, the theory was too simple; it had only enough detail to account for the main outlines of the process of growing old. By adding new elements and elaborating the basic propositions in more detail, I hope to be able to suggest a little of the complexity and diversity that we see among men and women in old age.

### The General Theory of Disengagement

The disengagement theory was developed during a five-year study of a sample of ageing people in an American city. The sample consisted of 275 individuals between the ages of 50 and 90 years; they were in good health and had the minimum of money needed for independence.[2] Briefly, the theory proposes that under these conditions normal ageing is a mutual withdrawal or 'disengagement' between the ageing person and others in the social system to which he belongs – a withdrawal initiated by the individual himself, or by others in the system. When disengagement is complete, the equilibrium that existed in middle life between the individual and society has given way to a new equilibrium characterized by greater distance, and a changed basis for solidarity.

Engagement is essentially the interpenetration of the person and the society to which he belongs. The fully-engaged person acts in a large number and a wide variety of roles in a system of divided labour, and feels an obligation to meet the expectations of his role partners. There are variations, however, in the type of engagement. It is possible to be broadly engaged in a number of social systems that exert little influence over the remainder of society, and it is possible to be deeply engaged in the sense of having roles whose function is to make policies that affect others in large numbers. It is possible to be symbolically engaged by epitomizing some valued attribute – by being a famous scientist, poet or patriot. A few men have roles that combine all three types of engagement and carry with them the extreme constraints that must accompany such a number and variety of obligations; presidents and prime ministers are among them. Roughly, the depth and breadth of a man's engagement can be meas-

Original publication: Cumming, Elaine, "Further Thoughts on the Theory of Disengagement," *International Social Science Journal* 15 (1963), pp. 377–93.

ured by the degree of potential disruption that would follow his sudden death.[3] The death of someone who has an important symbolic engagement with his society, however, can result in both loss and gain because the survivors can rally around the symbols he embodied and thus reaffirm their value. For many Americans, Dag Hammarskjöld's death brought into sharp focus the need for world order.

In its original form, the disengagement theory concerned itself with the modal case which, in America, is first, departure of children from families, and then, retirement for men or widowhood for women. It did not take account of such non-modal cases as widowhood before the marriage of the last child or of work protracted past the modal age of retirement. Most importantly, it did not, and still does not, concern itself with the effects of the great scourges of old age, poverty and illness.[4] This essay will modify and elaborate the theory somewhat and suggest some characteristics of ageing people that might make an important difference to their patterns of disengagement. Like the original statement, this modification has the status of a system of hypotheses. Some of the elements are close to being operational as they stand; others are still too general for testing.

Before proceeding further, an asymmetry in the earlier discussions of the theory must be dealt with. Disengagement has been conceived as a mutual withdrawal between individual and society, and therefore the process should vary according to the characteristics of both. In earlier statements, consideration was given to the different ways in which the environment retreats – retirement, loss of kin or spouse, departure of children, and so on – but the only individual difference to be considered in any detail was that between the sexes. Eventually, if the process is to be described adequately, we must have typologies of withdrawal and retreat. I suggest that deeply-rooted differences in character are a good starting point because it is reasonable to suppose that they colour all of life, including the disengagement process.

## Temperament and Disengagement

In its original form the disengagement theory did no more than suggest an ultimate biological basis for a reduction of interest or involvement in the environment. Variations in the process were attributed to social pressures, especially as they are differently experienced by men and women. A vital difference in style, however, can be expected between people of dissimilar temperaments, no matter what their sex. Combining biological and social variables within the framework of the disengagement theory, it might be possible to suggest a wider variety of styles of interaction in old age than would otherwise be possible.

A proposed temperamental variable, basically biological, is the style of adaptation to the environment. It seems well established that humans must maintain a minimum of exchange with the environment, or a clear anticipation of renewing exchange with it, in order to keep a firm knowledge both of it and of themselves.[5] There appear to be different modes of maintaining this relationship, which can perhaps be called the 'impinging' mode and the 'selecting' mode.[6] The impinger appears to try out his concept of himself in interaction with others in the environment and to use their appropriate responses to confirm the correctness of his inferences about himself, the environment, and his relationship to it. If the feedback from others suggests that he is incorrect, he will try to bring others' responses into line with his own sense of the appropriate relationship. Only if he fails repeatedly will he modify his concept of himself. In contrast, the selector tends to wait for others to affirm his assumptions about himself. From the ongoing flow of stimulation he selects these cues that confirm his relationship to the world. If they fail to come, he waits, and only reluctantly brings his own concepts into line with the feedback he receives. The selector may be able to use symbolic residues of old interactions to maintain his sense of self more efficiently than the impinger, and thus be able to wait longer for suitable cues.

We assume that temperament is a multi-determined, biologically based characteristic, and therefore that the temperamental types are normally distributed in the population with few people at the extremes. We also assume that the modal person can both impinge and select as the occasion demands, although perhaps favouring one style rather than the other. A normal person will shift to the alternate pattern when it becomes necessary either for appropriate role behaviour or for the prevention of 'diffusion feelings'.[7] If there are no complicating ego problems, a pronounced selector will probably be known as 'reserved', or 'self-sufficient', or 'stubborn', and a pronounced impinger as 'temperamental', 'lively,' or 'brash'. We would expect the impinger, as he grows older, to experience more anxiety about loss of interaction, because he needs it to maintain orientation.[8] The selector, being able to make more use of symbols, may have less difficulty with the early stages of disengagement.[9]

The disengaging impinger can be expected to be more active and apparently more youthful than his peers. His judgement may not be as good as it was, but he will provoke the comment that he is an unusual person for his age. Ultimately, as he becomes less able to control the situations he provokes, he may suffer anxiety and panic through failure both to arouse and to interpret appropriate reactions. His problem in old age will be to avoid confusion.

The selector, in contrast to the impinger, interacts in a more measured way. When he is young he may be thought too withdrawn, but as he grows older his style becomes more age-appropriate. In old age, because of his reluctance to generate interaction, he may, like a neglected infant, develop a kind of marasmus. His foe will be apathy rather than confusion.

These are not, of course, ordinary ageing processes; the extreme impinger and the extreme selector are almost certain to get into trouble at some crisis point because they cannot move over to the opposite mode of interacting when it is adaptive to do so. In general, in an achievement-oriented society, the impinger may be more innately suited to middle age, the selector perhaps to childhood and old age.

To sum up, some biologically-based differences among people may be expected to impose a pattern upon their manner of growing old. I shall now return to the theory, with this variable in mind, and at the same time suggest other concepts that it might profitably include.

## At the Outset of Disengagement

Disengagement probably begins sometime during middle life when certain changes of perception occur, of which the most important is probably an urgent new perception of the inevitability of death. It is certain that children do not perceive the meaning of death and it is said that 'no young man believes that he will ever die.' It is quite possible that a vivid apprehension of mortality – perhaps when the end of life seems closer than its start – is the beginning of the process of growing old. Paradoxically, a sense of the shortness of time may come at the height of engagement; that is, competition for time may draw attention to both its scarcity and its value. There may be a critical point beyond which further involvement with others automatically brings a sense of 'there is no time for all that I must do' which, in turn, leads to evaluations of what has been done compared to what was hoped for, and then to allocations and priorities for the future. If this process is common to many people, those who have never been very firmly engaged should feel less sense of urgency than those who are tightly enmeshed with society – all other things, including temperament, being equal.

Accompanying the need to select and allocate is a shift away from achievement. Achievement, as Parsons says,[10] demands a future; when confidence in the existence of a future is lost, achievement cannot be pursued without regard to the question, 'Shall it be achievement of this rather than of that?' Such a question is the beginning of an exploration of the meaning and value of the alternatives.[11] In American life, where achievement is perhaps the highest value, its abandonment has always been tinged with failure. We would, therefore, expect the relinquishment of achievement to be a crisis, and, indeed, general knowledge and some research tell us that in middle life competent men with a record of achievement feel sudden painful doubts about the value of what they have done.[12] Once any part of achievement is given up, some binding obligations are gone, and even if they are replaced with less demanding ties, a measure of disengagement has occurred.

Disengagement may begin in a different way, somewhat as follows: the middle-aged person who has not undergone an inner period of questioning reaches a point where losses, both personal and public, begin to outrun his ability to replace them. A friend dies, a business closes, his children move far away. For the healthy, ageing impinger these losses may be replaced; for the selector they may not, and an awareness of their permanence may be a turning point. With each loss, the ageing person must surrender certain potential feelings and actions and replace them with their symbolic residues in memory.[13] In a sense, this substitution of symbol for social action changes the quality of the self. Even if the role partners themselves are replaced, they cannot often substitute for the lost relationship because sentiments built up over the years cannot be copied.

The most crucial step in the disengagement process may lie in finding a new set of rewards. The esteem that achievement brings can be replaced by the affection generated in socio-emotional activity. The approval that comes from meeting contracted obligations can be replaced by the spontaneous responses of others to expressive acts. The inner rewards of weaving the past into a satisfactory moral fabric can partly replace the public rewards of achievement. Nevertheless, in America today there is a net loss because achievement is more highly valued than meaning or expression and because its symbols are more easily calibrated. To be rich is to be recognized a success; wisdom is often its own reward.

Finally, and perhaps most importantly, freedom from obligation replaces the constraint of being needed in an interlocking system of divided tasks. The fully engaged man is, in essence, bound; the disengaged man is free – if he has resources and health enough to allow him to exercise that freedom. The ability to enjoy old age may be the ability and the opportunity to use freedom.[14]

No matter how important the effects of the perception of time and the shift in rewards, the essential characteristic of disengagement is that once started it tends to be self-perpetuating. If the search for meaning becomes urgent, and the impulse toward seeking out others becomes less rewarding, there will be a tendency not to replace ties broken by loss.

Once withdrawal has begun, it may become more difficult to make new contacts. Not knowing quite how to behave under strange circumstances inhibits exploration, and this difficulty, in turn, can reinforce the disengaging process – many elderly people refuse to fly in aircraft, not because they are afraid but because they do not know airport etiquette! A sense of strangeness cannot, of course, in itself lead to withdrawal; any middle-aged adult feels discomfort if he finds himself in an unknown situation without a role. Prisoners of war must be helped to re-engage after long periods of isolation from their culture. For the ageing, such diffusion feelings enhance a process that is already under way – a process made inevitable by man's mortality.

Thus, empirically, we see ageing people interacting less and in fewer roles. Modally, ties to kindred become more salient, while more distant, impersonal, and more recent ties become less important and finally disappear. This process of reduction and simplification leaves the individual freer from the control that accompanies involvement in a larger number and greater variety of roles. Concretely, this means that the broadly engaged person receives fewer of the positive and negative sanctions that accompany and guide all interactions and control the style of everyday behaviour, and, therefore, idiosyncratic personal behaviour becomes possible. At the same time, ideas, removed from the scenes in which they can be tested out, become more stereotyped and general.[15]

It seems possible that those who have been deeply engaged in roles that influence considerable areas of society or those who have rare and valuable skills will remain engaged longer than those less deeply involved with the affairs of their generation. This is because the values that inform major decisions are slower to change than everyday norms, and those who have been consciously enmeshed with them may, in old age, symbolize their continuity for those who have not. Those who have been successful mathematicians, politicians, and poets can count on society remaining closer to them than those who have not influenced or represented their fellow men.

As the number of groups to which an ageing person belongs is reduced, his membership in those remaining becomes more important because he must maintain a minimum of stimulation. The memberships of old age – kinship, friendship, and perhaps church – are all marked by a high level of agreement among members and many explicit common values. In such groups, it is very difficult to deviate far from the common viewpoint. Thus, the more the elderly person disengages from a variety of roles, the less likely is he to take on new ideas. The conservatism of old age is partly a security measure, related to the need to maintain harmony among the remaining companions.

As withdrawal of normative control is an essential aspect of the disengagement theory, it must be asked why old people should enter a spiral of decreasing conformity when middle-aged people, except in extreme cases, are able to endure prolonged interpersonal disruptions and quickly reconstitute contact with the norms. Moving from one city to another is an interpersonal crisis, but it does not often set in motion a process that leads to a new orientation to life. The difference seems to be that for the ageing a combination of reduced biological energy, the reduction of freedom, preoccupation with the accumulated symbols of the past, and licence for a new kind of self-centredness cannot be resisted. Furthermore, all this is expected of the older person, and so the circle is further reinforced.

In contrast, if the middle-aged person feels that he is in a situation of reduced social control, he has both the energy and the opportunity to seek new constraints, and if he retreats too far from conformity he is sanctioned. In some ways, an ageing person is like an adolescent; he is allowed more freedom and expressiveness than a middle-aged adult. Later, when he is very old, he is permitted the dependency and individuation of the small child.

In this view, socialization is the encouragement of children to abandon their parochialism and individuation and to accept conformity to the demands of the major institutions of society, while disengagement is a permission to return again to individuation. In all, for the old person, the circular process of disengagement results in the social tasks getting harder and the alternatives more rewarding, while for the young person, the social tasks remain rewarding and the alternatives are felt as alienation. Were it not for the value placed on achievement, the chains that the adult so willingly allows to bind him might be put off at least as readily as they are taken on.

### Society's Withdrawal

The disengagement theory postulates that society withdraws from the ageing person to the same extent as that person withdraws from society. This is, of course, just another way of saying that the process is normatively governed and in a sense agreed upon by all concerned. Everyone knows how much freedom from constraint is allowable and where the line between the oddness of old age and the symptoms of deviance lies. There seem to be deeply-rooted reasons, in both the culture and the social structure, for this withdrawal process.

In the first place the organization of modern society requires that competition for powerful roles be based on achievement. Such competition favours the young because their knowledge is newer. Furthermore, the pressure of the young on to the highest roles cannot be met in a bureaucracy by an indefinite expansion of the powerful roles. Therefore, the older members must be discarded to make way for the younger. In America, a disproportionately large number of young adults will soon be competing for jobs that are becoming relatively fewer as industry moves toward complete automation.[16] If Americans are to remain engaged in any serious way past the seventh decade, as many observers insist they must, roles must be found for them that young people *cannot* fill.[17] Only an elaboration of available roles can accomplish this because it is impossible for a society organized around standards of achievement and efficiency to assign its crucial roles to a group whose death rate is excessively high. When a middle-aged, fully-engaged person dies, he leaves many broken ties, and disrupted situations. Disengagement thus frees the old to die without disrupting vital affairs.

Finally, at the end of life when one has outlived one's peers, social withdrawal consists in failure to approach. In this sense, the young withdraw from the old because the past has little reality for them. They cannot conceive of an old person in any but a peripheral role. Thus, they approach him with condescension, or do not approach at all because of embarrassment. This gulf between generations is a by-product of a future-oriented society; when it changes, America will have changed. In the meantime, it seems clear that the older person may find it more rewarding to contemplate a moment of past glory than to try to make new relationships, especially with the young. In the intimate circle, no such effort is needed; the only real social problem for the very old, given health and enough money, may be lack of such a circle.[18]

## Disengagement from Roles

Whether disengagement is initiated by society or by the ageing person, in the end he plays fewer roles and his relationships have changed their quality.

Socialization ensures that everyone learns to play the two basic kinds of roles that are known as instrumental and socio-emotional. In this essay, the instrumental roles in any given social system are those primarily concerned with active adaptation to the world outside the system during the pursuit of system goals. Socio-emotional roles are concerned with the inner integration of the system and the maintenance of the value patterns that inform its goals.[19]

Men, for reasons at once too obvious and too complex to consider here, must perform instrumental roles on behalf of their families, and this, for most men, means working at an occupation. Although men play socio-emotional roles, in business and elsewhere, they tend to assign the integrative tasks to women when they are present. In patriarchal societies, a man conceivably can live his whole adult life without playing a socio-emotional role, if, in both his family and in his work, others are willing to integrate social systems around him. A married woman, on the other hand, in addition to the socio-emotional role she plays in her family as a whole, must be instrumental in relationship to small children. Very few women, and those only perhaps among the wealthiest, can totally avoid instrumentality. Thus, women are in the habit of bringing either kind of role into salience with more ease than men.

Whether there is any inherent quality that makes it easier to play one role than another is obscure, although the impinging temperament may predispose toward socio-emotionality. Empirically, we see a spectrum that includes goal-directed men, all of whose roles are instrumental (officers in the regular Army whose wives tremble when they shout); men who play socio-emotional roles in some circumstances (comforting the baby when he falls), men who seek out socio-emotional roles (in America, perhaps the personnel man); women who play instrumental roles whenever the situation allows it (club presidents), women who shift from instrumental work roles to socio-emotional family roles, and women who play socio-emotional roles almost all the time (the helpful maiden aunt living in a relative's household).

Most married couples with children, no matter what secondary roles they may hold, have a basic division of labour in which the husband plays a core instrumental role *vis-à-vis* his family by working, and the wife a core socio-emotional one by maintaining their home and caring for their children. By the time the children have

72531

left home and the husband has retired, the original division of labour has lost much of its basis.

A man has no clear-cut role upon retirement. He may still play an instrumental role relative to his wife, but it loses its public label; there is no special place to go to perform it, and there is no paycheck that is the obvious consequence of his daily round. He must bring his capacities for integrative activity into salience much of the time and perhaps even share the instrumental roles that remain available with other retired men. For these reasons, the disengagement theory proposes that it is more difficult for a man to shift to socio-emotional roles and integrative activities than it is for him to assume new instrumentalities, both because it is a less familiar mode for him and because he is in danger of competing directly with his wife and possibly with his grandchildren for roles within kinship or friendship circles. Therefore, the theory predicts that retirement will bring a period of maladjustment to many American men.

A man's response to retirement may be coloured by the type of work role from which he withdraws. If his role has been part of a 'true' division of labour, such that he can see the contribution that he is making to the functioning of society, he is likely to have considerable ego involvement in his work – it is to him as children are to a woman, a persistent palpable achievement. If, on the other hand, the division of labour is such that the outcome of his contribution is invisible to him, he will tend to be alienated from the meaning of his work and will find his rewards in his personal relationships with his fellow workers. In the first case, his instrumental role has three facts: he can see his contribution to the larger society, to his immediate working group, and to his family; in the second case, he can see a contribution only to the primary groups, work and family. Men in these two situations may react quite differently to retirement. The first might be expected to suffer more sense of loss immediately upon retirement – as women do when children first depart – but eventually to take much satisfaction from recalling his contribution to social goals and perhaps seeing others build upon it. The second may be relieved at leaving a meaningless work role but eventually suffer from lack of the symbolic connexion with his own past, especially if he is a selector and accustomed to depending upon symbols for his orientation and sense of self.

Disengagement from central life roles is basically different for women than for men. This seems to be because women's roles are essentially unchanged from girlhood to death. In the course of their lives women are asked to give up only pieces of their core socio-emotional roles or to change their details. Their transitions are therefore easier[20] – the wife of a retired man can use her integrative skills to incorporate him in new groupings. She must, if she is tactful, become even more integrative through abandoning to him the more adaptive of her domestic tasks. Similarly, the problems raised by widowhood are more easily resolved than the problems raised by retirement. Moreover, the loss of status anchorage that women suffer at the time of a husband's death is less severe than the loss of status suffered at retirement because widowhood, unlike retirement, has no tinge of failure in it.[21] It is the blameless termination of a valued role. Furthermore, the differential death rate that leaves about 20 per cent of American women living without a conjugal bond by the age of 60, provides a membership group for them.[22] Men, in contrast, have difficulty finding memberships to compensate for work associations.

In general we might say that a woman's lifelong training to a role that is primarily socio-emotional but nevertheless includes adaptive skills leaves her more diffusely adaptable than a man's working career leaves him, because he does not automatically need integrative skills. Integrative skills are, in a sense, the *lingua franca* wherever people interact with one another. Adaptive skills, in contrast, tend to be more functionally specific and less easily transferred. The disposition toward the instrumental role can remain after retirement, but the specific skills lose relevance. Only rarely does a woman find herself with no membership group that can use her integrative contribution.

Finally, a retired man loses suitable role models – that is, role partners with whom he can try out patterns of adaptation and hence learn alternatives. He must seek out other retired men – who are themselves tinged with failure in his eyes – or learn from women. Women, again because of the differential death rate, have more models, and these are more familiar. For both men and women, however, the roles of old age must be learned from others who are themselves relatively free of constraints – unlike children who are taught the roles they anticipate filling by adults who are as fully engaged and constrained as they will ever be.

Among married couples, a crucial event after retirement may be a shifting of the representative role from the man to the woman. While he works, a husband endows his family with its position in society, but after he enters the socio-emotional world of women and leisure, his wife tends to represent their conjugal society at kinship gatherings and social affairs – even in church activities. In this regard, also, men are more freed by retirement than women are by widowhood.

If these differences between men and women are important, there should be a visible contrast in their ability to cope with the discontinuities of the disengagement process. Two obvious examples are available, that appear related, on the one hand, to women's abilities in finding roles in social systems and, on the other, to the sudden freedom from constraint of retirement. In table 2.1 we see the relative proportions of men and women in a study sample who, when seeking help from a public relief agency, were found to be homeless as well as in need of money. At no age are men who are in economic distress as able as women to maintain membership in a domes-

**Table 2.1**  Proportion of homeless* men and women in a time sample of applicants to two relief agencies

| Age and sex | Total | Percentage homeless |
|---|---|---|
| *Men* | 227 | 27.7 |
|   Under 60 years | 185 | 27.6 |
|   Age 60 and over | 42 | 28.6 |
| *Women* | 144 | 6.3 |
|   Under 60 years | 100 | 6.0 |
|   Age 60 and over | 44 | 6.8 |

* Excluding migrant workers, and those temporarily stranded away from home. These data are from a study of the division of labour among the integrative agents of society financed in part by NIMH (National Institute of Mental Health) Grant M4735, Principal Investigator Elaine Cumming.

**Table 2.2**  Living arrangements of 100 consecutive first admissions, aged 60 and over, to a mental hospital*

| Sex and marital status | Number | Percentage who had been living in | | |
| --- | --- | --- | --- | --- |
| | | Domestic unit | Hospital or nursing home | Shelter or home for aged |
| Men | 43 | – | – | – |
| Married | 16 | 81.3 | 12.5 | 6.2 |
| Non-married | 27 | 44.4 | 18.5 | 37.1 |
| Women | 57 | – | – | – |
| Married | 16 | 87.5 | 12.5 | 0.0 |
| Non-married | 41 | 63.4 | 26.8 | 9.8 |

* I am grateful to Mary Lou Parlagreco and John Cumming for permission to use these data from an unpublished study.

tic unit. Indeed, there is no female counterpart in America to the 'homeless man'. In table 2.2, we see that among a cohort of men and women over 60 years of age entering a mental hospital for the first time, one-third of the non-married men had been living in shelters and old people's homes, whereas less than one-tenth of the non-married women had come from such institutions. Women without husbands appear able to accommodate themselves to both the households of others and the hospital environment more readily than men without wives.[23] The differences in both tables are statistically significant at better than the 1 per cent level of confidence.

In figure 2.1, we see the rates of suicide, by age, for men and women. At the age that disengagement is postulated to occur, 65–75, the rate of suicide among women drops and continues to drop, while among men it rises persistently.[24] The figure leads to the speculation that women go from a little too much constraint to just the right amount of freedom while men go from too much of the one to too much of the other. In spite of this dramatic difference, it is unlikely that men who survive the transition crisis of retirement are as disadvantaged as these data make them seem; they are more likely to resemble Charles Lamb, who says of his sudden and unexpected retirement: 'For the first day or two I felt stunned – overwhelmed. I could only apprehend my felicity; I was too confused to taste it sincerely. I wandered about, thinking I was happy, and knowing that I was not. I was in the condition of a prisoner in the old Bastille, suddenly let loose after a forty years' confinement. I could scarce trust myself with myself. It was like passing out of Time into Eternity – for it is a sort of Eternity for a man to have all his Time to himself. It seemed to me that I had more time on my hands than I could ever manage. From a poor man, poor in Time, I was suddenly lifted up into a vast revenue; I could see no end of my possessions; I wanted some steward, or judicious bailiff, to manage my estates in Time for me. And here let me caution persons growing old in active business, not lightly, nor without weighing their own resources, to forego their customary employment all at once, for there may

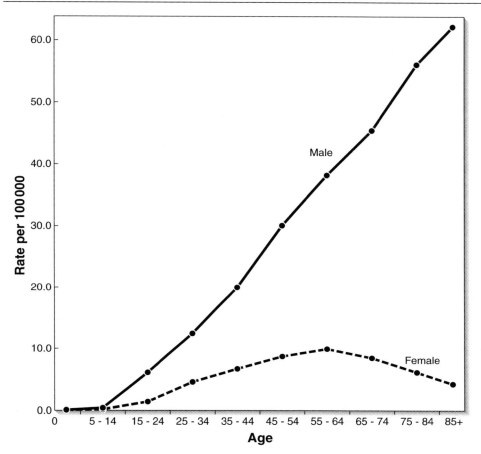

**Fig. 2.1**   Rates of suicide per 100,000 population for all white residents of continental United States, 1957. (Adapted from Table CO, *Summary of Mortality Statistics: United States, 1957*, Washington, D.C. National Office of Vital Statistics.)

be danger in it. I feel it by myself, but I know that my resources are sufficient; and now that those first giddy raptures have subsided, I have a quiet home-feeling of the blessedness of my condition.'[25]

### Changes in Solidarity

I have discussed disengagement as it affects temperamental types, as an inner experience, as a social imperative, and as a response to changing roles. Perhaps the most economical way of describing it is in terms of shifting solidarities that may have roots in middle life. In general, ageing brings change from solidarity bonds based on differences of function and hence on mutual dependency to bonds based on similarities and common sentiments. The post-retirement part of a man's life can be considered, therefore, in terms of a two-stage shift in the nature of his relationships with his wife, his kinsmen, and the rest of the world that starts with departure of children and retirement. On the one hand, the 'organic solidarity' of a divided labour that marked his conjugal life is weakened because after retirement he no longer has a clearly marked, publicly recognized, instrumental role; therefore, the 'mechanical solidarity' of common belief and sentiments that must precede and accompany the division of labour becomes more salient.[26] On the other hand, the man and his wife, as a unit, are no longer functioning as a factory for making adults from children and hence are now related to other segments of society through common characteristics. Thus, both men and women abandon the mutual obligations and power problems of a divided labour among themselves as well as between themselves and society. They move into a more equalitarian relationship with each other and with the world – a relationship in which solidarity is based almost entirely upon a consensus of values and a commonality of interest. Most importantly, the new segmental solidarity is marked by an essential redundancy of the parts.[27] Loss of a member from a system of divided labour disrupts the system. Loss of a member from a group of peers diminishes the society but does not disrupt it.

The second stage of old age comes when the old person is no longer able to carry out the minimum adaptive behaviour necessary to maintain health, or cleanliness or propriety. At that point, someone else must enter the conjugal society to perform adaptive functions for both man and wife, and thus they return to the asymmetrical social condition of infants – their contribution to the solidarity lies not in what they do but what they are – members by birthright of a family. A very old person with no family ties has the pathos of an orphaned child and society deals with him accordingly. This terminal dependency excludes all other social relations. Indeed, among the extremely aged, 'collective monologues' such as Piaget describes among children may replace conversation, for as Durkheim says – 'society has retreated from the old person, or what amounts to the same thing, he has retreated from it'.

Summarizing the shift in solidarity in more concrete terms, we may say that men at work are tied together by sentiments about the work itself and women by sentiments about children, schools[23] and domestic matters. After work ceases, the bonds between a man and those he worked with must literally be reforged if they are to survive, because they must have new substance. After children leave home, while much must be rewrought between women, it is less than for men because they still have in common the roles of spouse and mother – although the latter may be somewhat attenuated.

Among kindred there are values and sentiments arising from many common experiences, and, therefore, it is easy for solidarity to persist after disengagement. In other words, it is the diffusely-bonded solidarities that survive and the specifically-bonded ties that wither. If a specific bond involves some divided labour, the attachment is stronger, but once the conditions of mutual dependency are removed, it is weakened. In diffusely-bonded relationships, of which kinship is the prototype, common sentiments, values and traditions inevitably form around many activities and events. For this reason, such stable solidarities persist through role changes and become the salient relationships of old age. The energy to force such strong links as exist between siblings or very old friends because of common history, common experience, and interlocking membership, may be lost as soon as biological energy begins to fade.

It should be noted that there are certain 'atemporal' roles available to men that do not become outmoded and can be the basis of a divided labour until extreme old age. The clergyman's role, for example, is concerned with persistent values; it resists obsolescence because it ties society to its timeless values. The clergyman is the instrumental leader in his family but with the larger society as the social system of reference, he performs an integrative function in an important socio-emotional role. Such roles seem to perform for the whole society the function that women perform for the family – they maintain the pattern of values that inform the goals and they reduce the tension generated by the effort of adaptation. Their content is the *lingua franca* of the general culture.

## Implications

In this discursive account of the disengagement theory, I have raised more problems than I have begun to solve. The additions to the theory are untidily grafted on to the original formulation without regard to whether or not they contradict it or shift its focus. The next task is to formalize the propositions and wherever possible cast them in terms that can be tested – but this is another undertaking for another time. Given the choice, I have taken what is for me the pleasanter alternative of thinking widely rather than rigorously, and in doing so I have drawn attention to the theory's need for greater rigour.

## Notes

1   The theory was first suggested in 'Disengagement, a tentative theory of aging', by Elaine Cumming, Lois R. Dean, and David S. Newell, *Sociometry*, vol. 23, no. 1 March, 1960, and developed in greater detail in *Growing Old*, by Elaine Cumming and William E. Henry, New York: Basic Books, 1961.
2   This means that they were able to live on their incomes from whatever source without seeking public assistance.
3   Obviously this is an over-simplification. There are many structural safeguards in any society to keep this kind of disruption to a minimum; included among them is the rational-legal system of authority.
4   The population of study was a representative sample of the Greater Kansas City metropolitan area with the lowest and the highest socio-economic groups and all who could not fill their major roles on account of illness removed.
5   Philip Solomon et al., *Sensory Deprivation*. Cambridge, Mass.: Harvard University Press, 1961.
6   For a discussion of the implications of this typology of temperament for psychopathology, see, John Cumming and Elaine Cumming, *Ego and Milieu*, New York Atherton Press, 1962.
7   I use this phrase in the way that Erikson does in *Childhood and Society*, New York: W. W. Norton, 1950. Roughly, it refers to the anxiety that attends the doubt that others will confirm in the future either the relationship presently established or the identity currently implied by the interaction.
8   It is fairly obvious that these proposed temperaments are related to the psychological dimension, introversion-extroversion.

9   This raises a problem of the difference between the *appearance* of engagement and the *experience* of it. This problem is enhanced by a tendency to contrast disengagement with activity (see, Robert Havighurst, 'Successful aging', *Gerontologist*, vol. 1, pp. 8–13, 1961). In fact, activity and engagement are not in the same dimension. A disengaged person often maintains a high level of activity in a small number and narrow variety of roles, although it is doubtful if it is possible to be at once firmly engaged and inactive. In any event, the opposite of disengagement is engagement, a concept different from, though related to, the concept of activity. The result of confusing these two variables is that *active* people are judged to be *engaged*. They may, however, be *relatively disengaged impingers*. They may also, depending upon the type of activity, be exceptionally healthy or restless. There is no real way to judge because the issue has not been put to the test. Unfortunately, many of the populations used for gerontological studies are volunteers and thus can be expected to include a disproportionately large number of impingers. For example Marc Zborowski (in: 'Aging and recreation', *Journal of Gerontology*, vol. 17, no. 3, July 1962) reports that a group of volunteers reported little change over time of their recreational activities and preferences. The author concludes from this that the subjects are not disengaging, using the concept in Havighurst's sense as the opposite of active. His finding is only unexpected inasmuch as the disengagement theory would predict a rise in recreational activities after retirement among a population that might include numerous disengaging impingers. In contrast to this report is a careful study of a *general population* of older people in New Zealand (see, 'Older People of Dunedin City: A Survey', J. R. McCreary, and H. C. A. Somerset, Wellington: Dept. of Health, 1955) among whom only 10 per cent belonged to, or wanted to belong to, recreational groups, and only 9 per cent of those not working would seek work if the restrictions on their pensions would allow them.

10   Talcott Parsons, 'Toward a healthy maturity', *Journal of Health and Human Behavior*, vol. 1, no. 3, 1960.

11   Of course, at all times in the life span, priorities must be set up because it is impossible to do more than one thing in one space of time. But as long as there is the possibility of postponement until a later date, the problem of allocation has little poignancy.

12   William E. Henry, 'Conflict, age, and the executive', *Business Topics*, Michigan State University, no date.

13   No concept of 'economy of libido' is implied here. The inference is quite simply that a person with a store of memories is less likely to give full attention to the world around him than the person who has fewer symbolic residues to capture his attention. Of course, there are obvious limits on preoccupation with the past including some minimum level of interaction that seems almost mandatory for life itself.

14   See Emile Durkheim, *Suicide*, Glencoe, Ill: Free Press, 1951, pp. 157–9.

15   When the Kansas City respondents were asked the question, 'What do you think of the younger generation?' the middle-aged people gave concrete examples of youthful behaviour that they found compelling or unattractive while the older people answered in large generalizations, usually negative.

16   The whole problem of retraining for automation is complex. On the surface, retraining an older person seems wasteful, but if the rate of technical change remains the same, retraining may be necessary so frequently that older workers may economically be included in the programme. Retraining may not be necessary if Parsons is right in suggesting that as American society becomes more sophisticated there will be more variety of roles for old people just as there are more available to women past the childbearing age. If this is true, there should be demonstrable differences in the attitude toward older people between groups with different levels of sophistication and between countries with different kinds of cultural elaborations.

17   For a full discussion of this possibility, see Talcott Parsons, 'Toward a healthy maturity', *Journal of Health and Human Behavior*, vol. 2, no. 3, 1960.

18   It is interesting that American ideology holds that it is not good for an old person to live in his adult child's household. Nevertheless a very large number do so, and apparently successfully. In these cases there seems to be a tendency to define the situation as in some way extraordinary so as to keep honouring the shibboleth in the breach. See, Seymour Bellin, 'Family and kinship in later years', doctoral dissertation, Columbia University.

19   In this general statement, the word 'system' means any social system. In any particular case the system must be specified because the same acts can be part of an instrumental role viewed from one system and a socio-emotional role viewed from another. The clergy-man plays an integrative role in society in general, but an instrumental role *vis-à-vis* his family – and all his professional acts can thus be categorized differently according to the system of reference.

20   This point is strikingly made by Peter Townsend who has described (*The Family Life of Old People*, Glencoe, Ill.: Free Press, 1957) how working-class women in London pass smoothly through the roles of daughter, mother, and grandmother. The pattern in America may be somewhat less straightforward, but the disjunction for women still seems far less acute than for men.

21   When the data from which the disengagement theory was induced were gathered, the responsibility of women to feed their husbands in such a way as to avoid coronary heart disease had not appeared in the mass media. There may be a tendency since then for widowhood under some circumstances to be construed as role failure.

22   This does not mean that women go out and 'join' a group of widows. My impression is that they re-establish old bonds, or move closer to other women who have lost their husbands or never married. They probably tighten their ties to their children at this time also.

23   In the area of study, a shelter, which is really a 'poorhouse', and even an old people's home is considered much less desirable than a nursing home or hospital.

24   This may be an exaggerated phenomenon in America. In England, for example, the rates for men and women are more parallel.

25   Charles Lamb, 'The superannuated man', in *Aging in Today's Society*, eds. Clark Tibbitts and Wilma Donahue, New York: Prentice-Hall, 1960, pp. 99–100.

26   It is, of course, impossible to imagine a division of labour between people who are not bound by any common sentiments.

27   This is not so for the conjugal society toward the end of life. Immediately after retirement, husbands seem redundant to many women who have developed lives of their own since the termination of child raising. However, extremely old people, with no division of labour at all, become dependent upon one another to such an extent that if one dies the other is likely to follow quickly. This special case of a very binding mechanical solidarity is probably the result of these extremely old people being almost merged into one identity like twin infants.

28   American society strongly encourages women to belong to school-related organizations and thus to meet the mothers of other children.

# 4 A Current Theoretical Issue in Social Gerontology

*Arnold M. Rose*

A new field of research, especially one dealing with a social problem, is likely to emerge without using any explicit theory, and then gradually to adapt general theoretical formulations already in use in kindred fields. Thus, the earliest research in social gerontology was descriptive in character, but soon concepts like "adjustment," "role changes," "loss of roles," "changing self-concept" were borrowed from symbolic-interactionist theory in social psychology – a theoretical position to which many of the early social gerontologists adhered. Burgess, who probably can be considered to be the father of social gerontology, was also the source of the symbolic-interactionist concepts in some of the early research in the field. It was not until 1961, however, that systematic statements of symbolic-interactionist theory applied to the problems of social gerontology appeared. There were two such papers written independently (Cavan, 1962; Rose, 1961).

Much of the research in social gerontology today is explicitly or implicitly guided by interactionist theory, broadly conceived. The utility of this theory is thus constantly being tested in empirical research work. Research in social gerontology not guided by interactionist theory has tended to be descriptive or to interpret the facts of aging in an historical-cultural context.

There has been one major exception which has received considerable attention in recent years. This is the work of Cumming and her collaborators (Cumming, Dean, Newell, and McCaffrey, 1960; Cumming and Henry, 1961). The book, *Growing Old* (Cumming and Henry, 1961), is a major study in the framework of functionalist theory, a theory which has guided much empirical research in anthropology but very little in sociology; hence Cumming's work is a landmark in sociological functionalism. It is the purpose of the present essay to evaluate the Cumming and Henry book as a statement of theory and as a test of a specific theory. We are not here concerned with the research method or its manner of utilization in that book. But we shall be concerned with theoretical essays written by Cumming (1963), Henry (1963), and Parsons (1963) two years after the publication of *Growing Old*.

There has been such widespread misinterpretation of the theory of disengagement, as expressed in the Cumming and Henry book, that it is essential to state what it is before it be evaluated. It is *not* an hypothesis which states that, as people get older, they are gradually separated from their associations and their social functions. Such a hypothesis had been stated many times before Cumming and Henry and was generally assumed to be a fact. After all, this is what was meant by Burgess (1950) in his discussion of the "roleless role." Nor does the theory of disengagement state that, as

Original publication: Rose, Arnold M., "A Current Theoretical Issue in Social Gerontology," *The Gerontologist* 4(1964), pp. 46–50.

people become physically feebler or chronically ill, they are thereby forced to abandon their associations and social functions. This is a matter of logic and also long been assumed to be a fact.

Cumming and Henry (1961) wisely excluded from their sample any person who was in poor physical or mental health and explicitly denied that their conception of disengagement rests on ill health. Finally, the theory of disengagement does *not* say that because older people tend to have a reduced income in our society, they can no longer afford to participate in many things. That also would be a matter of logic and has long been known to be a fact. Cumming and Henry wisely excluded from their sample anyone who did not have the minimum of money needed for independence. To test *their* hypothesis, as distinguished from the popular misinterpretations of their hypothesis, Cumming and Henry must have made these exclusions.

The Cumming and Henry theory of disengagement is that the society and the individual prepare *in advance* for the ultimate "disengagement" of incurable, incapacitating disease and death by an *inevitable, gradual and mutually satisfying process of disengagement from society*. Each of these terms must be understood before the theory can be understood. Disengagement is inevitable, because death is inevitable, and according to a basic principle of functionalism, society and the individual always accommodate themselves to the solid facts of existence. Society and the individual always seek to maintain themselves in equilibrium and avoid disruption according to the functionalist. Since death must soon come to an older person, both society and the older person himself prepare for it sociologically and psychologically, so that when it comes the individual has divested himself of life's functions and associations and is ready for it. In this way, the death of an older person is not disruptive to the equilibrium of a society. The death of a young person, by accident or acute disease, *is* disruptive, and the society has a harder time accommodating to it.

Cumming and Henry compare the disengagement of an older person to the gradual and inevitable withering of a leaf or a fruit long before frost totally kills it. This total process must be gradual, in the sense that it involves a period of preparation for death, although disengagement from some *specific* association or function may come suddenly. It is mutually satisfying; society is pleased when the death of one of its members does not disrupt its ongoing functions (such as child-bearing, carrying on economic production, or the work of one of its voluntary associations). And the individual can face death with relative equanimity because he no longer has any social ties; he has said all his "goodbyes" and has nothing more to do, so he might as well "leave."

Because death is a universal fact, the social and psychological disengagement of the elderly must be a universal fact, according to the theory. It is thus not bound to any one culture, even though Cumming and Henry take all of their cases from Kansas City, Missouri. Of course, there are different degrees and speeds of disengagement among different societies, and within any one society some people resist disengagement while others start on its course even before they become elderly. Cumming and Henry say that the values in American culture of competitive achievement and of future orientation make this society especially negative toward aging and hence encourage disengagement. But the process itself must be understood to be inevitable and universal, according to the theory, and not limited to any one group in a society or any one society.

In her 1963 essay, Cumming expressed the need to recognize some of the complexities of aging as modifiers of the theory, but adhered to the "main outlines" of the earlier theory. She pointed out that the original study "did not take into account such non-modal cases as widowhood before the marriage of the last child or of work protracted past the modal age of retirement" (p. 378). She recognized that there are individual differences in disengagement, and even "typologies of withdrawal and retreat" based on deeply-rooted differences in character and in biological temperament. She went so far as to recognize that as lively oldsters were disengaged from their more important social roles, they might temporarily *increase* their recreational activities. She pointed out several other causes of disengagement besides the anticipation of death, such as rapid social change making obsolete some of the roles of older people, the gulf between generations in a future-oriented society, and the drastic shift in roles for men when they retire. While these latter points permit the distinctive characteristics of American society to modify the universal character of the theory, Cumming essentially has adhered quite closely to the basic outlines of the functionalist theory of disengagement.

Parsons (1963), the outstanding contemporary exponent of functional theory in sociology, accepted the Cumming theory of disengagement, while adding to it the idea that old age is the consummatory phase of life, a "period of 'harvest', when the fruits of his (the older person's) previous instrumental commitments are primarily gathered in."

Henry, however, in his 1963 discussion, deviated considerably from the theory. He started from the commonly observed *fact* of disengagement, rather than from the theoretical functional necessity of disengagement. In fact, he avoided functional theory altogether. His interest was primarily in the psychological rather than the sociological characteristics of disengagement, stating that, "engagement and disengagement become a general form of personality dynamic, and the disengagement of the aged, a special case" (p. 14). Further, he retreated from the notion that disengagement is inevitable (although he used the word "intrinsic") and he allocated a major role to the "culture's definition of the good and the bad." He agreed with certain critics of the theory of disengagement that "several styles of aging are possible" (p. 15). In general, one might say that Henry in 1963 was closer to certain critics of the theory of disengagement than he was to Cumming.

There have been three lines of criticism of the Cumming-Henry book. One questions the process of disengagement and holds that not only is it not inevitable but that non-engagement in the later years is simply a continuation of a *life-long* social psychological characteristic of *some* people. One finds this idea even in Henry's 1963 paper, and it has received empirical foundation in the researches of Reichard, Livson, and Petersen (1962), of Williams and Wirths (1963), and of Videbeck and Knox (1965). The latter authors, for example, show that 90 percent of those non-participant after 65 years of age were also non-participant 5 years earlier, while 90 percent of those participant after 65 were also participant 5 years earlier. Further, at each earlier period of life (since their research was not limited to the elderly but traced patterns of participation for a 5-year period among samples of people at all age levels), there is a comparably high correlation between degree of participation at the beginning and end of each 5-year period. For these authors, there is a type of person who throughout his life had limited or few social involvements, and they do not think of disengagement as a process characteristic of old age.

A second line of criticism of the Cumming-Henry book challenges their value judgment that disengagement is desirable for older people. Havighurst, Neugarten, and Tobin (1963) have stated this criticism most clearly and have provided empirical evidence that the engaged elderly, rather than the disengaged, are the ones who generally, although not always, are happiest and have the greatest expressed life satisfaction.

The third line of criticism of the Cumming-Henry book analyzes disengagement in a context of the social structure and social trends and finds the theory a poor interpretation of the facts. This point of view in which I am mainly interested and to which I shall devote the remainder of this essay, acknowledges that a large proportion of the older people in the United States tend to lose many of their adult roles. But it considers this fact to be a function of American culture in this phase of its organization, not a universal for all time. American culture accords a low status to the elderly; we have a youth-centered society. Many other societies accord special prestige and power to the elderly, do not disengage them from adult roles, or create new age-graded roles of importance for them. The situation of the elderly in the United States has been especially unfavorable in the last 50 years, with the decline of the self-employed occupations and the rise of compulsory retirement. These trends have meant that the major social role for men in the society is not open to most elderly persons. Forced disengagement in the occupational role has tended to cause disengagement in auxiliary roles, for example, in the occupational associations (trade union, businessmen's association, professional organization) and the "service clubs" which have a membership based on economic activity. Thus cultural values and economic structure have combined to create a condition in which a large proportion of the elderly people are non-participant.

Those men who remain economically active past 65 years do not disengage, even in the unfavorable cultural value system of the United States. The politician, the employer, the self-employed professional, do not disengage until they become physically or mentally feeble. In fact, they often take on additional membership and leadership roles after they pass 65 years.

The great bulk of the American people, however, are required to retire from remunerative occupations at about 65 years of age, and this situation is not likely to change. There are certain new trends, however, which are counteracting the forces which make for disengagement of the elderly. Most of these trends are not "inevitable," in the functionalist's sense; some are a product of deliberate organizational effort; others emanate from conditions that have nothing to do with the elderly but their influence will touch the elderly. We have arrived at the following list of such trends by examining the major changes now occurring in American society and forecasting their effects on the aging.

1   Modern medical science and health are allowing an ever-increasing proportion of those reaching 65 to remain in good health and physical vigor. It is doubtful that vigorous people will be as content to disengage as are those of the present generation of the elderly who have been weakened by earlier disease and by overly strenuous work. Loss of vigor may well be a factor in preventing many old people today from participating and, if that should be overcome, at least the motivation to disengage may diminish.

2   Social security legislation and private pension plans and annuities are slowly increasing the economic security of the retired. If older people have more money to spare from the bare necessities of life, which is true of only a small minority today, they may, like that well-to-do minority today, be more able and willing to continue their costlier participations.

3   I have elsewhere shown how older people in the United States are beginning to form a social movement to raise their status and privileges and that this movement is likely to gain an increasing number of adherents (Rose, 1962, 1965). Such a trend will influence the participation of the elderly in several ways: (a) It will provide a new engagement especially for older people; (b) It will inform the younger generations of the plight of the elderly, and may possibly make society less insistent that older people disengage (already we see, for example, a tendency of younger people to volunteer to transport older neighbors to meetings, church services, polling places, etc.); (c) It may raise the prestige and dignity of age, that is, reversing the negative cultural value mentioned earlier, and such a change would remove the major cause of present disengagement. If the elderly had high prestige, society would not force them to disengage, and the elderly themselves, like the few prestigious elderly today, would be less likely to disengage.

4   The trend toward earlier retirement from chief life role (occupation for men and child-rearing for women), while now a factor causing disengagement, may eventually become an influence for reengagement. Studies of the family life cycle (Glick, 1955) show that the average young woman today is having her *last* child at the age of 26, which means that her last child is ceasing to be dependent on her at the age of 40 to 45. Most women at this young age are just not going to be willing to disengage, even though they have lost their chief life role, and are going to have strong motivations to reengage. The same will be true of men if the age of retirement creeps downward, as some economists tell us it will, significantly below 65 years. The new reengagements have not yet emerged clearly, although for many middle-class women they seem to include voluntary associations and gainful employment. But it does seem probable that many of the new reengagements will be able to continue past the age of 65 years and not necessitate a second disengagement as old age is reached.

5   The types of engagements for which older people would be eligible have increased in number and openness. There are ever-new types of voluntary activities available in American society. There are many hobbies that have recently taken on an occupational aspect – such as stamp trading (Christ, 1965) – which provides satisfying and even prestigious roles for elderly men. There has also been an expansion in the cultural definition of the male role, so that men may today participate in artistic activities and hobbies that formerly were defined as feminine (including knitting, weaving, painting, etc.). Further, there has been a cultural redefinition of leisure-time activities as good in themselves, so that retired men do not necessarily feel a loss of status simply because they are no longer engaged in remunerative employment.

The disengagement theorists are completely oblivious to such trends and assume that a given cultural-social system, that of the United States today, is "inevitable" and more or less universal in the position it accords the elderly. Their ethnocentrism is pointed up more sharply, by evidence quite different from our own, by Talmon (1963). Talmon shows how, in the different, cultural system of the Israeli Kibbutz, there is little disengagement of the elderly but rather "a restructuring of roles and relationships and a shift in their relative importance rather than mere decline" (p. 10).

I believe it is no accident that the disengagement theorists, although they are sophisticated sociologists and may be skilled researchers, are ethnocentric and ignore major social trends. I believe that it is due to the general functionalist theory which underlies Cumming's work. With this approach, one largely ignores history, with its pointing up of trends from past to present and from present to future, and even minimizes cross-cultural variations by emphasizing the universal "functional prerequisites of culture" which Cumming extends to include the necessity of society to pre-adjust to death. The approach of the functionalist is to start with a certain observation about social life, in this case disengagement, exaggerate it so it seems to be characteristic of *all* persons in the category observed and then seek to demonstrate why it inevitably "must be" and cannot be changed.[1] The functionalists' assumption that "whatever is, must be" merely ruins an initially valid observation by exaggerating it and denying any possibility of countertrends by declaring its inevitability.

Two approaches have dominated research in social gerontology. One seeks to interpret the facts of aging in a historical-cultural context; the basic fact and factual trends of American society are considered to be the matrix for the social processes of aging. The second theoretical orientation is the interactionist, which seeks to interpret the facts of aging in terms of the interactions among the aging themselves and between the aging and others in the society. Cultural values and meanings are the most important elements in these interactions, and these are never assumed to be universal or unchanging. The neat, integrated "systems" of the functionalists may appeal to the esthetic sense of readers, but it seems to us that the facts of social life, in this case of the aging, are too complicated and varied to be encompassed in any notion of equilibrium. Cultural history and human interactions, organizing concepts which have thus far dominated research in gerontology, are better guideposts.

## Note

1   A comparable sequence can be found in Parsons' (1942) taking up the observation that the nuclear family has tended to replace the extended family in American society. This observation had been made earlier by Simmel and Park, but Parsons exaggerated it, ignored countertrends, and sought to show why the trend was inevitable. Since then, a spate of research articles have demonstrated factually that the trend never existed or has been reversed.

## References

Burgess, Ernest W. 1950. "Personal and Social Adjustment in Old Age." In *The Aged and Society*, edited by M. Derber. Champaign, Ill.: Industrial Relation Research Association.

Cavan, Ruth S. 1992. "Self and Role in Adjustment During Old Age." In *Human Behavior and Social Processes*, edited by Arnold M. Rose. Boston: Houghton Mifflin.

Christ, E. 1965. "The 'Retired' Stamp Collector." Pp. 93–112 in *Older People and Their Social World*, edited by Arnold M. Rose and Warren A. Peterson. Philadelphia: F. A. Davis.

Cumming, Elaine. 1963. "Further Thoughts on the Theory of Disengagement," *International Social Science Journal* 15: 377–93.

Cumming, Elaine, Lois R. Dean, David S. Newell, and Isabel McCaffrey. 1960. "Disengagement: A Tentative Theory of Aging," *Sociometry* 23: 23–35.

Cumming, Elaine and William H. Henry. 1961. *Growing Older: The Process of Disengagement*. New York: Basic.

Glick, Paul C. 1955. "Life Cycle of the Family," *Marriage and Family Relations* 17: 3–9.

Havighurst, Robert J., Bernice L. Neugarten, and Sheldon A. Tobin. 1963. "Disengagement and Patterns of Aging." Pp. 161–72 in *Middle Age and Aging*, edited by Bernice L. Neugarten. Chicago: University of Chicago Press.

Henry, William E. 1963. "The Theory of Intrinsic Disengagement." Paper presented at the International Gerontological Research Seminar, Markaryd, Sweden.

Parsons, Talcott. 1942. "Age and Sex in the Social Structure of the United States," *American Sociological Review* 7: 604–16.

Parsons, Talcott. 1963. "Old Age as a Consummatory Phase," *The Gerontologist* 3: 35–43.

Reichard, Suzanne, Florine Livson, and Paul G. Petersen. 1962. *Aging and Personality*. New York: Wiley.

Rose, Arnold M. 1961. "The Mental Health of Normal Older Persons," *Geriatrics* 16: 459–64.

Rose, Arnold M. 1962. "The Subculture of the Aging." Pp. 3–18 in *Older People and Their Social World*, edited by Arnold M. Rose and Warren A. Peterson. Philadelphia: F. A. Davis.

Rose, Arnold M. 1965. "Group Consciousness Among the Aged." Pp. 19–36 in *Older People and Their Social World*, edited by Arnold M. Rose and Warren A. Peterson. Philadelphia: F. A. Davis.

Talmon, Yonina. 1963. "Dimensions of Disengagement: Aging in Collective Settlements." Paper presented at the International Gerontological Research Seminar, Markaryd, Sweden.

Videbeck, R. and Alan B. Knox. 1965. "Alternative Participatory Responses to Aging." In *Older People and Their Social World*, edited by Arnold M. Rose and Warren A. Peterson. Philadelphia: F. A. Davis.

Williams, Richard H. and Claudine Wirths. 1963. "Styles of Life and Successful Aging." Paper presented at the International Gerontological Research Seminar, Markaryd, Sweden.

# 5 A Continuity Theory of Normal Aging

*Robert C. Atchley*

Continuity is an illusive concept. On the one hand, to exhibit continuity can mean to remain the same, to be uniform, homogeneous, unchanging, even humdrum. This static view of continuity is not very applicable to human aging. On the other hand, a dynamic view of continuity starts with the idea of a basic structure which persists over time, but it allows for a variety of changes to occur within the context provided by the basic structure. The basic structure is coherent: It has an orderly or logical relation of parts that is recognizably unique and that allows us to differentiate that structure from others. With the introduction of the concept of time, ideas such as direction, sequence, character development, and story line enter into the concept of continuity as it is applied to the evolution of a human being. In this paper, a dynamic concept of continuity is developed and applied to the issue of adaptation to normal aging.

A central premise of Continuity Theory is that, in making adaptive choices, middle-aged and older adults attempt to preserve and maintain existing internal and external structures and that they prefer to accomplish this objective by using continuity (i.e., applying familiar strategies in familiar arenas of life). In middle and later life, adults are drawn by the weight of past experience to use continuity as a primary adaptive strategy for dealing with changes associated with normal aging. To the extent that change builds upon, and has links to, the person's past, change is a part of continuity. As a result of both their own perceptions and pressures from the social environment, individuals who are adapting to normal aging are both predisposed and motivated toward inner psychological continuity as well as outward continuity of social behavior and circumstances. Continuity Theory views both internal and external continuity as robust adaptive strategies that are supported by both individual preference and social sanctions. Continuity Theory consists of general adaptive principles that people who are normally aging could be expected to follow, explanations of how these principles work, and a specification of general areas of life in which these principles could be expected to apply. Accordingly, Continuity Theory has enormous potential as a general theory of adaptation to individual aging (Blalock, 1982; Hage, 1972; Kaplan, 1964).

Researchers have shown that both internal and external continuity are very common aspects of aging (Atchley, 1987). Activity Theory (Havighurst et al., 1963; Havighurst, 1963; Rosow, 1963) was an early attempt to account for these findings. Like many social theories of its time, Activity Theory was a homeostatic or equilibrium model. It assumed that when change occurred, the typical response was to re-

Original publication: Atchley, Robert C., "A Continuity Theory of Normal Aging," *The Gerontologist* 29 (1989), pp. 183–90.

store the previous equilibrium. But aging produces changes that cannot be completely offset, so there is no going back to the prior state. Over the years, various bits and pieces of an alternative perspective called Continuity Theory have appeared (Atchley, 1971, 1987; Fox, 1981–2; Morgan, 1976; Rosow, 1963). Continuity Theory assumes evolution, not homeostasis, and this assumption allows change to be integrated into one's prior history without necessarily causing upheaval or disequilibrium. An evolutionary theory also allows the individual to have goals for developmental direction. Continuity Theory thus offers a parsimonious explanation for and description of the ways adults employ concepts of their past to conceive of their future and structure their choices in response to the changes brought about by normal aging.

The term *normal aging* refers to usual, commonly encountered patterns of human aging. Because there is a sociocultural overlay that interacts with physical and mental aging, normal aging can be expected to differ from culture to culture. Further, normal aging can be distinguished from pathological aging by a lack of physical or mental disease. In addition, there are individuals whose aging is anomalous in that it departs from the normal but is not pathological. For example, moving to a retirement community in later life is not typical, but it is not pathological, either.

A valid concept of normal aging must portray a general picture of aging that represents accurately the experience of aging for a large majority of people within a specific culture. For example, normal aging in the United States in the late 1980s implies no disabling chronic or acute disease. Normally aging people are independent adults with persistent self-concepts and identities. They can successfully meet their needs for income, housing, health care, nutrition, clothing, transportation, and recreation. They lead active, satisfying, and purposeful lives that involve adequate networks of long-standing social relationships. Continuity Theory contends that these positive outcomes of normal aging occur because large numbers of aging people use continuity strategies to adapt to changes associated with normal aging.

Aging people who cannot meet their own needs because they are disabled or poor are experiencing pathological aging, and external continuity is a less practical adaptive strategy for them. For this reason, Continuity Theory is not very helpful in understanding the external reality of pathological aging. Nonetheless, even in people who experience dramatic change in external circumstances, internal continuity may still be present (Lieberman and Tobin, 1983).

The goal of Continuity Theory is to abstract the essence of what continuity means and through concepts and relationships to reconstruct in summary form the underlying logic of continuity as an adaptive strategy. Continuity Theory is effective if it leads to better understanding of current research findings, leads to better research, and provides needed structure to thinking about adaptation to normal aging.

In this paper, a framework for Continuity Theory is presented, including definitions, classifications, relationships, and processes. To begin what is hoped will be a substantial new development in social gerontology, a large number of ideas have been compressed into a single article. This means that most readers will probably find something unsatisfying about the treatment. The goal is to focus debate, and one and all are invited to propose changes to this initial formulation.

## Defining Continuity

Fox (1981–2) criticized Continuity Theory on two grounds. First, she said, because continuity means sameness, and change is ever-present with aging, how could continuity be very important in explaining aging? Second, to find continuity, the study must be approached from a level of abstraction that she saw as defeating the operational definition necessary for adequate research and theory testing.

These criticisms are based on a static view of continuity. But what if specific changes only have significance in reference to a general construct that involves continuity over time? Indeed, the very concept of change implies that there is some baseline of comparison. And what if, to understand motives, attention must be concentrated exactly on relatively abstract perceptions of continuity and change rather than the more specific? Fox was correct in her assertion about the pervasiveness of change but wrong in her assertion about the unimportance of continuity because she looked at continuity at the wrong level of abstraction. She looked for continuity in objective specifics, not in the person's abstract perceptions.

Perhaps Fox's confusion about the prevalence of continuity came from the two meanings of continuity referred to earlier. If continuity is used to mean sameness, homogeneity, or lack of change, then there can be no doubt that continuity and aging are contradictory. But if continuity is used to mean coherence or consistency of patterns over time, then there is a great deal of continuity across adult life stages.

Continuity is not the opposite of change. Rather, change and evolution are usually perceived against a backdrop of considerable connection to the individual's past. Even substantial changes can occur in life without causing serious disruption in the stable directional context within which life's various episodes are played. Using a dramaturgical analogy, even if for most people there is an ebb and flow to the drama of everyday life, there is also substantial continuity of both character and plot. This sense of continuity is tied to the individual's perceived past. Continuity is thus an abstract cognitive construct into which dozens of specific changes easily could be incorporated.

Because of continuity, human development in later life is subtle. As Gutmann (1987) said, "Later-life development does not show itself so vividly, as in earlier adulthood – instead, it may cause no more than the quiet ripening of selected mental and spiritual capacities, or a gradual shift in appetites, interests, and occupations."

## Types of Continuity

Continuity is first and foremost a subjective perception that changes are linked to and fit with individual personal history (Cohler, 1982). Continuity can be either internal or external. Internal continuity is defined by the individual in relation to a remembered inner structure, such as the persistence of a psychic structure of ideas, temperament, affect, experiences, preferences, dispositions, and skills. Internal continuity requires memory. What is disconcerting to us about people with amnesia or Alzheimer's Disease is precisely their inability to use memory to present continuity of identity and self. They do not know who their character was or is, how it fits with other characters in the everyday drama, or even what the drama is about. Obviously, then, lack of internal continuity can be not only a source of distress to the individual, who has no orientation that can be used to get a sense of direction, make decisions, or take action, but also to those who are accustomed to interacting with him or her and expect a degree of predictability. Internal continuity is a healthy capacity to see inner change as connected to the individual's past and to see the individual's past as sustaining and supporting and justifying the new self (Lieberman and Tobin, 1983).

External continuity is defined in terms of a remembered structure of physical and social environments, role relationships, and activities. Perceptions of external continuity result from being and doing in familiar environments, practicing familiar skills, and interacting with familiar people. Individuals have everyday locations in social and physical space and behave in those locations in ways that are uniquely typical of them as individuals (Gutmann, 1987). External continuity is thus the persistence of a structure of relationships and overt behaviors. These patterns can be seen by others, but the existence of continuity in them can be validated only by making reference to the person's own internal set of ideas about what is typical for her or him. Using a dramaturgical analogy again, everyday life for most older people is like long-running improvisational theater in which the settings, characters, and actions are familiar and in which the changes are mostly in the form of new episodes rather than entirely new plays.

Whether internal or external, the extent of continuity is determined by a here-and-now assessment made by the individual based on her or his remembered past; therefore, continuity's existence and effects can only be studied by retrospection. The standards used to assess continuity reside in the personal constructs (Kelley, 1955) used by the individual to organize his or her perceptions. People construe the world around them by means of a personal repertory of concepts and it is this personal repertory, which may include social constructions of reality (Berger and Luckmann, 1966), that guides decision-making and evaluation. These personal constructs are organized, often non-consciously, into a theory of how the present is linked with both the past and the anticipated future.

The degree of continuity attributed by an individual to her or his life can be classified into three general categories: too little continuity, optimum continuity, and too much continuity. Too little continuity means that life seems too unpredictable to the individual. If lack of continuity comes to be defined by the individual as severe, then it can also be called discontinuity. Optimum continuity means that the individual sees the pace and degree of change to be in line with personal preferences and social demands and well within her or his coping capacity. Too much continuity means that the individual feels uncomfortably in a rut; there is not enough change to enrich life. Note that objective definitions cannot be used to classify people with regard to the degree of continuity. Instead, individuals must classify themselves based on their own interpretations of their own standards. Although there are regularities or normative standards within categories of people with regard to perceptions of continuity, the assessment itself must still be made by the individual.

## Pressures and Attractions Toward Continuity

Aging individuals are predisposed and motivated toward both internal and external continuity by identifiable pressures and attractions.

### Internal continuity

Individuals have strong motives for wanting to preserve internal continuity. To begin with, individuals perceive that internal continuity acts as a foundation for effective day-to-day decision making because internal continuity is an important part of individual mastery and competence. For example, continuity of cognitive knowledge is a major element of the individual's capacity to interpret and anticipate events. Without persistent cognitive knowledge, there is no predictability to the world. Without predictability, mastery (or even competence) is not possible.

Second, internal continuity is essential to a sense of ego integrity. Erikson et al. (1986) emphasized the importance of a sense of personal history and an acceptance of that history to a sense of ego integrity. Consistency and linkage amid change over time are necessary conditions for concluding that one's life has integrity. A perception of long-standing internal continuity, as opposed to discontinuity, increases the likelihood that the individual will also perceive his or her life as having integrity.

Third, internal continuity also helps meet the need for self-esteem. The continuity principle within the self contains the ideas used as the basis of self-esteem. Paraphrasing William James (1890), self-esteem is a function of one's perceived level of success in relation to one's ideal expectations of self. From this it follows that self-esteem can be raised either by increasing success or reducing expectations. For this formulation to apply over time, there must be a concept of continuity operating in the definition of both success and expectations. It then follows that it is impossible to have durable self-esteem without reference to some notion of continuity.

Fourth, people can also be motivated toward internal continuity as an effective means of meeting important needs. For example, most of us have ideas that quite effectively lead us to the food, housing, income, transportation, and clothing needed. Internal continuity also promotes easy maintenance of social interaction and social support. The predictability of an individual's identity, self, and temperament is seen as an important part of that individual's personal attractiveness because it makes him or her comfortable and predictable to be around. For example, predictable traits could be a good sense of humor and skill in articulating it or perhaps the capacity to sit with others and enjoy silence. Notice what is being talked about here are predictable general intellectual and affective qualities, not their specific manifestations.

### External continuity

Various pressures and attractions move people toward external continuity as well. First, as noted earlier, people are expected by others to present themselves in a way that is obviously tied to and connected with their past role performances. Older adults who have major social responsibilities such as jobs and childrearing are generally exposed to more pressures from others to show continuity compared to those who have retired or who are in the empty nest period of the family life cycle.

Second, external continuity of relationships is motivated by desire for predictable social support. Kahn and Antonucci (1981) drew attention to the "convoy" of social support, the inner circle of close family and friends who travel with us across our lifetime. The convoy of social support affirms individual identity, provides insurance against a potential need for instrumental dependency, and allows a sense of belonging (Atchley, 1987).

Third, external continuity increases the possibility that feedback received from others about the self-concept can be accurately anticipated. This anticipation increases the odds that the individual can concentrate his or her interactions among those who affirm his or her own view of self.

Fourth, external continuity is seen as an important means of coping with physical and mental changes that may accompany aging. For example, practice has been shown to offset negative effects of aging on various cognitive capacities (Botwinick, 1984; Salthouse, 1982).

Fifth, external continuity reduces the ambiguity of personal goals that can come with changes such as widowhood, retirement or the empty nest. The notion of continuity is an efficient way to narrow the field from which new goals are sought. For example, the most common pattern of adjustment to retirement is to maintain the same general set of personal goals (Atchley, 1982a, 1982b).

Thus, continuity is a preferred strategy for dealing with aging for a wide variety of reasons. Both internal and external continuity help individuals focus on and maintain their strengths and minimize the effects of deficits as normal aging occurs.

## Dynamics of Internal Continuity

As noted earlier, internal continuity involves the persistence of an inner structure. *Self* and *identity* are terms that refer to interrelated intrapsychic structures. *Self* refers to what we think and feel when we focus attention on our specific selves. The self concept is what we think we are like: our appearance, abilities, preferences, emotionality, personal goals, level of performance, attitudes, roles, and so on; the ideal self is what we think we ought to be like; self-evaluation is a moral assessment that depends on how well we see ourselves as having lived up to our ideal; and self-esteem is how much we like or dislike what we see. Self-esteem is a sum of the relative weights given to both valued and disvalued aspects of self-concept (Bengtson et al., 1985). The self-concept and ideal self are often tied to the social positions we occupy, the roles we play, and the norms associated with our social characteristics such as age, gender, race, ethnicity, social class, and so on.

*Identity* refers to those aspects of personality and self that the individual sees as remaining with him or her regardless of the social situation (Whitbourne, 1986). Some aspects of self are activated only under certain social circumstances, such as ambition and assertiveness at work, but those aspects that form identity tend to be with us across a variety of social situations. Identity also serves as the basis for incorporating new information about the self. Subjectively important changes occur mainly within identity. Identity also serves as the basis for the perception of both continuity and integrity. Thus, compared to the self, identity probably has a closer tie to the individual's concept of internal continuity.

Identity is not an either/or, black/white construct. Instead it is a holistic concept that tolerates contradictions. The dimensions of identity can be likened to a dozen teeter-totters in a line. The weight of perception usually causes most of the teeter-totters to come down on the positive side (Greenwald, 1980), but this does not make the negative perceptions disappear. We simply gloss over them in developing an abstract view of identity.

From middle age on, the evidence, although inconsistent, points clearest to a large amount of continuity in the global aspects of self and identity (Bengtson et al., 1985; Kaufman, 1987; Lieberman and Tobin, 1983; Maas and Kuypers, 1974; McCrae and Costa, 1982; Neugarten, 1964, 1977; Schaie and Parham, 1976). At the same time, there is substantial support that aging adults perceive a great deal of change in the details subsumed under these global conceptions (Bengtson et al., 1985; Kaufman, 1987; Lieberman and Tobin, 1983). The important point is that the global assessments and attributions the individual makes about himself or herself persist despite substantial changes in the details of everyday life. Once formed, identity tends to be resilient, and the components of identity can apparently contain a multitude of conflicting details without causing the individual to doubt the validity of the global assessment (Kaufman, 1987; Lieberman and Tobin, 1983). Let us now look at some of the processes that create and preserve perceptions of internal continuity.

Despite constant changes within the individual and the world around him or her, continuity of self and identity is not difficult to achieve. Over adulthood, people accumulate a vast storehouse of data about themselves. Early on they mainly use feedback from significant others to form their theory of self (Kelley, 1955). Such theories allow people to anticipate and predict, and personal experiences allow developing adults to refine their theory of self. Gradually, by confronting both successes and failures and incorporating them into their theory of self, developing adults come to more readily accept themselves as they are, not as they might like to be. This self-acceptance supports inner continuity. As the amount of data and number of observations increases, personal constructs about the self crystallize into global generalizations that form the core of identity (Neugarten, 1964, 1977; Whitbourne, 1986). Once this crystallization occurs, identity is relatively impervious to contrary feedback from others, especially strangers.

Perceptions of continuity are created in the very process of day-to-day identity evolution. Kaufman (1987) observed that older people had transformed certain experiences into themes such as "People can do anything if they only work hard enough," or "My family is my life." Themes are reformulated experiences that serve as building blocks for identity. Current identity is created from the present-time significance of selected symbols and events from the individual's past. People "select, define, classify, and organize experience in order to express the reality of their lives and permeate that reality with meaning" (Kaufman, 1987). Adults use these themes to justify their lives, to actively use the continuity contained within their constructed life history to infuse that history with inevitability, naturalness, and rightness (Erikson, 1963). Kaufman (1987) found that older people reinterpreted their current experiences "so that old values could take on new meanings appropriate to present circumstances." Lieberman and Tobin (1983) found similar processes at work among the participants in their study of institutionalization. Reinterpretation is an important adaptive process through which individuals create coherent pictures of the past and link the past to a purposeful, integrated present. Identity evolution is thus an active, cumulative, and lifelong process of restructuring ideas to fit current realities.

People tend to manage feedback actively, to support their identity by forming social support networks and maintaining them over extended periods of time. They also tend to interact mainly with people who support their personal constructs of self and avoid, or discount feedback from, people who do not provide such support.

The mentally healthy adult thus has a solid identity that persists over time. This continuity does not refer to obsessive clinging to the past. Instead, to go back again to the dramaturgical analogy, adult identity is like a stage play in which old sets are embellished and sometimes remodeled and new sets sometimes created to add new scenes to familiar acts. Familiar characters get new twists, some characters die or leave, and new characters get added although they are often superficial. However, the self, the perceiver, has absolutely no doubts about who is playing the title role.

Inner continuity occurs primarily in the relatively abstract self-attributions that form the core of identity. This continuity is not sameness, but rather is characterized by very gradual evolution in which new directions are closely linked to and elaborate upon already existing identity. Change occurs constantly, but in each of the components of identity new information usually can be absorbed relatively easily. As a result, life events such as retirement, the empty nest, and even widowhood often have had less impact on inner continuity than role theorists expected (Atchley, 1971; 1982b).

Morgan (1976) linked identity crises to severe discontinuities that required reorganization of identity and projected biography. But because discontinuity is defined in relation to personal constructs, various types of changes in objective circumstances such as widowhood or retirement cannot be assumed to cause identity crises automatically. We first must know how a specific change relates to a specific identity, then we might be able to predict effects.

Although internal continuity is generally a prerequisite for mental health, there are circumstances in which intrapsychic continuity can be maladaptive. It is important that current experiences be symbolically malleable so as to support continuity of identity, but it is also important not to deny genuine changes that need to be incorporated and reintegrated into a somewhat new identity. To refuse to acknowledge a real identity crisis is maladaptive because it hampers capacity to anticipate the future accurately (Lieberman and Tobin, 1983). If some important aspect of identity has fundamentally changed, then old ideas about that aspect of self will no longer lead to accurate expectations. Of course, it is also important to distinguish genuine from apparent or expected identity crises. Just because logic suggests that there ought to be an identity crisis connected with retirement, it does not follow that there will usually be one. Indeed, researchers have indicated that identity crises connected with retirement are relatively rare (Atchley, 1982a).

To maintain a perception of internal continuity, inconsistent details must be glossed over, as in the teeter-totter example given earlier. In addition, members of the support network must gloss over some amount of change in order to agree with the assertion that continuity of identity and self exists. If the amount of required glossing exceeds the willingness or capacity of others, then pressing others to support one's identity continuity can be maladaptive. When the convoy of social support is reluctant to affirm continuity, the individual has three choices: modify identity to take change into account, put up with negative feedback from the convoy of social support, or become socially isolated.

Not everyone in adulthood is in the happy position of having a positive identity to affirm. Sometimes expectations for one's own performance are impossibly high, which generally leads to low self-esteem. In such cases, inner continuity of unrealistic expectations is maladaptive.

Although the cards are very much stacked in the direction of internal continuity, people nevertheless do have times when no amount of mental redefinition will suffice to prevent the perception that discontinuity exists. However, Lieberman and Tobin (1983) reported that even institutionalization produced no discernible effect on older adults' capacity to maintain their perception of self-continuity. Thus, it would be a mistake to overestimate the internal effects of external change.

Discontinuity involves change seen by the individual as sharply diminishing her or his capacity for coherence in some aspect of his or her identity. Discontinuity thus alters identity, but both discontinuity and its impact on the individual cannot be known in the abstract. Instead, they must be assessed in relation to a particular identity. Lieberman and Tobin (1983) suggested that older people's self-continuity is not very vulnerable to changes in external environments.

To the extent that there are disvalued aspects of identity, there may be motivation to produce discontinuity in selected dimensions of identity. Psychotherapy is often concerned with helping an individual let go of disvalued patterns. Many self-help books are about how to change identity constructively. Continuity Theory would lead us to expect that neither psychotherapy nor self-help books would sell well among older people, and this is indeed the case.

Internal discontinuity, if severe enough, can destroy mental health. For example, lacking a perception of continuity can mean that the individual's life seems chaotic and unpredictable. Severe discontinuity means that the person has no standard with which to assess her or his life's integrity. The result can be severe anxiety and depression, a lack of hope born of the inability to project one's future with any confidence. This often happens to people with dementia, AIDS or other diseases with serious but uncertain outcomes.

## Dynamics of External Continuity

In the everyday lives of adults in their fifties, sixties, and seventies there is a great deal of continuity over time in skills, activities, environments, roles, and relationships. This has been found in a large number of research studies (Atchley, 1971, 1976, 1982a; Atchley and Miller, 1982–3, 1983; Bengtson and Black, 1973; Carp, 1978–9; Gordon et al., 1976; Lawton, 1983; Morgan, 1984; Oliver, 1971; Parnes and Less, 1983; Salthouse, 1984; Shanas, 1977; Streib and Schneider, 1971; Troll and Smith, 1976). We find older people using familiar skills to do familiar things in familiar places in the company of familiar people. Again, this continuity is not a boring sameness for most but rather a comforting routine and familiar sense of direction. No doubt part of the impetus for external continuity is related to restricted opportunity structures resulting from ageism and societal disengagement, but probably a majority of it results from the satisfactions people get from exercising mastery and the value of experience and practice in preventing and minimizing the deleterious effects of physical and psychological aging.

Through experience as adults, most people can separate the things they attempt to do into those they can do well and those they cannot. As changes such as the empty nest and retirement free people from external role demands, they are freer to concentrate their activities in areas they define as their strengths and to avoid areas they define as weaknesses. Continuity of activities, skills, and environments is a logical result of leading to one's strengths to get optimum satisfaction from life.

Experience and practice are powerful preventive and compensatory devices for minimizing the negative effects of aging on ability. Both require continuity of activities. Practice has been shown to maintain functioning and minimize declines in several areas of cognition (Botwinick, 1984; Salthouse, 1982, 1984) and in physical capacity (Buskirk, 1985). We need to know much more about the processes through which adults use practice and experience to maintain performance, but we can be sure that aging people will continue to use these strategies in the meantime.

But what about needs for new experience? Doesn't life amid all this familiarity become boring? Familiarity is not equivalent to sameness. Complex skills such as scholarship or art or music or organizational management or politics contain the potential for almost endless exploration and elaboration. In addition, constant change in the social world means that even within very familiar areas, adjustments must persistently be made. Continuity can support creativity. Indeed, Weisberg (1986) contended that creativity is the result of cumulative effort (continuity), not the instant flash of insight presumed in the stereotype of the creative genius.

When adults feel the need for stimulation, they look first to domains in which they have proficiency and for which they have a preference. Domains are general spheres of concern or function. The specific activity a person selects for stimulation may be new, but the domain usually is not. For example, people who see themselves as being good at one type of art or one area of sports, or one type of scholarship tend to see themselves as having the capacity to be good at other specific areas within the same general domain. We need to be more sensitive to abstract perceptions about domains of proficiency and preference that allow changes most people on the outside might view as significant to be defined by the individual as merely an offshoot from a well-established branch.

Continuity of environments is also important to adaptation. Environments condition us, and learning to cope with environments is an essential aspect of daily routines. We learn habits that allow us to cope routinely with environmental idiosyncrasies, but our habits are useful only within a particular set of idiosyncrasies. New environments can thus confront us with a drastic drop in our capacity to use habits to deal with mundane tasks of everyday living. We must instead pay attention to all sorts of trivial details, which takes valuable concentration and energy. This is one of the reasons why middle-aged and older people generally resist changing households or moving to different communities.

In addition, environments contain the physical and organizational infrastructure needed for continuity in meeting all sorts of needs. Most communities contain a wide array of facilities and services, but each community also has its own unique structure and way of functioning. Having successfully mapped the facilities and services in one community is often little help in securing services in another. Continuity of community or neighborhood environment means that one can take community structure and functioning largely for granted. Moving to a new neighborhood or community or type of household means starting over to find service providers such as physicians, dentists, lawyers, bankers, automobile mechanics, plumbers, carpenters, dry cleaners, grocers, insurance agents, and so on. Unfortunately, the Yellow Pages do not tell you whom you can trust to provide top-quality service. This is another important reason that middle-aged and older adults resist residential mobility.

Roles and relationships also show a high degree of continuity from middle-age on for most people. Friends and members of one's family with whom one has close ties tend to remain relatively consistent over time, even when contacts must be maintained by phone or mail over considerable distance. Maintaining relationships, especially with close friends, parents, and adult offspring, is a major goal for most older people. Indeed, next to being self-reliant, older people rank maintaining their relationships as their highest goal (Atchley, 1987).

Like familiar activities and thoughts, the company of familiar people provides a sense of comfort, security, and predictability. One's social support network consists of people one can count on for mutual aid, affirmation of one's identity and goal structure, a sense of belonging, and opportunities for intimate self-disclosure. Thus, external continuity of relationships can be seen as serving the needs of one's identity.

Aging allows the duration of adult relationships to increase, and duration is related to the degree to which relationships are highly personalized. For example, when relationships first begin, there is often a slightly formal quality to them. People tend to play roles straight while they steadily disclose personal information that can be used gradually to modify stereotyped role expectations. Hence, among spouses who self-disclose intimate aspects of self and identity to one another, the longer the duration of the marriage, the more the relationship is tailored to fit their respective personalities. That is, the relationship becomes highly personalized and may not resemble the cultural ideal for marital relationships very much at all. Of course, although increased duration may provide the opportunity for personalization and intimacy in a given relationship, it is not sufficient in and of itself. One must be willing to disclose one's actual identity, which means trusting the other not to use that information to do one harm. Highly personalized relationships are more likely to reinforce identity than are relationships with relative strangers. Likewise, formal role relationships, such as jobs that do not allow much personalization, are often easy to leave behind at retirement because they are rightly seen as having little reinforcement to offer one's identity.

Like internal continuity, external continuity is usually an effective adaptive strategy but can sometimes be maladaptive. External continuity generally becomes maladaptive only when there is a serious erosion of the physical and mental capacity necessary to continuity. For example, when a person becomes disabled to the point of needing assisted living, it is maladaptive for her or him to insist on continuing to live independently. Whether the subject is skills, activities, environments, roles or relationships, when the necessary competence for external continuity is no longer there, then insisting on external continuity is maladaptive because the customary fit between expectations and capacity has gone. Of course, what this means is that external continuity is not a very adaptive way to deal with pathological aging. Thus, external continuity has the potential to be much more problematic than internal continuity (Lieberman and Tobin, 1983).

Many gerontologists assume that role loss is generally a bad thing (Cumming and Henry, 1961; Rosow, 1974). We cannot pretend that role loss is seldom a problem. We can, however, view role losses in a larger context than is customary. For example, where is the tragedy in the widowhood of a person who hated her spouse? When people retire, they may no longer play the role, but they often retain the occupational identity (Atchley, 1971). Where is the loss? Aging often modifies what is expected in a role, but if the role relationship is one that has endured so long that no one is paying attention to the cultural ideal for the role anymore anyway, so what? The point is that specific relationships tend to grow in importance and traditional positions and roles tend to decline in importance as age increases through adulthood. Part of this shift is the release from the internal scrutiny of the "generalized other" that may come with the end of childrearing responsibilities and paid employment.

Nevertheless, external discontinuity can have serious implications for adaptation. Discontinuities in skills can cause discontinuities in the core of identity. For example, if being a performing musician is central to identity and the person loses the capacity to play, then identity may suffer. Whether this will happen depends to some extent on the potential remaining within the domain. In the case of the musician, for example, it may be possible for her or him to shift from playing to scheduling bookings, a change that preserves the identity with music and continuity of environment and relationships by shifting to another aspect of that domain. Of course, identity as a retired performing musician can also still be retained (Atchley, 1971).

Environmental discontinuities can be expected to trigger efforts to find external continuity in the new situation. At first, people attempt to preserve continuity by dealing with a new environment in familiar ways. A search for linkage and familiarity can be expected. Sometimes these attempts succeed, but more often the individual finds that meeting instrumental needs for housing, goods, and services becomes more problematic and that meeting everyday needs is filled with a new sense of ambiguity. Thankfully, such discontinuity is usually temporary, but the degree of stress connected with it can be substantial. The greater the disparity between the former and current environment, the greater the potential for external discontinuity. For example, we would expect moving from independent living in a household to assisted living in an institution to have a high potential for external discontinuity, compared to changing apartments in the same building.

If aging erodes competence, then there is not only a potential for internal discontinuity but for external discontinuity as well. For example, people with new impairments not only must cope with the impairment but also with pressure from the social system, especially family and friends, not to change. There may be a lessening of social support at a time when the person needs it the most. When discontinuities bring the need to get services from disinterested professionals, the result is often a reduction in the degree of personalization in role relationships and a reduction in the individual's capacity to control negative feedback. These are all important reasons behind the reluctance of middle-aged and older people to seek services from strangers and the preference for services from family and friends. They also speak again to the limits of Continuity Theory when dealing with pathological aging.

## Next Steps

A broad outline of a Continuity Theory of Normal Aging has been laid out. Initial statements of concepts, definitions, processes, and relationships have been provided. Refining, testing, and elaborating the theory itself will require the effort of many, but this should not be surprising because any general theory takes time to develop. This paper is intended as a beginning. The goal is to provide a rich array of ideas for further exploration.

## References

Atchley, R. C. (1971). Retirement and leisure participation: continuity or crisis? *The Gerontologist*, 11, 13–17.

Atchley, R. C. (1976). Orientation toward the job and retirement adjustment among women. In J. F. Gubrium (ed.), *Time, self, and aging*. New York: Behavioral Publications.

Atchley, R. C. (1982a). The process of retirement: Comparing women and men. In M. Szinovacz (ed.), *Women's retirement*. Beverly Hills, CA: Sage.

Atchley, R. C. (1982b). Retirement: Leaving the world of work. *Annals of the American Academy of Political and Social Sciences*, 464, 120–31.

Atchley, R. C., (1987). *Aging: Continuity and change*. 2nd edn. Belmont, CA: Wadsworth.

Atchley, R. C., and Miller, S. J. (1982–3). Retirement and couples. *Generations*, 7, 28–9, 36.

Atchley, R. C., and Miller, S. J. (1983). Types of elderly couples. In T. H. Brubaker (ed.), *Family relationships in later life*. Beverly Hills, CA: Sage.

Bengtson, V. L., and Black, D. (1973). Intergenerational relations and continuities in socialization. In P. B. Baltes and K. W. Schaie (eds.), *Life-span developmental psychology: Personality and socialization*. New York: Academic Press.

Bengtson, V. L., Reedy, M. N., and Gordon, C. (1985). Aging and self perceptions: Personality processes and social contexts. In J. E. Birren and K. W. Schaie (eds.), *Handbook of the psychology of aging*. 2nd edition. New York: Van Nostrand Reinhold.

Berger, P. L., and Luckmann, T. (1966). *The social construction of reality*. New York: Doubleday.

Blalock, H. M. (1982). *Conceptualization and measurement in the social sciences*. Beverly Hills: Sage.

Botwinick, J. (1984). *Aging and behavior*. 3rd edn. New York: Springer.

Buskirk, E. R. (1985). Health maintenance and longevity: Exercise. In C. E. Finch and E. L. Schneider (eds.), *Handbook of the biology of aging*. 2nd edn. New York: Van Nostrand Reinhold.

Carp, F. M. (1978–9). Effects of the living environment on activity and use of time. *International Journal of Aging and Human Development*, 9, 75–91.

Cohler, B. J. (1982). Personal narrative and life course. In P. B. Baltes and O. G. Brim (eds.), *Life-Span development and behavior, Volume 4*. New York: Academic Press.

Cumming, E. M., and Henry, W. E. (1961). *Growing old: The process of disengagement*. New York: Basic Books.

Erikson, E. H. (1963). *Childhood and society*. New York: Macmillan.

Erikson, E. H., Erikson, J. M., and Kivnick, H. Q. (1986). *Vital involvement in old age*. New York: W. W. Norton.

Fox, J. H. (1981–2). Perspectives on the continuity perspective. *International Journal of Aging and Human Development*, 14, 97–115.

Gordon, C., Gaitz, C. M., and Scott, J. (1976). Leisure and lives: Personal expressivity across the life span. In Binstock R. H. and E. Shanas (eds.), *Handbook of aging and the social sciences*. New York: Van Nostrand Reinhold.

Greenwald, A. (1980). The totalitarian ego: Fabrication and revision of personal history. *The American Psychologist*, 35, 603–18.

Gutmann, D. (1987). *Reclaimed powers: Toward a new psychology of men and women in later life*. New York: Basic Books.

Hage, J. (1972). *Techniques and problems of theory construction in sociology*. New York: Wiley Interscience.

Havighurst, R. J. (1963). Successful aging. In Williams, R. H., Tibbitts, C. and W. Donahue (eds.), *Processes of aging. Volume 1*. New York: Atherton.

Havighurst, R. J., Neugarten, B. L., and Tobin, S. S. (1963). Disengagement, personality and life satisfaction. In P. F. Hansen (ed.), *Age with a future*. Copenhagen: Munksgaard.

James W. (1890). *Principles of psychology*. Reissued Edition, New York: Dover.

Kahn, R. L., and Antonucci, T. (1981). Convoys of social support: A life-course approach. In S. B. Kiesler, J. N. Morgan, and V. K. Oppenheimer, (eds.), *Aging: Social change*. New York: Academic Press.

Kaplan, A. (1964). *The conduct of inquiry: Methodology for behavioral science*. San Francisco: Chandler.

Kaufman, S. R. (1987). *The ageless self: Sources of meaning in late life*. Madison, WI: University of Wisconsin Press.

Kelley, G. A. (1955). *The psychology of personal constructs*. New York: Norton.

Lawton, M. P. (1983). Environmental and other determinants of well-being in older people. *The Gerontologist*, 23, 349–57.

Liberman, M. A., and Tobin, S. S. (1983). *The experience of old age: Stress, coping, and survival*. New York: Basic Books.

Maas, H. S., and Kuypers, J. A. (1974). *From thirty to seventy*. San Francisco: Jossey-Bass.

McCrae, R. R., and Costa, P. T., Jr. (1982). Aging, the life course, and models of human development. In T. M. Field (ed.), *Review of human development*. New York: Wiley.

Morgan, L. A. (1976). Toward a formal theory of life course continuity and change. Los Angeles: Andrus Gerontology Center (mimeographed).

Morgan, L. A. (1984). Changes in family interaction following widowhood. *Journal of Marriage and the Family*, 46, 323–31.

Neugarten, B. L. (1964). *Personality in middle and late life*. New York: Atherton.

Neugarten, B. L. (1977). Personality and aging. In J. E. Birren, and K. W. Schaie (eds.), *Handbook of the psychology of aging*. New York: Van Nostrand Reinhold.

Oliver, D. B. (1971). Career and leisure patterns of middle-aged metropolitan out-migrants. *The Gerontologist* 11, 13–20.

Parnes, H. S., and Less, L. (1983). *From work to retirement*. Columbus, OH: Ohio State University Center for Human Resources Research.

Rosow, I. (1963). Adjustment of the normal aged. In R. H. Williams, C. Tibbitts, and W. Donohue (eds.), *Processes of Aging: Social and psychological perspectives. Volume II*. New York: Atherton.

Rosow, I. (1974). *Socialization to old age*. Berkeley, CA: University of California Press.

Salthouse, T. A. (1982). *Adult cognition: An experimental psychology of human aging*. New York: Springer-Verlag.

Salthouse, T. A. (1984). Effects of age and skill in typing. *Journal of Experimental Psychology: General*, 113, 345–71.

Schaie, K. W., and Parham, I. (1976). Stability of adult personality traits. Fact or fable? *Journal of Personality and Social Psychology*, 34, 146–58.

Shanas, E. (1977). *National survey of the aged: 1975*. Chicago: University of Illinois, Chicago Circle.

Streib, G. F., and Schneider, C. J. (1971). *Retirement in American society*. Ithaca, NY: Cornell University Press.

Troll, L. E., and Smith, J. (1976). Attachment through the life span. *Human Development*, 19, 156–70.

Weisberg, R. W. (1986). *Creativity: Genius and other myths*. New York: W. H. Freeman.

Whitbourne, S. K. (1986). *The me I know: A study of adult identity*. New York: Springer-Verlag.

## Further Reading to Part I

Bengtson, Vern L. and K. Warner Schaie (eds.). 1999. *Handbook of Theories of Aging*. New York: Springer.

Featherstone, Mike and Andrew Wernick (eds.). 1995. *Images of Aging: Cultural Representations of Later Life*. New York: Routledge.

Green, Bryan S. 1993. *Gerontology and the Construction of Old Age: A Study in Discourse Analysis*. Hawthorne, NY: Aldine de Gruyter.

Gubrium, Jaber F. and J. Brandon Wallace. 1990. "Who Theorizes Age?" *Ageing and Society* 10: 131–49.

Katz, Stephen. 1996. *Disciplining Old Age: The Formation of Gerontological Knowledge*. Charlottesville: University Press of Virginia.

Kertzer, David I. and Jennie Keith (eds.). 1984. *Age and Anthropological Theory*. Ithaca, NY: Cornell University Press.

Neugarten, Bernice L. and Dail A. Neugarten. 1986. "Changing Meanings of Age in the Aging Society." Pp. 33–51 in *Our Aging Society: Paradox and Promise*, edited by Alan Pifer and Lydia Bronte. New York: Norton.

Reinharz, Shulamit and Graham D. Rowles. 1988. *Qualitative Gerontology*. New York: Springer.

# Part II

## Aging and Identity

# 6 A Decade of Reminders: Changing Age Consciousness between Fifty and Sixty Years Old

*David A. Karp*

Documented are aging experiences shared in common by those between 50 and 60 years old. The fifties is a relatively neglected decade in the life course. Although social scientists have given considerable attention to identity transformations among those in their thirties and forties (Farrell and Rosenberg, 1981; Gould, 1978; Levinson et al., 1978; Vaillant, 1977) as well as to life transitions during the last years of work and retirement (Atchley, 1976; Barfield and Morgan, 1969; Rosow, 1974), little attention has been paid to the aging experiences of those in their fifties. Argued is that the decade of the fifties brings with it some distinctive changes in people's aging self-conceptions. As the respondents in this study were questioned about their current sense of aging, it became apparent that the pace of aging messages greatly increases and picks up momentum in the fifties. The fifties is a kind of fulcrum decade, a turning point in the aging process, during which people, more sharply than before, are made to feel their age. As the fifties progress it becomes harder to avoid the recognition of really growing older. Particular events occur, such as the deaths of parents and friends, being in the middle of three generations, being the oldest at work, and becoming grandparents, which inevitably make aging a prominent part of self-consciousness in the fifties. For this reason, the fifties can be characterized as a decade of reminders.

A fundamental assertion of social psychology is that human beings live in a world of symbols that they themselves create. The meanings attached to all aspects of social life are not fixed and immutable. Rather, human beings, in interaction with each other, confer meanings onto the world, including the meanings attached to age. So, like all meanings, those attached to being young, middle aged, or old also emerge out of the process of interaction. As Cooley (1909) described it long ago, other people become a "looking glass" in which individuals see themselves reflected and through these reflections come to have certain subjective definitions of the self. The self is formed and transformed through interaction with others. Through the reflected appraisals of others, people come to define themselves as certain kinds of persons. These definitions of self, of course, extend to and include the personal sense of aging (Karp and Yoels, 1982).

Original publication: Karp, David A. "A Decade of Reminders: Changing Age Consciousness between Fifty and Sixty Years Old," *The Gerontologist* 6 (1988), pp. 727–38.

Consistent with the perspective of symbolic interaction (Blumer, 1969; Hewitt, 1986; Mead, 1934), this research is about aging messages; it is about the distinctive communications people hear from those around them that contribute to clear commonalities of aging consciousness in the fifties. Some aging messages are subtle and others bring us up short, dramatically reminding us of how we appear to others. A few years ago, in my late thirties, I began to play basketball with undergraduates at Boston College. After a few months I became a "regular" on the courts and imagined that I was just "one of the guys." One day as I was walking off the court, feeling particularly good about a well-played game, a teammate turned to me and said, "Nice game, *sir*." That one communication disabused me of the "one of the guys" self-image. Everyone experiences similar moments during which age-related self-conceptions are called into question. Such events happen throughout life. My point here, however, is that messages of this sort become especially prevalent and powerful during the decade of the fifties. "Sirs" and their symbolic equivalents proliferate in the fifties. An often heard piece of conventional wisdom tells us that "we are as young as we feel." The more sociologically accurate idea that we are as young or old as other people make us feel is pursued here.

Although this article is about the common experiences and perceptions of people in their fifties, it departs conceptually from developmental aging theories positing uniform, invariant, and universal stages to adult life. Whereas the well-known developmental theories of Buhler (1968), Erikson (1963), Gould (1978), Levinson et al. (1978), and Vaillant (1977) differ on a number of points, they are united in their focus on the inevitability of the passage through various, universal life stages. In a popularized version of these approaches, Sheehy (1977) argued that crises regularly confront persons in predictable 10-year cycles. No doubt, part of the popularity of works such as Sheehy's derives from the influence that developmental theorists have had in shaping consciousness and expectations about the "normal" life cycle. In contrast, suggested by the data to follow is that such developmental theories inappropriately decontextualize the meaning of behaviors. In their recent, wide-ranging review of advances in research on adulthood, Datan et al. (1987) offered the opinion that life course study must give greater attention to "the contexts of change and continuity, and to the individual's construction of the life course." Just such a focus is central to this discussion.

Adult development is tied less to chronological age per se than to the timing of events within the contexts of work and family. Perhaps the argument is best put by saying that different features of life become more or less relevant at different points in the life course. Questions about intimacy, the meaning of work, the meaning of family life, and the meaning of aging become more or less insistent at different points across the life span. It is argued that questions about aging take on a particular significance and importance during the 50 to 60 year decade. The biological and contextual events that are generally characteristic of the fifties impose onto individuals problems of establishing coherence in their lives. Whereas events pile up in the fifties making reflection about age particularly likely during this decade, such events may occur earlier or later in the lives of different individuals. Others have made similar arguments about consciousness changes over the life course. For example, although a consciousness of finitude (Marshall, 1980; Munichs, 1980) is most characteristic of old age, certainly a terminal illness at a young age will require an effort to understand individual mortality at that time. The point is that contextual events giving rise to distinctive consciousnesses are correlated with age, but not determined by age.

The position outlined is similar to that of Gutmann (1987) in his recent book about the reorganization of male and female personalities in late middle age. Based on crosscultural data, Gutmann (1987) showed that "just as men in late middle age reclaim title to their denied 'femininity,' middle-aged women repossess the aggressive 'masculinity' that they once lived out vicariously through their husbands." Gutmann showed, however, that the consistently observed identity transformation of men and women in middle age is tied less to age itself than to a structural change in family life normally occurring in late middle life; namely, the end of the parenting period. The critical point of Gutmann's analysis is that the "post parental period" usually coincides with late middle age, but does not inevitably happen at this life moment. By specifying the social structural circumstances of personality change, Gutmann is able to identify broad and predictable patterns of adult development without maintaining a deterministic stance that equates age and identity transformation. In a similar fashion, the social-psychological approach taken here is meant to describe age-related regularities although avoiding the position that similar age cohorts march in a lockstep fashion through life cycle stages.

In short, this discussion is dedicated to an interpretive approach to aging and the life cycle. An interpretive approach tries to "illuminate how large social forces influence human destinies as well as tell us what the experiences mean on the individual level" (Marshall, 1986). According to this view, an adequate understanding of the aging process must account for the ways that individuals, through communication with each other, interpret the meaning of age at different points in life. Specifically, it is maintained that the decade of the fifties is characterized by a convergence of aging messages that require an intensification of interpretive work about aging during this period.

## Sample and Method

Between March 1982 and December 1984, 72 indepth interviews were conducted with Caucasian male ($n$ = 39) and female ($n$ = 33) professionals. These interviews were part of a study designed to learn how professionals between 50 and 60 years old think about themselves, their careers, and aging. The overall sample is the result of a snowball process. After each interview, the respondent was asked for additional names of persons whom it would be useful to interview. From these names a compilation of individuals that would reflect variation by gender and profession were chosen. Because the study was originally conceived to investigate academics beyond mid-life and only later expanded to study other professionals in the same age category, professors are disproportionately represented in the total sample (professors = 47, doctors = 8, business and industry professionals = 12, lawyers = 5). About two-thirds of the interviews were conducted at the respondents' offices and one-third in their homes. The taped interviews ranged from one and one-half to several hours in length. Each interview began by asking the individual to trace his or her occupational route. This broad opening question normally led to conversation that provided information about job history, personal background, the organizational context of work, work satisfaction, changes in the meaning of work over the life cycle, work and the sense of aging, and the connection between work and non-work life.

Like most qualitative research studies, the analytical foci of this project have evolved as data were collected. Consistent with the process of inductive grounded theory (Glaser and Strauss, 1967), the ongoing strategy was to write numerous theoretical memos on emerging themes in the data and then to refocus the interviews as necessary. This procedure required three revisions of the semi-structured interview guide. Unproductive questions were deleted and other questions included to obtain systematic data on important themes unanticipated at the outset of the project. A related strategy for getting close to the data was the construction of coding categories after approximately 30 interviews. The coding categories helped the author to stay close to the data and to clarify areas of greatest substantive richness.

Social psychology must be sensitive both to uniformities and variations in human behaviours. Earlier papers drawn from the interviews highlight systematic differences in the ways that the fifties are experienced. For example, men and women respond differently to the growing recognition that work time and life time are finite. The typical responses among male academics are to reduce the intensity of their research efforts, to become more selective in what they will do, to respond to their students in more humanistic terms, and to develop an exiting consciousness (Karp, 1986b). Women, on the other hand, most of whom began their careers later in life, experience an occupational vitality and sense of growth in their fifties that seems denied to men who have had comfortable and predictable careers (Karp, 1985). Differences also emerged in how satisfied men and women, as well as those in different occupational groups, feel with work in their fifties (Karp, 1987). From the data, reflection can be made on how their original "eth-class" membership (Gordon, 1964) influences people's perceptions and actions throughout their occupational lives. Class and ethnic background are important frames within which persons understand, experience, and create their careers (Karp, 1986a). Responded to here are the regularities in the data that transcend occupation, gender, and social class. Consciousness of age unfolds in response to the totality of messages heard at particular points in the life cycle. These messages, of course, are heard throughout life. Children acquire a sense of age in quite the same way that middle-aged or elderly people do. The distinctive kinds of messages that people hear in their fifties are detailed here.

## A Decade of Reminders

The men and women interviewed persistently expressed a paradox about aging. They repeatedly tried to convey that there is a contradiction between the way they feel inside and the way they know they appear to others. One way to capture this paradox is to use the metaphor of age as a stranger. The stranger notion was drawn from a quite different context in sociology. Among the several brilliant essays written by Simmel (1950) is one entitled "The Stranger." Simmel wrote about the stranger as a distinctive social type. As he conceived it, the stranger to a group or culture (for example the trader in the middle ages or the immigrant to a new culture) holds the distinctive position of being near and distant to a group at the same time. This idea of simultaneous nearness and distance captures well how many people feel about age and aging.

Over and again when asked "Into which age category do you fall?" Individuals acknowledged growing older, being middle-aged, and sometimes even old. They quickly added, though, that their feelings did not easily match up with their chronological age. They knew that they were no longer young, but still could not quite believe it. The fact of aging seems to be one of life's great surprises, a surprise that is most fully sprung in the fifties. One person told of a sense of surprise when he first heard the insurance salesman on television inquire, "Do you know someone between 50 and 80 years old?" His response was, "My God, he's talking about me." The idea that they are as chronologically old as they are seems foreign. Age, at least in the early fifties, is a stranger. It is psychologically near and distant at the same time. Many respondents tried to convey this contradiction or paradox of aging.

One is confronted with the world's external view of you. From the inside the world doesn't look very different, but from the outside it looks different. I've become much more aware of the fact recently that other people are seeing me as aging. . . . I don't feel particularly mortal, although I'm getting more mortal. As you grow older you get more mortal. In fact, one day you're going to cash it in. Up until a few years ago I always thought of myself as a kind of sophomore.

When I turned 50 I kept being perplexed because I knew I was 50 and I looked in the mirror and saw somebody with gray hair, but my picture of myself was, I think, more of somebody still getting her training and education. It is quite clear. My inner picture is quite different than, I would say, my chronological age. But I think it's shifting. I'm more seeing myself as not just a beginner . . . but as having arrived. And there's a part of that that I like and another part that I don't like (laughs).

As you age you sort of fight it. Like, there was a terrible TV program I saw a couple of years ago about someone about my age wanting to enter a marathon. And I understood. OK? It's like not being defeated by age. I'm 55 years old, right? I think that chronological age is not going to determine what I do or don't do . . . I mean, I'm aware of aging, but I don't accept it sort of.

I played on an "old man's" basketball team recently. I was playing full court basketball and killed my knees. And it's interesting because the way we talked about it with each other was that we felt about 15. And here we were. We knew our age and yet we felt 15 and in our minds we were 15. We could feel the aging in our bodies, but our minds didn't age at all. And that was kind of interesting to us.

I have been using the metaphor of the stranger. It might be said that during the course of the fifties especially, a recognition of aging becomes nearer and less distant. Age becomes less a stranger and more an intimate. Although the number of different age reminders contributing to a qualitatively new aging consciousness in the fifties is large, they tend to fall into several general categories. Described are some of the typical events or situations that clearly arouse the recognition of growing older. The kinds of events detailed collectively give rise to the recognition that work time and life time are finite. Each of the types of events described constitutes part of an overall aging mosaic. Although certain messages may jog consciousness more than others, aging events, experiences, or reminders work in conjunction with one another. Their mutual effect might be likened to that of drugs such as alcohol and tranquilizers which act synergistically, each magnifying the effect of the other when taken simultaneously. It is the concurrent experience of multiple reminders that fosters the sense of aging. The first reminder, universally experienced, is the reality that 50-year-old bodies speak their age.

## Body reminders

Most of the aging messages heard are external, arising from the social environment. Respondents, however, also talked about the internal messages conveyed by bodies that are aging. People may feel emotionally that they are still young. Some even jokingly describe themselves as adolescents. Nearly everyone, however, described changes in the way they experience their bodies, changes that they have most profoundly come to feel in recent years. In a few cases people have experienced major, life-threatening illnesses that have made them acutely aware of their mortality. Several have had heart attacks. Others have undergone surgeries in recent years. One woman is dying of cancer. Noteworthy is that some diseases especially are interpreted as signalling aging. One man, for example, reported that "The onset of my feeling old was two or three years ago. I had prostate trouble. I see that as an old man's disease." Most of the body reminders reported by respondents, however, are not of the major illness variety. Otherwise healthy people live in bodies that are discernibly slowing down.

> I'm getting more creakiness. I'm snoring at night. I can still appreciate beauty in a woman certainly, but you know, the testosterone is not quite there. I've also been noticing it with my kid over the last few years. My kid was playing baseball and I wasn't getting down for the ground balls as much. We'd go down to the field and I'd say, "John, instead of those ground balls, why don't you hit me some fly balls." And I wouldn't go out so far because it was harder for me to throw the balls in. I noticed those changes.

> You grow older. Maybe your stamina is less. Maybe you don't remember things as well as you used to. Maybe you have one illness or another which interferes with you. Those are all real things which happen to people as they get older. . . . They have to do with age and individual condition and they come on people at different ages, but as a common statement they tend to be evident in the fifties.

> I do not see the signs of old age, but I can see some of the clues. I have arthritis. You can't deny that. To me that's kind of old age. I've been running for 20 years and I didn't run last year. My arthritis caught up with me and a couple of other things like that. So, I see myself fighting it (age), but I'm only on the threshold of what I would call becoming old.

The last person quoted described himself as being on the threshold of old age. People know that they are no longer young, but neither do they yet see themselves as old. Not surprisingly, when asked "Into which age category do you fit?" nearly everyone describes themselves as middle aged. It is, however, a middleness that provides a clear preview of what is to come. In a significant sense old age itself begins to loom larger on respondents' subjective horizons. Although they still see old age as fairly distant (several saw old age as beginning at 70 and coinciding with retirement), they recognized their diminished physical abilities as a precursor of old age. Several said that old age will arrive when the kind of physical limitations they are already beginning to experience become serious enough to immobilize them. They see middle age as ending and old age as beginning when they become physically impaired.

I want to continue to call it middle age until I become physically impaired I guess. I'm still into having a good time – eating, drinking, traveling, rushing around. I'm not looking at old age, maybe not even when I am 60 or 65. I think I can still do what I'm doing now in the sixties.

I don't think I've ever felt particularly attached to a timetable. I've just sort of said, "This is what I want to do and the way I want to do it." And maybe that's the thing about old age. . . . I still think I have the power to do things if I want to. I haven't yet reached that point of saying "I don't have the power or the strength." If I really want it, I still feel that I can do it. When I can't, that will be the shift to old age.

In connection with the social psychological consequences of *middleness*, of being in-between things, comment should be made on the significance attached to the number 50. Although achieving age 50, from a strictly chronological, actuarial standpoint, puts one about two-thirds the way through life, it is nevertheless an age that strongly carries the connotation of being a mid-point. At age 50, after all, one has lived for half a century. All decade birthdays have significance as age benchmarks, but 50 seems especially symbolic of middle age. I did not specifically ask people to comment on that decade birthday, but several, now in their mid-fifties, spontaneously commented on the importance of having reached their fiftieth birthday. Many expressed sentiments similar to the man who said:

When I hit 50 it hit me like a ton of bricks. I felt at 48, this is terrific; this is the way I'd like it to be. I really knew my field and as a psychotherapist I thought "I'm much better than I was at 38." And I thought, "All that training is finally paying off." And I had 3 years until I hit 50 and I suddenly realized it's a down hill course. I think there's something symbolic about 50.

One of the reasons that it is hard to avoid attaching distinctive meanings to age 50 is that other people make a big deal out of that birthday. Spouses and friends often throw a big birthday party at this point. The very size of the fiftieth birthday party often contrasts with the more modest parties at earlier ages and directly signals a very significant change in age status. If others decide to throw a big bash at 50, it must be a special and important life point! Because of the size and unusual attention often given to the fiftieth birthday, it's difficult to see it as just another birthday. Such a birthday party functions as a kind of public proclamation, an affirmation of the fact that a major aging milestone has been reached. For this reason, the fiftieth birthday has somewhat the flavor of religious rituals such as confirmations and bar mitzvahs, directly calling attention as it does to a significant change in age status. Many experience the celebration of the fiftieth birthday as a kind of rite of passage.

When I turned 50 we had a party, a huge party. And I thought that half a century was kind of nice. And so we had a huge party and people asked me how I felt . . . I just became conscious of the fact that I had made it to a half a century.

My fiftieth birthday. It was a sort of a turning point. Fifty. People made a big deal of the birthday, big parties and whatever. So you were made conscious that you were 50 rather than 30 or 40 . . . very conscious of it and it sort of makes you think a little more about it.

*Generational reminders*

The middle age category is inextricably bound up with a host of social-psychological in-betweens. Those in their fifties are placed between their children and their parents. Earlier they worked to support a family and to get ahead. Now they must start thinking about the future retirement years. It is this bridging situation, this feeling of being suspended between several worlds, that lends a special poignancy to the interiorization of life that occurs in middle age. This turning inward is a frequently noted aspect of middle age existence (Gould, 1978; Levinson et al., 1978). The teenage children of middle-aged people are struggling to form their own identities and to establish independence from them. At the same time their parents, who are confronted with their own health and financial anxieties, are making new demands on them. In contrast to their children, the parents of middle-aged people are "apt to be struggling for a sense of connectedness rather than separation from the pivotal parental family" (Chilman, 1972). For many women there is the additional concern brought about by their transition out of the mother role into that of working wife. Each generation is likely, then, to have a different perspective on the meaning of family life. Respondents see their own aging reflected in the aging of their parents, children, and grandchildren. To use an earlier image, it is as though respondents have several mirrors before them. Each generation is a looking glass for self-reflection. An image that comes to mind is the maze of mirrors at amusement parks. There people see themselves reflected from so many different angles that they become confused. Generational mirrors do not so much confuse people as confront them. In one age mirror, people see part of themselves in their parents who are often failing:

> Since my mother has had this heart condition, she's slowed down a lot. My dad, he sometimes falls asleep in the middle of a conversation. I know my parents are not going to live forever. . . . You have to shout into the telephone when you talk to mother because her hearing is getting bad. She's slowing down every which way. . . . And I think when these things happen you're finding out that you're vulnerable.

> One of the things that makes me know that I'm probably going to get older is that one of my parents is still alive and I can see that my father is now at 81 going downhill, although he was for the longest time a pretty virile individual. So that makes me conscious of the age thing. That this can't go on completely forever. As I see my father becoming physically impaired I know it's going to happen to me eventually.

And when parents die the children become part of the oldest generation.

> Within the last 5 years both of my parents died. I became the oldest in the family. I'm the patriarch of the family now. Maybe that's when old age (begins).

In a second age mirror, people see part of themselves in their children. Although gerontologists and family sociologists have each developed an enormous literature in their respective fields of specialization, it is surprising that virtually no systematic studies exist on the effects of childrearing on parents' sense of aging. Children at home may force parents to acknowledge their own mortality in a very direct way. Wills may be drawn up and life insurance taken out. Important events in the life cycle of children, such as starting to talk and walk, entering school, being confirmed or bar mitzvahed, starting to date, leaving home, getting married, and having children also become significant transition points in the parents' awareness of their own journey through the life cycle. The simple fact that children come to inhabit their own social and cultural worlds calls attention to generational differences. One respondent felt his age in terms of a sense of disconnectedness from the concerns and interests of his children:

> I don't feel old. I don't think of myself as being old. Well, every so often there is almost like a little glimmer of it. . . . You know, "I'm old." Sometimes when I'm with my children . . . I say "Jesus." You know, I never thought of myself as being old-fashioned or old, out of step with the times, but when I'm with my children, I kind of get the impression that, "Yes, maybe I am a little out of step with the times."

And as two professors reported, it isn't necessary to have your own children to feel the impact of generational status. Their words call into question the validity of the conventional wisdom that working with young people helps to keep oneself young. It may certainly be the case that constant contact may keep one in touch with the ideas, feelings, consciousness, and popular culture of younger people. Equally likely, however, is that their presence will call attention to differences in generational status. The realization that one is old enough to be their father or even their grandfather reliefs differences rather than similarities between teachers and their students.

> This year (aging) hit me very poignantly as I was meeting students' parents at commencement and a lot of them are about my age. . . . When I started here I felt more like a big brother and then uncly and now more fatherly. But I felt it very poignantly this time. If I'd had kids, they'd be like this.

> More recently, I would say in the last 5 years. . . . When I meet the parents of students, it occurs to me that not only am I old enough to be their father, but I'm half way on the way to being their grandfather.

Usually, by the mid-fifties the children have left home and started their own families. Now, the grandparent role becomes a new family benchmark signalling a changed age status. Grandparenthood is an interesting case of a role in contemporary American society that can be viewed, in contrast to earlier historical periods, as ushering in the transition to old age. Although the popular mass media continue to portray grandparents as having all the characteristics and physical attributes stereotypically associated with elderly people, the significant fact is that grandparenthood is occurring increasingly among middle-aged segments of the population. An age range from the early fifties to the mid-sixties for grandmothers was reported in one study (Neugarten and Weinstein, 1973). In another sample of grandparents (Wood and Robertson, 1974), 44 percent became grandparents between the ages of 47 to 54. As more people become grandparents and see it as a natural part of the life cycle, they find themselves in a social role bridging middle and old age. Individuals explicitly mentioned the grandparent role as a salient reminder of age.

> What makes me conscious that I'm 51. . . . One of my children is married and I became a grandfather recently. So maybe I was going along feeling just as young as my children

until this other phase came along. And now he's married and has a family and I'm a grandfather, and so that makes me conscious that I'm 50 and not 30.

Over the last 3 or 4 years I have become more conscious of the division between me and the younger set. I look at my daughter. My oldest daughter is 36. Their children, my grandchildren, that tells me that I'm aging.

Having a son-in-law. . . . Having a daughter get married (reminds me of my age). And my daughter was talking about having a baby. That would make me a grandfather. "What are you crazy?," I told her. "If you're getting a baby, I'm getting a motorcycle" (laughs).

The fact that people in their fifties are in the middle of several generations is a rather new thing historically. People's sense of aging must be understood within the historical context in which they live. A category such as middle age is itself a social construction, the product of a particular historical era. As the demographer Glick (1977) has pointed out, a number of major demographic changes occurring over the last century have had a definitive influence in shaping people's sense of aging. For example, the so-called empty nest period is the product of increased life expectancy. It is indicated by the data that the time that couples spend alone after the last child has left home has been extended from 1.6 years in the early 1900s to 12.9 years in the 1970s, an increase of over 11 years. This means that where previously the death of a spouse usually occurred less than 2 years after the last child married, now married couples can plan on staying together for 13 years after their last child has left home. With retirement coming at 65 or so for most workers, those in their fifties still have another 15 to 20 years on the job. Consequently, the meanings attached to work earlier in the life cycle, such as supporting the family, take on a different hue. This situation is conducive to a great deal of inner mind work concerning the ultimate value and significance of occupational activities. Today, the sense of middle age is associated with a new and distinctly bounded period of life, a period in between the completion of child-rearing and retirement from work. Earlier generations in the nineteenth-century experienced no such clearly demarcated life period.

### Contextual reminders

Becoming the oldest! This is an important frame for aging throughout life. The subjective sense of feeling older, from childhood on, is contingent on age status relative to those immediately around us. In childhood, of course, being among the oldest is viewed positively. Children want to feel older. Being among the oldest bestows status. Much of children's lives involves alternating between being the youngest and the oldest. Everyone can remember the great feeling of being on top of the status system in grammar school. And then there was the plunge in status as we entered the next grade level and were viewed by others in the school as just a kid. In much the same way, the sense of age throughout life depends upon the demography of particular situations. Those in their fifties find themselves among the oldest, if not the oldest, in a number of contexts and this fact contributes mightily to a quickened sense of aging. Several of those interviewed have become part of the oldest generation or are anticipating that this will happen shortly. Equally important is the recognition, if not the shock, that they are now among the oldest at work. Respondents mention this contextual fact over and over again.

> It was depressing. I thought I was slipping. I was always the young, bright guy. Now I was the oldest in my group and slipping. As I was aging, young, bright folks began to appear and I was now the oldest one. . . . I kind of felt old and I was surprised at not being the young guy anymore.

> I'm a senior faculty member, at least in terms of longevity. I'm well aware of that, by the way. In the last couple or three years it has occurred to me that I have been around here longer than anyone except maybe two or three others. And they actually didn't go to medical school here. It makes me aware of how much time has gone by. It's a long time. I remember seeing alumni coming back for their twenty-fifth reunion. So you really do become aware of the fact that by many standards you're pretty old.

> There are in this department a number of us . . . of the same vintage. We are all in our early fifties, give or take a few years. . . . I am conscious of belonging to this group. . . . I like the fact that there are several of us. I didn't like for a while being the oldest person in the department. I just didn't like feeling old. I didn't like being the oldest. It's funny, this shift toward feeling older is on you.

One of the consequences of being among the oldest at work is that people are treated with a respect and deference that is clearly connected with their age. Younger workers seek the advice of the senior citizens at work. Older workers are seen as having special knowledge of the work organization. They know its history. They know where the skeletons are buried. And often they have greater power in the organization. Several respondents used a very evocative phrase when they said that they were now considered among a few elder statesmen in their organizations. A related occupational reminder was reported by a physician, an internist, who was feeling alienated at work. He reported that rather than being accorded deference and respect because of his advancing age, young people no longer wanted to be treated by an old doctor. As he described it, part of his malaise arose from the fact that the population of his patients has become nearly uniformly old.

> First of all, young people don't want to see you. You're old. To a 20-year-old, you're old. You look old to them at 45 and certainly at 55 you're old. . . . So, your practice gets much older. You get the seniors. My practice has aged tremendously. I have a lot of eighties, a lot of seventies. And I have some in the nineties. And it changes the nature of your day, not only in a strictly diagnostic sense. . . . Well, for example, when I was 30 I was seeing patients in their twenties or thirties and some people in their forties. And basically we were all in the same boat. We were building our careers and one interesting aspect of the practice was to talk to my patients about what they were doing and what they were interested in. And that was an interesting part of my day. Now when you see six 80-year-old people a day, some of them may be interesting, but you don't talk about what they are doing or planning on. For the most part, the ones you see in the office are complainers. They are very fearful of death and that's why they are there. And there is a tremendous increase in deaths in your practice. I can remember years where if I had three deaths it was a lot. Now I expect a lot of deaths.

The focus has been on the import of being among the oldest at work. Work contexts seem to be the source of particularly significant aging messages. To be among the oldest at work is a daily, repeated, institutionally-rooted reminder. Communications from work, however, are affirmed and strengthened by experiences in other contexts where individuals may be discomforted by being among the oldest. A few people expressed concern about going to parties, bars, or other places where the majority of people are likely to be young. For example:

> I may consider young people as colleagues, but they may not look upon me the same way. Suppose that I go to the Orson Welles theatre in Cambridge. And I look around and there are next to no gray heads. Anyway I'm quite conscious of the fact that I must be the oldest person there. Let's say that I might go to a bar or something like that. If I were, let's say in my twenties or early thirties, and there is a group of young people, I would feel very comfortable in saying, "May I join you?" I wouldn't feel comfortable at my age doing that because I'd be afraid of running the risk that they would say, "Hey, what are you doing here daddy?" They might show a lot of deference and go get a chair for you to sit down.

Coffee houses are only one of several contexts where people looked around and saw their own age reflected in the age of those around them. In the last case discomfort originated when a man felt he did not fit in contexts dominated by younger people. Discomfort can also arise when people are in circumstances where they fit in all too well. These are situations where people are surrounded by large numbers of people their own age. Particularly evocative of aging feelings are gatherings such as weddings and reunions during which people explicitly measure their own aging in comparison to a cohort of age peers. As everyone knows, much of the conversation during and after such events centers on how well or badly certain people, including ourselves, are aging. More than one person expressed sentiments similar to the woman who said, "I'm 30 years out of college. That would be another reminder. I didn't go to the reunion. I suspect I didn't go because I didn't want to see myself looking older by seeing my classmates." [One colleague, however, has pointed out that many of the contextual events described throughout this paper may provide some persons the opportunity to maintain a youthful self-conception. Events such as weddings and reunions may allow some the interpretation that they are aging much better than their chronological age peers. These events may, therefore, neutralize other communications about aging.]

Suggested by several of the preceding quotes is that in their fifties people are reminded that they must act their age. There is, however, some debate about whether norms surrounding age, particularly later in life, have become less influential in directing behaviors. Neugarten and Neugarten (1986) have argued that America is becoming a more "age irrelevant" society and that rigid norms about age-related behaviors are disappearing. She suggested that with the graying of America, the perceptions of the behaviors appropriate to given ages have loosened up considerably and that beyond adolescence, chronological age is becoming a poorer predictor of the way people will behave. Although it may be that the behavioral constraints associated with age are lessening, several respondents were very much aware of how people their age ought to act. Many were self-conscious about the possibility of acting too young at their age. This was most especially true for academics who deal routinely with younger people. Several described changed behaviors toward students in a way that speaks very much to the relevancy rather than irrelevancy of age.

I think I have a very good rapport with my students, yet I never fool myself into thinking that they look upon me as their buddy. I don't want them to in a sense. . . . I've always been very conscious of not wanting to be a middle-aged teenager. That role really turns me off. . . . Well, in a way I keep saying "Well, look, I'm almost 60 years old (and I should act it)."

You know, a lot of the appeal of teaching, it certainly was for me, is being young and "with it" in the eyes of the kids. Recently I have put a barrier between me and them because I don't think it was healthy to be as close as I was to the kids. I think I was using a lot of sex appeal as a younger woman. I've seen that happen with other women and I used to do that. . . . I mean, I would be using a lot of feminine charm in class; a lot of being sexy; sitting on a desk. Doing all these things. Because I started out young and it was an ego trip. I started very young and I was very close to the students. But then, I don't know, I realized that I'm older and that I had to play an older role. . . . You know now that you're close to the age of their mothers, so now you've got to act like a mother figure.

Other norms connected with age involve proper clothing and language. People use dress to give off certain messages and impressions of themselves (Stone, 1962). Popular writers (e.g., Molloy, 1976) have capitalized on the significance of clothed appearance with how to dress advice for aspiring executives, female as well as male. Politicians often employ consultants to advise them about the right clothes to wear for various occasions and different settings. The fashion industry exploits the desire of Americans to be considered up-to-date and to be acknowledged by others as sophisticated, interesting, important, and successful. Countercultural youth groups from the Bohemians of the 1950s to the hippies of the sixties and the punkers of the eighties have adopted unconventional clothing as a way of communicating their separateness from the conventional, adult world. It could be said that different age groups wear different uniforms. At a certain point people become sensitized to the impropriety of wearing the wrong uniform. One professor expressed disdain for colleagues who "adorned themselves in the plummage of the students." And another said.

I mean, I would never want to appear younger to my students. I would never dress like a student, to wear what a 21-year-old wears. I don't want to look old, but I certainly would not want to get the rapport with students that I had as a younger teacher. You know, closer age rapport. I would never want to wear blue jeans or what-have-you. I believe in propriety about the age I am and the way I look.

Another woman's comment illustrated that people are expected not only to look their age, but, as well, to talk their age.

I make speeches, and I make them fairly well, but anytime I use my current language, or use a cuss word, then I get this "Oh, grandmother, why are you acting like that?" And, of course, during the 1960s language got pretty dirty. . . . Everyone was saying fuck and everything. And I can remember my brother-in-law being horrified by my language. . . . It was because I was an older woman using young people's language. Oh, it just horrified him.

### Mortality reminders

Most persons have had to cope with death prior to their fifties. In the twenties, thirties, and even the forties, however, deaths and illness are relatively infrequent. In contrast, as one respondent cogently put it, there is a "momentum of mortality occurrences" in the fifties. People in their fifties find that members of their age cohort begin to die with some regularity. The obituary section of the newspaper routinely describes the deaths of people in their fifties. Learning of deaths among members of one's high school or college classes calls attention to the increased likelihood of one's own death. The deaths of same-aged friends, former college roommates, and work colleagues most profoundly intensify one's own recognition that life ends.

A month or two ago I read about a friend of mine who died at my age in Birmingham. Aah, I think that hits you with an awareness of your own mortality. I mean, we went to high school together; we went to Harvard together; we worked together for a couple of years. So we are in the life's stream together and he's gone. And that scares you a little bit. That's your reminder! Of your mortality. Of your aging. It frightens you a little bit. And it propels you, propels you for a period of weeks, months to take in as much as you can before it's too late. And so, you are carried by the momentum of the preceding unsettling event. Six months later something else will happen. A reminder. Almost a subconscious reminder. And so, it's always there. A momentum of occurrences, of reminders.

My college roommate with whom I was very close died in Mexico City about 3 or 4 years ago. And the only guy I was ever engaged to in college before I met my husband died at about the same time. Now, I don't really know anything about their deaths. I avoided it. These things have really made me think.

A few years ago my brother died and a friend of mine died. And if you don't die you have that experience. But I think particularly my brother's death. It affected me a great deal. He was 49. It was 6 years ago. It is a very vivid picture in my mind. At some point you begin to think "What the hell is it all about? If death is this, what is life? And what are you up to and what do you want?" You realize how fragile the whole thing is. Life is fragile and tenuous and relationships in the long haul are all that mean a goddamn thing.

As might be expected, anyone who has had a life-threatening illness such as cancer or a heart attack, reports a sharpening of their own sense of mortality.

Well, OK, there is an event when mortality awareness did hit me. Seven years ago, about. I had a little problem with my colon. It was misdiagnosed. I finally had it removed and it was a benign tumor. But it is also the type of tumor that is usually pre-cancerous if it's not removed. And it was the size of a pea. I had to go to Beth Israel Hospital to get it removed. I saw it in a jar and I said. "That little son of a bitch is going to kill me, a big man," and I was almost angry at it. I learned about my own mortality. I had to wait 5 days before I got the report from pathology – whether it was benign or malignant. It was a traumatic experience for me. I was very conscious of the fact that I might have cancer and the life expectancy for something like that is about 2 years. That was a jarring experience for me. I was depressed for a couple of months just from fear. I was angry at the tumor. It also taught me quick, before it's too late, to take it all in. That particular event had great teaching value.

## The Finiteness of Time

The various events, observations, and personal experiences that call attention, sometimes dramatically, to aging have been documented. Whether perceived positively or negatively, the cumulative effect of age fifties reminders is the development of a common orientation towards the meaning of time. All respondents acknowledged the finiteness of time in their lives. In their fifties, as never before, people confront the fact that there are time limits to their lives. The description of changing time perspectives in middle age offered by Neugarten and Weinstein (1973) was strongly supported by the data. Shown by their data collected from middle-aged men and women, was that

> Life is restructured in terms of time-left-to-live rather than time since birth. Not only the reversal in directionality but the awareness that time is finite is a particularly conspicuous feature of middle age.

Many respondents reported the relative recency of the feeling that time is beginning to run out. People may use different examples or metaphors to express their feeling, but there is extraordinary consistency to their thoughts.

> Now I can see that there is somewhere up there where in time there is an end. There is some kind of limit. . . . I'd like it to go on forever, but so would everybody. . . . I know also that when one does get older the risks of various debilitating diseases get greater. And I look around at 70-year-old people and 80-year-old people, some of whom are basket cases.

> I have the feeling that time is rushing by much faster. I mean, when I was a young mother, I thought the days were 48 hours long. They never ended. Now the days go by so fast. Time is collapsing and that's an important part of aging that I'm very much aware of.

> You know, somewhere along the line, in your fifties, you begin to realize that there is a finite number of years left. . . . If I have three score and 10, there's only ten or so years left.

Once time is recognized as a diminishing resource, people have got to decide what they are going to do with that resource. Inevitable questions arise about the nature of the contributions that can realistically be made at this life point.

> I remember talking with a colleague and somebody asked her whether she'd like to be the chair (of the department), or something like that, and she said, "You know, if I were 35 or something, but I'm 60. I only have 5 years left." And I remember listening to that and it touched something in my own psyche. . . . You know, if you really want to do something; if you really want to finish off and make a contribution. . . . How much time do you have? All of a sudden time becomes a factor.

About the nature of the projects that can reasonably be started at this life point.

> It's (time) an awareness that happens when you approach 60. Because then, you see, you're looking ahead. It's something that I don't recall being aware of before that. Be-

fore that, in a way, there is no limitation of time. In other words, when you're 40 or 45, you say "Well how long is it going to take me to finish *this* book." When you're 40 finishing a project is a convenience, a luxury, a status thing, but it's not really critical.

About the possibility of starting up new life ventures.

> I think the worst thing about growing old in your thinking is that you begin to realize that you're running out of time. There isn't enough time. I don't have time to start another business. I don't have time now. This thing about 60. You realize that life is coming to an end. . . . I even think of it in terms of marriage. I think about meeting another woman. I'd like to have a nice relationship. Then I think, "In 7 years I'll be 60." And yet I say that's silly because I know peoples have relationships after that. I know it, but it's in my mind. . . . I don't relate to the idea of being too old. I relate more to the idea that there's not enough time.

Generally, questions arise about the best way to prioritize things at this point in their lives.

> My wife's father died a couple of weeks ago, and we've had two other good friends die this summer. . . . The fact that there is a dark at the end of the tunnel has been, let's say, brought forward by the events of the summer. I'm enjoying coming to work and I'm not entirely sure what I would do if I retired. But you can begin to understand that there's some finite amount of time and there are things you wish you could have time to do.

People ask questions such as these throughout their lives. The point here, however, is that these questions become more persistent in the fifties and arise in consciousness as a correlate of multiple age reminders. As body reminders, generational reminders, contextual reminders, and mortality reminders become more prominent in the fifties, they foster the common sense that time is limited. There is a broad causal connection between the accelerating range of age messages heard in the fifties and the development of the recognition that life time and work time will run out.

## Liberation in the Fifties

There has been a somewhat negative cast to the discussion thus far. After all, mortality reminders, such as illness, bodies that betray, the experience of being in-between generations, and a sense of time running out have been discussed. These concerns do point up some of the difficulties associated with the fifties. When asked, "Which age would you choose to be if you could?," most respondents did not usually name their present age. This was especially so for men who felt that in their forties they were pretty much at the top of their occupational game, had their family life under control, and still enjoyed good health. Several individuals offered opinions similar to the person who said:

> In my opinion starting somewhere in your forties is the best period. You are out from under your kids, you're still healthy, and you have a reasonable level of income. You have the time and the money to do some of the things you're interested in and that can be very nice, professionally and personally.

Although preference for the forties is a distinctive pattern of response, it is certainly not all doom and gloom in the fifties. Many individuals also talked about the positive features of the fifties. The notion that people in their fifties feel an "enriched sense of self and a capacity for coping with complexity" (Neugarten and Weinstein 1973) was supported by the data. One word that came up frequently as people described themselves was *wisdom*. The attainment of a certain wisdom with age is one of the ways in which the fifties were considered a time of personal liberation.

## Wisdom

The idea that persons at mid-life become more reflective, introspective, and self-aware (Gutmann, 1980; Erikson, 1963; Neugarten and Weinstein, 1973) is indicated by a number of studies. Speaking of adult personality structure Neugarten and Weinstein (1973) commented that

> We are impressed with the heightened importance of introspection in the mental life of middle aged persons; the stock taking, the increased reflection, and above all, the structuring and restructuring of experience – that is, the processing of new information in light of experience . . . the handing over to others the fruit of one's experience.

Several people described a feeling of wisdom that they did not possess earlier. The similar thoughts of several are caught in the words of two scientists who said:

> I think that one good aspect of aging is the knowledge of accumulated experience. That translates into wisdom. In my own mind, I'm a far wiser man. I believe that, in my own mind, to be true. Now, I don't mean learned. I mean a far wiser man in most everything – priorities, values, judgments. Not a single thing, but in general. I think it's true of most persons. They gain from life's experiences and what they take out of it.

> I'm thinking of the philosopher, Bertrand Russell, who said that the idea is to be at the early stages like a rushing river making its path and then later it gets broader and gains wisdom and gently sort of flows through the whole terrain.

One theme in the words of respondents, certainly connected with the idea of wisdom, is that during the fifties things can be seen from a larger perspective. Individuals speak of seeing their lives in a larger, more holistic way. During the fifties they begin to review their life, to look for the larger themes in the meaning of life. Whereas earlier they might have been caught up in the details of everyday life, they are now more concerned with trying to see the whole of their lives. In a more philosophical way, many, like the man quoted, are looking to understand the larger picture of their lives.

> I do reflect on age and the way I do it is by trying to pull my life together. I think I'm more reflective than I ever was and I think that's part of the aging process. I think that I am far more concerned about understanding the meaning of my life. I have to put it together in an integrated, synthesized way. And I don't feel that I have to change the world any more. I feel like I have to see what all the pieces mean.

Others suggested that as a result of this broader turn of mind they are simply less irritated by things that would have disturbed them earlier. Now they are more laid back about life and they spend less time worrying about things. They find themselves fighting life less often.

> I think that I have very much come to terms with my work. I enjoy things about it that maybe frustrated me before. I don't try to fight my life the way I did a lot of it. I was always looking at my life in an idealized way. Where I would like it to be and how I would like it to be rather than living it the way it was. And I've very conscious of living it the way it is.

> When I was younger I always wondered if I did the right thing. You know, I made some terrible gaffes. But once I was 50, I thought, "Oh, what the heck." And now I really don't worry much any more about making mistakes, about doing the right thing, about saying the right thing.

### Enjoying the empty nest

The phase of the family life cycle termed *the empty nest period* has often been viewed as a stress-inducing time for parents, particularly for mothers (Rubin, 1979). Available studies, however, can be used to cast doubt on such assumptions. Lowenthal and Chiriboga (1972) conducted in-depth interviews with a number of men and women who were approaching the empty nest phase of parenthood. These researchers found that most of their respondents were favorably anticipating the departure of their children. They believed that this new phase in their lives held out the possibility for engaging in a less complicated life style. Lowenthal and Chiriboga (1972) concluded their research report by pointing out that the empty nest period "is only rarely a low point or even a turning point of any kind in their lives. . . . Viewed in the context of the past and the anticipated future, the present period appears to be a favorable one for both men and women." Consistent with Lowenthal's and Chiriboga's findings, both men and women in the sample viewed their children's leaving as liberating, as relieving pressure, and offering up new opportunities in their own lives.

> The big problem at 50 seems to be parents growing old and that kind of thing. On the other hand, the kids are grown for better or worse. Between my wife and I we have five children and they range from good kids to real stars. No problems with drugs, no broken marriages. What's done is done with the kids. So you don't have those pressures. So, the age I'm at isn't bad . . . and I'm pretty happy at this stage.

> In my early fifties, I was so preoccupied with my growing family and doing my job. There were too many balls to juggle. . . . Now I'm in my late fifties. All the kids are gone. They've all established themselves and my wife is settled and happy. . . . Now I have a grandchild. It's nice. I go visit. What the children do with their careers and so on is behind us.

> If I could choose any age to be maybe I'd go back to 50. I couldn't go back to 40 because I couldn't have had all these children and had a career and all this other stuff (that I have now). See, the kids are really great kids and they have meaningful careers and they're terrific people. I don't think they would have been quite this good if I hadn't stayed home some of that time. . . . I feel that it's what's inside that counts. When I was in my twenties I was looking good, but it doesn't make you feel that good. Staying at home during the thirties and much of the forties bringing up children was not such a big high for me.

It should be noted that although men feel a freedom to do things that their occupational lives have made difficult, many women feel an urgency about doing occupational things that their family lives have made difficult. Both men and women feel an urgency to do things, but often in different life spheres. Although systematic data on the issue is not included here, the stories of men and women in their fifties suggested an asymmetry of interests. Many men are interested in disengaging from work and recapturing intimacy with their wives. The wives, however, have only recently been liberated from family obligations and now wish to pursue careers. The dilemmas that can result from the fact that men and women in their fifties may have reversed aspirations from earlier years is evident in the words of a man who has spent most of his adult life building his business and now wants to reconnect with his wife.

> We discovered in recent years that we've had a real kind of going in opposite directions kind of thing . . . a really significant moving in opposite directions, and the marriage just really got kind of stressful a little bit over the last year or two over this kind of stuff. . . . I think really it is my need to have her closer to me. I've been doing more complaining. I'm looking for more time to spend with her. I think we have two different images of what it means for your kids to leave home. . . . My image is, "Oh, look, now we can spend more time together; kind of some of the courtship and some of the romance that we may not have had time to do when we were first married because we started a family, and so on. I'm really kind of looking forward to closeness and really getting to know her again and all that kind of stuff. But now she seems to be saying, "Good, now I've got the time to go out and work, learn to dance, sing in the church choir and be the treasurer of the church." I watched her mother and her do a lot of things and be distracted and not have time for me, and so forth. And I have this sort of need that men in their mid-fifties seem to suddenly have. I'm kind of aware that I'm not the only one that feels this way. I've talked to some other people and it sort of appears to me that I'm not the only one. I really find this to be a difficult time and so I've had to work with that.

## Conclusion

Having once observed that the 50 to 60 year decade is relatively and unjustifiably neglected in the life cycle literature, the symbolic interactionist dictum that all meanings arise out of the process of interaction is adopted as a broad explanatory frame. Such a view encourages the perspective that the emergence of people's subjective sense of aging arises from the range of communications from those immediately around them, as well as from those arising in the culture generally. Specifically, the central argument is that the frequency and intensity of aging messages increases in the fifties, fostering a quickened sense of aging during this decade. There is a momentum of messages that qualitatively distinguishes the fifties from earlier decades in the life course, messages giving rise to a common consciousness of accelerated aging. In the thirties, forties, and even the early fifties people experience aging as both near and distant simultaneously. During the course of the fifties, however, the aging process seems less remote and more immediate, less a stranger and more an intimate.

The distinctive types of aging messages heard in the fifties have been discussed. Although numerous discrete aging messages are characteristic of the fifties, they may be seen as falling into four general classes of reminders: body, generational, contextual, and mortality reminders. First, respondents uniformly reported becoming aware of the fact that the bodies are slowing down, that purely and simply they feel the physiologically concrete changes associated with aging in a more obvious way than earlier in their lives. Several interpret such changes as a preview of old age which will happen when their bodies no longer allow them to do as they wish. Second, those currently in their fifties are in the middle of several generations. Their parents, their own children, and often their grandchildren constitute multiple mirrors in which they see their aging selves reflected. A third and powerful set of reminders, contextual reminders, emerge from the fact that those in their fifties increasingly find themselves among the oldest in a number of settings. Especially potent is the recognition that they are often among the oldest at work. Finally, there are mortality reminders. Because of the sharp increase in the number of people who die in their fifties in contrast to earlier years, those between 50 and 60 feel a heightened sense of their own mortality. Taken together, these four generic types of reminders help to interpret the findings of earlier studies in which have been documented a universal sense of finiteness of time in the middle years. The pervasiveness of the four reminders described, however, does not imply that the fifties are experienced negatively. Respondents see the fifties as a time of liberation in their lives, a time during which they are able to view their lives in a broader, more holistic way than earlier. Several also experience the empty nest period, often beginning in the fifties, as liberating them from significant family responsibilities.

It is important to point out that although the discussion has been about widely shared aspects of consciousness in the fifties, it must be acknowledged that a common consciousness need not propel people to behave in identical ways. The manner in which a consciousness is translated into behavior will depend on other features of people's lives. For example, it seems safe to predict that those in different occupations will attribute different symbolic significance to the common recognition that their bodies are slowing down and will consequently respond differently to such a change, or that persons with different religious beliefs will respond differently to mortality reminders, and so on. The social-psychological perspective underlying the analysis has led to an appreciation of the basis for common aging experience in the fifties. That same perspective requires that the additional step be taken of learning how such social attributes as gender, race, ethnicity, occupation, and class are associated with different adaptations to a common subjective sense of aging. With such a research agenda proper respect can be accorded to both regularities in the life cycle and the diversity of responses human beings make to them.

## Acknowledgments

I wish to acknowledge John Donovan, Lynda Holmstrom and John Williamson for their help and suggestions on earlier versions of this article.

## References

Atchley, R. (1976). *The sociology of retirement*. New York: John Wiley.
Barfield, R., and Morgan, J. (1969). *Early retirement: The decision and the experience*. Ann

Arbor: University of Michigan, Institute of Social Research.

Buhler, C. (1968). The general structure of the human life cycle. In C. Buhler and F. Massarik (eds.), *In the course of human life*, New York: Springer Publishing Co.

Blumer, H. (1969). *Symbolic interactionism: Perspective and method*. Englewood Cliffs, New Jersey: Prentice-Hall.

Cooley, C. H. (1909). *Social organization*. New York: Charles Scribner's.

Chilman, C. (1972). Families in development at mid-stage of the family life cycle. In J. Wiseman (ed.), *People as partners*. San Francisco: Canfield Press.

Datan, N., Rodeheaver, D., and Hughes, F. (1987). Adult development and aging. *Annual Review of Psychology* 38, 153–80.

Erikson, E. 1963. *Childhood and society*. New York: W. W. Norton.

Farrell, M., and Rosenberg, S. (1981). *Men at midlife*. Dover, MA: Auburn House.

Glaser, B., and Strauss, A. (1967). *The discovery of grounded theory*. Chicago: Aldine.

Glick, P. 1977. Updating the life cycle of the family. *Journal of Marriage and the Family*, 39, 5–13.

Gordon, M. (1964). *Assimilation in America*. New York: Oxford.

Gould, R. (1978). *Transformations*. New York: Simon and Schuster.

Gutmann, D. (1980). The post-parental years: Clinical problems and developmental possibilities. In W. Norman and T. Scaramelia (eds.), *Mid-Life: Developmental and clinical issues*. New York: Brunner/Mazel.

Gutmann, D. (1987). *Reclaimed powers: Toward a new psychology of men and women in later life*. New York: Basic Books.

Hewitt, J. (1986). *Self and society*. Boston: Allyn and Bacon.

Karp, D. (1985). Gender, academic careers, and the social psychology of aging. *Qualitative Sociology*, 8, 9–28.

Karp, D. (1986a). You can take the boy out of Dorchester, but you can't take Dorchester out of the boy: Toward a social psychology of mobility. *Symbolic Interaction*, 9, 19–36.

Karp, D. (1986b). Academics beyond mid-life. Some observations on changing consciousness in the fifty to sixty year decade. *International Journal of Aging and Human Development*, 22, 81–103.

Karp, D. (1987). Professionals beyond mid-life. Some observations on work satisfaction in the fifty to sixty year decade. *Journal of Aging Studies*, 1, 209–23.

Karp, D., and Yoels, W. (1982). *Experiencing the life cycle: A social psychology of aging*. IL: Charles C Thomas.

Levinson, D., Darrow, C., Klein, E., Levinson, M., and McKee, B. (1978). *The seasons of a man's life*. New York: Knopf.

Lowenthal, M., and Chiriboga, D. (1972). Transitions to the empty nest. *Archives of General Psychiatry*, 26, 8–14.

Marshall, V. (1980). *Last chapters: A sociology of aging and dying*. Belmont CA: Wadsworth.

Marshall, V. (Ed.). (1986). *Later life: The social psychology of aging*. Beverly Hills: Sage Publishing Co.

Mead, G. H. (1934). *Mind, self, and society:* Chicago: The University of Chicago Press.

Molloy, J. (1976). *Dress for success*. New York: Warner Books.

Munichs, J. (1980). *Old age and finitude*. New York: Arno Press.

Neugarten, B. L., and Neugarten, D. A. (1986). Changing meanings of age in the aging society. In A. Pifer and Lydia Bronte (ed.), *Our Aging Society*. New York: Norton.

Neugarten, B., and Weinstein, K. (1973). The changing American grandparent. In M. Lasswell. and T. Lasswell (eds.), *Love, marriage, and family*. Glenview, IL: Scott Foresman.

Rosow, I. (1974). *Socialization to old age*. Berkeley, CA: University of California Press. *American handbook of psychiatry*. New York: Basic Books.

Rubin, L. (1979). *Women of a certain age*. New York: Harper and Row.

Sheehy, G. (1977). *Passages*. New York: E. P. Dutton.

Simmel, G. (1950). The stranger. In K. Wolff (ed.), *The sociology of Georg Simmel* New York: The Free Press.

Stone, G. (1962). Appearance and the self. In A. Rose (ed.), *Human behavior and social processes*. Boston: Houghton Mifflin.

Vaillant, G. (1977). *Adaptation to life*. Boston: Little, Brown.

Wood, V., and Robertson, J. (1974). The significance of grandparenthood. In J. Gubrium (ed.), *Time, roles, and self in old age*. New York: Human Sciences Press.

# 7 Identity Foreclosure: Women's Experiences of Widowhood as Expressed in Autobiographical Accounts

## Deborah Kestin Van Den Hoonaard

## Introduction

This article[1] presents findings from a study of women's experiences of widowhood that uses data from a largely neglected source – published autobiographical accounts of widows. This source first aroused my interest when a student lent me *When Things Get Back to Normal* (Dohaney 1989),[2] consisting of a journal of the author's first year as a widow. I spent two hours enmeshed in this book, for the first time sensing that I had a glimpse of what the experience of being a widow really felt like. This came as a surprise because I had spent much of the previous few years reading all of the research on widowhood I could get my hands on. What had been absent from virtually all work on women's experience as widows that I had read had been the voices of the widows themselves. Published autobiographical accounts of widowhood can allow us to hear these voices, and thereby learn not only which issues are most important to their authors but also the meaning that an important life event like becoming a widow has for the experiencer (Polkinghorne 1996: 82).[3]

Autobiographical accounts provide narrative data which researchers most often collect through in-depth interviewing. We are just beginning to recognise the significance of narrative data, which, as Polkinghorne (1996: 92) argues, 'provide researchers with the richest and thickest source of explicating their subjects' understanding of their own lives'. These stories are very moving and allow us to get a sense, however limited, of the emotional experience of losing one's husband. Listening to widows' stories, as they choose to tell them, gives us a glimpse of widowhood 'from the inside' (Birren et al. 1996). As Thompson et al. (1990: 13) discovered in their research, autobiographies and life stories can result in an openness and sense of wholeness that provide an advantage over surveys and other structured methods of data collection.

The British literature on widowhood contains classic works that include narrative accounts of both widowhood and ageing in general (most notably Townsend 1957; Marris 1958; Tunstall 1966; Blythe 1979). Marris (1958: 135), in collecting material for *Widows and Their Families*, specifically chose to ask 'indirect questions' which proved to elicit responses which were 'much more revealing' and moving than

Original publication: Van Den Hoonard, Deborah Kestin, "Identity Foreclosure: Women's Experiences of Widowhood as Expressed in Autobiographical Accounts," *Ageing and Society* 17 (1997), pp. 533–51.

prompted responses would have been. Blythe (1979) also included the evocative words of the people he studied. In contrast, Tunstall (1966) tells the story of his subjects in his own words with only the occasional quotation. I found that even this minimal move from the subjects' own words created a feeling of greater objectivity and less ability to 'feel' their situation from their perspective.

These accounts of widowhood speak not only to social scientists, but also to women who are experiencing widowhood. Widows, whom I have interviewed for a current study, have told me that they read these books both to help themselves adjust to their new situation and to learn what widowhood has meant to others. Thus, although it would be a mistake to assume that these narratives allow us to generalise about the experience of widowhood, they do, at least partially, shape the experiences of the widows who read them and how they define those experiences.

## The Accounts

The ten books that provided the data for this study were written by widows about their lives as widows. The accounts are American and Canadian and, thus, represent a North American perspective. Although beyond the scope of this article, it would be of interest to compare these accounts with others which reflect other cultures. The best known of these ten books is *Widow* by Lynn Caine (1974); the oldest was published in 1965 (Beck) and the most recent written in 1990 (Brothers; Rose; Rice; Graham). The widows who wrote these books range in age from Jane Seskin who was in her twenties when her husband died, to Joyce Brothers, Xenia Rose and M. T. Dohaney who, it would seem, were in their fifties.

The majority of the authors lost their husbands after long illnesses – primarily cancer. All the authors spend some time describing their experiences during their husbands' illnesses. They devote up to one-quarter of their books to this theme. For these women, the period of dying was an initial stage of widowhood.[4] Nonetheless, anticipatory grief did not lessen the shock for these widows. All felt completely unprepared for their husbands' deaths. Several (for example, Caine 1974) noted that they and their husbands had maintained a stoic composure which prevented them from sharing their pain and grief at the impending loss.[5]

The widows who wrote these books do not represent a cross-section of widows. Four (Caine, Dohaney, Brothers and Mooney) are writers or have ties to publishing. Although we know from Lopata's work that widows tend to idealise their dead husbands, it is clear that these women did have satisfying marriages. None report relief – there are no reports, for example, of abusive husbands. Not surprisingly, these authors are more highly educated than would be a representative sample. Nonetheless, although it would be inappropriate to generalise their experiences to other widows, the issues these widows raise should alert us to the importance of attending to what widows, themselves, feel is paramount.

Autobiographies are 'tantalizingly elusive' (Thompson et al. 1990: 45). They tease the reader with what they include and what they omit. The reader has no way of knowing what publishers have told the authors to remove. As well, these books are published with an audience in mind. Although they are not advice books, it is clear that the expected audience is, to a large extent, other widows. In that way, not only do they inform us about how these women experienced the loss of their husbands, but also what they feel is important to tell novice widows.

In this respect, the autobiography is an attempt to provide a 'coach' (Strauss 1959: 110) who can 'seek to move [a new widow] along a series of steps [which] are not entirely institutionalized and invariant . . . because some very surprising things are happening to [her] that require explanation.'[6] The books by Brothers (1990) and Rose (1990) highlight this problem. One wonders whether they feel a poverty of identity to the same extent as the others, or if they, as therapists, are attempting to echo the experiences of their patients and, thereby, very consciously, provide some coaching.

These ten accounts are told overwhelmingly from the author's point of view. Hence, we do not learn, for example, what the widows might have done – wittingly or un-wittingly – to force a change in their friends' perceptions of them. Nor can we inves-tigate the seeming paradox of their complaint that whilst couples felt uncomfortable when with them, they themselves felt awkward when with couples.[7]

Two of the accounts stand out from the others because their authors, Rebecca Rice and Laurie Graham, married considerably older (i.e. thirty-plus years) and highly accomplished men. Laurie Graham (1990: 42), for example, describes her husband as 'larger than life'. For both of these authors, their marriages to older men resulted in a distinctive type of marriage, very different reactions to becoming widowed and, therefore, focus on very different issues. Neither woman talks much about changing relationships with friends. Rebecca Rice spends about half her time writing about the way in which her parents and sister came to terms with her marriage to a much older man. This was still being worked out after his death. Laurie Graham's account uses the renovations to the house she and her husband had shared as a metaphor for her recovery. She does not refer to friends at all – in fact, unlike all the other accounts, she finally concludes that her dead husband will 'be the touchstone of the rest of my life' (1990: 173).

The striking difference between these two accounts and the other eight, suggests that a woman marrying a much older, highly successful, man results in a very differ-ent relationship between the couple and those who know them. This is a phenom-enon worthy of separate study.

I have analysed these ten books as if they were in-depth interviews with the writers. I have excluded books that are billed as 'Advice Books', for these have a different focus (e.g. Gates 1990). Through a close reading of the texts, I found that a series of themes emerge, primarily related to the widows' sense of identity. These themes are the loss of identity at the levels of self, personal and impersonal social relations, the process of building a new identity, and the transformed identity.

As Lund et al. (1986: 236) note, one's self-concept 'arises from and is maintained by social interactions and relationships with significant others'. These widows had lost their most significant other – their husbands. This loss meant that they could no longer reproduce social interaction in a meaningful way. Everywhere they went, and with everyone they interacted, they were treated differently; they even treated them-selves differently. The interaction they depended upon to credit their identity had disappeared, and their sense of 'authentic selfhood' with it (Weigart 1986: 169). It is this, the disappearance of validation of a sense of self at every level, that I refer to as 'identity foreclosure'.

### Identity Foreclosure

The ten authors focus on their experience as one of transformation, rather than as one of recovery or adjustment. Their stories give us a sense of how their changing relationships and circumstances have effected that transformation by stripping them of their identity and forcing them to see themselves differently.[8]

I describe this process as 'identity foreclosure'. This term refers to the fact that, although the writers of these books at first tried to hang on to their identities as wives, they no longer had the social resources to do so. They found themselves symbolically stranded on the sidewalk with their belongings (i.e. the elements of their identity) strewn about them. Even today, many women take their identity from their husbands and, because of this, these authors write evocatively of their loss of sense of self. Although Ann Martin Matthews (1987: 359) states that research on widowhood rarely acknowledges this centrality of the role of wife in women's lives and identities, these autobiographical accounts all take note of this.

Although 'identity foreclosure' may seem a strong term, it reflects the preponderance of comments in these books that the authors no longer knew who they were. Remarks of this sort also appear in advice books and books that recount histories of support groups. For example, Menton (1995: 15) quotes a woman in a support group as saying 'I don't know who I am any more'. Menton replied by asking 'Who do you feel like?' The response was 'No one.' Another woman in the group remarked: 'I look in the mirror and see only a partial person with no real identity' (Menton 1995: 16).

Identity foreclosure takes place on three levels: (1) widows do not know who they are to themselves; (2) they do not know who they are to their close friends; and (3) they do not know how they fit into society in general. I will use the words of the ten authors to illustrate each of these three levels. Their language communicates their distress, disorientation and, often, bewilderment.

Anselm Strauss (1959) discusses how the 'loss of world' can lead to a total loss of identity and the need to build a new one. The women who wrote the accounts have experienced this 'loss of world'. Their most important 'me' has disappeared and they are 'midstream between danger and discovery' (Strauss, 1959: 39) so that even though some parts of their identity (e.g. that of mother) may remain, they feel that they do not know who they are. Although a widow is still a mother, it may be that in her attempt to be both mother *and* father, she really is not even sure how to play that very familiar role. Lopata (1996: 130–41) discusses how a husband's death contributes to the disorganisation of a woman's mother role. Thus they no longer know how to act or what to expect in previously familiar situations. As a result, they foreclose on their identity to themselves.

### *Self-foreclosure*

These authors write evocatively of how they foreclosed on their identity:

> After Martin died, I had learned that my identity had been derived from him. I did not know who I was. (Caine 1978: 68)

My life was tuned to his and without him, the focus flickered out like a burnt match. (Mooney 1981: 22)

Who am I without Judd? Who will define my existence for me? (Seskin 1975: 170)

Even those widows who do not explicitly state that they had taken their identities from their husbands, had problems with figuring out who they were. Rose's comments conjure up Cooley's view of the looking-glass self (1902):

My sense of self, to a great extent, became linked to being Leonard's wife . . . We reassured, validated, reinforced, and encouraged. We mirrored the best part of each other. I lost that mirror when Leonard died. It was a double death. When he had said, 'You're wonderful,' I believed him . . . But with Leonard gone, I felt paralysed. It was as if he had taken a major part of me with him. (Rose 1990: 31)

This sensation of being only half a person pervaded these new widows:

Darling, I'm half living without you; half of me is dead. (Beck, 1965: 38)

After Milt died, wherever I was, whatever I was doing, I felt that I was only half of what had been a whole – and that whole was lost forever. (Brothers 1990: 142)

And so, not only was their way of life demolished, but the sense of who they were became blurred. Brothers (1990: 184) commented that her whole sense of self was shattered, that she became 'a sad Humpty Dumpty of a woman', while Rose searched for her identity in the concrete act of ordering personal stationery:

. . . as if the decision, once made would tell me who I was. All I'd have to do was open my stationery box and there I'd be. (Rose 1990: 15)

Perhaps one of the reasons they saw themselves as shattered 'humpty-dumpty women' is related to Ebaugh's account of role exit. In her study of people who voluntarily left roles (e.g. ex-nuns, and ex-doctors), she noted that there was some sort of 'hangover identity'. This referred to a 'role residual that is part of self-identity and must be incorporated into current ideas of self' (Ebaugh 1988: 5). How much more shocking must be the experience of these women who were thrust out of their role by circumstance. As Strauss (1959: 146) notes, 'It is the very lack of design that is reflected subjectively in feelings of personal discontinuity, of wrecked or abandoned selves'. Until a new concept of self was developed, these women did not have an identity; all that was left was this hangover identity, which, by itself, was incomplete.

### Identifying moments

The realisation of being a widow hit the writers of these books hard. Most commented on the shock of realising that the term 'widow' now referred to them. These 'identifying moments' (Charmaz 1991: 207) are 'telling moments filled with new self-images . . . telling because they spark sudden realizations [and] reveal hidden images of self . . .' They often occur when widows have to acknowledge their status officially when filling out a form:

> I was called a widow today. 'Sign here' the girl in the office of vital statistics said when I went to pick up a copy of your death certificate . . . 'Right here. In the block that says widow of the deceased.' The word pierced me like a lance and my sharp intake of breath was audible . . . Later as I walked home, I tried to give voice to my new label. Widow! Widow! I mouthed the word over and over and although I could hear it thundering in my head, no sound would leave my lips . . . Until two weeks ago, widow was only a word in the English language. Now it is me . . . (Dohaney 1989: 6–7)

> I try to fill in the answers on the application form for a charge plate: Name: Jane Seskin. I have trouble moving the pen and checking off the next question; Marital Status: Single——, Married——, Divorced——, Widowed——. After a time, I walk around the apartment and commit my status in life, to black and white print. (Seskin 1975: 175)[9]

Although these women may have felt shocked to realise that the term 'widow' now referred to them, they all knew what the connotations of the word were.[10] Each one described the image that the word widow conjured up for her. They used the following phrases to convey the despair they felt: 'a designing widow, a veiled threat' (Beck); 'leftover women, less fortunate' (Brothers); 'second-class citizen' (Brothers, Caine); 'empty' (Caine, Dohaney); 'dignified silence, brave' (Caine); 'alone, outsiders' (Caine); 'a woman with a bleak life' (Dohaney); 'life's losers . . . in the printer's world . . . something left over that nobody can figure out what to do with' (Mooney); 'Loneliness, gray hair, dependent on grandchildren and Walter Cronkite, bridge, matinees and fear' (Mooney); 'no husband equals no one . . . hearing the word made me feel as if I weren't there' (Rose); 'ignored' (Seskin). These connotations did not provide a 'self' that any of these widows wanted to embrace.

As they began to search around for a new identity, these authors discovered that in many ways they had not really acted as adults in their marriages. They became aware of their former identities as child-brides or wives:

> My philosophy is very different from my original childlike faith, yet it satisfies me. (Beck 1965: 8)

> If he had not died, I am sure I would have lived happily ever after as a twentieth-century child wife never knowing what I was missing. (Caine 1974: 181)

> No more the child wife, I have learned how to fight for what I want. I have learned to redefine who I am, give up the role in which I was cast for thirty-one years. (Mooney 1981: 309)

> The irony, of course, was that in marrying a man old enough to be my father, I had never relinquished that dependent, daughterly side of myself. (Rice 1990: 77)

### Foreclosure in personal relationships

As almost all research on widowhood has found, friendship does not often survive the widowhood of one of its members (e.g. Lopata 1973a, 1975, 1979; Matthews 1991; van den Hoonaard 1994). In fact, all but four accounts describe at some length the circumstances of the termination of friendships with couples after the deaths of their husbands and how they felt about it.[11]

This ending of friendships did not happen abruptly. It was usually accomplished when the widow slowly began to realise that her 'friends' had stopped phoning her or ceased inviting her to social occasions:

> I was hurt, as so many widows are hurt, to realize that a number of my married friends had dropped me. It took time for this to dawn on me . . . But even with my busy life, I slowly learned that I was being left out of all kinds of affairs that I would have been asked to if Martin had been alive. (Caine 1974: 145)

> The metamorphosis of married friends and acquaintances takes time and at first is not very noticeable. At first it is a matter of the phone not ringing as often with reports on bargain shopping . . . after a while, when I noticed that my party dresses hadn't been off the hangers in months, I was frightened . . . angry, bitter and scared. Where were they all when I needed them? Was it really possible that years of friendship can be wiped out by a change of social status? (Mooney 1981: 88)

> [My friends] became less and less available and quickly, quietly vanished. (Rose 1990: 11–12)

> The disappearance of friends was accompanied by surprise, hurt, and disappointment: Where are all the people who called so eagerly after the funeral to invite me out to dinner or to their home? I'm lonely. I still sleep with the light turned on, lying curled up on the right side of a double bed. (Seskin 1975: 174)

> So many people wrote, 'You must come and stay with us for a few days . . .' And I would have been very grateful for this respite. But no one extended a definite invitation, no one followed up with a date and a time. And this was hard. A widow feels so alone in the world, and then when friends seemingly let her down, it is just another blow making her feel even more alone. (Caine 1974: 87)

The explanations for the cessation of friendship focused on the widows' perceptions (whether true or not) that the friends of pre-widowhood days were actually their husbands' friends rather than theirs. It may be that their friends had previously not seen them as one individual and their husband as another but rather as a collective unit (McCall and Simmons 1966: 411, quoted in Lopata 1973b). Once that unit was destroyed through the death of one of its members, the identity of the remaining member was irrevocably changed. Wylie (1988: 35) in her book of advice for widows comments, 'two take away one doesn't equal one. Most of the time it equals nothing'. Other reasons that the authors gave included the inability of friends to understand or empathise with what the widow is experiencing; and the friends' feeling of discomfort or embarrassment around the new widow, especially if she is allowing them to witness her suffering:

> I had made the mistake that so many widows and divorcees make. I had believed that my husband's friends and business associates were my friends, too. They were not. They were my acquaintances, and when there was no common bond to hold us together, no focus for our relationship, no Martin, we drifted apart. (Caine 1978: 197)

> 'Can't you talk about anything else' . . . I felt as if I were being governed by an internal alarm clock that hadn't completed its run. My friends were in a hurry to put an end to my mourning. (Rose 1990: 82)

> To the friends of my former existence, I had entered a foreign country. I was still seeing them for card games on my days off, but the three days [at work] were outside their

sphere of interest . . . Nobody I knew in my 'Before this' could ever imagine finding herself [in my situation]. At first they met me for lunch, complaining that it was difficult to find my office. After a while they ceased to come. (Mooney 1981: 79–80)

Mooney had moved into a new 'social world' (Shibutani 1955: 565–7), a 'cultural area, the boundaries of which are set . . . by the limits of effective communication'. There was, therefore, no basis on which to maintain the intimacy of friendship; this widow had violated the group by becoming a different person living in a different social world and no longer validating others' identity, nor did they validate hers (Weigart 1986: 171).

As these new widows tried to hang on to their sense of self, they found that their friends began to treat them like second-class citizens and did not include them in social events that they had taken for granted. The authors of these books found themselves unprepared for the absolute change that they experienced:

. . . there are two fellows in the car pool that I hadn't met before, who are continually making remarks about widows. They know I am a widow, but they don't seem to take into consideration that I am human and have feelings too . . . it seems as if they can't resist making insinuations about widows in general . . . I can't even answer them; I can only retreat within myself . . . The hurt is too great. (Beck 1965: 61–2)

I had not expected to become a member of a minority group when Milt died, but I did. When a woman is divorced, there is a sense that she has failed. While people do not consider a widow to be a failure, they do view her as less fortunate than they, and for this reason they have less respect for her. The result is that old friends drop the widow, and families tend to treat her with less consideration. (Brothers 1990: 102).

Lower status often resulted in the widows being treated like servants or children by friends and family. Brothers provides an example of a widow she knew whose friends began treating her like a servant:

The winter my husband died, one woman started leaving her two kids with me on weekends so she and her husband could go skiing. 'I know you must be lonely', she would tell me as if she were the one who was doing the favor. (1990: 104–5)

Another widow wrote to Brothers commenting that her children now treat her like 'a child or someone who's not all there . . . they think they can run my life' (1990: 110).

Dohaney (1989: 63–4) notes that her friends 'refer me to widows now as if I'm a collector of them, as if I no longer want to be discriminating in my friendships'. These friends seemed to assume that widows simply belong together, that having lost a husband gives them enough in common to cancel out any differences in personality or interest that may have existed when they were married. This phenomenon is common for groups that suffer some form of stigma, which Parkes (1986) claims is suffered by all widows.

These widows were not only supposed to enjoy the company of other widows, any widows, but they were no longer welcome to occasions, like dinner parties, where it is awkward to have someone who is not a member of a couple present. It is not only that widows' friends excluded them from such social events, but the way in which they excluded them shocked and reinforced the feeling of having a lower status for these women:

> She had taken it for granted that I knew. The world has its rules, it is geared to pairs, to balanced numbers and married couples, and the misfits had better understand early that if they want to enjoy the rest of their lives, they should seek friendship among their own kind. (Mooney 1981: 18)

> I was really stricken when I found out that a dear friend had not invited me to her annual . . . dinner. This has been a tradition among our little group for a good ten years . . . the year after Martin died, I wasn't invited. In my naivete, in my self-centeredness, I thought at first the dinner had been cancelled because the hostess thought I would be too sad. But no, the dinner had been held. Instead of the Caines, another couple had been invited. Lynn Caine, widow, was no longer a desirable dinner guest. After that I became conscious of being left out of other gatherings of people whom I had always considered good, dear friends. (Caine 1974: 145–6)

Xenia Rose recounts a story of one of her patients (a new widow) being left out of a dinner party. The host of the party told the widow about the dinner party and 'suddenly' the widow 'realized she wasn't being invited. The incident made her feel like a nonperson' (1990: 10–11). It was not only when they thought about themselves and when they interacted with friends that these authors felt lost, but their experiences on an impersonal level also contributed to their feeling of having no place in the world.

### Foreclosure in impersonal relationships

These widows note the ways in which they fit into society also foreclose on their identity. First, the common practice of shared credit cards reinforced the feeling of nonexistence for some:

> Clip, clip, clip my credit card at Lord and Taylor as Booth's wife was dropping piece by piece into the trash . . . Over in the credit department I was now nobody's wife, but just another woman trying to establish credit late in life. (Mooney 1981: 267)

> VISA shredded my card and said I had ceased to exist. Because I had never established my own account, I now had no credit rating . . . This is just one more conspiratory indicator that you have stopped existing . . . (Rose 1990: 16–17)

Of course these women had not ceased to exist. Rather they had experienced a concrete example of foreclosure on their previous identity. It was also their perceptions of the world, as they had previously known it, as a coupled world, that made them feel like fish out of water on a broader level, this forced them to learn to break the unspoken taboo against women's going to public places, like restaurants and parties, alone:

> There comes a time when she discovers that she is ostracized by our couple-oriented society. When she is yearning for comfort, for companionship, to be included in the world of families where she used to belong so naturally, then she finds that she has been excluded from most of the intimacies of her old friends, the social life she used to take

for granted. (Caine 1974: 141)

My loneliness was overwhelming. 'Two by two marching into the ark', I said to myself as I sadly watched the rest of the world go by. 'Everyone is part of a pair except me'. 'Nonsense', responded my rational self, 'you're seeing things because you are feeling lost and raw'. But loneliness won over rationality, I continued to see a universe of couples. (Rose 1990: 89)

[I] ate dinner in my room the first two nights [in a resort hotel], afraid of entering the dining room and sitting at a table for one. I feel like I'm all alone in a coupled society – man and woman, woman and woman, man and man, and then there's me. (Seskin 1975: 178)

With this recognition of what they were, i.e. widows, and what they had been, the authors realised that they suffered from a poverty of identity and were ready to begin to develop a new one. They did this through taking on new responsibilities, learning to see themselves as 'one', and seeing themselves as 'new women'.

## Building a New Identity

The books I read focused on the great effort these widows made to take on new responsibilities and to learn to make decisions on their own.[12] All discovered how much they did not know. Most found that there were many jobs around the house that they had simply left to their husbands to do.[13] Brothers comments:

I always considered myself extremely competent in managing both my home and my career, but I was only competent in coping with my half. (1990: 87)

Some were initially immobilised with indecision while others got by at first by asking themselves what their spouses would have done in a particular situation. But all eventually learned to handle things themselves. Dohaney (1989: 77–8) ends her journal by listing a series of things she had learned to do in the twelve months of widowhood. She had learned:

to drive a car; to search a dark basement for intruders; to cut a squash; to fasten her own pearls; to warm her own feet; to change a ceiling light bulb; to sleep alone; to travel solo; to talk to service people.

Her list gives us a hint of the wide range of new responsibilities and emotional adjustments which gave her confidence. She had found a potential 'me' (Strauss 1959: 96) that she never knew was inside, one that moved from potential to actual through 'play[ing] a strange but important role and unexpectedly handl[ing] it well'.

One area not mentioned in Dohaney's list but present in all the accounts (including Dohaney's) is that of financial matters. Some of the widows had real money worries. Caine's husband had no insurance; Mooney needed to get a job in order to pay the tax bill on her house; Dohaney noted that her income potential was reduced by two-thirds; Seskin did not know anything at all about finance. These women report brooding about money more than was necessary. But more surprising is the fact that even those widows who were financially well off worried about money to an absurd degree. Caine (1988: 76–7) quotes a letter she received from a widow:

> I have a job as an office manager and I make a decent living and don't have big money worries. But suddenly I find myself terrified that I won't have enough money to pay the bills.

Most striking are the comments by Joyce Brothers. She comments that she has enough money to 'always live comfortably', but she still found that:

> What really upset me – to the point of losing sleep over it – was my financial situation . . . I felt financially insecure . . . more than insecure. I felt poor. I spent hours worrying at night writing down lists of my expenses and my earnings to make sure I had enough to get by . . . All I thought of was saving money. (1990: 138–40)

At the time of writing these books, none of these authors were destitute; all had mastered their fears about money and were making enough to get along. In addition, Brothers' reaction communicates the feeling that part of her sense of poverty was the poverty of identity – she tried to alleviate her lack of a concrete identity by focusing on tangible wealth.

## Transformed Identity

Through the loss of their identity and the various phenomena discussed above, these authors developed new identities. By the time they wrote of their experiences as widows they had been transformed. Almost all describe themselves as new women. Although they would not have chosen to be widows, they like the new women they have become better than the ones they were when they were wives:

> I have changed as well. I should put it even more strongly. I feel transformed. (Brothers 1990: 195)

> I can testify that while my grief has been a bitter burden, it has also changed me and made me more aware of the importance of living each 'minute of running time' to the utmost . . . I am another woman now. And I like this woman better. But it was a hard birth. (Caine 1974: 68)

These writers communicate a profound change in how they see themselves. They have discovered a potential 'me' that contributed to a completely different sense of who they are through the mastering of new tasks as well as learning how to function in the new 'social world' into which they have moved. This is in contrast to Strauss's (1959: 126) comment that when mourning is over, the bereaved becomes 'more or less himself again'. As these authors so eloquently communicate, they are never 'themselves' again. Dohaney's title, *When Things Get Back to Normal*, underlines this unanticipated phenomenon.[14]

As 'new women', these widows have different characteristics from those they had as wives. They identify a number of attributes, which they see in themselves, that are a direct consequence of their experience as widows. They are: 'more at peace [with] a quiet philosophy' (Beck 1965: 100); more serious (Caine 1974: 156); they 'feel pleasure in solitude' (Caine 1974: 156); are braver and more confident (Caine 1974: 159; Seskin 1975: 172); 'stronger' (Caine 1974: 182; 1978: 14; Mooney 1981: 309); 're-sponsible for myself . . . [able] to stand alone' (Caine 1978: 103; Mooney 1981: 148); 'more sociable, more tolerant, and more integrated' (Rose 1990: 176–7); 'more interested in people, much more sensitive to them' (Brothers 1990: 195); and perhaps most significantly, 'more independent' (Caine 1974: 155; Rose 1990: 176–7; Mooney 1981: 305). These characteristics not only denote change, they also tell us about valid adult qualities in North America, particularly those associated with self-reliance and independence.

## Implications

The empirical findings of this study include the recognition that widowhood is a process, the identification of the three levels of identity foreclosure, and the tension between self-definition and social expectations.

The autobiographies that I read for this article all chronicle a process that began either with the diagnosis of terminal illness or the sudden death of the authors' husbands and continued through their reporting of such a complete transformation that they felt like a different person. The books describe the closing off of the writers' previous identities (that of wives of particular people) at every level. It is almost as if their identity were composed of a pyramid of elements, and their husband's deaths have resulted in a bottom block's being removed – the other elements may still remain, but they need to be reassembled in a new way on a new foundation. It is the recognition of identity foreclosure that has allowed these women to construct a new identity brick by brick.

Lofland looks at what is lost when a husband dies by examining seven 'threads of connectedness' by which we are linked to others:

> by the *roles* we play . . . the *help* we receive . . . the wider *network* of others made available to us . . . the *selves* others created or sustain . . . the comforting *myths* they allow us . . . the *reality* they validate for us and . . . the *futures* they make possible. (1982: 231)

If someone counts on one person to provide all these connections, the result is devastating because 'all (or almost all) of the actor's connections are severed' (Lofland 1982: 235). For the women who wrote these books, it seems that although they might not have limited their connections to their husbands, all their threads of connectedness were mediated through their relationship with their husbands and their role as Mrs.———. Other roles were still there, but it was as if these authors had taken off their glasses – things seemed blurry, and they needed a new prescription in order to recognise and interpret even familiar roles in a new way.

The quoted excerpts from the autobiographies merely scratch the surface of the richness of the data which these widows have provided in their accounts.[15] Their evocative language puts us as 'inside' their experience as we can get and, as Homans

(1964) noted so many years ago, brings women back into our contemplation of a very common experience. These data also bring up issues which have not appeared in interview studies:

- The contribution that learning to do things they previously depended on their husbands for – making both for a sense of pride and for the embracing of a new sense of self;
- The briefness of the period which we give widows to grieve openly;
- The dislike of, and desire to distance themselves from, the term 'widow', and
- The use of new projects (such as house renovation) for the development of pride and a new, desirable identity.[16]

These issues may be explored in future studies in order to examine the extent to which they reflect women's experiences of widowhood, in general.

Yet, as powerful as the material is, there is still resistance to a study of women's experiences as widows. I have presented this material at academic conferences and to the general public a number of times. Each audience, professional or not, suggests that another group, for example the widows' children or divorced women, should be included in the study. I would argue as does Heinemann (1982) that widows are important to study in their own right both because so many women will one day share their experiences and because, as with any other group, these women's experiences shed light on the human condition.

## Notes

1   Parts of this paper were presented to the Qualitative Analysis Conference in Waterloo, Ontario, in 1993 and 1994. I appreciate comments offered by participants at those conferences as well as by Gary Kenyon, Robert Mullaly, Will van den Hoonaard, Sandy Wachholz, Sylvia Hale, and anonymous reviewers.
2   My thanks to Susan Breen, a student, who gave me this book to read.
3   I am grateful to Sylvia Hale for pointing out that published accounts also have to please publishers whose goal may be primarily to make money. Thus, *unpublished* diaries may give a clearer picture of what widows write primarily for their own purposes.
4   In a narrative-interview study currently in progress (1997), I have found that some women feel they need to talk about their whole married lives as well as the period of their husbands' dying in order to explain their experience of widowhood. As Silverman (1988) notes, in order to understand widowhood, we need to know 'what is lost when a spouse dies'.
5   This is contrary to Carey (1979–80) who found adjustment to widowhood easier for those whose husbands had been ill a long time. However, Connidis (1989:30) found that older persons 'do not prepare for the death of a spouse even when providing care during a terminal illness'.
6   The popularity of these books and the fact that many of the widows I have interviewed have told me that they have read these books (often given to them by friends) testifies to the fact that there is no 'coach' readily available for many widows.
7   My thanks to Sylvia Hale for these insights.
8   Silverman (1988: 189) notes the need to investigate just these issues in order to discover 'the impact of widowhood . . . beyond the first few years'.

9    In contrast, Smith (1991: 277) found that the women she interviewed wrestled with the realisation that they were widows and consequently described a more gradual process of closure of their 'wife' identity.

10    Glick et al. (1974: 220) comment that 25 per cent of their sample said 'spontaneously and emphatically that they disliked being referred to as a widow'. I had a similar experience when conducting research in a Florida retirement community (van den Hoonaard 1992, 1994), and one anonymous reviewer of this paper reported feeling the same way.

11    This includes the two accounts by Graham (1990) and Rice (1990) which are very different because the authors' husbands were much older than they.

12    Silverman (1988: 207) has looked at the differences in the way men and women change as a consequence of being widowed. She found that for the widows 'making decisions was one of the worst things that they had to deal with'. Men did not share this problem.

13    Although the range of things that widows needed to learn to do may seem very large, the widows that I am currently interviewing for another study generally feel they are more capable of managing on their own than their husbands would have been, had the situation been reversed.

14    A local bereavement counsellor tells widows that they should tell their friends that they are not new people but rather the same person in a new situation. I would suggest that the widows who have written these accounts would not agree with this.

15    Their words are even more powerful when read aloud. I cannot begin to recreate the atmosphere they have created in a room when I have presented this material orally.

16    My thanks to an anonymous reviewer for assisting me to list these points so succinctly.

## References

Beck, F. 1965. *The Diary of a Widow*. Beacon Press, Boston.
Birren, J. E., Kenyon, G. M., Ruth, J-E., Schroots, J. Jr. and Svensson, T. (eds) 1996. *Aging and Biography: Explorations in Adult Development*. Springer, New York.
Blythe, R. 1979. *The View in Winter: Reflections on Old Age*. Harcourt Brace Jovanovitch, NY.
Brothers, J. 1990. *Widowed*. Simon and Schuster, New York.
Caine, L. 1974. *Widow*. Bantum Books, New York.
Caine, L. 1978. *Lifelines*. Doubleday, Garden City, NY.
Caine, L. 1988. *Being a Widow*. Penguin Books, New York.
Carey, R. G. 1979–80. Weathering Widowhood: Problems and adjustment of the widowed during the first year. *Omega*, 10, 163–74.
Charmaz, K. 1991. *Good Days, Bad Days: The Self in Chronic Illness and Time*. Rutgers University Press, New Brunswick, NJ.
Connidis, I. A. 1989. *Family Ties and Aging*. Butterworths, Toronto.
Cooley, C. H. 1902. *Human Nature and the Social Order*. Scribner's, NY.
Dohaney, M. T. 1989. *When Things Get Back to Normal*. Pottersfield Press, Porters Lake, Nova Scotia.
Ebaugh, H. R. F. 1988. *Becoming an Ex: The Process of Role Exit*. University of Chicago Press, Chicago.
Gates, P. 1990. *Suddenly Alone: A Woman's Guide to Widowhood*. Harper and Row, New York.
Glick, I. O., Weiss, R. S. and Parkes, C. M. 1974. *The First Year of Bereavement*. John Wiley and Sons, New York.
Graham, L. 1990. *Rebuilding the House*. Viking, New York.
Heinemann, G. D. 1982. Why study widowed women: a rationale. *Women and Health*, 7, 17–2.

Homans, G. 1964. Bringing men back in. *American Sociological Review*, 29, 809–18.

Lofland, L. 1982. Loss and human connection: an exploration into the nature of the social bond. In Ickes, W. and Knowles, E. S. (eds), *Personality, Roles and Social Behavior* (219–42). Springer-Verlag, New York.

Lopata, H. Z. 1973a. *Widowhood in An American City*. Schenkman, Cambridge, MA.

Lopata, H. Z. 1973b. Self-identity in marriage and widowhood. *The Sociological Quarterly*. 14, 407–18.

Lopata, H. Z. 1975. Relationships in marriage and widowhood. In Glazer-Malbin, Nona (ed), *Old Family/New Family: Interpersonal Relationships* (119–49). D. Van Nostrand Company, New York.

Lopata, H. Z. 1979. *Women as Widows: Support Systems*. Elsevier, New York.

Lopata, H. Z. 1996. *Current Widowhood: Myths and Realities*. Sage, Thousand Oaks, CA.

Lund, D. A., Caserta, M. S., Diamond, M. F. and Gray, R. M. 1986. Impact of bereavement on the self-conceptions of older surviving spouses, *Symbolic Interaction*, 9, 235–44.

Marris, P. 1958. *Widows and their Families*. Routledge and Kegan Paul, London.

Matthews, A. M. 1987. Widowhood as an expectable life event. In Marshall, Victor (ed), *Aging in Canada: Social Perspectives*, 2nd Edition (343–366). Fitzhenry and Whiteside, Markham, Ont.

Matthews, A. M. 1991. *Widowhood in Later Life*. Butterworths, Toronto.

McCall, G. and Simmons, J. L. 1966. *Identities and Interactions*. The Viking Press, New York.

Menton, T. 1995. *Going Solo: Widows Tell Their Stories of Love, Loss and Rediscovery*. Running Press, Philadelphia.

Mooney, E. C. 1981. *Alone: Surviving as a Widow*. GP Putnam's Sons, NY.

Parkes, C. M. 1986. *Bereavement: Studies of Grief in Adult Life*, 2nd American Edition. International Universities Press, Madison, CT.

Polkinghorne, D. E. 1996. Narrative knowing and the study of lives. In Birren, James E., Kenyon, Gary M., Ruth, Jan-Eric, Schroots, Johannes J. R. and Svensson, Torbjorn (eds), *Aging and Biography: Explorations in Adult Development*. Springer, NY.

Rice, Rebecca 1990. *A Time to Mourn: One Woman's Journey through Widowhood*. Plume, New York.

Rose, X. 1990. *Widow's Journey: A Return to the Loving Self*. Henry Holt and Company, New York.

Seskin, J. 1975. *Young Widow*. Ace Books, New York.

Shibutani, T. 1955. Reference groups as perspectives, *American Journal of Sociology*, 60, 562–9.

Silverman, P. R. 1988. In search of new selves: accommodating to widowhood. In Bond, Lynne A. and Wagner, Barry M. (eds), *Families in Transition: Primary Prevention Programs that Work* (200–20). Sage, Newbury Park, CA.

Smith, L. L. 1991. *Journeying through Widowhood: The Crystallization of a New Reality*. Unpubl. Ph.D. Dissertation, University of California, San Francisco.

Strauss, A. L. 1959. *Mirrors and Masks: the Search for Identity*. The Free Press, Glencoe, IL.

Thompson, P., Itzin, C. and Abendstern, M. 1990. *I Don't Feel Old: The Experience of Later Life*. Oxford University Press, Oxford.

Townsend, P. 1957. *The Family Life of Old People: An Inquiry in East London*. Routledge and Kegan Paul, London.

Tunstall, J. 1966. *Old and Alone: A Sociological Study of Old People*. Routledge and Kegan Paul, London.

van den Hoonaard, D. K. 1992. *The Aging of Florida Retirement Community*, unpubl. dissertation, Loyola University of Chicago, Chicago.

van den Hoonaard, D. K. 1994. Paradise lost: widowhood in a Florida retirement community, *Journal of Aging Studies*, 8, 121–32.

Weigart, A. J. 1986. The social production of identity. *Sociological Quarterly*, 27, 165–83.

Wylie, B. J. 1988. *Beginnings: A Book for Widows*, 3rd Rev. Edition. McClelland and Steward, Toronto.

# 8 The Ageless Self

## Sharon R. Kaufman

> The old are unsure of a future, their past has grown stale so they are dependent on the sentience of the moment. It behoves us to be sentient. Or – the old live by recalling the past, and are fascinated by the query of what future is possible. Their present is empty. Or – there is nothing of interest to be said about the old, except that they are absorbed by age. Each could be true. One takes one's choice.
>
> Florida Scott-Maxwell, age 82. *The Measure of My Days*

The construction of a coherent, unified sense of self is an ongoing process. We have seen how old people express an identity through themes which are rooted in personal experience, particular structural factors, and a constellation of value orientations. Themes integrate these three sources of meaning as they structure the account of a life, express what is salient to the individual, and define a continuous and creative self.

The sources of meaning which themes integrate are continually reinterpreted in light of new circumstances. A person selects events from his or her past to structure and restructure his or her identity. Thus, themes continue to evolve from and give form to personal experience – making identity a cumulative process. At whatever point in time individuals construct their life stories, they pick and choose from a storehouse of memories and reflections. Reconstruction of the past and interpretation of one's self change as one grows older, as one has more experiences from which to choose and greater distance from which to evaluate past events. This is one reason themes "fit" together so well in a life story. Interpretations which have no explanatory or symbolic value at the time the story is told are weeded out and discarded. Continuous restructuring allows individuals to maintain a feeling of unity about themselves and a sense of connection with the parts of their pasts they consider relevant to who they are at present.

*Personal identity as a phenomenon can be studied only in the present; the researcher cannot know about those themes which have been altered or abandoned, because the integration of experience takes place only through presently existing frameworks of understanding.* The analyst cannot separate the past from the present in an oral life story; one can know the meaning of the past only through a person's current interpretation of it.[1] Because of this, the informant's identity (or major aspects of it) is shaped anew in the process of telling the story of his or her life.

Identity viewed as both cumulative process and current phenomenon may provide us with a way of understanding adult development over time and in a social context. Most theories of adult development implicitly assume that the individual life course follows a curve or trajectory – rising, arriving at a height of something (i.e., occupational success, social status, standard of living, positive self-image, etc.), and then

Original publication: Kaufman, Sharon R., "The Ageless Self," from *The Ageless Self: Sources of Meaning in Late Life* (University of Wisconsin Press, Madison, 1986), pp. 149–63.

falling back.[3] The concept of self often has been viewed from this paradigm with the aging individual seen as struggling to maintain a positive self-image – or succumbing to mental disorder or discontentment – in the face of declining health, social status, economic clout, power, and mobility. *The focus on themes in the lives of the elderly allows us to conceive of aging as continual creation of the self through the ongoing interpretation of past experience, structural factors, values, and current context.*

Identity is created and recreated over time as a person progresses through the life span. The structure and meaning of one's identity is established as experience is layered on experience and is simultaneously reflected upon, evaluated, adjusted to, and incorporated. But rather than being constructed to follow the rise and fall of an external trajectory through time, identity is built around themes, without regard to time, as past experiences are symbolically connected with one another to have meaning for a particular individual.

The elderly individuals I interviewed do not define themselves as being old. Study group members *know* they are old. They do not deny the fact. They are aware of the limits, physical and intellectual, imposed by old age, and they live within them. Moreover, they possess an awareness that their lives are without possibility: they unequivocally feel their lack of future. Nevertheless, they think of and describe themselves in terms of the themes they express as they reflect on their lives, rather than in terms of age. None of them has, at a certain juncture, created a new constellation of themes to coincide with the developmental stage of life called old age. The themes which appear to have evolved throughout the lives of these people are the themes through which they understand themselves and discuss their circumstances at present. Their conversations about their respective aging processes and the situations they must face as they grow older are framed in the thematic material they present.

Continuity of themes is, thus, a key element in the ageless identity of this particular elderly population and, I suspect, in the elderly in general. What can we say about the meaning of continuity in the individual life? Anthropologist Barbara Myerhoff notes that continuity in a life does not arise spontaneously, that it must be achieved. The individual *actively seeks* continuity as he or she goes through ordinary daily existence and interprets the circumstances with which he or she deals.[3] Millie, Ben, and Stella demonstrate the active search for continuity as they apply, adapt, and reformulate existing themes to new contexts so that a familiar and unified sense of self emerges in old age.[4]

## Millie

Millie speaks of starting a "new life" when she moved into the Home, and she sees herself "improving" and "learning" all the time. She perceives her own aging as a process of renewal that began when she arrived at the institution. I asked her to look in the mirror and describe her image. She said: "I go by what people tell me. They say I look 100 percent better than I did. I have changed considerably from what I looked like when I first came here, and I see a more pleasant expression in my face, and I'm more inspired about my routine . . ." Here, Millie's reference point for her self-description is other people's remarks about her improved morale and appearance since entering the institution.

In another interview, I asked Millie to describe herself. She replied: "I love people. I love the way they feel about me here, the attention." We know that she finds meaning in her relationships with people and that she thinks of herself only in terms of affective ties. Her current self-image is in keeping with this theme that is woven through her life story. As she views others in terms of their ties to her, so she sees herself as a product of social interaction. Continuous improvement and loving others are her specific self-descriptions at age 80. "Being old" – a state unrelated to other people – does not enter into her conceptual framework at all.

Millie's explanation of why she came to the Home, too, derives from her need for affiliation.

> Before I came here I was so lonely, I was afraid of going out of my mind. I'm not the type to sit around and watch TV and read magazines. That's why I came here. I like to mingle, to be around people, to have a room-mate, to have company. It's what my disposition needs.

Her family and physician probably would find the cause of her institutionalization elsewhere, most likely in the fact that she had a mild stroke and can no longer provide for all her physical needs.

Millie refers to her physical condition only when she feels she is being mistreated by others. In these instances, she uses her infirmities to manipulate interaction. Her body image is a device she employs to satisfy her needs and maintain other themes. For example, one morning she was quite distressed and complained to me that a nurse had offended her. She said: "I can't take it – in my condition. I'm a patient here. I don't have the strength to take that abuse." When someone does not treat her as she would like, she perceives herself as weak and ill, and then uses that identity as the reason she should not be abused. I never heard Millie refer to herself as a "patient" before or after this incident. This self-perception is clearly a survival tactic, and it is only called into play when needed to gain respect or take control of a situation.

As Millie describes her move to the nursing home, she speaks of taking control of her life for the first time. She claims to have changed her attitude and behavior in order to get what she wanted from her new environment. We have seen how she has been able to reorganize the institutional routine, structure her friendships, and invest casual encounters with affect through the creation of the theme self-determination. By establishing this new theme, Millie is able to maintain a viable self-image as she creates situations in which she acquires moral worth and social status.[5]

Another component in the formation of Millie's identity is her perception of her present relationship with her children. She says that she is happy living in the Home mainly because it pleases her children that she is there; she takes her cue for her own emotional state from them. For instance, she once stated to me: "When I tell my children of my accomplishments in classes, they say, 'Wonderful, Mother. I'm so glad to hear it.' . . . I'm so happy that they are thrilled because I'm here." She discusses her activities with them regularly by telephone and during their visits, and their reinforcement of her behavior seems to be crucial to the maintenance of her self-esteem and emotional well-being. She looks to her children for both feedback and encouragement for continuing with her specific pursuits in the Home and justification for living there at all. On several occasions, when she was depressed or angered by some incident in the Home, she broke down crying, and said: "If I didn't have my children to pull me through, I don't know what I'd do. They're everything to me." They provide her with a means of keeping up her morale and finding contentment in her present situation through an unspoken contract between them which reads: If my children are happy that I'm in the Home, then I must be happy about it too.

Yet, honoring the contract is not easy, for according to Millie, the relationship is far from satisfactory. Two children live in the same city as she does; they do not, according to her, visit enough. The other two live in another part of the country; apparently they do not communicate often enough by letter or telephone. Millie gets quite distraught if more than a week goes by without a visit and worries about her children's health, jobs, marriages, and children. Her peace of mind is forever being threatened by the perceived lack of attentiveness from them, and though she is surrounded by others who are sociable, she is lonely without constant communication from her children.

We recall that family members are devoted, attentive, and always available in Millie's thematic scheme, the worth of all relationships is measured by these qualities. In reality, the children do not always manifest all these traits. Though upset that her children do not meet her standards, Millie does not alter the theme to conform to their actual behavior or discard the theme outright. For it is the *theme*, not the children, which keeps Millie's identity intact. Through it, she is able to view her children as her primary and constant source of affection. This is her reason for living.

The theme also provides continuity. In order for Millie to continue perceiving herself as a loving and lovable person, her love for her children cannot falter, for they are the only stable outlet for her own love. Friends and acquaintances in the Home die or move away to hospitals. Staff members and volunteers come and go. But the relationship with children is permanent, whether or not they are visible. She can show her love for them in two ways – by honoring the unspoken contract, and by conceiving of her children in the ideal thematic framework she has constructed rather than focusing on their actual shortcomings.

## Ben

I asked Ben if he feels as though he is 74. He said: "No, I don't. I feel the same as I did when I was much younger. . . . And as a matter of fact, I have a strong desire since my wife died to relive my coed days." When he looks back on his life, the years he spent in college stand out as the closest he was able to come to his "carefree," "romantic" self. His arrival in the college town in his early twenties symbolizes both his break away from the small town where he was raised and forced into a religious mold that he did not fit, and his first exposure to "big city" life and freedom. He recalls those days: "What a thrill it was to be there, and see four street car tracks, and all the excitement. I got a little Chevy coupe, and I started to date girls. And I enjoyed life as a single person."

Ben yearns to become what he remembers about that self now. When I asked what he was going to do about it, he replied: "I'm not doing anything about it, because you have to be your age, you know. . . . I could easily get going with a younger person. But I realize that would be unfair to the younger person and make a fool out of myself." The dichotomy-of-self theme which informs Ben's interpretation of his past also informs his perception of being old, and the discrepancy between the two selves creates a sense of frustration and futility.

On the one hand, Ben does not identify with his chronological age. He is healthy and has no physical ailments. He feels like a college student and he wants to act that way. On the other hand, he knows that to be 74 and to act 21 is socially inappropriate. With such a strong sense of propriety, he cannot ignore a lifetime of moral values and transcend the cultural assumptions of age-graded behavior. His worry about what other people and his "sober," "responsible" side would think prohibits him from becoming involved with a young woman.

The maintenance into old age of the theme dichotomy of self is evident also in Ben's comments about sex. "When I hear these jokes and stories about sex at 70, it almost revolts me. But then I realize *I'm* 74. I still have sex on my mind." He accepts the cultural stereotype that sex and old age are incompatible and indeed repulsive. But he also knows that the stereotype does not fit his own identity. The conflict of *feeling* one age and *being* another age is unresolved.

I asked Ben if he had any expectations while he was growing up of what being old would be like. He answered: "Ever since I was a youngster, I have thought of old people as infirm and sick. It was not a cheerful picture. Debilitation, fear of poverty, dependency. It wasn't a nice thing to look forward to." His fears of catastrophic illness and destitution, formed by his image of his father and his early family life, have largely shaped his conception of the aging process.

Ben's picture of aging is not completely negative, however. We recall that the theme religion is the framework for Ben's past and sets priorities for his future. Religion was a limitation for Ben through his early and middle years; it provided an ideal which he could not achieve and a guide from which he deviated. It stifled the development of his "carefree" self. He could never change his image of religion to fit his behavior. Now, late in life, religion is Ben's framework for imagining what the future will be like, and as such, it is the only positive component in his conception of aging. I asked him what he was going to do for the next 20 years. He replied:

> The older I get, and the less I'm able to do for people and the less use I'll be to them, I'll be narrowed down to the time when I will be alone and helpless except for whatever visitors choose to come, which I know won't be very many. So, if I didn't have that final resource, life would look very bleak to me. . . . I don't see how people can get along, why they aren't driven to great sadness by the fact that people are going to desert them. . . . I would call on my religious aids, on the parish priest, and I would expect him to reinforce my hopes about the next life.

Religion injects the only optimism into his view of aging and dying, because it provides him with an explanation of both the purpose of life on earth and life after death.

Ben's assumptions about what aging and dying will be like reflect aspects of his disengagement theme as well. First, he supposes that he will become infirm and therefore will not be able "to do" for others: he fears he will end his life without fulfilling his need to be generous. Second, he expects to remain socially isolated until his death. And now in the context of the subject of aging, Ben explains his isolation as an outcome of his inability to help others. Third, he views "desertion" as a fact of aging. We know that Ben has no meaningful social relationships to give him a connection to the world of people. His feelings of ultimate abandonment stem from his lifelong experience of lack of permanence and supreme value in human relationships. Disengagement, the theme that emerges as Ben expresses his past and present style in the world, also defines his style, his sense of "expressive identifiability" (Goffman 1974) in the future, in his old age. The theme disengagement continues to have meaning for Ben, and though ultimately pessimistic, it provides an explanation of old age and a connection with his sense of himself at other times in his life.

## Stella

I asked Stella how she felt about growing older. She replied:

> Age doesn't mean anything to me. I don't ever feel like I'm getting any older. I usually feel like I'm going to live forever. If I don't go around falling and having accidents, I might. . . . I never feel old until something happens. When I had my automobile accident, it took me a long time to get over it. That to me is old – when you begin to feel weak and shaking, and you can't do what you had been doing. I didn't think I was ever going to be well again, and I was going to be that way the rest of my life. [When] you gradually get well and get back to work and you feel like yourself again – [you think] you're never going to be old.

Stella does not think of herself as old except when she cannot be active, when the expression of her achievement-orientation theme is blocked. Old to her means the limitation of activity and productivity. She views herself as ageless; only clumsiness on her part – "falling and having accidents" – can make her succumb to growing old.

Stella's ageless self is derived both from the themes she expresses as she describes her past and from her interpretation of her present environment. We recall that the people in her social world are at least a generation younger than she. Over a period of several months, I observed her interactions with the young people who work in the studio and found that they do not act toward her as if she were old; they do not assume her activity should be restricted or that she should be treated in a certain way because she is 82. Rather, they perceive her energy level and physical and mental capacities to be equal to theirs, and in fact, they are. Their behavior toward her reinforces her own view of self as ageless. She once said to me: "Somebody made the remark to me, 'You don't even talk like you're old; you talk like you're the same age as whoever you're talking to.' I said, 'That's the way I am.' I feel like I'm the same age they are when I'm talking to them."

Stella expresses her agelessness (and implied sense of immortality) in the promise to make better and better art all the time – way into the future. Productivity and excellence, regardless of the endeavor, are valued by the entire study group as we have seen, but Stella places more emphasis on these qualities at this stage of life than do any other informants. When I asked Stella what plans she has for the future, she replied with conviction, "I am going to make a masterpiece!" And when I inquired at the beginning of a new year what resolutions she had made, she answered, "I want to turn out 365 pieces of sculpture this year, one every day, and I'm already behind."

Stella's assertions are in marked contrast to the comments of other informants, many of whom stated to me: "I can't make any plans for the future now. I just live from day to day; that's the best I can do." Stella is trying to create something of lasting importance to the art world through tireless, creative effort.

The desire for continuity beyond her own life span extends to Stella's studio. She has poured herself into it and expects it will close when she dies. This is a major concern for her, and she spoke about it many times in our conversations. The studio is synonymous with life; she does not wish to see that life end. "My house and studio here – anybody I'd leave it to would sell it, just as soon as I die. But I don't want it to be that way. I don't want this place to be sold. I would rather I could make a permanent workshop out of it somehow." She discusses possible alternatives for keeping the studio a viable place after her death. Her wish for a permanent studio is not shared by others and she knows this. She talks about this problem in terms of the selflessness theme. "These kids, they only think of themselves. I suppose they think the studio will continue forever. They don't plan ahead at all." Just as she feels the daily upkeep of the studio rests ultimately on her, so she perceives its existence after her death as her sole responsibility.

Stella's preoccupation with a permanent studio underscores her selfless approach to life and the desire for continuity beyond her own life span; she envisions giving to others and creating art after she is gone. Preservation of the studio would immortalize these aspects of her identity. Moreover, Stella needs her personal efforts to be carried on by others just as she carried on her mother's productivity and her daughter's art. Since she has no living descendants to establish her biological continuity with the future, she needs "these kids" to act as her family, preserving what is important to her. In this way, they would symbolize a familial link with succeeding generations. Finally, the studio is her most important creation. Stella wants it, as a tangible object, to have an impact on the future as a work of art can. As the visible and symbolic edifice of her creative process, it could immortalize her identity as an artist. More than the other people I interviewed, Stella looks beyond her own life span as she seeks continuity.[6]

All research participants made it clear to me that *aging* per se is not a substantive issue in their own lives. They do not, now that they are over 70, conceive of themselves in a context of *aging* and act accordingly. Rather, they deal with specific problems, changes, and disabilities as they arise, just as they have been doing throughout their lives, and they interpret these changes and problems in the light of already established themes. It appears that the concept of aging is too abstract, too impersonal to be an integral part of identity. This is not to say that my informants ignore or deny their own aging and the discomforts and limitations which arise in that process. Nor does it mean that the changes experienced in old age have no psychological effects. But while dealing with the physical and mental manifestations of old age, old people also maintain an ageless sense of self that transcends change by providing continuity and meaning.

What is the meaning of this sense of timelessness for the field of gerontology? The concept of adaptation has traditionally channeled most research in social gerontology and has attributed certain characteristics to the nature of the aging process. The gerontologists George Maddox and James Wiley (1976:15) state, "The relationship between aging and successful adaptation (variously morale or life satisfaction or mental health) is perhaps the oldest, most persistently investigated issue in the social scientific study of aging." The meaning attributed to adaptation which has, by and large, shaped nearly 40 years of research is contentment. Simic (1978:16) has noted that research aimed at discovering and evaluating levels of contentment, problematic in itself, reflects an American ethnocentrism which supposes that "happiness" is what one strives for in old age. A basic premise of this view is that any state of being other than "happiness" is detrimental to the individual and is to be avoided if at all possible. Besides the empirical and methodological problems this view entails, the definition itself traps the investigator into looking at questions that deal with the presence, absence, and quantity of contentment in later life, a narrow scope for aging research.

In research formulated to define or measure adaptation, individual members of the population being studied are largely interchangeable; details of the individual life are of no consequence. However, if one investigates the individual life course and how meaning is obtained from it, the concept of adaptation can be broadened. Recent work in the field of lifespan development has contributed to a broader conceptualization of adaptation through studies of the subjective meaning of change and continuity in the individual life course (for example: Cohler 1982; Kotre 1984; Ryff 1984). These works and others lend support to the idea that *successful adaptation takes place when individuals symbolically connect meaningful past experiences with current circumstances.* Adaptation in late life must be conceived as more than striving for contentment; it is also the process by which a person creates meaning, organizes the past, explains events, and communicates with others. Adaptation viewed in these terms allows research in gerontology to address the operating frameworks of the elderly themselves. The thematic analysis of life-story material reveals the phenomenological understanding of self as ageless to show us that "morale" and "life satisfaction" are not necessarily key factors in the determination of behavior. Instead, construction and interpretation of experience as one grows older are found to be critical elements that give form and meaning to one's actions.

What does the concept of the ageless self tell us about the popular notion of aging as nothing but losses – sensory, functional, economic, social? In recent years, researchers have shown that the aging process is more than deprivation and forfeiture to which one must succumb and, it is hoped, adjust.[7] For old people continue to participate in society, and more than this, old people continue to *interpret* their participation in the social world. By looking at themes that emerge from their own stories, we can see how the old not only cope with the losses, but how they create new meaning as they reformulate and build viable selves. Thus, creating identity is a lifelong process.

## Notes

1 Psychoanalytic technique does aim to separate the meaning of the past from that of the present. However, free association, rather than the oral life story, is the vehicle used to accomplish that goal.

2 See Mandelbaum (1973) for a discussion and review of this concept.

3  Continuity is discussed at great length in Myerhoff, *Number Our Days* (1979), especially pp. 108–9; 221–2.
4  The active search for continuity may be described as an important adaptive mechanism for the study participants.
5  The idea of maintaining a self-image in which moral worth and social status are achieved is fully elaborated by Niels Braroe in *Indian and White* (1975).
6  Barbara Myerhoff (1979: 195–231) describes a similar situation in the case of Jacob Koved.
7  See especially G. Becker 1980; Clark and Anderson 1967; Hochschild 1973; Keith Ross 1977; Myerhoff 1979, 1984; Myerhoff and Simic 1978, and Plath 1980.

## References

Becker, Gaylene. 1980. *Growing Old in Silence*. Berkeley: University of California Press.
Braroe, Niels Winther. 1975. *Indian and White*. Stanford: Stanford University Press.
Clark, Margaret and Barbara Anderson. 1967. *Culture and Aging*. Springfield, IL: Charles C Thomas.
Cohler, Bertram. J. 1982. "Personal Narrative and Life Course." Pp. 205–41 in *Life-Span Development and Behavior*, edited by P. Baltes and O. Brim. New York: Academic.
Goffman, Erving. 1974. *Frame Analysis*. New York: Harper and Row.
Hochschild, Arlie Russell. 1973. *The Unexpected Community*. Berkeley: University of California Press.
Keith Ross, Jennie. 1977. *Old People, New Lives*. Chicago: University of Chicago Press.
Kotre, John N. 1984. *Outliving the Self: Generativity and the Interpretation of Lives*. Baltimore: Johns Hopkins University Press.
Maddox, George and James Wiley. 1976. "Scope, Concepts and Methods in the Study of Aging." Pp. 3–34 in *Handbook of Aging and the Social Sciences*, edited by R. H. Binstock and E. Shanas. New York: Van Nostrand Reinhold.
Mandlebaum, David C. 1973. "The Study of Life History: Gandhi," *Current Anthropology* 14: 177–96.
Myerhoff, Barbara. 1979. *Number Our Days*. New York: Dutton.
Myerhoff, Barbara and Andrei Simic (eds.). 1978. *Life's Career – Aging*. Beverly Hills, CA: Sage.
Plath, David. 1980. *Long Engagements*. Stanford: Stanford University Press.
Ryff, Carol. D. 1984. "Personality Development from the Inside: The Subjective Experience of Change in Adulthood and Aging." Pp. 243–79 in *Life-Span Development and Behavior*, edited by P. Baltes and O. Brim. New York: Academic.
Simic, Andrei. 1978. "Introduction: Aging and the Aged in Cultural Perspective." Pp. 9–22 in *Life's Career – Aging*, edited by B. Myerhoff and A. Simic. Beverly Hills, CA: Sage.

## Further Reading to Part II

Becker, Gaylene. 1980. *Growing Old in Silence*. Berkeley: University of California Press.

Eisenhandler, Susan. 1989. Chapter 10, "More Than Counting Years: Social Aspects of Time and the Identity of Elders." Pp. 163–82 in *Research on Adulthood and Aging: The Human Science Approach*, edited by L. Eugene Thomas. Albany, NY: SUNY Press.

Greenspan, Henry. 1992. Chapter 8, "Lives as Texts: Symptoms as Modes of Recounting in the Life Histories of Holocaust Survivors." Pp. 145–64 in *Storied Lives: The Cultural Politics of Self-Understanding*, edited by George C. Rosenwald and Richard L. Ochberg. New Haven: Yale University Press.

Kaufman, Sharon R. 1986. *The Ageless Self: Sources of Meaning in Late Life*. Madison, WI: University of Wisconsin Press.

Kenyon, Gary M. and William L. Randall. 1997. *Restorying Our Lives: Personal Growth Through Autobiographical Reflection*. Westport, CT: Praeger.

Matthews, Sarah H. 1979. *The Social World of Old Women: Management of Self-Identity*. Beverly Hills, CA: Sage.

Rosenfeld, Dana. 1999. "Identity Work Among Lesbian and Gay Elderly," *Journal of Aging Studies* 13: 121–44.

Ruth, Jan-Erik and Peter Öberg. 1996. Chapter 10, "Ways of Life: Old Age in a Life History Perspective." Pp. 167–86 in *Aging and Biography: Explorations in Adult Development*, edited by James E. Birren, Gary M. Kenyon, Jan-Erik Ruth, Johanness J. F. Schroots, and Torbjorn Svensson. New York: Springer.

# Part III

## Work and Retirement

# 9 Retirement as a Social Role

## Robert C. Atchley

It has been customary for sociologists to refer to retirement as a "roleless role" (Donahue, Orbach, and Pollak, 1960; Burgess, 1960). This somewhat contradictory expression refers to the popular notion that retirement is a position in society for which there are no corresponding rights and duties in the culture. As Burgess put it:

> In short, the retired man and his wife are imprisoned in a roleless role. They have no vital function to perform . . . This roleless role is thrust upon the older person at retirement and to a greater or lesser degree he has accepted it or become resigned to it. (1960: 20)

This simplistic view is incorrect, and on more than one level. Part of the problem comes from a confusion over the definition of *role*. First, *role* can refer to the culturally transmitted, general norms governing the rights and duties associated with a position in society (judge, woman, retired person, mother, etc.). The rights of a retired person include the right to economic support without holding a job (and without the stigma of being regarded as dependent on society as in the case of the unemployed), the right to autonomy concerning the management of one's time, and often more specific rights such as the right to use company or union facilities, to hold union office, to retain various privileges and so forth.

Concerning retirement duties, Burgess and those with a similar view have made a serious mistake. Burgess speaks of giving up one's "vital function." This is an obvious reference to the fact that job roles usually exist in a context of interdependent tasks, each of which is necessary to the operation of the system. Yet job roles are always more than merely instrumental tasks. To a greater or lesser degree, they also include mannerisms, ways of thinking, and generalized skills which the individual often incorporates as part of himself. He is expected by others around him to continue to be the same type of person after retirement as he was before. Expected continuity of behaviour is a major set of expectations facing the retired person.

In addition, the retired person is confronted with other general duties. The most universal and important of these is the expectation that the retired person will assume responsibility for managing his own life. For a great many job-holders it becomes customary to let the employer decide how much insurance is adequate, when to get up in the morning, when to go on a trip, what kind of clothes to wear, and even what to do for recreation. For a great many people, job-holding means following the rules, not only on the job but in other areas of life as well. For these people retirement means a great deal of added decision-making responsibility. This means also that part of the time formerly devoted to the job must be set aside for these new decision-

Original publication: Atchley, Robert C., "Retirement as a Social Role" from *The Sociology of Retirement* (Schenkman Publishers, New York, 1976), pp. 60–73.

making duties. Also, regardless of the level of retirement income, retired people are expected to live within that income, another reason that not all of the time of the retired person is available for leisure. For even the most responsible and autonomous job-holder, retirement forces an increase in decision-making about his *personal* life.

In these and many other areas of life, retired people are expected to manage their own affairs without assistance. Put another way, retired people are expected to avoid becoming dependent either on their families or on the community. And just as income without job-holding is a reward for retirement, denegration is a punishment for those retired people who become dependent. Some might say that this proscription on becoming dependent is a facet of aging and not of retirement, but consider the difference in reaction to the dependency of a fifty-five-year-old retired man as opposed to the reaction to the same dependency of an eighty-year-old retired man. We expect the retired man to fend for himself, but we allow the old man more dependency.

*Role* can also be defined as a *relationship* between a particular position holder and other position holders. In this framework, the retirement role is the relationship between the retired person and those who are still employed, either in a particular profession or in a particular organization. The crux of the relationship is the fact that both retired persons and the persons still on the job tend to identify themselves in terms of the same job or work organization. In this sense the position of retired person is similar to the position of alumnus. As with alumni of a given school, people recently retired from a job may be envied by those they left still on the job, and interaction centers around shared past experiences. However, the longer the elapsed time in the retirement role, the fewer the number of "old buddies" still on the job, and the relationship becomes characterized less in terms of shared past experience and more in terms of abstract notions of identity and loyalty. Loyalty to one's occupation, employer, or colleagues is an important aspect of retirement which has been the subject of too little research. The research literature indicates that contacts between retired people and those still on the job are not constant, but they are frequent enough that most retired people gain some experience with this particular aspect of the retirement role.

Thus, retirement does represent a role. However, the retirement role is usually defined in flexible, qualitative terms, whereas job roles are more often expressed in concrete, instrumental terms.[1] It was probably the absence of the instrumental element in job roles that led many investigators to view retirement as a "roleless role" and as an inevitable problem for the retired person. These people saw retirement as creating a gap which only a new instrumental or "functional" role could fill. Much of the retirement literature still contains discussions of possible functional alternatives to work (Miller, 1965).

However, other work (Schneider, 1964; Atchley, 1972; Streib and Schneider, 1971) indicates that instrumental norms may never need to develop around retirement. Schneider (1964) makes the point well.

> A clearly-defined role facilitates activity and gives a sense of security to a person involved in a network of impersonal universalistically-oriented judgments and evaluations. This may not be the kind of world in which many older people live. In the later years of life, the important persons in one's life – friends and relatives – know who the

older person is and, therefore, he moves in a world that is familiar to him, and with which he is familiar. He may not need a sharply defined extra-familial "role" to give him an identity or to facilitate his own activity in his everyday world. We suggest, therefore, that so far as the older person himself is concerned, his willingness to leave the work force and perhaps his satisfaction with other aspects of life are not dependent upon whether he has a clearly defined alternative role or not. (Schneider, 1964: 56)

Following this rationale, the retirement role, by its very vagueness, allows the individual a certain amount of flexibility in adjusting to his less consistent physical capabilities.

At this time, our ability to discuss the importance of social roles in later life is hampered by the lack of research and theory concerning the dynamics of role relationships in later life. Little attention has been paid to the impact of habit or reminiscence on the way people perceive their own performance of a role. There has been little examination of the effect of aging on the significance of fantasy in the role-taking process. And this work needs to be done, for until it is, our knowledge concerning retirement as a social role will remain incomplete indeed.

## Phases of Retirement[2]

When retirement is viewed as a social role, it is useful also to consider the various phases through which the role is approached, taken and relinquished. Yet because retirement has only very recently come to be viewed as a social role by sociologists, there has been little research on its phases. Accordingly, what follows is an attempt to sketch out the phases as we now know them, with the understanding that our knowledge is quite tentative in this area. Figure 8.1 gives an overview of the phases of retirement.

### Preretirement

The preretirement period may be divided into two phases: remote and near. In the remote phase, retirement is defined by the individual as a vaguely positive phase of the occupational career which is a reasonable distance into the future. This phase can begin even before the individual takes his first job. It ends when the individual nears retirement. Even in the remote phase, most people expect to retire. Very few expect to die before they reach retirement age and very few expect to continue working until they die. Few people dread retirement at this point. At the same time, few people see retirement as requiring rational planning. Information-gathering concerning retirement tends to be unsystematic and only rarely intentional. The exceptions to this are those whose employers expose them to some sort of formal program during the remote phase, but such programs are very rare. Thus, anticipatory socialization for retirement in the remote phase tends to be informal and unsystematic. It may include positive attitudes and beliefs gained through experience. It may also include exposure to negative stereotypes concerning retirement which have been carried over from an earlier period in the evolution of industrial culture. Because socialization in the remote phase is informal and unsystematic, the outcome is understandably unpredict-

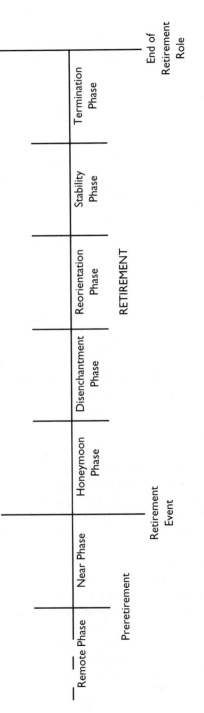

**Figure 8.1** Phases of Retirement

able. It also leaves to chance several issues which must be dealt with if the individual is to satisfy the prerequisites for successfully taking up the retirement role.

Socialization is intended not only to teach people how to play a role but also to alert them to the prerequisites of it. Thus, high school not only prepares students for college by teaching them (hopefully) how to learn but it also provides students quite systematically with knowledge concerning the SAT scores necessary for entrance to various types of colleges, the high school grades necessary for college, the funds necessary to attend various colleges, and sources of scholarships and loans. Most high schools attempt to provide this information early enough that students will know the prerequisites in time to satisfy them.

The retirement role also has prerequisites. The most important of these is a retirement income adequate for the style of life one wants to adopt in retirement. Prospective students from New York City who want to attend Princeton University have to do more financial planning than students who want to attend the City University of New York, where tuition is free to city residents. Likewise, people who want to lead an expensive life style in retirement must do more financial planning than those whose preferred life style can be maintained on Social Security benefits. Financing college educations is expensive and is best accomplished through long-range planning. The same is true of retirement, only more so. In retirement, the outlay is considerably larger and the time required to accumulate the necessary resources is much longer. Most people require a supplement to whatever retirement pensions they receive in order to sustain their desired life style. But in order to provide for this supplement, the individual must be aware of the need during the remote phase of preretirement.

Developing leisure skills is another prerequisite of the retirement role. These skills can sometimes be learned in later phases of retirement, but the literature on learning suggests that developing a wide variety of leisure skills is easier to accomplish during the early years of the remote phase of preretirement. The same can be said of developing ties with organizations in the community.

Smooth adjustment to retirement is associated with financial security and personal adaptability. At present, very little systematic effort is devoted toward developing these characteristics during the remote phase of preretirement. And a good case can be made for the need of such efforts, especially among working-class people. Yet, as haphazard as the socialization for retirement is during the remote phase of preretirement, people in general are not totally unprepared for retirement, they are merely inadequately prepared.

The near phase of preretirement begins when the individual becomes aware that he will take up the retirement role very soon. This phase is often initiated by an employer's preretirement program. It may also be initiated by the retirement of slightly older friends. For women, it is often initiated by their husband's retirement. At this point, attitudes toward retirement become more negative.

Attitudes toward retirement generally become more negative during the near retirement phase probably because the realities of retirement become clearer and because so many individuals currently are faced with not having met the financial prerequisites for taking up the retirement role. Yet there are many who remain quite positively oriented toward retirement during this phase. Preretirement planning programs help to offset the negative stereotypes concerning retirement, and there are many whose financial outlook is quite good. The leisure skill issue is particularly of concern to working-class people during this phase.

Preretirement programs most often are offered to people in the near phase of preretirement. The range of topics varies, but financial planning and the use of leisure time are the two most common topics. These programs are successful in reassuring people and reducing their anxieties about retirement. But at this late stage it is usually impossible to remedy large deficiencies in preretirement socialization. It is especially difficult to do much about inadequate financial planning at this stage.

During the near phase, the individual begins to gear himself for separation from his job and the social situation within which he carried out that job. He may adopt a "short-timer's attitude." He may begin to notice subtle differences in how he is viewed by others around him. As we said earlier, whether the person nearing retirement gets positive or negative reactions depends on the prevalent view of retirement on the part of those with whom he interacts.

Participation in retirement planning programs, retirement ceremonies, presence of an on-the-job trainee for replacement, and sometimes "promotion" into a less essential job are all mechanisms which serve to publicly define a person as being in the near phase of preretirement. In a job situation where retirement is viewed negatively, the individual can be expected to avoid these symbolic indicators of status decline. In a job situation where retirement is viewed positively, individuals can be expected to welcome these symbolic indicators of a gain in status.

During the near phase of preretirement, the retirer, to the extent that he normally engages in fantasy, will develop a fairly detailed fantasy of what he thinks retirement will be like. These fantasies may be quite accurate pictures of the future or they may be totally unrealistic. There is always an element of idealization in fantasy, but there is also a great deal of difference between pragmatic idealism based on knowledge, and romantic idealism based on wishful thinking. To the extent that fantasy is realistic, it can serve as a "dry run" which may smooth the transition into retirement by identifying issues requiring advanced decision-making. To the extent that fantasy is unrealistic it may thwart a smooth transition into retirement by setting up a detailed but unrealistic set of expectations. At this point, we know very little about the details of retirement fantasy during the near phase of preretirement and the role it plays in retirement adjustment. This is yet another promising area for research.

### The honeymoon phase

The retirement event is often followed by a rather euphoric period in which the individual wallows in his new found freedom of time and space. It is in this phase that people try to "do all of the things I never had time for before." The honeymoon period tends to be a busy time, filled with hunting, fishing, card-playing, sewing, seeing the grandchildren (or greatgrandchildren) and traveling, all at the same time. A typical person in this phase says: "What do I do with my time? Why, I've never been so busy!" The person in the honeymoon period of retirement is often like a child in a room full of new toys. He flits from this to that, trying to experience everything at once.

Not everyone has a honeymoon, however. For one thing, not everyone can afford it. For others, field of choices is pretty limited – by finances, by life style, by health, by family situation, or any of a number of other constraints.

The honeymoon period of retirement may be quite short or it may extend for years, depending on the resources available to the individual and his imaginativeness in using them. However, most people find that they cannot keep up the frantic pace of the honeymoon period indefinitely, and they then settle into some sort of routine.

The nature of the routine which follows the honeymoon period is important. If the individual is able to settle into a routine that provides a satisfying life, then that routine will probably stabilize. Many people whose off-the-job lives were full prior to retirement are able to settle into a retirement routine fairly easily. For these people, choices among activities and groups were made earlier. All that remains is to realign one's time in relation to those choices.

### The disenchantment phase[3]

However, for some people it is not easy to adjust to retirement. After the honeymoon is over and life begins to slow down, some people experience a period of let-down, disenchantment, or even depression. The depth of this emotional let-down is related to a number of factors. People with few alternatives, those who have little money or poor health, those who were over-involved in their jobs, those who are unaccustomed to running their own lives, those who experience other role losses in addition to retirement, those who leave communities where they had lived for many years – these are the people who are apt to experience deep and lengthy periods of depression following the honeymoon period.

In a sense, the honeymoon period represents a living out of the preretirement fantasy. The more unrealistic the preretirement fantasy turns out to have been, the more likely it is the retirer will experience a feeling of emptiness and disenchantment. Consequently, the failure of the fantasy represents the collapse of a structure of choices, and what is depressing is that the individual must start over again to restructure life in the retirement role. "So traveling constantly turned out to be a bore, now what?" This is the kind of question people face in the disenchantment phase.

In other cases, the disenchantment phase results from the failure of anticipatory socialization for retirement. Somehow the individual developed a concept of the retirement role that was either too unrealistic or too vague to be workable. Such failures are common. Quite often our fantasies of positions we are about to occupy are too unrealistic or vague to be workable, and we solve the problem by on-the-job training. Most people eventually work their way through the disenchantment phase, but some remain in this phase.

Because the bulk of the research is structured so as to measure people's reactions to retirement just before retirement, just after retirement, or all across the span of retirement, we have very little concrete data on the disenchantment phase of retirement. This would be an especially fruitful area for further longitudinal research.

### The reorientation phase

A reorientation phase is necessary for those whose honeymoons either never got off the ground or landed with a loud crash. During the reorientation phase, the depressed person "pulls himself together." This process involves using one's experience as a retired person to develop a more realistic view of alternatives. It also involves exploring new avenues of involvement. Very few people elect to become hermits in retirement. Most want to remain involved with the world around them.

Groups in the community sometimes help people during the reorientation phase. For example, many people become involved in Senior Center activities for the first time during this phase. Outreach programs of community agencies and churches also sometimes help.

But for the most part, the individual is on his own during the reorientation phase, and if he seeks help it is most often from his family and close friends. The goal of the reorientation process is a set of realistic choices which can be used to establish a structure and a routine for life in retirement which will provide for at least a minimum of satisfaction. People playing the retirement role do not aim for ecstatic bliss. They are quite willing to settle for an existence that is satisfying at least some of the time. This sort of criterion is used in other roles much earlier in life; therefore, applying it is seldom a problem for retired people. Most people who enter the reorientation phase of retirement pass through it to a stability phase, but some never quite achieve the needed degree of reorientation.

### The stability phase

Stability here refers not to the *absence* of change, but to the routinization of criteria for *dealing with* change. In the stability phase of retirement, the individual has a well-developed set of criteria for making choices, and these allow him to deal with life in a reasonably comfortable, orderly fashion. Life in the stability phase may be busy, and certainly it may have exciting moments, but for the most part it is predictable and satisfying. Many people pass into this phase directly from the honeymoon phase; others reach it only after a painful reassessment of personal goals; others never reach it. It is the ultimate phase in terms of role playing.

In the stability phase of retirement, the individual has mastered the retirement role. He knows what is expected of him, he knows what he has to work with – what his capabilities and limitations are. He is a self-sufficient adult, going his own way, managing his own affairs, bothering no one. Being retired is for him a serious responsibility, seriously carried out.

During the stability phase the individual inevitably encounters physical declines which change his level of functioning. But these changes too can usually be incorporated into the routine without changing the criteria for making choices. Sometimes, however, physical disabilities or losses of other roles are serious enough to cause a need for a new routine. At this point, the individual may regress back to the reorientation phase.

### Termination phase

Many older people die rather abruptly with no lengthy period of disabling illness. For these people, death may end the retirement role while they are still in the stability phase. But people can lose their retirement role in other ways. Most often, the retirement role is cancelled out by the illness and disability which sometimes accompany old age. When an individual is no longer capable of engaging in major activities such as housework, self-care, and the like, he is transferred from the retirement role to the sick and disabled role. This transfer is based on the loss of able-bodied status and the loss of independence, both of which are required for adequate playing of the retirement role. Another way that an individual may lose his retired status is to lose his financial support. At that point, he ceases to be retired and comes dependent. Of course, if he takes a full-time job, the individual loses his retired status.

The increasing dependence forced by old age usually comes gradually enough that the retirement role is given up in stages. Only upon institutionalization do independent choices begin to become so trivial as to totally remove the dignity inherent in the retirement role.

## Timing of Phases

Because there is no universal point of retirement, there is no way to tie the phases of retirement to a chronological age or to a period of time. These phases refer rather to a typical progression of processes involved in approaching, playing and giving up the retirement role. Any given individual may not experience all the phase or experience them in the order presented here.

## Retirement vs. Other Roles

Retirement affects other roles in at least three ways. It increases the time available for playing other roles. It changes the economic wherewithal available for playing other roles. And it changes the manner and quality of other role-playing.

The increase in time results from the fact that the personal decision-making and management functions which make up the retirement role do not require all of the time freed by loss of the job. This is particularly true once the stability phase of retirement is reached. This increased involvement may be wanted by the role-set or it may not.[4] For example, some wives welcome their husband's increased time spent around the house. Others do not. As one woman put it: "I married my husband for better or worse, but not for lunch."

Retirement income often necessitates curtailment of expensive leisure pursuits such as golf, boating or travel. It may also limit continued participation in voluntary associations which require dues. It may force the family to relocate.

Probably most important is the change which occurs in the *quality* of other role-playing, especially in the family. One of the things retired men inevitably seem to do is to take more part in taking care of the household. Middle-class wives usually welcome this trend, but working-class wives often do not. In general, however, retirement generally increases marital satisfaction (Rollins and Feldman, 1970).

## Summary

Retirement is not a void. It represents a valid social role which consists not only of rights and duties attached to a social position but also of specific relationships between retired people and other role players.

Like other roles, retirement involves a progression of processes through which the role is approached, played, and relinquished, and it interacts with other roles the individual plays.

Retired people are expected to remain the same type of person, to assume responsibility for managing their own lives, to avoid becoming dependent and to live within their incomes. Retired people receive pensions and various privileges. The relationships of retired people to their former work organization are similar to those of alumni to their school.

Socialization for retirement involves establishing prerequisites at least as much as it does developing specific knowledge or skills. This would ideally take place in the remote preretirement phase but it seldom does. In the near preretirement phase, the individual develops a detailed fantasy concerning retirement. In the honeymoon phase, he tries to live out that fantasy. If his fantasy is adequate, he moves into a stable phase typified by a detailed set of criteria for making routine choices and giving structure to retirement. To the extent that the fantasy is inadequate, the individual enters a disenchantment phase following the honeymoon. Eventually, he enters a reorientation phase in which a viable pattern for choice-making is sought. The termination phase of retirement is usually brought on by death or by a transfer to a sick and disabled role.

## Notes

1  Jobs also have important qualitative aspects, but these are seldom emphasized in "job descriptions" or in discussion about jobs, and this is perhaps a major oversight.
2  The initial outline for this section developed out of discussions with my colleague at the Scripps Foundation, Mildred M. Seltzer.
3  The term *disenchantment* was suggested by Vi Sobers, a lively retired nurse, who professed to be in this phase at the time she took my course on retirement at the 1973 Summer Institute for Study in Gerontology at the University of Southern California.
4  The *role-set* is the group of people with whom one must interact in carrying out a particular role.

## References

Atchley, Robert C. 1972. *The Social Forces in Later Life*. Belmont, CA: Wadsworth.
Burgess, Ernest W. 1960. *Aging in Western Societies*. Chicago: University of Chicago Press.
Donahue, Wilma T., Harold Orbach, and Otto Pollak. 1960. "Retirement: The Emerging Social Pattern." Pp. 330–406 in *Handbook of Social Gerontology*, edited by Clark Tibbits. Chicago: University of Chicago Press.
Miller, Stephen J. 1965. "The Social Dilemma of the Aging Leisure Participant." Pp. 77–92 in *Older People and Their Social World*, edited by Arnold M. Rose and Warren A. Peterson. Phildelphia: F. A. Davis.
Rollins, Boyd C. and Harold Feldman. 1970. "Marital Satisfaction Over the Family Life Cycle," *Journal of Marriage and the Family* 32: 20–8.
Schneider, Clement J. 1964. *Adjustment of Employed Women to Retirement*. Unpublished Ph.D. dissertation, Cornell University.
Streib, Gordon and Clement J. Schneider. 1971. *Retirement in American Society*. Ithaca: Cornell University Press.

# 10 The Unbearable Lightness of Retirement: Ritual and Support in a Modern Life Passage

## Joel Savishinsky

*Culture has often been thought of* in terms of tradition, but modern culture is more often noted for its inventions. The novelties of our time include not just the obvious and dramatic new technologies – the gene-splicers, CAT scanners, word processors, and spaceships of recent decades – but also new social forms. Feminism, single parenthood, nursing homes, rap music, psychobabble, and deconstructionism are just a few of these innovations. But, one of the most important developments has been in the life course itself where our century has seen the invention of retirement as a new stage of life with its own name, organizations, magazines, an economic and legal infrastructure, and full-blown planned communities.

Traditionally, when anthropologists have studied tradition, they have focused a lot on ritual, and many of the rituals they have addressed are rites of passage. These ceremonies help individuals move from one stage of life to the next by transforming their identities and by investing both the passage and the person with deep cultural meaning.[1] Societies that fail to provide timely and appropriate retirement rites may lay themselves open to intergenerational tensions and discontent among their elders (Foner 1984; Nadel 1952). In the culture of modernity, the potential dilemmas have been exacerbated: Rituals have been played down, and to act ritualistically is to risk being put down rather than socially elevated. Later life, in particular, is characterized by a dearth of expectations and ceremonies in industrial societies (Hazan 1994; Myerhoff 1984), and these deficits occur during a developmental period of great social discontinuity when rites of passage could potentially be the most helpful to individuals and the social order (Fortes 1984; Keith and Kertzer 1984). For most retiring employees, Maddox (1968) once observed, "this significant transition appears to be unceremonious, perhaps intentionally so, as though retirement were an event which one does not wish to mark especially" (p. 357). More recently, Manheimer (1994) has noted that retirement is still "a rite of passage we haven't figured out how to celebrate" (p. 44).

One of the most attentive students of retirement, Robert Atchley (1976, 1991), has observed that we do not know much about retirement ceremonies, how commonly they are held, or what part they play in this important transition. A similar point has

Original publication: Savishinsky, Joel, "The Unbearable Lightness of Retirement: Ritual and Support in a Modern Life Passage," *Research on Aging* 17 (1995), pp. 243–59.

been made by Linda George (1980), who comments that the "symbolism and subjective meaning of retirement as an event is a rich and largely unexamined area of study" (p. 56). Atchley notes that, unlike rituals such as weddings and graduations, retirement ceremonies are not standardized in our culture. Some rites are personal and informal events, others highly organized and elaborate; some honor one person, others feature a group of individuals; some are sponsored by employers, others by friends; some bestow meaningful gifts whereas others fail to; and although the atmosphere of such events is usually positive, the speeches and rhetoric focus on the past rather than on the transition that lies ahead (Atchley 1976, 1991).

Given the lack of careful attention to retirement rites, the absence of ceremonial standardization, and the uncertain significance of such rituals, several important issues remain to be addressed. What happens, ceremonially, when people enter the new life stage of retirement? Who organizes these events, and how are they arranged and put together? And what are the sources of meaning and support that retirees find, or hope to find, in these ritual experiences?

These are three of several questions I have been asking in a longitudinal study of retirement as a life passage in a rural American community. With the collaboration of my students and a developmental psychologist, I have been following a group of 26 people as they approach retirement and experience its first three years. Recruited through a combination of letters and notices to local employers and unions, and by a process of snowball sampling, study participants are equally divided by gender but represent a diversity of work backgrounds and personal circumstances. They include people who have been teachers, doctors, and professors, a lawyer, a secretary, a postman, a designer, an accountant, a human service worker, a biologist, a librarian, a musician, and a salesman. They are variously married, single, or divorced individuals, some of whom have children and grandchildren, and others who have neither. Their states of health vary, as do their financial situations. Their ages at the time of retirement ranged from 54 to 77, and about half have elderly parents or in-laws still alive. The methods involved in this project have emphasized formal and informal interviews, life-history analysis, and participant observation. The latter has included attendance at people's retirement rituals and parties, and the sharing of such mundane events as hanging out together at local coffee shops, shopping malls, and the weekly farmers' market (see the appendix). My concern in this article is with the way these people have experienced the public marking of their retirement with rituals, and with how these events reflect their social support systems, and the models they have developed of what this new state of life will be like for them.

## Formal Rituals

Retirement marks the end of work but not of responsibility, and one of those responsibilities is to mark retirement itself with ritual. Employers usually feel obligated to host farewell ceremonies, and prospective retirees feel compelled to attend them. The formal nature of these events tends to follow a fairly standard formula: advance announcements of the party's time and place; brief speeches by supervisors or senior personnel; the bestowal of a gift and a commemorative certificate or plaque; and the serving of food or a meal, accompanied by a toast. Although the course and content of such rites are fairly predictable, the expectations of workers, and the best laid plans of mice, men, and management are not always congruent. Nor are the results necessarily fulfilling.

At the age of 61, Martin Karler had been anticipating his retirement for months, and knew that it would only take one day in April to finish off the work of 37 years. For over three decades he had been employed in the production department of an appliance manufacturer. Rising slowly in its ranks, he wound up his career in charge of advertising and media. Martin was content with what he called his last promotion's "comfortable responsibility," and in the preceding five years had especially enjoyed the novelty of being a kind of model and mentor to younger workers just starting out in the division.

Martin saw himself as a very practical man. And – other than attending his children's college graduations and weddings – he was no lover of ritual. But with the end of work about to begin, he privately hoped that its public celebration would make the passage to retirement easier for him. He wanted some validation for what he had accomplished in the past and an acknowledgement of the brave new world he was about to enter. But the ceremony held to mark his last day of work was a disappointment. Like most retirees in the study, Martin found the formal ritual at his workplace to be "very nice" but also pallid and predictable. His boss said a few words, a plaque and a present were given, a toast was made, and people quickly turned to the buffet. Martin and other study participants have been witness to nearly identical ceremonies held for older coworkers, and what they had once seen was now what they themselves got. The climax to years of work was anticlimatic. There were, of course, minor variations in the content of speeches, the words on the card, and the value of the check or gift. In most cases, a few anecdotes were told by colleagues, and the retiree's history of work and contributions was recounted; but only the most general remarks were made about the person's family ties or future plans. The rhetoric and the proceedings followed a fairly standard formula, and in Martin's words, "even the laughter came on cue and sounded canned."

People retiring from some of the area's larger employers – a university in several cases, a financial corporation in others – were faced with another dimension, the fact of numbers. In these instances, the work year fell into well-defined periods, and there were clear junctures in time when groups of people, approaching retirement, were expected to leave and mark that event together. In such situations, retirees were forced to share an already weakened spotlight with others whom they either barely knew or who – in at least two cases – they actively disliked. These experiences underscored how distinct a social experience the retirement rite could be from a seemingly similar ceremony such as graduation, which often marked a person's entry into the world of work. Though adolescence and early old age parallel one another as times of transition, powerlessness, and identity confusion (Keith and Kertzer 1984), their rituals can differ in significant ways. Unlike a high school or college graduation, there was no collective or class identity at the end of work to bind retiring celebrants together. Employees generally began and lived their work lives as individuals, not as a cohort; and yet at the end of their careers, they were lumped into a collectivity of ceremonial convenience.

Even some of the people who felt negatively about the formal rites nevertheless felt compelled to attend them. In some instances, they did not want to disappoint those who desired to acknowledge their departure. In other cases, the compulsion was their own. Whether hollow or not, the rite was still an important form of closure these retirees preferred not to forego. In one case, that of Nate Rumsfeld, a public service employee was offered a window of time during which to take an early retirement. Encouraged by younger coworkers anxious to move up, pressured by his supervisors, and left to fend for himself by his union, Nate took the window at age 57 but did so with strong feelings of ambivalence and uncertainty. Although several others also made the same decision Nate did, none of these men or women was offered a party, and no one thought of organizing even the most minimal of departure rites for them. Although Nate felt he would not have especially enjoyed such an event, he nevertheless resented its absence. It was one more insult in a hurried, unsatisfying, and alienating process.

In a second case, that of Stefan Nokalsky, a man who chose to leave work in his mid-fifties was told by his employer of 20 years that this step could not technically be called a retirement. The personnel director insisted on the phrase "voluntary separation from employment." To call it a retirement, Stefan's superiors explained apologetically, would require the company to begin his pension and other benefits. Yet in Stefan's own mind, though he was not asking for early benefits, this was his retirement, and the withholding of that title felt like a betrayal. Feeling a hostage to language and bureaucracy, he worked hard to get his employer to at least include him in the end-of-the-year's retirement party because this event, when it happened, did finally allow him to lay personal and public claim to a status that those he called the "language police" had barred him from.

Another factor that made official rites of retirement so unfulfilling for many was that the organizers of these ceremonies – the bosses, supervisors, and administrators – only knew the retiree in a one-dimensional way, that is, as an employee or coworker. Because this was the only part of the person's identity they could speak to, they could not address all the other dimensions of the retiree's life that would be affected by this transition, such as family ties and friendships, personal dreams and life goals, and health status and finances. Only the people who knew the retiree in a more rounded, multifaceted way could relate to these other aspects of who they were. This was one reason why the informal rites that intimates organized for retirees were usually more meaningful.

## Informal Rites

One of these invented rituals reveals the structure and significance of such events. In the case of Alice Armani, retirement came at the end of 15 years of administrative work for a small, nonprofit human service agency – a very demanding, low-paying, yet high-profile position. This organization had only had two previous directors – neither of whom had retired after leaving – and so there was no institutional culture to frame a ceremonial tradition. When Alice decided to retire at the age of 67, her decision was prompted by a combination of burnout, a growing sense of her own age, and a feeling of diminished capacity and trust in her own memory and attentiveness. She was proud of what she had accomplished in her work but haunted by doubts of her own efficacy.

The retirement event created by Alice's staff, her board of directors, and the agency's volunteers included a dish-to-pass supper, the presence of Alice's adult children, a dance band featuring several of her colleagues, a song composed in her honor, and several speeches – brief but rich in detail – recounting episodes from Alice's career and highlighting the qualities of her character. There was also a memory book in which most of the six dozen people present wrote at some length about their feelings for Alice. Finally, there was a gift of a hand-carved easel, reflecting people's awareness of Alice's intention to focus her energy on her great passion, painting, once retirement began. The gift's presentation, which Alice's grown children participated in, focused specifically on the kind of painting Alice loved, and some of the actual landscapes she dreamed of visiting. Those who spoke obviously knew Alice's heart as well as her art. What also made the entire event so meaningful to Alice was not just the individual attention and the personal tone it embraced, but – as she put it – "The knowledge that my work had not been in vain, that I wasn't as incompetent as I feared I had become." The main reward, then, even more valuable than the easel, was the gift of reassurance and self-worth.

The very steps by which such informal rites were planned unveiled another of their important attributes, namely, the significance of process and selection. We found, for example, that preparing the guest list for a private celebration was itself a significant process in that it gave retirees a chance to sort through the people in their life and decide who constituted their real support system and circle of significant others. Ursula Chalfin, a biologist, reflecting on her recent party and the steps she had participated in to plan it, compared the experience of making the guest list to cleaning out her office and lab: The two processes had enabled Ursula – aged 63 – to figure out what and who was memorable and meaningful in her history, not just in a material, but also in an emotional way. She remarked that it "put things together by helping me put some things, and some dreams and people, away."

These informal or intimate rites revealed one other important dimension of retirement, namely, fantasy. In the safe and supportive company of friends, families, and colleagues, the more inventive and imaginative retirees articulated their vision of what they would have wanted their ideal departure to be like. At their party, sparked by the presence of confidants and a seasoning of alcohol, they spoke and joked about who they would have told off, for example, and in what words, or to what degree of drama and fanfare. Listening to them was like listening to people's fantasies of how they would have wanted to leave a bad relationship; it had all the theatricality, flair, and well-considered words that we come up with only in our dreams or on the morning after. A 63-year-old professor, Felix Davis, spoke at his party of wanting to hold his retirement rite on the main quad of his campus; in his fantasy he saw himself dressed in golfing clothes and awaiting a vintage Sopwith Camel that would fly low over the college, land on the quad, and taxi up to where he stood, surrounded by campus dignitaries. In Felix's dream he then saw himself mount the wing of the plane, hurl piles of bureaucratic forms and invective on the unprecedentedly silent college president, emit one huge fart, and roar off into the sunset. To be able to describe such dreams, mouth the words, and – in a few cases – even act them out before an appreciative group, lent a cathartic quality to the retirement event. Like court jesters, clowns, and other marginal figures licensed to express outrage and ridicule, ritualized fantasy also allowed these elders to use humor and their liminal status as platforms for social commentary and criticism (cf. Myerhoff 1984; Turner 1969). As Turner (1969) has emphasized, being marginalized does not necessarily disempower people. It is often from the margins that individuals can see, and voice, what those in the center of things may miss or choose to suppress. For retirees, ritual here was the opportunity for the repressed to find its voice, for intimates to become an audience, and for kin and colleagues to stand witness to an adulthood's accumulation of love and hate.

## Travel

In listening to people talk about retirement, and in following their lives during its first two years, we discovered an unexpected and unceremonious way that many of them had for dealing with this transition. Their method was travel. For quite a number of women and men, a major trip in the immediate postretirement period was not just a special reward that they gave themselves, it also served a number of significant social, emotional, and symbolic functions. Travel itself, beyond its inherent pleasures of leisure and excitement, allowed them to separate from work, home, hometown, the daily round of life, and the common flow of social ties. They found that when people persistently (and sometimes irritatingly) asked, "What are you going to do in your retirement?" they could simply answer, "I'm going to take a trip"; this would often satisfy others and shut them up. But, travel was more than merely a quick and convenient retort. New retirees used the time away not only to relax but to reflect on themselves and the past, put its immediacy behind them, and give thought to what they wanted from their future and their own life.

Teri Rogers, for instance, after her retirement at the age of 57 from teaching high school, took a long, leisurely, cross-country trip by train with her husband, visiting many of the national parks that she had dreamed about for years. The experience not only fulfilled a long-held ambition of Teri's but built on the growing sensitivity to environmental issues that she had developed while serving on her local civic association's executive board. By the time Teri returned home, she had decided to put her trip, her retirement, and her consciousness to work by devoting her energy to her town's fledgling efforts to develop a land preservation trust.

Teri's experience bears out the remarks of novelist and travel writer Lawrence Durrell (1957), who has observed that

> Journeys . . . flower spontaneously out of the demands of our natures – and the best of them not only lead us outwards in space, but inwards as well. Travel can be one of the most rewarding forms of introspection. (p. 1)

Several other participants said, as did Teri, that when they came back from their trip, their new identity as a retiree was "more real." They acknowledged that, except for the absence of work, the things around them were the same, yet they had changed. It was, in effect, easier to go away and come back as a different person than it would have been, in Teri's words, "to simply change in place."

These experiences add a special dimension of meaning to the role of travel in the period after people exit from the work force. Atchley (1991) has noted that one of the paths that some individuals follow after retiring is to actively pursue the activities they had not been able to engage in before. Among men and women who start out adopting this euphoric honeymoon approach, extended travel is a common feature for those with adequate income. Our study suggests that, for the persons on such a path, the pursuit of this particular form of pleasure is also a transformative process. Travel thus constituted a de facto rite of passage in the classic sense of that term; that is, the initial postretirement trip served as a mediator between statuses, and qualified as a transitional or liminal period between a person's separation from and subsequent reincorporation into the society at large. As Turner (1969) has so persuasively argued, the liminal phase of rituals needs to be more fully acknowledged and more carefully studied because it constitutes the period during which personal identity is actually reconstituted. This theme is congruent with the ritual emphasis on separation in retirement's broader meaning (Atchley 1976, p. 54). Thus, although many cultures have rites of passage (such as pilgrimages and the vision quest) that involve travel, here – for retirees – travel itself is ritualized, and helped them pass from an old to a new stage of life.

## Summary and Conclusions

Modern times have presented Western peoples with many forms of novelty in the domain of lifestyle as well as technology. These include important questions and new reflections on the idea that one's job is a central source of personal and social meaning (De Grazia [1962] 1994). Just as the Industrial Revolution and the nineteenth century gave birth to the weekend and modern forms of leisure (Rybczynski 1991), they have also restructured the life cycle of contemporary workers by creating the very concept of retirement (cf. Graebner 1980; Haber and Gratton 1993; Hannah 1986).

Studying how people cope with the transition to retirement is neither trivial nor esoteric: This passage is the gateway to a period of time that could amount to a third of their lives. The main findings of this study indicate, however, that the rituals held to mark people's entry into retirement take a number of different forms, and offer varying degrees of fulfillment. The key points may be summarized as follows.

1   For most participants in this study, the formal and public recognition of retirement was marred by the pale content of the official rituals meant to dramatize it. These ceremonies were formulaic, predictable, and clichéd; they were officiated over by individuals who did not know the retirees in a rounded way, and they sometimes lumped together a group of honorees who wanted to be acknowledged as individuals. These were the cases in which ritual did become "mere ritual." Because most of our subjects were in decent financial circumstances, what they were faced with then was not the culture of poverty but rather the poverty of their culture.

2   The private and informal ceremonies created for retirees were more fulfilling for a number of reasons. These included the content and tone of the rhetoric; the informed and sympathetic presence of people who knew the retirees, along with their histories and their dreams; the thoughtful process of selecting gifts and the reflective experience of formulating a guest list; and the opportunities provided for retirees to engage in fantasy, physical separation, and freedom of expression. The latter features of ceremonies opened the doors for catharsis and personal transformation.

All of these rewarding attributes suggest that the ritual entry into retirement is heavy with meaning and full of potential for people. Unfortunately, the language of the participants' culture and the rhetoric of formal ritual continue to convey the subtle and airy nature of this new phase of life, its aura of nothingness (Atchley 1976). People retire from work, which is an activity. They retire to bed or Florida, which are simply places. But there are still no prepositions or figures of speech to indicate what retirement is, for older individuals do not retire to a purpose, activity, or function. What they do in the place they retire to is ill-defined and largely up to them. Going through retirement strips people of a long-held identity and bestows nothing concrete to replace it (Hazan 1994). Personal uncertainty is compounded by the fact that retirement's impact can also vary with social class, gender, education, and work history, and so it is not "a single experience with a predictable consequence" (Maddox 1968, p. 364). Lacking a consensual model of retirement, most persons in this study tended to invent or seize on a metaphor that felt suitable to them: It was a "vacation" to those who anticipated its freedom; it was a "sentence" to those who could not escape its confinement; it was like "adolescence" to those who saw it, with either fear or hope, as a kind of "starting all over again." Like being, itself, whether retirees consciously followed the weighty philosophy of Sartre (1956) or floated along passively with the characters of Milan Kundera (1985), it was this undefined nature, this cultural lightness of retirement that made it so personally heavy to bear.[2]

Anthropologists and historians have shown how people, faced with the unexpected circumstances of modernity, commonly create new forms of behavior to pattern their unprecedented lives. The historian Eric Hobsbawm (1983), in fact, has pointed out how a good deal of what now passes for tradition is really of recent invention, created especially in the years since the start of the Industrial Revolution. And in Barbara Myerhoff's (1978) now classic study of elderly East European Jews in California, she observed how people created definitional ceremonies, that is, their own rites of passage, when their combination of New-and-Old World cultures failed to provide them with meaningful rituals. Private rites were here elaborated to compensate for the lack of effective public ones (Myerhoff 1984).

Our study has also shown that there are several positive ways in which the ritual handling of retirement can be made to work for people, just as it suggests that students of this life stage should give more careful regard to the details of its celebration. Indeed, it is the close observation and thick description found in other recent ethnographies of aging – such as Sankar's (1991) work on dying, and Gubrium's (1993) book on meaning – that demonstrate the power of qualitative gerontology for illuminating and critiquing the texture of older people's lives. In that spirit, and based on what retirees themselves have found in their own experiences, we would suggest that colleagues and kin pay more attention to the following five areas in planning people's retirement ceremonies.

*Informal rites.* The rites that people invent for their friends and family are a rich source of cultural creativity. They do, say, and provide more than the standardized rituals that have grown up in the American work place. Such private, intimate, and informal ceremonies should be encouraged, studied, learned from, and adapted to individual circumstances, and not be overshadowed by the pro forma events that usually occur at people's place of employment. As Martin's experience suggests, the transition to retirement is too important to be left to employers and managers, and – as Nate and Stefan's cases demonstrate – they are too critical to be allowed to suffer from the benign neglect of significant others.

*The gift.* The gift a retiree gets should have some direct relationship to his or her history and hopes. All-purpose presents, such as money or gift certificates, should be avoided: Retirement is a meaningful transition, and its meaning should be reflected and expressed in what is given. A gift that is connected to an activity that the retiree is looking forward to, such as Alice's easel, makes the ritual more personal, more future oriented, and thus more fulfilling.

*The guest list.* Although the gift for an informal event may be a surprise, the guest list should not be. Rather, it should be prepared with care, and the retiree should have a primary role in drawing it up. Family and friends who work on this process with the retiree should encourage her or him to talk about the reasons for including or excluding people. For some individuals, such as Ursula, this process becomes a valuable experience in sorting through one's social ties and work history. Some people find it helpful to begin with a very large list of potential guests – lots of colleagues, coworkers, family, and friends – and then winnow out those who are not meaningful, and identify those who are.

*Travel.* Travel turns out to be a potent, transformative experience for certain retirees, and its functional equivalent to a rite of passage should be recognized and reconsidered. Those planning their own retirement and those who help others plan for theirs might want to consider the efficacy of travel in this light, and think of ways to enhance its potential. Journeys should occur within a reasonable time (approximately 6 months) of actual retirement, and involve – as Teri's experience shows – a destination or itinerary that has some special meaning for the retiree.

*Fantasy.* Finally, retirement is a transition that brings out both memories and dreams and so it bears a strong link to the unconscious world of fantasy. The ritual celebration of this life passage offers a rich opportunity to express and act out those fantasies, and people should be given – or, as Felix did, they should give themselves – a chance to enjoy this possibility. If the American dream is one that has been built around the world of work, perhaps it is time for people to dream new worlds, and avenge themselves on old ones, when this time of transition is at hand.

## APPENDIX

### Sample and Methods

Study participants were recruited by means of letters and notices sent to major employers and unions in a rural county in upstate New York. Personnel departments also helped us to identify people who were likely to retire within a specific 12-month period. In addition, an article about the study in the area's major newspaper brought the project to people's attention. Once a core of participants was identified, individuals in this group told us of other women and men whom they thought would probably retire within the next 6 to 8 months. Such snowball sampling yielded a cohort of 26 people with the following characteristics at the start of the study (see table 9.1).

Methods employed in the study have included formal and informal interviews, life-

**Table 9.1**  Characteristics of study participants

| Gender and Age[a] | | Main Occupation | Family/Living |
|---|---|---|---|
| Male | Female | at the Time of Retirement | Situation[b] |
| 54 | | Engineer | Married |
| 57 | | Postman | Married |
| 57 | | Professor | Married |
| 59 | | Hotelier | Married (2nd time) |
| 61 | | Designer | Married |
| 61 | | Media consultant | Married |
| 61 | | Salesman | Married |
| 62 | | Accountant | Divorced; living with married daughter |
| 63 | | Professor | Married |
| 64 | | Lawyer | Married |
| 64 | | Fund-raiser | Married |
| 71 | | Doctor | Married (2nd time) |
| 77 | | Health educator | Married (2nd time) |
| | 57 | High school teacher | Married |
| | 58 | Musician | Married |
| | 59 | Lab Technician | Married |
| | 61 | Librarian | Married |
| | 61 | Bookkeeper | Married |
| | 62 | Secretary | Married |
| | 63 | Doctor | Married |
| | 63 | College administrator | Married |
| | 63 | Biologist | Single; living with partner |
| | 64 | Administrative assistant | Married |
| | 65 | College administrator | Married |
| | 65 | Elementary school teacher | Divorced; living with partner |
| | 67 | Human service specialist | Divorced |

[a]  Average age: 62.3.
[b]  All currently and formerly married participants have children and grandchildren, although only one individual resides with a grown child and her family.

history analysis, and participant observation. Initial structured interviews with all participants were held prior to their formal retirement: These occurred, on average, about 4 months before people retired. To date, two additional rounds of interviews have been held: The second round took place between 6 and 12 months after retirement, and the third round between 18 and 24 months of retirement. Formal and informal interviews, and casual conversations with retirees and family members, have also yielded a considerable body of life-history material. The specific topics we have collected data on include people's educational, work, and medical histories; their financial status; their family background and living situations; their expectations of, and reflections on, retirement; their mode of planning for retirement; their perceptions of individuals whom they feel constituted good and bad models of retirement for them; their views of how retirement has affected key relationships and activities; their involvement in travel, volunteer and paid work; and their views of the meaning of life.

The participant-observation component of the study has taken several forms. We have attended the formal and informal retirement parties and rituals held for people and have spent casual time with participants in coffee shops, shopping malls, the farmers' market, and other public settings where retirees tend to congregate. Furthermore, the very tenor of life in a small community has led to many unplanned contacts at dinners, at parties, in stores, and at such public events as concerts, ball games, school board meetings, and local fundraisers. In essence, there has been some approximation of the anthropologist's ideal of immersing oneself in the life of the people one is trying to understand.

## Acknowledgments

An earlier version of this article was presented at the 93rd Annual Meeting of the American Anthropological Association, Atlanta, Georgia, November 30, 1994 to December 4, 1994. The research reported on here is being supported by a grant to the Gerontology Institute at Ithaca College. I would like to acknowledge the help provided by the Institute, the cooperation of the study's participants, and the assistance of my students and my collaborator, Janet Kalinowski, of Ithaca College's Department of Psychology. To protect people's privacy, the names used in the text are pseudonyms, and some biographical details have been altered. For reprints, write to Anthropology Department, Ithaca College, Ithaca, NY 14850–7274.

## Notes

1   Important studies of rites of passage by early and more recent scholars include the works of Bateson ([1936] 1958), Gluckman (1962), Herdt (1981), Myerhoff (1978), Turner (1969), and van Gennep ([1909] 1960).
2   A caveat about retirement, issued many years ago by Maddox (1968, p. 363), continues to retain its relevance:

> Failure to conceptualize reaction to retirement as a variable (rather than as a social event with a single meaning) related to the particular configuration of experiences which constitute an individual's biography has been a crucial flaw in many studies of retirement.

One effort to address that flaw is Prentis' (1992) book that contains 40 brief case histories of individual women and men dealing with various phases of the retirement experience. Another approach is represented by ethnographies of communities of retired people, a number of which have appeared since the early 1970s, including Hochschild (1973), Jacobs (1974), Johnson (1971), Keith (1977), Myerhoff (1978), and Vesperi (1985).

## References

Atchley, R. 1976. *The Sociology of Retirement*. Cambridge, MA: Schenkman.
Atchley, R. 1991. *Social Forces and Aging: An introduction to Social Gerontology*, 6th ed. Belmont, CA: Wadsworth.

Bateson, G. [1936] 1958. *Naven*, 2nd ed. Stanford, CA: Stanford University Press.

De Grazia, S. [1962] 1994. *Of Time, Work and Leisure*. New York: Random House.

Durrell, L. 1957. *Bitter Lemons*. New York: E. P. Dutton.

Foner, N. 1984. *Ages in Conflict: A Cross-Cultural Perspective on Inequality Between Old and Young*. New York: Columbia University Press.

Fortes, M. 1984. "Age, Generation, and Social Structure." Pp. 99–122 in *Age and Anthropological Theory*, edited by D. Kertzer and J. Keith. Ithaca, NY: Cornell University Press.

George, L. 1980 *Role Transitions in Later Life*. Monterey, CA: Brooks/Cole.

Gluckman, M., ed. 1962. *Essays on the Ritual of Social Relations*. Manchester: Manchester University Press.

Graebner, W. 1980. *A History of Retirement: The Meaning and Function of an American Institution*. New Haven, CT: Yale University Press.

Gubrium, J. 1993. *Speaking of Life: Horizons of Meaning for Nursing Home Residents*. Chicago: Aldine de Gruyter.

Haber, C. and B. Gratton. 1993. *Old Age and the Search for Security: An American Social History*. Bloomington: Indiana University Press.

Hannah, L. 1986. *Inventive Retirement: The Development of Occupational Pensions in Britain*. Cambridge: Cambridge University Press.

Hazan, H. 1994. *Old Age: Constructions and Deconstructions*. Cambridge: Cambridge University Press.

Herdt, G. 1981. *Guardians of the Flutes: Idioms of Masculinity*. New York: Columbia University Press.

Hobsbawm, E. 1983. "Introduction: Inventing Traditions." Pp. 1–14 in *The Invention of Tradition*, edited by E. Hobsbawm and T. Ranger. Cambridge: Cambridge University Press.

Hochschild, A. 1973. *The Unexpected Community*. Englewood Cliffs, NJ: Prentice-Hall.

Jacobs, J. 1974. *Fun City: An Ethnographic Study of a Retirement Community*. New York: Holt, Rinehart & Winston.

Johnson, S. 1971. *Idle Haven: Community Building Among the Working Class Retired*. Berkeley: University of California Press.

Keith, J. 1977. *Old People, New Lives: Community Creation in a Retirement Residence*. Chicago: University of Chicago Press.

Keith, J. and D. Kertzen eds. 1984. "Introduction." Pp. 19–61 in *Age and Anthropological Theory*. Ithaca: Cornell University Press.

Kundera, M. 1985. *The Unbearable Lightness of Being*. Translated by M. H. Heim. New York: Harper & Row.

Maddox, G. L. 1968. "Retirement as a Social Event in the United States." Pp. 357–65 in *Middle Age and Aging*, edited by B. Neugarten. Chicago: University of Chicago Press.

Manheimer, R. J. 1994. "The Changing Meaning of Retirement." *Creative Retirement* 1:44–9.

Myerhoff, B. 1978. *Number Our Days*. New York: Simon & Schuster.

Myerhoff, B. 1984. "Rites and Signs of Ripening: The Intertwining of Ritual, Time, and Growing Older." Pp. 305–30 in *Age and Anthropological Theory*, edited by D. Kertzer and J. Keith. Ithaca, NY: Cornell University Press.

Nadel, S. F. 1952. "Witchcraft in Four African Societies." *American Anthropologist* 54: 18–29.

Prentis, R. S. 1992. *Passages of Retirement: Personal Histories of Struggle and Success*. Westport, CT. Greenwood Press.

Rybczynski, W. 1991. *Waiting for the Weekend*. New York: Viking.

Sankar, A. 1991. *Dying at Home: A Family Guide for Caregiving*. Baltimore, MD: John Hopkins University Press.

Sartre, J. 1956. *Being and Nothingness: An Essay on Phenomenological Ontology*. Translated by H. Barnes. New York: Philosophical Library.

Turner, V. 1969. *The Ritual Process: Structure and Anti-structure*. Chicago: Aldine.

van Gennep, A. [1909] 1960. *The Rites of Passage*. Translated by M. Vizedom and G. Caffee. Chicago: University of Chicago Press.

Vesperi, M. 1985. *City of Green Benches: Growing Old in a New Downtown*. Ithaca, NY: Cornell University Press.

# 11 "One of Your Better Low-Class Hotels"

## Joyce Stephens

When I moved into the Guinevere Hotel[1] the tenants, with an irony that is typical, informed me that it was "one of your better low-class hotels." The Guinevere is a deteriorating single-room occupancy hotel situated in the inner core of a large midwestern American city. Over a half-century old, the Guinevere reached its apogee in the 1920s, when it was considered to be one of the better hotels in the city, and catered to a wealthy if notorious clientele. Hoodlums, gangsters, and the like, "Legs" Diamond and members of the Purple Gang, were frequent guests at the hotel and earned it a certain notoriety.

With the decline of this turbulent era, the Guinevere fell upon lean times and began to deteriorate. During the forties and fifties, it was given the nickname of the "riding stable," as it became well-known in the area as a hotel catering to seekers of illicit sexual services. In addition, a physician operated a profitable abortion ring out of the hotel until he was convicted.

The present owners maintain a number of hotels in the city. They have attempted to arrest the rapidly degenerating operation of the Guinevere and to quell the scandal produced by the violent death of its previous owner, who was beaten to death in her room. They have been able to keep the Guinevere afloat by catering to a growing number of permanent, elderly occupants, so that at present less than two-thirds of the tenants are transients.

The surrounding neighborhood is honeycombed with rooming houses and hotels catering to transients, blacks, alcoholics, addicts, hustlers, prostitutes, recently migrated southern families, and the elderly poor. The economic character of the area is revealed in the high concentration of marginal businesses – nudie shows, nude photographic studios, resale shops, cheap cafes and restaurants, dry-cleaning stores, "we buy anything" shops, and bars. The area contains a heavy concentration of social and psychological pathology. Addicts and winos can be seen nodding off in alleys and in the backs of vandalized cars on the side streets. Street crime is common, even routine: muggings and robberies, frequently involving severe beatings and even killings, are a constant source of anxiety to the residents. Street brawls are a daily occurrence. Fires are so common in the cheap hotels and rooming houses that they scarcely stir the resident's interest. The bombing of a cafe adjacent to the Guinevere evoked minor expressions of regret that the cheapest cup of coffee in the neighborhood was now gone. The ubiquitous violence and the myriad forms of social and personal deviance have a direct effect on the attitudes and life styles of the people and give to the area an atmosphere of mutual suspicion and fear.

Original publication: Stephens, Joyce, "One of Your Better Low-Class Hotels," *Loners, Losers, and Lovers: Elderly Tenants in a Slum Hotel* (University of Washington Press, Seattle, 1976), pp. 3–13.

The Guinevere has eleven floors, with a total of 524 rooms. During my research, 371 rooms were occupied, of which 108 were rented to aged tenants. There are two wings, separated by two interconnected lobbies. Both lobbies have outside doors, but one is locked every evening at six o'clock. Anyone entering or leaving at night must use one door, which is in full view of the reception desk. Each wing is serviced by two self-service elevators that are inclined to frequent breakdowns.

In addition to the two lobbies, the Guinevere has a bar, a dry-cleaning service, a television room, a small room in one lobby out of which a bookie operates, and a restaurant that is physically connected to the hotel but is operated independently. In the lobbies are several vending machines that dispense coffee, cigarettes, candy bars, and soft drinks.

Rents are comparable to other hotels in the neighborhood ranging from sixteen dollars a week for a sleeping room to forty-six dollars a week for a two-bedroom suite. The expensive (by comparison) suites are usually vacant. Rooms fall into four categories: (1) sleeping rooms, which have no bath facilities, provide once-a-week maid service, and range in price from sixteen dollars weekly without television to eighteen dollars with black-and-white television to twenty dollars with color television; (2) connectors, which share a bath, provide once-a-week maid service, and range in price from twenty dollars weekly without television to twenty-two dollars with black-and-white television to twenty-four dollars with color television; (3) private rooms, which have a bath, daily maid service, and range in price from twenty-four dollars weekly without television to twenty-six dollars with black-and-white television to twenty-eight dollars with color television; and (4) suites, which have a bath, daily maid service, color television, and rent for forty dollars weekly for one bedroom and forty-six dollars for two bedrooms. The majority of the 108 elderly permanents live in the cheapest rooms and pay an average rent of $20.59 a week. Most live in sleeping rooms, although some live in connectors and a few have private rooms.

There are two public bathrooms (shower and commode) on each floor, one for men and one for women. However, more often than not the tenants disregard this sexual division of the communal bathrooms. This may not seem surprising in view of the sex ratio of ninety-seven males to eleven females. The units have neither cooking facilities nor refrigerators. All rooms contain a bed, a wash basin, a dresser, and a chair. The furniture is cheap and generally in need of repair. Paint is peeling off the walls, and cockroaches are abundant. During the winter months, rooms above the fourth floor are inadequately heated. The halls are dimly lit, and robberies and fights in these dark stretches are not uncommon. All doors have double locks.

The aged tenants are scattered throughout the hotel, although the manager attempts to put those with more severe disabilities (poor vision, paralysis) on the bottom four floors. In general, the hotel maintains a policy of not renting to elderly who are not ambulatory, although exceptions are made. The seventh floor is informally reserved for what the manager describes as his "nuts and mentals." There are four black tenants. The area has a high concentration of blacks, but the manager resolutely refuses to rent to them because "They're trouble-makers and they frighten my old people."

The average age is sixty-seven, and the oldest resident is ninety-one. The length of residence ranges from two to fifty-one years, with a mean of nine years. A significant proportion of the elderly tenants moved to the Guinevere from nearby hotels, and, indeed, this pattern of shuffling from one hotel to another is fairly common in the area. Among the males, over half have never been married, and the remainder are divorced or widowed. The females include a larger proportion of widowed or divorced.

Health problems are endemic in this group. The major core of diseases includes the geriatric illnesses (arteriosclerotic disease, stroke, and rheumatoid disorders), sensory deficits (poor vision, auditory loss), alcoholism, and various forms and degrees of paralysis. In addition, a significant minority suffers from mental illness, including schizophrenia, paranoid disorders, and the depressive syndromes. Many of them are in need of prosthetic devices (glasses, hearing aids, canes, dental appliances), but have neither the income nor the personal resources to obtain them.

Their work histories are generally episodic and encompass a variety of marginal work situations. Few had occupational careers in a formal sense: for the most part, they were concentrated in low-paying, intermittent types of employment – vendors, carnival hustlers, spot laborers, seasonal workers, petty criminals. For most, retirement was not an event that occurred on a particular day and terminated a career; rather, it happened gradually as they became less and less able to find even low-paying jobs, including street vending, spot labor, "go-fors," and the many forms of hustling. Over 80 percent are on some form of state assistance. Their income is low, with the major sources being Old Age Assistance (OAA), social security, disability insurance, and money picked up from occasional jobs. A small portion receive pensions.

Despite the prevalence of medical and psychiatric disabilities and the low economic status, a comparison of this group with other aged SRO tenants in the area would reveal that, as a group, they are not the most severely disadvantaged. The Union Hotel and the Lock Hotel, both adjacent to the Guinevere, house many former Guinevere residents. Tenants who become a problem to the management because of their accelerating alcoholic bouts, repeated failures to pay rent, or constant public brawling with other tenants, are eventually put out. Most likely they will seek lodging in one of these neighboring hotels. Thus, despite the comparable economic status of tenants, these nearby hotels contain many Guinevere rejects. As the manager and the tenants say, the Guinevere is "one of your better low-class hotels" in the area.

The attitudes of the elderly tenants toward the Guinevere betray a curious mixture of grudging appreciation and discomfiture. They are involved in a kind of love-hate relationship with the hotel and its functionaries. On the one hand, they view the "Rock" as their personal turf where no one will bother them and they can live their lives in privacy and autonomy; on the other hand, they are aware of the justifiably questionable reputation of this slum hotel. They are aware of the low repute in which such hotels, and by association their occupants, are held; however, they rationalize this stigmatizing attitude by pointing out that people from the "outside" cannot possibly understand or know what it is like in the hotel and that outsiders are guilty of accepting erroneous myths about the character of both the hotel and its residents. This strong ambivalence pervades their feelings about the hotel.

Undoubtedly, one of the major advantages of hotel living for these people lies in the autonomy that is characteristic of hotels – they are free to determine their own schedules; they may eat when they want, come and go as they will, without interference from anyone. Their only supervision is themselves, and they enjoy the continued opportunity to make their own decisions. In the words of one seventy-two-year-old woman who has lived in the Guinevere more than fourteen years: "One good thing about living here is you can live your own private life, and no one will bother you. You can be more private than if you lived in your own home. Outsiders think a lot of mistaken ideas about people in hotels. They can't know, they are wrong in those . . . er . . . opinions about the people in hotels. These are *our* homes, we live *here*."

Hotel life encourages personal freedom and privacy; in addition, it frees the tenants from certain tasks that are necessary in other private living arrangements, such as minimal housework. A sixty-eight-year-old man on OAA who has been at the Guinevere for six years put it this way: "Everything is right here. If I lived in the suburbs, what would I do, how would I get around?" A former carnival vendor had this to say: "I could live free in a house my niece has but I'll stay here, where things are cookin'. I'm independent. Some old people just give up, but I'm always plottin' and plannin' . . . and the 'Rock' has elevators. You don't have to walk up stairs." An elderly cabdriver who had moved out of the Guinevere, taken an apartment, and then later moved back into the hotel, gave his reasons for preferring to live in a hotel: "It was too quiet in my apartment, and too much work, washing and cooking and such. But, I missed the people here and the comings and goings."

There is an element of living there to "be with your own kind," which is sometimes expressed in the movement from another hotel to the Guinevere. A commonly held belief is that families and children do not really want to be bothered with the old people. Suburbs are for the young and for families; the old feel awkward there. In the anonymity of an inner-city slum hotel, absolute privacy and a high degree of personal freedom can be relished.

Further, the hotel situation provides access to services which the elderly tenants believe would constitute a problem in different living situations – transportation, proximity to the downtown area, maid service, company when desired and privacy when preferred, freedom, a certain anonymity, their "own kind," and "happenings." Many of these elderly people have been unable to live peacefully with their families, and the greater latitude permitted in the impersonal atmosphere of the hotel is an important factor in their continued residence. There they may act out behaviors that family members would have resisted, for example, excessive drinking, consorting with prostitutes, and other less extravagant behaviors which have been deemed as inappropriate for the old in our age-myopic society. In addition, for a number of them, relative isolation and unwillingness to enter into social commitments have been lifelong patterns.

Many elderly tenants express the attitude that the Guinevere is going to be the final period of their lives. They do not anticipate or plan on leaving:

> The Guinevere is the road of no return. Old-timers come to this point of their life. This is the last place they'll ever stay. When they get here, they don't never leave.

> A lot of us come down here to do this or that with the intention of leaving, but we keep coming back and at last, we never leave.

> This is a place where people come to die.

Generally, they view the Guinevere as "nicer" than other hotels in the area, pointing out that in the Guinevere people do not "jungle up." ("Jungling up" refers to the practice of communal cooking and eating of meals among hotel occupants, which occurs in some of the SRO hotels that cater to the most indigent groups of alcoholic elderly. The practice is virtually nonexistent in the Guinevere.) However, there are dissenting opinions on this matter, especially among the tenants who have lived at the Guinevere longer than a decade. They feel that the hotel has deteriorated, pointing out that undesirables are no longer screened out, that "they let anybody and everybody in, even prostitutes." They complain that the hotel's standards have gone down, and that many people who live there would have been turned away earlier. There is general agreement among all of the tenants that the neighborhood is deteriorating, and that inevitably the hotel will go downhill.

The manager acknowledges this loss of selectivity in clientele by noting that it was financially necessary to liberalize the policy regarding who would be allowed in, and that this has resulted in a gradual change in the type of people living there. This includes the acceptance of what the manager identifies as "welfare types," homosexuals, prostitutes, and drunks. The manager's formal policy is that prostitutes may live in the hotel as long as they do not ply their trade inside the hotel. In actual practice, the manager, like most managers of slum hotels, ignores prostitution unless it begins to encroach upon his business operation. Thus, when complaints become numerous or several tenants are unable to pay their rent, he checks, and if he finds that a prostitute in the hotel has been getting his rent money, he "cleans them out" of the hotel. In general, though, the Guinevere management is liberal and tolerant in its treatment of "hookers." Indeed, one of the tenants' more colorful nicknames for the Guinevere is the "whortel."

Specific dissatisfactions with the hotel include complaints about the inadequacy of heat in winter, noisy tenants, people throwing trash and debris from the windows, cockroaches, and fights in the elevators or halls. Some of the tenants feel that the current management has arrested the hotel's decline. They speak of the manager with grudging approval, for they see several changes that he has made which they interpret as efforts to provide services for them. Examples include vending machines in the lobbies, free ice to residents, and the inauguration of a Saturday raffle, at which time a tenant wins two free tickets to a current sports event and a five-dollar bill. This has generated a modest enthusiasm among some of the men. Another change effected by the manager was his handling of the hotel "hermits." These elderly tenants, many bedridden, never left their rooms and paid maids to bring them food. According to several sources, their fingernails grew to great lengths. The current manager had them moved into hospitals and nursing homes.

If there is ambivalence in their assessment of the relative advantages and disadvantages of living in the hotel, the tenants are unanimous in their evaluation that at least the Guinevere is a better place to live than the other hotels in the area, and that any hotel, however dilapidated, is superior to any nursing home. The common assertion is that the tenants at the Guinevere are a "better class of people" and that other nearby hotels are *really* "low-class." Since several of them have lived in these other hotels, they know from experience the relatively better treatment and services provided at the Guinevere. The Guinevere is cleaner, repairs are made sooner, there are fewer building code violations, and all rooms are equipped with telephones, yet the rent is comparable. The manager's attitude toward these people appears nearly benevolent when contrasted with that of some other SRO managers. The following excerpt from an interview with the manager of an adjacent hotel is revealing: "These old people! Who'd be interested in them? These old people are poor: they've always been poor; they elected it; they prefer it. They've never contributed to society. They're single, never even raised a family; they aren't even has-beens, they never were. They don't eat right; they never ate right. They've never been anywhere, never done anything. All they've done is take up space. I've contributed. At least, I've paid a lot of taxes."

The tenants are unanimously hostile and suspicious toward nursing homes. To these fiercely independent people, nursing homes represent the loss of autonomy they are determined to avoid. They frequently contrast their own independent living arrangements with their ideas of what nursing homes are like. Their basic view is that nursing homes exploit old people. A sentiment commonly expressed is that the time is approaching when old people will lose their independence, and the government will foist upon them programs that will serve not their interests but rather political aims. Nursing homes are the prime example, as far as they are concerned. The tenants regularly draw comparisons between the Guinevere and the two nursing homes in the immediate area. They call these homes "playpens" where "they tell you when to get up, when to eat, where to go, and take your money." By contrast, several Guinevere permanents characterized themselves as "lone wolves," "independent loners," and variations of this idea.

For these people, nursing homes also represent the tangible expression of society's rejection of old people. The following are representative comments of tenants on the subject:

They are the final humiliation for old people, the final humiliation.

Oh, the playpens, where people tell you when to get up, when to breathe. They take your money, yeah, I sold a rubber [balloon] to a woman lives at the Shady Glen, and they came out and said they'd arrest me if I came around again. Said she wasn't right and I took advantage of her. Ha, they said I couldn't take her money, couldn't sell her that rubber, but they take all her money.

Old people are not wanted. Nobody wants us old geezers. So, they, ah, segregate us, in nursing homes or ghettos. Oh, and the homes are terrible places where they tell you what to do. And what you want doesn't matter at all.

The specter of institutionalization looms as a reminder of the catastrophic consequences of loss of personal determination. It is an admission of dependency and physical and mental failure.

Interestingly, they make little mention of specific disadvantages or conditions (poor food, abuse, and so forth). In fact, few have actually lived in such places – although most know people who do. Rather, they object in principle to the very idea of homes for the aged, with their characteristic programs of regimented activities. Some distrust of social service agencies is generated by the issue of nursing home placement; some of the tenants fear that social workers will push them into a home. To quote a seventy-three-year-old retired cabdriver who has lived in the Guinevere since 1964: "Social workers would likely tell us this hotel is a bad environ [sic] for us, and we don't like it that they're always questioning our competences [sic], and saying this is a bad place, and we'd be better off in one of them homes."

The distrust and in some cases hostility of these elderly toward social workers was communicated to me in the early days of field work. Many of the tenants assumed that I was a social worker (an improvement perhaps on their initial belief that I was a hooker) and were consequently aloof and inaccessible. Fortunately, their suspicions relaxed as they observed my behavior, and later one elderly individual summed up their assessment of my presence there: "Oh well, that's all right. You're no social worker. Writin' a book that's O.K. You aren't going to hurt us."

*See end of chapter 12, pp. 149–50, for Notes.*

# 12 "Making It"

## Joyce Stephens

Truly, "It is a full-time job to be old and poor."[1] That these people are managing to retain their independence is no mean feat, when we consider their multiple physical and mental handicaps and disabilities, their meager economic resources, their lack of access to community services, their own internally atomistic pattern of social relationships. Such marginal patterns of living necessitate a disproportionate expenditure of energy and effort merely to get by, "to make it."

Making it is a constant preoccupation and a major goal for these elderly tenants; in order to accomplish this goal, they use several unconventional ways of supplementing their limited incomes. The Guinevere tenants refer to these unconventional ways of earning a living as hustling, and some sort of hustle constitutes the principal means of making it for most of them. Thus, to hustle is to make it, to engage in some kind of activity – legal or illegal, alone or with a partner – which brings in money to enable the individual to get by. Hustling includes a variety of work situations which, although operated on a stand-by and unstable basis, and capable at best of generating only sporadic and minimal funds, nevertheless allows these elderly hotel occupants to take care of their basic needs and maintain independent living arrangements.

The term "hustling" is a familiar one in the lexicons of many minority and subcultural groups in American society. It is a term indicative of the harsh realities of marginal status in the social structure of conventional society. It refers to some kind of effort that is aimed at obtaining desired ends, regardless of conventional ethics; often the hustle involves some risk, and by definition hustles are not stable kinds of work situations. They are operated on an ad hoc basis, and must adapt to the fluctuating conditions that characterize many forms of marginal living. Hustling differs from conventional work situations in that it lacks legitimacy and social approval and support; it confers no approved status within conventional society; and it is not a dependable source of income. The hustle work situation demands that the individual continually seek to manipulate and structure situations so as to serve his immediate interests. The extremely problematic character of hustling is demonstrated in this definition elicited from an elderly Guinevere tenant, who "hawks" balloons on the street: ". . . a way of working for people who can't get any steady employment. A guy does it because he's got no other thing to fall back on. He can't get no other job, no secure job. He does it cause he's got to, and he don't make no real money. He just gets by."

The elderly tenants in the Guinevere live in poverty; the majority are receiving public assistance. The monthly or biweekly check is insufficient for many of them, and they must find ways to supplement their incomes. They must, in short, find work.[2] However, there are strong deterrents to this. Discriminative hiring practices

Original publication: Stephens, Joyce, "Making It," *Loners, Losers, and Lovers: Elderly Tenants in a Slum Hotel* (University of Washington Press, Seattle, 1976), pp. 59–67.

with regard to the over-fifty worker are common enough throughout society. Many of these people have few or obsolete work skills. Additionally, poor health and mental and physical disabilities render some of them virtually unemployable. In the competitive sphere of job situations, these people are at the bottom of the heap. Many have poor work records and probably could not handle a steady job. Among them are heavy drinkers and chronic alcoholics who have histories of irregular work habits that have gradually eliminated employment opportunities for them.

A small number have found more or less steady conventional jobs in low-paying, low-skill services, working as waiters, dishwashers, cleanup helpers. Even these jobs, with their abysmally low pay scales, little security, and poor working conditions, are at a premium in the area. Most of these aged people cannot get conventional jobs; for them, the hustle is the only feasible alternative.[3]

The Guinevere tenants distinguish nine common types of hustling activity: (1) "conning," (2) "go-fors," (3) shoplifting, (4) scavenging, (5) "pushers," (6) prostitution (male and female), (7) "dingman," (8) begging or panhandling, and (9) peddling. Each kind of hustle involves an exchange of goods (with the possible exception of begging), requires the mastery of job-related skills, such as special argots, and in a minimal way permits the individual to realize the all-important goal of making it.

"Conning" has both general and specific meanings. The broad meaning is that the con is a strategy used to obtain some desired end by employing a verbal deception. Thus, the ruse to forestall the management from plugging one's room, and the manufactured life history to enhance social identity, are common uses of the con. In this sense, conning is a ubiquitous activity that serves a variety of personal aims in a number of different situations. In the more specific sense of the term, the con is a hustle designed to procure material goods. Then the con is most often employed in conjunction with another hustle. Examples would include the conning which the peddler does in persuading a prospective customer of the quality of his merchandise; the "poor me" story that the prostitute uses to garner a larger profit from her client; the efforts that the shoplifter makes to convince his customer of the legality of a particular item. The higher the degree of verbal skill – that is, the better the "con job" – the more successful the individual will be at gaining his desired end. There is considerable competition among them as to who can con better, and "telling a good story" confers prestige. Conning is a strategy used for the most part to obtain something from "outsiders" (prospective customers) or from the hotel staff. However, attempts to con each other are not uncommon.[4]

"Go-fors" or "runners" are individuals who engage in a certain kind of activity for money or alcohol. For a small amount of change – a dime, a quarter, rarely more – they go for small items, such as cigarettes, coffee, foodstuffs, wine. Many of the individuals who hustle in this fashion are chronic alcoholics who use the money earned to keep themselves supplied with liquor. In some cases, part of the agreement will be a share in the bottle brought back to the customer.

A number of the tenants practice shoplifting for the express purpose of selling the "hot items." Shoplifting for items that the individual plans to keep for himself is not considered a hustle. The hustle involves selling the goods to someone else. Items such as clothing, jewelry, and small appliances top the list. Buyers are usually other tenants in the Guinevere, or tenants in nearby SROs. The profession is not well developed and brings only a small return to those individuals in the hotel who do it. There is only one more venturesome and professional individual who shoplifts "on order" for specific items for buyers and also disposes of some items through a "fence."

Scavenging is a hustle in which the individual collects junk from trash cans and then carts his finds off to one of the "we buy anything" stores. Although the tenants know of such activities and know tenants at other hotels who do it, they insist that no one at the Guinevere has to resort to this way of earning a living. In fact, there are a small number of tenants in the hotel who sporadically collect and sell cast-off items to supplement their finances. Scavenging is a low-status hustle, and less common than the other unconventional work situations discussed thus far.

By "pushers" they mean individuals who sell narcotics illegally. They agree that "pushing" is a young person's hustle, and tend to link it with the "transients" and blacks in the area. The sentiment is usually expressed that elderly people are not interested or involved in the illegal market for drugs. There is a small market for certain painkillers and soporific drugs, however, and occasionally one of the elderly tenants might practice a hustle involving drugs.

Prostitution is a familiar hustle; the neighborhood abounds with "hookers" of both sexes. Some of the men may find themselves the victims of this hustle, for often enough a related hustle is the "rolling" of the client by the prostitute's "agent" (pimp). The elderly men are vulnerable to intimidation and force, and represent an easy "mark." It is interesting that the oldest profession can find a place in its ranks for some of the aged women in the hotel, who cannot find a place in the conventional job market. There are two elderly women living in the Guinevere who occasionally "turn tricks" to pay their rent. There are other instances of activities geared toward an exchange of goods, which are borderline and could be broadly defined as prostitution. For example, there is an elderly barmaid who goes out with the men and exchanges her sexual favors for what she calls her "tip money."

The "dingman" is an individual who sells Veterans of Foreign Wars pins and paper flowers to unsuspecting customers, who are led to believe that the profits go to charity. In fact, they are for the seller. The dingman may strengthen his appeal by wearing an old army outfit; he may con his customers by pleading with them to "give something for the boys." He may refer to his war wound. This hustle is practiced by both young and old tenants in the hotel and is exclusively a male hustle.

Begging or panhandling is a low-status hustle; it is something that *other* people at *other* hotels do. It is similar to scavenging in this regard, for none of the tenants openly admits to panhandling. (There is one notable exception. An elderly man in the Guinevere travels all over the country begging. He has lived in the hotel for a number of years and is regarded by the other tenants as a "real character." Since he has "style," the tenants define his begging as an activity above common panhandling.)

By far the most common hustle is peddling. Over a third of the elderly men in the hotel peddle more or less regularly to supplement their income. Various terms are used in referring to these individuals – peddlers, hawkers, hustlers, carnies. Reflective of the prevalence of peddling as the dominant type of hustling activity, the term "hustler" is often used synonymously with "peddler." They are also called "carnies," and many of them speak "carnese" or "carny talk," a mixture of pig latin and underworld slang spoken by the peddlers with prior connections with carnivals and circuses. The peddlers are dependent upon each other to realize economic gain; a person can peddle alone, but it is more efficient and profitable to establish working relationships. The work relationships established by the carnies display a stability not seen otherwise in the Guinevere society, and, indeed, these hustlers constitute the most identifiable and durable social grouping in the hotel. Also, as a group they enjoy the respect (and frequently envy) of the other tenants. It is one of those ironies of SRO life that these men who hawk balloons and plastic pennants through the city streets are engaging in what their social world considers to be a high-status hustle.

## Top Dogs and Underdogs

There exists a status hierarchy among these individuals that ranks hustles (and hustlers). The criteria for determining which hustles are high or low status are: (1) the more economically profitable, the higher the status of a specific hustle; (2) the greater the regularity and dependability of the hustle, the higher the status; and (3) the more individual autonomy afforded by a specific hustle, the higher the status.

Conversely, the less secure the hustle, the smaller the remuneration, the lower the status of the hustle and hustler. Exemplified in "go-fors," scavenging, and panhandling, such low-status hustles are avoided by the more resourceful individuals. Thus, the alcoholic "go-for," whose payoff entails only a swig from the client's bottle, is generally considered to be a fool.

The avoidance of dependency has a significant impact on the nature of the hustle employed, as evidenced by the fact that many hustlers operate as loners and are suspicious of shared endeavors. This preference for single person hustles, or at most hustles which require a minimum of partners, is a pattern that embodies several of the dominant norms of SRO society – independence, suspicion, and the manipulation of others to serve one's personal ends. Indeed, the latter is particularly revealing in its relation to status differences among hustlers. The carnies, in particular, are seen as the personification of the independent loners who make it, neither asking for quarter nor giving it, in the harsh world of the SRO. The panhandler, on the other hand, arouses contempt because of his subordinate position vis-à-vis his customer. Thus, the embodiment of the major SRO norms is a significant standard by which tenants rank hustling situations and each other as hustlers.

Certain job-related skills – such as amount of training necessary to master the hustle, the use of a special argot, and relative importance of "connections" – also figure in distinguishing between hustles. Some hustles require that the novice serve a kind of informal apprenticeship under someone more experienced, whereas other hustles can be done by almost anyone with little or no training. Those hustles that require a more formalized training period include peddling and shoplifting; "go-fors" and panhandlers, on the other hand, require almost no preparation or skill.

Another job-related skill is the mastery of a special argot. The carny talk of the street peddlers is the prototype, and other argots developed and used by individuals in specific hustle work situations are basically spin-offs from this colorful language derived from the carnival world. Further, mastery of carnese is indicative of the separation hustlers insist upon maintaining between themselves and "outsiders," that is, nonhustlers.

The importance of connections to the performance of the hustle varies greatly. The network of individuals involved in the carnie's business enterprise is (by SRO standards) dense. From the "backer" who "fronts" him money to buy stock, to the carny "boss," to the friendly merchant who charges only a nominal sum for the use of the "privilege," the carny uses a number of individuals to insure the success of his hustle. The beggar, however, works alone and can rely on no one to facilitate his hustle.

A final distinction between hustle situations involves the complexity of relationships and roles necessary to sustain different hustles. Hustle situations vary in the degree to which they are characteristically single-person endeavors or multiple-person operations. Those hustles that require more than a single individual working alone, typically require a clear-cut division of labor, with role rights and obligations. Thus, "ding-man," "go-fors," and panhandlers are carried out by individuals working alone. Shoplifting, as practiced in the Guinevere, is typically a single-person hustle. Prostitution and street peddling are usually multiple-person hustles. The carnies, whose hustle is more often a multiple-person endeavor, are able to maintain their favored status because their dependency upon others is confined to other carnies and does not extend beyond the economic contingencies of peddling. Of course, the fundamental reason for their high status rests upon the overall higher economic gain in their enterprise.

## Notes to chapters 11 and 12

*Chapter 11*    *"One of your better low-class hotels"*

1    All names and references to places have been fictionalized to insure the anonymity of individuals.

*Chapter 12*    *"Making it"*

1    Quoted from Curtin, *Nobody Ever Died of Old Age*, p. 56. Research into the occupational activities of elderly SRO tenants is urgently needed, as a shortcoming of previous studies lies in their almost total neglect of this issue. Members of the hotel society generate and sustain characteristic ways of making a living and providing for economic necessities. Unfortunately, we know very little about these matters.

2    The gerontological literature is replete with general studies of the fate of the older worker, the semiretired older worker, and the retired older worker. See Carp's study of the occupational characteristics of the aged slum dweller, for whom retirement – usually from menial jobs that provided no security, tenure, or fringe benefits – has not been an event that occurred on a given day, but was rather the culmination of increasingly frequent and lengthy periods of time during which these individuals were unable to obtain employment. Carp, "The Mobility of Older Slum-dwellers."

Several studies have found that the loss of the occupational role marks a dramatic turning point in the lives of the elderly. C. L. Preston, in a study of retired and nonretired aged, found that the retired group experienced more role confusion, shared the invidious stereotypes of older people which prevail in American culture, and were greatly lacking in confidence as to the possibility of their being included in meaningful social activities. Preston, "Traits Endorsed by Older Non-retired and Retired Subjects." C. L. Carp, in a study which included elderly persons who worked for pay, did volunteer work, or did not work at all, concluded that those who worked for pay more frequently identified themselves as middle-aged and were more likely to perceive themselves as useful and important. Carp, "Differences Among Older Workers, Volunteers, and Persons Who Are Neither." T. Meltzer found that the closer an individual gets to retirement, the more ambivalent he feels about his future status. With the advent of actual retirement, the individual is likely to perceive his role as unproductive and his status as not socially legitimized. T. Meltzer, "Age Differences in Happiness and Life Adjustments of Workers." Miller points out that the occupational identity of the individual establishes his position in the social system, allowing others to evaluate his status and role, and providing a context within which his social activity can be interpreted. On the other hand, the retired individual "finds himself without a functional role which would justify his social future and without an identity which would provide a concept of self which is tolerable to him and acceptable to others." Miller, "The Social Dilemma of the Aging Leisure Participant." The overall conclusions of many of these studies is that the giving up of the work role and the assuming of a leisure role involves nearly traumatic consequences for many elderly individuals. In some perverse fashion, the necessity for the Guinevere tenants to continue to work aids in their continued ability to function psychologically (as well as economically).

3   It should be stressed that I have defined hustling *not* in terms of external criteria – that is, not by referring to the sociological literature – but rather in terms of the definitions utilized by the tenants. For a discussion of the strategy of "grounding" concepts through the data-collection stage of a research project, the reader is referred to several works by Glaser and Strauss, namely. *The Discovery of Grounded Theory*; "Discovery of Grounded Theory": and "Discovery of Substantive Theory."

4   The reader is, no doubt, wondering if attempts to con and manipulate me were common. In answer, I might ask, "Is Los Angeles in California?"

## Further Reading to Part III

Allen, Katherine R. and Victoria Chin-Sang. 1990. "A Lifetime of Work: The Context and Meanings of Leisure for Aging Black Women," *The Gerontologist* 30: 734–40.

Ferguson, Karol Sylcox. 1989. Chapter 8, "Qualitative Research with Older Creative Adults." Pp. 127–40 in *Adulthood and Aging: The Human Science Approach*, edited by L. Eugene Thomas. Albany, NY: SUNY Press.

Jacobs, Jerry. 1974. *Fun City: An Ethnographic Study of a Retirement Community*. New York: Holt, Rinehart, and Winston.

Johnson, Sheila K. 1971. *Idle Haven: Community Building Among the Working Class Retired*. Berkeley: University of California Press.

Kaufman, Sharon R. 1995. *The Healer's Tale: Transforming Medicine and Culture*. Madison, WI: University of Wisconsin Press.

Unruh, David R. 1983. *Invisible Lives: Social Worlds of the Aged*. Beverly Hills, CA: Sage.

Voges, Wolfgang and Hannelore Pongratz. 1988. "Retirement and the Lifestyles of Older Women," *Ageing and Society* 8: 63–84.

Willigen, John Van. 1989. *Gettin' Some Age on Me*. Lexington, KY: University Press of Kentucky.

# Part IV

**Interpersonal Relationships**

# 13 Friendship Styles

## Sarah H. Matthews

While collecting and reviewing topical oral biographies, it became apparent that the taken-for-granted assumptions that informants held about the importance and meaning of friendships in their lives varied from one person to the next. Statements made about friendship that were "obvious" to some simply could never have been made by others. Given that friendship is a noninstitutionalized social relationship, this is to be expected. In this chapter, the different ways in which the informants approached friendships are elaborated.

For each of the individuals who were interviewed, a picture of his or her life course in relation to the acquisition and termination of friendships was constructed. A straight line representing the life span from birth to the age at the time of the interview was marked at the ages at which important turnings had occurred in the person's life – for example, significant events in childhood, deaths of parents, high school and college graduation, each job, each move, changes in marital status, and retirement. Below the straight "life line," lines representing friends were drawn, each one beginning at the age when, according to the informant, the friendship was established and at the age at which it ended, unless it was still ongoing at the time of the interview. If the friend had died this was noted. These "pictures" made it possible to focus on how many friends were claimed, the duration of friendships, and whether acquisition and termination of friendships were related to turnings in various "role domains" (Elder, 1978). From this analysis and from a careful reading of the interviews, three distinct ways of "doing friendship" (Lofland, 1976), or friendship styles, emerged – independent, discerning, and acquisitive. In this chapter each of these is described. Rather than attempt to explain why these informants adopted different styles of friendship, the concern here is with how they differ from one another and how each affected and continued to affect the social relationships and friendships of those who used them.

### The Independents

Because of the way they described friendships in their lives, 13 of the informants were classified as "independent." They did not identify any specific individual as a friend as they related their biographies, even when asked repeatedly to do so. Throughout the interview they talked generally about people whom they knew or had known but would not talk about anyone by name, unless it was a person with whom they currently interacted – someone whom they had met, in most cases, relatively recently. Even then, they were often quick to point out that the person was not really a friend.

Original publication: Matthews, Sarah H., "Friendship Styles," *Friendships Through the Life Course: Oral Biographies in Old Age* (Sage Publications, 1986), pp. 35–58.

It was clear that most of them were not isolated people, but instead considered themselves to be sufficient unto themselves. To illustrate this style of relating to people with whom they were not in institutionalized role relationships, but with whom they nevertheless had relationships, their descriptions of people they knew are cited.

Referring to his youth, one man said:

> Way back when we were children, going to school, I made a lot of friends with children, girls and boys. And as long as we were together, we enjoyed ourselves. We went to certain little functions that we had and we were always good friends. I wouldn't say there was any special friend. We just enjoyed what we used to do.

Another described his childhood friends in a similar way, referring to them as the "block bunch" and the "routine bunch." After identifying one boy who had died when he was 18 with whom the informant had "bummed around" in high school, he stated that after that he just "hung around" with people:

> I still do. No one in particular. I just have a number of friends, what you might call good friends, but no one that I would consider outstanding. They're just nice people to be with. They're helpful people. I help them, too, along the line, whatever they want, especially the older people. Somehow, they more or less depend on someone that's a little younger. I seldom turn anyone down. I guess it's my nature to be that way.

When asked by the interviewer if there was one friend who stood out about whom they could talk, one woman replied:

> No, I am a very private person. I always lived by the rule "no explain, no complain." When you say too much you are revealing too much about yourself. You should retain a little bit of your privacy and thereby you get pride and you get self-discipline. The very private things you keep to yourself.

Aside from her husband, there was no one whom she identified as being close to her except family members. She knew and admired many people and was not isolated, but there simply was no one whom she considered a close friend in the past or in the present.

Another informant said:

> I would prefer to be absolutely independent. There is a certain dependency involved in friendship relationships that I've noticed among my children, a dependency that I'm not very keen on for myself.

He also considered his spouse to be his best and only friend. One man who lived in a retirement complex replied when asked who his most recently acquired friend was:

> Oh, I consider all of them, most all of them, to be friends. There are some that I wouldn't give you a dime a dozen for them. But still you participate in the stuff that we do here. You have to go along with them, but I wouldn't call them friends.

In telling about his earlier life he expressed the same ambivalence:

Well, in 1923 I started working at a bakery and that was night work so you don't have many friends then. Well, you do and you don't. The only ones you have are the ones that were at work.

Like the other informants cited above, he allowed the situation to dictate who his associates would be. None was singled out as special and, again, he was careful to point out that he was a person who depended on no one. Another man described his associates in the town where he had lived before moving to his present location:

We had wonderful times there with people that we've never seen since. There were maybe eight or ten of us that used to go to a place where one of the men had a cottage, but there wasn't a close relationship as friends. It was more just that passing of time in a social way . . . But reviewing the situation, I really haven't had very many really close friends.

These informants, apparently beginning in childhood, were content to be with people who happened to be available wherever they were. There was no indication of commitment, and they were likely to identify themselves as loners who did not really need people.

One woman began the interview by making a statement that she had thought about and rehearsed:

Let me preface this by saying that I have been thinking a good deal about this since I knew you were going to talk to me about it. And I said, "Well, just how do you make friends?" It seems to me that one way is the neighborhood in which you live. You get acquainted with people. And some of them become your friends and others are just casual acquaintances. And then there is your school. From the time you are a youngster, you make contacts there. Again, it's selective. You pick out people who appeal to you because you have something in common, besides the fact that you are going to school. And then there is the church, another way in which you make friends, but there again, you are selective. But you form friendships because you are doing things together. And then the other things that occurred to me is the professional connections that you have. And then, of course, that makes me think of friends that I made when I was teaching. And what's become of them? Well, most of them have retired like I have and some of them have moved away. Some of them are gone. And then my last source of new friendships is the people that I have met here [retirement community]. And here, you see, circumstances have brought us together, but I'm still selective. I'm not friends with everybody. But I've made some very good friends with people that I never would have had any contact with if I hadn't been part of this group here.

In relating her biography, she remained true to her initial statement. Throughout her life she had allowed circumstances to provide her with friends, with only one singled out by name, a current one. In response to the query, "Do you have friends that you went to college with?" she replied:

No, not anymore. No, those years are so far behind me. I don't seem to keep close friends. The fact that I only mentioned one person here that I would say is a real friend. But, I'm sort of self-sufficient. I don't seem to need people the way some people do.

About a woman with whom she had lived for over a decade, when they both taught in the same grade school, she said:

> I guess we separated when I went to the other school to teach because I wanted to be within walking distance of the campus and, naturally, she wanted to stay where she was. I think that's what caused us to go our different ways.

And of other friends at the grade school, she said:

> When I left, I had to start all over again to get acquainted with people because I didn't see much of those teachers anymore. Some of the depth of your friendship depends on how much you see people and how you are brought together, whether circumstances bring you together or it's altogether a voluntary thing.

These two schools were within three miles of each other. Characteristic of informants who were classified as independent, friendships for her apparently were much more circumstantial than personal and would fall under the heading of "friendly relations" rather than "friendships" (Kurth, 1970) in the minds of many people, including those classified as discerning and acquisitive who are described below.

The specific associates of the independent informants were affected by the various turnings in their lives. They did not acknowledge ever having had a close friendship, so the commitment necessary to maintain a relationship after a turning was absent. As indicated earlier, they simply established ties with those with whom they were proximate. One man, for example, explained how his marriage had affected his relationships:

> You seem to get away from the people you knew, not entirely, but somewhat, and you make new friends, let's say among the married people, married couples. So, of course, the buddies that you chummed around with, you can't do that all the time. You no longer do that. In a sense you can – you can see them and all that – but you can't go out with them as often as you used to. [Did your wife's death affect your friendships?] Yes, you break away from those married people and you more or less start over, the way you were in your single days. Sure, you see the people and talk to them once in a while, but you don't associate with them like you did. People that were married, you break away from them.

The independent informants, then, allowed circumstances to dictate their associations.

Using the independent style of friendship did not necessarily preclude having known people for a long time. One woman who lived in a retirement community said:

> My best friend here runs the shop, and I support her and her work. Her husband is a lawyer, and they used to be in our church years and years ago, and then they went away. I think she's probably my best friend. I didn't see her until the last few years when he retired and came back to town. And then we renewed our acquaintance. [So you were friends at one time and then . . .] Oh, closer friends now because of the contact. They're close by. And our interests are very much the same. I have them to dinner over here once a week and she has me for dinner.

About another person she had known many years before, she said:

> Now one that I've revived recently is a girl that I was very friendly with at college. I've looked her up. She wrote to me, so now I write to her a couple of times a year.

Typical of those classified as independent, staying in one place, rather than commitment, meant that it was possible for her to have known associates over many years. About friendships through the life course, one man explained:

> It seems to me certain times of your life you have an opportunity to come close to somebody, whether it's teenage years or younger or older. And they move away or separation comes between you. I suppose you have to consider that as the normal process of growing up . . . After we got married I can't think of any particular friends off hand, after I was active in medical circles and so on that I had any real close friends. And I don't think I'm such a hard guy to get along with at that, but that is not . . . [I] just never had the opportunity to develop any close friendships.

However, he had spent his life since leaving medical school in the same community, which others might have seen as ample opportunity to establish friendships. For the most part, then, these independent informants left up to chance those with whom they would associate, and this apparently was a pattern that characterized their childhoods as well. It is going beyond the limits of the data, of course, to argue that the informants' memories matched what "really" happened. Nevertheless, the conviction with which they spoke is a testimony to their belief that they did.

The interview guide was structured so that each informant was asked to relate his or her biography and talk about friends at the same time. Needless to say, when they did not feel that they had ever had real friends, proceeding with the interview was somewhat problematic. In these cases the format was somewhat different, because informants were put in the position of having to explain as they related their biographies why they were not identifying anyone as a friend. In fact, four of them had prepared statements to read to the interviewer. For example, one began the interview by reading the following statement:

> At 76 years of age I realize that I have not made as many close friends as the majority of people for several reasons, as I will explain in my self-analysis.

The absence of friends to whom to refer in conversation led them to expound their own definitions of friendship more so than those who fell into the other categories. In addition, some felt that their position was an unusual one, although almost no one regretted having used this style, as is evident below.

A number of the independent informants applied such idealistic and rigid criteria to friendships that no one qualified. One man attributed his not having or wanting specific friends to an incident in late adolescence:

> I love friends. I love people. But I've been stung by friends, and I could never place myself in the position where I'd say, "Well, he or she is a *very* good friend of mine." I won't let myself get hurt anymore. [Can you say something about that?] Well, it happened when I met my wife. The boys that I used to go around with – we used to play

ball. And then, suddenly, just like I say, when you fall in love, your life changes. So I didn't have as much time to give them as I did to give her. I was the catcher on the team, and one day we were supposed to be playing and she was sick, so I didn't go to the ball game. We lost the game. I got blamed for it because I was doing something else. And I couldn't take that. I couldn't do justice to both of them. So I took what I wanted and that's what I went for. After we got married, we spent 55 years together.

About more recent associates he said:

I love 'em. I got a lot of friends, too, but I don't say they're friends that I would depend upon . . . I'm my own man. That's what I want to be . . . Do I have friends now? I have people that I know.

In this case, the informant's criteria for friendship appeared to include absolute commitment and this precluded friendships once he was committed to his wife. There simply was no room for competing relationships. It is interesting to speculate about how different his discussion of childhood friendships might have been had he been interviewed at the age of 15.

When asked who his best friend was, one man replied:

I have people that I've known for a period of a great many years, but I think friendship is a fairly rare thing in my life. So it would be hard to pick anyone out that was a real friend in the complete sense of the term.

Again, his criteria were so rigid and idealistic that no one qualified as a friend "in the complete sense of the term." It is instructive to compare these criteria with those for an institutionalized relationship. Spouses, for example, are not called upon to demonstrate that they are in fact spouses "in the complete sense of the term." Instead, agreed upon criteria exist so that the quality of the relationship and whether it in fact exists are separate issues.

Another man used a specific criterion:

I think there was one fellow who I chummed with quite a bit in high school. But I don't believe he had much influence on my life excepting that we were good companions, as boys will be at that age.

To have qualified as a friend, then, this "fellow" would have had to "influence" his life. Being his own person meant that few people – actually no one he could think of – really had influenced him, and during the interview no one was identified as a friend.

In some cases the informants offered explanations for why they had no friends:

This is a long way from friendship, but you can see that moving that many times I had to leave friends behind and pick up new ones. And my memory being what it is, I'd be away from a town, moved to a new one, maybe for a few months; and I wouldn't be able to tell you the names of some of the people that I knew there that I was most friendly with.

Many moves during his adult years, then, "explains" why he had no specific friends to include in the discussion. Extensive family obligations was another reason offered:

I don't have too many. You see, I have a lot of family, a terrific amount of family, and I write a lot of letters to family.

Another offered a similar reason:

But I didn't make very many really good friends there because I always had my older brother, and I think probably he took up the slack a lot of times. If I had been there by myself, it might have been different.

One man referred to his family in a somewhat different way to explain why he had had no friends during the course of his life:

Well, I might give you a little bit of background of my family life, which would set things up. My mother and father were divorced when I was about four, and that has made me probably a little bit more of a loner or an individual than I otherwise might have been. I had very few close friends when I was real young. I'm only trying to dwell on this because, as I interpret the whole thing looking back with an adult approach to it, I can see that it kept me from having a close contact; and since I was an individual who was earning his own way as a kid, I just didn't have the time for close relationships all the way through school. As far as high school relationships were concerned, I had some very good friends there but the relationship ended when we graduated. I never kept any of them afterward. They weren't that kind.

Although the woman who came with a prepared speech – her "self-analysis" – to explain why she had had no friends, did include her family, her explanation was much more wide ranging than that:

Psychiatrists will caution people not to become too attached and dependent on one person for companionship because it is so much more painful to bear the void when that relationship has ceased for one reason or another. I experienced that loss when my sister – two years my junior – married at 18. Because we had been inseparable, I had not developed more friends in my teenage years. At 18, I began my lifetime work for the electric company, retiring after 43 years of employment. Not being flexible, very dedicated to my job, my days began at 5:30 every morning in order to be able to make the 6:30 bus to avoid ever being late at my desk. With this lifestyle I was confined to dating only on Saturday nights. Curfew Sunday nights was 8:30, which made me very unpopular with friends of the opposite sex. The few friends I had developed during my school years were all married at an early age, while my first marriage did not take place until I was almost 30 years old. This fact caused a drifting apart because of the conflict of interests. My marriage only lasted 2½ years, since I continued to work and had no time to entertain or maintain a home for my husband. [Aside:] See, I can't bring out certain friends that I still see; of course, there's one gal that I went to school with that never married and she and I are on the same level because I had no children, though I've been married twice. [Reading:] My father preceded my mother in death by 20 years, at which time I developed a 'very close relationship with my mother, taking her with me everywhere on a companionship basis, including my job, my out-of-town business trips. Consequently, when she passed away in October 1965, I felt terribly alone again and married my second husband in 1971. Since I had retired from my job in 1967, I felt a little more relaxed and had a little more time to socialize with other married couples during my second marriage. But this continued only five years as my husband suddenly passed away in 1976, and again I felt alone because of a conflict of interest with my married friends. My lifestyle at present is satisfactory as long as I leave my apartment every day, spending time at the senior center, joining classes and attending lectures. I still cannot say that I have any "bosom friends," since I find entertaining too confining to stay home to do it, and refuse luncheon dates, having skipped lunch for the past 60 years, which is necessary to keep my weight down, so I refuse the luncheon dates. In summarizing, the well-known phrase "in order to make friends, one must first be one" does not always apply because so many of us are only "takers" and not "givers." In my opinion, after close observation, there are at least two sure-fire ways of attracting and retaining friends: First, own an automobile and be fortunate enough to be able to continue driving as you grow older; secondly, be active by accepting responsibility of being a chairperson or hold some office in club groups, etc. Become a leader instead of a follower, which I didn't do. This will attract attention to you as a person much admired and sought after.

A complicated set of circumstances, then, precluded and continued to preclude her having "bosom friends."

In summary, to explain why they had no specific friends, the independent informants in some cases indicated that they used very idealistic criteria in deciding whom to call a friend, so idealistic that no one qualified, and in some cases used biographical explanations such as commitment to or the impediments presented by family. The two explanations were not mutually exclusive. The life-course events that "explained" the absence of friends, however, were not different from those of the informants who were classified as discerning or acquisitive. Life events, then, are not adequate causal explanations. Clearly, the development of these styles is rooted in personality and thus beyond the explanatory power of these data.

Lest the reader come away with the impression that "independent" is equated with "lonely," it is important to point out that most of these informants were not isolated or unhappy. Addressing the issue directly one person said, "I know loads of people here, but I wouldn't say they're close friends. They're acquaintances, and yet I feel very happy." Another informant explained, "We have oodles of acquaintances – not that we're such popular people – but we have many acquaintances, friends, but I couldn't term them as being real deep down friends." The woman cited above included in her prepared statement that her life was satisfactory as long as she could "get out every day."

One reason that most of these independent informants were content with their relationships is that they did not expect them to be intense or intimate, but relatively superficial, especially in comparison with the expectations of those with the discerning style of friendship which are discussed below. One informant explained how to maintain smooth relationships:

It took me years to learn this. If you have an argument with a person, and maybe both are right. Maybe they're both wrong. So all right, you might part. At the moment you're very angry, see. But I think a person should be enough, let's say man enough, to go to the person and say, "If I'm wrong, I'm sorry." That's whether you're right or wrong, the very first thing you know, you're good friends again. That happened a couple of times to me. And now we're good friends. And then you usually wind up discussing the matter in a very friendly manner and then everything's patched up. I think that's the way it should be instead of being apart the rest of your lives.

Another explained:

> And I'm accustomed to the idea of a close acquaintance. I mean that I find that a very
> normal way to be.

A woman whose husband had been her best friend described one area of her life in which she missed him a great deal, revealing at the same time what she expected from relationships with others:

> My husband and I, we both loved and enjoyed dinner dances, parties, and then when we
> took the cruises we were the last ones to get off the dance floor. We enjoyed the music
> and it wasn't exhibitionism, but we enjoyed the rhythm and all the old-time songs. My
> husband played on the banjo and he sang beautifully. So we had a lot of rhythm and a
> lot of music. And when it happened that I didn't have a partner, I just didn't know what
> to do. And I couldn't go to any affairs; I mean, I just didn't know what to do. A lot of
> 50th wedding anniversaries I could not attend. I'd send my regrets, I'd send a gift, but I
> could not physically attend because of the great emotion. So then, about three years ago,
> I happened to get the book from the recreation board and it said no partners and line
> dancing and so on. And I said, well, I need the exercise and I need the music, and so
> that's where I attempted to go. Now I take the dance exercise class, and that gives me my
> exercise and feeling of music and I don't need to depend on other people.

She is not attracted to the dancing in order to meet people, possibly to acquire new friends to help ease the burden of her loneliness, but because it is a way to meet other needs.

Other independent informants indicated that they purposefully kept their relationships superficial, either because they did not trust people or because they did not trust themselves. As an illustration of the latter, one informant who felt that her life had been less than successful referred to a period in her life when she had tried to do something about it:

> I remember when I was 27 I went to see a psychiatrist. I knew my world was caving in,
> and that was when psychiatry was in its infancy. But I couldn't bare my soul to him. I
> did go; I didn't keep up with it.

Unable to "bare her soul" to anyone, she had been a loner all her life; but, unlike others classified as independent, she indicated that she was troubled by it, seeing in herself a flaw that prevented close ties.

The independent informants did not claim to have any close friends. Some of them could not be persuaded to include even one person. When someone was mentioned it was likely to be a relatively recent acquaintance with whom their relationship was far from intimate. Many of these informants had explanations for why they did not have friends, although not all indicated that they felt that justifications were necessary. Apparently, these informants had always depended on the circumstances in which they found themselves to provide them with friendly relations. One is left with the impression that they are surrounded by a sea of people, none distinguished from the others.

## The Discerning

All of the eight informants classified as discerning identified a small number of people to whom they had felt close, people who were very important to them. One woman began the interview by saying, "My two closest friends died quite a long, long time ago."

> I'd say that I formed very close friendships in high school within a group of girls . . . and there was a really close friendship with one of these girls. She died in her forties and so that ended that. And then another friend was a close friend in college and I married her brother, so that friendship was maintained. Really, it became a family relationship then, too. But she also died about ten years ago. After we were married, we went to live in New Hampshire and I didn't form any friendships there. Then we moved to Buffalo and I didn't form any friendships there either. And that was sort of hard, not to have any women to talk to. And then eventually we came back here and then I did form some new, close friendships here with two women particularly. But I would say that would be about it. We have a lot of more casual friends, for instance, that we play bridge with and that sort of thing, but not the type of friends that you are totally unreserved or honest with, that you can let down and say how you really feel about something. I'm pretty on guard most of the time with most people.

During the course of the interview, two other nonrelatives were mentioned as friends. One was a "friend of both my husband and me who was a really good friend whom we thought of as family." The other was a college friend who was jealous of her friendship with the woman who later became her sister-in-law. The informant felt that she was forced by the woman to choose between the two, and that this pressure disqualified her as a "real" friend. Both her husband and one of her daughters were described during the course of the interview as friends, which is in accord with Graham Allan's (1979:41) assertion that when kin are described as friends, it is to emphasize the quality of the particular relationship. For this woman, then, there was no question, no gray areas, about who her friends were. She speaks of her friends the same way one might speak of kin, as if there were institutionalized criteria that could be employed to place individuals in the category. In addition, once she had a friend or two, she saw no reason to look for more. Turnings in her life, then, were much less consequential for friendships than was the case for either the independent or the acquisitive informants.

A male informant identified only two men whom he considered friends, both of whom had had "an impact" on his life. About one he said, "We had a lot of interesting discussions over the years." About the other one – his best friend – he said:

> We had a lot of what we considered very serious discussions, you know, about our lives and the future and what our goals might be and that sort of thing. Then he moved, and I used to go down there during the late 1930s to see them and we visited back and forth; they'd come up here. We had a lot of interesting times together, had a lot of fun together. He had a good sense of humor as well as a rather keen mind and we had a very enjoyable time. We were very close and had a lot of discussions regarding our lives and friends and books we had read and things of that nature. Well, this went on until '62 or '63, and then they moved to a different city which isn't too far away, but there again, gradually

we've lost touch with one another. I've no idea where they are now. I've lost touch entirely.

In summary, he said:

Other than those two people – they've had the greatest impact. Oh, there were endless people that we knew as one another, but as far as close association, that sort of thing, or having any real interest in one another or real impact on one another's lives, there wasn't anything that close with one another. There are endless people you met, you went out with, out for dinners and that sort of thing, but not what you'd call a close friend. They're more or less a casual type of thing.

This discerning informant, then, described only two men as friends, both acquired when he was in his twenties, each of whom had had "an impact" on his life. Other relationships he found pleasant but not significant.

Another man who was classified as discerning struggled with defining friendship throughout the interview. He knew many men (and at the time of the interview was close to two women), but only one man qualified as "what I would call a true close friendship":

Now this is a man who is seven years older. My brother and I were seven years apart; my brother was seven years older. And this man, we grew up together, so he's known me ever since I was knee high to a duck and, in fact, he and my brother would have to take care of me. There was just the two of us in the family, so when I was about the age of three or four, why they were saddled with me. And this friendship has maintained itself all through the years and that's quite a few years. Now at least a couple of times a year I go to visit him and his wife and they come by here and visit with me.

He gave as an example of someone whom he did not consider to be a friend a man he had known for a long time and saw regularly at meetings of a group he attended:

There's one couple, one who's somewhat my counterpart in the banking business, he and his wife attend this. Now we've known each other a long time, but I don't consider him a friend. I guess there'd be lots of people you'd put in that category. Yes, you are glad to see each other and they know you, but you wouldn't just on the spur of the moment call them up or they call you; their social life might be in an entirely different arena.

Characteristic of the discerning informants, this man made clear distinctions between friends and friendly relations.

One man opened the interview by saying that he was the wrong person to talk to about friendship:

Because I am very suspicious of people. And I have a reason for it. When I was – as you can hear from my accent I was born on the other side. I was born in Germany. When I started on my doctorate I had a colleague. We studied together for the examinations and we were pretty close. I had no idea that he was a Nazi, an illegal Nazi. When they arrested all the Jews, he came to my house and said to me, "Here. I'm from the Gestapo. I arrest you because you make remarks against Hitler." [And he was a friend?] A close colleague I would call it. And then he arrested me and I was sent to a concentration camp, which is not a nice place to be. So ever since then I am very very suspicious about people. So I'm very distant with people now.

Later in the interview he accounted for his not having more friends:

I don't know how valid my experience is, but my experience is that the born Americans will not consort with foreign borns. They do not accept us. In all the years, it is now 40 years, I lived in the United States, we have not one American acquaintance. All our acquaintances – I don't call them friends, they're all just acquaintances – are German people which we met here that we didn't know over there.

He had two friends in the United States at the time of the interview and specific criteria for those who qualified as friends:

A friend in my opinion is somebody who has similar ideas. For me it means he would have to love classical music. He would have to have an interest in art, not in artists, but like to go to museums. Read good books, love nature, somebody you could have a serious talk [with], not just, "How is your car?" "Is your car [a] good running machine?" "How are the children?" and "How do you cook chicken cacciatore?" A serious conversation. People who have common interests with me. There are very few. [Can you think of any?] Oh, yes, this fellow who introduced me to my wife. He's my wife's cousin. We all lived together in New York. We saw each other two or three times a week. We spent our vacations together, which we still do. We went to Europe together. We went to the West Coast together. Every other year we visit. We were there in July. We take long walks together. I knew him before I knew my wife. I belonged to a group, a social club; we traveled together. He's a friend. I consider him a friend. And then I have a friend in Los Angeles. My wife knew her in Germany. She married an American fellow. They lived in New York, too.

This man, then, was classified as discerning because the only people he considered to be his friends at the time of the interview were two people, one whom he had acquired "on the other side" when he was in his early twenties and the other a woman, also from Germany, whom he had met through his wife. Earlier in his life, he had had more friends from the "social club" – one of his close friends who had lived in London had died during the year preceding the interview – but, at least partly due to his experiencing the Second World War in the way that he did, he was, in his words, "very suspicious of people." In addition, he characterized himself at another point in the interview:

I have the tendency never to ask anybody for a favor. I'd rather go without something than to ask somebody. It's fear, fear of being rejected, you know. I don't want to be rejected so I'd rather not ask.

Another person who was classified as discerning described his first friendship, which was with one of his professors in college:

Now what I call a friendship was when I was a young man, going to college and I met a man who was teaching there. Now that was a friendship that developed between an older man and myself. I did a lot of acting in school and he was head of the dramatic department. But I had read a great deal, practically all of the drama of English literature Norway, Sweden and German. And so we suddenly became very good friends. . . . It was a friendship that has completely penetrated and also changed most of my life. I formulated a lifestyle and a philosophy from this friendship. It gave me a sense of maturity and a little more character than I would have had if I hadn't had this relationship.

About his other relationships in college, he said:

I only had one college friend. I was a loner. Oh, I had a lot of acquaintances and people that I knew in class, but nobody that was very intimate.

He also described a friendship with a coworker that he had had in his mid-thirties shortly before and following his marriage:

He was a young man, a very good-looking fellow. And he had a great sense of humor, and he had a great appreciation for many things that I did. I don't think his interests were mine exactly, although he did have appreciation. Anyway, that relationship became very close because of the fact that he was such a joy to be with. We both sort of were able to find each other so compatible. And being young, we never took anything too seriously. We used to drink together and we used to go out to dinner together. And, yes, it was very close. I will say, however, there was not again the involvement of certain personal relations. I never took my involvement, my personal problems to him. Nor did he to me. And strangely enough, when I go back to this young boy I was going to college with, there again we didn't get into that, but it was a kind of joyous relationship, of friendship.

His friendship with an age peer in college and with his fellow worker five years his junior he regarded as not being of the same high caliber as that with his professor. He talked about only one other man whom he regarded as being as close a friend:

Now that friendship I'd just like to say was another friendship that developed very, very deep, for me – this was after we were married – because of his tremendous love for music. And we used to sit for hours and hours just listening to classical music. He liked a great deal of twentieth-century music and that built up a very, very important relationship. In fact, in the summertime when we all had our vacations, we would all go to the Cape. But this relationship, it was a good relationship. First of all, he mixed a marvelous martini. And that relationship was built on good drinking and good food and good conversation and a lot of good music. And that was a relationship that was based on an interest. However, he died. He died about seven years ago. When I put on a piece of music I immediately think of him, and when I buy a new record I think, "Good God, I wish he was around to hear this."

Although this informant was involved in many friendly relationships, according to him primarily because his wife was a very sociable person, only these two men were the ones that he considered close friends of his. In explaining the difference in relationships, he cited his experience with actors:

At the theater I made a great many friends because you know actors are bound together because of their insecurity. But remember that those friendships were always short-lived because in the theater people just come in or move out. You're very close to a person perhaps for a season; but the next season everybody's gone. You have a new group coming in. But nothing in a close, personal sense. . . . What I'm trying to say is friendship is not an acquaintance. And I think that you have to very, very definitely separate the two.

He had a great many friendly relationships which he enjoyed and was far from being isolated, even though his two close friends were no longer living; but he was classified as discerning because his ideal of friendship was embodied in two distinctive relationships.

Two men described only friendships in childhood or early adulthood, after which time they appeared to have "put away childish things." For example, one described two close friends, the first from childhood, the second from college:

My earliest friendship was with a boy in our home town. And we became very, very intimate. We were raised like brothers. And we continued our friendship as a matter of fact and we went to college together. And shortly after we got to college, he was taken ill and left. We saw very little of each other after that, although I was best man at his wedding. But there was quite a change in his personality. He became a stuffy, successful lawyer and we drifted apart. We saw very little of each other the last few years . . . When we were together on more or less infrequent occasions, I saw that the relationship I had had all those years was dead – he was a different person, a different human being. Now whether it was a result of his success, or certain things which I didn't see as a younger person or his marriage, I don't know. . . . We used to go around like twins. We were inseparable. We did everything together. Everything was always as a team and everyone in town regarded us that way.

In college, he acquired another friend:

And I had a very close friendship with a fellow with the same last name as mine. We were seated alphabetically in class and we became very, very close. And that lasted until a comparatively few years ago. And I never thought of it before. I had these two very, very close relationships. They're the only two in my life that were that close. And this one was almost a repetition of the one I had as a child. And this broke up just a comparatively few years ago.

This friend became a successful lawyer and a Presbyterian:

And I visited him a couple of times down there, and once when I was there he asked us to stay over to go to an Easter ceremony. Well, I didn't mind going, but I didn't like his sense of values. This selling of his birthright for a mess of pottage. I just couldn't take it. And of course his gentile wife, who was also socially ambitious, didn't help any. We haven't seen each other or talked to each other in 20 years.

From the perspective of the life course, it is interesting to note that in this man's mind, 20 years was "a comparatively few years ago." Friendships after these were "not as close, but I think, more mature":

We have some friends here and we have some friends in the town where we used to live who we feel very close to, but I think they are healthier friendships. The others became so ingrown.

As an adult, then, friendships as close as those in childhood and early adulthood were "immature" and, apparently, competitive with his marriage. He credited his wife with making him see the errors in his judgment.

The other man cited three specific individuals whom he considered to be friends; two were friends from adolescence, one from early adulthood. He described with warm feeling one of his adolescent friends: "He and I played together. He was, at that time, my very, very best friend." He had stayed in touch with both of these individuals until his early fourths when both had moved west. Included in the interview somewhat reluctantly was an individual with whom he was still in contact. He and this man had taken classes together in college, but he began to think of him, he supposed, as a friend when they both were colleagues in the early years of their professional careers. Among these three there was a clear ranking, with the "very best friend" from adolescence coming first, the other adolescent friend second, and the colleague a distant third. The first, then, was the standard against which the other two relationships were judged. In describing relationships with others in his life, he explained, "I try to be compassionate. I try to have concern. I try to be just to all the people with whom I am acquainted." With no one else in this man's life had he had a relationship which he would describe as friendship. Even identifying the third person as one may have been an artifact of the interview situation. As with the previous informant, the impression is that when this man reached adulthood he had put away childish things, friendships being one of them. During the course of his life, then, he had moved from the discerning style to the independent style of friendship.

Unlike the independent informants for whom others were an undifferentiated mass, the discerning identified, from this pool of others, only a very few people over the course of their lives whom they considered friends. Although not all of these informants had kept these friendships, those who had, valued them highly. With respect to friendships, these informants were the least affected by the turnings in their lives, although some of them, when they reached adulthood, had "put away childish things" and no longer expected to have close friendships. In adulthood, then, they were likely to resemble the independent or, in one case, the acquisitive. This style is the most difficult to maintain through time. It may well be that if the other informants included in this research had been interviewed much earlier in their lives, more of them would have been classified as discerning.

## The Acquisitive

The acquisitive are more difficult to characterize than informants who fell into the other two categories. These were people who moved through their lives collecting a variety of friendships, allowing circumstances to make possible the meeting of likely candidates but, then, committing themselves to the friendships once they were made, at the very least for the period of time during which they and their friends were geographically proximate. Unlike the independents, these informants indicated commitment to specific people with whom circumstances brought them into contact: "I'd say there is a core of half a dozen who are very, very special. Then you could take another group of 30 to 50 that we enjoy and bump into occasionally." Unlike the discerning, they were open to acquiring new friends as they met people with whom they felt some affinity:

> In the past three or four years we've met several couples that we see fairly often. Otherwise you become isolated. And the ones that die and the ones who move out of town, unless you make friends you're isolated. You have to make a conscious effort to make friends.

These informants, then, continued to acquire friends as they moved through their lives.

One informant who illustrates well the acquisitive style had five distinct periods into which she divided her life. The first period that she discussed was childhood. She had many school friends, but especially one girl with whom she had "kept in touch for many, many years, until she married a second time":

> We used to be very, very close friends even after we were both married. But circumstances change things. She's moved out to California and has a great deal of money. Her lifestyle is quite different from mine. I hear about her and she about me, but we're not close anymore. I still love her and have many happy memories of our times together.

After she married, she and her husband, a rising young lawyer eight years her senior, lived in the city and moved in a circle that included other lawyers and their wives, most older than she. Several women whom she had met during this period of her life she still regarded as friends, or did until they died: "They were our closest friends and right straight through until she died about two years ago."

The third period was marked by her move to the suburbs where she reared her four children. She described one friend: "We share lots of happy memories and confidences. I still talk to her. She calls me or I call her, and she came down to visit me last month." Her husband died just as her youngest child was launched, forcing a transition in her friendships which she spoke of with regret:

> The only thing I thought was kind of too bad when I left there was that I had built up a whole life with everything that you could possibly want. And then after my husband's death, I had to work all day long and I couldn't be chasing back to keep track of my old, original friends. That always pained me, hurt me, but there was nothing for me to do but start fresh. I could see that. They went on. They were busy. They couldn't wait. I couldn't. So we both had to break right off.

Her job, which she was offered by a man with whom she and her husband initially had been friends in the early years of their marriage, brought new friendships, one close one with a fellow employee and another with a nurse:

> When my aunt was living in a hotel, the last three years of her life she was paralyzed and was in bed and needed round-the-clock nursing. And one of her nurses, the three-to-eleven one, was this friend. And I used to come right out from my job to see my aunt and have dinner there. I'd have them bring dinner up on a table and the two of us would have dinner together. And we developed a good friendship. Now that was 1957. That's quite a few years. Nearly twenty-five years. And she has been marvelous to me. I introduced her to my friend from work, and we've had many, many good times together.

The final period of her life was the move to a retirement community:

> When I came I was a different person. I was so full of pep, I could dance all night. And when I came in, I didn't know anybody. Oh, I knew one woman slightly through girl scouts and another woman was an old, old friend, but I just met people all along and I made many friends and had something doing all the time.

With four other women who lived in the retirement community, she started an informal club. By the end of her life, then, she had participated in many of what she considered to be friendships, drawn from five distinct periods in her life. At each transition she acquired new friends, but she did not give up the old ones. Instead, she maintained affectionate ties and reactivated them when circumstances permitted. As she moved through her life, then, the number of people whom she considered to be friends grew, because new ones did not replace but added to old ones.

Other informants had not experienced such distinct transitions, especially in adulthood, but saw their lives as comprising relatively distinct spheres from which friends were drawn. One acquisitive informant, for example, after the interview had proceeded apace, stopped to review what had been said "I think, temporarily, that's it. It's church, clubs, school, retirement community, college, childhood. We've touched on all of these, haven't we?" In a similar vein an informant began with childhood friends whom he had met before he was five and then moved through each phase of his life – boarding school, college, military service in World War I, settling into a new community, occupation, military service in World War II, career changes, retirement and after – identifying friends. He had kept almost all of his early friends until they died, adding new ones as he advanced in age. These three informants, then, were typical of the acquisitive, who added friends as they moved through their lives and drew their friends from a variety of role domains.

There were differences, however, with respect to how many friends they felt were enough. Some people believed that an individual could never have too many friends. For example, one informant said, "I've always had a sufficient amount of friends but, still, if you have a thousand, you haven't got one too many." True to her word, in the year and a half since her retirement she had met at a senior center a number of new friends with whom she did things like shopping, baking, and going with them to visit relatives in nursing homes. This informant and those like her accumulated many friends because they kept the old while adding the new.

A somewhat different pattern is illustrated by a man who, when asked how many people from his former place of employment he considered close friends, responded:

> Oh, gosh, sometimes it's hard to draw the line between acquaintances and friends, but there must have been, I'd say, fifty or so of them, anyway, that I considered good friends, played cards with, just a lot of companionship.

Needless to say, being committed over time to this many people is not an easy task, as he explained:

> It's kind of hard to keep track of a lifelong friend, because your environment changes. It seems as soon as you go to work the whole picture is different. You immediately meet

new people. Of course, many of those become friends. But then you change jobs – as I say, my first three jobs all lasted about a year. It wasn't much time to grow good friendships. It wasn't until I got to the place where I stayed for 39 years that I got my roots into the ground.

The intensity of his relationships with friends also is reflected in the size of the group of people he considered friends. About his move to the retirement community in which he was living, he said, "I've never made so many friends so quickly in all my life as I made here." Although similar to the independents in that he relied on the situations he was in to provide him with friends, this man was also unlike them in looking for opportunities to engage in supportive ties with others. This informant replaced friends as the circumstances of his life changed.

The acquisitive informants accumulated enough friends to satisfy their own needs. One, for example, said, "I don't feel that I had many friends, but I didn't feel I had no friends." Another said, "I would say I have three lady friends I associate with." All three had been acquired during the ten years preceding the interview. About one she said:

Well, I would consider her my best friend. She lives just right across the boulevard from me. I met her when we were taking driving lessons together, about seven years ago. We had never known each other before but there again she's very friendly person and when I got to class, we would talk, you know; quite a bit when we would see each other at school. And then later when I passed my test, she was one of the first persons that I called to tell her about it. And I think that since then we started to be friends together. Now we call each other every day.

The other two friends, who are not as close, she does not see as often, although she has known both of them longer. As this informant moved through her life, she had close friends; but when circumstances changed for either one of them, the friendship "faded away" to be replaced by another.

The relationship between the acquisition of friendship and turnings for these informants was clear. With respect to terminations, however, there was a major difference which was evident in the figures constructed to represent each informant's life. For some, new friendships were added to the old ones so that an increasing number of parallel lines were pictured as one moved from left to right, from birth to the time of the interview, with the lines decreasing in number only as friends died. For others, fewer friendships were overlapping. Although quite often they continued to be committed to one or two friendships that were formed relatively early in life, they apparently were not as concerned with maintaining those added over the life course. In both cases, however, it is clear that turnings were important events that set the stage for the acquisition of friends.

According to David Mandelbaum (1973:181) turnings occur "when the person takes on a new set of roles, enters into fresh relations with a new set of people, and acquires a new self-conception." Especially for the acquisitive, such turnings – moving to new locations, changes in marital status, and new jobs – were used as benchmarks to describe when friends were acquired. One woman, for example, said,

I met both of them at parties when I first came to Cleveland in 1928. She is still one of my closest friends.

Another reported,

> I've known her now – this happened after my husband passed away – so I'd say I've known her maybe eight years and we're quite close and I see her maybe once in two weeks or so.

One woman spoke of her arrival in a new community after her marriage:

> Okay, my very first meeting, after he married me and we came over here, I went to a meeting of faculty wives. She was there and she was one of my closest friends. And this has gone on since I met her and we have been friends ever since.

One man explained that he had not had friends in high school, but after that:

> I had friends in college, particularly medical school, very close friends. But probably my closest friend I met in training.

A move to a new community also marked new friends for one woman who said,

> Yes, I did have childhood friends. [Do you still keep up with any of your friends?] I'm trying to think. I guess not, but I have the friends I met here when I first came.

The topical oral biographies of these informants clearly show the relationship between turnings and acquisition of friends.

The acquisitive, then, described very different patterns of friendship throughout their lives from those of either the independents or the discerning. Many maintained long-term friendships while adding to them; others replaced friends with new ones when circumstances changed. Not all of the acquisitive, then, had life-long friends. All were open to making new friends, however, and so continued throughout their lives to acquire friends. Turnings often provided that opportunity.

Three distinct ways of "doing friendship" have been elaborated in this chapter. Informants who were classified as independent, discerning, or acquisitive had different friendship patterns throughout their lives and, as evident in a later chapter, in old age. Their patterns of initiation, maintenance, and termination of friendships throughout life were quite different from one another. All social actors take into account past, present, and future in contemplating actions and in understanding social relationships. A major difference among these three styles is found in which period is emphasized. The independent informants lived almost entirely in the present. They associated with people who happened to be available. They did not expect necessarily that relationships would continue. For the discerning, the past was much more significant. The history of their relationships with a few individuals was very important. Those who had friendships in most cases projected them into the future, but those who had lost friends, saw ahead of them a life in which close friendships would not be a part. For some this was seen as tragic, while others apparently were resigned to it, accepting it as "natural." The acquisitive, in addition to having past and current friends, looked to the future as well. They expected and hoped that the friendships that they had would continue and at the same time were open to adding new ones as circumstances presented likely candidates.

## References

Allan, Graham A. 1979. *A Sociology of Friendship and Kinship*. Boston: George Allen and Unwin.

Elder, Glen H. 1978. "Family History and the Life Course." In *Transitions: The Family and the Life Course in Historical Perspective*, edited by Tamara K. Hareven. New York: Academic.

Kurth, Suzanne B. 1970. "Friendships and Friendly Relations." Pp. 136–70 in *Social Relationships*, edited by George J. McCall. Chicago: Aldine.

Lofland, John. 1976. *Doing Social Life*. New York: Wiley.

Mandlebaum, David B. 1973. "The Study of Life History: Gandhi," *Current Anthropology* 14: 177–96.

# 14 The Significance of Work Friends in Late Life

## Doris Francis

### Introduction

In advocating a critical gerontology, humanistic gerontologists have recently called for a refocusing of attention on the meaning of old age itself, an understanding of late life development grounded in concrete historical experience and self-reflexive interpretation (Cole and Gadow 1986; Moody 1988). The work of Myerhoff and Kaufman suggests how personal meaning is constructed in old age as individuals reinterpret the past to create a continuous self (Kaufman 1981, 1986; Myerhoff 1978). Plath calls for an expansion of the Western notion that human development is a process of individual biography and suggests, instead, that it be rethought as a problem of mutual endeavor and cobiography (Plath 1980a, 1980b, 1984).

Enduring consociate relationships are an essential psychological resource in the formation and confirmation of self-concept and its continuing change and development over the lifetime. Historical events, life stage and work context affect the composition, functions and tasks of this convoy of relationships (Kahn and Antonucci, 1980); individual and collective choices and their intersubjective interpretation are made against the background of life events, the life chances of the particular age cohort and the political economy (Moody 1988). This perspective forms the theoretical framework underlying this article's analysis of the patterns of friendship of seven working women who were among the first women chosen by the Metropolitan Housing Authority of a major American city as managers for the city's public housing projects. It analyzes these patterns before and after the retirement transition and examines the significance of age and employment to the friendship tie. This article assumes that the study of aging cannot be limited to an analysis of old age alone, but includes an understanding of old age in the context of earlier life experiences and ongoing social relationships, as well as the changing social and historical conditions affecting them.

Two of the major historical changes of the twentieth-century that helped mold the meaning of late life for today's elderly cohorts of women are the entry of women into the paid work force and the institution of retirement. This paper seeks to expand the critical gerontology literature on women and retirement by examining the nuturant role of work-based friends in late life. Through analysis of retrospective life history narratives, enriched by participant-observation and historical research, this article suggests how a convoy of female co-workers provided cumulative social and psychological support enabling the members to improvise new life designs and definitions of

Original publication: Francis, Doris, "The Significance of Work Friends in Late Life," *Journal of Aging Studies* 4 (1990), pp. 405–34.

self during a transitional historical period when there was no clear behavioral model for the shape of the female life course (Ginsburg, 1988), and thereby to bridge the culturally opposed spheres of workplace and home, as well as the discontinuities of work and retirement.[1] Here the importance of temporal factors is stressed, and the intersection of life-cycle and historical and social change is emphasized.

This article argues that through association with like-minded others who share socio-cultural understandings and historical context, consociates enable each other to adapt to the discontinuities of their lives by reconstructing experience to provide continuity between past and present and thereby to forge an integrated self. Friends of long-standing who have mutually witnessed each other's accomplishments over time continue to validate and affirm their claims to mastery and enable each other to deal with the disparities between expectations and experience to maintain self esteem. Through their shared dialogue, interaction and pooled memory, they enable each other to reinterpret the past in order to give coherent meaning and empowerment to the present and also to mark new directions for the future.

## Methods

The research on which this article is based was conducted over a four year period in a major eastern American city. During this time, I recorded the life history narratives of the five remaining members of this convoy and interviewed each member in depth about her personal support network. Frequently I discussed various possible interpretations of the recounted material to elicit further each woman's perspective and analysis. One of the consociates noted that my questions encouraged recall of the initial years of their friendship, and, by reaffirming early attachments, helped the members to feel closer. In addition to interviewing, I was a participant-observer on social outings, accompanied four of the women to a week-long Elderhostel, was introduced to many other friends and family members and occasionally joined the group for supper. Each woman critiqued an earlier draft of this article and then met with the others as a group to discuss and refine it further. They have accepted this final version as essentially accurate and meaningful, and many have shared it with daughters and nieces.

The group chosen for study was purposely selected because of their theoretical interest as long-standing work friends and as representatives of the professional, college-educated, female managers who began uninterrupted work careers in the late 1930s and retired in the mid 1970s. Their forty-year intimate relationship offered a unique opportunity for qualitative, longitudinal inquiry into the meaning, process and role of work-based friendship. (Most studies of co-worker networks have focused only on the scope of the network, the structural characteristics of members or the time spent in interaction.)

As an historically pivotal group, their noncompetitive interdependent friendships link back to late nineteenth-century models learned from female kin and were employed as a strategy for action to collectively challenge gender inequality at the workplace and bring about social change. As single career women and educated working mothers of young children, they were on the cutting edge of the long-range shift in female work force participation and helped formulate revolutionary patterns for working women. Their educational backgrounds, long work histories and careers in management also suggest comparison with future cohorts of working women who are similarly projected to achieve only limited occupational mobility in managerial positions despite technological and social change (Baron and Bielby 1985; Shaw 1986). The dynamics of gender inequality and sexual hierarchy which these women confronted, and which were significant in the formation of their group identity, remain issues on the contemporary feminist agenda. This article concentrates on the interpersonal context to better understand how these women's lives and images of self were shaped through and evolved within their relationships with significant others. The mapping of the stages in convoy membership and the types of resources provided furnishes a subtext for this analysis.

## The Forging of a Convoy of Relationships

*Friendship formation and occupational roles*

In 1939, during the Depression, an examination was given by the Metropolitan Housing Authority for positions as Manager's Assistant in the city's public housing projects. Despite the strong public hostility and condemnation of women workers for taking jobs away from male breadwinners (Margolis 1984; Ware 1982), this initial test was limited to female applicants. In the 1930s, the Housing Authority subscribed to the English social work model of Octavia Hill. Women, because of skills learned as part of the female role, were deemed especially qualified to collect rents by calling on female tenants in their apartments during the day, and also to discuss housekeeping and childrearing. Over 700 women took this examination; 28 passed. This group was proud to have been chosen specifically because they were female[2] and considered themselves a "select group" who would set the management standard for many years. In 1941 a second examination was given and an additional number of women joined the Housing Authority.

While a few of the woman already knew each other from college or through a mutual contact, others became acquainted by working at adjacent desks during their initial months on the job. They found they shared similar background experiences, values and attitudes. Many were daughters of German or Eastern European Jewish immigrants and they held a variety of leftist ideological and political views supporting social justice and equality, including the unstated assumption that women are autonomous individuals who should have rights equal to men. Many were trained to pursue a career in the professions or academic life, but in the 1930s, the doors to such careers did not open readily to Jews or women.[3] Civil Service, however, offered a viable, well-paying alternative to these women, who entered the labor force both for opportunity and to support themselves or their families. Work roles afforded the opportunity for friendship formation, and mutuality of status and values furnished the relational basis for the close friendship dyads that stemmed from this initial work period.

Participation in the "experiment" of public housing, which was lauded by politicians as "the wave of the future," was initially an exciting time for these women. They shared an interest in housing, and their work satisfied both their intellectual needs and their progressive commitment to social reform. One woman recalls:

> To enter the Housing Authority in those first ten years . . . you had the feeling of doing something important. You could see positive steps before you each day. I loved the work itself. It was really an introduction into urban understanding that one couldn't get from books . . . I developed a sense of the incredible variety of urban life.

After the war, the Metropolitan Housing Authority expanded rapidly, and in 1949 the first manager's examination was given. Of the 31 eligible candidates, twelve women and seven men passed.

It is important to note that, in recounting their early work histories, these women employ themes of historical context and gender opportunities and constraints as determinants of life course choices and as explanations for personal action. They discuss the broader historical, ideological and political context, note the intersection of their individual life course transitions and specific historical events, and view themselves as effectors of social progress who joined and remained in the workforce at a time when most women were not employed outside the home.

### Shared work experience; shared values

As the senior officer present, the manager of a housing project has complete administrative responsibility. Collection of rents – often for projects of 2,000 units – handling of tenant relations, keeping of records and preparation of the budget, supervision of the staff, maintenance of the physical plant and conducting of community relations are dimensions of the manager's job. In the early years of the Metropolitan Housing Authority, there were no preparatory courses or procedural manuals. "We were inventing the rules; there was no precedent," one woman recalls. Rather, resourcefulness, autonomy and acceptance of responsibility were what they perceived to be required. In describing the manager's job and its shared psychological impact and symbolic meaning to herself and her consociates, Elizabeth explains:

> It's more like being at sea in an open boat than being in an office building. You learned to size people up by how they can help you in the open boat, not by their dress or appearance . . . As a common experience, it leaves everyone else out. We're so used to being in the hard context of reality. That's the common bond, not because we worked together. If we had worked together in Saks Department Store, it wouldn't have any significance . . .

It is this sharing of a major role experience and the resultant common frame of reference that forms a bond of shared understanding and affirmation among these women. Their mutual role learning, noncompetitive problem sharing and mastery on the job are reinterpreted and recreated as a source for group- and self-validation in retirement. Their shared view of the world unifies them as a distinct occupational group whose members "speak the same language":

> To go through all this experience is a common basis that other people can't begin to share. You see life from a completely different point of view, and it's really that from which the friendships sprang. We're like the group of engineers I observed at a meeting the other night . . . They fight terribly, but it's like a family fight. They all understand each other; nothing has to be explained. (Elizabeth)

In developing her own management style, each woman used the authority of her position to enact a humanitarian philosophy of social justice, individualism and reform. Sheila, for example, got "involved with the tenants" and was awarded a foundation grant to work with dropouts and their mothers on a literacy and job training program. Every summer Riva developed a job program for her project's teens. Eva Paul was interested in fostering integration and held weekly staff seminars on race relations and civil rights. Earlier, just after the war, she had been in charge of vacancies, and used her position to counter a policy of segregated projects. A number of these women were also involved in trade union activities and helped organize unskilled workers.[4] In relating their early work experiences, it is these individual achievements and efforts to put their ideals of social justice and equality into reality that the women choose to discuss, and for which they praise and admire each other. Successive groups of women managers also tell stories about these senior women who are still considered to be "models of what a manager should be." Their achievements remain legendary, and are a continuing source of inspiration and challenge.

Here it is useful to explore further the complementary nature of social reform and women's issues, and to offer the interpretation that, by following the Octavia Hill dictum and using their management authority to promote growth and reaffirm social relationships, the women were extending the traditional domestic values of nurturance and communal concern into a broader social arena.[5] They, therefore, can be seen as redefining the cultural code linking women to home and housekeeping. Also, as working mothers maintaining the dual role of homemaker and wage earner, they further challenged the constraining ideology of gender where marriage and a career offering personal growth and satisfaction were mutually exclusive alternatives. Women's employment had meaning only in terms of the family economy or needs. But for these particular women managers, their management styles and their life-styles were more a counter-discourse to capitalist values than an assertion of feminist principles. They were more concerned with issues of socialism than feminism, although their concerns as women were an integral part of their larger political struggle.

### Friendship development: facing challenges

The women managers who had met during their initial months on the job kept in touch. Although they rarely worked together again, they dealt with parallel work situations and shared a common frame of reference about the workplace. These autonomous women rarely asked others for advice but functioned more as a source of expressive support, guidance and encouragement complementary to the innovative performance of their work roles. Elizabeth and Eva, for example, used each other as a sounding board and talked over administrative situations. "We were in constant contact; we had constant problems, the same ones," one recalled. Eva spoke daily to two of her other colleagues. They would recount their on-the-job ventures, gossip about fellow workers and supervisors, and devise strategies to resist the domination of their male supervisors. As Sheila noted, "We had a generic need to talk about the job, and conditions of work, and people on the job and our bosses. We talked about our lousy, nasty bosses and how to handle their pettiness. We talked to each other every day." As mutual role models, they esteemed each other's abilities, problem-solving skills and intellect, and encouraged competence and maturity. "Friends offer continuing testimony to who a person is beyond her roles, but also bear testimony to how well she handles her roles" (Plath 1984).

These telephone friendships carried over to nonwork times and places. Relationships grew beyond the role structure in which they originated, and came to be valued for additional reasons and extended to other contexts. It must be underscored, however, that the women managers did not yet function as a group, and socializing was confined to one or two friends getting together. Eva, for example, often invited two single friends over for supper with her family, and also included them at parties and holiday celebrations with her aunts. When her husband and young son were both ill, the friends reciprocated and took her daughter out on Saturdays. Two other working mothers lived on the same street and their children played together; another two families shared a summer rental. Through example these women calmed each other's concerns about leaving young children with a housekeeper, and also shared experiences about the double day of work in both the labor force and home production. Friendships grew in significance and intimacy as the managers shared personal feelings and asked new questions as liberated single women or working mothers of young children.

In 1940, only 15 percent of married women worked, and it was still unusual for women with very small children to work outside the home. Pervasive cultural values kept the vast majority of married women in the home (Ware 1982). These educated, independent and politically active women thought of themselves as unconventional, and were not bound by traditional socialization patterns of passivity and deference. As intimate friends, they offered each other both practical aid and emotional support in forging new social roles and new perceptions of self which meshed with economic circumstances rather than prevailing ideology.

During the 1950s, a number of these women faced personal and family challenges. Two were investigated by the House Committee on Un-American Activities. One woman divorced and remarried. Three husbands became seriously ill and the women became the sole breadwinners, supporting their families and caring for their spouses for many years. Career options and choices were buried beneath the full economic burden of their households. Again, intimate friendship provided an important coping resource and direct aid during these stressful times of adjustment to unanticipated crises. Close dyads of women managers continued "to meet each other's needs as best we knew how and as our needs changed." As Eva remarked about Elizabeth's friendship during her husband's illness and after his death, "She was very much a part of my life and very valuable in her support."

"We were all women on our own – single, widows, women with sick husbands – who were not taken care of in life." Elizabeth states, "and we shared this, although we didn't verbalize it." These economic and familial responsibilities, coupled with increasing occupational demands, further extended the resourcefulness and managerial capabilities of the women, even while taking their toll in physical wear and tear. It is this adaptational orientation, achieved with the support of friends, that the women managers took with them into retirement and old age. As Elder suggests, "successful coping builds confidence and resources for dealing with future trials" (Elder 1982, p. 78).

*Formation of a group identity: group action*

It was also in the 1950s, as the Metropolitan Housing Authority continued to expand in size, that all of the senior women managers, who were in their forties, were brought into contact through new work assignments or union involvements. Again, these new relationships were initially linked to occupational status, mutuality of experience and common values. Elizabeth and Sheila, for example, both became managers of nearby projects and met for lunch. Eva and Deborah, whose housing projects were in the same borough, would see each other at the newly instituted monthly district meetings. Others participated in union organizing or met regularly at the union's Managers Association meetings. These new relationships, which were initially connected to employment, also broadened into friendships as the women socialized outside of work.

In the 1960s, Riva's beach house became the meeting place for these women as this "endless hostess" offered generous hospitality. Here, those who had previously had only casual acquaintance through work or union meetings, became reacquainted and got to know one another better. Ties were established and affirmed between women who shared a linking friend in common or were coping with similar family and work experiences, such as caring for an ill husband and children and supporting the family financially. Thus, in addition to the intimate, long-standing friendships which they had made during their first months on the job, the women established a second, concentric circle of work friendships that they would extend and deepen ten years later in retirement.

In the 1960s, a crucial event in the formation of a group identity for these women occurred, played out against the historical background of contradiction between prevailing public ideology of the home and women's changing labor force participation. During this decade, women comprised more than 33 percent of the national labor force, but society still extolled the "feminine mystique" and the cult of domesticity (Margolis 1984). While it was grudgingly accepted that women worked to contribute to their families' welfare and to provide "extras," such as a college education for their children, career women and those who sought employment for their own wellbeing had no place in the social ethic (Margolis 1984). Women were not given access to equal economic opportunity, and possibilities for advancement and aspirations for success were explicitly limited. Women's employment preceded its approval, and the Metropolitan Housing Authority reflected this national consensus. Only in the 1970s did employers reevaluate their policies as the realities of female employment and the efforts of the feminist movement forced public opinion into accepting women's place in the job market.

Late in the 1960s, the regulations for municipal employee pension benefits were changed, and the women managers felt it was in their best interest to secure higher titles and salaries to guarantee an increased retirement income. Spurred on by this realization, and by the reemergence of feminism, the women assessed their attainments relative to those of the eight men who had taken the original manager's examination with them twenty years before, and had been promoted above the Civil Service ladder to positions of increased responsibility and authority. They felt betrayed. They were originally hired as women, yet were discriminated against in promotion based on their sex. They interpreted their experiences to suggest that once men and women had advanced far enough to vie for supervisory positions, women's chances diminished almost entirely (Baron and Bielby 1985). Elizabeth articulated their feelings:

> If you could have seen the men who were promoted. Not that they were men, but they were real jerks; and when they came round to supervising us . . . The last one, I never told him anything, because he would give me poor advice and if I'd follow it, I'd be in trouble for six months, straightening it out. In our group, the women had all the balls and the men were second-rate.

Nine women who had taken the original manager's test and had become acquainted through work and weekend socializing banded together to cosign a letter to the head of the Metropolitan Housing Authority protesting gender inequality in promotion. In their letter, the senior women managers stated that, despite seniority, they had been passed over repeatedly for promotion, and they requested that the discriminatory situation be rectified immediately:

> Let us state that we have each given a full lifetime of service to the Housing Authority and have been continually managing Public Housing Projects longer than any other persons in the United States. Twenty consecutive years in an assignment with face-to-face contact with the public certainly does not merit the kind of discrimination we have experienced.

The Metropolitan Housing Authority responded to their demonstration of solidarity, and three of the women were appointed to supervisory positions.[6] Two more filed discrimination suits. Elizabeth, who documented that she had been passed over for promotion twenty-five times in 24 years, won her case. Sheila lost her suit. In the following year, an examination for the title of Supervising Manager was instituted, and promotion to this position of administrative responsibility is now based on the objective criteria of the merit system, making upward advancement for future women possible.

Those who were promoted disliked the "meaningless paper work" and competitive bureaucracy of their new positions. They missed the autonomy of the projects and the contact with tenants and the surrounding community. As Brenda says, "I liked the work because when I was in the project I was in control. Later, after my promotion, the other was meaningless paper work. I was not effective. I was glad to get out at sixty-two." Others were exhausted after thirty years of work at large and challenging projects. All of the women retired within a few years when they were eligible to collect Social Security benefits.

At retirement, each woman was honored with a large retirement party attended by the Housing Authority hierarchy, union officials, fellow managers, friends, family and tenant representatives. Their careers, accomplishments and individual management styles were publicly acknowledged in formal speeches at these ritual occasions. At Sheila's retirement party, for example, an elderly Puerto Rican tenant said they should "erect a statue to this woman," and many other community members praised her activities on their behalf. Even though she had lost her discrimination suit, Sheila accepted their praise as justified. Even her supervisor acknowledged her outstanding contribution to their tenants' welfare. The women managers also spoke at each other's parties and publically reviewed and praised the retiree's accomplishments.

This public review of one's work life at retirement rituals and the accompanying subjective assessment of the significance of work comprises one of the main – yet often unacknowledged – tasks of the retirement transition, enabling one to assess issues of identity and integrity. The retirement transition is as much about one's past as it is about plans and goals for the future.

The group's united action to cosign the protest letter, their supportive involvement in the two ensuing discrimination suits and their retirement decisions forced each woman to reevaluate consciously the meaning of her work life. All of the women managers had invested time and self in their work roles, but only belatedly had their accomplishments been formally rewarded and acknowledged. Through conversations with consociates of similar work experience, outlook and strong self-concept, they constructed a shared interpretation that questioned their inferior occupational status and sought to rectify the situation through group action. The managers did not view their lack of promotion as symptomatic of personal inadequacy, fault themselves for their promotional failures, or see themselves as the source of discrimination (Margolis 1984). Rather, they constructed an account that explained the promotional limitations they faced in terms of old patterns of power and privilege and gender constraints.

## The Retirement Transition

### The continuity and ego integrity of individuals

Through this interpretation, the encouragement of cultural feminism and the social climate of the 1970s, which prompted a new view of adulthood as a time of growth and development, retirement after thirty-five years of work was not perceived as a negative transition, a final stage of life, or a time to return to domestic duties – the usual interpretations of women's retirement (Szinovacz 1982, 1983) – but rather as an opportunity to reassess and renew commitments, explore untapped avenues of creativity and reconstitute the self. As Deborah stated at her retirement party, "I want to discover who Deborah Berg really is, without all these trappings and titles." As individuals and as a group, these women were redefining the meaning of retirement when it was primarily a male life stage (Reinharz 1986; Stone and Minkler 1984).

In bridging the culturally discontinuous experiences of work and retirement and in assembling new life roles, each woman sought to clarify her earlier goals and dreams and to reassess her past work life as a meaningful resource in the present. As in the management of their housing projects and combined career and home roles, individual initiative and adaptability affected their selection of retirement activities. Many years of self-reliant decision making and autonomy in challenging work settings and home management are evidenced in their independent retirement choices. The retired female managers did not look to each other for direct aid while making the retirement transition, nor do they engage in voluntary activities as a group. Nonetheless, as in their occupational and home careers, friends again guided and learned from each other as each woman tested, shaped and affirmed her own choices against the innovative models of her friends. The women talked together about their plans and activities and clarified their thinking in repeated discussions and observations of the others. Consociates offered empowerment and validation as they reformulated their shared values of social action and social reform in new arenas.

Here significant others were a source of self-identity and adult continuity as they provided a reflective mirror enabling each convoy member to come to terms with who she is and what she has become. Friends, who had known each other a long time under changing circumstances, provided a bridge linking the old self with the new, and assisted one another in achieving a continuous sense of self across the adult life span. Here the individual life cycle can be seen as a group process in which these women's lives are mutually interrelated:

> Our biographies are formed most of all by our repeated encounters with those around us whose lives run close, and parallel to ours, by those who grow older with us. We grow as social persons by feeding upon nurturant others (Plath 1984, pp. 289–300).

Each woman saw the retirement transition as a creative challenge to redirect her life and to discover new patterns of meaning. Sheila, for example, reassessed her past work life and consciously decided to continue the positive dimensions of her managerial experience in community work and service to the aged, despite the loss of her discrimination suit. She spent the first years of her retirement rehousing 30 aged isolates living in the community where she formerly worked. Today she coordinates an interagency council for the aged, and lobbies for increased entitlements. She is also establishing an assistance network for the older residents of her own apartment building. "My way to change the world is to cultivate my garden; community organization and consciousness raising is the way to do it."

Elizabeth refocused the activities she initiated as part of her successful anti-discrimination case. She is active in the Women's City Club Housing and Status of Women Committees, where she fights for equality of rights and opportunities for women. Annually she compiles a report reviewing the employment status of municipal female workers. Serving with her on the committee are other recently retired women housing managers, who also actively promoted women's issues during their working lives, supported her suit, and acknowledge her abilities and achievements.

Two other women "came full circle" and returned to their original interest in academic pursuits. Eva took courses toward her doctorate and taught classes in education. But when the bottom dropped out of the academic job market, she withdrew and again acknowledged "the frustration of not being able to pursue the kind of work I should have. I really thought I was going to do some sort of teaching I'd have fun at." A second woman initially faced the classic symptoms of retirement (Atchley 1976). She found the early days of her retirement "terrible" and without structure and missed the daily interaction at the work place:

> It was very hard to stop being "Mrs. Sherman, Good-morning" and revert to a Waldbaum [supermarket] lady where you fight over whether the tomatoes are nice today. It's demeaning. When I worked, I organized my time, then when I retired I had all the time in the world. (Hope)

After pursuing a range of new intellectual interests through courses and reading, she has become a lecturer at her community's institute for retired professionals. She describes herself as "a good teacher with a regular following." A number of her work convoy attend her lectures both out of interest and support. They remark that she has always been a "smart woman," "a scholar," and that her class presentations are very thorough. Thus their comments confirm and ratify her self-concept and validate her claims to mastery.

A second dimension of the search for integration and self-understanding during the retirement transition was the women's reaching out to older family members. The retired managers purposely renewed contact with elderly aunts, asked about their place in family history and assumed caretaking responsibilities. Eva's aunt consciously talked to her about issues of autonomy and dependency in old age during her care-taking visits, and advised her to expand her own social support network as insurance against a time when friends and family grow old and she herself might require assist-ance. Eva followed her advice and assumed the role of family kinkeeper after her aunt's death. She has continued her lifelong practice of integrating her work friends into her family network and makes "family into friends and friends into family." Through her example and encouragement, her friends have become more closely involved with their own younger relatives, and exchange of family news occupies the opening part of the women's conversations and social get-togethers.

## The Continuity of the Convoy

In addition to consciously seeking involvement with voluntary associations and fam-ily to maintain social integration and prevent isolation, the women managers reached out to each other in retirement as their situation and needs changed. Relationships with intimate friends were intensified through increased interaction, and acquaint-ances with other female managers whom they had gotten to know over the past ten years were strengthened and extended. For these women, the retirement transition did not lead to discontinuity in relationship patterns, but rather to a reaffirmation of work-based friendships. In conversations they shared common concerns and experi-ences with retirement and widowhood, reinterpreted their occupational histories, reaffirmed their mutual outlook and value set, and joked about their Italian boy friends. Their relationships did not substitute for relinquished work roles, however, but rather offered companionship and support as insurance against loneliness.

It is only in retirement that the women managers truly view themselves as a group. This expanded relationship is facilitated by increased availability and free time and physical proximity. All of the women live in the same community, and two sets of women are neighbors in the same apartment building. Every few weeks or so, the women get together as a group for dinner.

In addition to these communal suppers, the women also meet individually in vari-ous dyads and speak a number of times weekly on the telephone.[7] These strong bonds of long-standing, intimate friendship hold the whole network together when there is a rare fallout, a feeling of disappointment or a loss of trust. The other members know and understand the history of the subtle frictions that occasionally flare up between certain consociates. No one is willing, however, to jeopardize the support of the others through defection or even prolonged anger, and the entire group soon gets together again for dinner even though there may be a polite coolness between two of the members. It is Eva who consciously plays the role of peacemaker, urging the others to accept peculiarities, to gloss over tensions and to give up their anger:

> Whatever our flaws and irritations, there is no question we need each other and we cannot allow any estrangement. We all gradually learned to work at it, to make sure to accept each other with all the peccadillos . . . You can't replace these people you have known for forty years, there's nobody around.

Acceptance and respect for various personality styles emphasize the women's positive valuation of personal autonomy and individualism. Each group member believes she has the security of acceptance and the knowledge that she will not be rebuffed. As Sheila explains:

> It's habit; we know each other; it's easy . . . I go to bed early and get up early. I don't have to apologize a thousand times because we know each other and we know our likes and dislikes. We don't step on each other in any way . . . We respect and we show that respect without even speaking about it and it's simply because of many years together.

The women feel that new friends made in retirement cannot replace their intimate, enduring consociates of almost fifty years. They believe that their life-course experiences, particularly the sharing of a major work role, are unique and cannot be understood easily by people of different occupational backgrounds or by women who never worked. For them, friendships are an "investment of the self" (Hess 1972, p. 390; Matthews 1986, pp. 147–48); here significant parts of the self from earlier periods of their lives are conserved, confirmed and made accessible. In their conversations, for example, the women discuss their mutually known parents, aunts and spouses, share stories about their children growing up together or joke about familiar work colleagues. Their friendship "represents their biographies," and their choice of new friends demonstrates a desire to preserve and affirm the significant history of the self.

While the retired managers enjoy the company of neighbors and other acquaintances they meet in voluntary organizations, they do not attempt to establish intimacy in these new relationships. The new friends they make are women who were also close friends of deceased convoy members, or fellow retired housing managers who share understanding of their historical context and shared experiences and know each other beyond their occupational roles. "These people sustain the prestige gained on the job as they know how that prestige was generated" (Atchley 1971, p. 15). There have also been shifts in the organization of the convoy over time; ties are realigned when members are seriously ill or die, and the remaining women deepen their friendship in an effort to replace the lost intimacy formerly shared with the ill or deceased consociate. Clearly these women's need is for long-term intimate friends who "provide continuity of experience and confirmation of a self which is valued" (Jerrome 1981, p. 193), rather than for new companions to share social activities, who know them only as elderly women in retirement.

It is clear from the following quotations that mutual value and esteem for intellectual competence, as well as shared experience, is a key to the meaning of these friendships for the women involved:

> These are not bridge friends. These are friendships from choice and we have a lot to say to each other: about life and how we feel about things. (Hope)

When we meet together . . . we let a few sparks of ideas fly and we're all stimulated. We're interested in things other than how to put curtains on the windows . . . We see a lot of each other and we can depend on each other. We shared the same place and the same time. (Sheila)

They're my peers. I value their opinions and world outlook. They were part of my life; they made a big difference in my life because they were part of my life. (Brenda)

## The Role of the Consociates in Reevaluating Experience

As the retired women managers grow older and deal with the late-life psychological tasks of ego integrity and achievement of a sense of completeness and personal wholeness, long-standing friends are well qualified to support their efforts. Consociates share retrospective knowledge of past life course experiences, cultural expectations and sociohistorical context, and their ongoing dialogue enables each woman to redefine and reconstruct her subjectively perceived past to achieve coherence and consistency with her current actions and beliefs. In conversations and shared discussion, each woman clarifies her own reinterpretation of the shared world of reference to forge a sense of identity and self incorporating past and current reality. In this process, both speaker and listener share social and cultural understandings and mutually provide mirrors for reflection which support and affirm each other's construction of self. Friends help each other to "determine the meaning of who we are as we grow and age" (Plath 1984, p. 302).

A key component in the achievement of ego integration for these retired managers is the reevaluation of their shared experience of working for the Housing Authority, an experience that involved many disappointments. In reexamining their work life, the former managers reevaluate two interrelated areas: (a) the experience of public housing, their belief in the possibility of social betterment, and their potential role in effecting social change; and (b) the experience of sex discrimination and lack of promotion.

In expressing ambivalence about the achievements of public housing and in voicing despair about the possibility of ever personally helping to bring about social reform, Hope claims to know the feelings of the other women: "These girls have been my friends for a hundred years and I know how they feel about things, about the Housing Authority." Her comments reflect the process of their shared dialogue:

I had a very fine mind, it was just a waste . . . I never had a feeling of great achievement . . . I've done nothing to make the world better . . . Ten years ago I realized "This is it, I'm never going to be any different, I'm never going to do anything more, that's all." It's a hard thing to come to grips with . . .

We were all very smart ladies and we worked at this job which to some was more fulfilling, to some less fulfilling, certainly never what we thought it would be. It was always a disappointment, because when we started in public housing, it was a new thing. It was going to solve many problems . . . We weren't able to create an integrated environment . . . and we really made an effort, and it's a very hard thing to come to grips with, the fact that white people don't want to live with Blacks or Hispanics. And there is always a certain percentage of people who really want to make it work; but never enough . . .

> The Housing Authority really made an effort to solve the problems. I give it credit. It's a fine agency, I have no regrets about working for it. And I made good friends . . . The income was there, but there was no feeling of accomplishment in the Housing Authority for many.

Thus there was a shared ambivalence with their hopes for public housing – "we were going to change the world" – and with the possibility of social change and integration that it promised. These feelings of existential remorse are poignantly felt when there is little time left in retirement for continued social involvement.

The second, interrelated issue concerns the reevaluation of the meaning of thirty-five years of hard work that were not rewarded with promotion. The women hold a range of views on the significance of their work experience that is consistent with their current retirement activities and coherent with their ongoing definitions of self. Thus the support of consociates, who share a common history, has enabled them to place their lives in perspective and knit the strands together to achieve a sense of wholeness and integrity (Kaufman 1986):

> The job of housing manager was nothing. I did it thoroughly. I did everything that was required and more. There was no intellectual challenge; I did it without much effort or interest. I never felt I belonged at the Housing Authority, especially in the passing over of women for promotion . . . I always felt I was at least as smart as any chairman in the Housing Authority, or anybody else. (Eva, who spent much of her early retirement in college teaching and pursuit of her doctorate)

> It was a terrible waste of energy, what I did. It was a worthwhile job and I did it properly . . . but on a lifetime basis to have put that much energy in for so little ultimate reward . . . The Housing Authority screwed us; it was not worthless, but we all felt we were treated like dogs, and we all share this. (Elizabeth, who successfully pursued her sex discrimination suit and devotes her energy in retirement to issues of urban housing and women's fight for equality)

> With public housing, there was some hope of good family life. I liked the job, I did not look down on the job. I thought we were doing something and to the limit of my ability I did . . . I thought the job was about the best I could have done . . . I was lucky to pass an exam and get into a field where there was hope of doing something useful. The Authority and Civil Service was one of the few organizations that gave you a chance for advancement and was not just a stultifying experience, as most of the Civil Service employment was. Work was the most productive time of my life. (Deborah, who is involved with the retiree division of her union and who travels extensively with fellow retired managers)

In valuing mental abilities, the consociates bear witness to each other's intellectual potential and support each woman's personal belief that in a different historical time she would have been better able to fulfill her dreams and ambitions. Friends are a bridge linking the old self and the new: "She knew me when, and she knows me now" (Rogers 1984).

In describing her ambitions, Hope noted, "School was always of supreme importance to me. I was always a student, a serious student. I thought I would have an academic career." Her friends enable her to deal with the existential issue of life turning out differently from what she anticipated. Through shared experiences, consociates know firsthand the constraints and limitations faced, and thus enable her to draw meaning from her choices. This support is clearly expressed in Elizabeth's description of Eva and Hope:

> In better times these women would have been college professors. This [Metropolitan Housing Authority] is where Eva ended up for lack of a better job. The only thing she wanted was to be a college professor, but this she never got. Instead she supported her family.

The question of Eva's lifelong but unrealized goal of becoming a professor surfaced again at her funeral last month. After many relatives and friends had spoken of her unstinting commitment to social justice and of her generative guidance and support, the Dean of her undergraduate college recalled her brilliance and the shared expectation that she would become a college president. He remarked that only after listening to the comments of others did he realize that she had fulfilled her promise as a teacher: guiding, nurturing and supporting others so that strength was fostered and possibilities for fulfillment increased. The meaning and integration of her life was clear. Through the encouragement of her consociates, she had adapted to the discontinuities and disappointments of her life and had improvised a life of meaning and wholeness.

These consociates thus help one another to deal with the discrepancies between their aspirations and the reality of their careers. They validate the course of each other's lives as the only possible course, given the limitations and opportunities faced at a particular historic time. As Eva says, "I feel we did okay. For who we were and when we were, we did okay."

## Conclusion

Through analysis of the retrospective life history narratives of a convoy of workplace friends who began work in the 1930s and retired in the 1970s, this article has attempted to answer questions about the meaning of old age in the context of earlier life experiences, ongoing interpersonal relationships, and the social and historical conditions affecting them. This article suggests that the role of workplace friends enables women in problematic life cycle and historical transitions to improvise new roles and to reconstruct experience to provide continuity between past and present, in order to forge a sense of identity. Through the nurturance and empowerment of friends, career women are able cognitively and socially to reformulate the symbolic oppositions between work and home as well as work and retirement to adapt to the discontinuites of their lives and the disparities between expectations and experience, and also to act in concert to challenge gender constraints and inequities in order to forge an alternative future.

Recent anthropological writings suggest that in times of historical transition, association with like minded others is required to make the self in new terms (Bateson 1989; Ginsberg 1988, 1989). This article extends this argument to suggest that ongoing association with friends who share historical context and sociocultural understandings provides the social and psychological resources that enable women to reconstruct a continuous sense of self within the discontinuous transitions and events of late life and to achieve a sense of meaning in old age.

## Acknowledgments

This article is a substantially reanalyzed and recast version of an earlier paper, "Friends from the Workplace," which appeared in *Growing Old in America*, fourth Edition, 1990, edited by Beth Hess and Elizabeth Markson for Transaction Books. I am grateful to Mark Luborsky, Sharon Kaufman, Maria Vesperi, Andrea Sankar and Chris Fry for their helpful comments and encouragement. I would like to thank the Retiree Division of Local 237, particularly Maggie Feinstin, Director, for support of this research from 1986 to 1989.

## Notes

1   The entry of these women into the labor force and their retirement from paid work must be placed against an enduring gender structure of home and workplace as separate male and female spheres. This structure developed with industrial capitalism and is being reinterpreted as women become a significant presence in the American work force.

2   Thus, ironically, these jobs, stereotyped as women's work, gave women a certain amount of hiring advantage and protection even in the midst of the Depression and saved them from the stigma of "taking jobs away from men."

3   "The proportion of women in the professions fell from 14.2 percent in 1930 to 12.3 percent in 1940, and the percentage of women earning doctorates declined relative to men. This loss of ground is evident in higher education. At the start of the decade women held 32 percent of the faculty positions in the nation's colleges and universities, but by the close of the decade their proportion had fallen to 26 percent" (Margolis 1984, p. 211).

4   "The growth and legitimization of the labor movement as a permanent part of the American political and economic system was one of the most significant changes of the 1930s, and women shared in this progress" (Ware 1982, p. 48).

5   For a fuller discussion of these issues in relation to the abortion controversy, see Ginsburg 1988, 1989.

6   The union was not actively involved as positions above the title of Manager were not in the bargaining unit. Conversations with top Housing Authority executives of the period indicate that the union was informally involved, however.

7   "I've talked to her every day on the phone for the last thirty-five years. Now we talk every other day, there's less to talk about" (Eva discussing her conversations with Hope).

## References

Adams, R. G. and Blieszner, R. (eds.) 1989. *Older Adult Friendship: Structure and Process.* Newbury Park: Sage.

Antonucci, T. C. 1985, "Personal Characteristics, Social Support and Social Behavior." Pp. 94–128 in *Handbook on Aging and the Social Sciences* edited by R. Binstock and E. Shanas, New York: Van Nostrand Reinhold.

Atchley, R. 1971. "Retirement and Work Orientation." *The Gerontologist* 11: 29–32.

Atchley, R. 1976. *The Sociology of Retirement.* New York: Halsted.

Atchley, R. 1979. "Interactions with Family and Friends: Marital and Occupational Differences Among Older Women." *Research on Aging* 1: 84–95.

Atchley, R. 1989. "A Continuity Theory of Normal Aging." *The Gerontologist* 29: 183–90.

Baron, J. N. and Bielby, W. T. 1985, "Organizational Barriers to Gender Equality: Sex Segregation of Jobs and Opportunities." Pp. 233–52 in *Gender and the Life Course* edited by A. S. Rossi, New York: Aldine.

Bateson, M. C. 1989. *Composing a Life*. New York: The Atlantic Monthly Press.

Blau, Z. S. 1961. "Structural Constraints on Friendship in Old Age." *American Sociological Review* 26: 429–39.

Blau, Z. S. 1973. *Old Age in a Changing Society*. New York: Franklin Watts.

Blumer, H. 1969. *Symbolic Interactionism: Perspective and Method*. Englewood Cliffs: Prentice-Hall.

Chodorow, N. J. 1989. "Seventies Questions for Thirties Women: Gender and Generation in a Study of Early Women Psychoanalysts." Pp. 199–218 in *Feminism and Psychoanalytic Theory* by N. Chodorow, New Haven: Yale University Press.

Cole, T. R. and Gadow, S. A.. (eds.) 1986. *What Does it Mean to Grow Old?* Durham: Duke University Press.

Elder, G. H. 1982. "Historical Experience in the Later Years." Pp. 75–107 in *Aging and Life Course Transitions: An Interdisciplinary Perspective* edited by T. K. Hareven and K. J. Adams, New York: Guildford.

Elder, G. H. (ed.) 1985. *Life Course Dynamics: Trajectories and Transitions, 1976–1980*. Ithaca: Cornell University Press.

Epstein, C. F. 1988. *Deceptive Distinctions: Sex, Gender and the Social Order*. New Haven: Yale University Press.

Erikson, E. H. 1963. *Childhood and Society*. New York: W.W. Norton and Company.

Erikson, E. H., Erikson, J. and Kivnick, H. 1986. *Vital Involvement in Old Age*. New York: Norton.

Francis, D. 1984. *Will You Still Need Me? Will You Still Feed Me? When I'm 84?* Bloomington: Indiana University Press.

Francis, D. 1990. "Friends from the Work Place." Pp. 465–80 in *Growing Old in America*, Fourth Edition, edited by B. Hess and E. Markson, New Brunswick: Transaction.

Geiger, S. N. G. 1986. "Women's Life Histories: Method and Content." *Signs* II: 334–51.

Ginsburg, F. 1988. *Contested Lives: The Abortion Debate in an American Community*. Berkeley: University of California Press.

Ginsberg, F. 1989. "Dissonance and Harmony: The Symbolic Function of Abortion in Activists' Life Stories." Pp. 50–84 in *Interpreting Women's Lives* edited by the Personal Narratives Group, Bloomington: Indiana University Press.

Hareven, T. K. and K. J. Adams. (eds.) 1982. *Aging and Life Course Transitions: An Interdisciplinary Perspective*. New York: Guilford.

Hess, B. 1972. "Friendship." Pp. 357–93 in *Aging and Society III* edited by M. Riley, M. Johnson and R. Foner, Russel Sage Foundation.

Hess, B. and M. Ferree. (eds.) 1987. *Analyzing Gender: A Handbook of Social Science Research*. Newbury Park: Sage.

Howe, I. (ed.) 1986. *Essential Works of Socialism*. 3rd edition. New Haven: Yale University Press.

Jerrome, D. 1981. "The Significance of Friendship for Women in Later Life." *Aging and Society* 1: 175–97.

Jerrome, D. 1984. "Good Company: The Sociological Implication of Friendship." *Sociological Review* 32: 696–718.

Kahn, R. L. and Antonucci, T. C. 1980. "Convoys Over the Life Course: Attachment, Roles and Social Support." Pp. 252–86 in *Life-span Development and Behavior*, vol. 3, edited by P. B. Baltes and O. Brim, New York: Academic Press.

Kaufman, S. 1981. "Cultural Components of Identity in Old Age: A Case Study." *Ethos* 9: 51–87.

Kaufman, S. 1986. *The Ageless Self: Sources of Meaning in Late Life*. Madison: University of Wisconsin Press.

Kessler-Harris, A. 1982. *Out to Work: A History of Wage-earning Women in the United States*. Oxford: Oxford University Press.

Leavitt, J. 1989. "Gender and Managing Public Housing." Unpublished manuscript.

McLaughlin, S. D., Melber, B. D., Billy, J. O. G., et al. 1988. *The Changing Lives of American Women*. Chapel Hill: University of North Carolina Press.

Margolis, M. L. 1984. *Mothers and Such: Views of American Woman and Why They Changed*. Berkeley: University of California Press.

Matthews, S. H. 1986. *Friendships Through the Life Course*. Beverly Hills: Sage.

Mead, G. H. 1934. *Mind, Self and Society*. Chicago: University of Chicago Press.

Moody, H. R. 1988. "Toward a Critical Gerontology: The Contribution of the Humanities to Theories of Aging." Pp. 19–40 in *Emergent Theories of Aging* edited by J. E. Birren and V.L. Bengston, New York: Springer.

Moore, H. L. 1988. *Feminism and Anthropology*. Minneapolis: University of Minnesota Press.

Myerhoff, B. 1978. *Number Our Days*. New York: E. P. Dutton.

Paine, R. 1969. "In Search of Friendship." *Man* 4: 505–24.

Personal Narratives Group (eds.), 1989. *Interpreting Women's Lives*. Bloomington: Indiana University Press.

Plath, D. W. 1980a. *Long Engagements: Maturity in Modern Japan*. Stanford: Stanford University Press.

Plath, D. W. 1980b. "Contours of Consociation: Lessons from a Japanese Narrative." Pp. 287–305 in *Life-span Development and Behavior*, vol. 3, edited by P. B. Baltes and O. Brim, New York: Academic Press.

Plath, D. W. 1983. *Work and the Lifecourse in Japan*. Albany: State University of New York Press.

Plath, D. W. 1984. "Of Time, Love and Heroes." Pp. 16–27 in *Adult Development Through Relationships* edited by V. Rogers, New York: Praeger.

Reinharz, S. 1986. " 'Friends or Foes' Gerontological and Feminist Theory." *Women's Studies International Forum* 9: 503–14.

Rogers, V. (ed.) 1984. *Adult Development Through Relationships*. New York: Praeger.

Rosow, I. 1967. *Social Integration of the Aged*. New York: Free Press.

Rossi, A. S. 1985. *Gender and the Life Course*. New York: Aldine.

Rossi, A. S. 1980. "Life-span Theories and Women's Lives." *Signs* 6: 4–32.

Sacks, K. B. and Remy, D. (eds.) 1984. *My Troubles Are Going to Have Trouble With Me: Everyday Trials and Triumphs of Women Workers*. New Brunswick, NJ: Rutgers University Press.

Shaw, L. B. 1986. *Midlife Women at Work: A Fifteen Year Perspective*. Lexington, MA: Lexington Books.

Stone, R. and Minkler, M. 1984. "The Socio-Political Context of Women's Reitrement." Pp. 225–38 in *Readings in the Political Economy of Aging* edited by M. Minkler and C. Estes, Farmingdale: Baywood.

Szinovacz, M. E. 1982. *Women's Retirement: Policy Implications of Recent Research*. Beverly Hills: Sage.

Szinovacz, M. E. 1983. "Beyond the Hearth: Older Women and Retirement." Pp. 93–120 in *Older Women: Issues and Prospects* edited by E. Markson, Lexington: Lexington Books.

Ware, S. 1982. *Holding Their Own: American Women in the 1930s*. Boston: Twayne.

# 15 Filial Obligations and Kin Support for Elderly People

## *Janet Finch and Jennifer Mason*

## Introduction

Research on the family care of elderly people has been a major growth area in recent years, in Britain as elsewhere. Underlying much of it – but often not addressed directly – are questions about the nature of obligation and responsibility within families, and how far these underscore the support which may be offered to elderly people who can no longer fully care for themselves. Research which has attempted to encompass these issues has tended to be conducted on a fairly small scale.[1]

This paper is based on a large research project, which includes qualitative and quantitative data on kin obligations and support. We have covered a wide range of life situations, but in this paper we are confining ourselves to discussing data upon the care of elderly people and upon the obligations of children in particular. The central focus of our research is support which passes between kin in adult life, and how far this is underpinned by concepts of obligation, responsibility and duty. We are therefore concerned with issues about norms and morality in family life, and how far these constitute explanations of what people do, or do not do, for their relatives. Other explanations of what people do are possible, of course: personal preference or liking, pragmatic considerations or patterns of exchange built upon reciprocity over a lifetime. We are not excluding any of these – indeed we are very interested in trying to understand how they mesh together – but our central concern in this paper is the issue of normative obligations and how they operate. To put it very simply, in what sense do people support their kin because they see it as 'the proper thing to do'?

Our discussion locates these issues in the context of contemporary Britain, because the study upon which we draw was based in the north-west of England. However, the issues which we raise are fundamental to understanding the nature of filial obligations in any society. Existing literature on kinship in Britain would suggest that if we are going to find a strong sense of duty or obligation anywhere, we will find it in parent–child relationships. It is variously described in this literature as the central kinship bond, the least ambiguous of adult kin relationships and the relationship most clearly founded upon a sense of obligation.[2] We can trace the evidence for that through the classic British kinship studies by Bott; Young and Willmott; Bell; Firth, Hubert and Forge.[3]

In this paper, we are looking at just one element of ongoing parent–child relationships, namely practical assistance and personal care given to parents when they are elderly. We also make some references to financial assistance, although this is not

Original publication: Finch, Janet and Jennifer Mason, "Filial Obligations and Kin Support for Elderly People," *Ageing and Society* (Cambridge University Press, Cambridge, 1990), vol. 10, no. 2, pp. 151–75.

explored in detail. The classic kinship literature indicates that it is widely seen as legitimate for parents who are elderly to make demands on their adult children, but that literature also suggests that it is possible for parents to overstep the mark by demanding *too much* and also by making demands in the *wrong way*. Alongside this we also have to place the substantial evidence that a situation of total dependence of elderly people on their children seems to be widely regarded as undesirable. Townsend's classic study of the family life of old people[4] popularised the phrase 'intimacy at a distance' to describe the desired relationships between elderly people and their children, and later studies do seem to keep confirming that.[5]

There are also predictable sources of variation in the support which passes between elderly people and their children, most obviously related to gender and ethnicity. The classic kinship literature documents the central role which women play in the maintenance of family relationships ('kin keeping'), and there is also ample evidence that when it comes to the more arduous of the practical tasks, these are usually performed by daughters, or indeed daughters-in-law, rather than sons.[6] Clearly that reflects the gender division of responsibility and labour in the performance of domestic tasks more generally, a division which itself varies in different ethnic groups. There is a separate, but linked, question abut whether women and men display a different sense of obligation and duty towards their parents, or their relatives more generally. Some feminist writers have argued persuasively that 'a sense of responsibility' permeates women's approach to family relationships in a way which is not replicated for men.[7]

These, then, are the kinds of issue which form the background to our study. The questions which we are raising in this paper are:

1   Do people in contemporary Britain clearly acknowledge that parent–child relations are founded upon norms of obligation (rather than personal preference, pragmatic considerations, etc.)?
2   What is the substance of these norms? Is there anything approaching a consensus about what parents can expect from their children?
3   How do norms operate in practice?


## Public Norms about Filial Obligations

We begin with some of the data from the Family Obligations survey. This was conducted in the Greater Manchester area in late 1985 and involved interviews with 978 adults of all ages (representing a 72 percent response rate), drawn as a random sample from the electoral register. This represented the first phase of our data collection. The second was a smaller-scale qualitative study, based on in-depth interviews.[8]

The purpose of the survey was to investigate how far it is true to say there is a public normative consensus about obligations between adult kin. We wanted to see if there is any level of agreement among a random sample of the population about what counts as 'the proper thing to do' for relatives in specified circumstances. We were not trying to use the survey to generate data about what people *actually* do for their own relatives – that came at the second stage of the study, which was based on in-depth interviews with some of the people who had been in the survey, and some of their relatives. Nor were we wishing to make any prior assumptions about the relationship between beliefs and values expressed in our survey and the ways in which people arrive at commitments to their own relatives. Again, it is in the second stage of the study that we have tried to explore the extent to which people are guided by a sense of 'the proper thing to do' in relationships with their own relatives. In the survey, our method was to assess whether there is agreement about proper forms of obligation between kin, mainly by using questions about hypothetical situations concerning third parties, in which people were invited to indicate what the participants 'should' do. Some of the questions were in the form of longer vignettes, where we were able to specify the circumstances quite precisely.[9]

### Do people give assent to the idea of filial obligations?

At the most general level, our survey data suggest that most people do give assent at this normative level to the idea of filial obligations (i.e. that adult children are obligated to their parents), but that this assent is neither universal nor unconditional. When presented with a bald attitude statement: 'Children have no obligation to look after their parents when they are old', 57 percent of our sample disagreed and 39 percent agreed. Disagreement with this statement indicates assent to the idea of filial obligations, and we can see that although a majority fall into this category, a sizeable minority do not.[10]

In various other more specific questions concerned with examples of middle-aged or elderly people needing assistance, again a majority seemed to give approval to the idea of filial obligations. We had a whole series of questions in which we spelled out a situation, asked respondents to presume that some relative was going to provide assistance and invited them to say *which* relative this should be. Respondents were not presented with a list of options so that, in effect, they could propose any permutation of relatives they wished. In all circumstances where a child could be presumed to exist, children were the clearest targets. Tables 13.1–13.4 give some examples from these questions, which are concerned both with financial and practical assistance.

A number of points could be explored in relation to these tables – for example, the variations in people's responses according to the type of assistance needed. However, we use them here for a fairly limited purpose: to focus upon what is being said about *who* should offer help. Although there is some variation in the preferences expressed, it is noticeable that they remain concentrated in a very narrow genealogical range. Of course there is nothing startling about this pattern, but it does confirm empirically that, at the level of publicly expressed norms, most people do see children as the people who should step in first and offer assistance even when other relatives are presumed to be available. A few people did mention siblings, grandchildren or more distant relatives, but they were in a very small minority.

Thus the data contained in these tables suggest fairly strong support for the idea of filial obligations specifically – the special responsibilities of children over other relatives. This seems to hold for all the questions where we asked our respondents to assume that *some* relative was going to provide assistance for an elderly person. These answers have to be understood in the light of knowing that a sizeable minority of our survey population would not necessarily have wanted care to come from relatives at all – or at least did not regard this as the optimum solution. That is illustrated

**Table 13.1**   Caring for an elderly woman: which relatives should offer assistance

I would like to ask you about some situations in which people might need personal care. This time, let's suppose that the help is going to come from a relative.* In each case, the person has a lot of relatives living nearby who could help.

An elderly woman who can manage well living alone but who needs help getting up and going to bed. Which relative should be the first to offer help?

|  | Number of respondents | Percentage |
|---|---|---|
| Daughter | 663 | 67.8 |
| Children | 102 | 10.4 |
| Son | 43 | 4.3 |
| Sister | 42 | 4.2 |
| Brother/sister | 10 | 1.0 |
| Other named relative | 18 | 1.8 |
| Whole family/all equally | 33 | 3.3 |
| Immediate/closest | 9 | 0.9 |
| Who is available/can cope | 8 | 0.8 |
| Other | 16 | 1.6 |
| DK/NA | 34 | 3.4 |
| Total | 978 | 100.0 |

* Respondents had been asked to consider these same situations earlier in the interview, but had been asked different questions about them.

**Table 13.2**   Caring for a woman recovering from a hip operation: which relatives should offer assistance?

Introductory statement – see table 13.1

An elderly woman who lives alone and who has to stay in bed all day for the next few months following a hip operation. Which relative should be the first to offer help?

|  | Number of respondents | Percentage |
|---|---|---|
| Daughter | 646 | 66.0 |
| Children | 94 | 9.6 |
| Son | 33 | 3.3 |
| Sister | 59 | 6.0 |
| Brother/sister | 9 | 0.9 |
| Other named relative | 12 | 1.2 |
| Whole family/all equally | 53 | 5.4 |
| Immediate/closest | 12 | 1.2 |
| Who is available/can cope | 4 | 0.4 |
| Other | 13 | 1.3 |
| DK/NA | 43 | 4.3 |
| Total | 978 | 100.0 |

**Table 13.3**   Caring for an elderly and confused man: which relatives should offer assistance?

Introductory statement – see table 13.1

An elderly man who can move about well, and who lives alone, but who gets confused and who needs someone to go in regularly several times a week to check that everything is safe. Which relative should be the first to offer help?

|  | Number of respondents | Percentage |
| --- | --- | --- |
| Son | 382 | 39.0 |
| Daughter | 299 | 30.6 |
| Children | 90 | 9.2 |
| Brother | 46 | 4.7 |
| Sister | 28 | 2.8 |
| Brother/sister | 7 | 0.7 |
| Other named relative | 19 | 1.9 |
| Whole family/all equally | 43 | 4.3 |
| Immediate/closest | 9 | 0.9 |
| Who is available/can cope | 7 | 0.7 |
| Other | 15 | 1.5 |
| DK/NA | 33 | 3.3 |
| Total | 978 | 100.0 |

in table 13.4, for example, where 35 percent thought that relatives definitely should not offer money to pay for decorating. In relation to the situations posed in table 13.1–3, earlier in the interview between 56 percent and 70 percent of our respondents had opted for some solution other than family care, when they were given the choice of State care, privately paid for care, care by relatives or care by friends. Presumably what these respondents were telling us is: I would prefer the responsibility not to fall on the family, but if it *has* to be relatives, then it should be children.

However, although our data suggest that people generally see it as appropriate that adult children should do *something* to support their parents, there is less broad agreement as to exactly what children should do. In fact, our data often point to different ways of fulfilling obligations legitimately. One of our questions which illustrates this particularly well is concerned with a middle-aged couple facing the dilemma of what to do about the husband's parents who live several hundred miles away, and who have been seriously injured in a car accident. Proportions of our sample choosing the various options were as follows: move to live near the husband's parents 33 percent; have the parents move to live with them 24 percent; give the parents money to help them pay for daily care 25 percent; let the parents make their own arrangements 9 percent. Only the last option suggests that the couple have no filial responsibility, and even there people may well have expected that they would, in fact, provide some kind of support. Viewed in this way, we can say that 82 percent of our sample were assenting to the notion of filial responsibility, but were acknowledging different ways of fulfilling it.

**Table 13.4**   Decorating an elderly couple's house: should relatives help to pay?

(a) Suppose an elderly couple need money to redecorate their home. Do you think that relatives should offer to pay to have the work done?

|  | Number of respondents | Percentage |
|---|---|---|
| Yes | 538 | 55.0 |
| No | 342 | 35.0 |
| Depends | 98 | 10.0 |
| Total | 978 | 100.0 |

(b) Respondents who said 'Yes' or 'Depends' – up to three answers post-coded. Assuming that they could all afford to help which relatives, if any, should be the first to offer money?

|  | Number of responses | Percentage |
|---|---|---|
| Son | 247 | 38.8 |
| Children | 138 | 21.7 |
| Daughter | 27 | 4.2 |
| Other named relatives | 24 | 3.8 |
| All equally/whole family | 113 | 17.7 |
| Whoever can afford it | 32 | 5.0 |
| Immediate/closest family | 11 | 1.7 |
| DK/NA/Other answer | 44 | 6.9 |
| Total | 636 | 100.0 |

*Do people distinguish between children in relation to their filial obligations?*

We did not have any questions in the survey which explored in detail whether people distinguish between different children when allocating responsibility for parents, but our data do give us some clues here.

First, there does not seem to be any significant inclination to distinguish children by birth order. We had expected that people might see the obligations of an eldest son or daughter as 'stronger' than the rest, but very few specified this on those open-ended questions where we invited them to name a relative (as above).

Second, there is a clear sense in the data of people wanting to follow an 'equal shares' principle if at all possible. Tables 13.1–13.4 all have substantial proportions of respondents who say that the 'children' should assist the elderly people in question, without making any further distinction, or who specify that it should be 'the whole family' or 'all equally'. This occurs in questions where people were asked to say who should offer *first*, directing them to name a single individual, so we take this to be quite a strong response.

Third, there is clearly some tendency to distinguish between sons and daughters in the allocation of responsibilities, although this is not as straightforward as stereotypes would predict. The equal shares principle suggests that many people see both sons and daughters as targets for providing assistance to parents, although in the case of providing money (table 13.4) a substantial proportion of our respondents specify that it should be a son. When it comes to providing care (tables 13.1 to 13.3), the question of where the responsibility should fall apparently depends upon the gender of the person needing care, at least for some of our respondents. Where an elderly woman needs care (tables 13.1 and 13.2), a daughter is the clear preference of two-thirds of our respondents. For an elderly man both daughters and sons are regarded as appropriate to take prime responsibility. (What 'taking responsibility' means could, of course, be different for daughters and sons, but we cannot explore that on the basis of these data.) This pattern is repeated elsewhere in our survey data. Although the pattern of preferences expressed in all these questions is quite complex, and certainly does not just follow gender stereotypes, there are some situations in which gender does seem to have a clear impact upon people's normative judgements: daughters are rarely chosen as the appropriate people to provide money, and sons are rarely chosen as the people who should provide care for an elderly woman.

### Do filial obligations have limits?

One important way to test out the significance of publicly expressed norms about filial obligations is to consider whether they have limits and, if so, of what kind. Our data enable us to make two points about this.

First, the quality of the relationship between a parent and adult child does not seem to have much impact upon the way responsibilities are allocated – at least not at this level of publicly acknowledged norms. We asked one question about whether a person should be prepared to make daily visits to look after his or her elderly father, even if they have never got on well together (table 13.5); 72 percent of people said 'yes'. Neither respondents' gender nor their social class was apparently related to the answers they gave, although there was a small tendency for people over the age of 65 to answer 'yes' more frequently than younger people. Table 13.5 also shows that, for about half of those respondents who thought that a child should visit despite a poor relationship, a key consideration was the fact that the relative in question was a *father* since, when we substituted 'uncle' for 'father', the proportion saying 'yes' dropped to 40 percent.

This 'strong' view of filial obligations is supported elsewhere in our survey data. For example, one of our longer vignettes concerned an elderly woman and her daughter, who had never got along well. They had quarrelled, and the older woman had cut the daughter out of her will. Yet in this case, 37 percent of people still thought that the daughter should offer her mother a home when she needed it – a proportion very similar to answers given in other questions about children giving a home to elderly parents, where the circumstances were less contentious. So it appears that the particular circumstances in this question, including a very poor relationship between mother and daughter, have little effect on the number of people prepared to endorse the principle of filial obligations. In general, people do not seem to 'count' the quality of the relationship as a factor which legitimately puts limits upon the obligations of children to their elderly parents.

**Table 13.5**   Obligation to visit and 'getting on'

(a) Should a person be prepared to make daily visits to look after his or her elderly father, even if they have not got on well together?

|  | Number of responses | Percentage |
|---|---|---|
| Yes | 704 | 72.0 |
| No | 220 | 22.5 |
| Depends | 49 | 5.0 |
| NA | 5 | 0.5 |
| Total | 978 | 100.0 |

(b) And should a person be prepared to make daily visits to look after his or her uncle, even if they have never got on well together?

|  | Number of respondents | Percentage |
|---|---|---|
| Yes | 390 | 39.9 |
| No | 486 | 49.7 |
| Depends | 90 | 9.2 |
| DK/NA | 12 | 1.2 |
| Total | 978 | 100.0 |

Second, the fact that the quality of the relationship does not set limits does not mean that there are no limits at all to filial obligations. In another of our longer vignettes, we set up a situation where a middle-aged couple would be torn in two directions – between moving several hundred miles away to care for the husband's parents, or staying put because their own children were at a crucial stage in their education (coming up to 'O' levels). Here there was much clearer agreement about the proper thing to do: 78 percent said that they should stay put, and 20 percent that they should move, which we interpret to mean that four out of five of our respondents thought that the needs of the younger generation should take precedence over the older. Thus there *are* normative limits upon filial obligations and, in this instance, these are set by the need to fulfil other responsibilities which are seen as taking precedence.

In summary, our findings do seem to confirm the normative strength and importance of filial ties, but also underline that they do not entail unconditional responsibilities.

## Norms and Negotiations about Filial Obligations in Practice: A Case Study

It seems then that there is a degree of public normative consensus (although by no means universal) that children should do *something* to assist their parents in these types of circumstances, but it is not always clear what that should be, who should do it, or what limits might apply to filial obligation. If various different courses of action *could* constitute the 'proper thing to do', then two consequences follow. First, on an individual level, each person necessarily has to engage in a task of 'working out' what to do for his or her own parents in a given set of circumstances. The appropriate course of action does not present itself as obvious, as if it were a well-defined rule where the only choice left to the individual is to obey it or break it. Second, there is the task of presenting one's actions publicly and getting other people to accept that they lie within the legitimate range of filial obligations. These two processes might be consecutive (you decide what you are going to do first, then you sell it to other people), but equally they might operate in parallel (your assessment of what other people will accept as legitimate may well influence precisely what you decide to do for your parents).[11] On the basis of our survey findings, it seems likely that both processes have to be worked at actively, but clearly we need quite different kinds of data to get further with understanding that.

At this point we turn to the other part of our data, based on 119 interviews with 88 individuals.[12] Almost all of those interviewees had some experience, directly or indirectly, of questions arising in their own kin relationships about the care of elderly people. In fact, the data which we are using in this part of the paper come principally from a set of seven interviews with six members of one family. We built the strategy of interviewing several members of the same family into our methodology, because it produces accounts of family events and responsibilities from different angles. By analysing the accounts in relation to each other, we can begin to get to grips with the *processes* involved in negotiating sets of obligations within families. It is only with these types of data that we can begin to understand the legitimacy of each person's account and position *vis-à-vis* other family members. We are going to focus our discussion principally around one of a potential eleven 'kin group' case studies in our data set, because we need depth of analysis to be able to understand the processes operating in that (or indeed any) family. We shall draw on other examples from our study population in a more limited way.

### The Mansfield family case study[13]

We have selected the Mansfield family case study as a way of discussing filial obligations, because it enables us to look both at the actual care of Vic Mansfield (who died in 1985, before our interviews) and the future care of Nan Mansfield, who was part of our study. Figure 13.1 shows a simplified family tree for the Mansfields.

Every family has distinctive features, and we will point out briefly some of those which apply in this case. There are six adult children in this family, none of whom had been geographically mobile outside Greater Manchester. Nor had there been much social mobility: like their parents, they worked in a mixture of skilled and unskilled manual occupations or were self-employed – including one who owned a classic corner shop. From the point of view of the story which we are going to tell, it is also important to know that the Mansfield parents had an unhappy marriage. All our interviewees acknowledged this, including Nan herself, who said that her husband had 'led me a dog's life'. Their marriage had been characterised by periods of separation and reconciliation.

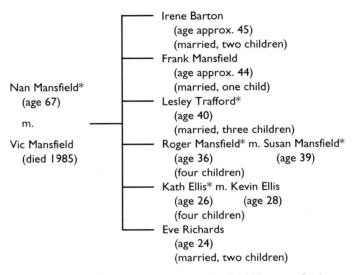

Nan Mansfield*
(age 67)

m.

Vic Mansfield
(died 1985)

Irene Barton
(age approx. 45)
(married, two children)

Frank Mansfield
(age approx. 44)
(married, one child)

Lesley Trafford*
(age 40)
(married, three children)

Roger Mansfield* m. Susan Mansfield*
(age 36)                    (age 39)
(four children)

Kath Ellis* m. Kevin Ellis
(age 26)        (age 28)
(four children)

Eve Richards
(age 24)
(married, two children)

* Interviewed in the second stage of the Family Obligations Study.

**Figure 13.1**    Mansfield kin group: simplified family tree.
(Ages as at time of interviews in 1987.)

Vic Mansfield had died about eighteen months before our interviews, having been unable to care for himself for about a year previously. At this point he and Nan had been separated for some time. We were told that he 'wasn't really ill' and that he was 'just senile'. He was admitted to hospital at one point but was apparently very unhappy and the children believed that his condition deteriorated. For the last few months of his life he was cared for principally by two of his children, Roger and Kath, and their respective spouses, Susan and Kevin. These two couples lived in adjacent streets and shared his care on a day-to-day basis. He lived first in one house then in the other, in both cases making conditions very overcrowded in their small Victorian terraced houses. He moved for a brief spell back into his own home, to be cared for by his elder son, Frank, who was living there temporarily, then finally to the flat of his estranged wife, Nan. This arrangement seems to have lasted a rather short time before he was readmitted to hospital, where he died.

We were interested also to explore with members of this family whether they had begun to think and talk about the future care of Nan. It was clear that this question was on their minds and negotiations about it were under way, albeit indirectly. One of her daughters, Lesley Trafford, said that they have 'skirted around' the topic. Nan herself says that she has told them all to 'put me into a home', but the one thing which all are agreed upon is that this will not happen. Roger says that it is an 'unwritten rule' in the family that one of them will look after her. Both Lesley and Kath say that she does not really expect to end her days in a home and that when the time comes, 'she would expect to be with one of us'.

Having outlined the circumstances of the Mansfield kin group briefly, we will now look in more detail at how the processes of defining filial obligations worked in this family, linking our discussion at appropriate points with other cases in our data set and with the survey data.

### Rules of conduct about filial obligations

Our survey was concerned with establishing whether people acknowledge publicly, at the normative level, clear 'rules' about filial obligations. In looking at the Mansfield case, we can ask: in practice, do people have the idea that there are well understood rules about how you should behave towards your parents? When faced with the actual needs of their father, or the anticipated needs of their mother, is it obvious to the children what is 'the proper thing to do'?

The only person who uses the word 'rule' is Roger, when he talks about the 'unwritten rule' that his mother will be cared for by her children. We think that he is using the word 'rule' here to mean a shared understanding that the family as a whole will take responsibility for the care of the mother. But he is not saying that each individual is subject to a rule that he or she must do this. That becomes clear as he goes on to elaborate a future scenario. When we ask him whether it would be the same people who looked after his father who would care for his mother, he says yes, it probably would be the same ones, but adds:

> The thing is, you don't know when it would happen, you know and what, what would happen if it did . . . families are a moving thing really, aren't they? Circumstances at one time are not necessarily the same at another time . . . So you really don't know what would happen.

He seems to be saying that it would be open to negotiation at a particular point in time to decide precisely who should do what. Thus the precise application of the 'unwritten rule' is rooted in specific circumstances, which are seen as subject to change.

Roger's position seems to be that responsibility for the care of an infirm parent lies with the children, rather than, say, with State services. The other members of his family whom we interviewed also seem to share this view, using phrases like, 'I think families should really look after their own'. However, they also endorse his view that 'circumstances' are relevant in deciding precisely what should happen. The two sides of this particular coin come across very clearly in the following extract from Lesley Trafford's interview, where she is talking about why she was not involved in caring for her father.

*Lesley*: I think if I'd have been at home all day, or had a part-time job or something, then definitely I would have got, would very much have liked to get involved.

*Interviewer*: Yes, yes. Your earlier answers to my questions about families taking responsibility for older people were – presumably you felt that was the right thing to do for your father at that time, did you?

*Lesley*: Oh yes, yeah. I think it's wrong that you should just shove them into a home. I wouldn't like that you know. I wouldn't like mine to do that to me (laughs). But it all depends on circumstances.

In summary, the Mansfield case suggests that, in this family at least, a clear 'rule' is recognised: children should take responsibility collectively for the care of their parents. But that strong view of filial responsibilities is made much more ambiguous by their view that a consideration of 'circumstances' is legitimate and relevant. This makes negotiations inevitable, but they may not necessarily be completely open-ended. We need to pose a further question: are there other rules which give clear guidance about *which* child should perform the active work of caring for a parent, exercising a responsibility which is perceived as collective? There are two obvious possibilities here, if we take other recent studies of elderly people as a guideline: that the responsibility will be allocated to women rather than men; that there is a hierarchy of responsibilities within the family, defined in genealogical terms. We will explore each of these in relation to the Mansfield case.

### Is there a hierarchy of obligations in this case?

The concept of the hierarchy of obligations has come though quite strongly in recent British work on the care of elderly people. Implicit in some earlier work, it has been made explicit in Quereshi's Sheffield study.[14] The hierarchy is said to be: spouse, relative living in household, daughter, daughter-in-law, son, other relative. Ungerson's smaller scale study in Canterbury[15] shows that people may be acutely aware of normative hierarchies precisely because they are being pulled in another direction, and that hierarchies can thus be competing and reorderable. In relation to the care of Vic Mansfield, we should note (i) he lived alone, so the 'person in the household' category was not relevant, at least initially, (ii) he had a spouse but they were estranged, (iii) he had more than one daughter, son and daughter-in-law.

Did the responsibility for his care get allocated on the basis of this hierarchy? We do not think it did, at least not in a straightforward way. The spouse was initially bypassed, and two of the children, one son and one daughter, seem to have accepted the major responsibility. The other son as well as the other daughters were also regarded as legitimate targets for caring. However, if we look a bit more carefully, we can see that there *was* a residual notion of the hierarchy, which in a sense the people most immediately involved (Roger, Susan, Kath and Kevin) were attempting to mobilise and adapt to their particular circumstances.

An important distinction here is between the long and the short term. In the short term the daughter and the son who had kept closest contacts with their father assumed direct responsibility. They felt he was deteriorating in hospital and would not 'make him go back' after a weekend visit. However, once this situation went on beyond a couple of weeks, and presumably looked set to continue for an unknown length of time, they began to consider questions about whether these arrangements were 'proper' in normative terms – fair to them as well as to him. Quite apart from any other considerations of fairness, it would have been difficult to deny that both houses were already overcrowded and could accommodate a dependent, elderly man only with great difficulty. At this stage, looking round for an alternative to a semi-permanent arrangement based on their present one, they do seem then to have started to think about who 'ought' to take responsibility in a fairly formal way. The terms in which they thought look very like Qureshi's hierarchy. Certainly they mobilised the normative principles built into that hierarchy, even if they did not neatly work down the list in consecutive order. In considering whether another of the siblings would be more suitable than themselves to take responsibility for their father, they looked to the one who was 'sharing' a household, in the sense of currently living in the father's house. And above all, they mobilised the principle that part of the marriage bargain is to take responsibility for a sick spouse, even though their parents were unhappily married and had been living apart.

The events leading up to Nan's agreeing to care for her estranged husband are described to us in various ways in the interviews. It was clear, eighteen months afterwards, that they all still felt keenly the difficulties of negotiating with each other in this situation. Nan expressed herself as having been 'perfectly willing' to look after Vic, although plainly she was relieved that she did not have to do so for long. Roger's account of these events presents his mother as more reluctant. Whatever happened in reality, the accounts given to us about this decision make explicit the importance of the normative principle that the responsibilities of spouses are stronger than those of children. Roger said that he told his mother at one point, 'I still feel it's your responsibility' and also – in a comment which encapsulates neatly the notion of hierarchy – 'If you were dead, then we'd have to do it.' This is obviously all the more striking in that the spouses were actually living apart, yet all parties seem to have regarded it as legitimate, if necessary, to mobilise this principle in the care of a dying man.

This is the clearest example in our data set of ranking the responsibilities of a spouse above filial responsibilities – the factor of estrangement makes it explicit in a distinctive way. But certainly there are echoes of it in other cases. For example, Dorothy O'Malley, a woman in her sixties caring for a husband with multiple sclerosis, told us that she had recently learned to drive and passed her test, so that she would have to rely less on her daughter for assistance. Her daughter, Jill (whom we also interviewed) had a strong sense of filial responsibilities and had been visiting her parents every day once her father developed his chronic condition. Her mother had been 'mithering about how she kept coming up' and felt that 'she had enough to do at home'. In a context quite different from the Mansfields, the same principle was being mobilised. Dorothy's learning to drive was a means to establishing that she herself should be accorded the prime responsibility for the care of her husband.

What we take from the Mansfield case study in particular is that there *is* a concept of hierarchy of obligations at a normative or ideological level, but it by no means gets straightforwardly applied (as some usages tend to suggest). In the Mansfield case it would not have enabled us to predict what actually happened in practice. But it *is* important as a tool with which people negotiate and, as Ungerson suggests, awareness of one's place in a hierarchy can make one vulnerable to feelings of guilt for not fulfilling responsibilities. We want to suggest that for the Mansfields a hierarchy was used or constituted in the practice of working out family responsibilities as though it were part of a more general public morality.

### Are obligations gender-specific in this case?

The other 'rule' which one might expect to find, and which would give clear guidance about *which* child should be the one to exercise the family's collective responsibility, is concerned with gender. In the Mansfield case, are obligations to parents gender-specific?

Again, the answer seems to be: only in part, with one exception. The exception concerns physical taboos about touching, an issue which has been identified as non-negotiable in other studies, principally those of Ungerson. In the Mansfield case, Roger was the one who bathed his father and this seems to have been considered normatively appropriate. Certainly it was seen as inappropriate to put pressure on daughters or daughters-in-law to do this. As Susan put it:

> It was very awkward because he needed to be bathed, you know. Well [pause] Roger, my husband, did that, the others couldn't [pause]. I suppose it's something in you isn't it? Some things you can cope with, some you can't. So he used to bath him because Kath couldn't.

Other than on the question of bathing, the gender divisions in caring are perhaps a bit more blurred in this case than one might expect. The situation was presented as one in which a son and a daughter took more or less equal responsibility, and were pretty equally involved, along with their spouses. However, we would argue that this is because we are talking about the care of an elderly *man*. It would be consistent with our survey findings that 'the normative guidelines' about who should care are less clear in the case of a man than a woman, where a daughter is clearly targeted.

This seems to be borne out by the way in which the future care of Nan Mansfield is shaping up. One can detect the possible use of the principle of gender as a negotiating tool in that future situation. For example, Susan says:

> I think now she's got a bit of rheumatism, she's not as fit as she used to be – won't be long before she can't manage, you know. But I think that will be a different case than when, his Dad. Because I think people will, well her daughters in particular won't find it such a burden as, as a man.

Other cases in our data set tend to support the idea that gender-specific rules operate more clearly where an elderly woman needs care. For example, Barbara Arkright was involved, with her three sisters, in supporting her elderly mother by visiting and staying with her regularly. 'The four girls' had evolved this arrangement, but her brothers had not been drawn in. It was a considerable commitment for Barbara, since her mother lived in the Irish Republic, whilst her own home was in Manchester. Another of our respondents, Avril King, had been involved in the terminal care of her mother at a point where she also had a full-time job. She indicated that her two brothers gave little active assistance and that these arrangements were never questioned.

*Avril*: I think if there are brothers and sisters – they automatically think that the girl or girls should, should do it.
*Interviewer*: Yes. Did anybody ever say anything to you, or was it just a sort of feeling you picked up?
*Avril*: Oh no, oh no. But I mean they never even offered to, you know, help or anything like that. It was, it was as though I was just left to it.

Although our data on these two cases are much less rich than for the Mansfields, they do seem to confirm the general point – identified, of course, by other researchers

– that in the British cultural context gendered obligations seem to be particularly clear in the case of mothers and daughters. Against that, however, we need to set evidence from some of our respondents who were of Asian descent, whose experience must at least lead us to modify this general statement. Whilst it may be true of the white majority that daughter-to-mother assistance has a particularly strong quality of obligation, the tradition of sons taking the main responsibility for their mothers remains an important dimension of filial obligations acknowledged by other parts of the British population. This introduces further complexities into our understanding of the gendered nature of obligations, especially since we always have to distinguish between public normative expectations and what is negotiated in practice.

Our general conclusion on the question of gender is that we can detect some substantive rules which get evoked, but they do not come in a non-negotiable form (except possibly the taboo about physical touching). That does not, however, imply that they are unimportant. Their significance is that they represent resources to be used in negotiation. This is apparent, for example, in the way that people talk about the future care of Nan Mansfield.

## Procedural Rules in Negotiating Filial Obligations

We have suggested that the Mansfield case leads us to modify the straightforward idea that there are 'rules' of obligation in that, in given circumstances, people do not appear to have a clear sense of precisely what constitutes the proper thing to do in respect of their parents. This is something which needs to be negotiated. However, we also believe that the Mansfield case reveals 'rules' of a slightly different kind, which we are calling procedural rules. Essentially these are rules about *how you should work out* the proper thing to do. In many senses these seem clearer to identify than substantive rules indicating precisely what you should do.[16] We shall discuss briefly four procedural rules which seem to operate in this case.

### *The need to respond collectively to a parent's need for care should supersede interpersonal considerations within the sibling group*

None of the Mansfields actually used the phrase 'rally round' but that seems to express appropriately what we mean here. Roger was the one who most explicitly articulated it, but all the others certainly gave the impression that difficulties between siblings should not affect their cooperative efforts on behalf of a parent. Roger said:

> I think then the hatchet's usually buried [laughs]. You know, everyone pulls together for whatever time is necessary for that. Certainly it was in my family and I imagine it would be in most.

In fact, even by Roger's own account, and certainly in other people's, the whole sibling group did not 'pull together' and additional resentments were caused as a result. But Roger is giving expression to a procedural normative rule which indicates that hostility *should* be suspended – anyone who does not do that would then legitimately be defined as acting improperly.

*The burden should be shared equitably, if not equally, between all those in an equivalent genealogical position*

Roger's concept of 'pulling together' hints at the principle of sharing the burden. So too does the actual procedure which they went through in relation to the father's care, where each of the siblings was regarded as a *possible* carer – a position from which none of them apparently dissented (or, at least, any such dissent was not reported to us). The question of who *actually* should do it is a matter of bringing additional procedural rules into play (see below). If those other rules did not produce a definitive answer that one individual was clearly more suitable than the rest, then this particular procedural rule would suggest that the parent should literally be shared out between them, that is, passed round from one to the other. Lesley Trafford actually does suggest this literal application of the sharing the burden principle, in relation to the future care of Nan Mansfield. Having been through all the reasons why Nan would not enjoy living at various of her children's houses, she says, 'I think she'd have to go to each one and just sort of do the rounds' (laughs).

The idea of 'doing the rounds' may seem an excessively literal way of working out how the burden can be shared, but mechanisms like this do sometimes get used, indicating the importance of this principle. We have already quoted the case of Barbara Arkright, who took turns with her sisters in going to stay with her mother. A similar, and even more demanding, arrangement was reported to us by another of our respondents, Maureen Vickers, who for approximately two years had shared the care of her mother with her sister. Neither of them lived nearby, and they both travelled to their mother's home to take weekly 'turns'. In Maureen's case, this meant a journey from London to Barrow-in-Furness (a distance of some 300 miles) on the overnight coach.

The importance of the principle of sharing the burden is also indicated where people talk about resentment against other siblings. To return to the Mansfield case, we asked Kath about whether there was any feeling that some of them were not pulling their weight over her father's care. Her answer was a bit ambiguous, but she said, 'We did have bits of rows over it, you know, in between the family.' Roger also refers to this kind of resentment, telling a story against himself concerning an earlier stage of his father's illness when his two younger sisters felt that they were carrying the burden and that Roger should be doing more.

We conclude that the principle of sharing the burden constitutes an important procedural rule in negotiations about filial obligations. However, common adherence to the principle of sharing does not necessarily translate straightforwardly into agreement about who does what and when. Other procedural guidelines are invoked in deciding that.

*Who has prior commitments? These lessen the claims of the parent upon them specifically*

The claim to prior commitments seems to be one of the most important procedural rules which comes into play in deciding who should take responsibility. As the group as a whole (i.e. all those who acknowledge that they hold collective responsibility) attempts to reach an understanding of which of them should be regarded as reasonably available to care for the parent, people's claims to be excluded from that list are importantly (though not exclusively) established in terms of prior commitments. A good example of this being put into practice comes from Roger Mansfield's account of why he felt it was reasonable for his mother to resume responsibility for the care of his father, although they were estranged.

> He [father] wanted to stay in his own house but, er [pause] that would mean somebody living with him. But we all had our own houses and things. We were all married and all had our own houses, families and all the rest of it [pause and sigh]. The only solution really was that my mother went back.

The emphasis here is upon the prior commitments of the children: 'We had our own houses, families and all the rest of it.' It is not necessarily easy (it certainly was not in this case) to get the agreement of all parties about what should count as the kind of prior commitment which makes someone unavailable to provide care. We suspect that there may be systematic differences in people's ability to get prior commitments recognised as legitimate, and that these are quite closely related to gender. But, in general terms, the principle that prior commitments take precedence does not seem to be challenged, or at least anyone who does try to challenge it is on weak ground (Nan, after all, did eventually agree that she should be the one to care for Vic).

The same principle can be seen in a number of other cases in our data set, where it has had some influence upon the level of responsibilities for parents which people had accepted. In the majority of these cases (12 in all) responsibilities to children specifically are seen as taking precedence over obligations to parents. In some other cases, respondents have used less precise phrases like 'your own home' or 'your own family' (as did Roger Mansfield) in describing what counts as a prior claim. Men seem sometimes to use this phrase to indicate the distinctiveness of their own prior commitments. This is clear in the following extract from our interview with Derek Thompson, a man in his twenties of Caribbean descent, who compared the more optional nature of his own filial obligations with those of his sister.

*Interviewer*: Do you think you can see a time when you might be responsible for helping to look after someone in your family for instance?

*Derek*: I've got a family to look after though. I mean I'm even getting married . . . So I've got my family as such. And in the future, yes, if it comes to it, you have to . . . [But] I've only got a certain amount of time. It depends on what's happening at the time with the rest of them. I mean the one who's really going to get the brunt of it is my sister, isn't it? . . . You know, if it comes to it and I can't help, my brothers can't help – you know. It'd go down the line wouldn't it, and she'll get it [laughs].

### The quality of relationships between particular individuals should be one consideration in deciding who should provide care

The issue of quality of relationships is somewhat ambiguous in the Mansfield case. In relation to caring for their father, it appears not to have been cited as a reason why one sibling rather than another should take this responsibility. On the other hand, Susan implies this principle when she talks about the daughters currently having a good and close relationship with their mother and therefore being the most appropriate people to provide for her care in the future.

It is also interesting that both Susan and Kevin – the two in-laws who were involved in caring for Vic Mansfield – indicated that they positively liked him. They do not make the link that they cared 'because' they liked him, and we cannot rule out that this was a *post hoc* rationalisation or, at least, a result of the experience of caring for him. But, in a set of interviews where everyone says what a difficult person Vic was, they both say quite appreciative things about him. Susan indicates that she had always had a good relationship with him and that she respected his advice: 'You could confide in him and he'd listen to you and give you advice. I miss his Dad.'

Kevin says that he had a difficult relationship with his father-in-law for most of the time, but that in his last illness he grew to enjoy his company, liked talking to him, and began to appreciate him:

> As much as we didn't get on, um, I still had quite a lot of respect for him [pause] you know, I quite liked him but I just didn't agree with him a lot of times and he probably didn't agree with me [pause]. But all of a sudden we just seemed to be able to talk about anything, or maybe it was that I had the time to listen.

The fact that it was the children-in-law who emphasised their good relationship, whereas Vic's own children tended to say that he was a difficult man, points to an important facet of this procedural rule. We suspect that, where there is the possibility of a parent moving into the household of one of their children, the quality of their relationship with the son/daughter-in-law is treated as a more legitimate consideration than the quality of their relationship with their own children. The implication is that it is much less reasonable to expect a son/daughter-in-law to take in a person whom they find difficult. Elsewhere in our data set, we can document some other situations in which the quality of the relationship with children-in-law seems to have been a decisive consideration – or at least is seen as a legitimate way of presenting the reason why an elderly parent was not offered a home. Even where children have taken (or are expecting to take) a parent into their own home, the relationship between the parent and their spouse is treated as a matter to be taken very seriously. For example, Sally Brown, another of our interviewees, was really worried about the relationship between her husband and her father, and what would happen if he moved in with them. Although she thought it would eventually happen, she obviously regarded her husband's preferences and feelings very much as a legitimate consideration and returned to this topic several times in the two interviews which we conducted with her.

In negotiations about who is going to take active responsibility for the care of an elderly person, it seems that the quality of relationship is a factor to take into consideration in relation to some people but not others: of marginal relevance between spouses (as we saw in relation to Nan and Vic Mansfield), possibly more so between children and their parents, and more clearly so for children-in-law. Another possible interpretation is that the quality of relationship operates differently as a procedural rule according to whether it is good or bad. If children or children-in-law have a good relationship with their parents, then this makes them particularly appropriate carers. However, if someone who is the 'obvious' carer on other grounds – in our example, a wife – has a poor relationship with the person to be cared for, that does not exempt her.

## Conclusion

There is much more that could be said about the Mansfield case, but let us draw the threads together here. In our study, we have tried to get behind data on who actually cares for whom (which is now quite well documented) to understand how far such arrangements are founded on a sense of obligation of children towards their parents, in the context of contemporary Britain. In exploring this complex issue, which raises considerable challenges for research, we have used different methods of investigation. In a sense we are trying to capitalise upon the different logics which underlie survey methods and case study methods, that is, the way in which explanations are built from case studies is different from survey data.[17] We are trying both to look at different elements of a complex research issue, as well as to make different claims of representativeness. In the survey, we have a representative sample, and wish to make generalisations on that basis. In our case studies, our sample is not representative in any statistical sense, but we are trying to gather in a range of experiences, and to probe to the limits our understanding of processes and negotiations. Any generalisations we might wish to make from this part of the study will be on the basis of the validity of our inductive logic, rather than the representativeness of the sample.

One thing that we certainly have illustrated is that the two types of data do pick up some similar themes, albeit in different ways. For example, the principle of 'equal shares' in designating obligations; the fact that obligations to parents do have limits; the importance of seeing one set of obligations (e.g. of children for parents) as locked into a broader set, in which some obligations can legitimately take precedence over others.

To come back to the questions which we posed at the beginning, we think we have provided some answers, although we have by no means exhausted the issues. We can say that relationships between parents and children *are* importantly founded on a sense of obligation, but one which recognises definite limits. There is not a clear consensus about what it is reasonable to expect. However, there are well understood principles which can be mobilised when you are working out 'the proper thing to do' in practice. People do have an understanding of what would be generally accepted as proper, but they use it as a resource with which to negotiate rather than as a rule to follow.

## Acknowledgments

We are grateful to the Economic and Social Research Council who funded the project discussed in this paper (Grant number GOO 23 2197). The authors would like to thank Gillian Parker and Clare Ungerson for their comments upon a draft of this paper. Our thinking has also benefited from discussions in the following departments, where we have presented some of these data in seminar papers: Department of Anthropology, University of Manchester; Social Policy Research Unit, University of York; BSA Postgraduate Summer School, University of Warwick; Department of Social Administration, University of Lancaster.

## Notes

1   For example, Ungerson, C., *Policy is Personal*. Tavistock, London, 1987; Lewis, J. and Meredith, B. *Daughters Who Care*. Routledge, London, 1988.

2   Morgan, D. H. J., *Social Theory and the Family*. Routledge & Kegan Paul, London, 1975.

3   Bott, E., *The Family and Social Network*. Tavistock, London, 1957; Young, M. and Willmott, P., *Family and Kinship in East London*. Routledge, London, 1957; Willmot, P. and Young, M., *Family and Class in a London Suburb*. Routledge, London, 1960; Bell, C., *Middle Class Families*. Routledge & Kegan Paul, London, 1968; Firth, R., Hubert, J. and Forge, A. *Families and their Relatives*. Routledge & Kegan Paul, London, 1969.

4   Townsend, P. *The Family Life of Old People*. Routledge & Kegan Paul, London, 1957.

5   Firth et al. *Families and their Relatives*. Routledge & Kegan Paul, London, 1969; Allan, G., Kinship, responsibility and care for elderly people. *Ageing and Society*, 8 (1988), 249–68.

6   Firth et al. *Families and their Relatives*. Routledge & Kegan Paul, London, 1969; Wenger, G. C., *The Supportive Network*. Allen and Unwin, London, 1984; Qureshi, H. and Simons, K., 'Resources within families: caring for elderly people', in Brannen, J. and Wilson, G. (eds), *Give and Take in Families*. Allen and Unwin, London, 1987.

7   Graham, H., 'Caring: a labour of love', in Finch, J. and Groves, D. (eds), *A Labour of Love: Women, Work and Caring*. Routledge & Kegan Paul, London, 1983; Cornwell, J., *Hard Earned Lives*. Tavistock, London, 1984; Ungerson, C., *Policy is Personal*. Tavistock, London, 1987.

8   The two-stage research design, which was fairly complex and reflected the conceptual framework within which we were working. We are not discussing this here, but have written about it elsewhere: Finch, J., 'Family obligations and the life course', in Bryman, A. et al. (eds), *Rethinking the Life Cycle*. Macmillan, London, 1987; Finch, J. and Mason, J., 'Decision-taking in the fieldwork process', in Burgess, R. G. (ed.), *Reflections of Field Experience*. JAI Press, London, 1990.

9   For discussion see: Finch, J., The vignette technique in survey research. *Sociology*, 21, 1 (1987).

10  This and other attitude statements in our survey were taken from another study, in Scotland in 1982, directed by Patrick West. Patterns of response to this question were similar on both surveys: (See West, P., the family, the welfare state and community care: political rhetoric and public attitudes. *Journal of Social Policy*, 13, 4, (1984) 417–46). There were some differences among our survey population in answering the attitude statement about filial obligations. Notably, older people were more divided in their views than younger people. In the 18–29 age group, 65 per cent supported the principle of filial obligations.

11  Finch, J., *Family Obligations and Social Change*. Polity, Cambridge, 1989.

12  The procedure for selecting interviewees at this second stage was complex and we have not provided details in this paper. It is discussed in Finch, J. and Mason, J., 'Decision-taking in the fieldwork process', in Burgess, R. G. (ed.), *Reflections of Field Experience*. JAI Press, London, 1990.

13  Our policy on maintaining confidentiality is as follows. All interviewees are referred to by pseudonymns, which we invited them to choose themselves. In some instances certain details of people's circumstances, which might make them recognisable, have been changed as a further guarantee of anonymity.

14  Qureshi, H., 'Responses to dependency: reciprocity, affect and power in family relationships', in Phillipson, C. et al. (eds), *Dependency and Interdependency in Old Age*. Croom Helm, London, 1986; see also Qureshi, H. and Simons, K. 'Resource within families:

Caring for elderly people, in Brannen J and Wilson, G (eds), *Give and Take in Families*. Allen and Unwin, London, 1987.

15   Ungerson, C., *Policy is Personal*. Tavistock, London., 1987.

16   We see the same phenomenon in our survey data and are exploring this point elsewhere. See Finch, J. and Mason, J., *Family Responsibilities in Britain*. Unwin Hyman, London, forthcoming.

17   See Finch, J. and Mason, J., 'Decision taking in the fieldwork process', in Burgess, R. G. (ed.), *Reflections of Field Experience*. JAI Press London, 1990.

## Further Reading to Part IV

Allen, Katherine R. 1989. *Single Women/Family Ties: Life Histories of Older Women.* Beverly Hills, CA: Sage.

Adams, Rebecca G. 1985. "People Would Talk: Normative Barriers to Cross-Sex Friendships for Elderly Women," *The Gerontologist* 6: 605–11.

Frankfather, Dwight. 1977. *The Aged in the Community: Managing Senility and Deviance.* New York: Praeger.

Groger, Lisa. 1992. "Tied to Each Other Through Ties to the Land: Informal Support of Black Elders in a Southern U.S. Community," *Journal of Cross-Cultural Gerontology* 7: 205–20.

Hazan, Haim. 1980. *The Limbo People: A Study of the Constitution of the Time Universe Among the Aged.* London: Routledge & Kegan Paul.

Hazan, Haim. 1992. *Managing Change in Old Age.* Albany, NY: SUNY Press.

Lopata, Helena Znaniecki. 1973. *Widowhood in an American City.* Cambridge, MA: Schenkman.

Myerhoff, Barbara. 1978. *Number Our Days.* New York: Simon and Schuster.

Vesperi, Maria D. 1985. *City of Green Benches: Growing Old in a New Downtown.* Ithaca, NY: Cornell University Press.

# Part V

## Living Arrangements

# 16 Parental Dependence and Filial Responsibility in the Nineteenth Century: Hial Hawley and Emily Hawley Gillespie, 1884–1885

*Emily K. Abel*

During the twentieth-century, the proportion of elderly people living by themselves has risen dramatically. By 1988, almost a third of all people 65 and over were living alone (Commonwealth Fund Commission, 1988). Although the proportion of the elderly residing with spouses has remained constant, the proportion sharing households with adult children has plunged from 60 percent in 1900 to 40 percent in 1960 and just 22 percent in 1984 (Congressional Budget Office, 1988; Smith, 1986).

Living alone has numerous disadvantages. As the Commonwealth Fund Commission (1988) states, "among elderly people who live alone are some of the most fragile, vulnerable and neglected members of America's aged population" (p. 16). A high proportion have poverty-level incomes and suffer from serious disabilities. Although some older people welcome their independence, others experience acute loneliness and isolation. And they often find themselves bereft of assistance when in need. Aged people living by themselves also rely disproportionately on community and home-based services and tend to enter nursing homes prematurely. At a time of increased alarm about our ability to support the burgeoning frail elderly population, the rising incidence of solitary residence among the aged has prompted deep concern (Commonwealth Fund Commission, 1988; Congressional Budget Office, 1988).

Some Americans look back nostalgically to the nineteenth-century, when people 65 and over often moved in with their children. But we know little about the quality of life in shared households (Dahlin, 1980). I recently found diaries describing one instance of intergenerational living from the perspective of the caregiving daughter. In 1884, Hial Newton Hawley went to live with his daughter Emily Gillespie, an Iowa farm woman. Their story alerts us to the problems joint living arrangements can produce.

In addition, it helps to illuminate three general themes. The first is the impact on adult children of financial responsibility for elderly parents. Since the passage of the 1935 Social Security Act, the principle of filial economic responsibility gradually

Original publication: Abel, Emily K., "Parental Dependence and Filial Responsibility in the Nineteenth-Century: Hial Hawley and Emily Hawley Gillespie, 1884–1885," *The Gerontologist* 32 (1992), pp. 519–26.

has been whittled away in the United States (Axinn and Stern, 1985; Callahan, Jr. et al., 1980; Crystal, 1982; Quadagno, 1988). But when Hial Hawley stayed with his daughter, she had to provide financial as well as social support.

The second is the response of elderly people to structures of subordination. It has become commonplace to note that older people lost status in the United States at some point between 1800 and 1914 (Achenbaum, 1974; Cole, 1980; Fischer, 1977; Gratton, 1986; Haber, 1983). But historians direct little attention to the ways in which the elderly resisted their devaluation. A basic premise of the new social history is that subordinate groups – women, ethnic and racial minorities, and poor people – do not passively accept external constraints; many actively seek to shape their lives (see Sklar and Dublin, 1991). This case study reminds us of the importance of focusing on the agency of the elderly as well.

Finally, this episode highlights the need to examine hierarchies of gender as well as generation. A variety of factors reinforced female dependence during the nineteenth-century. Women were denied citizen rights and barred from many occupations. Although many women worked for pay (Kessler-Harris, 1982), the prevailing ideology confined the great majority of women to the domestic sphere. We will see that Hial Hawley sought to counteract his powerlessness as an old person by taking advantage of his privileges as a male.

### Hial Newton Hawley

Born in New York in 1807, Hial Newton Hawley moved to Michigan as a young man. In 1836, he married Sarah Baker, who had just turned 20. Emily was their first child, born in 1838. (See figure 14.1 for family tree.) She was followed by Edna in 1840, Henry in 1842, and Harriet in 1845. Their farm grew less rapidly than their family. The property was worth just $1,000 in 1860, when most surrounding farms were worth at least twice as much (Lensink, 1989).

By 1884, the 77-year-old Hial Hawley suffered from a number of physical problems. His most serious affliction was lameness. Although he still tried to do farm labor, he experienced difficulty and had to lie down a substantial part of every day. In addition, he needed economic help. He had transferred his property to his son Henry, but the latter had sold the farm and then squandered the proceeds; as a result, Henry no longer could support his father. In the absence of either public or private income maintenance programs, Hial was forced to rely on Emily, his one child with a substantial income.

### Emily Hawley Gillespie

Emily had left home in June 1860 to work as a housekeeper for her uncle, who owned an inn in a small Iowa town. In September 1862, she married James Gillespie, a 25-year-old farmer. Although he still lived on his parents' land, he grew increasingly prosperous. Emily and James were able to move to their own land in 1864 and to build a new house in 1872. Their farm thrived during the agricultural depression of the 1870s, when many others failed.

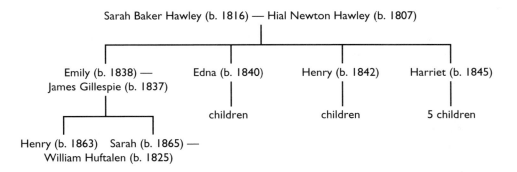

**Figure 14.1**  Family tree of Emily Hawley Gillespie and Hial Hawley

But Emily was ill-prepared to care for her father in other ways. Her own health was declining. In 1882, she had begun to suffer from dropsy, a condition of having an abnormal accumulation of serous fluid in any bodily part, especially the abdomen. In 1884, her condition grew considerably worse. Moreover, she was determined to concentrate her resources on upward mobility for herself and her two children. She hated the circumscribed and exhausting life of a farm woman. Riley argues that many nineteenth-century Iowan women aspired to the prevailing ideal of a true lady despite its irrelevance to their lives (Riley, 1981; see Riley, 1988; Schlissel, Ruiz, and Monk, 1988). This code was predicated on the assumption that women no longer were responsible for productive labor (see Ryan, 1981; Ryan, 1982), but the survival of farm families depended on women's willingness to engage in grueling work. Although Emily's chores were far more arduous than those of most middle-class urban women (see Strasser, 1982), she tried to surround herself with the trappings of gentility. Like many other farm women, she assumed that the money she earned on eggs and poultry was hers to spend alone (Elbert, 1987; Jensen, 1981). In 1880, she improved her home with $50.40 worth of new carpets (EHG, Dec. 16, 1880). She adorned herself and her children as well, buying silk, cashmere, and velvet to make clothes. In February, 1887, her daughter's new dresses cost $43.84 (EHG, Feb. 17, 1886). Whenever she had extra cash, Emily bought special presents for her children, including jewelry, pens, albums, and ink wells. In addition, she paid their tuition at a private academy, where they could associate with "young ladies & gentlemen" (EHG, Nov. 10, 1879). Her great regret was that she lacked sufficient money to send them to college. Helping her impoverished father, however, had no place on her agenda.

By the spring of 1884, furthermore, Emily's conjugal relationship had reached a nadir. She viewed James as a danger to her physical and emotional well-being. According to her account, he was subject to both deep depressions and uncontrollable rages and threatened her with physical abuse. Money was a major source of marital strife. Emily and James fought over who made the greatest economic contribution to the farm and who should be responsible for paying their joint expenses. During the spring of 1884, their fights focused increasingly on Emily's possession of the deed to the farm. Earlier, in 1874, Emily had written exultantly in her dairy, "James gave me

a Deed of his farm, indeed I can hardly express my feelings of gratitude for his placing so very much confidence in me as to entrust to my honor the keeping of his hard
earned property" (EHG, Jan. 4, 1874). Eleven years later, she acknowledged that
James's action represented fear of potential creditors more than faith in his wife (see
Lebsock, 1984). Regardless of James's motive, however, Emily viewed possession of
the deed as no mere formality, and she was determined to keep it.

Because this deed occupies a central position in this story, its significance requires
detailed discussion. A major focus of nineteenth-century feminist activity was the
property rights of married women. As Basch (1982) notes, feminists believed that the
legal disabilities of wives constituted one of the most egregious examples of women's
inferior status. During the middle decades of the century, some states began to expand the rights of married women to own and control property in their own names
(Basch, 1982; Shammas, Salmon, and Dahlin, 1987); Iowa enacted such a statute in
1851 (Riley, 1981). Although historians debate the extent to which this legislation
affected women's status, contemporaries attached enormous significance to it (see
Basch, 1982).

Emily was a strong supporter of the women's movement and a fervent proponent
of the rights of married women. Although suffrage began to replace the marital property system as the most critical feminist issue by the end of the nineteenth-century,
the legal disabilities of wives continued to consume Emily's attention. In her diary,
she wrote frequently about the need for all women to achieve economic independence. Her struggle to keep the deed must be viewed within this context. Possession of
the deed did not allow her to control the operation of the farm (Lensink, 1989), but
she believed it would give her a say in any intergenerational transfer. Above all, she
wanted to divide the property equally between her two children. Although her father
had followed tradition in giving the farm to his son alone, Emily believed she had
suffered a grave injustice. By ensuring that her daughter received her fair share of the
Gillespie property, Emily could prevent such an injustice from recurring.

Possession of the deed also had another meaning for Emily. As her marriage deteriorated, she grew increasingly terrified that if James regained legal title to the land,
he would expel her and her children. We will see that Emily's father was partly responsible for making this prophecy come true.

Emily's most satisfying relationships were with her children. In 1884, Henry was
21 and Sarah 19. Like other women who attach great importance to their maternal
duties, Emily made an enormous investment in her offspring, expecting them to fill
the void left by the absence of other significant bonds. By the spring of 1884, however, her children had begun to leave home. In September 1882, Henry was the first
to go, spending 6 months as a peddler in Nebraska County, 120 miles from the farm.
During the winter of 1883–4, he spent a term at a college in Michigan. At other
times, he found work reasonably close to the farm but still had to board away from
home at least part of the time. Sarah followed the "escape route" of large numbers of
other young Iowan farm women, beginning a teaching career in 1883 (see Riley,
1981). Like other nineteenth-century rural school teachers, she boarded at the homes
of her students during the term (Kaufman, 1984). Although both Henry and Sarah
returned home repeatedly, Emily's grief increasingly dominated her life. In January
1884, she wrote, "My children – *they are gone – they that are so dear. How lonely it
is here in this big house all alone, the tears will start for I do miss them so much*"

(EHG, Jan. 30, 1884). Her sorrow diminished her resources for coping with her father's demands.

Emily's alienation from her family of birth was still another factor affecting her ability to render care. In the absence of telephones, automobiles, and paved roads, mobility often severely disrupted familial relationships. After leaving home at the age of 22, Emily corresponded with her parents and visited them twice in Michigan, but she considered herself outside the family circle.

The only sibling to whom she remained close was her sister Harriet; by 1884, however, this tie also had fractured. Harriet had come to Iowa in September 1869 and stayed with Emily for 2 years. Although Harriet taught school, she also helped with the housework. Emily's two children were young, and she was grateful for her sister's assistance. When Emily went to nurse her dying mother-in-law for two days in November 1869, she noted, "Hattie does all my work. – how good she is" (EHG, Nov. 6, 1869). After Harriet married John McGee and moved to his farm, the two women preserved an intimate bond and continued to exchange goods and services. Emily assisted Harriet during each of her five confinements as well as after an abortion; Emily's children occasionally spent the night with Harriet. In November 1873, Emily reported that she was sewing a cloak for Harriet's baby; Harriet, in turn, would knit for her. Emily also relied on Harriet for emotional support. "We all go & make Harriet a visit," Emily wrote in January 1874, "How glad I was to go – yes indeed! I rather visit her than any one else this side of the Mississippi" (EHG, Jan. 28, 1874). Six months later, she wrote, "Harriet here most all day, *was glad* she came for I had the blues" (EHG, Aug. 21, 1874). And in June 1875 she reported having had "a *good* visit with Harriet all day" (EHG, June 8, 1875).

The relationship cooled considerably when Harriet's fortunes declined during the agricultural depression of the 1870s. Although large numbers of farms failed at this time, Emily blamed Harriet for her plight. When Harriet and John owed "debts to the amount of *twenty-six hundred dollars*" in October 1876, Emily noted that they had been "advised to do different" (EHG, Oct. 1, 1876). Emily's sympathy eroded still further after Harriet and her husband lost their farm. When Harriet failed to return a garden tool promptly, Emily wrote, "I wanted to dig some roots in the garden this afternoon, our potatoe-fork was down to Harriets. I was provoked that I had to go after it – when I was so tired . . . when I work & get things to use I do not like to have them gone when I want them . . . I hope . . . it may learn them a lesson that they can not always expect some one of their relatives to help them, they must work to a better advantage for them-selves" (EHG, May 9, 1881).

Emily also chastised Harriet for losing the middle-class life-style that she herself strove so hard to cultivate. "Oh dear!" Emily wrote in August 1883, "She does seem to have fallen from all the refinement she ever had . . . she looks more like a beggar than any thing else . . . indeed I am sorry. I do think women ought to retain enough of their pride to keep themselves in a shape proper to their sex" (EHG, Aug. 15, 1883). Although the two sisters continued to visit back and forth, they never reestablished their former intimacy.

The death of her mother in 1882 increased Emily's sense of isolation from her family. Their attachment had been especially strong, and her grief engulfed the pages of her diary for several months. The death also precipitated a major clash between Emily and her siblings. In July 1882, she had responded angrily to a suggestion from her brother Henry that Harriet receive the bulk of their mother's clothes and other personal items. As Emily wrote in her diary, "Henry seems to think that most of her things ought to be given to Harriet for he thinks she needs them. It may be she needs them yet I think what belongs rightfully to [me] should not be given to some one else. except by the owner of such things" (EHG, July 30, 1882). When their mother's effects arrived in Iowa in October, Emily was shocked to discover that Harriet's box contained five times as much as her own. The sale of the family farm occurred nine months later, adding insult to injury. Because Emily had considered herself entitled to receive a portion of her parents' property, she felt especially aggrieved when Henry kept the proceeds of the sale himself. In May 1883, Emily recorded her anger:

> Brother Henry wrote . . . "*they had sold their place* and it gave him *a chance to look for* a home." More likely it gives him a chance to spend the rest of *What Father & Mother worked for*, I feel as if tis the last of their earthly possessions, gone, gone – though I wish Henry no harm it seems to me he cannot prosper with that which is not rightfully his, had he have let us girls each have $200.00 – it would have been no more than right. (EHG, May 23, 1883)

Emily's six-week visit to her family in Michigan in March and April 1884 did little to heal the breach with her siblings. Soon after her arrival, she learned that Harriet had written a letter to the rest of their family "slandering" Emily and her children. The contents of the letter were too "horrid" to be recorded in her journal (EHG, March 6, 1884). Her brother Henry's economic situation was even more desperate than Emily had feared. Although he was responsible for the support of a wife and several children as well as his father, he had lost most of the proceeds from the sale of his parents' farm. "Everywhere I go," Emily wrote, "I hear of Henry drinking & playing pool, *it is too bad*" (EHG, March 10, 1884). He claimed to be searching for work, but she believed he had deserted his family.

Although the other sister, Edna, worked hard, Emily was almost as contemptuous of her. Married to a struggling farmer, she used poor grammar, had few ambitions for her children, shunned "the best" society, and had "lost all her pride in keeping things tidy and clean" (EHG, April 10, 1884). Moreover, Edna expressed "unpleasant feelings" toward Emily. "I try to make all agreeable," Emily complained, "but Edna acts as if she had orders what to do and say" (EHG, April 10, 1884).

## Father and Daughter

This was Emily's first meeting with her father in 18 years. Although she pronounced him "real glad to see me," he failed to recognize her at first (EHG, March 6, 1884). In some ways he was unchanged. His views on women's rights, for example, remained antithetical to hers: "He is just the same as ever to talk [to] on subjects of Religion, Politics, Temperance and Woman-Suffrage, he still thinks it is not quite in place for a lady to vote" (EHG, March 7, 1884). But he also had become an "old man" who walked "with two canes" (EHG, April 2, 1884; May 7, 1884). Although he tried to help with the household labor, it was "pretty hard work for him to do the chores," and he lay "on the couch a good share of his time" (EHG, March 10, 1884;

April 5, 1884). Because he had exhausted his resources and could no longer rely on Henry, his future looked bleak.

Emily had first expressed a desire to assist her father when she entered a lottery in January 1884, two months before her trip to Michigan. "Should I be so fortunate as to draw a prize I shall try to take care of Father the rest of his life," she promised (EHG, Jan. 23, 1884). When she failed to win, she wrote nothing further about caring for him. When she visited her father in March, she assured him that he always "would have a place" with her (April 2, 1884); but she was confident that he would not take up her offer.

She was stunned, therefore, when he appeared on her doorstep six weeks later. On May 15, Emily's daughter Sarah described the shock of his arrival: "Last night just as we had retired, and were about to enter in the sweet slumber of ten o'clock: we were quickly awakened by a loud knock, and who should appear but Grandpa Hawley" (SGH, May 15, 1884). Emily recorded her own dismay in her diary:

> I feel it an imposition upon us all – after Henry has squandered *all* he had, then leave him, poor old man, in the streets. . . . I will do the best I can and see what we can do about it, most surely I do not feel able to take care of him, my health is too poor and I can not conscientiously [sic] keep Sarah at home to do the work, she wants to teach and earn something for herself. And it would cost more than we could earn to hire help. (EHG, May 15, 1884)

She was even more enraged when his possessions followed: "Fathers *box* of things came, he went with James after them . . . his big arm chair came too, it looks to me as if there was something wrong about him coming here as he has for a genuine visit, can it be he is deserted by them who has had his property?" (EHG, May 26, 1884).

Despite Emily's feminist sympathies, she believed that she and her daughter – rather than her husband and son – were responsible for providing domestic services. Although she nourished high hopes for her daughter's career, she assumed that women should do all the housework. Moreover, she would have liked to conform to the reigning concept of a dutiful daughter. Just as she had felt obliged to invite her father to stay, now she believed she owed him decent care. But she also assumed that her responsibility was narrowly circumscribed. According to custom, the duty to care accompanied the inheritance (see Osterud, 1991). Because Henry was the only son and had received the family land, Emily believed that the onus fell most heavily on him. Gilligan (1982) argues that women tend to subscribe to an ethic of care, men to a morality of rights. But Emily thought in terms of equity and justice, not human connectedness and personal responsibility. Because she had received less than her share of the parental property, her moral obligation was proportionately small. In addition, Emily believed that her first loyalty was to her children, and she wished to husband her resources to further their mobility.

If Emily viewed her father as an "imposition," she also realized that her sister resented her responsibility. Harriet was jealous that Hial had chosen Emily's home rather than her own, claiming that Emily had known beforehand of their father's visit but kept it secret. Sarah wrote that when Hial refused Harriet's invitation to spend a week at her house, "she started off crying" and accused Emily of stopping him (SGH, May 16, 1884). Harriet's sense of anger and betrayal suggests that, at least at this point, responsibility for their father was an honor as well as a burden.

At first Emily tried to behave like a good daughter. Hial's plight aroused her sympathy. When he seemed "despondent," she comforted him, promising to "make it as pleasant for him as I can" (EHG, May 18, 1884). She also welcomed him by making up "a nice bed" for him in the sewing room and carefully putting away his clothes and papers. When he tried to work around the farm, she encouraged him to rest. She refused payment for making him a coat.

Emily, in turn, received Hial's support. He gave her a $1,000 note he held against his son Henry and expressed the hope that she "would collect every cent interest and all" (EHG, May 28, 1884). He also told her that he had defended her against the criticisms of her siblings in Michigan. And he took her side against Harriet. After he paid his first visit to Harriet's house, Emily reported, "he does not approve of Harriet talking as she does about me & the children" (EHG, May 18, 1884). A week later Emily wrote that her father found Harriet's family "too noisy for him" (EHG, May 24, 1884). At the end of August, he declared himself "perfectly disgusted with the way Harriet talked" (EHG, Aug. 31, 1884).

Hial's support of Emily's claim to her mother's bureau was especially gratifying. This bureau arrived at the Gillespie house along with Hial's possessions on May 26. Although Harriet argued that their mother had left the bureau to her, Emily found an inscription on the bottom, proving her ownership. On May 27, she wrote, "When I was washing the last drawer (the small one that I kept my trinkets in when I lived at home) I beheld on the underside of it where Mother had written on two different times that she wanted me to have her beauro [sic] when she was dead & gone, it seems to me as from the dead" (EHG, May 27, 1884). Because Emily cherished material possessions and demonstrated affection through gifts, this bequest symbolized her mother's love. "I have always felt that Mother loved me above all others. but could not know it until to day," she wrote, "it seemed almost when I read her gift to me that she came to tell me" (EHG, May 27, 1884). She was even more delighted when her father expressed his pleasure at the resolution of the dispute. "Now Father loves me, too – best of his children," she proclaimed (EHG, May 28, 1884).

It is not clear why the relationship between Emily and her father soon soured. She claimed that both James and Harriet turned him against her, portraying her as lazy and deceitful. Because we have no access to Hial's version of events, we can only speculate about how he perceived their relationship. We do know, however, that by the time he came to Emily's house, he had suffered several major blows. Historians frequently note that nineteenth-century men experienced a precipitous drop in status when they forfeited their positions as household heads (Gratton, 1986; Hareven, 1986; Smith, 1979; see Haber, 1983). After relinquishing his farm, Hial Hawley no longer could wield power over his children; instead, he was dependent on them. The death of his wife, his departure from Michigan, and his failing health also represented major losses. He could not rely on his son for assistance and was terrified that he soon would have no place to live. Edna and Harriet were too poor to take him in. As Emily acknowledged, she was his "last resort." But the evidence indicates that Hial hated his dependency. As we have seen, he sought to pay his way in so far as possible and contribute to the work of the farm.

Although we cannot know how Emily treated her father, her diary suggests that she did little to bolster his dignity and self-esteem. He remained an object of pity in the pages of her journal. "Poor old man," she wrote often, or "I feel so sorry for him." A cardinal principle of contemporary gerontologists is that the elderly are not children; whatever disabilities they suffer, they deserve all the rights and privileges of adults. But Emily repeatedly implied that her father had regressed to childhood. When reminded of his financial situation, for example, he "cried like a child" (EHG, May 17, 1884). Emily also demonstrated her low esteem for her father by placing his needs beneath those of her offspring. Emily's principal injury to his pride seems to have been her disparagement of his work. His labor, she repeatedly claimed, was primarily therapeutic; he worked only because "he wants something to do." And he had difficulty accomplishing the chores he undertook. He hoed "too close" to the strawberry vines (EHG, May 22, 1884). When he sawed wood, "his cane went into a hole, – he fell against a post & hurt his face" (EHG, June 6, 1884). Two months later, he "fell down three times" while pulling weeds in the garden (EHG, Aug. 12, 1884).

But Hial did not passively accept the subservient status his daughter assigned him. If she belittled him because of his age and infirmities, he expressed contempt for all women. According to Sarah, he continued to argue that women should be denied the vote, and he expressed disapproval of Sarah's driving a carriage. "Grandpa can't bear to see a woman be anybody," Sarah complained (SGH, Sept. 6, 1884). Hial also asserted his independence by allying himself with James. The two men spent their days together, and Hial increasingly took James's side in the conflicts that raged within the household. On July 31, both men "laughed" at Emily's account of her attempts to make money (SGH, July 31, 1884). Emily displayed less and less sympathy for her father. Just as she blamed Harriet for her misfortunes, so Emily held her father responsible for his impoverishment. In giving up his farm, she noted, he had disregarded the sound advice he had received. Emily also feared that her siblings had conspired to send their father to her and now were ridiculing her. And Emily complained that Hial increasingly resembled James. He withdrew repeatedly into silence. On the rare occasions when he spoke, he was "sarcastic and cross" (EHG, Oct. 22, 1884). On November 1, she wrote, "it is sometimes as much as I can endure . . . continually being obliged to be on my guard to be able to be calm at all times – two such men to deal with" (EHG, Nov. 1, 1884). Communications with her father – like those with her husband – began to consist solely of mutual recriminations.

Her son Henry's accident in October may have weakened Emily's ability to tolerate her father's actions. Henry had been helping to rebuild a church spire when he fell 74 feet. Emily nursed him around the clock for 2 weeks. Although he recovered, she worried for many months that he would be permanently disabled.

By the end of October, Hial was spending increasing amounts of time at Harriet's house. Early in November, Emily lamented, "When he first came he said . . . that Harriet tried to set him up against me and make trouble between him & me but she could not & now he has sided with her" (EHG, Nov. 2, 1884).

On November 7, seven months after his arrival, Hial announced that he would move permanently to Harriet's house. Although stung by his defection, Emily agreed to pack his possessions. But conflicts continued to erupt after his departure. He asked for the two dollars he had given her to buy a present; she responded that the amount was just $1.75. When he demanded the return of Henry's $1,000 note, she asked for compensation for the sheep she had lent him 25 years earlier. Their worst fight concerned the bureau. He insisted on taking this heirloom to Harriet's house, but Emily refused, reminding him that it had been passed down through the female line. She had received it from her mother, who had bought it with money she received from her own mother. When he threatened to sue, she finally admitted defeat. "Dear-a-me," Emily wrote on December 16 when he came to collect the bureau, "I felt as if he stole it from me & from the dead & that I believed it would haunt him every night of his life" (EHG, Dec. 16, 1884). As she later commented, the loss of this cherished possession demonstrated the legal power of men. "Father took it just because he could," she wrote in January 1885 (EHG, Jan. 8, 1885).

Hial was indirectly responsible for inflicting a still more grievous injury on Emily. In March 1885 James informed her that she would remain liable for her father's financial support unless she relinquished the title to the farm. (In many states, children had economic responsibility for their parents [see Achenbaum, 1978].) Just as James once had signed over the deed to her as a way of hiding from potential creditors, so Emily now had to return it in order to avoid liability for her father's support. But she remained terrified of the consequences. "I dare not give James a deed," she wrote, "for fear he may in one of his spells turn us all out of door" (EHG, March 12, 1885). Her daughter shared her concern. "Pa now thinks we are in his clutches," Sarah commented (SGH, March 12, 1885). Although Emily consulted her own lawyer, she was advised to surrender the property, and on April 2, she returned to the lawyer's office to do so. "*I gave James a deed of the farm*," she wrote, "*indeed I felt as though it was signing myself out of a house*" (EHG, April 2, 1885). She placed the primary blame on her father; as she wrote months later, Hial "has finished up my ruin" (EGH, Sept. 28, 1885).

Emily and her children continued to live on the farm for two-and-a-half years after she relinquished title. In the summer of 1886, however, Emily and James separated, and the following summer James forced Emily and her children to leave the farm and rent rooms in town. Here her children cared for her until she died in March 1888.

Hial's departure had still other negative consequences. Emily had to confront her own feelings of guilt and failure. She found it difficult to preserve her self-image as a good woman in the face of her father's refusal to acknowledge her existence. The experience also damaged Emily's reputation in the community. According to James, a rumor circulated that she had expelled her father after making him work at her house all summer.

Hial's situation remained difficult. Although Harriet initially was jealous that her father chose to live with Emily, she also found him a trial. In February 1885, Emily wrote that Harriet was having a "terrible time with Father" (EHG, Feb. 13, 1885). In June, having exhausted his children's good will, he was compelled to apply to the local authorities for assistance (EHG, June 6, 1885). (Since the first English colonies in America, care for destitute elderly people had been a local government responsibility [Quadagno, 1986].)

### Discussion

Despite our sentimental image of several generations living harmoniously under one roof in the nineteenth-century, Hial Hawley's 7-month stay at his daughter's house was marked by rancor and acrimony. The two fought with increasing frequency and bitterness. Although Hial remained in the neighborhood after leaving Emily's home, all communication between them soon ceased. His visit also intensified Emily's ongoing battle with her sister Harriet. The women competed for their father's affection and contested his one valuable possession. And Hial's presence exacerbated Emily's marital conflict. She accused James of slandering her to her father; James charged that her poor filial relationship was further proof of her difficult personality. The accidents of personal history can help to explain how this story unfolded. Emily's intense desire for upward mobility made her reluctant to share resources with any extended kin. Her alienation from her natal family weakened her sense of filial responsibility. And both the decline of her health and the deterioration of her marriage undermined her ability to render care.

But, if some aspects of this story expressed the particularities of Emily's and Hial's personalities and the idiosyncracies of their relationship, this episode also reveals larger patterns. Jealousy about the division of parental property and household goods is common. Even when nineteenth-century parents followed traditional practices, sibling rivalries frequently erupted (see Osterud, 1991). Moreover, although Emily's concern with exercising control over her property may have been extreme, she was not alone in her desire to influence inheritance. The marital property system was one of the most fiercely contested issues in nineteenth-century gender relations, and many wives struggled for power over the intergenerational transfer of land.

This episode suggests that the elderly did not gracefully accept their degradation. I have noted that many Americans viewed old people as useless and unproductive by the end of the nineteenth-century. Hial Hawley's desire to participate in the farm work demonstrates his determination not to be consigned to the ranks of the superannuated. When Emily refused to respect his dignity or value his labor, he responded by joining James in belittling Emily and depriving her of a cherished heirloom.

In the end, Emily's economic responsibility for her father and legal subordination to her husband combined to reduce her to Hial's level. In order to avoid her financial obligation, Emily had to surrender the deed to the farm. Two-and-a-half years later, her husband forced her off it. Without a home of her own, she became dependent on her children for support.

The inferior status of women and the elderly in the late 1800s can help to explain why neither Emily nor Hial could win their struggle for control. Each could undermine the other's limited power but neither could escape the structures of subordination.

In many ways, the position of women and elderly people has improved dramatically since that time. For example, the phenomenal rise in female labor force participation allows at least some women to achieve the economic independence denied to Emily Gillespie. A variety of income maintenance and health care programs established since 1935 insulate the great majority of elderly people from many of the problems besetting Hial Hawley. But structural barriers of age and gender remain intact. The physical attributes of women and elderly people continue to serve as rationalizations for trivializing their activities and devaluing their contributions. The mutually destructive relationship between Hial and Emily highlights the need to create a society that accords greater respect to both groups.

This case study also illuminates the impact of financial obligations on intergenerational relationships. Had Emily been responsible only for ministering to her father's physical and emotional needs, she still might have resented the burden he imposed. But his need for economic support clashed with her desire for financial independence, creating unbearable strains, exaggerating her sense of deprivation, and aggravating the anger and bitterness she harbored toward her siblings. During the early 1980s, the Reagan administration tried to reinstitute filial economic responsibilities (Scott, 1983; see Callahan, 1985; Rivlin and Wiener, 1988). Proponents of such obligations often view them as a means of promoting family solidarity (see Quadagno, 1986). This story reminds us that financial responsibilities can fracture as well as consolidate family relationships.

It also underscores the need to provide far greater support for caregivers. A host of recent studies demonstrate that daughters caring for elderly parents continue to experience physical, emotional, social, and financial problems. In many cases, caregiving responsibilities reignite family conflicts, encroach on other activities, and impose stress. Although few daughters provide economic assistance to their parents, some quit their jobs in order to render care, and others reduce their hours of work (see Abel, 1991). As long as filial responsibilities demand enormous personal sacrifice, many adult daughters will find it difficult to provide decent care to aging parents.

## Acknowledgment

This research was funded by the UCLA Center for the Study of Women. The diaries of Emily Hawley Gillespie and Sarah Gillespie Huftalen are quoted with permission of the State Historical Society of Iowa. The author also wishes to thank Judy Nolte Lensink and Suzanne Bunkers for their help.

## References

Abel, E. K. (1991). *Who cares for the elderly? Public policy and the experiences of adult daughters*. Philadelphia: Temple University Press.
Achenbaum, W. A. (1974). The obsolescence of old age in America, 1865–1914. *The Journal of Social History*, 8 (Fall), 48–62.
Achenbaum, W. A. (1978). *Old age in the new land*. Baltimore: Johns Hopkins University Press.
Axinn, J., and Stern, M. J. (1985). Age and dependency: Children and the aged in American social policy. *Milbank Memorial Fund Quarterly/Health and Society*, 63(4), 648–70.
Basch, N. (1982). *In the eyes of the law: Women, marriage, and property in nineteenth-century New York*. Ithaca: Cornell University Press.
Callahan, D. (1985). What do children owe elderly parents? *The Hastings Center Report*, April, 32–37.
Callahan, Jr., J. J., Diamond, L. D., Giele, J. Z., and Morris, R. (1980). Responsibility of families for their severely disabled elders. *Health Care Financing Review*, Winter, 29–48.
Cole, T. R. (1980). *Past meridan: Aging and the northern middle class*, 1830–1930. Unpublished doctoral dissertation, University of Rochester, Rochester, NY.
Commonwealth Fund Commission on Elderly People Living Alone (1988). *Aging alone: Profiles and projections*. Baltimore: Author.
Congressional Budget Office, Congress of the U.S. (1988). *Changes in the living arrangements of the elderly*: 1960–2030. Washington, DC: U.S. Government Printing Office.
Crystal, S. (1982). *America's old age crisis: Public policy and the two worlds of aging*. New

York: Basic Books.

Dahlin, M. (1980). Perspectives on the family life of the elderly in 1900. *The Gerontologist*, 20, 99–107.

Elbert, S. (1987). The farmer takes a wife: Women in America's farming families. In L. Benerea and C. Stimson (Eds.), *Women, households, and the economy* (pp. 173–97). New Brunswick: Rutgers University Press.

Fischer, D. H. (1977). *Growing old in America*. New York: Oxford University Press.

Gillespie, Emily Hawley, Diary, State Historical Society of Iowa, Iowa City, (EHG).

Gilligan, C. (1982). *In a different voice: Psychological theory and women's development*. Cambridge, MA: Harvard University Press.

Gratton. B. (1986). The new history of the aged: A critique. In D. Van Tassel and P. N. Stearns (Eds.), *Old age in a bureaucratic society: The elderly, the experts and the state in American society* (pp. 3–24). Westport, CT: Greenwood Press.

Haber, C. (1983). *Beyond sixty-five: The dilemma of old age in America's past*. Cambridge: Cambridge University Press.

Hareven, T. (1986). Life-course transitions and kin assistance. In D. Van Tassel and P. N. Stearns (Eds.), *Old age in a bureaucratic society: The elderly, the experts and the state in American society* (pp. 110–25). Westport, CT: Greenwood Press.

Huftalen, Sarah Gillespie, Diary, State Historical Society of Iowa, Iowa City (SGH).

Jensen, J. M. (1981). *With these hands: Women working on the land*. Old Westbury, NY: Feminist Press.

Kaufman, P. W. (1984). *Women teachers on the frontier*. New Haven: Yale University Press.

Kessler-Harris, A. (1982). *Out to work: A history of wage earning women in the United States*. New York: Oxford University Press.

Lebsock, S. (1984). *The free women of Petersburg: Status and culture in a southern town, 1784–1869*. New York: W. W. Norton.

Lensink, J. N. (1989). *"A secret to be burried": The diary and life of Emily Hawley Gillespie, 1838–1888*. Iowa City: University of Iowa Press.

Osterud, N. G. (1991). *Bonds of community: The lives of farm women in nineteenth-century New York*. Ithaca: Cornell University Press.

Quadagno, J. (1986). The transformation of old age in a bureaucratic society. In D. Van Tassel and P. N. Stearns (Eds.), *Old age in a bureaucratic society: The elderly, the experts and the state in American society* (pp. 129–55). Westport, CT: Greenwood Press.

Quadagno, J. (1988). *The transformation of old age security: Class and politics in the American welfare state*. Chicago: University of Chicago Press.

Riley, G. (1961). *Frontierswomen: The Iowa experience*. Ames: Iowa State University Press.

Riley, G. (1988). *The female frontier: A comparative view of women on the prairie and the plains*. Lawrence: University Press of Kansas.

Rivlin, A. M., and Wiener, J. M. (1988). *Caring for the disabled elderly: Who will pay?* Washington, DC: Brookings Institution.

Ryan, M. P. (1981). *Cradle of the middle class: The family in Oneida County, New York, 1790–1865*. Cambridge: Cambridge University Press.

Ryan, M. P. (1982). *The empire of mothers: American writings on women and the family, 1830–1860*. New York: Haworth Press.

Schlissel, L., Ruiz, V. L., and Monk, J. (Eds). (1988). *Western women: Their land, their values*. Albuquerque: University of New Mexico.

Scott, J. L. (1983). Associate Administrator for Operations, Health Care Financing Administration, Statement before the House Select Committee on Human Services, May 16.

Shammas, C., Salmon, M., and Dahlin, M. (1987). *Inheritance in America from colonial times to the present*. New Brunswick, NJ: Rutgers University Press.

Sklar, K. K., and Dublin, T. (1991). Introduction. In K. K. Sklar and T. Dublin (Eds.), *Women and power in American history: A reader*, Vol. I. Englewood Cliffs, NJ: Prentice Hall.

Smith, D. S. (1979). Life course, norms, and the family system of older Americans in 1900. *Journal of Family History*, 4(3), 285–96.

Smith, D. S. (1986). Accounting for change in the families of the elderly in the United States, 1900–present. In D. Van Tassel and P. N. Stearns (Eds.), *Old age in a bureaucratic society: The elderly, the experts, and the state in American society* (pp. 87–109). Westport, CT: Greenwood Press.

Strasser, S. (1982). *Never done: A history of American housework*. New York: Pantheon Books.

# 17 An Old Age Community

## Arlie Russell Hochschild

Mrs. Clark's Typical Day:

"(Morning) I get up about seven in the morning. Then I fix a little breakfast and have my breakfast. Then I clean the dishes and start in cleaning the house. Dust, scrub, washin' and just general house-cleaning. Sometimes I wash or iron and do things like that.

(Afternoon) A little before noon I prepare a little lunch. I usually have lunch about noon. I clean the dishes, and if I can, I gad about. I usually visit (a relative). Sometimes I just watch TV or sometimes I straighten things around the house.

(Evening) I usually prepare a little supper to have it ready by about five. Then I wash the dishes and usually watch TV the rest of the evening."[1]

> "Utterly boring. I certainly hope that won't be my typical day at 69."

> "She's in a rut. She should get involved in the community around her. Why doesn't she do something constructive?"

> "It's kind of wasteful, but if that's what she wants to do – let her do her own thing."[2]

## Evolution of a Subculture

Most of the widows who moved into Merrill Court had lost their husbands within the last five years. Aside from five who knew one another casually, the widows were strangers before 1965.[3]

The story of how a collection of near-strangers became a community has several versions. Almost from the start, there was a structure of parallel leadership, as in the nineteenth-century British and French colonies. As Freda, the first "indigenous" leader tells it, "There wasn't nothin' before we got the coffee machine. I mean we didn't share nothin' before Mrs. Bitford's daughter brought over the machine and we sort of had our first occasion, you might say." There were about six people at the first gathering around the coffee machine in the Recreation Room. As people came downstairs from their apartments to fetch their mail in mid-morning, they looked into the Recreation Room, found a cluster of people sitting down drinking coffee, and some joined in. A few weeks later the Recreation Director "joined in" for the morning coffee, and as she tells it, the community had its start at this point. She had formerly worked at a bowling alley nearby and, as she put it:

> I went to see Ted at the alleys and I worked out a special season rate for the seniors. We organized teams and always got Lanes 6 and 7 from 2 to 3 on Tuesdays. People actually got to know each other bowling. I drove them there and back and at the end of the year we had a "do" for the winning team and the best bowler.

Original publication: Hochschild, Arlie Russell, "An Old Age Community," from *The Unexpected Community* (University of California Press, Berkeley, 1973), pp. 37–71.

Half a year later Merrill Court was a beehive of activity: meetings of a Service Club, which was soon set up; bowling; morning workshop; Bible study classes twice a week; monthly birthday parties; and visits to four nearby nursing homes. Members donated cakes, pies, and soft drinks to bring to the nursing home, and a five-piece band, including a washtub bass, played for the "old folks" there. The band also entertained at a nearby recreation center for a group of Vietnam veterans. During afternoon band practice, the women sewed and embroidered pillow cases, aprons, and yarn dolls. They made wastebaskets out of discarded paper towel rolls, wove rugs from strips of old Wonder Bread wrappers, and Easter hats out of old Clorox bottles, all to be sold at the annual bazaar. They made placements to be used at the nursing home, tote-bags to be donated to "our boys in Vietnam," Christmas cards to be cut out for the Hillcrest Junior Women's Club, rag dolls to be sent to the orphanage, place cards to be written out for the bowling league banquet, recipes to be written out for the recipe book that was to go on sale next month, and thank you and condolence cards.

All this activity had a special meaning for the widows. Through it they defined what was work and what was leisure, what was "on" time and what was "off" time. This meaning could easily be lost in a behaviorist study. A behaviorist doing research[4] at Merrill Court might note the following. At 9:00 o'clock, one woman entered the Recreation Room, gathered materials, and began making yarn dolls. At 9:10, two other women entered the room, sat down, and did the same. Within half an hour, nine or ten others were assembled at the table, cutting pieces of yarn, wrapping and tying them into different shapes, and putting them in a large pile. One woman with a lame arm, who had been sitting and watching, was handed some of the finished dolls, which she wrapped with one hand. The women looked at one another, talked, laughed, and continually handled the yarn. One woman patted two others on the back. Another entered the room, was hugged and kissed, took off her coat, and began to handle the yarn. At 10:00 o'clock two got up, made coffee, and served it to the rest. At 10:30 they all went out to the mail room and returned with letters. Several read their letters aloud. One woman began singing and was watched while the others continued handling the yarn. At noon, four or five women left the room and returned with dishes of food.

What was going on? What meaning did this activity have for the people involved? Was it work or was it leisure? All the women were living on social welfare, social security, or pensions, and in the eyes of society they were not workers. They earned no pay and had no employer, paid no taxes, and punched no time clocks. They came to the Recreation Room voluntarily and a decision to come downstairs to work was a decision about what to do with their leisure. But if you asked them, they would tell you they were working. They jokingly talked about being on "company time" and talked about what they would do when they were "free" to attend to their own affairs. It was written into the weekly schedule on the bulletin board as "workshop" and if one of the regulars failed to come down, she was called and reminded. If people came only to talk, they were quietly handed work.

I should say at this point that what follows is not written from a behaviorist perspective, since the focus of this study is not on behavior *per se* but on its meanings. In particular, it focuses on the meaning of roles and relationships – the formal ones downstairs and the informal ones upstairs; the ones at the top of the social ladder and the ones at the bottom; the ones based on earned status and the ones based on "luck" status. Having described these, I will then play back over the descriptions, showing how they illustrate aspects of the special "sibling bond" that emerged between social equals and that forestalls the isolation of the old.

Thus, the morning's activities downstairs meant work. The residents also described them as "enjoyable," but the enjoyment was incidental to getting the yarn dolls finished and ready to sell at the annual bazaar. The money from the sale was used to "have fun" seeing a movie or the Ice Follies, dining out, or touring California. The official principle was "work now to have fun later." Yet the work itself was interspersed with eating, talking, and (as the woman in the behavioral description above was doing), singing ballads.

Strung on this web of sociability, then, was a value on work, on being productive. Even the dead, once they were gone, were evaluated according to their work. For example, when one widow died, people mentioned that she had worked all year on the bazaar and had died just before the trip to the Ice Follies. They regretted her absence but posthumously praised her for being "such a good worker," not for her ability to enjoy things. Irma, a farmer's widow from West Texas, compared the work downstairs to an old-fashioned "workin' in." As she put it,

> Neighbors would come in and help out if you were takin' in a harvest or doin' some cannin'. One time our barn burned down and we had another one up in two days. Doin' it together we got more done, see? I met my husband at a workin' in.[5]

Other occasions were for "pure" fun. There were, for example, the parties to celebrate birthdays, Thanksgiving, Christmas, Easter, Halloween; and there was some dispute about what to do with St. Patrick's Day. By the third year there was a potluck luncheon every other week for residents only and on alternate weeks, luncheons for outsiders. Following the potluck dinners there were post-potluck luncheons to use up leftovers. Also, food salesmen, kitchenware sellers, hobby experts, and hairdressers came to demonstrate their goods. After the demonstrations, tin-working or basket-weaving classes might be established, only to disband a month or so later. Once a week there was "Recreation Day," which was called "Game Day" until objections were voiced: "That sounds like kid stuff. We're not children, you know." On this day they played card games such as Cheat Your Neighbor, Aggravation, or Canasta. Only eight were regular players. A number did not play because "their religion was against it," although they would nonetheless sit on the sidelines each week making comments to that effect: "I never played a game of cards nor touched a drop of liquor."[6]

Both work and play were somebody's responsibility to organize. The Merrill Court Service Club, to which most of the residents and a half-dozen non-residents belonged, set up committees and chairmanships that split the jobs many ways. There was a group of permanent elected officials: the President, Vice-President, Treasurer, Secretary, and a Birthday Chairman, in addition to the Recreation Director. Each activity also had a chairman and each chairman was in charge of a group of volunteers. Offices that were rotated during the year included the Chairman of the Flower Fund, Chairman of Publicity, "Sunshine" Chairman (who sent out condolence and get-well cards). "Secret Pal" Chairman (who arranged for gifts to be given anonymously on birthdays and at Christmas), and the Chairman of the Bowling League banquet. Only four club members did not chair some activity between 1965 and 1968; and at any time about a third were in charge of something. There was an annual election of officers by secret ballot followed by installation of officers – the biggest affair of the year. Outgoing officers usually stood up to accept a long round of applause; and those who had been applauded became, in time, vigorous applauders.

## Issues

As activities gradually became more communal, certain customs, in competition with others, became known as "our way" of doing things. Consensus on what was "our way" was questioned only when an issue arose; or rather, a disagreement became an issue when it was unclear whose side others would take.

For example, Ada, a former shipyard cleaning woman in World War II and an acknowledged hard worker, was making wastebaskets. She made them from discarded paper towel rolls that the residents donated and with glue, paint, and scissors that the Recreation Department donated. The wastebaskets were to be sold at the annual bazaar, the proceeds of which went to the Service Club's kitty (called "mad money"), which in turn financed the members' excursions. An issue arose when Ada asked if she could keep two of the twenty baskets she had made, to give her children for Christmas. Ernestine, a Canadian carpenter's wife, complained: "I've knitted twelve pairs of socks and I gave every one to the bazaar. If we all took what we made, there'd be a small heap to sell. How far could we get on that kind of money?" Every day for a week thereafter conversations usually got around to "Ada's basket problem." Some people, especially those who made items for the bazaar, sympathized with the aggrieved, and others did not. The issue questioned the boundary between public and private property, between public and private time.

The solution – that the baskets were public property – was at first accepted only by the five important officers. After an incubation period, during which other opinions were privately assessed, a tentative consensus emerged. Only after the bazaar and the trip following it did most others come around on the issue. By the time of the next bazaar, the principle "What you make here is public property" was not publicly questioned and the issue had, in the meantime, fallen into the realm of recent tradition: "We've always done it that way."[7]

Other issues – such as whether or not to have formal bylaws, whether to keep the Club's money in a cigar box in the Treasurer's apartment or whether to put it in the bank, whether chairs could be borrowed from the Recreation Room by other organizations without permission, whether non-dues-paying members could go on trips, whether a 40-year-old woman who came to meetings could join the Club, at what age to set the limit for membership, how many potlucks to restrict to residents only – all seemed to follow the same course on the way to becoming precedents.

Whose opinion counted most depended on who knew the most, cared the most, and had the most elaborate suggestions. Only a few had been more than casually involved in voluntary clubs before coming to Merrill Court. These few "old hands" became the culture-carriers from one (age-integrated) sector of society to another (age-separated) sector. Not only she who had experience but she who advocated the most elaborate and official-seeming ritual usually won her point. For example, what was to happen at the yearly Installation of Officers banquet was not entirely a settled matter even by the third year. Harriet, a widow from Wisconsin, suggested to the group a few months before the affair:

> Why don't we have Floyd circle once around and usher Freda (the outgoing officer) to her seat. Then he can circle once around and usher Delia (the incoming President) to the front where Freda was sitting. It looks real nice. That's the way the VFW (Veterans of Foreign Wars) does.

There were a few supportive remarks ("If that's how they do it, that's how it's supposed to be done." and "It looks right to me.") Some suggestions were made about the number of circles Floyd was to make and from which side Freda was to exit and Delia to enter before the ritual settled into people's memories. The few who opposed the "hocus pocus" were reminded that Harriet "knew about these things," and they did not care enough to object.[8] In the same way, details about signing the guest book, handling coats, seating people, and rising for the flag were suggested by a voluntary cultural advisor and ratified by the group. Thus was the social architecture gradually built up and passed into the realm of things "as they have always been." The prehistory of these customs is vague in almost everyone's mind and no one takes responsibility or credit for them now.

In his analysis of secret societies, the German sociologist Georg Simmel made an interesting comparison of the late-nineteenth-century American and German Freemasons. In the United States, where the individual enjoyed relative freedom in the general society, Freemasonry had the most rigorous internal rules and rituals. In Germany, where there was less freedom in the general society, the lodges were internally freer of ritual and more independent from one another. Simmel concluded that man

> . . . needs a certain ratio between freedom and law . . . when he does not receive it from one source, he seeks to supplement what he obtains of the one by the missing quantity of the other, no matter from what additional source, until he has the ratio he needs.[9]

The ritual of Freemasonry is itself, as Simmel points out, objectively often senseless, but it fills a social void.

In society at large, what old people ought or ought not to do is only vaguely defined. The former "should's" and "shouldn't's" that applied to a wife, a worker, or a mother have faded with time. But this was clearly not the case in Merrill Court. If one was no longer a mother to a brood of small children, or a wife, or provider, one was at least the Birthday Chairman or the Treasurer or a member of the Flower Committee. For friends lost through death there were replacements; whenever an apartment was vacated, it was immediately filled by the first on a long list of applicants at the housing agency. If there was no longer work that "had to be done," something like it was there. With each new role came new customs and new notions of the right and wrong of them.

At least in the case of old people, Simmel's fixed ratio of freedom to constraint holds only under certain conditions. The neatly carved roles and finely embroidered rituals might well be what the late American sociologist, Howard Becker, called a "normative reaction to normlessness." This reaction occurs, according to Becker, when one urban sector of society too brusquely invades another, more rural sector,[10] exactly what has happened to the rural farm wives in urban Merrill Court. Merrill Court is a strange mixture of old and new, of a vanishing Oakie culture and a new blue-collar life style, of rural ways in urban settings, of small-town community in mass society, of people oriented toward the young in an age-separated subculture. These internal immigrants to the working-class neighborhoods of West Coast cities and suburbs indeed perceived their new environment through rural and small-town eyes. For example, one woman who had been dress shopping at a department store observed "all those lovely dresses, all stacked like cordwood."[11] Another habitually said, "What d'ya think of them apples?" as a way of saying "What do you think of that?" A favorite saying when one was about to retire was, "Guess I'll go to bed with the chickens tonight." But the farm life they had known was nowhere in sight. They would give directions to the new hamburger joint or hobby shop by describing its relationship to a small stream or big tree. What remained of the old custom of a funeral wake took place at a new funeral parlor with neon signs and printed notices.

It may be that the communal life in Merrill Court had nothing to do with rural ways in an urban setting. Had the widows stayed on the farms and in the small towns they came from, they might have been active in community life there. I do not know. I do know that those who had been involved in community life before remained active, and with the exception of a few mentioned earlier, those who previously had not, became active.

For whatever reason, the widows built themselves an order out of ambiguity, a set of obligations to the outside and to one another where few had existed before. Perhaps this result could be described in Herbert Marcuse's terms[12] as "surplus repression." It is possible to relax in old age, to consider one's social debts paid, and to feel that constraints that do not weigh on the far side of the grave should not weigh on the near side either. But in Merrill Court, the watchfulness of social life, the Protestant stress on industry, thrift, and activity added up to an ethos of keeping one's "boots on," not simply as individuals but as a community.

## Social Patterns

The social arrangements that took root early in the history of Merrill Court later assumed a life of their own. They were designed, as if on purpose, to assure an *ongoing* community. If we were to visually diagram the community, it would look like a social circle on which there are centripedal and centrifugal pressures. The formal role system, centered in the circle, pulled people toward it by giving them work and rewards, and this process went on mainly "downstairs." At the same time, informal loyalty networks fluctuated toward and away from the circle. They became clear mainly "upstairs." Relatives and outsiders pulled the individual away from the circle downstairs and network upstairs although they were occasionally pulled inside both. We will look at the social arrangements both "downstairs" and "upstairs."

## Downstairs: The Biography of a Formal Role

A minor but interesting role "downstairs" was the Secret Pal chairmanship, which in 1967 was filled by a shy, thin woman named Rubie. I shall describe this role to show what it did both for Rubie and for the community. This role, like others, changed hands the Monday after New Year's. After calling for a round of applause for the outgoing chairman, the Recreation Director asked for volunteers. Several tentatively suggested someone else, and Rubie, the first to respond to being nominated, with laughter and side-talk to a neighbor, was declared the Secret Pal Chairman for the year.

She was to see that everyone received a small gift worth no more than $2.00 each Christmas and birthday. Since the gifts were anonymous (given by a secret pal), every anonymous donor had to know the recipient's birthday and what he or she would like in the way of a $2.00 gift. Rubie inherited from her predecessor a roster of names that she updated. People knew whom they gave gifts to, but not whom they received them from, and the Secret Pal Chairman thus manipulated a network of secrets that she gave out selectively. She worked "behind the scenes" and her roster was a point of much joking: "What you got on that list there? Make sure I get somethin' nice."

The arrangement itself resembled the incest taboo in prohibiting emotional alliances between particular pairs of people and inhibiting rivalry. It was an emotional insurance policy, distributing the feeling of "being remembered" evenly throughout the group. It also replaced the family, or tried to, in those cases when a grandmother was forgotten on her birthday.

The work was seasonal. Just before Christmas those who had forgotten asked Rubie who their secret pal was and what she wanted for Christmas. One conscientious former chairman kept an inventory of what each resident received the preceding Christmas and what she wanted the next. As each gift was received, Rubie was called and received part of the credit; or if a birthday went by without a gift being received, part of the blame. There was some dispute about how much responsibility Rubie bore for a forgetful donor. She received many telephone calls and visits from donors and recipients alike, and, in this way, the job enmeshed her in a social network.

Rubie's role was mainly important within Merrill Court, where she was applauded after presents were distributed; outside it, the status was not transferable. Most widows had to explain to uninitiated relatives precisely what a Secret Pal Chairman was and did.[13] Ironically, when insiders went outside, the role diminished in importance; but when outsiders came inside, it shone forth. When, for example, the mayor and head of the Recreation Department attended the Christmas Party, there was a round of speeches praising the industry and dedication of club officers. Outside the subculture, the women were pensioners without major functions in life, and to step outside the subculture was to step down socially, or at least to withdraw from a source of social rewards. This situation might account for the fact that even those with low status inside the community (for example, Beatrice the piano player) preferred to remain stigmatized within rather than to become nothing outside.

The role of Secret Pal Chairman never lasted more than a year, and most roles lasted the three months from one banquet to another.[14] Or rather, the roles lived on but their occupants retired after three months. Hence, responsibility and involvement were widely distributed and new work was always coming up. Over a period of three years, of the six deaths in the building, four of the deceased had jobs, which immediately became available. When Emma returned from the hospital after a minor heart attack, she was offered a role just vacated. The system of offices seemed designed to deal with a "transient" population; if informal friendships were lost through the death of one Secret Pal Chairman, the Secret Pal chairman*ship* lived on impervious.[15]

## Upstairs: The Informal Social Web

Shadowing the formal circle was an informal network of friendships that formed over a cup of coffee in the upstairs apartments. The physical appearance of the apartments told something about the network. Inside, each apartment had a living room, kitchen, bedroom, and porch. The apartments were unfurnished when the women moved in and as one remarked, "We fixed 'em up just the way we wanted. I got this new lamp over to Sears, and my daughter and I bought these new scatter rugs. Felt just like a new bride."

For the most part, the apartments were furnished in a remarkably similar way. Many had American flag stickers outside their doors. Inside, each had a large couch with a floral design, which sometimes doubled as a hide-a-bed where a grandchild might sleep for a weekend. Often a chair, a clock, or picture came from the old home and provided a material link to the past. Most had large stuffed chairs, bowls of homemade artificial flowers, a Bible, and porcelain knickknacks neatly arranged on a table. (When the group was invited to my own apartment for tea, one woman suggested sympathetically that we "had not quite moved in yet" because the apartment seemed bare by comparison.) By the window were potted plants, often grown from a neighbor's slip. A plant might be identified as "Abbie's ivy" or "Ernestine's African violet."

The apartments were so alike to me (although not to the residents) that I was reminded of Leo Tolstoi's short story, "The Death of Ivan Ilych," in which Ivan found and decorated a house just as he himself had fantasized an ideal house, room by room. Although Ivan considered the house an expression of his individuality, it exactly resembled the houses of others in the same social class, with the same aspirations and taste.

There were photographs, usually out of date, of children and grandchildren, and Woolworth pictures of pinkcheeked children on the walls.[16] Less frequently there was a photo of a deceased husband and less frequently still, a photo of a parent. On the living room table or nearby there was usually a photograph album containing pictures of relatives and pictures of the woman herself on a recent visit "back east." Many of the photographs in the album were arranged in the same way. Pictures of children came first and, of those, children with the most children appeared first, and childless children at the end.

The refrigerator almost always told a social story. One contained homemade butter made by the cousin of a woman on the second floor; berry jam made by the woman three doors down; corn bought downstairs in the Recreation Room, brought in by someone's son who worked in a corn-canning factory; homemade Swedish rolls to be given to a daughter when she came to visit; two dozen eggs to be used in cooking, most of which would be given away; as well as bread and fruit, more than enough for one person. Most of the women had once cooked for large families, and Emma, who raised eight children back in Oklahoma, habitually baked about eight times as much corn bread as she could eat. She made the rounds of apartments on her floor distributing the extra bread. The others who also cooked in quantities reciprocated, also gratuitously, with other kinds of food. It was an informal division of labor although no one thought of it that way.

Most neighbors were also friends and friendships, as well as information about them, were mainly confined to each floor. For example, according to Ernestine, "There was a lot of to-do when Mr. Hill decided to remarry. They say Irma (whom he did not marry) was really, you know, disappointed. But now I don't know. I don't live on that floor."

All but four had their *best* friends on the same floor and only a few had a next-best friend on another floor. The more one had friends outside the building, the more one had friends on *other* floors within the building. That is, the wider one's social radius outside the building, the wider it was inside the building as well.

There was a distinction between socializing over a cup of coffee and socializing over a meal. As Irma commented, "Sometimes I see Rosy in the elevator and she says, 'Come on over for a cup of coffee' or else she calls and I shuffle over in my housecoat and slippers." But she added, "There's a problem, when you invite a person to lunch, you can't know where to stop." Potential guests were not hurt not to be invited for a cup of coffee, but meals were a different matter.

Apart from the gratification of friendship, neighboring did a number of things for the community. It was a way of relaying information or misinformation about others. Often the information relayed upstairs influenced social arrangements downstairs. For example, according to one widow,

> The Bitfords had a tiff with Irma upstairs here, and a lot of tales went around. They weren't true, not a one, about Irma, but then people didn't come downstairs as much. Mattie used to come down, and Marie and Mr. Ball and they don't so much now, only once and again, because of Irma being there. All on account of that tiff.

Often people seated themselves downstairs as they were situated upstairs, neighbor and friend next to neighbor and friend, and a disagreement upstairs filtered downstairs. For example, when opinion was divided and feelings ran high on the issue of whether to store the Club's $900 in a cigar box under the Treasurer's bed or in the bank, the gossip, formerly confined to upstairs invaded the public arena downstairs.

Relaying information this way meant that without directly asking, people knew a lot about one another. It was safe to assume that what you did was known about by at least one network of neighbors and their friends. Even the one social isolate on the third floor, Velma, was known about, and her comings and goings were talked about and judged. Talk about other people was a means of social control and it operated, as it does elsewhere through parables; what was told of another was a message to one's self.

Not all social control was verbal. As I mentioned before, since all apartment living rooms faced out on a common walkway that led to a central elevator, each tenant was usually seen coming and going; and by how he or she was dressed, one could accurately guess what they were about. Since each resident knew the visiting habits of her neighbor, anything unusual was immediately spotted. One day when I was knocking on the door of a resident, her neighbor came out:

> I don't know where she is, it couldn't be the doctor's, she goes to the doctor's on Tuesdays; it couldn't be shopping, she shopped yesterday with her daughter. I don't think she's downstairs, she says she's worked enough today. Maybe she's visiting Abbie. They neighbor a lot. Try the second floor.

Neighboring is also a way to detect sickness or death. As Ernestine related, "This morning I looked to see if Judson's curtains were open. That's how we do on this floor, when we get up we open our curtains just a bit, so others walking by outside know that everything's all right. And if the curtains aren't drawn by mid-morning, we knock to see."[17] Mattie perpetually refused to open her curtains in the morning and kept them close to the wall by placing potted plants against them so that "a man won't get in." This excluded her from the checking up system and disconcerted the other residents.

The widows in good health took it upon themselves to care for one or two in poor health. Delia saw after Grandma Goodman who was not well enough to go down and get her mail and shop and Ernestine helped Little Floyd and Mrs. Blackwell who were too blind to cook their own meals. Irma took care of Mr. Cooper and it was she who called his son when Mr. Cooper "took sick." Even those who had not adopted someone to help often looked after a neighbor's potted plants while they were visiting kin, lent kitchen utensils, and took phone messages. One woman wrote letters for those who "wrote a poor hand."[18]

Some of the caretaking was reciprocal, but most was not. Three people helped to take care of Little Floyd, but since he was blind he could do little in return. Delia fixed his meals, Ernestine laundered his clothes, and Irma shopped for his food. When Little Floyd died fairly suddenly, he was missed perhaps more than others who died during those three years, especially by his caretakers. Ernestine remarked sadly, "I liked helping out the poor old fella. He would appreciate the tiniest thing. And never a complaint."

Sometimes people paid one another for favors. For example, Freda took in sewing for a small sum. When she was paid for lining a coat, she normally mentioned the purpose for which the money would be spent (e.g., bus fare for a visit to relatives in Montana), perhaps to reduce the commercial aspect of the exchange. Delia was paid by the Housing Authority for cleaning and cooking for Grandma Goodman, a disabled woman on her floor; and as she repeatedly mentioned to Grandma Goodman, she spent the money on high school class rings for her three grandchildren. In one case, the Housing Authority paid a granddaughter for helping her grandmother with housework. In another case, a disabled woman paid for domestic help from her social security checks.[19]

## Elite and Masses

Downstairs and up, the residents' relations had a comradely side-by-side quality, expressed in the names they called one another. Downstairs people went by last names: Judson, Whitcock, Farmer, Raymond, reminiscent of a roll call in the shipyards. To her relatives Bernice Judson was Bernice and to outsiders, Mrs. Judson; but downstairs it was "Hey, Judson, come here." Only those on the margins of communal life were called by their formal names. For example, Mr. Cooper, who was defined as slightly senile and was treated as a non-person, was called "Mr. Cooper" never plain "Cooper." Others had pet names; for example, "Grandma Goodman." The 70-year-old blind man called "Little Floyd" was no younger or smaller than any other resident.

Like sisters, their relations were tinged with as much rivalry as friendly support. The rivalry took several forms. In the eyes of the outside world, all at Merrill Court were social equals, but within the community there was an elite, a counter-elite, and the masses. What were coexisting friendship networks in time of peace became rivaling juntas when an issue arose. Although there were many separate friendship duos and trios, nearly all of them sided with either the elite or the counter-elite. It was perhaps no accident that the two groups were divided by region, the first including people from Virginia, Oklahoma, and Tennessee, the second, from Wisconsin and Montana. The two cliques also worshipped at different Baptist churches.

How an issue divided the group depended on the whereabouts of gossip or "meta-gossip" (talk about gossip). In this "meta-gossip," malicious or unkind words were not in themselves forbidden or worried about, only unkind words spoken in public. On one occasion some unkind words were spoken downstairs, and people began to trouble over "the gossip problem." The very same unkind words had been spoken upstairs, in my presence, and had not been defined as "a problem" then.

According to each junta, the other was a source of "bad tales."[20] The leader of the counter-elite was Mrs. Farmer. As Treasurer for three years running, she was the Talleyrand of the community's political life. Other officeholders would come and go but Mrs. Farmer was always Treasurer. She was also a main source of disaffection and as the stratum of "underdogs" (non-officeholders) changed, so would the membership of the junta centered around her. She apparently started the "rumor" that a woman was taking trips to Reno to deposit extra money in a bank there in order to avoid exceeding the maximum income to qualify for welfare. The elite, figuring that the woman in question had been on A.D.C. for twelve years, decided that the rumor was false and so accused the rumor-spreaders. The same happened to a rumor about another member who was said to have smuggled in an expensive sewing machine that might have disqualified her for welfare. The same information or misinformation ran both circuits but what was fact to one was rumor to the other. It did seem that the counter-elite, which had only one officeholder and was thus more socially on the bottom, was the source of more rumors. The elite, composed entirely of club officers, seemed to spend more time squelching rumors. However, my own association with the elite junta may have biased my observations.

The elite more often stressed "service to others" whereas the masses were more isolationist, stressing rewards "at home." Delia, who like past club presidents, came from a small town, summed up the situation from her viewpoint:

Since I've become president here, I feel we are part of Verada just like the VFW and the Eagles. "Why do they come to us [referring to other organizations]?" some of the women ask. They come and say we want 50 favors to be made for the Mayor's conference. They come to us because they think we can do the job; they wouldn't come to us if they didn't think that. It's an honor. But so many here feel we shouldn't have any truck with that. They don't want our mad money used on anyone else. They don't want to pay $40 for a self-portrait of Reena [the Recreation Director who fell ill]. They don't want to have to pay for a dinner to honor her. What has she done for us? they ask. If I tell them all the contribution she made to the community outside of us, they think she shouldn't be rewarded for that, only for what she's done for us. They're always wanting a special dinner price for relatives. They don't care beans about what we can do for others. You might call it selfish.

On the other hand, the out-group complained that Delia and her henchmen were "hobnobbing" with those people in the Recreation Department, and being exploited by them. "We work and she gets the credit. Is that any way to run a ship?" The pattern persisted in the face of three turnovers in leadership, so that the three succeeding club presidents came, in turn, to espouse the "contribution" view while the masses tended more to the "rewards at home" view.

Both the "foreign aid" and the "isolationist" policies seemed to be linked to the distribution of rewards for aid offered outside organizations. Delia was directly rewarded on *behalf* of Merrill Court; the isolationists symbolically rewarded only *through* their leader. When the club did a good turn for the Cancer Society or the boys in Vietnam, thank-you letters were addressed back to the club President. It was the President and the two officers next in line who were invited to visit a "beautification" program, or to lunch with other presidents of voluntary organizations such as the Garden Club, the Daughters of Rebecca, and the Hillcrest Junior Women's Club. On one occasion the President and her officers were invited by the Recreation and Parks Department to view a cemetery on which trees were sold for $3 each. The President, Delia, bought a tree not for the club but for herself in memory of her deceased husband. The counter-elite and the masses, who had not been invited, began finding fault with Delia and complaining about "thankless chores" shortly thereafter.

The masses more often mentioned the fact of age, which democratized the group. For example, as Mrs. Farmer frequently brought out, "We're all elder people here. The club President isn't a day younger than any of us. There's no reason for her to be feeling so special." On the other hand, the ruling elite, *while* it was that, seldom mentioned age. They equated themselves, rather, with the Veterans of Foreign Wars and the Lions Club, whose memberships are not based on age.[21] Outside of Merrill Court, the residents were all "the senior citizens over at the project," and there was no distinguishing between the masses and their representatives.

## The "Poor Dear" Hierarchy

Parallel to the distinction between elite and masses was an informal status hierarchy that had little to do with the formal social circle. If within the formal social circle there was a status hierarchy based on the distribution of *honor*, there also was a parallel hierarchy based on the distribution of luck. In fact, "luck" is not entirely luck. Health and life expectancy, for example, are often considered "luck,"[22] but an upper-class person can expect to live ten years longer than a lower-class person. The widows of Merrill Court, however, were drawn from the same social class and they saw the differences among themselves as matters of luck.

There was a shared system of ranking according to which she who had good health won honor. She who lost the fewest loved ones through death won honor and she who was close to her children won honor. Those who fell short on any of these criteria were often referred to as "poor dears."

The "poor dear" system operated like a set of valves through which a sense of superiority ran in only one direction. Someone who was a "poor dear" in the eyes of another seldom called that other person a "poor dear" in return; but seldom did anyone accept the label from "above." Rather, the "poor dear" would turn to someone felt to be less fortunate, perhaps to buttress a sense of her own achieved or ascribed superiority.[23] Thus, the hierarchy honored residents at the top and pitied "poor dears" at the bottom, creating a number of informally recognized status distinction among those who, in the eyes of the outside society, were social equals.

It is a tricky business to link feelings, which psychologists mainly deal with, with social distinctions, which mainly concern sociologists, but I offer the following. How one fares in the distribution of luck can be compared to how one fares in the distribution of "earned" honor. In both cases, the unequal distribution has to be socially handled. How one fares in the distribution of luck has by definition nothing to do with merit. One cannot help it if one's husband dies or one has a heart attack. But luck, once it *has* been unequally distributed, and becomes ascribed, is also socially handled much as the earned honor is socially handled.

In both cases, the haves experience different emotions toward the have-nots than the have-nots experience toward the haves. The haves of fate often experience pity or its negative companion, scorn, for the have-nots. And the have-nots, in turn, feel envy for the haves. In the distribution of honor, on the other hand, the haves feel charity looking down, and the unhonored feel respect, which includes an element of fear, looking up.[24] Perhaps the have-nots of respect feel envy like the have-nots of fate, but envy in the first case is less legitimate since there is the ideological cushion that respect is earned, whereas luck is not. If one has not earned respect, it is thought to be one's own fault. Insofar as luck is concerned, envy is more readily and legitimately felt since there seems to be no justice in the distribution of luck. As regards both luck and respect, those feelings probably exist only in relation to those to whom one is, in *other* respects, socially equal and thus comparable. In both cases there is social distance between the respected and unrespected, lucky and unlucky. Although the unlucky do not blame themselves for bad luck, and do not accept a stigmatized status, the lucky impose it on them, especially the *relatively* lucky. The unlucky (or pitied), perhaps to avoid the unpleasant emotion of envy, turn to others whom they themselves can pity. In behavioral terms, the unlucky receive solicitous behavior from above, ward it off, and in turn are solicitous toward others still less fortunate.

The distinctions made by residents of Merrill Court are only part of a larger old age status hierarchy based on things other than luck. At the monthly meetings of the countywide Senior Citizens Forum, to which Merrill Court sent two representatives, the term "poor dear" often arose with reference to old people. It was "we senior citizens who are politically involved versus those 'poor dears' who are active in recreation." Those active in recreation, however, did not accept a subordinate position relative to the politically active. On the other hand, they did not refer to the political activists as "poor dears." Within the politically active group there were those who espoused general causes, such as getting out an anti-pollution bill, and those who espoused causes related only to old age, such as raising social security benefits or improving medical benefits. Those in politics and recreation referred to the passive card players and newspaper readers as "poor dears." Old people with passive life styles in good health referred to those in poor health as "poor dears" and those in poor health but living in independent housing referred to those in nursing homes as "poor dears." Within the nursing home there was a distinction between those who were ambulatory and those who were not. Among those who were not ambulatory there was a distinction between those who could enjoy food and those who could not. Almost everyone, it seemed, had a "poor dear."

At Merrill Court, the main distinction was between people like themselves and people in nursing homes. Returning from one of the monthly trips to a nearby nursing home, one resident commented:

> There was an old woman in a wheel chair there with a dolly in her arms. I leaned over to look at the dolly. I didn't touch it, well, maybe I just brushed it. She snatched it away, and said "Don't take my dolly." They're pathetic, some of them, the poor dears.

Another woman, a 69-year-old widow, noted:

> I like to talk to old people (referring to a 105-year-old woman in a nursing home). It's not boring. They have a lot of interesting things to say. I talk to them and every so often I break in, you know. But mostly I just let her talk. She likes to have someone to tell things to.[25]

Even within the building, those who were in poor health, were alienated from their children, or were aging rapidly were considered "poor dears." It was lucky to be young and unlucky to be old. There was more than a twenty-year age span between the youngest and oldest in the community. When one of the younger women, Delia, age 69, was drinking coffee with Grandma Goodman, age 79, they compared ages. It was Grandma Goodman who dwelt on the subject and finished the conversation by citing the case of Mrs. Blackwell, who was 89 and still in reasonably good health. Another remarked about her 70th birthday:

> I just couldn't imagine myself being 70. Seventy is old! That's what Daisy said too. She's 80 you know. It was her 70th that got her. No one likes to be put aside, you know. Laid away. Put on the shelf you might say. No sir.

She had an ailment that prevented her from bowling or lifting her flower pots, but she compared her health to that of Daisy, and found her own health a source of luck.

Old people compare themselves not to the young but to other old people. Often the residents referred to the old back in Oklahoma, Texas, and Arkansas with pity in their voices:

Back in Oklahoma, why they toss the old people away like old shoes. My old friends was all livin' together in one part of town and they hardly budged the whole day. Just sat out on their porch and chewed the fat. Sometimes they didn't even do that. Mostly they didn't have no nice housing, and nothin' social was goin' on. People here don't know what luck they've fallen into.

They also compared their lot to that of other older people in the area. As one resident said:

Some of my friends live in La Casa [another housing project]. I suppose because they have to, you know. And I tried to get them to come bowling with me, but they wouldn't have a thing to do with it. "Those senior citizens, that's old folks stuff." Wouldn't have a thing to do with it. I tried to tell them we was pretty spry, but they wouldn't listen. They just go their own way. They don't think we have fun.

On the whole, the widows disassociated themselves from the status of "old person," and accepted its "minority" characteristics.[26] The "poor dears" in the nursing home were often referred to as childlike: "They are easily hurt, you know. They get upset at the slightest thing and they like things to be the way they've always been. Just like kids." Occasionally, a widow would talk about Merrill Court itself in this vein, presumably excluding herself: "We're just like a bunch of kids here sometimes. All the sparring that goes on, even with church folk. And people get so hurt, so touchy. You'd think we were babies sometimes."

If the widows accepted the stereotypes of old age, they did not add the "poor dear" when referring to themselves. But younger outsiders did. To the junior employees in the Recreation and Parks Department, the young doctors who treated them at the county hospital, the middle-aged welfare workers, and the young bank tellers, the residents of Merrill Court, and old people like them, were "poor dears."

Perhaps in old age there is a premium on finishing life off with the feeling of being a "have."[27] But during old age, one also occupies a low social position. The way the old look for luck differences among themselves reflects the pattern found at the bottom of other social, racial, and gender hierarchies. To find oneself lucky within an ill-fated category is to gain the semblance of high status when society withholds it from others in the category. The way in which old people feel above and condescend to other old people may be linked to the fact that the young feel above and condescend to them. The luck hierarchy does not stop with the old.[28]

## The Sibling Bond

Rivalries and differences there were in Merrill Court but not alienation and not isolation. A club member who stayed up in her apartment during club meetings more often did it out of spite than indifference. More obvious were the many small, quiet favors, keeping an eye out for a friend and sharing a good laugh.

There was something special about this community, not so much because it was an old age subculture, but because the subculture was founded on a particular kind of *relationship*, the sibling bond. In what follows I will describe the sibling bond, show how it appeared in Merrill Court, and then discuss the link between the sibling bond and social trends. The link is briefly the following: (1) the faster the rate of social change, the more society is stratified by age; (2) the more it is stratified by age, the larger the pool of potential social siblings; (3) such pools can sometimes coalesce into peer communities such as this. However, this happens only under certain conditions, as relations between old people in nursing homes and in hospital wards show.

There are two basic types of relations[29] and all bonds in some way resemble one or the other: the parent–child and the sibling bonds.[30] These are what German sociologist Max Weber called "ideal types" or abstract models against which one can compare every day, real relationships. They do not necessarily refer to relations between *actual* siblings or *actual* parents and children. Actual siblings are likely to have a "sibling bond" but they may not, just as actual parents and children may not, have a "parent–child bond." The sibling bond involves (1) reciprocity, and (2) similarity between two people.[31] Reciprocity implies equality; what you do for me I return to you in equal measure. We can depend on each other a lot or a little but we depend on and give to each other equally. If the exchange is not always even, the feeling is that it should be. The sibling bond also involves similarity between people: I have the same things to offer and the same needs to fill that you have. On one hand, this relationship opens up the potential for community based on similar interests, and on the other hand, feeds the potential for rivalry based on the competition to fulfill similar needs. Like the relationship between real siblings, it can reflect feelings (hostility, for example) that have their roots in another (parent–child) relationship.

By contrast, the parent–child bond is not based on reciprocity or similarity. What you do for me I cannot return in equal measure. I depend on you more than you depend on me. And what is exchanged is different, not similar. Very old people often need care and their mature children may have a (not quite commensurate) need to nurture. In the parent–child bond, there are fewer similar needs, resources, or experiences and more different resources exchanged, different needs met, and different experiences shared.

Speaking about the relations of real parents to children, and brothers to sisters, Freud wrote: "We find an absence of love far more repellent between parent and child than between brothers and sisters. In the former case we have, as it were, made something sacred which in the latter we have left profane."[32] Freud discusses social substitutes for this profane sibling relation in his *Group Psychology and the Analysis of the Ego*. Each follower in a group has a parent–child relation with the leader but a sibling bond to his fellow followers. This brotherhood of followers is governed by the rule of justice and equality. As Freud put it, "No one must want to put himself forward; everyone must be the same and have the same."[33]

The sacred and more indispensable parent–child bond fills complementary needs and binds polarities. The profane sibling bond provides a fellowship to shore up one end of the complementary relationship, often reducing aloneness in a different way, with laughter more than comfort, conviviality more than the act of being needed. The sibling bond seeks for other "me's" rather than "you's." In psychological terms, in the sibling relationship, one identifies with the other sibling more but takes that other sibling as an "object" less.

Most residents of Merrill Court are social siblings. The custom of exchanging cups of coffee, lunches, potted plants, and curtain checking suggest reciprocity. Upstairs, one widow usually visited as much as she was visited. In deciding who visits whom, they often remarked, "Well, I came over last time. You come over this time." They traded, in even measure, slips from house plants, kitchen utensils, and food of all sorts. They watched one another's apartments when someone was away on a visit, and they called and took calls for one another.

There are hints of the parent–child bond in the *protégé* system, but protectors picked their protégés voluntarily and resented taking care of people they did not volunteer to help. For example, one protector of "Little Floyd" complained about a crippled club member, a non-resident:

> It wasn't considerate of Rose to expect us to take care of her. She can't climb in and out of the bus very well and she walks so slow. The rest of us wanted to see the museum. It's not nice to say, but I didn't want to miss the museum waiting for her to walk with us. Why doesn't her son take her on trips?

The quality of a relation was reflected in their telephoning voices. I began to notice that when they answered the phone, as I was sitting in their apartments, I could predict the category of the person at the other end of the line. Their tone of voice was soft and receptive and they listened longer when it was a child. It was louder, gayer, and there was more talk interspersed with listening when it was a peer. Also, the content of the talk was different. With relatives, they might ask after relatives, or a granddaughter might ask what to do after the rolls in the oven have risen once. With peers it was more likely to be a comment such as "What are you wearing tonight?" or "Wasn't that something about Rose and the museum?" or a comment explaining the outcome of a visit to the doctor. The comments with relatives involved a dissimilarity of experience, those with peers a similarity.

The widows were not only equals among themselves, they also were remarkably similar. They all wanted more or less the same things and could give more or less the same things. They all wanted to *receive* Mother's Day cards. No one in the building *sent* Mother's Day cards. And what they did was to *compare* Mother's Day cards. Although there was some division of labor, there was little difference in labor performed. All knew how to bake bread and can peaches, but no one knew how to fix faucets. They all knew about "the old days" but few among them could explain what was going on with youth these days. They all had ailments but no one there could cure them. They all needed rides to the shopping center but no one among them needed riders. There was little of the complementarity that goes with the parent–child relation.

Their similar functions meant that when they did exchange services, it was usually the same kinds of services they themselves could perform. For example, two neighbors might exchange corn bread for jam, but both knew how to make both corn bread *and* jam. If one neighbor made corn bread for five people in one day, one of the recipients would also make corn bread for the same people two weeks later. Each specialized within a specialization, and over the long run the widows made and exchanged the same goods.

Hence the "side by sideness," the "in the same boat" quality of their relations. They noticed the same things about the world and their eyes caught the same items in a department store. They noticed the same features in the urban landscape – the pastor's home, the Baptist church, the nursing homes, the funeral parlors, the places that used to be. They did not notice, as an adolescent might, the gas stations and hamburger joints.

As a result, they were good listeners to one another. It was common for someone to walk into the Recreation Room and launch into the details of the latest episode of a mid-afternoon television drama ("It seems that the baby is not by artificial insemination but really Frank's child, and the doctor is trying to convince her to tell. . . ."). The speaker could safely assume that her listeners also knew the details. Since they shared many experiences, a physical ailment, a death, a description of the past, an "old age joke" could be explained, understood, and enjoyed. They talked together about their children much as their children, together, talked about them. Each shared with social siblings one side of a parent–child bond.

This similarity opened up the possibility of comparison and rivalry,[34] as the "poor dear" hierarchy suggests. In the same way, distinctions between the "elite" and "masses" were based on the assumption that people were similar and that everyone was equal to start with. Whether the widows cooperated in collecting money for flowers, or competed for prestigious offices in the Service Club, bowling trophies, or front seats in the bus, their functions were similar, their status roughly equal, and their relations in the best and worst sense, "profane."

Not all groups of old people form this sibling bond – for example, old people in institutions do not. All things being equal, we might expect subcultures to also arise in nursing homes, certain hospital wards, or convalescent hospitals. To begin with, all things are not equal; the institutionalized tend to be older, physically weaker, poorer, and initially more isolated than their peers in the population at large.[35]

But even among the fairly healthy and ambulatory within institutions, the likes of Merrill Court is rare. It is not enough to put fairly healthy, socially similar old people together. There is clearly something different between institutions and public housing apartments. Perhaps what counts is the kind of relationships that institutions foster. The resident of an institution is "a patient." Like a child, he has his meals served to him, his water glass filled, his bed made, his blinds adjusted by the "mother-nurse." He cannot return the service. Although he often shares a room or a floor with "brother" patients, both siblings have a non-reciprocal relationship to attendants or nurses. Even the research on the institutionalized focuses on the relation between patient and attendant, not between patient and patient. If there is a strong parent–child bond, it may overwhelm any potential sibling solidarity. If the old in institutions meet as equals, it is not as independent equals. The patient's relation to other patients is like the relation between *real*, young siblings, which may exaggerate rather than forestall narcissistic withdrawal.

The widows of Merrill Court took care of themselves, fixed their own meals, paid their own rent, shopped for their own food, and made their own beds; and they did these things for others. Their sisterhood rests on adult autonomy. This is what people at Merrill Court have and people in institutions do not.

## The Sibling Bond and Age-Stratification

The sibling bond is delicate and emerges only when conditions are ripe. Rapid currents of social change lead to age-stratification, which, in turn, ripens conditions for the sibling bond. Tied to his fellows by sibling bonds, an individual is cemented side by side into an age stratum with which he shares the same rewards, wants, abilities, and failings.

French sociologist Emile Durkheim, in his book *The Division of Labor*, describes two forms of social solidarity.[36] To over-simplify, in organic solidarity there is a division of labor, complementary dependence, and differences among people. In mechanical solidarity there is no division of labor, self-sufficiency, and similarity among people. Modern American society as a whole is based on organic solidarity, not only in the economic but in the social, emotional, and intellectual spheres.

Different *age strata* within the general society however, are more bound by *mechanical* solidarity. This is important both for the individual and the society. Although division of labor, complementary dependence, and differences among people describe society's network of relations as a whole, they do not adequately describe relations among particular individuals. An individual's complementary dependence may be with people he does not know or meet – such as the person who grows and cans the food he eats, or lays the bricks for his house. Again in his most intimate relations, an individual may have complementary relations[37] (either equal or unequal) with his spouse and children. But in between the most and least intimate bonds is a range in which there are many sibling relationships which form the basis of mechanical solidarity.

In fact, many every-day relations are with people similar and equal to oneself. Relations between colleague and colleague, student and student, girl friend and girl friend, boy friend and boy friend, relations within a wives group, or "the guys at the bar," the teenage gang, the army buddies are often forms of the sibling bond. These ties are often "back up relations," social insurance policies for the times when the complementary bonds of parent and child, husband and wife, student and teacher, boy friend and girl friend fail, falter, or normally change.

From an individual's viewpoint, some periods of life, such as adolescence and old age, are better for forming sibling bonds than are other periods.[38] Both just before starting a family and after raising one, before entering the economy and after leaving it, an individual is open to, and needs, these back up relationships. It is these stages that are "problematic," and it is these stages that, with longer education and earlier retirement, now last longer. It is in precisely these periods that social siblings are sought.

From society's point of view,[39] the sibling bond allows more flexibility in relations between generations by forging solidarity *within* generations and divisions *between* them. This divides society into age layers that are relatively more independent of one another, so that changes in one age layer need not be retarded by conditions in another. The institution that has bound the generations together – the family – is in this respect on the decline. As it declines, the sibling bond emerges, filling in and enhancing social flexibility, especially in those social strata where social change is most pronounced. The resulting social flexibility does not guarantee "good" changes and continuity is partly sacrificed to fads and a cult of newness. But whether desirable or not, this flexibility is partly due to and partly causes the growing importance of the sibling bond.

Thus, the times are ripe for the sibling bond, and for old age communities such as Merrill Court. In the social life of old people it is not the sibling bond versus the parent–child bond. Rather, the question is how the one bond complements the other. The sisterhood at Merrill Court is no substitute for love of children and contact with them; but it offers a full, meaningful life independent of them.

## Notes

1  From *Growing Old: The Process of Disengagement*, by Elaine Cumming and William Henry. Basic Books, Inc., Publishers, New York, 1961.
2  Selected questionnaire responses, Sociology I Class, University of California, Berkeley, Spring 1968.
3  However, the apartments that were vacated through death were taken by people who had previously joined the community and were known to the original residents.
4  Let us assume that the behaviorist does not include verbal datum as behavior. See Homans, 1950.
5  They talked over the possibility of having a "workin'-in" to can some peaches, which one of the sons of a resident had brought in. But, as they complained, sugar cost too much and they had thrown out the jars when they moved into the small apartments.
6  Mr. Farmer, for example, stated that "his" God was against card playing, although, as everyone pointed out, he was an avid pool player. Freda, who attended the same Southern Baptist church, did permit herself a game of cards.
7  Ada did not come down to meetings for a month but she finally rejoined the group, although privately she felt the decision unjust. A number of issues seemed to jeopardize collective life and highlight the importance of quasi-private friendship networks. When a hot issue remained unsettled, the public norm that "everyone is welcome here" in the Recreation Room was substituted by, "This table is reserved for our close friends." Thus, issues affected the fluctuating boundary between private and public, formal and informal, status arrangements.
8  Some characteristics of the age peer community are common to other working-class voluntary organizations, although they perform unique functions for older people. Other characteristics appear to be unique to an age-segregated setting.
9  See Wolf, 1950, p. 361. As Simmel put it, ". . . the internal, ritual regimentation of secret societies reflects a measure of freedom and severance from society at large which entails the counter-norm of this very schematism, in order to restore the equilibrium of human nature."
10  See Becker, 1960, p. 805.
11  Another warned me to come early to the Christmas party they were having, "because it gets dark awful early these days," even though the party was to be held indoors.
12  See Marcuse, 1955. One might also interpret this pattern as "escape from freedom." See Fromm, 1941.
13  A work role, even if others do not know precisely what it involves, is transferable outside the work context, and even more transferable is the money that results. Roles in voluntary organizations seldom have that legitimacy outside the organization.
14  Exceptions were the presidency, secretaryship, and treasurership.
15  See Blauner, 1968, for an incisive analysis of how the social structure accommodates death. In Merrill Court, the formal role structure did not have to change to accommodate death.
16  Their preference in art objects was for what Marshall McLuhan calls "hot media." That is, what they liked was realistic, spelled out, unambiguous. They seemed to like flat visual designs rather than sculptural art or paintings with a sculptural dimension. They also liked intricate small objects rather than simple or large objects.

17   The function of "keeping an eye out" is more impersonally handled when a peer community is absent. For example, the *St. Petersburg Times* (Florida, August 9, 1969), noted ". . . homebound older persons living alone here, either permanently or temporarily, are eligible for a free 'Reassurance Telephone Program.' It is offered by the Senior Citizens Referral and Guidance Center . . . Volunteers call individuals seven days a week (about 5 calls a day) to be sure they're okay, between 9:30 A.M.–3:30 P.M." Also see Clark and Anderson, 1967.

18   The average had six years of school, but some had not passed the third grade.

19   Among neighbors there was an informal code of etiquette about borrowing money. It was understood that an individual never refused to lend money, but if she didn't want to lend it, she gave a more acceptable reason, such as not having money on hand. In one instance, a neighbor called Delia to borrow three dollars for a taxicab. Delia did not have three dollars, but she borrowed three dollars (from me) to lend to the neighbor. As she explained, "If I said I didn't have the money, she'd have thought I didn't *want* to lend it to her. I didn't want her to think that." Delia borrowed money to lend in order to avoid having her behavior misinterpreted as accepted subterfuge.

20   Gossip seemed to be a constant threat to public occasions, barred from them only by the fear of reprisal. That fear may be an important dimension of what we mean by social solidarity. In the case mentioned above, a widow had commented, "Due to feeling so poorly I'm resigning from the birthday chairmanship. There are those who say I haven't been doing a good job . . ." Others responded to the accusation and a crisis arose. The comment itself seemed harmless enough, except insofar as it publicly accused some gossipers.

21   Age was also occasionally invoked as an explanation for disharmony. For example, when there had been a series of feuds concerning the annual bazaar, the women informally diagnosed the situation; "We're none of us getting any younger. Some of us can't work as well as before. Last year we had Alma with us. She was a real worker." However, a month later when the issue had been resolved, age was never mentioned, nor were the deaths that had occurred since the last bazaar.

22   Even the number of children one has, and one's relation to them, are not entirely matters of "luck." For a short story that touches on this general question, see J. F. Powers, "The Poor Thing," in *The Presence of Grace* (1956). For a study of the relationship between social class and life expectancy, see Mayer and Hauser (1953).

23   One does not always respect those one fears, but I suggest there is almost always an element of (legitimated) fear in respect.

24   The respected person is free to protect himself from social encounters by invoking the fear in others that is his due. On the other hand, he is also free to undo the fear, and reduce social distance. The non-respected have no such choice.

25   Clark and Anderson note that many of their older respondents liked to help those less fortunate (1967, p. 315).

26   Most old people do not consider themselves as old. Kutner et al., found that relative to most people their age, 65 percent felt younger, (1956, pp. 94, 98). Relative to their actual age, over 40 percent of those over 65 think of themselves as younger, while less than 20 percent think of themselves as older. Only a minority (less than a third) of those 60 and over think that people they care most about think of them as old. Feeling old is also linked to low socioeconomic status (Kutner et al., 1956, p. 94) and to loss of major roles – the retired, and widowed (Phillips, 1957, p. 216).

27   This comes close to what Erik Erikson calls a sense of integrity, which wins over a sense of despair in the successful resolution of the final life crisis (Erikson, 1959).

28   As Memmi points out, "It is a fact that misery consoles misery. Is it surprising then that the racist takes a rest from his own misery by looking at the next man's? He even goes one

step further, claiming that the next man is more miserable, unfortunate and perverse than he really is." See Memmi, 1968, p. 202. Also, Thorstein Veblen in *The Theory of the Leisure Class* discusses the belief in luck, noting its importance to economic efficiency (Veblen, 1953, p. 184).

29    Any relationship has many more dimensions than I am talking about here; for example, the extent to which it is intimate or impersonal, based on one specific thing in common or many things in common. I am focusing here on two dimensions – complementarity and reciprocity.

Since there are two dimensions, we have four theoretically possible combinations: (1) complementary and reciprocal (e.g., Grandma Goodman who pays Delia to do work for her), (2) complementary and non-reciprocal (*e.g.*, Mr. Cooper who needs help but can't return the favor), (3) similar and reciprocal (most relations in Merrill Court), and (4) similar and non-reciprocal (two people who need the same service, though only one can give it).

30    These two bonds crosscut the distinction between primary and secondary relations since both bonds can be either. They may be useful in analyzing social change. A hundred years ago, most primary relations were confined to a circle of kin. Parent–child and sibling bonds were found within kinship circles. Today, the nuclear family probably absorbs fewer of all primary relationships. These relational models, held as constants, can enable us to compare the structural context of an individual's relationships at Time$_1$ with that at Time$_2$. Taking the relationship rather than the family as a unit of analysis, we can trace social change not by looking at institutions, but by looking at the component relationships that build them up or tear them down.

31    See Alvin Gouldner's excellent article. "The Norm of Reciprocity" (1960). Gouldner distinguishes between reciprocity and complementarity. Only in some cases do complementarity and reciprocity overlap (p. 164). ". . . complementarity connotes that one's rights are another's obligations and vice versa. Reciprocity, however, connotes that each party has rights *and* duties" (p. 169). This is crucial because if we mesh complementarity with reciprocity, we wrongly assume that when two parties divide labor they get equal returns.

32    See Freud, 1966, p. 205. Freud had little to say about social siblings in relation to rivalry, but he notes in his *Introductory Lectures* the potential for rivalry between biological siblings; "A small child does not necessarily love his brothers and sisters; often he obviously does not . . ." (1966, p. 204).

33    Richman, 1957, p. 197.

34    There is the notion that comparisons between people are only "fair" when a number of factors are held constant. A parent may not compare his own performance with that of his child because the comparison is "unfair." They differ in too many ways to make the comparison meaningful. When a widow says of another. "She is doing well," she means "She is doing well for a 69-year-old lower-class white widow."

35    The institutionalized are generally older, more likely to be female, widowed, white, to not have living children, to live alone prior to institutionalization, to be poor and physically impaired, and to be put there by "mistake." Goldfarb found that only 89 percent of the patients over 64 in mental hospitals "should" be there (Goldfarb, 1961, p. 253).

Townsend's study of 530 new residents in British old age homes showed only 18 percent with close friends inside the institution (Townsend, 1962, pp. 343, 347).

36    See Cumming and Henry, 1961, p. 65, to whom I am indebted for their application of Durkheim to age-grading theory.

37    It may be that rapid social change tends to accent the sibling bond between husband and wife and between parent and child. It has been noted that wife and husband are more equal and more similar (their roles are less differentiated) and more like siblings than

husbands and wives used to be a hundred years ago. The parent too is less "parental," and more of a "pal" and companion than an authority.

38    Two authors have suggested that organic solidarity prevails in childhood, mechanical solidarity in adolescence, organic solidarity in adulthood, and mechanical once again in old age. At the very end of life there is sometimes a reversal to vertical solidarity similar to that of childhood. See Cumming and Henry, 1961.

39    In modern society, there is a special premium on the sibling bond. As I see it there is a tension between two trends. On one hand, rapid social change calls for social flexibility. On the other hand, the declining death rate and the aging of the population means that more generations are alive at any given time in 1960 than was true in 1900. This reduces social flexibility, since the old (for whatever reasons) tend to be more committed to old ways of doing things and less open to new ones. Mannheim remarked in his essay, "The Question of Generations," that if birth and death were not natural facts, we would have to invent them. Birth and death, he notes, are forms of collective remembering and forgetting. I suggest that the functional equivalent to death *has* been devised in the sibling bond. The solidarity within generations and the divisions between them split society into layers of perspective and layers of experience, thus enhancing social flexibility by making the younger layer more independent of the older one. *See* Mannheim, 1952, and Ryder, 1965.

## References

Becker, Howard. 1960. "Normative Reactions to Normlessness," *American Sociological Review* 25: 803–9.

Blauner, Robert. 1968. "Death and Social Structure." In *Sociology and Everyday Life*, edited Marcello Truzzi. Englewood Cliffs, NJ: Prentice-Hall.

Clark, Margaret and Barbara Gallatin Anderson. 1967. *Culture and Aging*. Springfield, IL: Charles C Thomas.

Cumming, Elaine and William Henry. 1961. *Growing Old: The Process of Disengagement*. New York: Basic.

Erikson, Erik. 1959. "Identity and the Life Cycle," *Psychological Issues*, Monograph 1. New York: International Universities Press.

Freud, Sigmund. 1966. *The Complete Introductory Lectures on Psychoanalysis*. New York: Norton.

Fromm, E. 1941. *Escape from Freedom*. New York: Holt, Rinehart, and Winston.

Goldfarb, A. 1961. "Current Trends in the Management of the Psychiatrically Ill Aged." Pp. 248–65 in *Psychopathology of Aging*, edited by Paul H. Hoch and J. Zubin. New York: Grune and Stratton.

Gouldner, Alvin W. 1960. "The Norm of Reciprocity," *American Sociological Review* 25: 161–77.

Homans, George. 1950. *The Human Group*. New York: Harcourt, Brace and World.

Kutner, B. et al. 1956. *Five Hundred Over Sixty*. New York: Russell Sage Foundation.

Mannheim, Karl. 1952. "The Problem of Generations." In *Essays on the Sociology of Knowledge*. New York: Oxford University Press.

Marcuse, Herbert. 1955. *Eros and Civilization*. New York: Vintage Books.

Mayer, Albert. J. and Philip M. Hauser. 1953. "Class Differentials in Expectation of Life at Birth." In *Class, Status, and Power*, edited by Reinhard Bendix and S. M. Lipset. Glencoe, IL: Free Press.

Memmi, Albert. 1968. *Dominated Man*. New York: Orion Press.

Phillips, Bernard. 1957. "A Role Theory Approach to Adjustment in Old Age," *American Sociological Review* 22: 212–17.

Powers, J. F. 1956. *The Presence of Grace*. New York: Atheneum.

Richman, James. (ed.). 1957. *A General Selection from the Works of Sigmund Freud*. Garden City, NY: Doubleday.

Ryder, Norman. 1965. "The Cohort in the Study of Social change," *American Journal of Sociology* 60: 239–338.

Townsend, Peter. 1962. "The Purpose of the Institution." In *Social and Psychological Aspects of Aging*, edited by C. Tibbitts and W. Donahue. New York: Columbia University Press.

Veblen, Thorstein. 1953. *The Theory of the Leisure Class*. New York: Mentor.

Wolf, Kurt H. 1950. *The Sociology of Georg Simmel*. New York: Free Press.

# 18 Resisting Institutionalization: Constructing Old Age and Negotiating Home

## Pia C. Kontos

## Introduction

In this article I seek to contribute to critical gerontology by broadening the discussion of "place" and its inextricable link with the body. Following Agnew (1993), the concept of place is interwoven with three elements: locale, location, and a sense of place. Locale is the setting in which an activity and social interaction occur. Location is the social, economic, and political processes which affect locales. Sense of place is the subjective territorial meaning of a locale, or "structure of feeling". A key tenet of Agnew's definition of place is that it is not just a locale, a setting in which social relations are constituted, but also a source of emotional and experiential meaning for its inhabitants.

A growing body of research is focusing on important experiential dimensions of a home environment as they apply to the elderly. An important theme to emerge from this research is that place, construed as home, plays a critical role in maintaining a sense of personal identity (Rowles 1983, 1993; Rubinstein 1989). This is because home, unlike many other accommodation options available to frail older people, does not compromise their independence. Home is a place where control over one's own life can be freely exercised (Fogel 1992; Rutman and Freedman 1988). The home environment as both a physical entity and a meaningful context for everyday life has significant implications for how old age is experienced by its inhabitants.

In this article I explore the significance of home space for a group of senior tenants living in a supportive housing building. Drawing upon twelve months of anthropological field research conducted at Home Frontier[1] in 1995, I describe the nature and meaning of the linkages between the senior tenants and their living space.[2] "Locating" seniors within their living environment (house, apartment, seniors' residence) identifies physical, emotional and experiential realities which their home holds for them. Understanding how their lived environment is constructed and negotiated, and how it signifies meanings of home, enriches our understanding of the senior tenants for whom home is integral to a meaningful existence and their sense of independence. Home is an invaluable resource to senior tenants in adjusting to physical decline that

Original publication: Kontos, Pia C., "Resisting Institutionalization: Constructing Old Age and Negotiating Home," *Journal of Aging Studies* 12 (1998), pp. 167–84.

comes with old age and in sustaining their independence and a sense of personal identity.

Rules and regulations which are enforced by the staff of Home Frontier are perceived by the tenants as features of institutional living. These constraints compromised the tenants' independence and effectively threatened their personal identities. Home Frontier became a struggle between a vision of home-as-place and place-as-institution. This is confirmed and dramatized by the tenants' relentless efforts to resist staff directives and to negotiate with staff their own terms of existence.

Home Frontier is more than a physical setting and a functional environment. It is a home setting that shapes and maintains personal identity by maximizing a sense of personal competence and control; it is also a "place" in that it is a shifting social space maintained through resistance, negotiations, and collective social life. Home Frontier is a home-place: both a space which facilitates independent daily living, and a local construction that is negotiated and contested in the practice of its use.

Localizing changes in personal capabilities and faculties which are inherent in the experience of growing old, captures what is all too often absent from gerontological and geriatric accounts of old age – the complex engagement between biological change, place, self-identity, and meaning. My argument is that culture[3] and place are important and valid indicators of the experience of old age, as are the biological and physiological changes which are an inherent part of the aging process. All aspects of the interaction between biology, culture and place are essential to the very constitution of old age as a human reality.


## The Medical Model of Old Age

In the nineteenth century, geriatrics and gerontology emerged as medical specializations in an era of Big Science (Achenbaum 1995). Important developments in the theory and practice of medicine had a significant effect upon the emergence of these medical specializations and the perception and treatment of the elderly (Haber 1983). Reflecting a preoccupation with scientific progress, researchers of old age endeavored to credentialize their field as a science (Katz 1996). Approaches generated by the micro-perspectives of biology, chemistry, immunology, and other "hard sciences" were embraced in order to achieve this endeavor. The meanings of old age were aligned to definitive physiological, pathological, and biological signs of senescence; the construction of old age derived from an analysis of bodily structure, process, and products. The terrain of these scientific researchers was restricted to what could be seen of old age in the body (Katz 1996).

With the biomedical model's focus on individual organic pathology and physiological etiologies, medicine became the pervasive force in the definition of and the approach to the aging process and the aged body (Estes and Binney 1989). The entire phenomenon of old age was brought within the domain and control of biomedicine because it was regarded as a process only of biological decline; as such, it was regarded as individual pathology (Robertson 1990). Medicine positioned the aged body in pathology thereby investing it with meanings linked only to disease and decline.

Geriatrics and gerontology ". . . arose in the wake of medicine's remaking the body into a precise field of signs whose referents were internalized, naturalized, and essentialized" (Katz 1996, p. 22). Medicine focuses on the anatomical body (Turner 1987; Katz 1996) engendering an act of closure and finitude, establishing cultural boundaries and securing biological norms. The body, with its physiological changes and organic functions, became the central focus for an understanding of old age. As geriatrics and gerontology developed, despite the diversity of interests among biologists, chemists, immunologists, and other researchers of old age, all assumed the biomedical model unquestioningly. It is the organizing principle of this model, which maintains a severance of biology from culture, and a decontextualization of the body, that is the focus of my critique.

## Gerontology

As social scientists, gerontologists recognized that geriatricians' exclusive focus on physiological changes produced a limited social construction of old age. Gerontologists therefore sought ways to broaden their discourse. They distinguished their field from geriatrics by incorporating studies of sociology, psychology and demography (Katz 1996).

Despite their efforts to move beyond a strictly biological reading of old age, gerontologists retained many of the reductionistic tendencies characteristic of geriatrics and the biomedical model. Notwithstanding the considerable differences among conventional gerontological theories, all fall short of capturing a full contextual perspective of old age. In addition to abstracting sociocultural processes and variables from place, there is the common underlying presumption that such factors can be studied independently from biological processes. For example, in both disengagement theory and activity theory, the individual is the primary unit of focus. This inevitably renders both theories inattentive to structural or political factors. To transcend this limitation, age stratification theory, modernization theory and political economy theory focused on macro-structural relationships between the aged and capitalist society. However, in doing so, these theories tended not to consider cultural factors and individual intentionality.

All of these conventional theories seem to either focus exclusively on ". . . external influences affecting the observable behavior of the aged . . ." (Hazan 1994, p. 49) or make ". . . unsubstantiated inferences about the internal processes shaping the aged self" (Hazan 1994, pp. 49–50). In either case the body is accepted as a dichotomous, decontextualized form.

## Critical Gerontology

There is widespread unease in gerontology today that conventional styles of research and practice – the conventional positivism and empiricism prevalent in the field – are inadequate (Cole 1993). Sociological theories of old age have become exceedingly dynamic and comprehensive, and have taken a more critical turn. As Katz notes (1996, p. 4): "Critical gerontologists admonish gerontology for its narrow scientificity, advocate stronger ties to the humanities, endorse reflexive methodologies, historicize ideological attributes of old age, promote radical political engagement, and resignify the aging process as heterogeneous and indeterminate."

According to critical gerontologists the experience of old age in the scientific discourse is treated as part of the natural order to the exclusion of the cultural order (Dannefer 1989). This natural order produces an image of the individual as a passive being processed through an objectively factual life-course lacking any intentionality. Such a narrow postulation denies the importance of agency, choice, and context, and mutes the voice of the individual. It also neglects political and social surroundings, and culturally constituted meanings (Dannefer 1989). Critical gerontologists argue that knowledge of old age should come from the aged themselves. The focus is often on collecting personal narratives in order to give voice to experience. Friendship circles, residential settings, and the collaborative meaning-sharing activities of the aged serve as discernible contexts for elucidating meanings of old age (Gubrium 1993).

It is against the conventional positivism and empiricism in geriatrics that there has been a decided surge of interest in personal meaning in everyday life (Gubrium 1993). The aged individual is seen not as an object of social practices but as a subject constituted through individual experiences. The central thrust of this qualitative work ". . . emphasizes a view of the individual as . . . participating actively in fashioning a life course" (Marshall 1986, p. 13). Personal accounts represent a previously suppressed "voice" now speaking out and telling how it "really" is to experience old age. Personal accounts become the basis on which an alternative interpretation of knowledge of old age is possible. By providing gerontology with a critical subjective dimension it is possible to counter the claims of positivistic social science and its neglect of the subjective dimension. The goal is to make visible variety, contingency, and inventiveness in old age while resisting the temptation to produce an analytically consistent text that privileges certain voices and silences others (Gubrium 1993).

Old age has biological, psychological and sociological aspects, and the challenge of conceiving old age as both authentically human and culturally located has been a central concern of critical theorists in gerontology (Hendricks and Leedham 1987). Theoretical developments in critical gerontology have emerged with increasing sophistication and insight. Nevertheless, while these critical perspectives do provide valuable critiques of medical theories, they reproduce a problem inherent in geriatric and mainstream gerontological theoretical formulations of old age: culture is understood as being externally related to a universal human form. Culture, within this dichotomous framework, explains variation in surface meanings and shared beliefs while the depths of each individual are presumed to involve the same physiological and organic processes and changes.

Thus the field of aging studies in its medical and gerontological configurations represents an articulation of human characteristics that denies the ongoing dynamic interaction between the body and intentionality, the body and culture, and the body and its physical and social surroundings. It is the influence of these dichotomous paradigms, and the reluctance to explore the interface between them, that leads even critical gerontology discourse to hold that the natural body is generalizable to all human beings in all social contexts. This ultimately denies the intimate exchange between biology and culture, and consequently denies a full contextual perspective.

## Locating the Body

The theme of localizing biology, that is, contextualizing the interrelationship between biology and culture is championed by Margaret Lock. In her rich ethnographic account of Japanese experiences of menopause (1993), she interprets processes of aging in relation to the social and political order in Japan and to the medical discourse about female mid-life in North America. Using data from field research conducted in Japan in 1983–4, Lock questions the universalism underlying biomedical studies on menopause and its symptoms. In exposing contradictions between individual narratives about menopause in Japan and professional discourse about a universal Menopausal Woman, Lock challenges the assumption that menopause is a universal experience at *any* level – social, psychological or biological. She argues that even at the level of chemistry and physiology there are extensive biological variations within and between populations. Such variations result from an extraordinarily complex process of engagement between biology, individual sentience, culture, and history. Though Lock acknowledges that this exchange may be difficult to articulate, perhaps of more importance is that such a dynamic can never ". . . be assumed to be manifest in virtually the same way for everyone" (Lock 1993, p. 372).

Lock deconstructs representations of aging which treat the body as an entity distinct from any cultural meaning. She moves beyond the biology/culture dichotomy and acknowledges the plasticity of biology and its interdependence with culture. She argues that though there is a biological reality to the etiology of menopause, a full understanding of menopause calls for its contextualization in the complex and dynamic interaction of biology, individual subjectivity, culturally infused expectations, and social and physical surroundings. By placing an interpretation of the experience of the body at the centre of her analysis, Lock argues that biology both constrains and shapes human experience but, "aging realities" are never merely reflections of biology. Lock asserts that we must contextualize interpretations of the body through local histories, local politics and local knowledge; what she ultimately terms "local biologies" (Lock 1993, p. 39). Lock rejects a universal aging body and posits in its place aging *bodies*.

The theme of plurality finds support in other disciplines. In feminist thought (Butler 1993; Haraway 1991; Benhabib 1992) and sociology (Featherstone et al. 1991; Turner 1987; Shilling 1993) knowledge about the body is being called into account and deconstructed, and its interconnections with culture, power, and discourse are being explored. Universal knowledge claims about biology are challenged, deconstructed and thus "located."

Such critical theoretical leads take the study of old age to a new frontier where the temporal and situational diversity of the cultural and social intersections of the aged make it impossible to totalize old age into a single essential unity. Indeed, such unity has largely been defined by biological or social conditions exclusively. It is a new frontier where biology and culture are indivisible, culture and meaning become one, body and mind merge. To proceed as though the dichotomies between biology and culture, and mind and body are divorced from each other is to deny their mutual mirroring and their modifying effects upon each other. However, to observe how they inform each other, interact, clash and readjust is to provide the key to a more accurate understanding of old age as experienced and constituted by the aged within their social milieu (Hazan 1987). Neither biology nor culture nor place exists independently, and it is in their exchange that each acquires its properties from its relation to the other. All are elements that the aged appropriate to infuse their experiences with meaning.

Lock's notion of "local biology" illuminates the complex and dynamic interplay between biology, meaning and sentience. From this understanding that the body is always located in place, and hence a local phenomenon, flows the premise that informs my analysis of Home Frontier as a *home-place*.

## Experiencing Old Age at Home

In the following section I unravel some of the stratagems employed by the tenants in their attempt to build a community that manages deterioration associated with the process of aging. This is a community that the senior tenants themselves constructed in a place they call home.

Contact Agency and Resources for the Elderly (CARE)[4] is a pioneer agency in the development of a range of supportive housing options for seniors with various needs which delay or even eliminate the need for institutionalization of the frail aged. CARE coordinates the delivery of a wide range of services which allow elderly people with different levels of competence and capacities for independent living to remain in community settings. Seniors are able to remain in community settings by progressively receiving greater input of service support as they become more vulnerable. One of CARE's supportive housing buildings, Home Frontier, was the site of my field research.

Home Frontier, located in the east end of Toronto, opened in 1990. It is an eight-story brick building with 174 apartment units. Of the 234 tenants, 162 are women and 72 are men; the average age is 74. The tenants are mainly first or second generation United Kingdom immigrants. There is also a large number of Chinese tenants. The great majority share a background of low socioeconomic status resulting from minimal schooling and having assumed low income occupations. Osteoporosis, diabetes, Parkinson's, and arthritis are the most common degenerative conditions of the tenants.

Of the 35 tenants with whom I spoke, I interviewed ten for interview periods of several hours, six of whom I visited more frequently during the entire fieldwork period. Of the ten whom I interviewed, nine were women and one was a man. Four of the ten tenants whom I interviewed, all women, were regarded as the core group of tenant leaders and three of them I visited frequently. I also interviewed four staff members, two women and two men, and the Executive Director of CARE, a woman.

At Home Frontier home is the context that figures significantly in the construction and experience of old age. The significance of home brings to the foreground the importance of coping strategies that seniors use, and the length they will go to avoid relocation to an institutional care facility (Sixsmith 1990). An important issue for senior tenants of Home Frontier is maintaining their independence in the face of mounting illness and disability. Their desire to remain independent and in control of their own lives is linked to home living and to what home signifies to them. In fact, it is their independence that facilitates their claim to home. At the same time, home is a valuable resource to senior tenants in adjusting to physical changes that come with old age. In terms of independence, home is therefore significant for seniors as it fosters their awareness of physical decline and provides a forum to negotiate that decline (Sixsmith 1990). Home is a way of ". . . preserving independence, both instrumentally and as a symbol of continuing individuality" (Sixsmith and Sixsmith 1991, p. 189).

## Managing Health Deterioration: Shared Fate and Interdependence

Good health is relative for the tenants of Home Frontier as it is for many seniors. Most have at least one chronic condition and some degree of illness or bodily malfunction. Their main concern is with avoidance of health deterioration and its management and stabilization when it occurs.

There is an overriding concern with health, and numerous strategies are developed in order to avoid or minimize the occurrences of illness and accident. One is sure to take any prescribed medication. Eating regularly and watching one's diet are also very important. Diabetics must keep a daily record of their blood sugar level and, depending on the type of diabetes, either insulin injections are required or through diet and exercise levels of blood glucose can be controlled. Sometimes it is difficult not to eat foods one likes, despite warnings of their consequent effects. Sometimes succumbing to the temptation and eating what one pleases is favored over strict abstinence. But this may cause suffering for having done so. As Audrey[5] comments: "There is a price for everything I do. I go for a walk and my legs hurt, I eat a beautiful meal and I suffer inside."

The variation of individual circumstance and condition regarding health at Home Frontier is substantial. Yet the problem of maintaining health and managing deteriorating health is common to all tenants. It is dealt with by taking medication, watching one's diet and being cautious so that falling accidents in particular, and accidents in general, can be avoided. As Sylvia explained:

> Sometimes I'm sitting on the sofa and I want something from the kitchen. I have to decide if it is worth the trouble of getting up and using the walker. It is exhausting business moving this walker around. I don't go anywhere because it is quite an effort and I'm afraid of falling. Beyond reading and watching television there is not much that I can do. I can't paint or do clever things like that because my hand shakes. That's the Parkinson's.

Yet even the best precautions sometimes fail and the possibility of becoming ill or suffering an injury is something with which one must live. These problems are partially solved by socializing mechanisms and various strategies for maintaining health. Illness is so prevalent and accidents are such common occurrences that many tenants are engaged in adapting themselves to deterioration and change associated with the aging process. Deterioration and other changes associated with old age are dealt with and incorporated into the ongoing life at Home Frontier.

At Home Frontier many tenants are involved in assisting others who are disabled, convalescing or are experiencing the loss of their physical abilities. Nobody is comfortable with the prospect of leaving Home Frontier because of poor health since the next move would be to a nursing home or other residential care facility. As Margaret comments:

> All I do is sleep. I'm tired all the time. It gets me down when I can't do things. I do love living here. I have a nice view and the sun shines through. The people in this place keep me going. I'm confined to this chair for the most part because I can't walk good. I keep my mind busy by planning parties, starting knitting projects and thinking. I am afraid of having to move to a nursing home because it will kill me.

Neighbors and friends together form an informal support network that provides assistance for those individuals who become less able to manage on their own. Tenants confined to wheelchairs or with other infirmities are helped through the day by neighbors and friends with meal preparation, dressing and doing household tasks. The tenants who help others feel that they are reciprocating for favors which had been done for them when they were in need. Enid explained that:

> I was very sick for a while. They thought that I was going to die. People here took good care of my cat when I was in the hospital. I don't have much in terms of money but I love the seniors here and I help out where I can. Sylvia is a sweetheart and I take care of her. It's funny that I feel responsible for her, but I do. She helps me too. I think that's what my life boils down to in the end. Helping others.

Friends and neighbors exchange various kinds of help based on special skills. Individuals with particular expertise do work for friends or neighbors in exchange for other forms of work that others, with their own particular skills, do for them. For example, Claire, a former seamstress, sews, hems, and mends for Sophie who knitted her a blanket. Harry, who is especially skilled at carpentry, built a stool and a coat rack for his neighbor who in return, had his wife Sophie share recipes with Harry's wife Judith. Women often do mending and ironing for widowers who in turn help out with household repairs.

Margaret told me that when she came home from the hospital after having had surgery she was deluged with offers to help her with cleaning her apartment, food preparation, and laundry. Sylvia is financially sound but her Parkinson's progressively reduces her capacity to do things on her own. Sylvia's neighbor Enid is in good health, but her income is minimal, and she barely gets by each month. Each has a valuable resource; Enid has her health and Sylvia has money. They have created a reciprocal arrangement that serves to balance each other's weakness. Sylvia helps Enid financially, and in return, Enid assists Sylvia by helping her to dress each morning, picking up groceries for her, washing and cutting up vegetables, and keeping the apartment tidy between visits by the homemaker. Enid also takes Sylvia for "walks," by pushing Sylvia's wheelchair, and accompanies her to activities in the building.

Exchanging items or services is not the only means of reciprocation between tenants. Often reciprocations take the form of invitations to dinner. Margaret has a dinner party once a month in return for favors done by friends and neighbors.

In addition to material assistance, emotional caring is another important kind of caretaking. A special solidarity developed between Eleanor and Emily, a pair who have come to be recognized by other tenants as "mates" who rely on each other for a wide range of assistance, emotional support and company. As Eleanor explained:

Emily is my dear friend. She's my confidant. She's my pal. She's everything to me. I've never had a friend like Emily. We do our shopping together, we go to movies, parks and concerts. She'll call me and say "What do you have in your fridge?" I'll say "Wait a minute and I'll look." I'll fill a basket and take it over to her place or she will bring things here. We get busy in the kitchen together. It's really nice. Neither of us like to eat alone so this works out well. We take care of each other. We know one another's kitchen as well as we know our own. We talk about things and that helps us manage.

The tenants continuously provide social and emotional support for each other. For example, Sylvia was congratulated by the Breakfast Club[6] when they realized that she had socks on. For a woman with Parkinson's, this is not a small accomplishment. They all knew that she had been wearing closed slippers for some time since she had been unable to put a pair of socks on by herself. At a bingo game everyone applauded when Pearl took a bow and announced that she had seen her doctor that day and received a clean bill of health. When Sylvia got her automated wheelchair it attracted a lot of attention; everyone was very patient with her unfamiliarity with its operation. Often she would bump into people, miscalculating distances, or hold people up in the elevator as she had trouble maneuvering the wheelchair into narrow spaces. Comments made by those tenants witnessing her difficulties were of a humorous nature, indicating understanding rather than irritation: "You need a license to drive that," or "Slow down, you might get a speeding ticket." Enid would go for "walks" with Sylvia while she practiced on her new machine.

A number of customary practices such as sending "thinking of you," "welcome home," "get well," "birthday," and "bereavement" cards, or daily telephone calls let tenants know that they are cared for by others and provide a continuous monitoring of physical and emotional states. There is genuine concern for each other that plays a significant role as a source of support and emotional sustenance.

At Home Frontier, the development of mutual support, reciprocal dependence, shared experiences and feelings, are sources of community and cohesion, and are the basis for social organization. Life at Home Frontier is largely dominated by mutual and community care. This care is extensive and significant since illness and handicap occur and recur with regularity. The tenants' construction of home is intimately tied to their common struggle to live independently. Interdependence is indeed an important source of community the tenants have created for themselves.[7] Extending and receiving assistance amongst tenants is by far preferred to making bureaucratic requests which emphasize the tenants' dependence on staff. This observation finds support in Hazan's ethnographic study of a London England day center (1980). In an elaboration of this study Hazan states that only dependency on nonmembers of the center, and particularly on staff members ". . . became a threat to the idea of self-sufficiency and autonomy" (Hazan 1986, p. 314).

There are significant areas of collective meanings at Home Frontier centered mainly upon the world of the building and the tenants' "shared fate." This world unites the tenants and founds commonality. Tenants together define Home Frontier as their home. Friends and neighbors provide one another with practical and emotional support, and help one another find appropriate ways of adapting to the personal, physical, and social changes that occur in old age. Interdependence, mutual assistance and community care together highlight the tenants' common desire to remain independent. Living at home symbolizes their independence and represents victory over deterioration and dependency.

The tenants' understanding of Home Frontier as home is threatened by staff and management's policies, procedures, guidelines, and constraints which restrict the tenants' independence. Home Frontier is a *home-place* by virtue of its contested constructions. This contestation reflects conflicting experiential realities that Home Frontier holds for both the tenants and staff. The following section turns to the ways in which the tenants' social existence is constructed through a complex dynamic of resisting staff directives and negotiating with staff. More precisely, there is a complex relation between tenants accepting and managing their physical decline in a home environment and resisting their perception of staff's conversion of their home environment to an institutionalized care of their decline. The tenants struggle to establish and maintain certain social arrangements in their home world in an effort to negate any perceived features of an institutional world.

## Resistance and Negotiation

On the lower level of Home Frontier there is an office for staff. A property manager is there to speak with tenants concerning their lease or other matters having to do with the building. A life skills coordinator gives support to tenants who have special needs. Three programming staff can be met regarding recreational activities, and three Case Managers are available to coordinate other services for tenants such as transportation, shopping and assistance with government forms.

The staff's enforcement of rules and regulations in order to ensure the smooth operation of the apartment building, creates a particular tension for tenants between notions of home and institution. Funding constraints, planning requirements, policies, procedures, safety standards and operational guidelines – all features of an institutional setting – are perceived as negating home space and converting it into institutional space. Tenants' identities are therefore the stake of their struggle to assert their independence and resist a premature dependence that bespeaks of loss of personal competence.

At Home Frontier tenants are encouraged to assume a great deal of managerial work such as working as desk receptionist, organizing and running the daily activities in the building, and planning and scheduling events and programs in the Tea Room. CARE's objective at Home Frontier is to enhance the possibility for tenants to control their own lives and to participate in the decision-making processes governing their social environment. As the Executive Director of CARE commented: "We want to encourage these people to run things for themselves and give them some interest in life now that they have retired. We don't want them to become candidates for our 'frail' housing option."[8]

Tenants are encouraged to participate and share in the control of events affecting their lives. This creates the opportunity for some tenants to make administrative demands such as to take part in scheduling the program calendar and deciding on the allocation of certain funds. Yet, since the opening of the building four years ago, many if not all of the activities requiring some degree of cooperation between tenants and the staff have led to conflict.

Tenants demand that their feelings be recognized, they insist on being heard, demand recognition on their own terms, and insist on entitlements. In encounters with the staff, the tenants put forth points of view and explanations that are intended to persuade staff, interpreting their own demands and actions as fair and reasonable. Thus they create situations in which the assertion and confirmation of their self-identities remain in their control.

Home Frontier is the total life world for many tenants. It is only the world of work for staff. Staff operate at Home Frontier on an eight-hour day and are socially integrated in other worlds, in other realities, and are therefore often seen by tenants as having divided loyalties. This makes their position appear paradoxical. Staff set out to organize Home Frontier within a philosophy of care that explicitly aims to provide a supportive environment for seniors. Yet the fact that they are not living at Home Frontier makes their presence a subtle threat to the success of their efforts to create a comfortable and rewarding experience for the tenants. Staff work at Home Frontier but tenants live there. Tenants struggle to make it into, and maintain it as, the kind of community they want. It is after all their home.

In the face of staff's preoccupation with administrative priorities tenants are constantly engaged in a battle of wills to get their concerns addressed. Tenants organized programs that better satisfied their interests as opposed to those of programming staff, they fought to have the Tea Room[9] redecorated, and they always challenged and resisted rules imposed by staff. Even the smallest victory is significant to the active tenants, and is also appreciated by the less active tenants. This is because active tenants are using their energy to do things that others may not have the energy or inclination to do. Tenants who try to improve the situation at Home Frontier are appreciated for not becoming discouraged by the frequently paltry results. Resistance and negotiation dramatize and confirm the significance of home space for the tenants' sense of personal identity, self-confirmation, and for a meaningful existence.

A number of programs were in place when the tenants moved into the building in June of 1990. Tenants were hostile toward programming staff, claiming they did not really represent the tenants' interests, that the staff simply wanted power and enjoyed being important, and never solicited ideas for activities from tenants. Grace commented on an encounter with programming staff when she expressed to them her anger about their initiating activities without any input from tenants:

> We are adults and would like to be consulted before activities are scheduled, especially since these are projects that are supposed to involve us. You don't even take an active part in anything so why are you implementing activities? We can make our own decisions. I don't believe you have asked us about any of these activities. You think we're beyond the age of creativity or even competence. We're not senile.

Some tenants felt that their potential for initiating activities was underestimated by the staff. They resented being excluded from the decision-making process regarding activities that are designed specifically for them. They claimed to be capable of making decisions of their own rather than being passive recipients of decisions made by others. Over the summer of 1990 this group of tenants talked amongst themselves about their own ideas and concluded that they had a better sense of what their interests were. They came up with euchre, bingo, pub night, singing classes, and the Breakfast Club. All of these activities were implemented in the Fall of 1990.

In February 1992, a new issue emerged. It was recounted to me that tenants wanted to redo the wallpaper in the Tea Room because they found the existing wallpaper dull and unattractive. The property manager's response to their request was "no" since the wallpaper had just recently been changed, and therefore the expense of redoing it could not be justified. The tenants saw things from an entirely different perspective. They argued that since the tenants *live* there and don't like the paper, that should be reason enough to change it.

Because the tenants initiated activities they assumed it was their right to manage the earnings these activities generated. They felt that they should be permitted to manage the money they were making, and because they consider the Tea Room part of their home, they should be able to decide what the room needs and doesn't need without seeking approval. In fact, tenants felt they should advise the staff of Home Frontier how funds should be spent. Contrary to such claims to ownership, the staff insist that the Tea Room belongs to CARE, and as such, *they* are entitled to oversee what transpires there. The wallpaper was not changed.

By January 1993 tension between tenants and the staff had increased further. My informants recounted that rules became tighter. Permission from programming staff was necessary for the use of the Tea Room and restrictions were placed on the duration of time the Tea Room could be used. Also notices had to be approved before being posted up on the bulletin boards.

The tenants reflected that they experienced all these rules as features of institutional control. Sophie insightfully commented: "It got worse. Too much of what we wanted to do was regulated, sanctioned, and judged." Tenants agreed that it was impossible to accept the new rules. The staff's strict rules gave rise to bitter jokes about needing their permission to, for example, use the bathroom or empty garbage.

Tenant leaders began to plan new strategies to challenge and resist the constant sanctioning that was causing dissension. They attempted to reverse the new changes by appealing to the board members of CARE. Grace recounted that at a Tenant/Management meeting Sylvia and she spoke out on the issue of the Tea Room hours. They asked that it be open from 9:00 a.m. to 9:00 p.m. Sylvia explained to the board members that "people complain bitterly that they can't get into the room and use it. Often we want to get a book from the library at our convenience. Maybe there's nothing on T.V. and I'd like to come up and get a book. Others like to come in with a friend and chat over a cup of tea." At the same meeting Grace and Claire offered to assume the responsibility for locking up the room at 9:00 p.m. One of the board members turned down this request explaining that when the building first opened and the Tea Room was accessible at all times, lamps and small items from the kitchen disappeared. As a result, she said that "as landlords we have to protect our property. The door must be locked for security reasons."

Regarding the rule that notices needed prior approval to be posted, tenants told me they agreed with the claim made by a tenant at the Breakfast Club that "this makes us feel like children that someone has to read our notices before they can be posted." Competition began for bulletin space between the staff's events and those organized by the tenants. This eventually became problematic since it is the staff who assumed authority in determining what got posted, and their notices often took precedence over those of the tenants. There was a decline in participation in the evening programs organized by the tenants. This was explained to me by those tenants in charge of running the evening activities as a result of not being able to post notices to remind people of upcoming social events. The tenants' solution to this was to lobby for their own bulletin board.

Understanding why the tenants continue their struggle for control over the Tea Room cannot be separated from their notion that the Tea Room, in particular, and the building as a whole, is their home. Hence their persistent suggestions at meetings with CARE to make their home more attractive and comfortable. Hanging framed prints of some kind in the lobby, mounting a mirror, getting a new desk for the lobby reception area, and installing brighter lights are the most common suggestions. One woman at a Tenants' Association meeting said "the lobby looks like an institution but this isn't an institution, it is our home." When the issue turned to the matter of money another woman shouted "don't ask CARE because they'll say they don't have the money. Besides they only work here but we live here." Another woman said "we should be willing to do the work and invest the money because this is our home." Everyone applauded in response.

This sentiment was echoed at the first Tenant/Management meeting. Grace recounted that she stood up and made the following opening statement:

> Over at CARE you seem to feel that you have a lot of smart, intelligent clever people, and I grant you that you have. But let me tell you what we have over here. We also have a lot of smart, intelligent and clever people, but we have a hell of a lot more than you because we have experience on our side. We hope that cooperation is possible because *you only work here but we live here.*[10] This is our home and as such we want it to be as nice as possible. Let's please start this meeting with that understanding.

The idea of home is a dominant theme of the senior tenants' existence. Tenants' resistance and negotiations reaffirm and further elucidate the significance of home. In the process of negotiation a clash emerged between the way in which the staff conceived of Home Frontier as an administrative territory and the way the seniors conceived of themselves as a home community. Particularly troubling to the tenants was when the staff attempted to frame the nature of their problems as purely administrative dilemmas. The staff did not realize that the exercise of their administrative tasks was perceived by the seniors as a prematurely harsh reminder of what might be their future. The tenants redefined the issues that the staff perceived to be exclusively administrative as experientially and emotionally significant realities of home.

## Discussion

"Locating" the senior tenants within their social milieu highlights the inadequacy of the assumption that old age is primarily a natural phenomenon whose course is predetermined. Such a construction ignores any physical or sociocultural location, self-identities, and self-defined social roles. Indeed it is the failure to acknowledge self-identities "that generates the concept of the old person as sick and in need of medical care" (Hazan 1994, p. 14).

My central argument has been that place is integral to how old age is experienced and constructed. Home affords independence by defining a space that is controlled by and is uniquely the domain of the individual. Home is a space in which to pursue personal interests and also, as it is resonant with experiences and expectations, it is a vital facet of self-identity. Understanding the senior tenants' experiences of old age at Home Frontier must therefore include an exploration of how and why they construct a home community, including their experiences of ambiguity and conflict regarding their home community.

The tenants' construction of home largely hinges on their pragmatic responses to the exigencies of their functional, economic and social conditions. These pragmatic responses become apparent in their "adjustment" tactics. The tenants adopt strategies which allow them to retain control over many aspects of their lives and maintain the fabric of home at standards they recognize as being appropriate for themselves. Strategies for coping with declining health involve the construction of home as a meaningful context, one that affords independence, and shapes and maintains seniors' self-identities. Declining health does not lead inevitably to the disintegration of self-identity.

Tenants justify their existence and assert their self-identity through the process of resistance to the staff. In terms of identity, the ability to control intrusions into "home territory" is a salient issue. Home plays an important part in framing the experience of independence, since independence is so intimately linked to control. Tenants resist the staff's efforts to control the Tea Room and, in essence, their lives at Home Frontier. The tenants are claiming the legitimate control exercised in the home domain. Jackson et al. stress the significance of personal control over one's living space by arguing that functional capacity is largely determined by the "... physical or dispositional competency to negotiate one's living environment ..." (1991, p. 306).

The seniors living at Home Frontier engaged in strategies to oppose what they perceived as staff interference. This is because staff interference was not merely the painful negation of home for the seniors, but the conversion of "home space" into "institutional space." This perceived conversion symbolically represented a confirmation of their deterioration and dependency. What the senior tenants feared most is their future inability to care for themselves which would call for institutional care.

Symbolic approaches to understanding the built environment as an expression of culturally shared meanings contributes to my analysis of the "territorial stakes" (Lawrence and Low 1990) in the Tea Room. As an expression of culture, the Tea Room played a communicative role, embodying and conveying meaning. It was therefore far more than a point of reference; it was a "socially constructed product" of "interests, needs and ideas" (Rodman 1992). In this sense, for the senior tenants, the Tea Room was both a locale for social activities and it was invested with a "sense of place" (Agnew 1993) as home. Ironically, for the staff too, the Tea Room was invested with symbolic value which transcended the activities and events that took place there. It symbolized their work at Home Frontier. The Tea Room therefore embodied fragmented multivocal meanings which rendered it a contested space in the practice of its use.

The senior tenants' social existence is constructed, contested and affirmed through the conflicting territorial stakes in the Tea Room. When staff obstruct the tenants' self-direction and control of the home domain, this has direct implications for the tenants' experience of that place as home. The staff's sanctions, perceived by the senior tenants as interference, challenge the seniors' personal connection with home and thereby undermine the seniors' independence, control and sense of identity.

## Conclusion: Theoretical Implications

Given that knowledge is produced and reproduced in context, it follows that knowledge about old age must be culturally relative and socially diverse. However, in geriatrics the category of the aged is read as exclusively biological; in gerontology it is read as exclusively socio-cultural. By contrast, I suggest that old age does not permit any exclusive reading.

There are complex and dynamic interactions among biological changes, social surroundings, and individual cognition. This extraordinarily complex engagement is revealed at Home Frontier in personal narratives, socialization mechanisms, resistance and negotiation. The argument in this article is that place is inextricably linked to the experience of old age. By implication, how old age is constructed is variable depending on the context. The tenants at Home Frontier are living the experience of old age in a place that they constructed as home.

Place is much more than just a setting. Home Frontier is an agent that by definition plays a significant role in the tenants' self-identities. It is perceived as home and tenants constantly project this interpretation in their fight to have a voice in determining the organizational framework and administration of Home Frontier. Their resistance and negotiations show most clearly how home as a physical place and a meaningful context for everyday life carries meaning and sentiment and frames the tenants' construction and affirmation of their experiences of independent living.

I have argued that a dynamic relationship ensues between the body, meaning and place. It is a dialectical process in which cultural beliefs influence the interpretation and experience of physiological processes associated with old age which then inform the cultural construction of place. Thus, the tenants' construction of home is intimately tied to their struggle for independent living which involves "adjustment" tactics to cope with physical decline and incapacity. The immediacy of illness and handicap occurring and recurring with such regularity is the "body's insistence on meaning" (Kirmayer 1992).

The body is by no means a "mute objective biological substrate upon which meaning is superimposed" (Csordas 1994, p. 287). The tenants, in attending to the "body's insistence on meaning", socially organize their home community such that it is informed by mutual support, reciprocal dependence, and boundless care. The home community at Home Frontier is largely the meaningful effect of the senior tenants' interpretation and response to exigencies of their physical decline.

The contextualization of the tenants' chronic conditions and physical decline further reveals that self-definition and the sociocultural construction of the community at Home Frontier has "corporeal existential significance" (Csordas 1994, p. 288). Thus, the place where the last stage of life is lived is prominent in how old age is experienced and interpreted. The tenants create informal support networks which provide assistance to those who become less able to manage on their own. For many this assistance sustains their independence. Through the support they give and receive they confirm one another's self-identity. Helping one another find appropriate ways of adapting to the physical changes that occur with old age shapes how these changes are experienced.

Tenants are experiencing old age in a particular environment, an environment that is largely the product of their activities and construction. Place and the experience of old age are related since the distinct definition of social organization at Home Frontier can be traced to the tenants' interpretation and management of biological changes.

Through observation, interviews and analysis I have found that these senior tenants' identities are what is at stake in the struggle to construct and assert their independence and control, and to resist any premature loss of function or ability. Therefore there is a complex relation between senior tenants accepting their physical decline, interpreting and managing it, and simultaneously resisting the conversion of their home into an agent of institutionalization of their decline. This perceived conversion effectively threatens their sense of place symbolized as home and, in turn, their personal identity in old age.

The ethnographic research presented here opens up an analytic space to reformulate a theoretical perspective on old age and its relations with culture and experience, with the body at its center. Understanding the body as "a vehicle for thinking, feeling and acting" (Kirmayer 1992, p. 325), as the "seat of subjectivity" (Csordas 1994, p. 9), is a challenge to geriatric and gerontological perspectives in which culture is deployed in parallel with or in contrast to biology.

Just as Young asserts that disease episodes are grounded in the order of social relationships, meaning, belief, and human understanding (Young 1976), I argue that the same applies to old age. The claim that the body in old age has its grounding in the order of meaning and human understanding is the source for critical theorizing in this article. It is the basis for exploring the relation of biology and culture. Following the lead of critical theorists in anthropology, sociology, and feminist thought, it is most constructive to conceive the body as subject of knowledge, experience, and meaning, rendering old age knowable only through an interpretive scheme. The body's insistence on meaning interacts with social, psychological, and physiological processes to produce distinct lived experiences of old age. The body's universal quest for meaning can only be fulfilled within a particular place, and hence there can only be an array of meanings as opposed to a universal, permanent, and timeless meaning of old age.

The task of this article has been to problematize the boundary erected between biology and culture in the discipline of gerontology and geriatrics, and to consider the implications of that boundary. My argument casts doubt on claims of a static universal bodily condition of old age by alluding to the impossibility of a placeless old age. Localizing narratives and the body in old age clearly captures the particularity as opposed to the universality of this multidimensional phenomenon.

## Notes

1   The name of this building is a pseudonym.
2   For the full account see P. C. Kontos 1995. *Constructing Old Age in a Place Called Home*. Unpublished M.A. Thesis. York University, Department of Anthropology. Toronto, Canada.

3   In the context of my argument presented here, the term culture is regarded as primarily an ideological phenomenon, providing a means for interpreting the world.
4   The name of this agency is a pseudonym.
5   The names of tenants living in Home Frontier, referred to in this article, are pseudonyms.
6   This is an open drop-in organized and run by tenants at which coffee, tea, toast and muffins are available for all tenants for one dollar.
7   The tenants' interdependence does not contradict their desire to be independent. Tenants of Home Fronteir are living "independently" in the sense that they presently are not in need of an institutional care facility.
8   This is a housing option for the more frail individuals. This option accommodates those with more severe levels of impairment by providing a more complete package of on-site services.
9   The Tea Room is located at the end of the lobby and is used by the tenants for parties, card games, the Breakfast Club, movies, information seminars, and special entertainment events. It is also used by the staff for afternoon and evening meetings.
10  The emphasis reflects the speaker's tone.

## References

Achenbaum, W. A. 1995. *Crossing Frontiers: Gerontology Emerges as a Science*. Cambridge: Cambridge University Press.
Agnew, J. 1993. "Representing Space: Space, Scale and Culture in Social Science." Pp. 251–71 in *Place/Culture/Representation*, edited by J. D., and D. Ley, London: Routledge.
Benhabib, S. 1992. *Situating the Self: Gender, Community and Postmodernism in Contemporary Ethics*. New York: Routledge.
Butler, J. 1993. *Bodies That Matter: On the Discursive Limits of "Sex"*. New York: Routledge.
Cole, T. R. 1993. "Preface." Pp. vii–xi in *Voices and Visions of Aging: Toward a Critical Gerontology*, edited by W. A. Achenbaum, P. L. Jakobi, and R. Kastenbaum. New York: Springer Publishing.
Csordas, T. J. 1994. *Embodiment and Experience: The Existential Ground of Culture and Self*. Cambridge: Cambridge University Press.
Dannefer, D. 1989. "Human Action and its Place in Theories of Aging." *Journal of Aging Studies* 3(1): 1–20.
Estes, C. L., and E. A. Binney. 1989. "The Biomedicalization of Aging: Dangers and Dilemmas." *The Gerontologist* 29(5): 587–96.
Featherstone, M., M. Hepworth, and B. S. Turner (eds.). 1991. *The Body: Social Process and Cultural Theory*. London: Sage.
Fogel, B. S. 1992. "Psychological Aspects of Staying at Home." *Generations* 16(2): 15–9.
Gubrium, J. F. 1993. "Voice and Context in a New Gerontology." Pp. 46–64 in *Voices and Visions of Aging: Toward a Critical Gerontology*, edited by T. Cole, W. A. Achenbaum, P. L. Jakobi, and R. Kastenbaum. New York: Springer Publishing.
Haber, C. 1983. *Beyond Sixty-Five: The Dilemma of Old age in America's Past*. New York: Cambridge University Press.
Haraway, D. J. 1991. *Simians, Cyborgs, and Women: The Reinvention of Nature*. New York: Routledge.
Hazan, H. 1980. *The Limbo People: A Study of the Constitution of the Time Universe Among the Aged*. London: Routlege & Kegan Paul.
Hazan, H. 1986. "Body Image and Temporality Among the Aged: A Case Study of an Ambivalent Symbol." *Studies in Symbolic Interaction* 7(A): 305–29.
Hazan, H. 1987. "Myth into Reality: Enacting Life Histories in an Institutional Setting." Pp.

441–8 in *Aging: The Universal Human Experience,* edited by G. L. Maddox, and E. W. Busse. New York: Springer Publishing.

Hazan, H. 1994. *Old Age: Constructions and Deconstructions.* Cambridge: Cambridge University Press.

Hendricks, J., and C. A. Leedham. 1987. "Making Sense of Literary Aging: Relevance of Recent Gerontological Theory." *Journal of Aging Studies* 1(2): 187–208.

Jackson, D. J., C. F. Longino, R. S. Zimmerman, and J. E. Bradsher. 1991. "Environmental Adjustments to Declining Functional Ability: Residential Mobility and Living Arrangements." *Research on Aging* 13(3): 289–309.

Katz, S. 1996. *Disciplining Old Age: The Formation of Gerontological Knowledge.* Charlottesville: University Press of Virginia.

Kirmayer, L. J. 1992. "The Body's Insistence on Meaning: Metaphor as Presentation and Representation in Illness Experience." *Medical Anthropology Quarterly* 6(4): 323–46.

Kontos, P. C. 1995. *Constructing Old Age in a Place Called Home.* Unpublished M. A. Thesis. York University, Department of Anthropology.

Lawrence, D. L., and S. M. Low, 1990. "The Built Environment and Spatial Form." *Annual Review of Anthropology* 19: 453–505.

Lock, M. 1993. *Encounters with Aging: Mythologies of Menopause in Japan and North America.* Berkeley: University of California Press.

Marshall, V. W. 1986. "A Sociological Perspective on Aging and Dying." Pp. 125–46 in *Later Life: The Social Psychology of Aging,* edited by Victor W. Marshall. Beverly Hills: Sage.

Robertson, A. 1990. "The Politics of Alzheimer's Disease: A Case Study in Apocalyptic Demography." *International Journal of Health Services* 20(3): 429–42.

Rodman, M. C. 1992. "Empowering Place: Multilocality and Multivocality." *American Anthropologist* 94(3): 640–56.

Rowles, G. D. 1983. "Place and Personal Identity in Old Age: Observations From Appalachia." *Journal of Environmental Psychology* 3: 299–313.

Rowles, G. D. 1993. "Evolving Images of Place in Aging and 'Aging in Place'." *Generations* 17(2): 65–70.

Rubinstein, R. L. 1989. "The Home Environments of Older People: A Description of the Psychosocial Processes Linking Person to Place." *Journal of Gerontology, Social Sciences* 44(2): S45–53.

Rutman, D. L., and J. L. Freedman. 1988. "Anticipating Relocation: Coping Strategies and the Meaning of Home for Older People." *Canadian Journal on Aging* 7(1): 17–31.

Shilling, C. 1993. *The Body and Social Theory.* London: Sage.

Sixsmith, A. J. 1990. "The Meaning and Significance of Home in Later Life." Pp. 172–92 in *Welfare and the Ageing Experience,* edited by B. Bytheway and J. Johnson. Aldershot: Gower.

Sixsmith, A. J., and J. A. Sixsmith, 1991. "Transitions in Home Experience in Later Life." *The Journal of Architectural and Planning Research* 8(3): 181–91.

Turner, B. S. 1987. *Medical Power and Social Knowledge.* London: Sage.

Young, A. 1976. "Some Implications of Medical Beliefs and Practices for Social Anthropology." *American Anthropologist* 78(1): 5–24.

## Further Reading to Part V

Climo, Jacob. 1992. *Distant Parents*. New Brunswick, NJ: Rutgers University Press.

Cohen, Carl I. and Jay Sokolovsky. 1989. *Old Men of the Bowery: Strategies for Survival Among the Homeless*. New York: Guilford.

Gubrium, Jaber F. 1991. *The Mosaic of Care: Frail Elderly and their Families in the Real World*. New York: Springer.

Gubrium, Jaber F. 1997 [1975]. *Living and Dying at Murray Manor*. Charlottesville, VA: University Press of Virginia.

Jaffe, Dale. 1989. *Caring Strangers: The Sociology of Intergenerational Homesharing*. Greenwich, CT: JAI Press.

Smithers, Janice A. 1985. *Determined Survivors: Community Life Among the Urban Elderly*. New Brunswick, NJ: Rutgers University Press.

Ross, Jennie-Keith. 1977. *Old People, New Lives: Community Creation in a Retirement Residence*. Chicago: University of Chicago Press.

Rubinstein, Robert L., Janet C. Kilbride and Sharon Nagy. 1992. *Elders Living Alone: Frailty and the Perception of Choice*. Hawthorne, NY: Aldine de Gruyter.

# Part VI

## The Aging Body

# 19 Managing Aging in Young Adulthood: The "Aging" Table Dancer

## Carol Rambo Ronai

According to several strip bar owners and other bar personnel in a large metropolitan area in the Southwest where this study was conducted, strip-tease dancers are getting old at a younger age. Studies conducted well over a decade ago (Boles and Garbin 1974a, 1974b, 1974c; Carey, Petersen, and Sharpe 1974; Gonos 1976; McCaghy and Skipper 1969, 1972; Salutin 1971; Skipper and McCaghy 1970, 1971, 1978) report a median age of 23. Those interviewed for this study consider the average age to be 19 or 20. An explanation is succinctly offered by Santino;[1] a respondent and bar owner:

> It used to be that dancers catered to older customers, but now, younger and younger customers are coming into the bar all the time. When customers are forty to fifty years old, it's okay for a dancer to be thirty years old, but when the customers are in their twenties, they are interested in younger dancers, not older ones.

Asked why he thinks younger customers are going to strip bars, Santino explains:

> These guys come here instead of going to a singles bar. Girls in singles bars are too much trouble for them; they're difficult to start talking to, stuck-up, and you don't get to see them undressed. Here, it's their [the dancers] job to talk to you. Plus, these guys think there is a better chance of taking out one of these women, than a woman you meet in a regular bar.

This article considers the social and personal consequences of an aging process experienced in the late teens and early twenties by strip-teasers known as "table dancers." While occupational identity is tied to biological aging, it is also social construction. If one traces the career routes and occupational transitions of the table dancer, one can readily see that she has the ability to manage the definitions of age and usefulness assigned to her. Based on the table dancer's experience in exotic dance bars, I contend that since most of the aging literature and its theoretical formulations are limited to the latter end of the life course, namely, old age, the experience of aging as a descriptive category of earlier years is ignored, in particular as this applies to the meanings assigned to age at various times and in various contexts of life. In relation

Original publication: Ronai, Carol Rambo, "Managing Aging in Young Adulthood: The 'Aging' Table Dancer," *Journal of Aging Studies*, 6 (1992), pp. 307–17. (Reprinted with permission from Elsevier Science).

to gerontology, this perspective is a way of arguing that aging is neither a clear matter of final disengagement nor a particular activity level, but something used, situated, and managed (Holstein 1990).

The concept "managed utility" is introduced to convey how dancers manipulate the definitions assigned them regarding age-appropriateness for their occupation (Neugarten and Hagestad 1976). For dancers the definition of old is both bodily and socially contingent, the dancer herself being active and reactive in her ability to control the contexts and conditions contributing to definitions of her age. It is my hope that separation of aging from old age, a distinction often conflated in gerontology, will add an important dimension to formulating a general processual approach to aging as an experience across the life course.

## Table Dancing and Aging

In exotic dance bars, "dance" refers to a staged stripping routine as well as a one-on-one individualized "turn-on." Appearing in full costume on stage, the stripper gradually removes her clothing while dancing. Depending on local ordinances, the stripper disrobes until she is clothed in a full bikini top and bottom, pasties and t-back panties, or nothing. Between acts, strippers stroll the floor and fraternize with customers. In some bars, strippers make money when customers buy them drinks, but the main source of income is table dancing.

Table dances are "sold" in a complicated negotiation process, the aim of which is to convince the individual customer that he is "turned on" to her and/ or that she is "turned on" to him, that is, being sexually attracted. The table dancer controls the situation so that she is not caught disobeying "house" or bar rules, many of which spill over the edge of what local authorities would consider illegal. For example, at two of the bars studied, "charging" for a table dance is considered soliciting. Like the "word games" used by the masseuse to bypass direct solicitation (Rasmussen and Kuhn 1976), dancers regularly "suggest" a donation, called a "contribution," usually an amount ranging from five to twenty dollars a dance, depending on what is locally customary.

Persuaded to buy a dance, the customer is led to a dark secluded area of the bar designated for table dancing. Depending on the dancer's interpretation of local ordinances, she leans over her seated patron, her legs inside his, and sways suggestively to the rhythm of the music playing in the bar. Customers are allowed to touch the hips, waist, back, and outsides of a dancer's legs. Many men try and some succeed in gaining greater advantage. Customers attempt to touch dancers' bodies by inserting fingers into briefs or fondling breasts. In practice, the range of sexual activity in the bar includes infrequent "hand jobs" (the dancer masturbating the customer), oral sex, and, less frequently, sexual intercourse. Commonly, the dancer and customer engage in body-to-penis fiction, a form of which is humorously called "talented knees" by participants in the stripbars.

Staged stripping routines and individual table dances put considerable emphasis on physical attraction, but more importantly, sexual appeal. First impressions are derived from the dancer's appearance, in particular, the appearance of her body. Loss of physical attractiveness risks loss of credibility and influence. Unlike the aging athlete, where physical performance is declining, aging for the dancer means that she is no longer persuasive sexually (Salutin 1971). While she still may be an adept dancer, her body loses appeal as a sexual object. Sustaining the resources she formerly possessed – youth and beauty – becomes strained and in the eyes of customers has diminished sexual utility, that is, a form of aging.

How does a dancer know she is too old to dance and what does a dancer do when she is showing her age? Popular theories of aging such as the disengagement (Cumming et al. 1960) or activity theory (Cavan et al. 1949) lack in explanation. They take aging and retirement to be marked events that happen towards the latter part of the life course. Aging is presumed to happen in old age. Even symbolic interactionists, who commonly treat life events as contextual and definitional matters, presume the existence of an inevitable "life courses" with regular age-related markers (Marshall 1979). Accordingly, the aim is to predict or understand the factors that produce or enter into aging in old age.

The gerontological conception of aging seems to have ignored the variety of situations and structures – besides chronological age – that engage participants in the *experience* of aging. A dancer's activities, for one, are informed by her own and others' underlying conceptions about aging in particular contexts. What is more, aging research has been too focused on conventional contexts (Stephens 1976). The strip tease literature, on its own, has not subjected its data to the analysis of "normal" experience, thus eclipsing questions of aging, role transformations, and the like. The literature portrays stripping as a *deviant* activity, focusing on contingencies of a deviant career (Skipper and McCaghy 1970), deviant patterns in early life (McCaghy and Skipper 1972), and structural factors facilitating lesbian and other deviant behavior (McCaghy and Skipper 1969; Salutin 1971).

## Procedure

Consideration of the aging table dancer's experience as "normal" evolved from reflections on data gathered in a field study of interaction strategies among strip tease artists (Rambo 1987; Rambo Ronai and Ellis 1989; Rambo Ronai 1992). For eight years, I have had insider access to the table dancing scene in the region where the study was conducted. Access began as part of dancing for employment. Opportunistically using an available social setting (Riemer 1977), I became a "complete-member-researcher" (Adler and Adler 1987) and undertook a field study of the dancers everyday world. I subsequently left the occupation, but over the years maintained contacts in the field by occasionally re-entering it as a participant.

A growing interest in body image and self-conception led to consideration of the place of an aging process in the table dancers' self-acceptance and acceptance by others. "Aging" table dancers were interviewed and asked about the process of getting old in the occupation. The first three dancers approached were offended by the question, and, in turn, asked me questions like "Why are you asking *me* this?" and "What are you *really* saying?" The third dancer was so offended that she terminated the interview with "I haven't got time for this bullshit." In time, however, by talking casually with younger and older dancers, informing each of other dancers I had spoken with, and by asking what kinds of options they generally thought older dancers in the bar setting had, I was able to avoid what could have been an insurmountable barrier to data collection.

With a few exceptions, most of the dancers were unwilling to discuss their thoughts and feelings about their own aging. They were willing, though, to tell stories about other dancers whom they felt had "gotten old." Together with field observations, these and other stories form the data base of this study. The stories suggest how serious the consequences of aging are for the dancer's acceptance, and how active the dancer can be in managing the process. Stories, other accounts, and observations were recorded in the form of field notes, as close as possible to their actual expression. Altogether, over thirty dancers, fifteen customers, three bartenders, four managers, and four bar owners were interviewed and their stories obtained.

## Aging as Managed Utility

A dancer manages the definitions assigned the physical consequences of aging by shifting her resources to either leave the occupation or continue working in the bar setting. Leaving the occupation or "getting out" is a clear exit. It is rare and usually needs planning. Remaining in the setting requires a dancer to carve out a niche that either does not rely on attractiveness or depends on a rearrangement of attractiveness as the priority of a new role.

At no point can it be confidently said the dancer has quit, or retired, even though there are gradual transitions or situated "disengagements." A dancer's career path is dynamic in character, highly responsive to definitions of utility negotiated or managed in the context of her particular experience. "Retirement" is more a matter of what roles evolve from her situation than a matter of leaving, departure, or final exit.

### Getting out

A popular way out of the dance world is to find a so-called "sugar daddy," which is an older, wealthy man willing to take care of a woman in exchange for companionship and/or sexual favors. As one dancer observed of two friends:

> It was like one minute they weren't interested in settling down and the next, boom! They started dating lots of older guys instead of the young ones they used to. It was really gross. But maybe it'll be different when I get older. Anyway, they both got married to these guys like 20 years older than them. One is divorced now and she is out at Mammy Larry's [a strip bar] datin' round for another one.

According to Santino, a bar owner, "shopping" for a sugar daddy can start for some as young as twenty-one years of age, adding:

> They look for someone old enough to always consider them young so they won't be abandoned later for a younger woman. Also, the guy has to have money and he has to treat her "well."

Santino relayed a story of a woman who found a sugar daddy at twenty-three and quit stripping. After ten years, she divorced and started dancing again at thirty-three, in search of another man. According to Santino, she was open about her mission and often joked with him, "I'm going to blow this joint as soon as I find myself a man." She subsequently left the bar a second time after moving in with another man.

Some dancers attempt to save money to buy a business or support themselves while attending school. Few are successful. According to most stories, even if a dancer manages to get out, she usually returns to the stripping business. One dancer who returned worked a hot dog cart that she and her boyfriend bought together. She was only earning $50.00 a day. As she commented:

> I worked my ass off out there in that hot sun. I spent more time with that fuckin' cart than I would spend dancing in a cool air-conditioned bar where I could earn a couple hundred dollars. I can even drink – its part of the job – if I want.

She left her boyfriend, a bar manager trying to get her out of the business and stuck him with the hot dog cart. Referring to another dancer who tried to leave the trade, a young woman who had recently received her state board cosmetology license, Mae, an older dancer, explained to the young woman while changing in a dressing room:

> Don't worry, you'll be back. Mark my words. They all come back some time. You won't make enough money, especially when you're used to this. You're spoiled on that money. You'll see.

### No one just quits

Many contextual factors keep dancers dancing. Aging in the stripper's world is more a matter of leaving and returning than retirement per se. When asked if he knew anyone who quit the business, Santino remarked:

> This business spoils you – male, female alike. No one just quits dancing or any other job around it. There is too much money to be made. I know of a bar manager right now trying to buy this bar. I've hired lots of guys as bouncers that have gone on to manage at other clubs. I started out with a B.A. in business, managed this bar for a while and a religious bookstore I inherited. I sold the bookstore and used the proceeds to buy this bar. There is just too much money here to get out of it. I'm trying to get out now, before I get in too deep. Talk to me in a year. We'll see.

"No one just quits" is a common phrase among dancers, customers and bar workers. Money is said to be the primary inducement to strip, in addition to easy hours, easy work (no responsibility), and gifts (Skipper and McCaghy 1970). Many dancers are supporting a husband, a boyfriend, children, or a combination of the three. One woman danced to support a bisexual girlfriend who acted as a housekeeper and nanny for her child, and a boyfriend who was a part-time bouncer at the bar where she worked as well as being the cook at home. The need for easy money to support such lifestyles keeps them "in the life" (Salutin 1971). Other than attractive bodies and performance routines, most dancers have limited skills. Few have sufficient training or education to make as much money in other occupations as they do now (Carey, et al. 1974; Skipper and McCaghy 1971).

Dancers are typically aware of the public's negative conception of the trade (Salutin 1971). The stigma of a deviant identity drives them closer together in defense against outsiders negative conceptions. The longer a dancer stays in the trade, the more likely she will be entangled by its associations, activities, and relationships. Relatedly, in a discussion of prostitutes, Prus and Vassilakopoulous (1979) state:

> With each overlapping set of interests – namely, financial, friendship, and intimacy – the involved persons are not only likely to find that contact with "straight society" becomes less important, but that disengagement "from the life" even when so desired, becomes more difficult and costly.

### Carving out a niche

One response to bodily aging or uselessness is to seek a promotion to a role not as dependent on physical attractiveness. Take Marge in this regard. Coy about her age, Marge was a night manager estimated to be in her late forties. An ex-dancer who was fond of such items of the trade as whips, paddles, blonde wigs, and evening gowns, she went on stage once a night and danced, much to the delight of other dancers and the customers. She sat and drank with customers and occasionally did table dances. Regarding her situation, she once noted:

> I've been in this business in one shape or form for a long time. I was a dancer when this bar was located at the corner of Fifth and Main. I started waitressing after a while, you know, a couple days a week, and dance a couple days. I've tended bar, waited tables, even been on the door [as a bouncer]. Finally, it seemed like all the girls would listen to me any way. So they just went ahead and made me night manager. It's easy for me now. I can dance if I want to, but I don't gotta do anything if I don't feel like it. One thing about this business – if you prove yourself, they take care of their own.

At first blush, this might suggest that Marge and the bar's owner mutually contributed to an inevitable disengagement from dancing. Marge gradually withdrew from her role as a dancer, but it was not an automatic, nor inevitable process. She carved out a niche for herself in the bar setting. She was free to dance if she chose, while being able to literally shape her environment to do as she pleased. She disengaged from dancing by trading the role of sex object for a managerial role. The reconstructed role with its related age identity did not produce a genuine or final disengagement from the bar scene or her dancer role, but, locally redesigned her circumstance and the consequent meaning of usefulness.

Some dancers are recognized alcoholics. They carve out their niche by drinking with customers. At several bars, dancers were required to "sell," that is, have a customer pay for a certain number of drinks. If dancers fell below their quota, they were required to pay for the drinks themselves. If they sold over the requirement, they earned a dollar for every drink sold. In this scheme of things, it was relatively easy to become habituated to alcohol. Besides, as some women put it, "You can handle the bullshit better with a buzz on."

As this type of dancer gets older, she usually gets heavier and becomes less active on stage because of her fear of falling while drunk. She gradually cuts back on table dances. But she can carve out a niche at the bar, waiting for customers to offer her a drink as a way of having someone in turn, sit and talk. Eddie, a heavy drinker, said of Nancy, an aging dancer:

> I like her. I take care of her; she takes care of me. She ain't nothing to look at but she's good people, good company. We have a good time. She's got moxie. She likes to bet with me on stuff. She'll say like, "I'll bet you ten bucks that broad will stand on her head on stage." She's great!

It was said that Nancy drank so much that the management put her on a limit of five half-shots of liquor per hour, thus curtailing her particular form of adaptation.

Some dancers have impressive social skills, used to cultivate regular customers. Women who carve out their niche in this way tend to be in their thirties and forties. The dancer interacts with the customer in a manner to make him feel as if some type of involved, long-term relationship were taking place. This is called "getting them going." Mae was well known for her ability in this regard. One evening Mae was given a mink coat by a customer, but she returned it to him. Asked why she returned the coat, Mae answered, "I couldn't hock it for very much, and I won't use it here in Florida. I'd rather get money." Asked how, then, she would earn money, she explained, "I'll get more money from him by being the type of person who gives this stuff back than if I keep it. I have lots of customers who give me stuff nicer than that mink." As a bouncer/ drinker who knew Mae explained further, "It's true, Mae can really get them going." Referring to one of Mae's more impressive gifts, he remarked, "That necklace was a grand, easy."

As the dancer grows older and her appearance becomes less desirable, attractiveness as a component in self-management takes on a lower priority. She may make up for declining visual sex appeal with wholesale sexual activity. There are many stories about the older dancer who "does tricks" to get by, something most younger dancers need only leave to customers' imaginations. Younger and more attractive strippers are not as compelled to perform sexual favors to make money. Trina was exemplary in this regard. She was considered pretty but "rough around the edges," being about ten pounds over what was considered desirable and having a few extra lines on her face. Regarding aging and sexual favors, she noted:

> The longer you dance, the more bullshit you'll have to put up with. You'll gradually start to let them get away with stuff. You know, for the money. When you get older you have to work on getting them [the customer] into it.

That older dancers typically recast their situation into a compromise of necessity, was tacitly understood by regular customers. As one customer cryptically put it, "Guys sometimes prefer older dancers because they work hard for you." I once spoke with a dancer named Maxine about this. She was "near 50" and only sat with "certain customers."

CR: I noticed that you don't sit with too many customers. Is that intentional?
*Maxine*: You bet. You can't be too careful with some of the jokers that come in here. I don't put up with any shit, you know what I'm saying here. No shit. You never know who could be a cop. I only sit with guys I know, guys I've known for years.
CR: I don't want you to get offended . . .

*Maxine*: Then don't say nothing you might regret.

CR: How can you make any money if you don't meet new people?

*Maxine*: [Laughing] Oh that. Well, you see, I got my regulars. I got their phone numbers. When I go to a new bar, they follow me. I give 'em a call. When you start out, well, you're young, you know what I mean. You can handle their crap. Out of all those guys you meet you find a few you treat "special" and they stay with you. You saw me with that one guy yesterday? [I nod agreement] Well he gave me five hundred dollars. Now later today I'm expecting Sam in. He's usually good for a hundred or two between his Friday and Saturday visits. Even if I don't see another customer all week, I'm set for a while. You follow this? [I nod].

I later observed some of Maxine's "special" treatment. During a table dance, she allowed Sam to make oral contact with her breasts while his hands roamed her body. By catering only to regulars, Maxine protected herself from potential arrest from undercover agents while making a great deal of money from the few men who visited her in the bar, even though she was "elderly."

The constant onslaught of propositions, paired with an increased performance of sexual favors, tempts some older dancers into prostitution. Salutin (1971) implies that the general population regard them as prostitutes anyway; so there is nothing to lose in terms of status. Yet those who turn occasional "tricks" insist they are not like full time "whores" or "street walkers." They claim to engage in sexual activity only when they need the money. Still, older dancers can make a satisfactory, relatively safe living by using the bar as a place of contact for prostitution (Prus and Irini 1980). A schedule of "regulars," whom the older dancer "tricks for" outside the bar, provides security and predictability. She need not worry about where her money is coming from or being arrested.

When a stripper ages, she may find herself fired from a bar where she has worked for a long time, or forced to quit because she no longer makes money at the location. Aging dancers who cannot create a niche for themselves in bars where they are currently employed wind up in lower status clubs (Salutin 1971). Bars have reputations in this regard. A bar may be known for its "celluloid queens," where every physique in the house is perfect because all the dancers have had plastic surgery to enhance bodily attractiveness such as liposuction or breast and buttocks implants. Some bars are known to have beautiful "stuck up" girls, others for their friendly average-looking girls, and still others for "sleazy" women with whom anything is said to go.

Accordingly, the "demotion" of aging dancers who can't carve a niche goes from beautiful to friendly to, finally, sleazy. Related stories form a kind of social control in their own right. Santino, for one, often took misbehaving dancers on "the circuit," visiting other bars in descending order of status for an "attitude adjustment." He stated that dancers usually were sobered by the experience and "straightened up their act."

The status of a bar and physical attractiveness work in tandem to define aging. A dancer may be too young, or too attractive to work a particular bar. A "elderly" twenty-five-year-old dancer in the company of nineteen-year-olds may find herself broke. But if she moves to a lower status bar, she may regain her youth and rejuvenate her earning potential, until she has aged there as well. Managers also work the age angle. A manager or owner of a "dive" will hire on older, attractive dancer who is younger than his other dancers in hopes of luring clientele and other attractive dancers. Other dancers may become angry because the younger, more attractive dancer monopolizes the business in the bar. Management may become wary if many dancers in their bars become "rough around the edges." Too many unattractive women working a higher status bar will bring down that bar's public standing. Bar owners have been known to ask young attractive dancers if they have young attractive friends who would like to dance. They solicit help with stories typically beginning "If this bar gets a bad reputation for old ugly dancers, you stop making money because the customers will stop coming." What managers fail to mention is that young attractive dancers can move on to better bars.

## Separating Age from Aging

Aging is a process both physical and social. Experientially, there is not set definition for what or who is old, even while there seems to be general agreement among gerontologists that old age occurs in the later years. The aging experience is socially constructed by individuals and through contexts that assign meaning to the physical body.

Meanings change over time because contexts change, something eminently social. The bar's physical setting may be the same, the people employed in the bar and those who patronize it may be the same, but the dancer starts to exhibit external signs of unattractiveness. As chronologically young as she may be, she can be old. Her body is not as supple and her dance not as animated as it once was. Her gestures towards customers are construed to be abrupt, demanding, nagging, less patient than before. A dancer's sexual utility and the sincerity of her presentation come into question. Appearing and acting like an old dancer breaks the tacit rule that women who sell their bodies in one form or another should be selling young, attractive, and cooperative commodities.

Popular theories of aging fail to account for the processes examined here. Dancers' and others' stories and accounts suggest that aging is an experience not necessarily just of later life, nor socially automatic or inevitable. In separating age from aging, and making visible the management of an aging experience, we learn the life course contingencies of being old.

## Acknowledgments

An earlier version of this article was presented at the Gregory Stone Symposium on Emotions and Subjectivity held in St. Petersburg Beach, Florida, January 1990. I thank Carolyn Ellis, Michael G. Flaherty, Jaber Gubrium, Danny Jorgensen, Hernan Vera, and two anonymous reviewers for their comments and suggestions.

## Note

1   The names of persons and places have been fictionalized.

## References

Adler, P. A. and P. Adler. 1987. "The Past and the Future of Ethnography." *Journal of Contemporary Ethnography* 16: 4–24.

Boles, J. and A. P. Garbin. 1974a. "The Strip Club and Customer-Stripper Patterns of Interaction." *Sociology and Social Research* 58: 136–44.

Boles, J. and A. P. Garbin. 1974b. "The Choice of Stripping for a Living." *Sociology of Work and Occupations* 1: 110–23.

Boles, J. and A. P. Garbin. 1974c. "Stripping for a Living: An Occupational Study of the Night Club Stripper," Pp. 312–35 in *Deviant Behavior: Occupational and Organizational Bases*, edited by Clifton Bryant. Chicago: Rand McNally.

Carey, S. H., R. A. Peterson, and L. K. Sharpe. 1974. "A Study of Recruitment and Socialization in Two Deviant Female Occupations." *Sociological Symposium* 11: 11–24.

Cavan, R. S., E. W. Burgess, R. J. Havighurst, and H. Goldhammer. 1949. *Personal Adjustment in Old Age*. Chicago: Science Research Associates.

Cumming, E., L. R. Dean, D. S. Newell, and I. McCaffrey. 1960. "Disengagement: A Tentative Theory of Aging." *Sociometry* 23: 23–35.

Gonos, G. 1976. "Go-Go Dancing: A Comparative Frame Analysis," *Urban Life* 9: 189–19.

Holstein, J. A. 1990. "The Discourse of Age in Involuntary Commitment Proceeding." *Journal of Aging Studies* 4: 111–30.

Marshall, V. W. 1979. "No Exit: A Symbolic Interactionist Perspective on Aging." *International Journal of Aging and Human Development* Pp. 345–58.

McCaghy, C. H. and J. K. Skipper. 1969. "Lesbian Behavior as an Adaptation to the Occupation of Stripping." *Social Problems* 17: 262–70.

McCaghy, C. H. and J. K. Skipper. 1972. "Stripping: Anatomy of a Deviant Life Style," Pp. 362–73 in *Life Styles: Diversity in American Society*, edited by S. D. Feldman and G. W. Thielbar. Boston: Little, Brown.

Neugarten, B. L. and G. U. Hagestad. 1976. "Age and the Lifecourse," in *Handbook of Aging and the Social Sciences*, edited by H. B. Binstock and E. Shanas. New York: Van Nostrand Reinhold.

Prus, R. C. and S. Irini. 1980. *Hookers, Rounders and Desk Clerks: The Social Organization of the Hotel Community*. Salem, Wisconsin: Sheffield.

Prus, R. C. and S. Vassilakopoulos. 1979. "Desk Clerks and Hookers: Hustling in a 'Shady' Hotel." *Urban Life* 8: 52–71.

Rambo, C. 1987. "Negotiation Strategies and Emotion Work of the Stripper." Unpublished Masters Thesis, Department of Sociology, University of South Florida.

Rambo Ronai, C. and C. Ellis. 1989. "Turn-on's for Money: Interactional Strategies of the Tabledancer." *Journal of Contemporary Ethnography* 18: 271–98.

Rambo Ronai, C. 1992. "A Night in the Life of an Erotic Dancer/Researcher: the Emergent Construction of a Self," in *Subjectivity in Social Research: Windows on Lived Experience*, edited by Carolyn Ellis and Michael Flaherty. Newbury Park, CA: Sage.

Rasmussen, P. and L. Kuhn. 1976. "The New Measure: Play for Pay." *Urban Life* 5: 271–92.

Riemer, J. W. 1977. "Varieties of Opportunistic Research." *Urban Life* 15: 467–77.

Salutin, M. 1971. "Stripper Morality." *Transaction* 8: 12–22.

Skipper, J. K. and C. H. McCaghy. 1970. "Stripteasers: The Anatomy and Career Contingencies of a Deviant Occupation." *Social Problems* 17: 391–405.

Skipper, J. K. and C. H. McCaghy. 1971. "Stripteasing: A Sex Oriented Occupation," Pp. 275–96 in *The Sociology of Sex*, edited by James Henslin. New York: Appelton-Century Crofts.

Skipper, J. K. and C. H. McCaghy. 1978. "Teasing, Flashing and Visual Sex: Stripping for a

Living," Pp. 171–93 in *The Sociology of Sex*, edited by James Henslin and E. Sagarin. New York: Schocken.

Stephens, J. 1976. *Loners, Losers and Lovers: Elderly Tenants in a Slum Hotel*. Seattle: University of Washington Press.

# 20 Narratives of the Gendered Body in Popular Autobiography

*Mary M. Gergen and
Kenneth J. Gergen*

One of the commonplace truths of contemporary culture is that people are born either male or female, and that these two groups of people exhibit differing characteristics related to their sexes across the life span. Except for rare instances, people identify themselves in the most profound ways as either male or female, and become acutely aware of qualitative changes in what it is to be a man or a woman as they age. Yet, how we understand these matters is subject to broad debate. Let us contrast two positions, the one stressing *essence* and the other *meaning*. It is frequently presumed that facts about gender differences, along with views about human development more generally, are (or should be) derived from systematic observation of behavior. What we believe about gender development is, ideally, a reflection of the actual essence of gender differences across the life span (cf. reviews of sex difference research in Maccoby and Jacklin, 1974; Money and Ehrhardt, 1972). Scientific knowledge on this account represents a distinct advancement over folk psychology because scientific observation of essential differences is more systematic and rigorous.

Yet, though the essentialist view is commonplace, it is also delimited. A growing body of scholarship now places central emphasis on the formative effects of understanding itself. That is, what we take to be knowledge of gender and development over the life span are not reflections of the essences; rather, our presumptions of knowledge enter, reflexively, into daily affairs to shape the contours of human activity (cf. Steier, 1991). On this latter account, the possession of full breasts or a bald head is of no necessary consequence in itself – no more, let's say than other observable facts, such as having brown eyes or large toes. However, if full breasts and a bald head come to demark discrete stages of development, and the members of such classes are thereby defined as more or less emotional, rational, passive, sexy, or moral, then having full breasts or a bald head may importantly shape one's life chances, activities, and satisfactions.

Further, as people live out their lives, engaging in various courses of action, they often support the matrix of preexisting meanings attached to various physical characteristics. In this way the current cultural meanings, whatever they are, exert their effects on others, even into future generations. In a broad sense, one is thus born into

Original publication: Gergen, Mary M. and Kenneth J. Gergen., "Narratives of the Gendered Body in Popular Autobiography," from (ed. Ruthellen Josselson and Amia Leiblich) *The Narrative Study of Lives*, vol. 1 (Sage Publications Inc., Newbury Park, CA, 1993), pp. 191–218.

a culture composed of interlocking patterns of meaning and action (Bruner, 1986). These meanings give specific significance to various biological characteristics, rendering them socially visible or insignificant, deeming them valuable or debilitating, using them to designate differences or similarities. The result of this process of cultural construction is a deep sense of the *natural* differences between men and women as they develop and age over the life span.

From the social constructionist perspective, meanings are not private and subjective events, but public and shared.[1] Meanings are generated through the discursive practices of the culture, transmitted from adults to children within various cultural contexts. Because such practices are inherently fragile and subject to continuous alteration, various significations can be foregrounded in one cultural enclave but overlooked in another. Cultural patterns of speaking and acting at any time may be viewed as a patchwork of discourses, each with its different history and context of usage.[2] In order to carry out relationships, it is thus necessary to borrow from various repositories of discourse to achieve mutual coordination of action.[3] At the same time, most recognizable cultures also contain a body of more or less interdependent, enduring, and broadly sustaining discourses. Thus, for example, in the United States a common discourse on justice may enter into relationships in the courtroom, the classroom, or the living room. In this case, each localized usage may support a more or less pervasive array of cultural meanings.

In the present offering we explore a small repository of discourse within the culture; although relatively insignificant in the literary landscape, this body of writing provides significant bearings for negotiating the life course. Our particular interest is in narrative construction, and most focally, the stories people tell about their lives. In our view, the narrative is the central means by which people endow their lives with meaning across time.[4] Thus, as people are exposed to the popular narratives within the culture; they learn how to regard themselves, how to make themselves intelligible to each other, and how to fashion their conduct. In Paul de Man's (1979) words, "We assume that life produces the autobiography . . . , but can we not suggest, with equal justice, that the autobiographical project itself may produce and determine life?" (p. 920).

To the extent that narratives are gendered, furnishing different structures of meaning for men as opposed to women, so do they contribute to cultural patterns that differentiate between the genders and prescribe both what is likely and unlikely during a lifetime. Thus, as men and women tell the stories of their bodies – what they mean and how they should be considered – so do these stories affect the course of their relationships with others, their career potentials, and their life satisfactions. If the stories of embodiment differ importantly between men and women they may also generate estrangements. To live in a different story of the body from another can render an impasse of understanding. Male and female actions toward each other may be misunderstood, and relationships dwindle into lonely alienation.

## Autobiography and the Fashioning of the Life Course

One of the most accessible forms of narrative available to contemporary North American readers is the autobiography. Highly marketable in the United States, the best-seller list each week usually includes at least two autobiographies in the top ten non-fiction books (cf. *New York Times*, 1990–92 booklists). These autobiographies vary in their instantiations, but best-sellers are frequently based on formula formats prescribed by publishing houses. These forms allow celebrities, often abetted by professional writers who specialize in this form, to tell their life stories in a revealing and engrossing way. Despite their mass appeal, we believe the popular autobiography is far more than a mode of public entertainment. Rather, such works operate much like secularized primers for the "good life" (Stone, 1982). They provide an idealized model of the life course – furnishing direction, sanctioning deviation, and providing benchmarks against which the common person can measure and judge their development. Autobiographies such as these are not, of course, the only such sources for rendering the life course meaningful. However, because they bear an intertextual relationship with other popular sources of narrative – television documentaries, Hollywood films, and magazine stories, as well as other fictional fare – their significance is noteworthy.

The function of the autobiography as a life course model is revealed in the narrators positioning of self vis-à-vis the reader. As Eakin (1985) points out, the autobiographer typically takes "the stance of the wise and fatherly elder addressing the reader as son or niece" (p. 29). The principal form of the autobiographical relationship is expert to novice, elder to younger, master to apprentice, or powerful to powerless. The edifying principle behind autobiographies is also revealed in their central themes and the personages selected to write about themselves. The central emphasis of the autobiography is on success and failure, and particularly how to achieve the former and avoid the latter. The authors are typically figures widely recognized for their cultural achievements (Olney, 1980). Classical autobiographies almost exclusively delineate the life of cultural heroes – those who have achieved greatness through their accomplishments (Jelinek, 1980). Readers benefit by being able to fantasize about the pleasures of escaping their humdrum circumstances and learning the ways and means to a notable life.

## The Emergence of the Female Voice

What kind of image of the life span does the popular autobiography present? There has been no systematic study of this question, but the answers can be ascertained, in part, by reference to the historical development of the autobiographical form itself. Although the history of autobiography is in its infancy, scholars suggest that its particular form took shape with the rise of the bourgeoisie, and the accompanying concept of the self-made man (Lejeune, 1975, Pascal, 1960). Similarly, Weintraub (1978) argues that the development of autobiography is closely linked in Western culture with the emerging value of the unique and independent individual. "The fascination with individual specificity leads to deep intrigue with life stories" (Eakin, 1985, p. 204). In this view, autobiographical figures represent a culturally and historically situate model of an ideal self.

With the emphasis on individual achievement, autobiographies tend to follow the classical lines of the "monomyth," a form that Joseph Campbell (1949/1956) has designated as the most fundamental in Western civilization. In its clearest form, the monomyth is the saga of a hero who triumphs over myriad impediments. When applied to the life span, the monomyth is a heroic trajectory. It thus tends to recognize youth as a preparatory period, early and middle adulthood as induction and struggle to attain one's goals, and mature adulthood and old age as full achievement and later consolidation and appreciation of one's successes. The form of the heroic life span is indeed like a skewed arc, with the apex at the climactic moment of highest attainment. The particular time in the life span is dependent upon the goals, but in the popular autobiography it is usually formed so that this point is approximately three quarters of the way through the text. In the autobiography, the form of the story is singular, linear, and progressive to the climax, and usually stable thereafter.

Yet, it is also clear that this account of the autobiography is most relevant to – if not the unique provenance of – prominent public figures; in almost all cases, the high status man. The chief features of the monomythic tale speak most directly to the life span of a man, not a woman (Gergen, 1992). As Mary Mason (1980) has described, "the self presented as the stage for a battle of opposing forces and where a climactic victory for one force – spirit defeating flesh – . . . simply does not accord with the deepest realities of women's experience and so is inappropriate as a model for women's life-writing" (p. 210). Included in the monomythic story are several women's roles, none of which is considered heroic. Women are cast in roles that are defined as stable, passive, or service oriented. Women are thematized as fair maidens to be wooed and won, mothers and wives, witches and sorcerers.[5] Women tend to be objects of quest, or forces that impede the hero in pursuit of his quest.

Earlier work on gendered forms of autobiography (M. Gergen, 1992; in press) indicates that in contrast to men's accounts, women's story lines are multiple, intermingled, ambivalent as to valence, and recursive. Whereas men's stories concentrate on the pursuit of single goals, most often career oriented, women's are more complex. Women's stories usually weave together themes of achievement, along with themes of family obligations, personal development, love lives, children's welfare, and friendship. Whereas men's stories are rarely revealing about emotional experiences, traumas, self-deprecation, self-doubt, and self-destructiveness, women's stories often express these aspects. Because of these multiple themes and self-expressions, the tone or movement of women's stories are never unidirectional, focused, or contained. Thus the content and the form of men's and women's autobiographies are distinct. The men's stories, however, exhibit the cardinal characteristics of the idealized form of autobiography. Women's forms are deviant.

## Gendered Narratives of the Embodied Self

Although there are substantial differences in the narrative forms located in male as opposed to female autobiographies, our special interest is in a specific form of content, namely embodiment. As reasoned above, the body doesn't "speak for itself." Rather, as a culture, we invest it with meaning – giving it importance (or not), treating its changes as significant (or not), and elaborating these meanings in such a way that life satisfactions blossom or are obliterated. The question, then, is how these culturally acclaimed authors embody themselves over the life span. How do they define, elaborate, and give significance to their physical being? How do males and females differ in the model they provide for the experience and treatment of one's body through the life course?

To explore these issues we shall consider how famous men and women account for their bodies from their youth through adulthood and old age. A sample of autobiographies of 16 men and women published in the United States in the past 7 years will serve as the basis for this discussion. These books were chosen to reflect the range of autobiographies available in the popular market. This selection includes people who have accomplished noteworthy activities, and are not merely associated with or related to famous people. The authors of this sample do vary in age, primarily because many of them – in particular the athletes and performers – became famous in their youth. The male autobiographies include those of: Ansel Adams, John Paul Getty, Lee Iacocca, T. Boone Pickens, Ahmad Rashad, Donald Trump, Jr., Thomas Watson, Jr., and Chuck Yeager. The female autobiographers are Joan Baez, Sidney Biddle Barrows, Nien Cheng,[6] Linda Ellerbee, Gelsey Kirkland, Martina Navratilova, Joan Rivers, and Beverly Sills. Although the full complexity of these accounts cannot be conveyed in this chapter, illustrative quotations will allow dominant themes to become apparent.

## Bodily Inscription from Childhood to Puberty

Remarkable differences between men's and women's accounts of their bodies begin to emerge from their earliest reminiscences of childhood. Two facets of this difference deserve notice. First, men have very little to say about their physical beings, except to note how effective their bodies were in attaining their goals. Second, men display little affect when making these descriptions. Perhaps the time lag between event and reportage has stifled any sense of connectedness that once may have existed for the author, and/or the inclusion of any emotional reactions might seem inappropriate. In any case, the body is virtually an absent figure in their reminiscences. Women's stories tend to be far more embodied. Beginning with the early years, women include greater detail in the descriptions of the body, and they are often emotional in describing their embodied lives.

A typical example of the "indifferent" male author is Thomas J. Watson, Jr. (1990), powerful long-term boss of IBM. After looking at a homemade film of his first grade class in 1921, Watson (1990) reports only, "I'm the tallest, long boned and ungainly" (p. 4). More poignant to the reader, but apparently not to the owner, is photographer Ansel Adams's (1985) account of how he acquired his misshapen nose:

> On the day of the San Francisco earthquake [April 17, 1906] . . . I was exploring in the garden when my mother called me to breakfast and I came trotting. At that moment a severe aftershock hit and threw me off balance. I tumbled against a low brick garden wall, my nose making violent contact with quite a bloody effect. The nosebleed stopped after an hour, but my beauty was marred forever – the septum was thoroughly broken. When the family doctor could be reached, he advised that my nose be left alone until I matured; it could then be repaired with greater aesthetic quality. Apparently I never matured, as I have yet to see a surgeon about it. (pp. 7–8)

For Adams, the contorted nose that punctuated his face simply became irrelevant to his life.

For women, the physical tribulations of childhood are often felt strongly and deeply, sometimes for many years. Feelings of present day self-worth seem strongly conditioned by the physical nature of the person they were. For example, comedienne Joan Rivers (1986), now a Barbie-doll look-alike, has made a career out of comic references to her misbegotten self. As she describes a family photograph:

> When I make jokes . . . about being fat, people often think it is just my neurotic imagination. Well, on the right, with her mother and sister during a vacation trip to Williamsburg, Virginia, is the thirteen year-old fat pig, wishing she could teach her arms and hips to inhale and hold their breath. (p. 183)

Fat also plagued the prima ballerina, Gelsey Kirkland (1986). She describes her dancing debut at camp as a form of self-defense for her misshapen body: "The other children taunted me about the disproportions of my body. I never let them know how much I was stung by their disparagements . . . I turned my abdominal bulge to advantage by performing a belly dance to amuse those in my cabin" (p. 10). Tennis star Martina Navratilova (Navratilova and Vecsey 1985) had the reverse problem: being too small. "I was tiny, not an ounce of fat on me – nothing but muscle and bone – just sheer energy. In school I was kind of embarrassed about being so small, but on the tennis court it didn't really matter that much" (p. 24).

In terms of development over the life span, the impact of physiognomy for both boys and girls often turns on the extent to which its effects are intensified or altered in puberty. For men in contemporary Western culture, the adolescent challenge largely takes place within the arena of athletics. The body's abilities to measure up to the competition is all-important in athletics particularly. For these males, it is in this period that body and identity are more closely linked than at any other time in the life span. Chuck Yeager (Yeager and James 1985), the man with the "right stuff," looks back with pleasure: "By the time I reached high school, I excelled at anything that demanded dexterity . . . In sports, I was terrific at pool and pingpong, good in basketball and football" (p. 11). Having an athletic body also helped ease a racially tense social scene for footballer Ahmad Rashad (1988), as well as contributing to his self-esteem. "If you lived in my neighborhood, . . . you tended not to go to Eastside – they would kick your ass over there. Because of my brother and my athletic ability, the law of the street didn't apply to me" (p. 47). T. Boone Pickens, Jr. (1987), the billionaire "take-over" tycoon describes himself: "Fortunately, I was well coordinated . . . Only five feet nine inches tall, . . . but a basketball player" (p. 17). In effect, being short was a threat to adolescent identity; being coordinated was a fortunate compensation. Donald Trump (Trump and Schwark 1987), New York's bad-boy builder, avoids any physical description of himself as a youth, except to relate that he was physically aggressive, to the point of giving a music teacher a black eye when he was in second grade "because he didn't know anything" (p. 71).

Lee Iacocca (Iacocca and Novak 1984) turned the story of his youthful illness into gains in the realms of gambling and sex. "I came down with rheumatic fever. The first time I had a palpitation of the heart, I almost passed out – from fear. I thought my heart was popping out of my chest . . . But I was lucky. Although I lost about forty pounds and stayed in bed for six months, I eventually made a full recovery" (p. 16). While convalescing, he started playing poker and reading books. "All I could remember about the book [*Appointment in Samarra*] was that it got me interested in sex" (pp. 16–17).

An exception to the bravado and self-assuredness of the vast majority of autobiographers, Watson (1990) portrays himself as unathletic. "While I was skinny and taller than most other kids, I was no athlete. My eye-hand coordination was terrible, so I hated baseball." Late in his life he proves himself by going sailing in dangerous waters away from medical supports, in part to overcome his fears of dying following a heart attack. A theme of overcoming his bodily and psychological defects is a stronger undercurrent in his book than in others. His success in mastering himself is illustrated, however.

For the adolescent girl, character is not made so much on the playing fields as in private chambers. Because girls seem more fully identified with their bodies, bodily changes at puberty become an enormous issue for identity formation. It is as if the body, which seemed a reasonably stable and controllable aspect of the girlhood self, begins to undo one's identity in adolescence. Spontaneously, it can make one hideous or desirable, both of which are problematic shifts in identity. Unlike men, it is a rare woman whose personal narrative is not concentrated on the unsettlement of adolescent transformation. As Navratilova (Navratilova and Vecsey 1985) comments, "The girls started to fill out in the sixth or seventh grade, but I didn't wear a brassiere until I was fourteen – and God knows I didn't need one then. I was more than a little upset about developing so late" (p. 24). Later she gains in stature: "My new weight gave me some curves I never thought I'd have, and they gave me the idea that I was a full-grown woman at seventeen" (p. 122). Joan Baez (1987) described her entry into junior high school as marked by rejection, which stemmed from her physical appearance. Without much pathos she recounted her image: "Joanie Boney, an awkward stringbean, fifteen pounds underweight, my hair a bunch of black straw whacked off just below my ears, the hated cowlick on my hairline forcing a lock of bangs straight up over my right eye" (p. 30). In high school her self-evaluation echoed a degree of self-confidence, mixed with doubt: "On the one hand I thought I was pretty hot stuff, but on the other, I was still terribly self-conscious about my extremely flat chest and dark skin" (p. 43). Beverly Sills (Sills and Linderman 1987), the great opera singer and director of the New York City Opera, describes her anguish:

> I developed breasts earlier than any of my classmates, and that was a great source of anguish for me. I was already feeling tall and gawky, and when it became obvious in gym class that I was the only girl who needed a bra, I didn't just become miserable, I became *hysterical*. I was so unhappy with the sheer size of me that my mother bought me a garter belt, which was about seven inches wide, and I wore it around my chest. (p. 17)

As a more general surmise, through the period of childhood and adolescence, boys and girls develop dramatically different interpretations of their body. Boys describe their bodies as separated from self, and as more or less useful instruments to attain their will. Whereas the male's identity is alienated from physical form, females tend to define themselves in terms of their body. This tendency is congenial to the views of many object relations theorists who hold that daughters are much more strongly linked to their mothers' identities through the similarities of their bodies, but sons are taught that they are distinct and separate from their mothers. Boys must suppress their identification with their mothers and cleave to the unknown world of men outside the home (cf. Chodorow, 1978; Dinnerstein, 1977). To elaborate in the context of autobiography, it is possible that the distinctiveness that men acquire of self from mother becomes fulfilled in their alienation from their own bodies. That is, they echo their mother's actions in regarding their bodies as "other." In support of this complex relationship, theorist Jane Flax (1990) speculates that men desire the unity with the mothering figure that characterizes girl-mother relationships, and their rejection of the "female" in themselves and others [including their embodied natures] is a constant discipline required "to avoid memories of, longing for, suppressed identification with, or terror of the powerful mother of infancy." She cites "a long line of philosophic strategies motivated by a need to evade, deny, or repress the importance of . . . mother-child relationships" (1990, p. 232).

## The Adult Years: Living Within and Beyond the Body

The tendency in narrative for men to distance themselves from their bodies intensifies in adulthood. The major plot in adult male autobiographies is focused on career development; these careers are typically defined independently from the body. The discourse of career tends toward the transcendent – emphasizing ideals, goals, values, and aspirations as opposed to organicity. The body, if mentioned at all, tends to be characterized as servant to the master's plans and purposes, whether for career or pleasure. For most of one's activities the body is simply taken for granted; it seems not to be a matter of particular interest or concern. Metaphorically, the body is considered a machine possession, and like one's automobile, its normal operation should enable one to get on with the real business of life. Only on occasion does the body enter the register of meaning, and that is when it serves as an asset or a liability to ends that lie beyond. Thus, as Yeager (Yeager and James 1985) describes, "Being in our early twenties, we were in good physical shape and at the height of our recuperative powers – which we had to be to survive those nights. That was our Golden Age of flying and fun. By the time we reached thirty, our bodies forced moderation on us" (p. 180). In effect, one simply goes on until the machine begins to break down. Watson (Watson and Petre 1990) describes an attempt to turn a disenabling threat into a career gain: "I developed a pain in my right side that turned out to be appendicitis. Getting operated on gave me a chance to postpone taking the exams by six weeks, so I was able to study and pass" (p. 47).

At times the male autobiographer is surprised to find the body makes a difference. Donald Trump (Trump and Schwark 1987), commenting on his early efforts to join a prestigious Manhattan club (with a lack of modesty about his body that is not found in women's autobiographics), is shocked to find his body is a consideration: "Because I was young and good-looking, and because some of the older members of the club were married to beautiful young women, [the officer of the club] was worried that I might be tempted to try to steal their wives" (p. 96). Having a good body can thus be a career impediment. It can also cause other troubles, especially for the man who takes too much pride in his athletic abilities. Consider J. P. Getty's (1986) attempt to pass himself off as a boxer. Enticing his friend Jack Dempsey to spar with him, he finds himself in difficulty in order to impress some young ladies:

A few moments after we began to spar; I realized that Jack was pulling his punches. My *macho* was taking all the punishment, for there were two or three very attractive young women friends watching at ringside. I wanted not only to test my ability as a boxer but also to prove myself . . . "Damn it, Jack, treat me just as you would any professional sparring partner." . . . I swung my lefts and rights as hard as I could. Jack . . . moved back a pace or two.

"Okay, Paul," he said, "If you insist . . ."

The first punch was hard. Jack swung again – and connected. That was that . . . I picked myself up off the canvas, fully and finally convinced that I would thenceforth stick to the oil business. (pp. 276–7)

One might also note from this little tale that Getty was willing to subject his body to abuse in order to satisfy his "macho" needs.

Because the body as an asset is taken for granted – much like the beating of a heart – it is only its potential for failure that must be confronted. The male reaction is expressed in two major ways: *anxiety* and *denial*. Among autobiographers, overtly expressed fear of dysfunction is largely reserved to men whose career success is closely linked to physical condition. Thus Rashad (Rashad and Bodo 1988) comments:

injuries are the ultimate reality for a pro athlete – they throw a shadow over your days . . . Football is like the army in that you know that a third of your men will become casualties. You just hope it isn't you that gets hit. Football is not just a job, it's an adventure – until it comes time to get killed. (pp. 118–19)

However, by far the more common reaction to the threat of dysfunction is denial. Again consider Rashad:

On a pass play early in the game, Ferguson threw to me . . . As I caught the ball, cornerback Jimmy Marsalis undercut me, rolling with his full body weight on my left knee.

The pain was excruciating, but the invulnerable Keed did the natural thing: I bounced up off the turf, pretending nothing was wrong. I didn't want to be hurt, and I insisted on walking it off. That provided the next real sign that something was wrong: I couldn't put my foot down . . . As the trainers came out, I insisted to them, "Nah, it ain't too bad. It'll be all right. There's nothing wrong with this baby." (p. 179)

A more dramatic illustration of defensiveness at work comes from Chuck Yeager's (Yeager and James 1985) account of his emergency exit from a crashing plane. Yeager's parachute caught on fire as he ejected himself from the cockpit. Upon hitting the ground, he wanders toward a passerby who has seen him land:

My face was charred meat. I asked him if he had a knife. He took out a small penknife . . . and handed it to me. I said to him, "I've gotta do something about my hand. I can't stand it anymore." I used his knife to cut the rubber lined glove, and part of two burned fingers came out with it. The guy got sick. (p. 360)

Yeager himself registers no reaction.

Women's accounts of embodiment in the adult years stand in marked contrast to men's. The woman's sense of identity remains closely tied to her physical condition. It is not so much that the body is used instrumentally – as a means to some other end outside the body. Rather, to be in a certain bodily condition is to "be oneself." Consider the detail in which Joan Baez (1987) describes her bodily being as she readies herself for a major performance:

> I am in my room by two o'clock, tired, wired, and thinking about what to wear. I turn my suitcase upside down, littering the floor from wall to wall to get a good look at my entire out-of-date collection of rags and feathers. By three o'clock I have finally ironed a yellow parachute skirt and cobalt blue blouse, dug out the belt with the big silver circles and the necklace made of spoon ladies linked together, and the nineteen-dollar black sandals bedecked with rhinestones. I spend an extra twenty minutes hunting down my half slip . . . They escort me to the green room. All the saliva in my mouth evaporates on the way. I have to go to the bathroom desperately, but it's too far and won't do any good anyway, so I sit tight, sip water, and ask Mary not to let anyone talk to me. (pp. 355–7)

This is not to say that women do not speak of using their bodies as instruments of achievement. For women, appearance constitutes an integral part of every story they tell and they are often keenly aware of shaping their bodies for ulterior ends. In the dramatic tale of survival in a Chinese detention prison during the era of the Cultural Revolution, Nien Cheng (1986) described the day her long ordeal with the Red Guard began. Two men from her company arrive unannounced at her home to take her to her "trial." She delayed going downstairs to have more time to think what she should do to preserve herself in this tense situation. She strives to create an impression of herself through her appearance. "I put on a white cotton shirt, a pair of gray slacks, and black sandals, the clothes Chinese women wore in public places to avoid being conspicuous . . . I walked slowly, deliberately creating the impression of composure" (p. 8). Effects of appearance on career goals continues to be especially relevant to women in the public eye. Comments by Linda Ellerbee (1986), a television journalist, are telling:

> I was told to lose weight if I wished ever to anchor again at NBC News. I wonder if anyone's ever said that to Charles Kuralt . . . Regarding my hair – I have lots of hair – I've paid attention to commands to tie it back, bring it forward, put it up, take it down, cut it, let it grow, curl it, straighten it, tame it – and I stopped doing so before someone asked me to shave it off . . . Maybe I'd just gotten older, not mellower, or maybe I'd had it up to here with men telling me to do something about my hair. (p. 119)

Because women describe themselves as deeply embodied, they are more often candid than men about the discomforts and threats to their bodies. A typical example is furnished by Beverly Sills (Sills and Linderman 1987), as she describes her bout with ovarian cancer at the age of 45: "I was lucky. I had a tumor the size of a grapefruit, but the doctor removed it entirely." Then she adds a gratuitous aside from a medical standpoint: "After my operation, I probably weighed about 125 pounds. I don't think I'd weighed 125 pounds since I was four years old" (p. 264). Returning to the stage very quickly, she mentions the pain she suffered. "To be blunt about it, I was in agony . . . the pain was almost unbelievable," but she did it anyway. "The plain truth is that if I had canceled, I would have worried that I was dying" (p. 267).

After her arrest and imprisonment, Nien Cheng (1986) minutely describes her experiences in prison as embodied ones of privation. Her description is rich with details of her bodily states, her illnesses, and her deteriorating condition: "After some time, hunger became a permanent state, no longer a sensation but an ever present hollowness. The flesh on my body slowly melted away, my eyesight deteriorated, and simple activities such as washing clothes exhausted my strength" (p. 185).

Given women's close identification with their bodies, it is also possible to appreciate why violations of the body are so unsettling for the woman: They represent invasive negations of one's identity. Consider Sidney Biddle Barrows's (Barrow and Novak 1986) account of how nude photos were taken of her and published in national newspapers. With a boyfriend in Amsterdam:

> We went to the houseboat and sampled our new friend's excellent hashish. After a while, [the friend] tactfully disappeared, leaving us together in the shimmering afternoon sun . . . I was delighted to have him snap some shots of me in my skimpy summer clothes. Pretty soon, he started flattering me: I looked so terrific, the light was just right, so why didn't I take off my clothes and let him shoot some nude photographs? (p. 22)

Later when Barrows was arrested for running a high-class escort service, her former boyfriend sold the photos to the *New York Post*:

> I was devastated. I could live with being called the Mayflower Madam, and I could even tolerate having my real name known. But now nude photographs of me were being splashed across two of the largest newspapers in the country! I couldn't believe that Rozansky had so shamelessly betrayed me, and I was disgusted that I had ever given him the time of day. (p. 290)

Other intimacies of the body were shared by Ellerbee (1986), who describes her illegal abortion:

> I'd been one of those women . . . who'd gotten pregnant, then gotten the name of someone through a friend of a friend, paid six hundred dollars cash, and waited, terrified, at my apartment until midnight when a pimply-faced man showed up, exchanged code words with me, and came in, bringing cutting tools, bandages and Sodium Pentothol – but no medical license I could see. I was lucky. I did not bleed uncontrollably. I did not die. I recovered. I was no longer pregnant. But I wasn't the same, either. No woman is. (p. 96)

From the standpoint of the unity of mind and body, it is also possible to understand why women's stories – and seldom men's – often contain instances of bodily alteration, mutilation, or destruction. When a woman is unhappy with her identity – feeling like a failure, wishing for a change in identity – the frequent result is some form of bodily obliteration. Ballerina Gelsey Kirkland (Kirkland and Lawrence 1986) described a period of despair: "I wanted to lose my identity . . . [at night, sleeping] I was able to dream my way into somebody else's body. I was no longer Gelsey" (p. 205). At another point, when she has lost her boyfriend, "I went through another round of cosmetic surgery. I had my earlobes snipped off. I had silicone injected into my ankles and lips" (p. 126). Joan Rivers (Rivers and Meryman 1986) turned such events into comedy:

That winter, in fact, suicide become one of my options; a way to strike back at all the people who did not appreciate me, a way to make them pay attention and be sorry . . . I wanted to do something terrible to myself, expend my powerless rage on my body, so I went into the bathroom and with a pair of scissors crudely chopped off my hair. (p. 249)

Summing up the narratives of embodiment for the adult years, we find that the man's bodily self fades even more into the background as career interests expand. The career is typically tied to ideas and ideals, power and prestige, and not to corporality. In contrast, women typically remain wedded to their bodies regardless of their career interests and abilities. In their identification with their bodies, self and bodily activities are one.

## Embodiment in the Latter Years

Because popular autobiographies tend to embrace the traditional criteria of the well-formed narrative,[7] their endings are extensions of that which proceeds. Especially for the male, the story line is a coherent one, with the writer describing early events in such a way that later outcomes are almost necessitated. Thus, in accounting for the body in the later years, much of the groundwork has already been laid. For the younger male autobiographer, the life account will be notable for its absence of body talk. Discursively, career success serves almost as an epiphany, enabling the male to achieve a state of the pure ideal. For males who do write from a more elderly position, however, matters are more complex. For here there are pervasive signs of what the culture defines as bodily deterioration. Issues of embodiment, then, begin to break through the seamless narrative of career advancement.

Three primary reactions tend to dominate the male autobiography. First, there is a *self-congratulatory* theme. If one's body has remained in reasonably good health, one may offer it (as separated from "I, myself") some form of adulation. Like a motorcar that has outlasted those of one's friends, one may feel proud to be the owner of the machine. This orientation flavors Getty's (1986) commentary on aging: "I am eighty-three. Cold, damp winters do bring on attacks of bronchitis . . . I can't lift weights or swim for hours or walk five miles at the brisk pace I did ten years ago . . . Luckily, I can afford the best medical care available" (p. 275). With a "touch" of the "chronic," Getty appears to revert to the earlier defensive posture.

Among those writers who are not so fortunate as Getty, two other orientations are taken toward the body. One is *begrudging admission* that one has a body, and that it must be given its due. This approach is taken by Chuck Yeager (Yeager and James 1985):

My concession to aging is to take better care of myself than I did when I was younger . . . Nowadays, I hunt as much for the exercise . . . as for the sport . . . I'm definitely not a rocking-chair type. I can't just sit around, watch television, drink beer, get fat, and fade out. (pp. 422–3)

This begrudging interruption of the heroic narrative is more dramatically illustrated in Ansel Adams's (1985) revelations of his chronic and increasingly disabling problems: "As I cleared the decks for future projects, I found an ever-present complicating factor: Health. My mind is as active as ever, but my body was falling farther and farther behind" (p. 365). (The reader may note that the "real" Adams is the mental form, and the body is a recalcitrant fellow-traveller who is lagging behind.) Adams (1985) describes his heart surgery (a triple bypass and valve replacement). "Without surgery I was fast reaching an embarrassing state of inactivity; I could not walk a hundred feet without the crippling symptoms of chest pains and shortness of breath" (p. 366). Yet, the sense of bodily infringement on the idealized masculine narrative is revealed in Adam's (Adams and Alinder 1985) description of recovery: "My only complaint was a pestiferous vertigo . . . In two months the vertigo vanished and I was able to drive the late Congressman Philip Burton to Big Sur for his first view of that marvelous region; he soon became one of the leaders in the fight for its preservation" (p. 366). Back to business as usual.

A third orientation to the aging body is often encountered in the male autobiography, essentially a *trauma of broken defenses*. Because of the ravages to the body in the later years, the picture of the self during the middle years – detached from natural anchors – can no longer be maintained. With the disruptive sense of being the victim of "a dirty trick," the male at last confronts the possibility of finitude. Watson's (Watson and Petre 1990) description of his heart attack is illustrative:

> In mid-November, I was in my office and Jane Cahill, my executive assistant, started to come in the door. Then she stopped cold, because I had my head down on the desk, "Are you all right?" she asked.
> "I'm fine. I'm tired."
> That night I woke up with a pain in my chest. It wasn't very intense but it wouldn't go away. Olive was in the Caribbean with friends, so I drove myself to the emergency room at Greenwich Hospital . . . having a heart attack. (p. 392)

Employing the metaphor of the body as the serviceable machine, Watson also reveals his sense of vulnerability; "When you have a heart attack, you realize how fragile your body is. I felt that mine had let me down, damn near entirely, and for several months I had very volatile reactions to insignificant things" (p. 394).

It would be useful to make broad comparisons between older male autobiographies and those written by older women. Unfortunately, however, few women write popular autobiographies when they are past 60. For this genre of literature, women's reputations tend to result from achievements of the early years. Lifetimes that culminate in professional heroics are rarer for women than for men. For those older women who do contribute to the genre, the body continues to figure importantly in two ways. First, although one might anticipate a drawing away from bodily identification as it become more problematic, this does not seem to be the case with women. Instead, the writers continue to "live their bodies," in spite of the body's transformation. Beverly Sills's (Sills and Linderman 1987) account of her body's reaction to her chores in the management of the opera company after her retirement as a diva is illustrative: "I was working like a horse, my blood pressure was way up, and I was eating six meals a day . . . I came into my job as general director weighing 150 pounds; on June 16, 1984 when I visited the endocrinologist, I weighed 220 pounds" (p. 345).

There is a second theme located in the accounts of women, including those in later years, that is far more subtle in its manifestation, but pervasive and profound. Because the woman's body is so closely identified with the self, one's bodily relations with others essentially extend the self. In the same way that violations of the body are defacements of identity, so are investments of the body in others' modes of unifying self and other. Thus, in pondering the preceding years and the meaning of one's life, women are more given to thinking about their children, lovers, and parents – those with whom the body has been intimately shared – and others, such as friends, who are now part of oneself. Nien Cheng's (1986) autobiography is a continuous knitting of her life to her daughter's especially. After the memorial service for her daughter, killed by the Red Guard, she describes a night without sleep:

> Lying in the darkened room, I remembered the years that had gone by, and I saw my daughter in various stages of her growth from a chubby-cheeked baby . . . to a beautiful young woman in Shanghai . . . I blamed myself for her death because I had brought her back to Shanghai in 1949. (p. 495)

This recounting of significant connection is not wholly reserved for the old age, however. Even when the younger women think back on their lives, their ruminations tend to center on those related through extensions of the body. When Navratilova (Navratilova and Vecsey 1985) won the Wimbledon Championship, she expressed her first thoughts on winning as: "For the first time I was a Wimbledon champion, fulfilling the dream of my father many years before. . . . I felt I was on top of the world" (p. 190). Joan Baez (1987) writes an epilogue in which she describes her family and friends, those who have been important in her life. In the final pages she talks of going to a party in Paris with her son. When she returns home:

> Mom will have a fire going in the kitchen and perhaps a Brahms trio on the stereo. Gabe will fall into bed, and I will sit in front of the fire, dressed like a Spanish princess, telling Mom how the sun rose, piercing through the mist over the lake . . . and how there was peace all around as the castle finally slept. (pp. 377–8)

For men, rumination about the significance of intimates plays but a minor role in their stories. When one is on the grand highway of monomyth, it is important to travel light. Thus Yeager and Getty, for example, speak only in passing of deaths and illnesses within the family; Trump describes himself, his family members, and his then wife, Ivana, as "rocks." The major exception to this general disregard is the father's death, which often receives considerable attention. The importance of the father's death can be traced to the threat it symbolizes to the male portrayal of invulnerability. Because one can see within the father's death the possibility of one's own finitude, added attention is needed to keeping the defenses strong. There is no male autobiographer who could write as Nien Cheng (1986), who is an old woman when she is finally allowed to leave China. Leaving Shanghai harbor she continues to speak of bodily sensations, the feeling of the heavy rain, her lack of umbrella or raincoat, her "staggering up the slippery gangway," the "wind whipping my hair while I watched the coastline of China receding." She ponders her daughter's fate. "I felt guilty for being the one who was alive. I wished it were Meiping standing on the deck of this ship, going away to make a new life for herself" (pp. 534–5).

## Embodied Selves over the Life Span

The popular autobiography is both a repository of cultural meanings and a model for future lives. As the present analysis indicates, autobiographical stories differ dramatically in the meanings they impart to the male as opposed to the female body over the life span. The male autobiographer suggests that the man should be "above bodily concerns," more invested in culture than nature, in rationalities and values as opposed to the corporal.[8] To be fixed on one's body would be unmanly, narcissistic, and perhaps effeminate. To put matters of corporality aside is also highly functional for the male in terms of career. More hours can be devoted to achievement, and with fewer complaints. It is only in the later years that the male autobiographer admits an important relationship between self and body, and it is often an admission of shock, fear, and sorrow. The grand story is being brought to a close by a secret villain, and that villain dwells within.

Female autobiographers present a life story in which body and self are more unified. To be a woman is to be embodied; to fail in attending to one's corporality would be to ignore the cultural codes of being. Bodies serve a more central role in women's lives and consciousness than they seem to in men's. As Adrienne Rich (1977) has put it: "I know no woman – virgin, mother, lesbian, married, celibate – whether she earns her keep as a housewife, a cocktail waitress, or a scanner of brain waves – for whom her body is not a fundamental problem" (p. 14). This embodiment lends itself to a far greater sense of unity with others – particularly with those who have shared the flesh. To be embodied in this way is thus to be in significant relationship with others. At the same time, the discourse of embodiment sets the stage for deep unsettlement during puberty, for self-mutilation during periods of disappointment, and for a more profound sense of aging in the later years.

Inevitably an analysis such as this raises questions of the cultural good. For if one lives the life course within frameworks of meaning, and these meanings invite and constrain, celebrate and suppress, then one may ask whether it might be otherwise. If we could alter the forms of meaning – whether in autobiography or elsewhere – should we do so? From the female standpoint, there is much to reject in the male version of life and the practices that they favor. The male life course seems a strange "out of body" experience, one that devalues potentially significant aspects of human life. For the male, the female's mode of indexing life seems often irrelevant to the tasks at hand, and lends itself to emotional instability. However, rather than conceptualizing themselves as participants in "the longest war," perhaps both genders might benefit from new syntheses that would expand life story options for all. At the same time, however, further attention is needed to the cultural patterns in which these discourses are embedded. So long as the power relationships between men and women appear to favor the male version of reality and value, so long as the workplace makes little allowance for embodied selves, and so long as relationships are treated in a utilitarian manner, new stories might not be able to survive. Yet, one might hope that within dialogues, through reciprocal and reflexive endeavors, and via political and social changes, new stories might encourage new practices and prospects – and we might hope that embodied stories would be available to all (see K. Gergen, in press).

## Notes

1   For further discussion of meaning as discursive rather than psychological, see Gergen (1991).
2   See Bakhtin's (1981) concept of *heteroglossia*.
3   For more extended accounts of the mutual management of meaning, see Pearce and Cronen, 1980.
4   See also Bruss (1980), Rabuzzi (1988), Russ (1972), Sprinker (1980), and White (1978).
5   See Frye (1957) and Rich (1977).
6   Nien Cheng's (1986) autobiography, *Life and Death in Shanghai*, is exceptional within this group because she was not well known before her book was published, and she did not write with the help of a professional writer. Her volume was selected for inclusion in this sample because it was a best-seller and, in addition, she was a businesswoman and an older woman author. These characteristics are difficult to find in best-selling autobiographies by women.
7   See Gergen and Gergen (1983, 1988) for further discussion of these criteria.
8   It should be emphasized that the subject of concern here is how embodiment is described in autobiographies. It is possible that in private spheres men express their embodiment much as women do in print. This possibility remains to be explored.

## References

*Autobiographical*

Adams, Ansel, with Mary Street Alinder. (1985). *Ansel Adams. An autobiography*. Boston: Little, Brown.
Baez, Joan. (1987). *And a voice to sing with: A memoir*. New York: New American Library.
Barrows, Sydney Biddle, with William Novak. (1986). *Mayflower madam*. New York: Arbor House; London: MacDonald.
Cheng, Nien. (1986). *Life and death in Shanghai*. New York: Penguin.
Ellerbee, Linda. (1986). *And so it goes: Adventures in television*. New York: Berkley Books.
Getty, J. Paul. (1986). *As I see it: An autobiography of J. Paul Getty*. New York: Berkley. (Original work published 1976)
Iacocca, Lee, with William Novak. (1984). *Iacocca. An autobiography*. New York: Bantam Books.
Kirkland, Gelsey, with Greg Lawrence. (1986). *Dancing on my grave*. Garden City, NY: Doubleday.
Navratilova, Martina, with George Vecsey. (1985). *Martina*. New York: Fawcett Crest.
Pickens, T. Boone, Jr. (1987). *Boone*. Boston: Houghton Mifflin.
Rashad, Ahmad, with Peter Bodo. (1988). *Rashad*. New York: Penguin.
Rivers, Joan, with Richard Meryman. (1986). *Enter talking*. New York: Delacorte.
Sills, Beverly, and Lawrence Linderman. (1987). *Beverly*. New York: Bantam Books.
Trump, Donald, with Tony Schwark. (1987). *Trump: The art of the deal*. New York: Warner Books.
Watson, Thomas J., Jr., and Petre, Peter. (1990). *Father son & co. My life at IBM and beyond*. New York: Bantam Books.
Yeager, Chuck, and Leo James. (1985). *Yeager, an autobiography*. New York: Bantam Books.

*General*

Bakhtin, Mikhail. (1981). *The dialogical imagination: Four essays* (Michael Holquist, ed.). Austin: University of Texas Press.

Bruner, Jerome. (1986). *Actual minds, possible worlds.* Cambridge: Harvard University Press.

Bruss, Elizabeth W. (1980). Eye for I: Making and unmaking autobiography in film. In J. Olney (ed.), *Autobiography: Essays, theoretical and critical.* Princeton, NJ: Princeton University Press.

Campbell, Joseph. (1956). *Hero with a thousand faces.* New York: Bollingen. (original work published 1949).

Chodorow, Nancy. (1978). *The reproduction of mothering: Psychoanalysis and the sociology of gender.* Berkeley: University of California Press.

de Man, Paul. (1979). Autobiography as de-facement. *Modern Language Notes, 94,* 920.

Dinnerstein, Dorothy. (1977). *The mermaid and the minotaur: Sexual arrangements and the human malaise.* New York: Harper & Row.

Eakin, Paul John. (1985). *Fictions in autobiography: Studies in the art of self-invention.* Princeton, NJ: Princeton University Press.

Flax, Jane. (1990). *Thinking fragments.* Berkeley: University of California Press.

Frye, Northrup. (1957). *Anatomy of criticism: Four essays.* Princeton, NJ: Princeton University Press.

Gergen, Kenneth J. (1991). *The saturated self.* New York: Basic Books.

Gergen, Kenneth J. (in press). *Social construction: Critique and re-creation in the postmodern community.* Chicago: University of Chicago Press.

Gergen, Kenneth J., and Gergen, Mary M. (1983). Narrative of the self. In T. Sarbin and K. Schiebe (eds.), *Studies in social identity.* New York: Praeger.

Gergen, Kenneth J., and Gergen, Mary M. (1988). Narrative and the self as relationship. In L. Berkowitz (ed.), *Advances in experimental social psychology* (Vol. 21). San Diego, CA: Academic Press.

Gergen, Mary M. (1992). Life stories: Pieces of a dream. In G. Rosenwald and R. Ochberg (eds.), *Telling lives.* New Haven, CT: Yale University Press.

Gergen, Mary M. (in press). The social construction of personal histories: Gendered lives in popular autobiographies. In T. Sarbin and J. Kitsuke (eds.), *Constructing the social.* London: Sage.

Jelinek, Estelle C. (1980). *Women's autobiography. Essays in criticism.* Bloomington: Indiana University Press.

Lejeune, Philippe. (1975). *Le pacte autobiographique.* Paris: Seull.

Maccoby, Eleanor, and Jacklin, Carol. (1974). *The psychology of sex differences.* Stanford, CA: Stanford University Press.

Mason, Mary G. (1980). Autobiographies of women writers. In J. Olney (ed.), *Autobiography. Essays theoretical and critical.* Princeton, NJ: Princeton University Press.

Money, John, and Ehrhardt, A. A. (1972). *Man & woman. Boy & girl.* Baltimore, MD: Johns Hopkins University Press.

Olney, James. (1980). *Autobiography. Essays theoretical and critical.* Princeton, NJ: Princeton University Press.

Pascal, Roy. (1960). *Design and truth in autobiography.* Cambridge, MA: Harvard University Press.

Pearce, W. Barnett, and Cronen, Vern. (1980). *Communication, action, and meaning.* New York: Praeger.

Rabuzzi, Kathryn Allen. (1988). *Motherself. A mythic analysis of motherhood.* Bloomington: Indiana University Press.

Rich, Adrienne. (1977). *Of woman born: Motherhood as experience and institution.* New

York: Norton.

Russ, Joanna. (1972). What can a heroine do? Or why women can't write. In S. Koppelman Cornillon (ed.), *Images of women in fiction*. Bowling Green, OH: Bowling Green University Popular Press.

Sprinker, Michael. (1980). Fictions of the self: The end of autobiography. In J. Olney (ed.), *Autobiography: Essays theoretical and critical*. Princeton, NJ: Princeton University Press.

Steier, Frederick. (ed.). (1991). *Method and reflexivity: Knowing as systemic social construction*. London: Sage.

Stone, Albert E. (1982). *Autobiographical occasions and original acts. Versions of American identity from Henry Adams to Nate Shaw*. Philadelphia: University of Pennsylvania Press.

Weintraub, Karl J. (1978). *The value of the individual: Self and circumstance in autobiography*. New York: Random House.

White, Hayden. (1978). *The tropics of discourse*. Baltimore, MD: Johns Hopkins University Press.

# 21 Stigmatizing a "Normal" Condition: Urinary Incontinence in Late Life

## Linda S. Mitteness and Judith C. Barker

Urinary incontinence is of major concern for a relatively large proportion of the community-living elderly and for a majority of the institutionalized elderly. As a health condition it has received surprisingly little attention despite its documented prevalence, cost, and associated morbidity (Resnick and Ouslander 1990). This article demonstrates how beliefs about the causes and consequences of urinary incontinence in the elderly lead to the linking of incontinence with incompetence. Urinary incontinence in old age symbolizes a loss of control that is incompatible with adulthood in US society. This set of beliefs militates against the success of preventive and interventive strategies for urinary incontinence, unless those strategies focus first on disentangling continence and social competence in the minds of health care providers and the elderly themselves.

Continence has a broad meaning of self-restraint or abstinence, especially in regard to sexual activity, as well as the narrower, physiological meaning of the ability to control discharge of urine or feces. Responses to physiological incontinence in US society are heavily laced with connotations of the broader definition of continence, focusing on self-restraint, temperance, moderation, self-control. Loss of continence has moral consequences that go far beyond physiological impairment to cast strong doubt on a person's social competence.

Incontinence is a classic case of a stigmatizing condition in that it discredits a person's social identity and provokes responses of fear, stereotyping, and social control (Coleman 1986; Goffman 1963). Incontinence, however, is unusual in that while it is discreditable, it is also considered by many to be a normal part of aging. This linkage of the discreditable with normal aging helps explain the difficulties that many people in the United States have with aging and the social disadvantages that elderly people experience.

Incontinence in younger people – those in early adulthood who suffer from spinal cord injury, neurological deficit, or birth defect – is aggressively treated and managed (Mandelstam 1980). The rehabilitation literature places great emphasis on returning these younger people to their usual social world as soon as possible. Removing any possibility of stigma and keeping a young person socially connected is a major therapeutic aim. Urinary incontinence for young people is discreditable, but it is not a

Original publication: Mitteness, Linda. S and Judith C. Barker, "Stigmatizing a 'Normal' Condition: Urinary Incontinence in Late Life," *Medical Anthropology Quarterly* 9: 1 (1995), pp. 188–210.

"normal" part of young adulthood; thus, intervention or amelioration is called for.

Until recently, no such emphasis existed in the literature on the therapeutic management of urinary incontinence in the elderly. While the shamefulness and embarrassment attendant on incontinence was acknowledged, the emphasis was clearly on keeping the incontinent person and his or her surroundings dry (e.g., Caldwell 1975; Willington 1976). In the social imagination, incontinence in the elderly is linked with frailty, disintegration, incompetence, and a general discrediting of old age. The logic for intervention, even though it is expressed in the current specialist geriatric medicine literature (e.g., Resnick and Ouslander 1990), is out of touch with common understandings that incontinence and incompetence are linked in old age.

## Models of Urinary Incontinence

The view of urinary incontinence found in the specialist literature of geriatrics is in sharp contrast to the view held by other health professionals and by laypeople. In the specialist literature, urinary incontinence is seen as a problem that is amenable to treatment and the serious consequences of which are avoidable (NIH Consensus Development Conference 1990). Most physician-authors agree that a large portion of urinary incontinence in the elderly can be reversed or markedly improved (Urinary Incontinence Guideline Panel 1992). The picture of urinary incontinence drawn by our studies of primarily white, urban American elderly people and their nonspecialist health care providers is in stark, pessimistic contrast to the presentations in the geriatric medical literature. For the nonspecialist, incontinence in old age is irreversible, untreatable, and virtually inevitable.

### The geriatric medicine model

One widely accepted definition of urinary incontinence is that it is an objectively proven condition in which involuntary loss of urine is a social or hygienic problem (Bates et al. 1979). This definition makes no reference to pathophysiology or etiology.

The physiology of normal micturition is highly complicated, involving several organs as well as a range of muscular and neurological controls. Consequently, the causes of incontinence in the elderly are multiple and complex, including environmental, introgenic, and behavioral factors as well as impairments of neurological and muscular controls (Resnick and Yalla 1985).

Classification schemes for urinary incontinence focus either on duration (transient versus established) or on pattern of urine loss (stress, urge, overflow, mixed) (Diokno 1990). Treatments for these different types of incontinence differ in both variety and effectiveness (Burgio and Engel 1990; Fantl et al. 1990; Raz 1990; Welm 1990; Wells 1990). Accurate diagnosis of type of incontinence affects not only choice of therapy but also its likelihood of success. A wide variety of treatment strategies is used, ranging from correcting underlying disorders to behavioral and biofeedback methods, drug therapy, and surgery (Urinary Incontinence Guideline Panel 1992).

It is estimated that 15 to 30 percent of the noninstitutionalized elderly have some loss of control of bladder function (Herzog and Fultz 1990). Over 50 percent of the institutionalized elderly are incontinent of urine (Ouslander 1990; Ouslander et al.

1982). The costs of incontinence in the elderly population are truly staggering. Medical costs include cystitis, urosepsis, pressure sores, perineal rashes, and falls (Resnick and Yalla 1985). Financial cost estimates suggest that at least $10 billion annually (in 1987 dollars) goes toward incontinence care (Hu 1990). Social consequences of urinary incontinence range from embarrassment, depression, and confusion to extreme social isolation and vulnerability to institutionalization (Hunskaar and Vinsnes 1992; Lagro-Janssen et al. 1992; Mitteness 1987a, 1987b; Norton 1982; O'Donnell et al. 1992).

The frequency of discussions about the importance of diagnosis and treatment of incontinence in the elderly has increased in recent years, both in prestigious academic medical journals, such as the *Annals of Internal Medicine* and the *New England Journal of Medicine*, and in practice-oriented journals, such as the *American Family Practitioner*. The medical literature on urinary incontinence now focuses on protocols for the evaluation and treatment of the incontinent patient with the goal of reversing or substantially improving incontinence.

### The cultural model

The cultural model of urinary incontinence, as derived from our research over the past decade, differs from that found in the geriatrics literature on three dimensions: beliefs about the causes of incontinence; ideas about the range of appropriate responses to incontinence; and beliefs and perceptions about the consequences or sequela of incontinence. We must emphasize here that what we have termed "the cultural model" is not restricted to laypeople but is widely shared by physicians and other health care providers as well.

## Methods

Six interrelated projects have formed the background of our analysis, although most of the data presented in this article come from two studies of incontinent community-living elderly people. The six projects include two studies with samples of community-living elderly people, two studies with samples of health care professionals, and two with samples of social service providers and apartment managers, both groups having some degree of influence over the ability of frail elderly people to remain community resident.

### Studies with community-living elderly people

The first of the projects with community-living elderly people focused on the management of incontinence in subsidized housing for elderly people (Barker and Mitteness 1988; Barker, Mitteness, and Wood 1988; Mitteness 1987a, 1987b; Wolfsen et al. 1988). This study began with participant observation (by a team of researchers) of social activities in the public places of three subsidized apartment buildings. All residents of the buildings were then invited to participate in a survey of health problems of residents. A subsample of all residents who were observed to be or reported being incontinent (n = 30) and a sample of their neighbors (n = 18) were interviewed repeatedly over a six-month period.[1] This first study resulted in the observation that the experience of incontinence appeared to be quite different for those with and without multiple concomitant health problems.

The second study of community-living elderly people focused on a sample of new clients of a very large home health care agency. While the majority of the respondents in the first study were female and all had moderate to low incomes, the second study covered the full range of economic groups and the sample was stratified by gender.[2] The home health care agency selected for study is the largest in this urban area, serving over 500 people per month, the majority of whom are elderly. For a 22-month period, from February 1987 through November 1988, home health nurses were asked to complete a short survey on every new elderly client on the first visit. These surveys were collected and provided the pool of eligible persons from which a stratified random sample was asked to volunteer for the study. Stratification by gender resulted in an oversampling of men (46 percent of the sample), who comprise only 35 percent of clients over 65 years of age. Similarly, incontinent people were oversampled, as only 26 percent of agency clients were known to be incontinent at the time of the first nursing visit. Because large numbers of incontinent people never report their incontinence to health care providers, however, the degree of oversampling is less than these numbers indicate.

A total of 255 elderly clients agreed to a first visit for interviews in their homes. Of the 255 visited, 211 (83 percent) agreed to participate in the study for a six-month period. To assess the bias inherent in less than perfect response rates, we examined the initial survey data on the 4,421 elderly clients collected by the nurses and selected at random an additional 126 people from among all those who were not contacted or who refused to participate, to have medical records at the home health agency anonymously recorded and examined. Most important, gender, age, and continence status were not associated with response status. Those who refused or were lost to participation were no different in these respects from those who agreed to be interviewed. Nor was participation associated with ethnicity or socioeconomic status. Clients who were nonwhite or who lived in wealthy neighborhoods were no more or less likely to refuse participation than were people who were white or lived in poor neighborhoods.

The 211 home health care clients were interviewed face-to-face at two time periods – at recruitment to the study and again six months later. While some people's interviews were completed in one meeting, it was more common for informants to be visited in their homes on two to four occasions upon recruitment to the study and one occasion at six months. Monthly telephone calls and occasional visits were made between the first and last time periods to maintain contact with people and to check for significant changes in health and functional status. The interviews included structured, formal questions, as well as open questions followed by probes. Six broad topics were covered at both time periods: (1) demographic characteristics; (2) a description of the person's current and past health conditions, including beliefs about the causes of these health problems, daily management strategies, and evaluations of the seriousness and troublesomeness of each health problem; (3) a detailed interview concerning bladder control disturbances, including descriptions of symptoms and management strategies; (4) an assessment of the informant's social, mental, and physical functioning, using a variety of established assessment tools; (5) a description of the size and functioning of the informant's informal social support network; and (6) the informant's use of both agency and other health and social services. Home health care agency records were examined to confirm informant reports for demographics, major diagnoses, functional status, and services received.

### Health professionals

The projects focusing on health care professionals consisted of one study of community nurses (Barker and Szkupinski-Quiroga 1991) and one of physicians (Barker, Mitteness, and Heller 1991; Barker, Mitteness, and Muller 1993). The study of nurses involved a survey of 41 home health care nurses, drawn from five agencies in the local area. In semistructured interviews we explored their beliefs and attitudes about urinary incontinence, mobility impairment, and dementia as three common health problems in the elderly. The study of physicians was a telephone survey of the physicians of a subsample of 54 of the clients in the home health care agency sample. In a brief interview we obtained their perspectives on diagnoses, functional status, prognosis, and treatment goals for our informants.

### Social workers and housing managers

Early pilot work suggested that uncontrolled urinary incontinence was often thought to be a risk factor for institutionalization. We were therefore interested in the perspectives of people who could potentially contribute to decisions to move elderly people to other types of housing. We focused on two groups – social workers and apartment managers. The first study involved 20 medical social workers who worked for home health care agencies with frail, homebound elderly clients (Mitteness and Wood 1986). Semistructured interviews focused on attitudes, beliefs, and management strategies used in dealing with clients who had mobility impairments, dementia, or urinary incontinence. The second study consisted of interviews with 34 managers of apartments and residential hotels for older persons (Barker, Mitteness, and Wood 1988; Mitteness et al. 1995).

### Summary

The data we discuss in this article come primarily from the two studies of elderly people, although the other studies provide corroborative evidence. Since we focus on cultural beliefs, it is important to note that not every segment of society is represented here. We do, however, have data from people of a variety of ages and occupying a variety of social roles that are relevant to the question at hand. Within these constraints, the cultural model being proposed is consistent. Since US society is tremendously complex, we make no claims that every subgroup in society would fit this model, merely that certain significant subgroups do fit this model relatively well. Work by other researchers has supported, replicated, and expanded our findings (see, for example, Herzog et al. 1988, 1989; Hunskaar and Vinsnes 1992; Lagro-Janssen et al. 1992; Norton 1982; Norton et al. 1988; O'Donnell et al. 1992; Simons 1985; Wells 1984; Wyman et al. 1990).

## Results

### Types of bladder problem

Generally, older people do not claim to have urinary incontinence, or even a *problem* with bladder control (Mitteness 1987a). What they do claim to have are various types of bladder control disturbances, for which they don't always have a single name or term, and which do not always match biomedical labels. For instance, the medical definition of nocturia, though imprecise (Barker and Mitteness 1988), implies excessive urination during the night. The layperson rarely knows or uses the term "nocturia"; rather, this phenomenon is usually simply described as "having to get out of bed to pee, over and over again."

Six categories of bladder control disturbances were described by elderly informants (Barker and Mitteness 1988; Mitteness 1987a). Most older people experience more than one kind of bladder control disturbance, with the most common combination being nocturia and diurnal frequency.

*Frequency.* Quantity and frequency of urination varies widely from individual to individual and is much influenced by type and quantity of diet, fluid intake, medications, exercise, and sweating, not to mention a host of pathophysiological conditions, such as prostate enlargement in men, neurological damage due to cerebro-vascular accidents, or infection (Resnick and Yalla 1985). Urinating as many as six to eight times per day is regarded as normal. More than this is termed "frequency," a phenomenon older people describe simply as "having to *go* a lot." Some older people report diurnal frequencies of 16 to 20, or having to urinate every 20 to 30 minutes. In many such cases people report being literally imprisoned in their homes by their bladder condition.

*Nocturia.* The need to get out of bed to urinate is very common among the elderly. Making more than two trips to the bathroom per night is usually regarded as evidence of nocturnal frequency. Some older people report urinating as often as every hour during the night, which severely disrupts sleep and daytime functioning.

*Nighttime accidents.* Nocturnal urinary events during which the bed gets wet are nighttime accidents. These are usually occasional rather than constant problems, largely because people use pads or other means to prevent the bed from getting wet. Wetting a pad intended to catch urine is not usually regarded as an "accident." Mobility impairments contribute significantly to nighttime accidents.

*Lack of warning.* The biomedical term for this is urgency, which means that a person has only a short interval between receiving a signal that his or her bladder needs emptying and involuntarily voiding. People can normally ignore such signals (also called "holding on") for 20 minutes or more. For some older people, the ability to hold is reduced to less than two minutes, making "accidents" virtually inevitable.

*Dribbling.* Constant leakage is another kind of bladder condition that affects the lives of a few older people. This usually involves small amounts of urine and is controlled by use of pads or diapers.

*Sneezing and urine loss.* Nearly half the women reported losing some urine when they sneezed, coughed, or laughed. Although embarrassed if this happens in public or results in visible wet spots on clothing, for some women this is so much a "fact of life" that they also laugh about it and matter-of-factly deal with it.

*Beliefs about the causes of incontinence*

When asked to explain the causes of bladder disturbances or incontinence, the initial response of older respondents was generally one of confusion and surprise that such a question would even be asked. When these informants did dredge up explanations, they tended to be vague and difficult to articulate beyond the overwhelmingly prevalent belief that incontinence is the utterly predictable and inevitable result of a normal process of the body's weakening with age.

The disintegration of bodily systems was seen to be a normal part of the aging process, about which the individual and the medical care system could do nothing. More than half of the informants considered normal aging to be the primary explanation for incontinence. Even among those who presented disease or damage explanations, normal aging was considered to be an important corollary cause (Mitteness 1987a). With these words of resigned acceptance, two women epitomize the responses to questions about "why" incontinence occurs:

> It's just that the body's wearing out, that's all. I just consider that it's my age and it's to be expected.

> [Incontinence is] part of getting older, I think. I don't think it's a disease . . . just a body change.

One-third of the independently living incontinent people in the sample reported that they had never mentioned their incontinence to a physician. Their reasons for not seeking medical care indicated that incontinence was "not important enough" to bother a doctor with and that treatment for incontinence was only appropriate for younger people (Mitteness 1987a, 1987b).

This belief that incontinence is a normal, irreversible part of the aging process was often bolstered by interactions with health professionals. Two-thirds of independent community-living incontinent elderly people reported that they had mentioned their incontinence to their physicians (Mitteness 1987a). They then used the response of the physician as further evidence to support their belief that incontinence was normal.

Of those incontinent people who did mention their incontinence to a physician, nearly half (48%) reported that the doctor had not responded to their report, either by ignoring the statement of symptoms or by providing a dismissive explanation (Mitteness 1987a, 1987b). They did not send patients for diagnostic evaluations and offered few interventions. This nonresponse by physicians has been reported by other authors as well (Eastwood 1978; Newman 1962; Simons 1985).

> The doctor years ago told me that they can't do anything for it because I was too old. They can't operate on anything like that.

> He said that sometimes when a person gets older you have different weaknesses. And he says, "Your bladder, it sounds to me like you've lost some of your muscle tone." And he said, "This happens quite often in elderly people." . . . And I just accepted that: What can they do for the bladder?

> This doctor didn't give me much encouragement. He said he still wants me to drink a lot of water, you know, which is important . . . But he seemed to indicate that this [incontinence] is a part of the machinery wearing out.

Of course, these statements represent what the patient heard the physician say, not necessarily what the physician intended to communicate. Nevertheless, it is clear that whatever occurs in the consulting room has the effect of normalizing incontinence – suggesting that, by its very commonality, it is a predictable, and hence normal, part of aging.

Why are people content with physicians who appear not to respond effectively to their complaints? One reason is that these elderly people did not expect a cure for their incontinence. After all, they usually had two to five other major health problems that were not "curable" by medical treatment. Others consulted a doctor in hopes of receiving advice about the most appropriate urine collection devices. In the same spirit, they occasionally consulted medical social workers or home health care nurses for advice. Incontinent people considered the physician's non-response or dismissal of incontinence as a reaffirmation of their own belief that incontinence is a normal, irreversible part of the aging process, which must be accepted and managed rather than reversed or cured.

Medical social workers (Mitteness and Wood 1986) explained the causes of urinary incontinence in terms that were very similar to those used by elderly laypeople. Explanations ranged from "just because they're old" or "muscle tone weakening with age," through references to a "weak bladder," "weak sphincters," or "emotional stress," and on to specific lists of diseases thought to cause or be closely associated with incontinence. These lists commonly included dementia, psychiatric problems, stroke, infections, and mobility problems. Multiple explanations for incontinence were provided by 65 percent of social workers, along with frequent admissions that "lots of times it's a mystery." Despite the existence of several explanations for incontinence, half of the social workers reported that the most important underlying factor was "the weakening of the body with age." Along with this strong belief in the age relatedness of incontinence went corollary beliefs that incontinence in the elderly was neither preventable nor reversible (Mitteness and Wood 1986).

Nurses delivering in-home health services to the frail elderly and physicians also tended to come up with disease-specific causes for urinary incontinence, such as dementia, neurological disorder, infection, aftermath of stroke, immobility due to Parkinson's disease or arthritis (Barker and Szkupinski-Quiroga 1991). Many times these causes were then associated with old age, that is, urinary incontinence was the result of a disease process that was alleged to be common only among older age groups and therefore irreversible.

Thus laypeople and general health professionals alike tend to attribute incontinence to old age. "So what do you expect when you're 85?" is neither a flippant nor an ignorant statement when made by doctors, nurses, social workers, or patients. It is a concise statement of an important piece of cultural knowledge: loss of control of the bladder is caused by getting old.

*Management strategies*

Although urinary incontinence is thought to be the result of aging, this does not mean that people happily accept having this disorder. It assaults their sense of adulthood through its association with early childhood, when bladder control had not been established, and it compromises their ability to participate fully in normal social life.

Incontinent older people are ashamed, embarrassed, and distressed by this disorder (Mitteness 1987a; Norton 1982; Wyman et al. 1990).

Effective management (i.e., concealment) of incontinence is absolutely vital if incontinent people are to maintain their social position and self-esteem. Central to this management is the control of information about the self, through care taken to not reveal the problem to any but the very closest others, and hypervigilance with respect to "wetness" or other evidence of "accidents." This is a classic instance of the responsibility stigmatized people have to manage themselves so as not to offend "normal" people (Freidson 1970; Goffman 1963).

Fears – and stereotypes – associated with public incontinence come early in life. Gaining control over the urinary bladder is a key marker of the transition from baby to child and is usually achieved in the first several years of life. Maintaining such control is a central aspect demanded of "normal" people. Any hint that bladder control is fragile or tenuous is fiercely guarded lest it become public knowledge. In his "ethnography of peeing," Oring (1979) talks about the fear engendered in (young) men by the possibility that they may display visible signs of wetness after urination.

> The fear is not that you have contaminated yourself, but that others will notice. [Visible wet spots on clothing] challenge an important aspect of the masculine image, the feeling of being in control . . . It goes without saying that he should . . . be able to control his own bodily functions.[1979:20–1]

Thus, older people devise mechanisms and techniques to maintain a public image of being in control of their bladders for the same reasons as do younger people. Even the kinds of strategies they resort to are not very different. What is different is the deliberation, the awareness, the calculatedness with which older people experiencing bladder control problems set about managing this condition.

The types of management strategies available to incontinent people are varied and range from sophisticated medical interventions to environmental strategies. As we have already seen, however, few incontinent elderly make use of medical intervention. Most people, therefore, rely on the other types of strategies. For those who have the skills and resources to use them, all these approaches enhance secrecy and prevent public disclosure of their incontinent status. In general, planning strategies and attempts to provide physiological control aim at preventing episodes of urinary incontinence through the manipulation of time and of body functioning whereas environmental strategies concern space/location issues and deal more with the aftermath of urinary "accidents."

### Planning ahead

These strategies make conscious and very deliberate the techniques and plans that are done automatically by "normal" people. Available strategies for the incontinent elderly include (1) developing cognitive maps of every publicly or easily accessible toilet in one's neighborhood; (2) scheduling activities by their proximity to toilets; (3) hypervigilance so as not to be caught in public without sufficiently easy access to a toilet. Each of these efforts requires much advance planning and attention to detail. Spontaneity is risky for incontinent people depending on planning strategies.

### Improving physiological control

These strategies vary from those aimed at dealing directly with the presumed causes of incontinence to those focused on coping with wetness and odor. When one's understanding of incontinence is that it is a result of weakness, then exercise may become an important management effort. Exercise may take the form of Kegel's exercises (Kegel 1952), as learned from health professionals or women's magazines, which specifically strengthen the muscles of the pelvic floor. But exercise also often includes general strengthening exercises such as yoga and tai chi.

If incontinence is thought to be caused by some impairment in a bodily hydraulic system, then the control of fluid intake is attempted as a means to reduce output. Variations on this theme include "preventive peeing" (Barker and Mitteness 1988), making frequent trips to the toilet regardless of sensed need to void so as to prevent public disaster. Ironically, this strategy can actually exacerbate bladder dysfunction.

### Environmental control

If prevention of urinary "accidents" is unsuccessful, then management efforts shift from prevention to coping with the results of incontinence; that is, if time and body management fails, then a move is made to control the location (space) in which bladder disturbances happen. Now the focus is on wetness and odor: both must be prevented or minimized.

People may begin to wash massive amounts of laundry to cope with the results of urinary accidents. In efforts to collect urine in a way that prevents wetness and odor, people resort to using a variety of urine collection devices, ranging from rags, pads, adult diapers, and absorbent sheets (often referred to by their brand name, Chux) to cans, pots, or urinals. The enhanced housekeeping, in particular, is merely an exaggeration of existing control mechanisms, substituting hypervigilance and housekeeping skills for the physiological control that is assumed of all people past infancy.

Just as physician responses (or, rather, nonresponses) boistered the beliefs of the elderly about the cause of urinary incontinence being "old age," so other health professionals bolster environmental control as an appropriate management strategy. Interventions routinely offered to incontinent elderly by medical social workers and community nurses delivering in-home health care services were devices to collect urine or control wetness and odor (Barker and Szkupinaski-Quiroga 1991; Mitteness and Wood 1986). This effectively reinforces the idea that the central task is to manage wetness and odor, not to diagnose or treat urinary incontinence.

A key aspect of environmental control is redefinition of what comprises adequate control. This recategorization requires major psychological and behavioral changes and, basically, occurs through a process of stimultaneously restricting and expanding space; that is, restriction of activities to private space is accompanied by a concomitant expansion of the number and type of locations or receptacles in which it is legitimate to urinate. People isolate themselves in their homes, withdraw from public activities so that they will not be observed to have "accidents." Control becomes avoidance of wetness and odor in public.

*Examples*

*Case 1.* One incontinent informant is in her mid-sixties, has multiple sclerosis, and is rather severely impaired, using bilateral elbow canes to get around. She has a difficult form of incontinence that results in the unpredictable voiding of large amounts of urine. Despite her several severe impairments, she maintains an active social life, even so far as taking long trips each year. Her technique for managing incontinence is multifaceted and extremely complex. She takes oxybutynin chloride, a medication to improve bladder control, and her physician is using bladder cystometry to train her bladder to hold more urine. She does Kegel's exercises in an attempt to strengthen her pelvic floor muscles and takes exercise classes in the belief that fitness helps her manage her incontinence. She uses, washes, and reuses kitchen towels as pads because she feels she has too little money to buy disposable pads; for special occasions she uses several layers of disposable pads and rubber pants. Finally, she does two to three loads of laundry per day, traveling from her apartment to the basement laundry on elbow canes and carrying a basket of laundry.

Her incontinence management regimen is very time and energy consuming. These complex strategies are quite successful, as no other residents of the apartment building where she lives appeared to realize that she was incontinent.

*Case 2.* An 86-year-old woman, also living on her own, is another example of a person with a complex set of strategies, even though she has few financial and physical health resources. Because of mobility and vision impairments, she is homebound.

She has to get up three to four times a night. Using a walker to get around, she doesn't always make it to the bathroom in time. Thus she surrounds the toilet with rags to soak up any urine that gets spilt, and places a small towel between her legs to prevent dripping on the hall floor as she slowly makes her way there. Every time she goes past the bathroom she uses it, whether or not she feels an urge to urinate. If she feels she can't make it as far as the toilet, she will urinate into a hospital-supplied fracture pan and empty the urine into a bucket that she keeps by the bed. When she can afford it (which is not often), this woman wears an absorbent pad during the day. Usually, however, she uses small towels or rags, which she washes herself by hand and reuses. Piles of these towels are tucked out of sight behind the furniture in her living room so she always has them on hand. Though she tried Kegel's exercises, they did not afford her any relief. As insurance against wetting the bed she keeps an absorbent pad under the bottom sheet. In addition, she carefully controls the timing and quantity of fluid and diuretic ingestion. A large and diverse set of helpers come to her apartment, to help her manage her finances, to deliver groceries, and to undertake housekeeping chores such as laundry. None of these people knows she is incontinent.

*Case 3.* A 73-year-old white woman, living in her family home and caring for a sick husband, has suffered from slight urinary incontinence for ten years. She is homebound after a recent stroke, which also considerably worsened her incontinence. Now, she not only has urgency and frequency but dribbling/leakage of urine especially at night. She copes by putting a plastic garbage bag over the bed and layering adult-sized diapers on top of that. She wears disposable pads, day and night. By avoiding fluid intake after midafternoon, and reducing the number of diuretic medications, she tries to reduce the quantity of urine voided. She is not entirely successful, however, as a distinct odor of stale urine pervades her house.

*Case 4*. Another informant, 77 years old, has difficulty getting to the toilet on time at night. She simply refuses to have a commode in the bedroom even though there is a long hallway between bedroom and bathroom, and she does not always make it in time. She prefers to wet her pajamas. When this happens, about three to four times a week, she mops up the floor, changes pajamas, and launders the soiled ones. When she goes out during the day, she carefully times herself so that she is not away too long. She also delays taking her diuretic medication till she gets back home, a tactic that exacerbates her nighttime problems. She frequents places only where she knows there are public restrooms and makes sure that she uses these before traveling home. Despite these preventive actions, a major problem still confronts her once she reaches home: she still has to get up the stairs to her apartment and down the long hallway to the toilet without beginning to leak urine. At this, she rarely succeeds.

*Case 5*. One 75-year-old woman told us that dealing with her incontinence is like having a full-time job. She always wears a pad but complains that it does not always contain all the urine she involuntarily voids. Partly because she has trouble keeping her diabetes under control, she experiences frequency, especially at night. She suffers from urgency, too, along with occasional bouts of diarrhea. All this creates a need for constant housekeeping and laundry, and makes keeping herself clean and dry a major task. On good days she is able to accomplish these tasks; on bad days, which are becoming more and more frequent, she cannot do everything that is required. She puts her efforts into trying to stay clean and dry herself rather than trying to maintain total control of her environment. Towels are strewn all over her tiny studio apartment – over the floors, the bed, and the chairs. The furniture is stained from her frequent "accidents," which now happen at least once a day. Over the six months we visited with her, on every visit her home always smelled strongly, of either urine or feces, or of powerful cleaning fluids. A home health aide comes twice a week for two hours each time to assist her. It then becomes a choice as to what assistance she most needs at the time – does she most need help to clean the apartment, do the laundry, or go grocery shopping?

She recounts being greatly ashamed of and embarrassed by past "accidents" on the street, which "just happened all of a sudden with no warning." She curtails trips outside of her home even when her urinary and bowel problems are under reasonable control, because of the very short time (maybe an hour and a half) she has available between trips to the toilet, and because of her fear of "accidents." Now, she leaves her home about once a month to transact business that cannot be otherwise accomplished. She wears a coat when out, even in the hottest weather, so wetness and stains on her clothing will not be visible. She is afraid to have people come to her home because of her embarrassment over the state of her furniture and floors and anxiety about whether she will have an "accident" while they were there. She gets groceries delivered but only to the door. Banking and most other ordinary business she conducts by telephone or mail or goes without.

*Case 6*. An 82-year-old black man has a great deal of difficulty with urinary frequency, needing to urinate every 30 minutes. Since his last hospitalization for heart problems, his urinary frequency has increased and so have the number of "accidents." He is severely depressed by his failing health, especially his incontinence, and now rarely leaves his bed. He refuses to even try using adult diapers. An external (condom) catheter was unsuccessful, so now he uses a portable urinal. When full, he dumps the contents of this urinal into a bucket next to his bed. A plastic sheet lies on top of the mattress, and on top of it are a couple of bath towels. In his wife's words: "He done plum give up, because he do it in the bed." Previously, on the rare occasions when he left the house he would not use any protective device and always returned with wet clothes.

*Case 7.* Living in a neighborhood close to a small complex of stores, an 83-year-old informant is able to shop and do business with the aid of a motorized scooter. He has several different kinds of urinary problem: frequency (needing to urinate every 20 minutes), inability to hold his urine for more than two minutes, and dribbling or leakage. He does not use pads, diapers, or other devices, and does not manipulate the time of ingestion of diuretic medications. When out, he cannot get through a trip without needing to urinate, and is not always in a store or business that has a restroom available or accessible. His solution is simply to urinate – in his words, to "let 'er rip" – wherever he happens to be and to not worry about having wet clothing or leaving puddles on the floor. "Accidents" like this happen, on average, once a week. He described several instances of urinating while in the bank and in the grocery store, to the dismay of other patrons, and ended his commentary by saying, "I don't care. They'll get old one day."

*Case 8.* One older woman in her mid-sixties completely ignores her bladder control problems. In fact, she gives the impression that she is unaware of having such problems. Her clothing is very often wet and she is continually malodorous. She is a universal source of gossip in her senior housing apartment building and, though an extremely gregarious person, is rebuffed at every turn. In the public dining room, which forms the center of social life in the building, she has been refused permission to sit at almost all tables, finally being forced to share the table of a small group of residents who speak no English. Gossip about her is rife and focuses on her "craziness," for which her wetness and odor are primary pieces of evidence, and there is considerable interest in persuading her to move out of the building. Her incontinence has been socially devastating and has resulted in very strong negative sanctions. Early in our study, sustained vocal complaints about her by her neighbors forced her out of the apartment building into a more "sheltered" living environment.

## Control and Visibility: A Continuum

It should be obvious from the survey of management strategies and examples that not all incontinent people use or have access to all strategies for control of incontinence. Some strategies require income, social status, and social skills that are beyond the reach of many – finding the right urologist in the right tertiary care center to do the right kind of surgery to effectively cure stress urinary incontinence, for example, or having enough money to buy commercially made absorbent pads. Other strategies require levels of cognitive focus and energy that are daunting. Others require physical or social resources that are differentially available to older people.

The combination of resources required and strategies used leads to an ordering of people on a continuum of outcome: from successfully managed and totally invisible to highly visible, unmanaged incontinence. Figure 19.1 presents this continuum, including a summary of the resources required and consequences of controlling the visibility of incontinence.

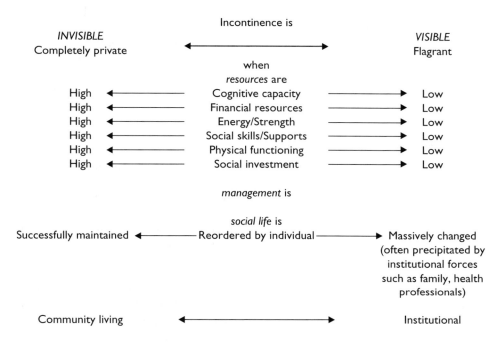

**Figure 19.1**  Model of the resources needed for and consequences of effective control of the visibility of urinary incontinence.

There is a continuum of success at managing urinary incontinence created by the complex interplay of resources, skills, motivation, physical and mental health and functioning, and social and environmental factors. These are not so much new issues in the lives of older people who become incontinent as exaggerations of strategies used regularly but not so consciously through the earlier adult years (Oring 1979).

Some people are more successful than others at managing incontinence. Three distinct types of management emerged from our data: supercompetence, isolating competence, and incompetence. Because most urinary incontinence is successfully hidden from public view and not revealed except to intimate others, we have only estimates of the relative proportion of incontinent elderly who fall into each category of management. It is fairly certain, however, that most people are somewhere between supercompetent and isolating, and that the proportion who are incompetent managers is low – probably around 10 percent or less.

### Supercompetence

The person who has relatively few coexisting medical problems as well as many cognitive, social, and economic resources can marshal all of these resources to very effectively keep the secret of incontinence. These people are capable of doing (or having other people do) heavy amounts of laundry; of planning time very carefully so that "accidents" occur in privacy; of searching for management tools, such as urine collection devices; of "keeping secrets," of not letting others know about their incontinence; of developing cognitive maps of the community so that they are never far from a toilet; and of rescheduling toileting so that the opportunity for accidents is minimized. Any elder who can manage all these tasks that are necessary to keep incontinence a secret is truly supercompetent. This supercompetent incontinent person is able to spend the vast amount of time necessary to manage incontinence while maintaining a social and public persona and self-esteem.

### Isolating Competence

A second set of management strategies becomes necessary when the elder has fewer resources, whether he or she is physically ill or just less able to plan or work so effectively. The incontinent elder who isn't supercompetent is still able to maintain self-esteem and a persona but at a greater cost – that of increasing social isolation.

This elder redefines control. Redefining control consists of extending the definition of appropriate locations for voiding, beyond the toilet to clothing or the floor of one's own private space. It is by this process of redefinition that an elderly woman is able to say that she does not really have "accidents" because she holds a towel between her legs and urinates into it as she makes her way to the toilet. In the same way, residents of subsidized housing often refuse to use the public toilets near the common dining rooms, preferring to rush to their own apartment toilets after lunch. Wetting the floor of a public toilet is considered shameful; wetting the floor of one's own apartment, as long as others do not see it, is relatively acceptable.

The sharp distinction between public and private and the reorganization of one's life that this strategy demands lead to increasing social isolation. This association of urinary incontinence with social isolation has been documented in a number of studies since our initial work was first published (e.g., Grimby et al. 1993; Lagro-Janssen et al. 1992).

An incontinent elder isolates himself or herself at home, where loss of bladder control is tolerable, and avoids visitors because their presence would threaten these "normalizing" strategies (Strauss and Glaser 1984). Because a strategy of redefining control leads to a greater frequency of wet or stained clothing and the possible odor of stale urine in one's apartment, visitors to the apartment frequently will have access to evidence of the elder's incontinence. This observed evidence of incontinence is a failure of the management strategy and can result in negative sanctioning. This concern for public appearance and the risk perceived to exist in public accidents is similar to the concern surrounding public seizures expressed by respondents in Schneider and Conrad's (1983) study of epilepsy. Both epilepsy and incontinence carry implications of lack of social competence as well as larger meanings of disgrace and shame.

For some people, secrecy becomes less important at some point. For people who have given up on independence, who acknowledge their frailty and dependence on others, secrecy is sometimes no longer a primary consideration. In these cases, urinary incontinence may become *less* important as other, more overwhelming health problems take priority. These people continue, however, to be reluctant to appear in public for fear of accidents, of being exposed as incontinent.

*Incompetence*

Finally, there is a group of people who are too impaired even to manage the social isolation necessary to retain public competence. These form a small portion of the incontinent elderly, but their flagrant incontinence is public information, due to their physical or cognitive inability to keep it secret. The consequences of this inability to keep a secret are truly profound. These are the incontinent people who are subject to gossip, hostile actions, and other forms of severe social ostracism and who are clearly at risk for institutionalization.

## Stigmatizing Urinary Incontinence

That urinary incontinence is severely stigmatized and compromises both a person's social standing and the customary presumption of competent adulthood is evidenced by the reactions of others to the incontinent. Incontinent people are alleged to be less able, less competent, less attractive, less desirable companions. Even those who are themselves incontinent make negative attributions about and express little sympathy for generalized, anonymous incontinent others whom they do not know, while denying such attributions apply to them personally or to incontinent family or friends (Mitteness 1987a). These responses to incontinent people are classic examples of responses to stigmatizing conditions, as discussed by Goffman (1963) and others.

Managers of apartment buildings or residential hotels claim that urinary incontinence in an elderly tenant is a reason for eviction, for having the person move to a less independent living environment, even institutionalized. In discussing actual cases of incontinent tenants, a variety of helping strategies were often utilized. However, if the incontinent person was not successful in eliminating public accidents, wetness, and odor, or was not willing to make an effort, apartment managers nearly universally said they could not stay in the building (Barker, Mitteness, and Wood 1988; Mitteness et al. 1995).

Of three common conditions among the impaired elderly – confusion, mobility impairment, and urinary incontinence – urinary incontinence received the most negative evaluations and emotional responses from medical social workers and home health care nurses (Barker and Szkupinski-Quiroga 1991; Mitteness and Wood 1986). At least half the sample could find something positive to say about the other two conditions, but only one or two respondents had positive or even neutral emotional responses to incontinence. Most interventions offered by these health care professionals focused on the control of wetness and odor. Some respondents "blamed the victim" if the incontinent elder was unable to use or unsuccessful with these interventions, saying, for example. "If she'd just use the pads, then she wouldn't be incontinent." Thus, confused or immobile older people can expect some sympathy from these health providers and are exempted from responsibility for their condition; not so the incontinent.

As we have already seen, physicians often abdicate from diagnosing or treating incontinence. Not only do they tend to turn over control of this problem to nurses and other ancillary medical staff, but there is a general tendency among physicians to assume that once incontinence becomes flagrant, that is, public and therefore no longer able to be ignored, institutionalization is the best – or only – treatment option available.

Responses by incontinent people to the discreditability of incontinence focus on keeping incontinence a secret. The supercompetent incontinent person is able to prevent becoming discredited by using a wide variety of strategies. This work of managing stigma is common to many stigmatized conditions, although specific strategies differ by condition and by person (Davis 1973; Goffman 1963; Herskovits and Mitteness 1994; Shifflet and Blieszner 1988; Wiener 1975).

## Cultural Linkages

Who are the discredited, not merely discreditable, incontinent people? Elderly incontinent people who are incompetent managers are the only incontinent elderly whose incontinence is public, and they are incompetent; that is, they have concomitant difficulties that make the control of information about the self an extremely difficult or impossible task. They either willfully flout convention, are victims of circumstance, or are incompetent to perform that which is required of adult persons because of psychiatric, cognitive, or physical impairments. When incontinence occurs repeatedly in public, then the competence of the person is seriously called into question.

Underlying all of these management strategies, then, is the recognition by the incontinent elder that the major potential social consequence of incontinence is the attribution of incompetence. Loss of bladder control is linked with loss of control of other aspects of life, and to be out of control is to be incompetent.

Because of the very success of the other types of management strategies in keeping things secret, from the viewpoint of the general populace, the only incontinent people about whom one knows anything are those who are publicly incontinent. Therefore, they come to represent *all* incontinent people. In a sense, then, an incontinence–incompetence linkage in beliefs about incontinence is not unreasonable since the only incontinent people who are *seen* to be incontinent are those whose other physical or mental health problems impair their competence. Public incontinence is proof of incompetence. Unfortunately, when it is assumed that all incontinence is visible and that this small number of flagrantly incontinent people constitutes all incontinent people, then it becomes far too easy to assume that all incontinent people are this incompetent.

Loss of bladder control, then, is a cardinal sign of impending incompetence, which creates an attendant concern for keeping incontinence a secret to prevent reprisals such as social ostracism or forced institutionalization. While urinary incontinence is seen as a normal part of the aging process, it is by no means an acceptable or comfortable part of aging. Incontinence is linked to incompetence and decrepitude to a degree that makes secrecy and control of information about the self (odor and wetness) an absolute imperative. The competent incontinent elder can and does control wetness and odor. The incompetent elder is visibly incontinent.

This association of incompetence and incontinence is not intrinsic. It is a social construction, a linking together of various attributes and ideas into a culturally relevant value package. That this association is strong and widespread was brought home to us by the anonymous reviewer of another manuscript in which the phrase "competent incontinent person" appeared. The reviewer circled this phrase in red ink and wrote in the margin "a contradiction in terms; there are no competent incontinents."

## Conclusion

The cultural model of urinary incontinence described here is one that depicts life as beginning as an unfinished fabric, which is then woven into a proper adult; as one lives longer and longer, the threads become worn and the adult fabric unravels again. There is incredible power and symmetry to this model that is very difficult to counter. Incontinence, because of its seeming link to the lack of bladder control of infancy (consider the meaning of baby diapers and "adult diapers"), along with cognitive impairments that make some older people as illogical and undependable as a child, fit distressingly well into this symmetric model of the cycle of life.

Older Americans frequently report fears of becoming dependent or incompetent, of "losing it" (Clark and Anderson 1967; Kalish 1969). Incontinent elderly people are under a double threat: age alone makes their competence socially suspect, and public knowledge of their incontinence would confirm that suspicion. By not offering the elderly the opportunity for cure or effective treatment of urinary incontinence, social institutions reinforce the suspect competence of the elderly based on their age. Further, this lack of opportunity for treatment puts incontinent people "on probation," forcing them to continually prove their competence by effectively hiding from others evidence of their incontinence, of their dependency.

Francis Hsu (1961) referred to the "American blind spot" – our failure to recognize the inordinate moral and ethical value placed upon complete self-reliance and self-control in this culture. Williams (1959) has said that our definition of freedom is founded on an incredible confidence of the individual in his or her own competence. Bellah et al. (1985) repeat this theme in a more contemporary format. Clark and Anderson's (1967) classic study described the stresses and strains of US aging in terms of these cultural demands for autonomy in conflict with societal institutions that force the dependency of elderly people. Callahan (1987) describes the dilemma of fears of the illnesses of old age and fears of medical technology that threaten self-control. It is no wonder, then, that incontinence, with its associated implications of incompetence, is so feared.

Continence and competence are *not* logically linked; they are culturally linked through an insistence on control of oneself and one's environment as requisite for adulthood. The emphasis on control and mastery is relevant to the frequent stereotyping of old people as being infirm, senile, childlike, and worthless (Butler 1975). Maintaining bladder control is, then, more than physiological; it is central to the maintenance of a sense of self. To lose control of one's bladder is to lose control of one's life, to become dependent.

Incontinence and certain other age-related disorders appear to differ from other stigmatized chronic conditions in the type of threat they pose to the social fabric. Incontinence is not a disease in the common understanding but rather is seen as a normal, irreversible part of the aging process. Its perceived universality, combined with its dirt and disorder connotations (Mitteness 1987a), makes incontinence especially fearful for Americans.

The marginality, indeed liminality, of old age has been commented on by other authors (Barker 1990; Bever 1982; Solomon 1986). The morally suspect nature of "in between" people (in this case, old people in between life and death) is often demonstrated culturally through their association with dirt, filth, disintegration, and decay (Herskovits and Mitteness 1994). In the case of urinary incontinence the connections between incontinence and incompetence are overdetermined; that is, there are myriad social, psychological, and symbolic reasons to affirm that incontinent old people are different, are incapable, are beyond the bounds of acceptability. To live a long life is to reach a final stage of great and irreversible disorder. Incontinence symbolizes this disorder and is proof that the elder is no longer an adult person but is on the road to the ultimate in disorderliness and decrepitude, to becoming a nonperson.

## Acknowledgments

The research on which this article is based was supported by a National Institute on Aging Research Grant (#AG03471) and an NIA Research Career Development Award (#AG00274) to the first author. The authors also gratefully acknowledge the collaboration of Connie Wolfsen, R.N., M.S., who has been integrally involved in most of this research.

## Notes

1  The demographic characteristics of Study A are as follows: mean age – 74 (s.d. = 10.2); 25% men; 61% high school education or less; 83% annual income less than $10,000 (median = $6,000); 17% annual income $10,000–$19,999; 91% Euro-American.
2  The demographic characteristics of Study B are as follows: mean age = 79 (s.d. = 8.7); 46% men; 48% high school education or less; 47% annual income less than $10,000, 29% annual income greater than $20,000 (median = $12,500); 65% Euro-American, 22% African American, 7% Hispanic, 6% other.

## References

Barker, Judith C, 1990. Between Humans and Ghosts: The Decrepit Elderly in a Polynesian Society. In *The Cultural Context of Aging: Worldwide Perspectives*. Jay Sokolovsky, ed. Pp. 295–313. New York: Bergin and Garvey.
Barker, Judith C., and Linda S. Mitteness, 1998. Nocturia in the Elderly. *Gerontologist* 28 (1): 99–104.
Barker, Judith C., Linda S. Mitteness, and Karen Heller, 1991. Physicians' Knowledge of Adult Day Health Care for the Elderly. *Gerontology and Geriatrics Education* 12 (1): 1–16.
Barker, Judith C., Linda S. Mitteness, and Hayyah Muller, 1993. Relationship between Older Patients' and Physicians' Assessments of Functional Status. Manuscript in authors' files.
Barker, Judith C., Linda S. Mitteness, and Sandra J. Wood, 1988. Gate-Keeping: Residential Managers and Elderly Tenants. *Gerontologist* 28 (5): 610–19.
Barker, Judith C., and Seline Szkupinski-Quiroga, 1991. Community Nurses' Responses to Three Common Illnesses in the Elderly. Final Report to Standford Teaching Nursing Home Project. Manuscript in authors' files.

Bates, P., W. E. Bradley, E. Gien, D. Griffiths, H. Melchior, D. Rowan, A. Sterling, N. Zinner, and T. Hald, 1979. The Standardization of Terminology of Lower Urinary Tract Function. *Journal of Urology* 121: 551–4.

Bellah, Robert N., R. Madsen, W. M. Sullivan, A. Swidler, and S. M. Tipton, 1985. *Habits of the Heart: Individualism and Commitment in American Life.* Berkeley: University of California Press.

Bever, E., 1982. Old Age and Witchcraft in Early Modern Europe. In Old Age in Preindustrial Society. P. N. Stearns, ed. Pp. 150–90. New York: Holmes & Meler.

Burgio, Kathyrn L., and Bernard T. Engel, 1990. Biofeedback-Assisted Behavioral Training for Elderly Men and Women. *Journal of the American Geriatrics Society* 38: 338–40.

Butler, Robert N., 1975. *Why Survive: Being Old in America.* New York: Harper & Row.

Caldwell, K. P. S., ed., 1975. *Urinary Incontinence.* New York: Grune & Stratton.

Callahan, Daniel, 1987. *Setting Limits: Medical Goals in an Aging Society.* New York: Simon and Schuster.

Clark, M. Margaret, and Barbara G. Anderson, 1967. *Culture and Aging: An Anthropological Study of Older Americans.* Springfield, IL: Charles C. Thomas.

Coleman, Lerita M., 1986. Stigma: An Enigma Demystified. In The Dilemma of Difference. S. C. Ainley, G. Becker, and L. M. Coleman, eds. Pp. 211–32. New York: Plenum Press.

Davis, Marcella, 1973. *Living with Multiple Sclerosis: A Social Psychological Analysis.* Springfield, IL: Charles C. Thomas.

Diokno, Ananies C., 1990. Diagnostic Categories of Incontinence and the Role of Urodynamic Testing. *Journal of the American Geriatrics Society* 38: 300–5.

Eastwood, H., 1978. Incontinence in the Elderly. *Health and Social Services Journal* 88: 550.

Fantl, J. A., J. F. Wyman, S. W. Harkins, and E. C. Hadley, 1990. Bladder Training in the Management of Lower Urinary Tract Dysfunction in Women: A Review. *Journal of the American Geriatrics Society* 38: 329–32.

Freidson, Eliot, 1970. *Profession of Medicine.* New York: Dodd, Mead and Co.

Goffman, Erving, 1963. *Stigma: Notes on the Management of Spoiled Identity.* Englewood Cliffs, NJ: Prentice-Hall.

Grimby, A., I. Milsom, U. Molander, I. Wiklund, and P. E. Kelund, 1993. The Influence of Urinary Incontinence on the Quality of Life of Elderly Women. *Age and Ageing* 22 (2): 82–9.

Herskovits, Elizabeth J., and Linda S. Mitteness, 1994. Transgressions and Sickness in Old Age. *Journal of Aging Studies* 8 (3): 327–40.

Herzog, A. Regula, and Nancy H. Fultz, 1990. Prevalence and Incidence of Urinary Incontinence in Community-Dwelling Populations. *Journal of the American Geriatrics Society* 38: 273–81.

Herzog, A. Regula, N. H. Fultz, B. M. Brock, M. B. Brown, and A. C. Diokno, 1988. Urinary Incontinence and Psychological Distress among Older Adults. *Psychology and Aging* 3 (2): 115–21.

Herzog, A. Regula, N. H. Fultz, D. P. Normolle, B. M. Brock, and A. C. Diokno, 1989. Methods Used to Manage Urinary Incontinence by Older Adults in the Community. *Journal of the American Geriatrics Society* 37: 339–47.

Hsu, Francis L. K., 1961. *Psychological Anthropology: Approaches to Culture and Personality.* Homewood, IL: Dorsey Press.

Hu, Teh-wei, 1990. Impact of Urinary Incontinence on Health-Care Costs. *Journal of the American Geriatrics Society* 38: 292–5.

Hunskaar, S., and A. Vinsnes, 1992. The Quality of Life in Women with Urinary Incontinence as Measured by the Sickness Impact Profile. *Journal of the American Geriatrics Society* 39 (4): 378–82.

Kalish, Richard A., ed., 1969. The Dependencies of Old People. Occasional Papers in Gerontology, 6. Institute of Gerontology, University of Michigan – Wayne State University, Ann Arbor, MI.

Kegel, Arnoid H., 1952. Stress Incontinence and Genital Relaxation: A Nonsurgical Method of Increasing the Tone of Sphincters and Their Supporting Structures. Ciba Clinical Symposia 4: 35–51.

Lagro-Janssen, T., A. Smits, and C. Van Weel, 1992. Urinary Incontinence in Women and the Effects on Their Lives. *Scandinavian Journal of Primary Health Care* 10 (3): 211–16.

Mandelstam, Dorothy, ed., 1980. *Incontinence and the Management*. 2nd ed. London: Croom Helm.

Mitteness, Linda S., 1987a. So What Do You Expect When You're 85? Urinary Incontinence in Late Life. In The Experience of Illness: Research in The Sociology of Health Care Series, 6. Julius Roth and Peter Conrad, eds. Pp. 177–219. Greenwich, CT: JAI Press, Inc.

Mitteness, Linda S., 1987b Management of Urinary Incontinence by Community-Living Elderly. *Gerontologist* 27 (2): 185–93.

Mitteness, Linda S., Judith C. Barker, and Emily Finlayson, 1995. Residential Managers' Experience with Urinary Incontinence in Elderly Tenants. *Journal of Applied Gerontology*, in press.

Mitteness, Linda S., and Sandra J. Wood, 1986. Social Workers' Responses to Incontinence, Confusion, and Mobility Impairments in Frail Elderly Clients. *Journal of Gerontological Social Work* 9: 63–78.

National Institutes of Health Consensus Development Conference, 1990. Urinary Incontinence in Adults. *Journal of the American Geriatrics Society* 38: 265–72.

Newman, J. L., 1962. Old Folk in Wet Beds. *British Medical Journal* 1: 1824–7.

Norton, C., 1982. The Effects of Urinary Incontinence in Women. International Rehabilitation Medicine 4: 9–14.

Norton, P. A., L. D. McDonald, P. M. Sedgwick, and S. L. Stanton, 1988. Distress and Delay Associated with Urinary Incontinence, Frequency, and Urgency in Women. *British Medical Journal* 297 (6657): 1187–9.

O'Donnell, B. F., D. A. Drachman, H. J. Barnes, K. E. Peterson, J. M. Swearer, and R. A. Lew, 1992. Incontinence and Troublesome Behaviors Predict Institutionalization in Dementia. *Journal of Geriatric Psychiatry and Neurology* 5 (1): 45–52.

Oring, Elliot, 1979. From Uretics to Uremics: A Contribution toward the Ethnography of Peeing. In Culture, Curers and Contagion. Norman Klein, ed. Pp. 15–21. Novato, CA: Chandler and Sharp.

Ouslander, Joseph G., 1990. Urinary Incontinence in Nursing Homes. *Journal of the American Geriatric Society* 38: 289–91.

Ouslander, Joseph G., Robert L. Kane, and Itamar B. Abrass, 1982. Urinary Incontinence in Elderly Nursing Home Patients. *Journal of the American Medical Association* 248: 1194–8.

Raz, Shlomo, 1990. Vaginal Surgery for Stress Incontinence. *Journal of the American Geriatric Society* 38: 345–7.

Resnick, Neil M., and Joseph G. Ouslander, eds., 1990. National Institute of Health Consensus Development Conference on Urinary Incontinence. *Journal of the American Geriatrics Society* 38: 263–386.

Resnick, Neil M., and S. V. Yalla, 1985. Management of Urinary Incontinence in the Elderly. *New England Journal of Medicine* 313: 800–5.

Schneider, Joseph W., and Peter Conrad, 1983. *Having Epilepsy: The Experience and Control of Illness*. Philadelphia: Temple University Press.

Shifflet, Peggy A., and Rosemary Blieszner, 1988. Stigma and Alzheimer's Disease: Behavioral Consequences for Support Groups. *Journal of Applied Gerontology* 7 (2): 147–60.

Simons, J., 1985. Does Incontinence Affect Your Client's Self-Concept? *Journal of Gerontological Nursing* 11 (6): 37–42.

Solomon, Howard M., 1986. Stigma and Western Culture: A Historical Approach. In The Dilemma of Difference. S. C. Ainley, G. Becker, and L. M. Coleman, eds. Pp. 59–76. New York: Plenum Press.

Strauss, Anselm, and Barney G. Glaser, 1984. *Chronic Illness and the Quality of Life*. 2nd ed. St. Louis, MO: C. V. Mosby.

Urinary Incontinence Guideline Panel, 1992. Urinary Incontinence in Adults: Clinical Practice Guideline. AHCPR Pub. No. 92-0038. Rockville, MD: Agency for Health Care Policy and Research, Public Health Service, U.S. Department of Health and Human Services.

Welm, Alan J., 1990. Pharmacologic Treatment of Incontinence. *Journal of the American Geriatrics Society* 38: 317–25.

Wells, Thelma J., 1984. Social and Psychological Implications of Incontinence. In *Urology in the Elderly*. J. C. Brocklehurst, ed. Pp. 107–26. New York: Churchill Livingstone.

Wells, Thelma J., 1990. Pelvic (Floor) Muscle Exercise. *Journal of the American Geriatrics Society* 38: 333–7.

Wiener, Carolyn L., 1975. The Burden of Rheumatoid Arthritis: Tolerating the Uncertainty. *Social Science and Medicine* 9: 97–104.

Williams, R. M., 1959. *American Society: A Sociological Interpretation*. New York: Alfred A. Knopf.

Willington, F. L., ed., 1976. *Incontinence in the Elderly*. London: Academic Press.

Wolfsen, Connie, Linda S. Mitteness, and Judith C. Barker, 1988. Adverse Consequences of Urinary Frequency and Urgency. Paper read at Gerontological Society of America meetings, San Francisco, November.

Wyman, Jean F., Stephen W. Harkins, and J. Andrew Fantl, 1990. Psychosocial Impact of Urinary Incontinence in the Community-Dwelling Populations. *Journal of the American Geriatrics Society* 38: 282–8.

## Further Reading to Part VI

Becker, Gay. 1997. *Disrupted Lives: How People Create Meaning in a Chaotic World.* Berkeley: University of California Press.

Becker, Gaylene. 1994. "The Oldest Old: Autonomy in the Face of Frailty," *Journal of Aging Studies* 8: 59–76.

Barker, Judith C. 1997. Chapter 21, "Between Humans and Ghosts: The Decrepit Elderly in a Polynesian Society." Pp. 407–24 in *The Cultural Context of Aging,* edited by Jay Sokolovsky. Westport, CT: Bergin and Garvey.

Charmaz, Kathy. 1991. *Good Days, Bad Days: The Self in Chronic Illness and Time.* New Brunswick, NJ: Rutgers University Press.

Deppen-Wood, Monika, Mark R. Luborsky, and Jessica Scheer. 1997. Chapter 23, "Aging, Disability and Ethnicity: An African-American Woman's Story." Pp. 443–51 in *The Cultural Context of Aging,* edited by Jay Sokolovsky. Westport, CT: Bergin and Garvey.

Furman, Frida Kerner. 1997. *Facing the Mirror: Older Women and Beauty Shop Culture.* New York: Routledge.

Gubrium, Jaber F. and James A. Holstein. 1999. "The Nursing Home as a Discursive Anchor for the Aging Body," *Ageing and Society* 19: 519–38.

Öberg, Peter. 1996. The Absent Body – A Social Gerontological Paradox," *Ageing and Society* 16: 701–19.

# Part VII

## The Aging Mind

# 22 Geriatric Ideology: The Myth of the Myth of Senility

## James S. Goodwin

> But our first most important function, the reason the people need us and keep us, is to preserve the purity of all sources of knowledge.
>
> Hermann Hesse, *Magister Ludi*.

Ideology has been defined in various ways. The term was introduced at the time of the French Revolution by the philosopher A.L.C. Destutt de Tracy; he described it as possessing five characteristics:

1  An ideology contains an explanatory theory of a more or less comprehensive kind about human experience and the external world.
2  It sets out a program, in generalized and abstract terms, of social and political organization.
3  It conceives the realization of this program as entailing a struggle.
4  It seeks not merely to persuade but to recruit loyal adherents, demanding what is sometimes called commitment.
5  It addresses a wide public but may tend to confer some special role of leadership on intellectuals.

Over the past two centuries the term ideology has kept much of the meaning originally ascribed to it by Destutt de Tracy. An ideology is a "system of ideas that aspires both to explain the world and to change it."[1] The concept of ideology has attracted many critics, including Albert Camus, who was revolted by the violence committed in its name, and Karl Popper, who criticized its fundamental theses. Popper saw the scientific method as involving continual trial and error in which ideas or conjectures are put to experimental test; those that are not falsified are provisionally accepted. In other words, there is no definitive knowledge in science, only provisional knowledge that is constantly being corrected.[2] In an ideology, science is a tool, as are education and politics, by which the goals of the ideology are achieved. Popper criticized ideologists' affinity for certainty; their scientific postulates were in actuality prophesies, with no scientific validity.

Original publication: Goodwin, James, S., "Geriatric Ideology: The Myth of the Myth of Senility," *Journal of the American Geriatrics Society*, 39 (1991), pp. 627–31.

## Geriatric Ideology

In this article I will discuss the ideological aspects of geriatric medicine. My thesis is that much of the content of academic geriatrics is ideological. To a certain extent, we perceive ourselves as in a struggle against ageism, against the forces in medicine and society at large that do not value old age and the elderly. Such a struggle promotes the growth of ideology. Ideology introduces a moral context to scientific discussions. In other words, ideas or discoveries are good or bad, not just right or wrong. In an ideology one is likely to hear "I disagree with the results of that research because the findings imply . . ."[11] Needless to say, an ideological context inhibits the growth of knowledge.

There are several ways to describe geriatric ideology. One overall ideological concept is that aging is good, that bad things do not inevitably accompany aging. Perhaps the most extreme statement of geriatric ideology is that if we all do the right thing, we will never die. Since this statement is absurd on inspection, it is never clearly enunciated. Nevertheless, I feel that it forms the basis for many of the less absurd but equally ideological concepts that underlie geriatrics. In the remainder of this discussion I will describe one example of geriatric ideology, the concept that senility is a disease, and then summarize other manifestations of ideology in geriatrics. I will then return to a discussion of the causes and adverse consequences of geriatric ideology.

## The Myth of the Myth of Senility

An underlying tenet of geriatrics is that senility is a disease. We emphasize this in many ways, not the least of which is in our vocabulary. The terms "senility" and "senile" have been banished, replaced first by dementia and then by Alzheimer's disease. Patrick Fox has traced the rapid transformation in the late 1970s in the US of the term Alzheimer's disease from describing a small number of patients with presenile dementia to almost everyone of any age with progressive loss of global cognitive function.[3] Robert Butler, the first director of the National Institute of Aging, coined the term "myth of senility" to identify what he considered to be the prevalent and fallacious notion that dementia is a natural consequence of aging. Dementia, or Alzheimer's disease, was a disease, similar to diabetes or pneumonia. Seen as such, Alzheimer's disease has a cause (or causes), and it should be theoretically possible both to prevent and successfully treat: "When we eliminate Alzheimer's disease, the polio of geriatrics, we will empty half of our country's nursing home beds."[4] The transformation of senility into Alzheimer's disease has been credited with focussing research on this problem: "That made it a disease you could work on . . . It was not aging. This was a disease. This was not senility."[5]

This concept that dementia is a disease and not a natural consequence of aging was stressed in every recent geriatric textbook that I reviewed. Indeed the concept has been broadened to include many other conditions afflicting the elderly. "We must begin by systematically analyzing the many myths and distortions about aging. Too much is attributed to age that is actually due to disease, disability, social adversity, personality, educational level, alcoholism, lifestyle, or the environment."[4] I will return to the issue of this broadening of the message later. One point I would like to make here is that the tenor of the above quotations would appear to satisfy the third characteristic of an ideology, that the realization of the program is conceived as entailing a struggle.

One might rightfully ask, what is wrong with the proposition that dementia is a disease? If it were only a proposition, or a hypothesis, then nothing would be wrong with it. Indeed, it may turn out to be correct. But it is more than that; it is a fundamental tenet of the geriatric belief system. As such, it is not questioned or subjected to experimental test. Actually, there is evidence to suggest that senile dementia of the Alzheimer's type (SDAT) may be part of the normal aging process. Cognitive function clearly declines with age, and there is no evidence among the elderly at any given age for a bimodal distribution of cognitive function, a finding that might suggest a disease process. Instead, those subjects who are below a certain point in the normal distribution of cognitive function are diagnosed as having dementia. The prevalence of this condition rises strikingly with age.[6,7] A recent community-based study estimated the prevalence of Alzheimer's disease to be 3 percent in those 65 to 74, 19 percent in those 75 to 84, and 47 percent in those aged 85 and older.[6] There are few associations in medicine as strong as that between dementia and advanced age. When the term Alzheimer's disease was limited to those with true presenile dementia, the pathological findings of plaques and neurofibrillary tangles were used to support the concept of a distinct disease process, but these plaques and neurofibrillary tangles are commonly found in autopsy specimens of individuals over age 75, regardless of whether their premorbid diagnoses included dementia.[8] Some Alzheimer's disease runs in families, and this may be associated with a gene on chromosome 21. This is not strong evidence that Alzheimer's is a "disease." Aging, or life expectancy, also runs in families and is under clear genetic control. Another argument made in favor of the concept of Alzheimer's "disease" is that subjects with this diagnosis have a markedly reduced survival. If the appearance of clinically apparent dementia is an indicator of the rate of brain aging, it is not surprising that individuals aging at a relatively faster rate would have a shortened survival. In addition, a markedly decreased survival associated with dementia is actually not well documented; results from longitudinal studies show little or no decrease in life expectancy associated with impaired cognition after controlling for age.[9–12]

Let me propose a hypothesis regarding the occurrence of what we now call Alzheimer's disease. Alzheimer's disease is the clinical expression of an aging brain. Brain function declines with age, though as with other organ systems, the rate of decline varies among individuals in the species. Thus, true presenile dementia represents the extreme of the normal distribution of decline in brain function with age. The average rate of decline in brain function is such that by age 90 approximately 50 percent of individuals will be clinically demented. External factors, such as nutrition, cardiovascular disease, or drugs, can accelerate the onset of clinical dementia by their additive (or perhaps synergistic) effects with the aging process on decline in brain function.

What is wrong with the hypothesis outlined in the last paragraph? In a scientific context it is either right or wrong, or somewhere in between. One can think of various ways of testing the hypothesis. In an ideological context, however, this hypothesis is bad. It has adverse implications. If senility is the manifestation of an aging brain, then perhaps this will encourage lack of respect for the elderly; perhaps it will discourage expansion of federal funding for research on the problems of aging; perhaps it will encourage a sense of fatalism and an avoidance of health-promoting activities in our older patients. All of these concerns are real. However, they have absolutely no bearing on whether the hypothesis is correct or incorrect. Nevertheless, geriatric ideology dictates that the potentially negative implications of the hypothesis preclude even its consideration, much less its acceptance. The concept that dementia may be the clinical manifestation of an aging brain is not to be found in any recent textbook of geriatrics. Perhaps this idea is incorrect; perhaps dementia is a disease. My point is that this should be an issue that is discussed, debated, and subjected to experimental validation rather than included as part of geriatric ideology.

## Other Manifestations of Geriatric Ideology

As mentioned above, the concept that dementia is a disease has been broadened to the point where all age-associated physiologic deterioration is seen as a disease. This ideology is quite recent in its inception and can be traced at least in part to a series of novel and attractive hypotheses introduced by James Fries in an article entitled "Aging, Natural Death, and the Compression of Morbidity", published in 1980[13] and expanded upon in a later monograph.[14] His message can be summarized as follows. Human life span is fixed; human life expectancy is increasing; physiologic changes with age possess "plasticity" and are subject to modification by interventions such as exercise; as human life style and general health continue to improve, we will see a compression of morbidity and a rectangularization of the survival curve, wherein the great majority of individuals will maintain good health into advanced old age and then sicken and die over a relatively brief period.

Similar concepts were propounded by Walter Bortz, who described the similarities between the biologic changes associated with aging to those associated with physical inactivity.[5] He proposed that increased physical activity might slow the aging process and the appearance of aging-induced loss of physiologic function. The ideas of Fries[13] and of Bortz[15] were reformulated by Rowe and Kahn[16] who proposed a distinction between "usual" and "successful" aging. These authors noted that, given the increase in variance with age in the measurement of almost any physiologic parameter (bone density, cardiac output, cognition, etc), it was possible to find elderly individuals whose function in one or another organ system was still within the normal range for young adults. This was then termed "successful" aging; all others were examples of "usual" and, by inference, unsuccessful aging. It is in the translation of Fries' and Bortz's concepts by Rowe and Kahn (and by many others; Rowe and Kahn provide the clearest example) that we see the emergence of ideology from hypothesis. What we used to consider normal aging is in actuality a disease, a failure of the individual to age successfully. "The effects of the aging process itself have been exaggerated, and the modifying effects of diet, exercise, personal habits, and psychosocial factors have been underestimated."[17] Once again, this statement may be correct or incorrect. If it is stated as a hypothesis in a scientific context, specific experimental tests of its validity can be easily generated. If it is stated in an ideological context, it becomes a moral guideline used to judge other concepts.

Examples of this ideology abound in the recent geriatric texts. My principal source will be the *Geriatric Review Syllabus*[18] for several reasons. It is recent; it was compiled by a committee and thereby presents consensus views; and it was organized and published by the American Geriatrics Society. Three representative examples follow.

1   One manifestation of geriatric ideology is that "old age" has been eliminated as a cause of any problem in the elderly. For example, the discussion of causes of failure to eat adequately does not mention the concept that many very old people decrease and sometimes stop eating in the weeks before they die ([18], pp 105–6). The clear implication of the discussion is that it is always to be regarded as abnormal when elderly individuals stop eating.

2   A corollary of the loss of "old age" as an explanation for problems is that just about every problem in the elderly can be successfully treated. For example, "urinary incontinence is curable in many older patients . . . Even when not curable, incontinence can always be managed in a manner that will keep patients comfortable, make life easier for caregivers, and minimize costs of caring for the condition and its complications ([18], p. 75)." Always – not sometimes, not usually, but always.

3   Whatever is good medicine for a younger adult must be provided for the elderly. For example, the treatment of hypertension represents one of the major successes of preventive medicine. The underlying rationale for its treatment is that, first, the presence of hypertension is associated with increased morbidity and mortality and second, the treatment of hypertension is associated with a lowering of that morbidity and mortality, particularly from cerebrovascular disease. Neither aspect of this rationale has been documented in the very old. Several studies have failed to find an association between blood pressure and mortality in those over age 80 ([19–21]). In addition, the only prospective controlled study of treatment of hypertension in the very old found decreasing benefit in treatment of those over age 75 and no benefit associated with treatment for those aged 80 and older.[22] It is interesting to speculate why the very strong association between hypertension and mortality disappears, or even reverses,[21] in the very old. However, this subject goes unmentioned in the Geriatrics Syllabus and other recent texts. According to geriatric ideology, the undertreatment of hypertension and other medical conditions in the elderly is *de facto* evidence of ageism.

## Reasons for the Emergence of Geriatric Ideology

The causes of the rise in geriatric ideology are similar to those behind most ideologies. There was a clear need for action. The special problems of the elderly were largely ignored by the academic and practicing medical community. Many physicians were (and many still are) ignorant about basic aspects of geriatrics.[23] However, geriatric ideology has a more fundamental stimulus. We are all aging. It is as if all oncologists had cancer. Personal involvement tends to distort scientific objectivity. We all want to believe that the aging process can somehow be made better, that we might avoid the particularly devastating and unpleasant consequences of aging. For example, here is a prominent researcher explaining her initial incentive to study cognitive function in the elderly. "I didn't want to believe our intelligence would go down from then on. It didn't seem like a good thing to face for the rest of your life."[24] This is not the usual approach to or motivation for examining a question in science. There is nothing intrinsically wrong with this motivation; most of us share it in some form or another; I certainly do. It would be foolish, however, not to recognize the potential for a loss of scientific objectivity.

## Consequences of Geriatric Ideology

The consequences of geriatric ideology are not all bad. Ideology facilitates communication. There has been a clear increase in awareness of and concern about the special problems of the elderly within the medical community and in society at large. In addition, concepts generated in an ideological context may still turn out to be correct. For example, geriatric ideology has promoted research that has demonstrated that severe osteoporosis is not a normal consequence of aging. Also, research demonstrations that exercise does indeed slow or reverse age-related declines in skeletal muscle and cardiovascular function can be seen as stimulated by geriatric ideology. However, many effects of geriatric ideology have been harmful.

First, geriatric ideology inhibits scientific progress because it distorts our thinking. It hinders our ability to formulate important research questions. Experiments designed within an ideological construct frequently lack critical controls.[25] Important results can be overlooked because they do not "make sense."[26] I recently participated in meetings sponsored by the National Academy of Sciences Institute of Medicine, the purpose of which was to define and prioritize research goals for geriatrics in the next decade. However, we were told at the outset that we should focus on distinguishing changes in the elderly due to disuse or disease from changes due to true aging; thus, the "usual versus successful" ideology was imposed *a priori*. What if the "aging vs disease" dichotomy is an unhelpful way of conceptualizing research problems in gerontology?[27] How can we begin to determine this if all research questions are formulated within a paradigm that incorporates this dichotomy?

A second consequence of geriatric ideology is an emphasis on comprehensive evaluation at the expense of long-term primary care of frail elderly men and women. It is easier to adhere to geriatric ideology if one is not confronted with the realities of day-to-day care of frail elderly. No one providing primary care to those over age 80 can subscribe to geriatric ideology without precipitating a large dose of cognitive dissonance. We in academic geriatrics are painting ourselves in a corner. On the one hand, we want to promote humane, compassionate care for frail elderly men and women. On the other hand, our ideology is forcing us to see normal human aging as a series of diseases to be rigorously evaluated and treated. Surely part of what we do in geriatrics is to care for people whose bodies are getting ready to die. Geriatric ideology hinders us in that task. Where in geriatric ideology is the concept of a natural death? The clinical manifestation of brain aging is seen as a disease. The clinical manifestations of an aging heart are seen as due to past dietary and lifestyle indiscretions. Indeed, the emphasis on successful versus usual aging may provide physicians and others with a club with which to beat their "unsuccessfully" aging patients.

A third deleterious effect of geriatric ideology has to do with our ability to train future leaders of academic geriatric medicine. This particularly involves the fourth characteristic of an ideology, recruiting loyal adherents. Many if not most of the current leadership in geriatrics have come from other disciplines. We have a background in rigorous scientific investigation. It is not clear to me that geriatric trainees are receiving that same experience. Indeed, the mandated requirements of geriatric fellowships are such that it is difficult to include the type of in-depth laboratory or clinical research experience necessary to produce independent investigators. As I have mentioned elsewhere,[28] the unit of currency in academic geriatrics is becoming the review article, the position paper, the opinion piece, not the scientific report. Who will be designing and conducting fundamental research in geriatrics in the next generation?

## Conclusion

One could make the argument that geriatric ideology is only for external consumption. Fox has traced how the medicalization of dementia and the Alzheimer's movement was a major help in securing federal funds for aging research in the early 1980s,[3] and the concept of aging as a disease to be conquered is at least partly responsible for the recent dramatic rise in congressional appropriations for geriatric research. Thus, it may be argued, we are only fooling Congress with this ideology; no one is hurt; we benefit from it. I would disagree. Scientific investigation is a tenuous undertaking.[2] We cannot handicap ourselves by subscribing to an unexamined belief system.

And we are not fooling our patients. I have encountered very few people over age 75 who subscribe to the geriatric ideology outlined above. On the other hand, we do risk burdening our patients with guilt for acquiring their age-related "diseases."

The issue that we have not been able to come to grips with in geriatrics is that everyone dies. Death is inevitable for every living organism. If all "disease" is eliminated, all humans will still die. In the process leading up to death, our bodies will gradually fail. Within an organism, organ systems fail at different rates. These failure rates clearly can be influenced and modulated by many external and internal factors, but to deny the fundamental fact of organ failure in old age is absurd and somewhat sad.

The dominance of geriatric ideology may recede as quickly as it appeared. We have witnessed evidence of change in the past year, with articles by Curb et al.[29] questioning the clinical utility of the "successful aging" paradigm and by Blumenthal and Premachandra[27] challenging the validity of the aging-versus-disease dichotomy. The task for academic geriatrics is straightforward. We need to identify what we know and what we do not know about aging. The primary goal of geriatric medicine cannot be to promote societal change. We need to allow ourselves and each other to ask any question, and we need always to speak the truth.

## Acknowledgments

Mary Carnes, Harvey Cohen, Edmund Duthie, James Fries, Clifford Goodwin, Jean Goodwin, and John Morley reviewed an earlier version of this manuscript. While all of these individuals did not agree with all the points I make, they all made helpful suggestions, and I thank them.

## References

1   Ideology. In: *The New Encyclopedia Britannica*; Macropedia Vol. 9. 1981, 194–8.

2   Hempel, C. G. *Philosophy of Natural Science*. Englewood Cliffs, NJ: Prentice-Hall Inc, 1966.

3   Fox, P. From senility to Alzheimer's disease: the rise of the Alzheimer's disease movement. *Milbank Q* 1989; 67: 58–102.

4   Butler, R. N. A disease called ageism. *J Am Geriatr Soc* 1990; 38: 178–80.

5   Davies, P. *Philosophy of Natural Science*. Englewood Cliffs, NJ: Prentice-Hall, Inc, pp. 88–9.

6   Evans, D. A., Funkenstein, H., Albert M. et al. Prevalence of Alzheimer's disease in a community population of older persons. *JAMA* 1989; 262: 2551–6.

7   Henderson, A. S. The epidemiology of Alzheimer's disease. *Brit Med Bull* 1986; 42: 3.

8   Poirier, J., Finch, C. E. Neurochemistry of the aging human brain: In: Hazzard, W. R., Andres, R., Bierman, E. L., Blass, J. P. eds. *Principles of Geriatric Medicine and Gerontology*. New York: McGraw-Hill, 1990, pp. 905–12.

9   Sayetta, R. B. Rates of senile dementia Alzheimer's type in the Baltimore Longitudinal Study. *J Chron Dis* 1986; 39: 271–86.

10   Gruenburg, E. M. The epidemiology of senile dementia. In: Schoenberg, B. S. ed. *Neurological Epidemiology: Principles and Clinical Application*. New York: Raven Press, 1978, pp. 437–55.

11   Wang, H., Whanger, A. Brain impairment and longevity. In: Palmore, E., Jeffers, F. eds. *Prediction of Life Span*. Lexington, MA: Heath and Co, 1971, pp 95–105.

12   Radebaugh, T. S., Gruenberg, E. M. Cautions re: study of senile dementia. *J Clin Epidemiol* 1988; 41: 307–8.

13   Fries, J. F. "Aging, natural death, and the compression of morbidity." *N Engl J Med* 1980; 303: 130–5.

14   Fries, I. F., Crapo, L. M. *Vitality and Aging: Implications of the Rectangular Curve*. San Francisco: W. H. Freeman and Co. 1981.

15   Bortz, W. Disuse and Aging. *JAMA* 1982; 248: 1203–8.

16   Rowe, J. W., Kahn, R. L. Human aging: usual and successful. *Science* 1987; 237: 143–9.

17   Rowe, J. W. Toward successful aging: limitation of the morbidity associated with "normal" aging. In: Hazzard, W. R., Andres, E., Bierman, E. L., Blass, J. P. eds. *Principles of Geriatric Medicine and Gerontology*. New York: McGraw-Hill, 1990, pp 138–41.

18   Beck, J. C. ed. *Geriatric Review Syllabus: A core curriculum in Geriatric Medicine*. New York: American Geriatrics Society, 1989.

19   Sourander, L., Ruikka, I., Kasanen, A. A health survey on the aged with 5-year follow-up. *Acta Soc Med Scand* 1970; Suppl 3: 1–41.

20   Andersson, F., Cowan, N. R. Survival of healthy older people. *Brit J Prev Soc Med* 1976; 30: 231.

21   Mattila, K., Haavisto, M., Rajala, S., Heikinheimo, R. Blood pressure and five year survival in the very old. *Brit Med J* 1988; 296: 887.

22   Amery, A., Birkenhager, M., Bulptir, C. et al. Efficacy of antihypertensive drug treatment according to age, sex, blood pressure and previous cardiovascular disease in patients over the age of 60. *Lancet* 1986; 2: 589–92.

23   Goodwin, J. S. Knowledge about aging among physicians. *J Aging Health* 1989; 1: 234–43.

24   Jarvik, L. quoted by Siegel, L. (Associated Press). "Is losing it part of old age?" *Milwaukee Journal*, part I, p. 3, Sunday, Sept. 17, 1989.

25   Goodwin, J. S., Goodwin, J. M. The use of cement controls in evaluating assumptions

about etiology and mechanism of action. *J Clin Epidemiol* 1988; 41: 803–4.

26  Goodwin, J. S., Goodwin, J. M. The Tomato Effect: rejection of highly efficacious therapies. *JAMA* 1984; 251: 2389–92.

27  Blumenthal, H. T., Premachandra, B. N. Bridging the aging-disease dichotomy. The amyloidosis model. *Perspect Biol Med* 1990; 33: 402–20.

28  Goodwin, J. S. Citation Classic: Regulation of the immune response by prostaglandins. *Current Contents* 1990; 33: 21.

29  Curb, J. D., Guralnik, J. M., LaCroix, A. Z. et al. Effective aging: meeting the challenge of growing older. *J Am Geriatr Soc* 1990; 38: 827–8.

# 23 Bringing the Social Back In: A Critique of the Biomedicalization of Dementia

## Karen A. Lyman

Alzheimer's disease emerged as an illness category and policy issue in the 1980s, more than 70 years after Alois Alzheimer documented the first case. Dementing illnesses only recently have received attention from researchers and policymakers because "senility" previously was viewed as an inevitable part of normal aging (Ruscio and Cavarocchi, 1984).

Today, Alzheimer's disease is identified as the most common of the dementing illnesses, progressive brain disorders characterized by gradual deterioration of memory, language, other intellectual abilities, and general competence over a 7- to 15-year period until death. There is as yet no cure. A clinical diagnosis results only in a prescription for basic custodial care, perhaps assisted by drugs for symptomatic relief of "agitation."

The clinical manifestations of dementia are associated with many other conditions that may be reversible or treatable. Differential diagnosis, however, is unequivocal only postmortem. Neuropathological analysis often reveals a misdiagnosis of Alzheimer's disease, and autopsies of healthy adults who functioned without symptoms of dementia reveal that approximately 10 percent show the classic Alzheimer's neuropathology (Bergmann, 1985; Brody, 1982; Lauter, 1985; McKhann et al., 1984; Mortimer and Hutton, 1985; Mortimer and Schuman, 1981; U.S. Government Office of Technology Assessment, 1987; Zarit, Orr, and Zarit, 1985).

Alzheimer's disease and related disorders arouse a sense of urgency with policymakers and federal research funding agencies because of the prospect of staggering health care costs for a large population of severely impaired older people (Shanas and Maddox, 1985; Terry and Katzman, 1983). Although dementing illnesses affect less than 5 percent of people over 65, approximately 20 percent of people 80 and older are affected. Therefore, the rapid population increase among the oldest old represents escalating numbers of those most at risk from dementia (Brody, 1982; Gilhooly, Zarit, and Birren, 1986, pp. 2–4; Lauter, 1985; Mortimer and Schuman, 1981).

Many other more prevalent and treatable conditions of old age have not received as much attention, largely because Alzheimer's is now viewed as an epidemic, an

Original publication: Lyman, Karen A., "Bringing the Social Back In: A Critique of the Biomedicalization of Dementia," *The Gerontologist* 229 (1989), pp. 597–605.

emerging problem of increasing magnitude. The "discovery" of Alzheimer's disease has involved a political process more than simply biomedical discovery. Consciousness raising about Alzheimer's disease is addressed later in this paper. This consciousness is reflected in the title of a 1987 Office of Technology Assessment publication, *Losing A Million Minds: Confronting the Tragedy of Alzheimer's Disease* (U.S. Government Office of Technology Assessment, 1987).

The growing public consciousness of Alzheimer's as "the disease of the century" has refuted the myth that senility is an inevitable condition of old age, and has legitimized research and policy interests that offer hope for a cure. Funds for Alzheimer's research through the National Institutes of Health and National Institute of Mental Health have dramatically increased in the 1980s. Fruits of this research include increasingly precise assessment tools that differentiate treatable from nonreversible dementias and the promise of clinical markers that may identify patients by disease stage for inclusion in new treatment trials. Clearly, dementing illnesses involve disease processes for which biomedical research may hold the key to an eventual cure. But while awaiting a cure, care occurs in social settings and relationships that are seldom examined in regard to their contribution to dementia. It is this neglect of the social component of dementing illness that should be of interest to social gerontologists.

The argument presented here is that reliance upon the biomedical model to explain the experience of dementing illness overlooks the social construction of dementia and the impact of treatment contexts and caregiving relationships on disease progression. The neglect of social factors in dementia will be addressed by this analysis: first, a historical perspective on the medicalization of senility; second, a critical analysis of the prevailing biomedical model of dementia; third, an examination of the impact of the biomedical model in research on caregiver strain; and finally, an outline of a model that acknowledges social factors in dementing illness.

## The Medicalization of Senility

Throughout this paper, the problem of dementia is viewed as an example of the "medicalization of deviance," which refers to explaining and treating personal and social troubles as medical problems (Conrad and Kern, 1986; Conrad and Schneider, 1980; Zola, 1972). Troublesome behavior is explained by pathological conditions of somatic origin subject to treatment by medical authority. In regard to dementia, difficulties in caring for increasing numbers of impaired older people are commonly defined as medical problems, and difficulties in the caregiving relationship are explained by the progression of the disease. Recently the "medicalization of senility" has become the "biomedicalization of senility," with the emergence of biomedicine as a medical specialty (see Estes and Binney in this issue).

Conrad and Schneider's historical overview (1980) of the emergence of concepts of mental illness, the "medicalization of madness," includes definitions of dementia prior to the 1980s. In the Middle Ages, dementia was not distinguished from other forms of madness, which was interpreted within the prevailing theological model that identified various dissidents and deviants, especially older women, as witches. Some physicians argued that witches really were mentally ill persons, including melancholy (depressed) old women, but they were largely ignored until the seventeenth century. Meanwhile, of the half million people hanged, drowned, or burned at the stake as witches during the Middle Ages, large numbers were old women who today would be identified as suffering from a dementing illness and/or depression.

The first direct reference to *dementia* identified by Conrad and Schneider was an 1801 psychiatry text by Pinel, a director of French asylums. His classification of mental diseases precurses the American Psychiatric Association's Diagnostic and Statistical Manual of Mental Disorders (DSM), in its third – revised – edition in 1987 (DSM-III-R). Pinel's classification comprised only a handful of mental diseases, including *dementia, melancholy* (depression), *mania*, and *idiocy*. DSM-III, on the other hand, contains more than 250 labels and symptomatic descriptions of mental disorders (a dramatic increase from 60 psychiatric conditions in the 1952 DSM-I).

The nineteenth century was a period of humanitarian reform in the asylums. Moral restraints were substituted for chains and other physical restraints. Moral treatment for madness consisted of establishing a constant, stable daily routine, "careful coercion," and work therapy. During this period, there was little scientific evidence to support the claims of doctors that madness was a "mental illness." But, Conrad and Schneider argue that the definition of mental illness supported the expansion of medical turf and professional dominance (Freidson, 1970) to include the "moral treatment" of madness. Doctors became the administrators of asylums. By the end of the nineteenth century, asylums had become simply custodial institutions, in an era of somatic pessimism in which no cure for mental illness was expected. And although there was yet no scientific evidence of somatic origin or medical treatment for mental illness, it was in this period that psychiatry was established as a medical specialty, essentially a "tinkering trade" (Goffman, 1961) practiced by asylum administrators.

Early in the twentieth century, the first evidence of somatic origin for at least one form of mental illness encouraged further development of the medical concept of madness, including dementia. Third stage syphilis was found to produce neurological breakdown resulting in "general paresis." This discovery renewed interest in the classification of mental illness. During this period, the first specific classification of dementia was made, "dementia praecox," a reference to "early senility" (Conrad and Schneider, 1980). It is important to note that only *premature* senility was considered an illness earlier in this century. Senility in old age was considered normal. Thus, the very definition of dementia was an instance of medicalized deviance. The violation of age norms was the basis for the medical label.

There are parallels between the emergence of Alzheimer's disease as a diagnostic category in the 1980s and Peter Conrad's account of the "discovery of hyperkinesis" in children (Conrad, 1975). Until recently, hyperactivity in children, like senility in old age, was considered to be within the normal range of behavior. Now there is biomedical ownership of these recently discovered "diseases" of childhood and old age, which are attributed to biological causes and subject to medical treatment. An explanation for this trend may be found within Estes' framework of the "political economy" of the "aging enterprise" and the "biomedicalization of aging" generally (Estes, 1979; Estes et al., 1984; and Estes and Binney in this issue). Also, political scientist Neal Cutler provides an analysis of the politics of Alzheimer's disease (Cutler, 1986), which may be seen as a process of "claimsmaking" in which "facts" are constructed by "moral entrepreneurs" who have an interest in the creation of a new disease category (see Becker 1973; Conrad and Schneider, 1980; Freidson, 1970; Gusfield, 1967; Spector and Kitsuse, 1977).

The "facts" generally accepted about Alzheimer's disease today have been defined by the America Psychiatric Association, specified further by several national research organizations. In the 1980s, DSN III has identified the criteria for diagnosing "primary degenerative dementia," and a joint work group of the National Institute of Neurological Communicative Disorders and Stroke (NINCDS) and the Alzheimer's Disease and Related Disorders Association (ADRDA) has specified standards for a probable diagnosis of Alzheimer's disease and related dementing illnesses (Dick, Kean, and Sands, 1988; Mace, 1987). The primary criteria of senile dementia of the Alzheimer's type (SDAT) include global cognitive impairment, more specifically a *decline* in intellectual functioning. The question of decline is crucial, most often answered by the family's or other caregiver's retrospective assessment rather than prospective studies of community samples.

Conrad and Schneider (1980) argue that the medicalization of hyperactivity in children shifts attention from the school and family situation of the child to an individual/physiological deviance designation. The recent conceptualization of dementing illness results in a similar shift, with consequential limitations on the research questions that are asked about dementia and caregiving. In *Oldtimers and Alzheimer's*, Jay Gubrium (1986) presents a critical review of the evidence (or lack thereof) for the "discovery" of Alzheimer's as a disease category. Gubrium's argument is that it is not yet possible to clearly differentiate dementing illness from normal aging, and that the attempt to do so is a social construction to create order from the disorderly aspects of living with dementia (Gubrium, 1987).

Viewing dementia as a biomedical condition helps bring order to dementia care. Like other chronic illnesses, dementia is characterized by an "uncertain trajectory" (Strauss, 1975). Dementia typifications, medical labels, and medical authority (carried out by paraprofessionals and family caregivers, supported by medical diagnosis and, in some cases, prescribed pharmacological restraints) ease the stress of dementia care by increasing the sense of predictability and control for caregivers. Particularly with dementing illness, there is an overriding "therapeutic nihilism" (Cohen, 1988; Mace, 1987) in regard to the inevitability of intellectual decline and self-deterioration. "Losing" people long before they die is one of the most stressful aspects of dementia care. A model of stagelike disease progression can make more tolerable the difficult role of caring for and deciding future care for a demented loved one. If the illness can be defined as having a beginning and middle, the end may be predicted.

In some respects, the myth of "senility" has been replaced by the myth of "Alzheimer's disease," the ready acceptance by clinicians, service providers, and families of an oversimplified diagnosis and prognosis (Gubrium, 1986; Lynott, 1983). Observations of caregivers in several settings have found that, once the label *Alzheimer's* is applied, even normal behavior is interpreted in terms of disease stages (Gubrium, 1987; Gubrium and Lynott, 1987; Lyman, 1988, 1989; Smithers, 1977). The result may be a self-fulfilling prophecy of impairment. "Excess disabilities" (Brody et al., 1971) and "learned helplessness" (Hofland, 1988) may result because the person is expected to decline, and few opportunities are provided to continue meaningful activity.

## The Biomedical Model of Dementia

Most of the social and behavioral science research on dementia gives little consideration to social factors affecting disease progression, including the power relationship of caregiving and dependency. Greater attention to this relationship and to the sociophysical context in which care is provided is required to understand caregiver stress and the distress of demented persons.

The major features of the biomedical model of dementia are outlined below, within the framework of the "medicalization of deviance" perspective (Conrad and Kern, 1986; Conrad and Schneider, 1980; Zola, 1972) and Estes and Binney's discussion of the "biomedicalization of aging" (in this issue). Dementia is now in this domain.

Dementia has fallen through the cracks between social gerontology and medical sociology, with neither specialty paying much attention to the social forces that affect the conceptualization and experience of the disease. A *Journal of Health and Social Behavior* associate editor recently explained that research on dementia has not yet been published by the *JHSB* because dementia is "at the cusp of gerontology and medical sociology" (Radelet, 1987). No articles on dementia have appeared in *Social Science and Medicine* from 1984–8 either. Apparently, the social context surrounding dementia has been of little interest to mainstream medical sociologists.

Social gerontologists have also had little to say about dementia. A review of recent work (1984–8) on dementia in *The Gerontologist*, the *Journal of Gerontology*, *Research on Aging*, and the *Annual Review of Gerontology and Geriatrics* finds little social and behavioral science research on dementing illness, except in *The Gerontologist*. Dementia research in these publications occurs primarily within neuropsychology, contained by the biomedical model. Even the large literature on dementia "caregiver strain" is framed by the biomedical model, focusing primarily on the medicalization of troublesome behavior problems attributed to disease progression.

The biomedical view of the behavior referred to as "senile dementia" includes three features. First, dementia is pathological and individual, an abnormal condition of cognitive impairment, dysfunction, and mental disorder. Second, chronic dementia is somatic or organic in etiology, caused by progressive deterioration of brain regions that control memory, language, and other intellectual functioning, resulting in stages of increasingly severe impairment. And third, although there is currently no cure, dementia is to be diagnosed by biomedical assessments of brain disease and clinical functioning, and treated and managed according to medical authority, including the possible prescription of chemical and/or physical restraints.

The widespread acceptance of the biomedical model of dementia has countered the longstanding ageist assumption that senility is an inevitable condition of old age, has legitimized research and policy interests that offer hope for a cure, and has offered caregivers some degree of order and control in the difficult work of dementia care. However, the biomedical view of dementia is narrow, limited, and sometimes distorted in its ignorance of social forces that affect the definition, production, and progression of dementia. Employing only the biomedical model to explain dementia often results in the paradigmatic dilemma Kuhn described as "a strenuous and devoted attempt to force nature into conceptual boxes . . ." (Kuhn, 1962, p. 5). In reality, the psychosocial experience of a dementing illness often cannot be contained within biomedical concepts of brain disease.

This critique addresses all three parts of the biomedical model of dementia: the definition of pathology; disease stage attributions; and the legitimation of medical control over persons with dementing illnesses.

### Pathology versus normalcy

First, if senile dementia is a pathological condition, what is normal? How might we distinguish dysfunction from the degree of memory loss associated with normal aging? In the epidemiologic literature, "mild" dementia is only vaguely defined and prevalence rates range from 5 to 50 percent. It is very difficult to distinguish mild dementia from the stable condition of normal aging known as "benign senescent forgetfulness" (Kral, 1978) or "everyday memory problems" (Cutler and Grams, 1988). Also, in community studies in the United States and Scandinavia, mild dementia has been found not to be predictive of progressive dementia (Bergmann, 1985; Lauter, 1985).

Second, how might we distinguish mental disorder from behavioral quirks and eccentricities developed over a lifetime that are found within the normal range of heterogeneity in aging? (This question is developed in more detail by Gubrium, 1986; and Shomaker, 1987). Aberrant behavior, continuous over a lifetime, including memory problems that are normal for a given person, may be erroneously attributed to a dementing illness. And, behavior that would not be considered abnormal if displayed by others is often attributed to dementia if exhibited by someone "known" to be impaired, someone with a clinical diagnosis of dementia (Gubrium, 1986; Lyman, 1988; Shomaker, 1987).

For example, consider behavior known as "wandering," one of the most frequently identified "behavioral problems" associated with dementia (Mace, 1987). Wandering has been defined as "frequent and/or unpredictable pacing, with no discernible goal" (Dawson and Reid, 1987). The relativity of this definition becomes clear if it is applied to a young man pacing the halls of a maternity ward. The definition of wandering and many other behavioral problems associated with dementia indicate social deviance or misbehaving more than pathological dysfunction.

Two recent articles make it apparent that wanderers are viewed as deviant because they behave *more* normally than other impaired elderly persons. In one study, wanderers are distinguished from nonwanderers in a long-term care facility primarily by something called "hyperactivity," which included these traits: "not withdrawn, hearing normal, good gait, perpetual motion, socially skilled" (Dawson and Reid, 1987). Another recent study found that these "problem" patients are "often mistaken for visitors" because they are "quite physically able and appeared mentally alert" (Rader, 1987). Both studies reveal that wanderers are difficult to distinguish from normal people, leading the staff in one facility to mark these residents with a red dot on their clothing between the shoulder blades (Rader, 1987). Clearly, the conceptualization of wandering and other misbehavior involves social definitions of deviance not explained by the biomedical model.

Even the neuropathological changes associated with Alzheimer's disease do not neatly distinguish normal from pathological. Alzheimer's-type brain lesions are found at autopsy in many intellectually preserved normally functioning elderly (Mortimer and Hutton, 1985; McKhann et al., 1984). Additionally, the pathologic criteria used by neurologists to identify an "Alzheimer's brain" vary by age. With increasing age, a microscopic examination of tissue samples within the neocortex finds an increasing number of neuritic plaques and neurofibrillary tangles. The increasing number of plaques and tangles may be within a "normal" range, not associated with disease or dysfunction. For a patient over 65, an Alzheimer's brain is identified by twice the number of plaques and tangles than for a patient under 50. However, the standard number may be revised downward if the older patient is "known" to be demented, with a clinical diagnosis of a dementing illness (Henderson, 1988). If even the diagnosis and neuropathology of dementia is subject to such negotiation and interpretation, pathology must be framed within a sociocultural as well as a biomedical definition.

The biomedical definition of abnormality begins a process Goffman has called the "moral career" of people who are officially labeled abnormal (Goffman, 1961, pp. 127–30). The effect of being identified and treated as if one were demented must be seen as distinct from the effect of traits stemming from a pathological condition. Whether by misdiagnosis or in the medicalization of deviance, medical labels designating irreversible chronic impairment result in limited social opportunities.

Charmaz (1983) and Strauss (1975) have identified the severe blows to self-esteem that accompany chronic illness, largely as a result of social isolation and negative expectations of others. Particularly for persons with a dementing illness, the self-deterioration accompanying the disease is exacerbated by negative experiences in social relationships. For example, in one day care center, once persons suffering from dementing illnesses were identified as "the dementias," very little was expected of them compared with other nonimpaired day care clients, and staff frequently took over activities they could have managed by themselves (Lyman, 1989). For persons labeled demented, the outcome may be "excess disabilities" (Brody et al., 1971), "learned helplessness" (Hofland, 1988), or other forms of social impairment.

Those labeled demented often are aware of and embarrassed by their stigmatic condition and its social consequences. Illustrations are provided from field notes in an ongoing study of dementia day care.

> The director at Metropolitan Day Care told me about the family situation of several clients. One man was neglected, given no new clothes, and was infrequently bathed. "It's as if he already were dead."

> The wife of another man strips his dignity; she pulls his pants down in front of others to give him shots.

> A woman told me her husband would not buy her new clothes because he said, "No one wants to look at you anyway."

> Another man told me how he felt in his relationship with caregivers at home and at day care. Searching for memory of his own age, he said, "I'm . . . 80 or 90 something . . . and I'm like a ten-year-old . . . I don't want to do much because . . . people about 40 something . . ." He didn't complete the sentence, but it was clear he was referring to his powerlessness relative to younger caregivers.

These examples indicate an awareness of loss, as a result not only of dementing illness but also of being identified and treated as a demented person.

*Disease stage attributions*

Sociological questions also may be addressed to the causal analysis of the biomedical model: that stages of progressive brain deterioration result in corresponding clinical stages of impairment. The epidemiologic and medical knowledge about the causes of chronic dementia is still very limited (Bergmann, 1985; Freed, 1987; Mortimer and Hutton, 1985; Secretary's Task Force, 1984). Also, there is considerable evidence contradicting the assumption of universal stages of progressive impairment, mainly from longitudinal community surveys in the United States, Great Britain and Scandinavia (Bergmann, 1985; Brody, 1982; Lauter, 1985). Nonetheless, even in writings that acknowledge flaws in the stage theory of dementia, progressive staging is the framework for the discussion. (For a recent example of this contradiction, see Mace [1987], who identifies three stages in the "progression of dementia," just after stating that there is considerable variability among people with dementia, and nonconformity to stagelike progression.) Perhaps more important, caregivers and service providers who interact daily with persons identified as demented often characterize dementia in terms of typical stages of decline, and attribute most of the demented person's behavior to the presumed clinical condition (Gubrium, 1986; Lyman, 1988). The person's disease progression often is reconstructed retrospectively to fit the rational stage model (Lynott, 1983).

Even persons identified as demented adopt the biomedical perspective in attributing behavior to disease. In field notes from one day care center, this conversation was recorded between two clients:

> One client asks (about another who rubs her hands): "Why does she do that?"
>
> The second responds: "Just nervousness, I say."
>
> The first persists: "No, I think its a disease, maybe a brain disease . . ."

The attribution of behavior to disease progression sets the stage for limited opportunities based on expectations of increasing incompetence. A kind of social death accompanies the diagnosis of Alzheimer's disease, a sense of hopelessness given visual expression by an Alzheimer's Disease and Related Disorders Association poster showing the demented person gradually fading away, in successive frames (or stages) of the picture. According to the assumption of typical disease progression, no new learning takes place in "later stages" of dementia, and the person is expected to become increasingly incompetent. However, even those who employ the biomedical model recognize that "there is significant variability" and "there are no noticeable hallmarks that mark a person's passage from one stage to the next" (Mace, 1987). And so, it is never entirely clear who is in which stage, or what kind of treatment is appropriate for people presumed to be in the same stage.

Research with institutionalized elderly has found that "iatrogenic treatment" and other environmental factors result in increased dependency (Hofland, 1988). Further research is needed to examine the impact of situational conditions on the demented elderly, in families as well as institutional settings. For example, clinical depression is common in old age and is difficult to differentiate from senile dementia (Thompson et al., 1987). The hopelessness associated with clinical depression impairs intellectual performance; an Alzheimer's diagnosis may lead to depression because the disease seems hopeless.

Even the assessment procedures used to determine degree of impairment may depress the demented person. On several occasions during an ongoing field study in dementia day care centers, I have overheard clients who were concerned about "failing" the "tests" (such as the Mini Mental State Exam) used by day care providers to report client characteristics to the California Department of Aging. Also, if caregivers have low or negative expectations of persons diagnosed with dementia, depression and further intellectual decline may occur. Therefore, an erroneous Alzheimer's diagnosis, distressing assessment procedures, or negative expectations by caregivers may produce depression, resulting in behavior that may be attributed to dementia. A staff member in one dementia day care center observed, "People think 'agitation' is inevitable, but it's because they're depressed about how they're being treated!" The biomedical model, focusing only on disease stage progression, precludes the possibility that diagnostic error or iatrogenic treatment in the caregiving relationship contribute to dementia.

The widespread acceptance of the notion of disease stages is understandable for caregivers and service providers, who seek structure, order, and control in their attempts to "do something" for the demented person and the family (Gubrium, 1987). Making plans for the future is not possible unless the disease course is somewhat predictable. Researchers also find the conceptual boxes of the biomedical model attractive. Staging of the disease would allow researchers to compare different individuals at similar stages of the illness, and would allow measurement of the effects of experimental interventions in postponing the next stage (Mace, 1987). However, this narrow biomedical view neglects social factors in disease progression.

### Medical control

The assumption that dementia is to be treated according to medical authority raises a number of sociological questions. Medical authority and control is exercised over the demented person by medical practitioners, paraprofessionals, and family caregivers as well. This power relationship in which "caregiving" takes place should be of primary interest to social gerontologists. For example, physical and chemical restraints still are commonly used to control wanderers and other "troublesome" demented elderly in long-term "care" facilities in the United States (Dawson and Reid, 1987; Rader, 1987).

Generally, dependency is encouraged and acts of independence are either ignored or punished in long-term care facilities (Hofland, 1988), and perhaps in the family as well. When caregivers are under stress, they may increase their control over demented persons, restricting care receivers' self-determination and increasing their dependency. In contrast, if caregivers encourage self-determination, the functioning of demented persons may improve. A field experiment with nursing home residents in which choice and personal responsibility were encouraged for the experimental group found significant improvements in alertness, active participation, and general well-being as a result of increased self-determination (Langer and Rodin, 1976). Whereas this group became more responsive, the control group became more debilitated.

A recent review of similar intervention studies and related research on autonomy in long-term care settings concludes that self-determination for impaired elderly is a primary characteristic of quality care (Hofland, 1988). However, the emotional exhaustion associated with caregiver stress often results in increased control over demented persons, as illustrated by this example from field notes in one dementia day care center:

> The design of the facility at Inland Day Care created problems in supervising "wanderers." There were many exits, and a highly visible locked gate was the main entrance. Some clients persisted in requesting that the gate be unlocked, and the staff grew weary of answering these requests. The program often was short staffed, so that workers could not accompany clients on walks outside the gate. On one particularly difficult day, after another round of repeated requests by a persistent client to go for a walk outside the gate, an exasperated staff member responded, "I'm going to give her a pill. I'm going to give her *five* pills! I'm getting a a headache!" Pharmacological control over the clients seemed to be the only recourse, rather than changing the design of the facility.

Medicalization, through medical labels, disease typifications, and medical authority, justifies control as appropriate treatment for the good of the patient.

The biomedical model does not consider ways in which the caregiving relationship and conditions in the caregiving context affect stress for the dementia caregiver as well as the impaired person. If dementia is viewed only as a biomedical condition, the behavior of the demented person is individualized and power relationships involving the elderly and their caregivers are depoliticized. Thus, the impact of power relationships on illness production and disease is not examined.

## Caregiver Strain: The Impact of the Biomedical Model

In the new field of dementia caregiving, families are a major component of the long-term care delivery system (George and Gwyther, 1986). Families provide free services to the rapidly increasing number of impaired older adults. It is understandable, then, that their burnout or strain is a concern to policymakers concerned with curtailing health care costs. If family caregiver strain can be minimized, demented persons may be maintained in the community longer than they are now.

Caring for persons with dementing illnesses is difficult work, in institutional settings as well as in families. Much of the strain is associated with what Strauss has called the "uncertain trajectory" associated with some chronic illnesses (Strauss, 1975), the fact that disease progression most often does not conform to predictable patterns.

To cope with the uncertainty surrounding dementing illness, both family and paid caregivers readily adopt the biomedical model of dementia. The biomedical model predicts stagelike disease progression and inevitable deterioration, and rationalizes certain treatment strategies by caregivers. For families, the possibility of institutionalization as a last resort is deemed appropriate in the "later stages." Institutionalization may seem to be the only alternative, as families become drained by the financial and emotional burden of dementia care. Families may find some comfort in making the institutionalization decision if "disease progression" is the reason for this difficult choice.

Strauss has described similar "abandonment rationales" for other "stigmatic . . .

or terribly demanding" diseases (Strauss, 1975, pp. 56–7). For families and service providers, the expectation of regression to a childlike state of dependency rationalizes the management of "behavior problems" presumed to be caused by the dementing illness. And so, for either paid or family caregivers, the biomedical model offers a "knowledge" base to face some of the uncertainty associated with caring for the demented.

There is greater certainty in facing the future task of caregiving within the biomedical framework. The result may be a reduction in stress for caregivers. However, the biomedical model includes disease typifications that limit the self-identity of demented persons, overgeneralizations Strauss has referred to as "identity spread" in describing other chronic illnesses (Strauss, 1975). Research in family caregiver support groups by Gubrium and Lynott (1987) finds a similar pattern of overgeneralization about dementia: once the family member has been diagnosed, people see "impairment everywhere."

The literature on family caregivers presents a onesided view of the caregiving relationship and illustrates the "medicalization of deviance." Caregiver strain is explained by the deterioration of the demented care recipient. The source of trouble in caregiving is located in the misbehavior of the demented person, which is explained by the progression of the dementing illness.

The large gerontological literature on the health and mental health of family caregivers portrays families as the "second victims" of Alzheimer's disease, the "hidden victims" of dementing illnesses (for the most comprehensive work on this question, see: Brody, 1981, 1985; Cantor, 1983; George and Gwyther, 1986; Ory et al., 1985; Zarit, Orr and Zarit, 1985; Zarit, Reever and Bach-Peterson, 1980). Most of the articles on dementia in *The Gerontologist* in recent years have focused on the "burden" and "strain" of providing care for persons with dementing illnesses. Also, of the three articles on dementia that have appeared in *Research on Aging* from 1984–8, two concerned caregiver burden. The first was a review of current knowledge about Alzheimer's disease and family caregiving (Ory et al., 1985). This is one of the few articles to consider the social and behavioral aspects of age-related chronic diseases and disabilities, including the impact of the family on demented persons. The second article was more typical, discussing caregiver strain and lack of social support as primary factors in the desire to institutionalize demented family members (Morycz, 1985).

Certainly, families suffer as their loved one slowly deteriorates and requires increasingly demanding care. However, in much of the recent literature, family troubles become medical problems, reflecting what Michel Foucault has called "the medicalisation of the family" and of the caregiving relationship (Foucault, 1976, pp. 166–76). While "the first wave of this offensive bears on the care of children" in the eighteenth century (ibid., p. 173), the last wave in the medicalization of family relations is the care of the old, especially those with dementing illnesses.

Much of the recent gerontological literature on caregivers as "victims" of dementia perpetuates the medicalization of the family, and neglects important questions about the social dynamics of families in which one member has a dementing illness. George and Gwyther (1986) review current research on caregiving and find weaknesses in sample selection and research design. There is little awareness of heterogeneity among caregivers and no longitudinal research on the dynamics of caregiver burden. George and Gwyther propose a multidimensional model of caregiving, since they have found that caregiver strain and institutional placement are better predicted by characteristics of the caregivers and the caregiving context than by the impairment and behaviors of demented patients.

There are problems in much of the caregiver burden literature in regard to the conceptualization and measurement of burden and strain (Ory et al., 1985). Much of this research equates impairment with burden, and predicts a decision to institutionalize at higher levels of impairment. Gubrium and Lynott (1987) are critical of these assumptions, finding there is no uniformity of impairment, and no equivalence to burden in the institutionalization decision. All are part of a "care equation." Caregiver burden is the product of the ongoing dyadic relationship between caregiver and care recipient (Johnson and Catalano, 1983; Montgomery, Stull, and Borgatta, 1985). However, this reciprocal relationship most often is not examined in the caregiver strain literature.

Ironically, the interest in the "victims" of Alzheimer's disease generally does not include an interest in the perspective of the person with dementia (Rakowski and Clark, 1985). Changes in the caregiving relationship are traced to disease progression, rather than examining disease progression as a consequence of changes in the caregiving relationships. The demented person is viewed as burdensome but not burdened by the illness or by changes in relationship. The demented one is viewed as a stressor, not as one who is experiencing stress. As a result, people with dementia are largely invisible in most of this literature; they are merely disease entities, independent variables. (Two recent exceptions are Cohen and Eisdorfer, 1986, and Shomaker, 1987, which take the perspectives of both the person with a dementing illness and the caregiver.) From a review of this research, it becomes clear that it is those suffering from the impairment, not their caregivers, who are still "hidden victims" of dementia.

In the caregiver strain literature, one consistent finding is that it is not cognitive decline that is most burdensome, resulting in a decision to institutionalize the demented family member; it is troublesome behavior (Diemling and Bass, 1986; Mace, 1987; Morycz, 1985). A poignant irony is that many of the "behavior problems" associated with dementia may be traced to problems in the caregiving relationship, which are overlooked if the behavior is attributed to disease. The medicalization of senility shifts attention from problems in the social situation of caregiving to locate problems in the pathology and misbehavior of the demented person. This focus overlooks the impact of the treatment context and caregiving relationship on the experience of dementing illness.


## Social Factors in Dementia

Eliot Freidson (1970) has charged that sociologists should study the development of social conceptions of illness, as well as social causes of illness behavior. Among social scientists who study dementia, few have examined either the cultural definitions of brain disease or the experience of a dementing illness within caregiving relationships. There are some exceptions in the recent social gerontological literature on dementia, research that pays some attention to individual variation, autonomy, and negotiation, and to the effects of power relationships and other socioenvironmental factors in disease progression (see Cohen and Eisdorfer, 1986; Diamond, 1983; Gilhooly, Zarit and Birren, 1986; Gilliland and Brunton, 1984; Hanson, 1985; Lawton, 1980; Ory et al., 1985; Rader, 1987; Shomaker, 1987; Winogrand et al., 1987). For example, a recent supplement of *The Gerontologist* is devoted entirely to articles on "autonomy and long-term care." Three of the articles specifically address questions of autonomy for mentally impaired elderly (Cohen, 1988; Hegeman and Tobin, 1988; Stanley et al., 1988).

Within sociology, Jay Gubrium and Robert Lynott are exceptional for their critical contributions concerning the social construction of dementia by family caregivers and service providers (Gubrium, 1986, 1987; Gubrium and Lynott, 1987; Lynott, 1983). However, social gerontologists generally have had little to say about dementia, except that it is a dysfunctional disease with profoundly negative consequences for caregivers and the larger society.

What is missing from most of the current social and behavioral science research on dementia and caregiver strain is an analysis of the impact of cultural definitions, care settings, and the caregiving relationship on the experience of dementing illness. These social factors in dementia may be identified within the "sociogenic" model proposed by Dannefer (1984) to replace the predominant "ontogenetic" normative/developmental "stage theory" of aging. The sociogenic model counters the view of "medicalized deviance," in which the impaired elderly become mere disease entities, deviants, who cause social and interpersonal problems.

The sociogenic perspective recognizes that all human experience involves intentional social action and interaction, in socially structured environments, in the context of taken-for-granted socially constructed knowledge about aging, development, and disease. Employing the sociogenic model in research on dementia would view demented persons as social actors who live with impairment and interact with others in caregiving relationships, within a variety of socially structured environments such as long-term care facilities, day care centers, and in families. Within this framework, shared "knowledge" of dementia is a collective definition, part of the sociocultural world of the demented and their caregivers, not a fixed biomedical reality. For example, in dementia day care facilities, I have heard caregivers assert that they "know" there is only a "decline" in functioning, "no new learning," which results in these caregivers expecting very little from demented persons. If demented people withdraw from interaction to save face, their nonresponsiveness is taken as confirmation of the negative dementia expectations, a classic example of the self-fulfilling prophecy.

Schmidt (1981) identified a similar pattern in other care settings for the aged, from an exchange theory perspective. The sociogenic model suggests that when caregiving is stressful, for either caregivers or recipients, an explanation may be found within the sociocultural care context and caregiving relationship, rather than located only within the condition of impairment.

The biomedical paradigm offers a nearsighted view of dementing illness, focusing only on those aspects that can be explained as brain disease. The predominance of this view in social and behavioral science research on dementing illness neglects much of the daily experience of chronic illness and intellectual impairment, both for demented persons and their caregivers. Social gerontology should offer a broader vision of the social forces involved in dementia: cultural definitions of illness, the socioenvironmental context in which impaired people receive care, and the dynamics of the caregiving relationship.

## Acknowledgments

This work is supported by Grant #IIRG-87-055 from the Alzheimer's Disease and Related Disorders Association. An earlier version of this paper was presented to the 1988 meetings of the American Sociological Association in Atlanta, Georgia. Very helpful comments on earlier drafts were provided by: Gary Albrecht, Vern Bengtson, Dale Dannefer, Jaber Gubrium, Victor Marshall, Jon Miller, David G. Morgan, Judith Treas; Carol Warren, Michael Viera, and four anonymous reviewers.

## References

Becker, H. S. (1973). *Outsiders: Studies in the sociology of deviance*. New York: Free Press.

Bergmann, K. (1985). Epidemiological aspects of dementia and considerations in planning services. *Danish Medical Bulletin*, 32, 34.

Brody, E. M. (1981). Women in the middle and family help to older people. *The Gerontologist*, 21, 471–80.

Brody, E. M. (1985). Parent care as a normative family stress. *The Gerontologist*, 25, 19–29.

Brody, E. M., et al. (1971). Excess disabilities of mentally impaired aged: Impact of individualized treatment. *The Gerontologist*, 11, 124–33.

Brody, J. A. (1982). An epidemiologist views senile dementia: Facts and fragments. *American Journal of Epidemiology*, 115, 155–62.

Cantor, M. (1983). Strain among caregivers: A study of experience in the United States. *The Gerontologist*, 23, 597–604.

Charmaz, K. (1983). Loss of self: A fundamental form of suffering for the chronically ill. *Sociology of Health and Illness*, 5, 168–95.

Cohen, D., and Eisdorfer, C. (1986). *The loss of self: A family resource for the care of Alzheimer's disease and related disorders*. New York: W. W. Norton.

Cohen, E. S. (1988). The elderly mystique: Constraints on the autonomy of elderly adults with disabilities. *The Gerontologist*, 28 (supplement), 24–31.

Conrad, P. (1975). The discovery of hyperkinesis: Notes on the medicalization of deviant behavior. *Social Problems*, 23, 12–21.

Conrad, P., and Kern, R. (1986). *The sociology of health and illness: Critical perspectives*, 2nd edn. New York: St. Martin's.

Conrad, P., and Schneider, J. W. (1980). *Deviance and medicalization: From badness to sickness*. St. Louis: C. V. Mosby.

Cutler, N. (1986). Public response: The national politics of Alzheimer's disease. In M. L. M. Gilhooly, S. M. Zarit and J. E. Birren (eds.), *The dementias: Policy and management*. Englewood Cliffs, NJ: Prentice-Hall.

Cutler, S. J., and Grams, A. E. (1988). Correlates of self-reported everyday memory problems. *Journal of Gerontology*, 43, 582–90.

Dannefer, D. (1984). Adult development and social theory: A paradigmatic reappraisal. *American Sociological Review*, 49, 100–16.

Dawson, P., and Reid, D. W. (1987). Behavioral dimensions of patients at risk of wandering. *The Gerontologist*, 24, 104–7.

Diamond, T. (1983). Nursing homes as trouble. *Urban Life*, 12, 269–86.

Dick, M. B., Kean, M., and Sands, D. (1988). The pre-selection effect on the recall facilitation of motor movements in Alzheimer-type dementia. *Journal of Gerontology*, 43, 127–35.

Diemling, G. T., and Bass, D. M. (1986). Symptoms of mental impairment among elderly adults and their effects on family caregivers. *Journal of Gerontology*, 41, 778–84.

Estes, C. L. (1979). *The aging enterprise*. San Francisco: Jossey-Bass.

Estes, C. L., Gerard, L., Zones, J. S., and Swan, J. H. (1984). *Political economy, health and aging*. Boston: Little-Brown.

Estes, C. L., and Binney, E. A. (1989). The biomedicalization of aging: Dangers and dilemmas. *The Gerontologist* (this issue).

Foucault, M. (1976). The politics of health in the 18th century. In C. Gordon (ed.), 1980, *Power/knowledge: Selected interviews and other writings 1972–77 by Michel Foucault*. New York: Pantheon.

Freed, D. (1987). Long-term occupational exposure in the diagnosis of Alzheimer's disease. Lecture to the Andrus Gerontology Center Director's Series. University of Southern California, Los Angeles.

Freidson, E. (1970). *Profession of medicine*. New York: Dodd, Mead & Company.

George, L. K., and Gwyther, L. P. (1986). Caregiver well-being: A multidimensional examination of family caregivers of demented adults. *The Gerontologist*, 26, 253–9.

Gilhooly, M. L. M., Zant, S. M., and Birren, J. E. (eds.). (1986). *The dementias: Policy and management*. Englewood Cliffs, NJ: Prentice-Hall.

Gilliland, N., and Brunton, A. (1984). Nurse's typifications of nursing home patients. *Ageing and Society*, 4, 45–67.

Goffman, E. (1961). *Asylums*. Garden City, NY: Doubleday.

Gubrium, J. F. (1986). *Oldtimers and Alzheimer's: The descriptive organization of senility*. Greenwich, CT: JAI Press.

Gubrium, J. F. (1987). Structuring and destructuring the course of illness: The Alzheimer's disease experience. *Sociology of Health and Illness*, 9, 1–24.

Gubrium, I. F., and Lynott, R. J. (1987). Measurement and the interpretation of burden in the Alzheimer's disease experience. *Journal of Aging Studies*, 1, 265–85.

Gusfield, J. R. (1967). Moral passage: The symbolic process in the public designations of deviance. *Social Problems*, 15, 175–88.

Hanson, B. G. (1985). Negotiation of self and setting to advantage: An interactionist consideration of nursing home data. *Sociology of Health and Illness*. 7, 21–35.

Hegeman, C., and Tobin, S. (1988). Enhancing the autonomy of mentally impaired nursing home residents. *The Gerontologist*, 28 (supplement), 71–5.

Henderson, V. (1988). Neocortical symptoms of Alzheimer's disease. Lecture to the Andrus Gerontology Center Director's Series, University of Southern California, Los Angeles.

Hofland, B. F. (1988). Autonomy in long term care: Background issues and a programmatic response. *The Gerontologist*, 28 (Supplement), 3–9.

Johnson, C. L., and Catalano, D. J. (1983). A longitudinal study of family supports to impaired elderly. *The Gerontologist*, 23, 612–18.

Kral, V. A. (1978). Benign senescent forgetfulness. In R. Katzman, R. D. Terry. and K. L. Bick (eds.), *Alzheimer's disease: Senile dementia and related disorders (Aging, v. 7)*. New York: Raven Press.

Kuhn, T. S. (1962). *The structure of scientific revolutions*. Chicago: University of Chicago Press.

Langer, E., and Rodin, J. (1976). The effect of choice and enhanced personal responsibility for the aged: A field experiment in an institutional setting. *Journal of Personality and Social Psychology*, 34, 191–8.

Lauter, H. (1985). What do we know about Alzheimer's disease today? *Danish Medical Bulletin*, 32, 1–21.

Lawton, M. P. (1980). Psychosocial and environmental approaches to the care of senile dementia patients. In J. O. Cole and J. E. Barrett (eds.), *Psychopathology in the aged*. New York: Q. V. Raven Press.

Lyman, K. A. (1988). Infantilization of elders: Day care for Alzheimer's disease victims. In Dorothy Wertz (ed.), *Research in the sociology of health care*, v. 7. Greenwich, CT: JAI Press.

Lyman, K. A. (1989). Day care for persons with dementia: The impact of the physical environment on staff stress and quality of care. *The Gerontologist*, 29, 557–60.

Lynott, R. J. (1983). Alzheimer's disease and institutionalization: The ongoing construction of a decision. *Journal of Family Issues*, 4, 559–74.

Mace, N. L. (1987). Characteristics of persons with dementia. In U.S. Congress, Office of Technology Assessment, *Losing a million minds: Confronting the tragedy of Alzheimer's disease and other dementias*. OTA-BA-323. Washington, DC: U.S. Government Printing Office.

McKhann, G., Drachman, D., Folstein, M., Katzman, R., Price, D., and Stadlan, E. M. (1984). Clinical diagnosis of Alzheimer's disease: Report of the NINCDS-ADRDA work group. *Neurology*, 34, 939–44.

Montgomery, R. J. V., Stull, D. E., and Borgatta, E. F. (1985). Measurement and the analysis of burden. *Research on Aging*, 7, 137–51.

Mortimer, J. A., and Hutton, J. T. (1985). *Senile dementia of the Alzheimer's type*, pages 177–96. New York: Alan R. Liss.

Mortimer, J. A., and Schuman, L. M. (1981). *The epidemiology of dementia*. New York: Oxford.

Morycz, R. K. (1985). Caregiving strain and the desire to institutionalize family members with Alzheimer's disease: Possible predictors and model development. *Research on Aging*, 7, 329–61.

Ory, M. G., Williams, T. F., Emr, M., Lebowitz, B., Rabins P., Salloway, J., Sluss-Radbaugh, T., Wolff, E., and Zarit, S. (1985). Families, informal supports, and Alzheimer's disease: Current research and future agendas. *Research on Aging*, 7, 623–44.

Radelet, M. L. (1987). Response to questions in roundtable session 80, Review criteria for the Journal of Health and Social Behavior. American Sociological Association annual meeting. Chicago, IL.

Rader, J. (1987). A comprehensive staff approach to wandering. *The Gerontologist*, 27, 756–60.

Rakowski, W., and Clark, N. M. (1985). Future outlook, caregiving and care receiving in the family context. *The Gerontologist*, 25, 618–23.

Ruscio, D., and Cavarocchi, N. (1984). Getting on the political agenda: How an organization of Alzheimer families won increased federal attention and funding. *Generations*, 9, 12–15.

Schmidt, M. G. (1981). Exchange and power in special settings for the aged. *International Journal of Aging and Human Development*, 14, 157–66.

Secretary's Task Force on Alzheimer's Disease, U. S. Department of Health and Human Services (1984). *Alzheimer's Disease*. Washington, DC: U.S. Government Printing Office. DHHS Pub. No. (ADM) 84–1323.

Shanas, E., and Maddox, G. M. (1985). Health, health resources and the utilization of care. In R. H. Binstock and E. Shanas (eds.), *Handbook of aging and the social sciences*, 2nd edn. New York: Van Nostrand Reinhold.

Shomaker, D. (1987). Problematic behavior and the Alzheimer patient: Retrospection as a method of understanding and counseling. *The Gerontologist*, 27, 370–5.

Smithers, J. A. (1977). Institutional dimensions of senility. *Urban Life*, 6, 251–76.

Spector, M., and Kitsuse, J. (1977). *Constructing social problems*. New York: Bejamin Cummings.

Stanley, B., Stanley, M., Guido, J., and Garvin, L. (1988). The functional competency of elderly at risk. *The Gerontologist*, 28 (Supplement), 53–8.

Strauss, A. (1975). *Chronic illness and the quality of life*. St. Louis: C. V. Mosby.

Terry, R. D., and Katzman, R. (1983). Senile dementia of the Alzheimer's type. *Annals of Neurology*, 42, 50–4.

Thompson, L. W., Gong, V., Haskins, E., and Gallagher, D. (1987). Assessment of depression and dementia during the later years. *Annual Review of Gerontology and Geriatrics*, pp. 295–324. New York: Springer.

U. S. Government, Office of Technology Assessment (1987). *Losing a million minds: Confronting the tragedy of Alzheimer's disease and other dementias*. OTA-BA-323. Washington, DC: U. S. Government Printing Office.

Winogrand, I. R., Fisk, A. A., Kirsling, R. A., and Keyes, B. (1987). The relationship of caregiver burden and morale to Alzheimer's disease patient function in a therapeutic setting. *The Gerontologist*, 27, 336–9.

Zarit, S. H., Orr, N. K., and Zarit, J. M. (1985). *The hidden victims of Alzheimer's disease: Families under stress*. New York: NYU Press.

Zarit, S. H., Reever, K. E., and Bach-Peterson, J. (1980). Relatives of the impaired elderly: Correlates of feelings of burden. *The Gerontologist*, 20, 649–54.

Zola, I. (1972). Medicine as an institution of social control. *Sociological Review*, 20, 487–504.

# 24 The Mask of Dementia: Images of "Demented Residents" in a Nursing Ward

## Hava Golander and Aviad E. Raz

### Introduction

'Dementia' is dually constituted by psycho-biological pathologies and social processes of labelling. The latter are examined here through an ethnographic look at the social construction of 'demented' residents in a nursing ward. In addition, the impetus for writing this paper was generated by a recent account of the construction and deconstruction of self in Alzheimer's disease (AD) (Sabat and Harre 1992). In their paper, Sabat and Harre suggested that while personal identity persists far into the end stage of AD, the multiple personae which constitute one's social identity can be lost as an indirect result of the disease. This paper sets out both to extend and criticise this intriguing hypothesis. It describes the construction of social identity in AD as it takes place in an institutional setting, presenting data on how AD patients are labelled with former social identities by fellow residents who do not have cognitive impairments. On the theoretical level, it is argued here that since the 'I' and the 'me' are split in dementia, conventional psychological perspectives on the interconnectedness of personal and social identity are no longer directly applicable to its analysis. We therefore try to question whether, in the case of 'demented residents,' social identity is indeed always lost, and whether we can oppose it to the preservation, or otherwise, of personal identity.

### The Setting

The setting for this study is a nursing ward of a large Israeli long-term care geriatric centre, where observations were conducted by one of the authors from 1984 to 1985 as part of her dissertation study. In addition, a follow-up study was conducted with several key-informants until all residents who originally participated in the study had died. Everyday institutional life experiences were examined using participant observation methods. The nursing ward chosen provided observations of residential life, capturing the general conditions inherent in the institution, mainly physical depend-

Original publication: Golander, Hava and Aviad E. Raz, "The Mask of Dementia: Images of 'Demented Residents' in a Nursing Ward", *Ageing and Society* 16(3), 1996, pp. 269–85.

ency, social segregation and identity transformation, in their extreme (see also Golander 1995a, b). Both nursing care and ward cleaning were performed by nursing assistants working in three daily shifts under the supervision of a head nurse. Physiotherapy and occupational therapy were not offered to the nursing ward residents, who were considered, according to institutional criteria, to be 'beyond rehabilitation'. Instead, there were some activities on the ward, though only a few participated. The administration of pain medication, on the other hand, was seen as the predominant nursing task on the nursing ward, compared to the other wards of the two other centre wings – the 'independent' and the 'frail' – where observations were also conducted for purposes of comparative analysis. In what follows, however, we focus on the specific population of demented residents found within the nursing ward.

At the time of the study, the geriatric centre consisted of approximately 1,000 residents and employed some 200 personnel. The nursing ward chosen for this study comprised 33 residents average age of 81, with the majority of residents being women (73%), of Ashkenazi (Western Europe/US) origin (73%), and with children (81%). During the time of the study, almost half of the nursing ward residents were diagnosed, according to their medical record, as suffering from OBS (Organic Brain Syndrome) and were commonly referred to as demented, or Alzheimers, by other residents as well as carers.

## Symbolic Interaction and Dementia

Our understanding of dementia is predominantly shaped by biomedical concerns. These include efforts to link histopathic findings with neurobiological factors, to manage undesirable behaviours through medication, and to study the impact of the disease on caregivers and families (for critical discussions see Lyman 1989; Cotrell and Schultz 1993). An alternative approach, however, would emphasize the social and inter-personal nature of any illness, dementia included. This approach focuses on such concepts as 'the local culture of dementia' (Kitwood 1993), the 'social construction of "senility"' (Gubrium, 1986), and on processes such as 'infantilisation' (Hockey and James 1993), 'labelling,' 'stigmatisation' and ultimately 'banishment' (Kitwood 1990). These constructs and processes hinge on a symbolic interactionist perspective (Cooley 1902; Mead 1934) whose view of the social construction of (mainly mental) illness was later articulated in the framework of 'labelling theory' (Lemert 1951; Becker 1963).

Social constructionism, in a manner quite parallel to symbolic interaction, contends that one's identity depends on inter-personal give-and-take. Social identities, it further argues, are created and maintained primarily in the process of engaging in certain types of spoken discourse (Shotter 1983; Harre 1983; 1991; Urban 1989). If demented patients are socially ascribed, or denied, certain forms of discourse, this can therefore lead to a 'loss of self.' The fact that such mechanisms of social ascription generally constitute the 'elderly' as a social category is well documented (Hazan 1994; Featherstone and Hepworth 1989, 1991). This 'loss' in fact refers to and can be deduced only, according to the methods and outlook of social constructionism, from what can be termed 'the spoken self.' We will return in the conclusion to a criticism of the inherently problematic manifestation of the 'spoken self' in old age in general and dementia in particular. In the following section we consider the general acceptance of the 'demented' label as both a behavioural and a medical category, to prepare the ground for discussing the importance of symbolic interaction in constructing the protean image of dementia.

## Labelling Dementia

Alzheimer's disease or senile dementia is a little-known but surprisingly common disorder that affects the brain cells, causing a progressive and irreversible 'senility', starting with memory loss and continuing to the point where patients can no longer recognize their own families . . . There are many different patterns – in fact, no distinctive patterning – in the type, severity, and sequence of changes . . . The cause, prevention or cure of the disease are yet unknown . . . It is truly the 'disease of the century.'

This passage, taken from Gubrium (1986:1), is a representative collage of statements characterising the Alzheimer's disease literature. The factual status of Alzheimer's as a distinct disease entity separate from the varied experiences of normal ageing is not obvious. Gubrium's (1986) book is a brilliant account of the descriptive construction of AD as a 'gray area' – a term which could also be taken as an ironic allusion to the neuritic plaques which serve as post-mortem indicators of the disease. However, this 'characteristic' neuro-organicity of AD as opposed to dementia, or normal ageing, is quantitative rather than a difference in kind (Terry 1978; Katzman 1983). As Tomlinson et al. argue,

finally it is clear that great caution is needed in the interpretation of 'senile' changes of the kind described in the pathological investigation of any disease in old age, since . . . they are likely merely to reflect the age of the patient. (1968:355)

Ageing itself can therefore be pathological, perhaps acting as a catalyst the genetic change which produces AD (Reisberg 1981). Other possible etiological factors for AD, except genetics and ageing itself, have been traced to toxic substances such as the accumulation of trace metals (especially aluminum) (Wells 1978) in the brain, and to viroids (e.g. a slow virus) (Kaufman 1982). This could mean that AD, senile dementia or any other type of 'senility' (see Wang 1977 for a discussion of this terminological confusion) are not to be regarded as disease entities but rather as a 'normal' part of the biology of ageing.

Diagnostically, physicians are nowadays commonly concerned with telling Alzheimer's-type from multi-infarct dementia. These two 'diseases' are the most common causes of dementia in old people. However, because they occur together in a significant proportion of elderly people and separately present similar types of intellectual deficit, the clinician is faced with a diagnostic problem (Katzman 1982:8). The widespread use of mental status examinations or questionnaires (MSE/MSQs) adds to the confusion, ignoring the fact that 'differentially demented patients may score identically but, upon further clinical investigation, show signs of contrasting symptom histories' (Gubrium 1986:12). Recently, one paper appearing in a mainstream neurological journal has argued that the controversy throughout the century over the identity of presenile (AD) and senile dementia is historically based on 'anecdotal clinical observations . . . [and] that competition among universities was one of its underlying determinants (Amaducci et al. 1986:1497). Medically undecided, 'dementia' – whether Alzheimer's type or other – becomes a matter of description and labelling. It enters the realm of public culture, defined as a 'social problem,' prescribed with procedures of care and institutionalisation in order to provide practical answers for worried families and busy caretakers.

The nursing ward residents under study relied neither on clinical measures nor on mental status questionnaires in order to label other residents as demented. They saw things in behavioural terms, and nurses as well as other caretakers usually followed their lead. Most of the demented residents – designated as such by 'normal' residents as well as in their medical records – spent much of their time snoozing, their heads against the table with their eyes closed. However, other demented residents used to wander around the ward relentlessly and in what seemed to be a purposeless manner. Demented residents usually did not reject offers of help or treatment, but did not initiate requests for care. This, along with medical diagnoses of Organic Brain Syndrome and failures in social performance (especially conversation), were key factors in the demented labelling process.

Most of the demented residents spent their time with other similarly-labelled residents of the same sex ('among their like' as several 'normal' residents put it). Staff separated normal and demented residents – necessary for the maintaining of these categories – by means of several kinds of spatial segregation. Demented residents were seated, for example, around separate tables, which were separately reserved for men and women, located at the rear side of the entrance hall. During rest hours and at night demented residents were returned to their rooms, located at the far ends of the ward. The rooms reserved for the demented, compared with those of normal residents, were bigger and more crowded. Demented residents often shared their room with three or more others, while rooms for normal residents had no more than two to three beds. While spatially and socially segregated in a depersonalising manner, demented residents nevertheless differed among themselves. They were stereo-typed neither on the basis of medically clinched diagnoses nor on common behavioural characteristics.

Demented residents differed, for example, in their remaining physical skills and mental faculties. The ability to feel pain, for instance, was completely lacking in some of them, while others exhibited what could be described as over-sensitivity. The meaning of pain presentation, therefore, had to be decided by the carer. Carers often ignored certain demented residents who were moaning and rocking because 'that was their normal behaviour' (see Marzinsky 1991 for a parallel description of the vague assessment of pain in the demented elderly). One of the major differences among demented residents was the degree of their involvement in the social life of the ward. While some of them were completely divorced from such involvement, others were engaged in a wide range of relationships with residents, carers and families. However, it should be noted that while the latter presented the relative physical competence of motor, linguistic and emotional skills, they lacked the ability to find a normal place in the social structure of the ward. In other words, they maintained the formal appearance of social proficiency without the ability to exercise it contextually and functionally. This difference, however intricate, was noticed by normal residents and led to the labelling of these socially active residents as 'demented.' The following section illustrates the interactions involved in the process of such labelling.

## The Performance of *Dementia*

A concise description of several typical cases of demented residents could perhaps illustrate the meaning of social involvement which neither hinges on an existing social structure nor seems to improve one's life satisfaction. Shimon (male, age 84), for example, used to invade other residents' personal territories and take their personal possessions. He would sit on his neighbour's bed wearing wet pyjamas, and while moving around, often bumped into wheelchairs, hurting painful limbs and causing havoc. He followed occasional visitors around, asking questions about their car model, requesting permission to hold the car keys and making comments on the car's appearance. He used to open cars whose doors were left unlocked and sit inside. He often stayed awake at nights, and joined the carers' night meal while talking loudly. One day he entered the carers' cloakroom and put on a caretaker's clothes. At other times his trousers would fall down, but this he ignored and kept walking around naked. All these activities interrupted life on the ward, but also served to revive things a little. Residents, therefore, looked forward to Shimon's next folly with both fear and anticipation.

The picture was complicated as a result of Shimon's disappearances from the ward. He used to leave the nursing ward and wander around the centre, forcing the carers to go out and search for him. When accused by them of 'running away,' he replied 'how can you accuse me, when I am trying so hard to do my best.' On one cool October night Shimon disappeared from the ward and was not found for several hours. Aided by the local police, the searchers found him safe and sound, but wet and trembling from the cold. They said that Shimon did not connect the havoc of that night to the fact that he had 'disappeared.' He did identify the searchers, who wore police uniforms, as officials and – perhaps sensing the urgency of those around him – called the whole event a 'turmoil,' but endowed it, however, with his own meaning. His finders reported that his first reaction was: 'What is this turmoil? Where are all these soldiers going? Have they caught Arabs sneaking over the fence? What did the greedy scoundrels do this time?' In the morning following his escape, a few residents approached Shimon, who was sitting in his chair, a thoughtful expression on his face, murmuring 'if only I could, if only I could . . .' When asked by another resident: 'if only you could . . . what?' he replied, immediately and confidently: 'find a buyer for my cow'! Thinking that perhaps his disappearances were somehow connected with this purpose, one of the authors asked him whether he went to look for a buyer this last night. Shimon kept quiet, looking puzzled as if he had no recollection of that last night or as if he did not remember mentioning any cow.

Shimon's activities could be seen as having a logic of their own. However, being (a fragmented) part of a private language, any attempt to decode their 'real' meaning is problematical. Rather than attempting to decipher Shimon's world, which of course deserves to be studied in its own right, we focus here on the meaning given to his activities by those around him: residents, carers and families. In endowing Shimon's activities with meaning, the ward collectively acted as an 'interpretive community' (Fish 1980). In other words, the act of interpretation hinged on shared conventions, which the case of Shimon exemplifies, and which the following account sets out to illustrate. We first describe briefly Shimon's history in the institution.

At the time of his application, to the nursing ward in the geriatric centre, Shimon and his wife concealed from the committee his tendency to wander and disappear from home. Later, as Shimon's disappearances became routine, he became a target for inspection. Residents were asked by carers to watch over Shimon and report on his movements. Several hypotheses were posed in the ward regarding his behaviour. The most popular among them argued that there was some sort of connection between Shimon's disappearances and his wife's visits. Carers had found that Shimon usually attempted to 'escape from the ward' after his wife's visits in the afternoon. They hypothesised that he was searching for his wife, walking after her, but could not find his way back. To test this, Shimon's wife was asked not to visit the ward for a week, after which time she would limit herself to regular hours agreed with the staff. This programme appeared logical and applicable to all parties involved. Shimon, however, kept disappearing, and it was even harder to find him. During this period staff and residents began to talk about him in terms such as 'confused,' 'does not know his way around,' and 'senility strikes again.' The ground was prepared for the final labelling. However, at the same time communication between Shimon and other residents was kept alive and residents even conveyed to me that they liked Shimon. In fact what they liked was a social identity constructed by them to account for Shimon's incongruent behaviours. The following illustrates this claim.

Shimon's past biography, known to residents partly from personal relationships with him in the past and partly from his wife's accounts, was re-assessed to explain his behaviour. His occasional work in the cowshed was emphasised, serving to explain his disappearances as resulting from a deep urge to complete certain unfinished tasks from the past (i.e. finding a buyer for his cows). Shimon's respected background as a 'pioneer' (halutz), one of the first to cultivate the land of Israel at the beginning of the century, was offered to account for his 'understandable distaste for enclosed spaces' such as the ward. The mistaken conviction that his 'escapes' began only after his institutionalisation (in fact he had done the same at home, but this information had been concealed) was brought up by residents as evidence for this. The confused disappearances of the demented resident were therefore also seen as a portrayal of the pioneer's yearning for the 'free land.' Shimon's speech, which preserved the distinct vocabulary and diction of the pioneers' language, contributed to the social construction of his persona. His articulation, however, was undermined by a disorientation in time and space. His idiosyncratic intentions – whatever these might have been – were therefore re-oriented by those around him. It was not his intentions that mattered, but their social interpretation and manifestation. The case of Pinhas, another demented resident of the ward, illustrates a parallel situation.

Pinhas (male, age 78) was admitted to the ward in a condition described as 'advanced dementia.' In his case, therefore, labelling was part of the admittance process. He had severe deficiencies in his memory, orientation and judgement, as well as in physical abilities such as bowel control, eating and swallowing. When being fed, he did not chew his food and a special carer had to 'persuade' him to swallow. Often he would, 'play around' with his excreta. Despite these considerable inadequacies, Pinhas was viewed as one of the most honorable residents in the ward's history. His famous past identity, life-achievements and the type of visitors he still attracted all contributed to the social fabrication of his present persona (the original meaning of the word 'persona', in Greek, is in fact 'mask'). Residents were proud to tell their families and visitors about their famous neighbour. In their tales they focused on Pinhas's well-known public career as a researcher, adventurer and a Don Juan. These past attributes were used equally by residents, families and carers to explain Pinhas's daily behaviour in the ward. When Pinhas stared for hours at his neighbouring Ethiopian resident or at the television set, this was accounted for by saying that 'he is interested in the subject of immigration from Ethiopia,' 'the language interests him,' 'once a researcher, always a researcher,' 'he was a scholar, he cares what happens in this country', and so on. Other instances of apathetic staring would precipitate such remarks as 'he's thinking,' or 'father was always a stoic.' When Pinhas was caught staring at female carers, this led to remarks such as 'once a Don Juan, always a Don Juan', 'still interested in girls', and 'he reacts better to women than to men'.

A group of normal residents, formed in order to attend gym classes, was later joined by Pinhas. His acceptance into that gym class, despite his obvious failure to participate in its activities, further illustrates the significance of labelling by residents. Upon hearing the instruction 'raise your hands up in the air and then lower them', Pinhas, who was sitting nearby, would move his hat in time with the instructions. His behaviour, while presenting a failure to participate in class activities, attracted positive remarks such as 'see how he pretends to exercise . . . still pulling everyone's leg'. As with Shimon, Pinhas's remaining articulation helped to sustain his esteemed social identity. His linguistic 'skills,' however, were largely evident in their formal – syntactic, rather than contextual–semantic, aspects (for discussions of this assumed 'first' stage of linguistic deterioration in old age, see Bartol 1980; Hier et al. 1985). The following excerpt, which is quite typical of communication with Pinhas, illustrates this. One evening the following exchanges occurred between Pinhas and a carer:

*Carer*: Would you like something to drink?
*Pinhas*: To drink!
*Carer*: Tea? or Something cold?
*Pinhas*: Something cold!
*Carer*: I did not hear you, do you want cold or tea?
*Pinhas*: Tea!

The social identity constructed for Pinhas in the ward included neither his inability to present those features attributed to him, nor the inconsistency and disorientation of his utterances and behaviour (for similar findings regarding the strategies family members use to 'hang on to' their respective loved ones as they were once known, see Orona 1990). There were other 'demented' residents in the ward whose presentation of self was far more consistent and informed than that of Pinhas. However, as these residents did not have any well-known or reliable biographies, their social identity was deconstructed rather than re-constructed by residents and carers.

## The Involvement of Family Members and Carers in Constructing Identities

While the involvement of normal residents in the labelling of 'demented' residents was probably the most significant, family members as well as carers were also involved. As mentioned in the cases of Shimon and Pinhas, re-edited biographies played a significant part, in the creation of social identities for 'demented' residents. As they could not themselves recount their biographies, this task was taken over mainly by their families. Family members assumed the role of 'editors'; they interpreted the patient's behaviour in the light of various biographical clues. Many family members used their visits to convey their 'demented' relative's sense of his or her past, as reconstructed. The following typical exchange illustrates this:

*Daughter* (to her mother, considered a 'demented' resident, during visit time): Mother, do you remember the shirt I am wearing?
*Bellah* (her mother, age 80): No.
*Daughter*: You knitted it after Rami was born. To this very day it looks great and everybody asks me where I bought it. I tell them proudly it was you.
*Bellah* (excited): You really tell them so? I have completely forgotten that I once knew how to knit.
*Daughter*: What do you mean 'knew how to knit'; when we lived in Jerusalem, and the winter was extremely cold, you used to knit shirts for half of Jerusalem's population.
*Bellah*: Me? We lived in Jerusalem?
*Daughter*: We moved to Jerusalem from Tiberias in 1935. We lived there in a huge house with beautiful roses in the entrance?
*Bellah*: Right, I remember the roses now . . . There were lots of people there.

Bellah's daughter, it should be noted, repeatedly told staff and residents about Bellah's 'motherly qualities', accentuating, for example, her expertise in knitting. Knitting was thus made a key leitmotif in what Kaufman (1986) would call the resident's 'ageless self.' It was the ageless self of a demented resident as mother. That ageless self, however, was not a personally re-constructed past 'core identity', as Kaufman argues. Rather, it was a socially re-edited biographical fragment with which the resident was labelled. In the cases of Pinhas and Shimon, whose biographies were well-known to the public, this re-editing had more alternatives and was relatively easy. In many other cases, such as Bellah's, however, the re-editing of a past biography which took place in the domestic (rather than public) domain, was more limited and resulted in emphasis on a single, stereotyping element, such as 'knitting'.

Carers were primarily involved in the construction of identity for the 'demented' residents through their role in defining 'pain presentation'. When a carer ignored a resident's call for help, explaining it as a 'false alarm', this would no doubt contribute to the resident's labelling as a demented person. In the private talks we had, many of the carers complained about the unreliability of communication with 'demented' residents, who often 'say one thing and mean another.' One carer illustrated this with the following dialogue she had had with a 'demented' resident named Zvi (male, age 84). Zvi used to moan loudly and repeatedly, making the other residents angry. One time, when the moaning became particularly loud, the carer approached Zvi, saying

*Carer*: your cries made a hole in everyone's heads. All day long you cry. What is it that hurts you so much?
*Zvi*: Nothing!

*Carer* (taken by surprise): If there is nothing the matter with you, why do you keep moaning all the time?

*Zvi*: Do I have anything better to do? Oy, Oy, Oy . . .

Other carers mentioned that many 'demented' residents, who often complained, were 'cured' when their mind was distracted by speaking about their family and other topics which were of interest to them as well as by taking placebo tablets (vitamin C). Carers, however, could also have a much more 'creative' role in constructing identities for their 'demented' residents. This construction of identities for demented people was no less important, taking into account the carers' authority in the ward. The following examples serve to illustrate the creation of identities by caters for 'demented' residents.

Yevgeni (male, age 81) was a new immigrant from Russia. He spoke Russian only and the staff was unable to communicate with him. Yevgeni was considered by the carers to be a 'problematic' resident. He often wandered about, could become aggressive, and would often burst into cursing. His family members scarcely visited him. On one of their visits, they told the carers that Yevgeni was a high-ranking officer in the Red Army. Ever since, carers used to call Yevgeni 'the General', and would greet him with a military salute, which he would return. According to the carers, the new identity ascribed to him helped to moderate Yevgeni's aggressive behaviour.

Another example involved a passive, isolated 'demented' resident whose relatives refrained from visiting him. One of the carers, who knew he was a doctor, decided to 'take him under her patronage', as she put it. She began to cultivate his identity as a doctor, giving him a stethoscope and a suitcase with sheets inside, to be completed as medical records. Gradually she even dressed that resident with a doctor's white uniform, and asked him to accompany her during (the real) doctor's visits in the ward. During these visits, she pretended to consult the resident, using medical terminology in order to communicate with him. We shall not analyse here the full implications, including the ethical ones, of that carer's behaviour, but shall return to it in the conclusion as an example of 'validation therapy'. It is presented here in brief in order to illustrate the involvement of carers in the construction of identities for 'demented' residents. In line with the argument developed thus far, it serves to illustrate how the social identity of demented people is re-constructed by those around them by appropriating a biographical fragment and enlarging it into a 'personality leitmotif'. The carer involved in the labelling of the former 'demented' resident as a doctor claimed that the new occupational identity given to him was a blessing. 'For him', she said, 'it was a sort of awakening. It filled him with new life. His behaviour in the ward changed completely. He pretended to scramble things in his sheets. He used the stethoscope to check other residents, who cooperated and referred to him as 'doctor'.'

## The 'Demented Role': The Adaptive Image of Dementia

The 'demented role' is a concept denoting the functional, adaptive aspects attributed by 'normal' residents to those labelled by them as 'demented'. The term 'demented role' was coined by us as an allusion to Parsons' (1951) 'sick role'. The two roles have several components in common. They are both prescribed to certify illness in order to explain the patient's failure to comply with social expectations. These roles therefore legitimate social withdrawal from various obligations. However, while this exemption is only temporary (and therefore socially 'functional') in the case of the sick role, it becomes chronic in the case of the demented role. Some 'normal' residents thus conveyed to me a view of 'the demented role' as a beneficial resource which exempts its owners from social responsibilities without committing them to seek recovery. In the nursing ward, where all residents suffer from various mental and physical impairments, and the future promises nothing but further decline (and ultimately death), even dementia may have its bright side. The 'demented role' should therefore be read here as another example of the social construction of the attributes of dementia by residents who do not have cognitive impairments. The following examples illustrate this.

When referring to 'demented' residents, almost all 'normal' residents with whom we talked preferred to concentrate on various 'side benefits' supposedly entailed by the state of dementia. The social construction, or labelling, of dementia therefore involved, for residents as well as others, not only scapegoating but also 'halo effects'. It was thus said to me that many 'demented' residents were better nourished since they had been taking food items from other residents' drawers. While no one ventured to state clearly that 'demented' residents did that on purpose; still the unspoken implication hung in the air. Other residents emphasised the 'adaptive' value of dementia. As dementia could afflict each and every resident, perhaps it was a form of denial of the worse parts of the illness. In the opinion of many 'normal' residents, dementia made life simpler, releasing one from 'the burden of the past and the premonitions of the future'. Several residents said that 'perhaps if my head had also been fucked up, it would have been easier for me. I would not know where I was.' Family members in particular accentuated what they called 'the merits of confusion'. A common phrase was 'mother is better off this way, at least she does not know what is happening to her. Those whose mind still works have a much more difficult time'. In this way both residents and carers reflected on the meaning that they distilled from the behaviour of the 'demented.'

## Conclusion: The Disappearing 'I' of Dementia

Old age, sociologists argue, is an apparition conjured up under society's gaze. 'Old age' is represented by and to middle aged society through the so-called 'mask of ageing' (Featherstone and Hepworth 1991; Harré 1991). Mass media, welfare criteria and social stereotypes provide programmes of talking about the old which are further validated by selectively-induced expressions uttered by elderly people. Old age is masked behind images of senility, crime, social abuse, poverty, nonproductivity, family neglect and medical illtreatment. Pre-assumptions as to the pathological nature of ageing, for example, play a major part in medicalizing almost all forms of communication by and with the old. All this applies just as well to the masking of dementia by society at large as well as by 'normal' elderly people. For the larger society, 'dementia' epitomises the most bewildering conditions of old age. For elderly people, however, dementia seems to capture a more intricate symbolic space. If elders are society's others, then demented elders are elderly people's others. It could be expected that 'demented elderly people' would therefore be constituted as scapegoats by those designated 'normal'. This is indeed the case in some old-age homes previously studied, where the criteria of 'functioning' would determine the social death of individuals (Hazan 1992). In the nursing ward studied, however, 'demented' residents were also endowed with positive images. We chose to focus on these positive images since this is the less predictable aspect of the social construction of dementia among elderly people.

There is, therefore, both a duality and an ambivalence towards dementia in the attitude of those on the outside. Dementia, as this paper has attempted to demonstrate, was viewed by non-demented residents as both a blessing and a curse. Demented people are a nuisance, but they are also exempted from social responsibilities; they have neither friends nor obligations. They lose their memory and awareness of the future, but who needs these anyway? If the goal of many elderly communities, as Hazan (1980) has so convincingly argued, is to 'arrest time,' then dementia achieves this in an enviable manner. Demented residents can therefore be depicted by non-demented as existing in a reality of their own, a 'time-capsule' which is, in the eyes of the non-demented residents of the nursing ward, also a kind of escape pod. Within 'dementia,' the existential ruptures of ageing no longer exist. Personal and social, mind and body, become one again. This is the imagined 'freedom' attributed to dementia and to the so-called demented role. Accentuating this attribute undoubtedly also serves as a mechanism for denial and distancing.

The perception of dementia by old people as a (successful or otherwise) 'escape attempt' can also serve to throw into relief the ruptures, or dilemmas, daily confronted in normal ageing. Old age, where the personal is split from the social and the body betrays the person, is a world shot through with dilemmas and paradoxes where middle age, taken-for-granted coordinates no longer hold. One such midlife convention is the Western cultural postulate regarding the inter-connectedness of social and personal identities. But if old age splits between these two constructs, and dementia further distances the 'I' from the external world, then what can we say about this I, the I of dementia? Practically very little.

Sabat and Harré (1992) claim that '[this] self is not lost even in much of the end stage of the disease (p. 460)'. This of course depends on how exactly one defines, or measures, 'the self'. Sabat and Harré locate it within self-referential formal expressions in discourse (e.g. first person indexicals such as 'I', 'me', 'myself', 'my'). However, as the examples given in this paper show, first person indexicals (indeed discourse in general) could be imitated in the formal, syntactically-preserved but content-lacking speech of demented residents. In order to argue that indexicals are 'meaningful', one should be able to expose their 'intention'. This difficult task becomes highly problematic in the case of dementia. It is also undermined by the insignificance of intention (meaningful or otherwise) in the ward. What mattered to the ward residents and their carers was how 'intentions' were socially interpreted and accounted for. Intentions were appropriated and endowed with meaning by those surrounding the demented resident. This is arguably also the rationale underlying the methods and outlook of 'validation therapy' as it has been used regarding dementia (Kitwood and Bredin 1992). However, what validation theory does not take into account is that positive social identities can possibly be validated (or fabricated; the difference is very subtle) even with a demented patient whose personal I is fading. This was shown to exist in the two cases of 'the General' and 'the Doctor' cited above.

The findings of this paper show that in re-constructing social identities for demented people, individual agency is imitated and prescribed, and fragments of past biography are magnified to serve as 'personality leitmotifs'. This dubbing of the social identity of demented people is conducted by their fellow residents, who do not have cognitive impairments, in much the same way as the latter are 'dubbed' by middle-aged society (see Raz 1993, 1996). In both cases, dubbing – or the collective prescription of personal meanings – is so strongly manifested because it allows the obliteration of the speaker's personal, idiosyncratic intentions. It can therefore be used as a means of normative control. Within such discourses of normative control as manifested in the ward, dementia – as seen by those not yet subjected to it – can be (surprising as it may seem) masked as a 'role', and through positive images.

## References

Amaducci, L. A., Rocca, W. A. and Schoenberg, B. S. 1986. Origin of the distinction between Alzheimer's disease and senile dementia: how history can clarify nosology. *Neurology*, 36, 1497–9.

Bartol, M. A. 1980. Dialogue with dementia: non-verbal communication in patients with Alzheimer's disease. In Stilwell, E. (ed.) *Readings in Gerontological Nursing*. Charles B. Black, Thorofare, N.J.

Becker, H. 1963. *The Outsiders*. Free Press, Glencoe, IL.

Cooley, C. H. 1902. *Human Nature and the Social Order*. Scribners, N.Y.

Cotrell, V. and Schultz, R. 1993. The perspective of the patients with Alzheimer's disease: a neglected dimension of dementia research. *The Gerontologist*, 23, 205–11.

Featherstone, M. and Hepworth, M. 1989. Ageing and old age: reflections on the post-modern life course. In Featherstone, M., Hepworth, M. and Turner, B. (eds) *Becoming and Being Old: Sociological Approaches to Modern Life*. Sage, London.

Featherstone, M. and Hepworth, M. 1991. The mask of ageing and the post-modern life course. In Featherstone, M., Hepworth, M. and Turner, B. (eds) *The Body: Social Process and Cultural Theory*. Sage, London.

Fish, S. 1980. *Is There a Text in this Class? The Authority of Interpretive Communities*. Harvard University Press, Harvard.

Golander, H. 1995a. Rituals of temporality: the social construction of time in a nursing ward. *Journal of Aging Studies*, 9, 35.

Golander, H. 1995b. Old, chronically sick and institutionalized: being a nursing ward resident. *Community and Health Care*, 17, 63–79.

Gubrium, J. F. 1986. *Oldtimers and Alzheimer's; The Descriptive Organization of Senility*. JAI Press, Greenwich, CT.

Harré, R. 1983. *Personal Being*. Blackwell, Oxford.

Harré, R. 1991. The discursive production of selves. *Theory and Psychology*, 1, 59–63.

Hazan, H. 1980. *The Limbo People: a Study of the Constitution of the Time Universe Among the Aged*. Routledge & Kegan Paul, London.

Hazan, H. 1992. *Managing Change in Old Age*. SUNY Press, Albany.

Hazan, H. 1994. *Old Age: Constructions and Deconstructions*. Cambridge University Press, Cambridge.

Hier, B. D., Hagenlocker, K. and Shindle, G. A. 1985. Language disintegration in dementia. *Brain and Language*, 25, 117–33.

Hockey, J. and James, A. 1993. *Growing up and Growing Old: Ageing and Dependency in the Life Course*. Sage Publications, London.

Katzman, R. 1982. The complete problem of diagnosis. *Generations*, 7, 8–10.

Katzman, R. (ed) 1983. *Banbury Report 15: Biological Aspects of Alzheimer's Disease*. Cold Spring Harbor Laboratory, N.Y.

Kaufman, M. 1982. Treatable dementias. Topics in geriatrics. *Massachusetts General Hospital Newsletter*, 1, 1–2.

Kaufman, S. R. 1986. *The Ageless Self: Sources of Meaning in Late Life*. The University of Wisconsin Press, Wisconsin.

Kitwood, T. 1990. The dialectics of dementia: with particular reference to Alzheimer's disease. *Ageing and Society*, 10, 177–96.

Kitwood, T. 1993. Towards a theory of dementia care: the interpersonal process. *Ageing and Society*, 13, 51–67.

Kitwood, T. and Bredin, K. 1992. Towards a theory of dementia care: personhood and well-being. *Ageing and Society*, 12, 269–87.

Lemert, E. M. 1951. *Social Pathology*. McGraw-Hill, N.Y.

Lyman, K. 1989. Bringing the social back in: a critique of the biomedicalization of dementia. *The Gerontologist*, 29, 597–605.

Marzinsky, L. R. 1996. The tragedy of dementia: clinically assessing pain in the confused, non-verbal elderly. *Journal of Gerontological Nursing*, 17, 25–30.

Mead, G. H. 1934. *Mind, Self and Society*. Chicago University Press, Chicago.

Orona, C. J. 1990. Temporality and identity loss due to Alzheimer's disease. *Social Science and Medicine*, 30, 1247–56.

Parsons, T. 1951. *The Social System*. Routledge and Kegan Paul, London.

Raz, A. E. 1993. The reinherited self: a case study in the dynamics of a social world. In Denzin, N. K. (ed). JAI Press Inc., Greenwich, CT.

Raz, A. E. 1996. (forthcoming). The discourse of aging and other age-related languages: how selves are authorised in the post modern world. In Denzin, N. K. (ed) *Studies in Symbolic Interaction*, JAI Press Inc., Greenwich, CT.

Reisberg, B. 1981. *Brain Failure*. Free Press, N.Y.

Sabat, S. and Harré, R. 1992. The construction and deconstruction of self in Alzheimer's disease. *Ageing and Society*, 12, 443–61.

Shotter, J. 1983. *Social Accountability and Selfhood*. Blackwell, Oxford.

Terry, R. D. 1978. Aging, senile dementia and Alzheimer's disease. In Katzman, R., Terry, R. D. and Bick, K. (eds) *Alzheimer's Disease, Senile Dementia and Related Disorders*. Raven Press, N.Y.

Tomlinson, B. E., Blessed, G. and Roth, M. 1968. Observations on the brains of demented old people. *Journal of the Neurological Sciences*, 7, 331–56.

Urban, G. 1989. The 'I' of discourse. In Lee, B. and Urban, G. (eds) *Semiotics, Self and Society*. Mouton de Gruyter, N.Y.

Wang, H. S. 1977. Dementia of old age. In Lynn Smith, W. and Kinsbourne, M. (eds) *Aging and Dementia*. SP Books, N.Y.

Wells, C. E. 1978. Chronic brain disease: an overview. *American Journal of Psychiatry*, 135, 1–12.

## Further Reading to Part VII

Downs, Murna. 1997. "The Emergence of the Person in Dementia Research," *Ageing and Society* 17: 597–607.

Gubrium, Jaber F. 1986. *Oldtimers and Alzheimer's: The Descriptive Organization of Senility*. Greenwich, CT: JAI Press.

Gubrium, Jaber F. 1986. "The Social Preservation of Mind: The Alzheimer's Disease Experience," *Symbolic Interaction* 9: 37–51.

Gubrium, Jaber F. 1988. "Incommunicables and Poetic Documentation in the Alzheimer's Disease Experience," *Semiotica* 72: 235–53.

Gubrium, Jaber F. and Robert, J. Lynott. 1985. "Alzheimer's Disease as Biographical Work." Pp. 349–67 in *Social Bonds in Later Life*, edited by Warren Peterson & Jill Quadagno. Beverly Hills, CA: Sage.

Lyman, Karen A. 1993. *Day In, Day Out with Alzheimer's: Stress in Caregiving Relationships*. Philadelphia: Temple University Press.

Mills, Marie A. 1998. *Narrative Identity and Dementia: A Study of Autobiographical Memories and Emotion*. Aldershot: Ashgate.

Sabat, Steven R. and Rom Harré. 1992. "The Construction and Deconstruction of Self in Alzheimer's Disease," *Ageing and Society* 12: 443–61.

# Part VIII

## Caring and Caregiving

# 25 The Dependent Elderly, Home Health Care, and Strategies of Household Adaptation

## Steven M. Albert

### Introduction

Ethnographic research has shown how household organization plays an important role in a wide variety of health contexts, such as sanitary practices, nutrition, responses to morbidity, decisions to seek medical care, and the interpretation of symptoms. In particular, anthropologists have stressed the ways that variation across households *mediates* the effect of disease transmission or attempts to improve health. For example, variation in task allocation and the organization of work within households makes some households more efficient in preparing food and securing adequate nutrition for family members (Pelto and Pelto, 1984). The anthropological emphasis on household organization is equally relevant in assessing the ways that households marshal resources to meet a health crisis, such as acute illness or chronic disability in a family member. Mobilization of the material and psychological resources required for such caregiving also differs across households; one task from an ethnographic perspective on the home care experience is to document the range of variation in this *household production of care*. How do households meet the disruptions in family life associated with illness? What makes family caregivers more or less successful in coping with these challenges? What adaptation strategies emerge within households for managing care demands?

A wide range of research has shown that the household is the key element in the organization of care for the chronically ill and impaired elderly. Families, organized as households, provide 80 to 90 percent of the medical and personal care required by the elderly (Brody, 1985). This is true even for severely impaired, older adults whose functional limitations and care needs are virtually identical to those of the institutionalized, nursing home population. For example, nearly one quarter of the elderly in the United States are functionally disabled and require assistance with personal care (bathing, dressing, toileting), help with the instrumental activities of daily living (shopping, cooking), and nursing care of the kind typically provided by a skilled nurse or health aide (changing dressings, administering oxygen). Yet only one in five

Original publication: Albert, Steven, M., "The Dependent Elderly, Home Health Care, and Strategies of Household Adaptation," from (ed. Jaber F. Gubrium and Andrea Sankar) *The Home Care Experience: Ethnography and Policy* (Sage Publications Inc., 1990), pp. 19–36.

of these elders receives care in a nursing home; the other four are cared for at home (Doty, 1986). Use of the formal support system of nursing, homemaking, and counseling services is usually delayed until family resources have been stretched as far as possible; even when formal services are engaged, households always combine formal support with family supports. Likewise, nursing home placements are normally an option of last resort. Among the small number of families that do institutionalize an elder, nursing home placements are usually sought only when the elder's health declines dramatically (and quickly, before a family has had time to adapt), or when some change in the household (divorce, illness of the caregiver) affects the capacity to render care. As Brody puts it, "the family, virtually unnoticed, had invented long term care well before that phrase was articulated" (Brody, 1985).

Given the deep-seated commitment of families to care for impaired parents at home, it would be valuable to know more about the ways households adapt to the demands of caregiving. In accommodating household organization to the needs of an impaired elder, families make a continuing, often implicit appraisal of the *disruptiveness* of an elder's impairments and the caregiving demands bound up with them: Is my mother's condition such that caregiving can be peripheral to normal, ongoing household activity? Does giving her effective care now require that the household be thoroughly reorganized around caregiving tasks? It must be stressed that this appraisal process is only partly determined by the severity of an elder's impairment. The bedridden elder who is moved to the first-floor living room certainly becomes newly prominent in household activity, as patterns of interaction, contact with friends, and utilization of space are all altered. Yet it is striking that in some households the same living rooms are hardly altered and remain the focus of family life despite the presence of the elder. Caregivers and their families continue to gather there to watch television at night, to converse, or simply to relax. Other households respond differently, either by refusing to relocate the parent to the center of the home or by taking the living room out of circulation once the parent has been moved.

This chapter reports on ethnographic data gathered within caregiving households to explore variation in adaptation to caregiving demands and parental impairment. A major finding of the research concerns the importance of particular *adaptation strategies* that evolve within households and which allow them to render care more effectively. As we will see, such strategies in fact often evolve explicitly to *prevent* the radical reorganization of the household that is threatened by overwhelming caregiving demands. In a phrase that recurs again and again, caregivers say they "draw lines" between caregiving tasks and the noncaregiving component of the household. After a brief discussion of the source of these data, we shall explore the nature of parental impairment as a disruption of household organization and the ways households prepare for such disruption, and actual strategies used by caregivers to adapt household organization to caregiving demands. We conclude with a discussion of the ways that knowledge of such adaption might be useful in designing interventions to help caregivers.

## Subjects and Method

To pursue these above-mentioned questions, semistructured interviews with a pool of 75 caregivers were conducted. These interviews typically lasted 90 to 120 minutes.

A smaller sample of 15 households participated in repeated interviews stressing adaptation to caregiving. These were conducted one a month over a 6 month period, with two interviews conducted in the respondent's home and three conducted as follow-up telephone calls. The interviews drew on a "care diary" that caregivers filled out to keep track of their parent's changing health needs and their own caregiving responses. Unfortunately, the diary was only partly useful as a source of data. Many caregivers found it onerous to record what seemed to them to be "more of the same old thing" – doctor's visits for chronic minor illnesses; successive alterations of medications; and continued bouts with a parent's constipation, refusal to drink water, sleeplessness, etc. The result was that only few households produced reliable data on the frequency of changes in household routine. However, the diary elicitation was useful in stimulating caregivers to think about the ways they respond to caregiving demands.

The interviews were part of a larger, ongoing study of caregiving as a cultural system (Albert, 1990), which represents the ethnographic portion of the Philadelphia Geriatric Center's program project on caregiver mental health and the dependent elderly. Subjects were recruited through word of mouth; public service announcements; and fliers sent to caregiver support groups, adult day care centers, and related social service and medical facilities. In addition, tapes and transcripts from two prior studies conducted by the Philadelphia Geriatric Center were reviewed. Interview material was supplemented by direct observation of household organization and material culture.

For this study, we restricted caregiving households to those of daughters, daughters-in-law, and sons of the impaired elder. We did not require that caregivers and impaired elders be coresident. Also, a number of caregivers reported on caregiving that had taken place prior to a nursing home placement or death of the parent. We reasoned that a degree of distance from the caregiving might allow retrospective insight on the ways the household had changed in response to caregiving demands.

The interviews yielded a great deal of verbal transcript material concerning caregivers' progressive socialization into the role of caregiver, their interpretation of when they had become a caregiver, and their perception of key markers in the periodization of their caregiving career. A number of open-ended questions were also asked of informants specifically to elicit caregivers' perceptions of household adaptation to caregiving demands. These included the following:

1   Do you have any special tricks or techniques that make caregiving easier? What are they? Can you remember how they first got started?
2   Would you say your caregiving has gotten easier with time? What has gotten easier? What has made it easier?
3   Are there certain family routines that seem to have emerged in response to the demands of caregiving?
4   What has gotten you through the hard times of caregiving? What do you do when you feel you need to get away from it all?

## Parental Impairment as a Disruption of Household Organization

In what sense do caregiving demands disrupt a household? Beyond the obvious, changes in the utilization of space in a home and alterations in a family's activity patterns are more subtle and complex forces of change. Relocation of a newly impaired parent to a caregiver's home is both more and less disruptive than one might expect, or more accurately, it disrupts the different components of the household regime to varying degrees.

### Household Preadaptation

The unexpected rapid decline of a parent, who then lands in the lap of a family unprepared for the event, is quite rare. Households begin their adaptation to caregiving demands long before acute illness forces a relocation of the impaired elder (or the relocation of a caregiver to the parent's home), just as households continue to care for a parent who has been removed from the home and placed in a nursing home. Sensory and cognitive deficits, functional limitations associated with chronic illness, and loss of the parent's informal support system (e.g., through the death of a spouse) usually precede the acute crisis that results in the actual relocation of the parent. This gradual decline leads future caregivers to alter schedules and begin their socialization into the role of caregiver *before* caregiving demands precipitate major changes in the household. With such increasing parental dependence, we find that caregivers and impaired parents begin to form *quasi-households*: For example, a daughter's occasional food shopping or preparation of meals for her mother becomes a regular feature of the week; after the death of her father, an unmarried working daughter begins to stay at her mother's house on weekends so that trips back and forth are less onerous; occasional visits with a daughter's family become more frequent and begin to lengthen in duration, so that when the heater at the parent's house finally breaks, it seems easiest and most appropriate to formalize the relation and admit that the parent really lives with the daughter's family.

When the impaired elder suffers a health crisis that finally precipitates a family gathering to discuss, as one caregiver put it, "who's gonna do for Mom," the outcome of these meetings is mostly decided in advance. One adult child has usually already assumed the role, though such people, on reflection, are often surprised to see how much they have altered their household routine even before they finally define themselves as caregivers. This moment of recognition – the realization that one is a caregiver rather than someone who simply helps out once in a while – is quite complex. Research shows a great deal of variation in the thresholds of such self-definition. A parent's deficits are compared to his or her prior level of competency, which also changes over time. Caregivers find themselves comparing the parent's current disability to a more restricted functional competency. This allows caregivers to deny that the parent is as impaired as he or she really is. Many caregivers, particularly spouses, also cover up for the elder's deficits, often in ways not completely conscious to themselves. Since in some families a father never cooked or did laundry, or a mother never balanced a checkbook or paid bills, a standard for pre-impaired competency may also simply be lacking. Of course, when an adult child finally recognizes herself as a caregiver, she may have to admit that the parent has irrevocably changed and that the relationship between them has been fundamentally altered. One daughter, for example, reported that she knew she was a caregiver when her father collapsed and her mother stood by confused and unable to take action; the daughter realized that she alone possessed the wherewithal and concern that could keep her parents alive. It is significant, however, that a great many caregivers reach this point only after a long history of adaptation and selective recognition.

Another source of such preadaptation involves caregivers' *self-selection* to the role of caregiver. While many say "there was no one else" in explaining why they became caregivers, quite often there is in fact someone else. This yields another clue as to how households preadapt to caregiving demands. Research reveals that one child becomes the primary caregiver, and that being female, single, nonworking, and living near the parents all predict selection to the role of caregiver (Ikels, 1983). This has been shown to result in a bias toward youngest adult children, who may still reside with the parent when functional limitations become apparent and who may delay a move out of the home because of anticipated caregiving obligations. Less often remarked in the process of caregiver selection is the active role of one child in excluding siblings who might also become caregivers. While active competition between siblings over who will become the caregiver is rare, our research reveals that the child who becomes caregiver often pre-selects him- or herself by taking a greater interest in the parent's welfare, by staying near or moving near the parent, and by preparing her household in advance for the parent's eventual relocation. These adult children are not always the favorite children of the parents; in fact, some seek increased intimacy with the parent through such overtures. Preselection in this sense ranges from quite conscious planning to a more or less implicit coadaptation within families, a relationship in which a set of siblings allocates different caregiving responsibilities among themselves while reserving primary responsibility for the one who has already shown the greatest interest. The pre- or self-selected caregiver often is motivated by a desire to provide the parent with a *family*, quite apart from caring for the parent's needs or illness.

This exclusion of rivals and stress on the family links caregiving to other processes in which a single family member makes a sacrifice for another family member. A striking parallel, for example, can be seen in the case of kidney transplantation. Research by Simmons and her colleagues has shown that the person who donates a kidney to a family member often takes actions that give other potential donors an excuse to bow out (Simmons, Klein, & Thorton, 1973). Likewise, a family member feels a greater obligation to donate when he or she is the only one available (as determined by medical evaluation), when he or she has fewer family obligations, and when he or she adopts the spontaneous norm-directed decision style that is consistent with commitment to family as a paramount value. Thus the caregiver who states that she offered to have her mother join her household without any concern as to whether her siblings would make the offer is behaving quite similarly to the kidney donor. This caregiver has already taken a series of antecedent steps that has given her siblings an opportunity *not* to provide care.

The upshot of this preadaptation to caregiving and the formation of quasi-households involving the elder is that the transition to caregiving is less disruptive than one would expect. The majority of caregivers in our sample *expected* to share their household, once they noted that their parents were beginning to need help. And, as we have seen, many alter their routines in anticipation of doubling up with a parent, going so far as to take actions that give their siblings an opportunity not to get involved.

### The Limits to Preadaptation

While the decision to become a caregiver appears to be relatively easy and straightforward in its implications, putting a limit on such care – that is, knowing when one has done enough – is not so easy. Rendering care *to* a parent quickly becomes a sign of how much one cares *about* a parent. Caregivers assert that if you care for someone (definition one, if you love and show concern for that person), then you must be caring (i.e., you provide nursing care for that person when you or she is infirm). Since care (definition two) is normatively unbounded, many feel that being caring must be similarly unbounded, even when it exceeds one's resources and affects the health of the caregiver – even, we might add, when the demented recipient of such care bears only the most remote relation to one's mother or father. For many, to do anything less means that one's care for the parent was not deep enough or true. The anxiety caregivers feel on this score is summed up well in an adage often recited by caregivers: "A parent can take care of many children, but many children can't take care of even one parent." The shift in meaning between the two senses of *care* is elided.

Intensive interviews with caregivers reveal that this uncertainty regarding the limits of one's obligation to render care is perhaps the greatest source of disruption in household organization. If one is always on call, always expected to do more, and never sure one is doing enough, it is impossible to plan for the future or maintain any interest outside caregiving. Caregiving in this case absorbs all household resources. The caregiver who can say, "I know I've done all I can possibly do, a 100 percent plus," is usually one who has allowed her household to be maximally disrupted by caregiving demands. The same caregiver, for example, also claimed that she was continually unsteady on her feet because of the loss of sleep and daily fatigue brought on by caregiving demands. Even caregivers who do expend all their resources on caregiving may doubt themselves. For them, the impaired parent must die at home; otherwise the child's loyalty to the parent and commitment to caregiving are suspect.

Preparing oneself to become a caregiver in the ways outlined above does not seem to be associated with an ability to set limits on such care once one has become a caregiver. This ability to set limits must be learned. However, if caregivers are differentially predisposed to learn how to set these limits, one significant factor predicting their ability to do so appears to be their own status as parents (Albert, 1990). Caregivers who are parents themselves are evidently more likely to set limits on what is enough in caregiving. It would seem that being a parent is associated with some degree of psychological distance from one's own parents, or perhaps having children leads to a greater sense that one has obligations that rival commitment to parental care. More research is required on this point.

Having made the choice to care for a parent at home, how do caregivers set limits to caregiving demands? Our research shows that households have evolved two broad sets of strategies for limiting the disruptions caused by caregiving demands. The first involves establishing *routines* for caregiving tasks, a strategy that limits disruptions of temporal and spatial order. The second strategy involves *role redefinition*, which limits disruptions of social organization. The two together allow members of caregiving households, as many say, "to balance our lives," to establish a boundary for their obligation to render care. In practice, this means imposition of a routine for caregiving tasks and a redefinition of one's relation to a parent.

## Routines and Ritualization of Caregiving Tasks

One can easily imagine the value of a *routine* for performing caregiving tasks. Imposition of a routine means fixity in timing, place, and sequence – in short, more certainty with respect to what the task consists of and a clearer sense of when it is complete. A routine for bathing, feeding, or administering medications establishes regular borders and patterning. It makes caregiving more finite: something is done in a certain way, it is then completed, and one can go on to other things. Such routinization is an obvious candidate for limiting the disruptiveness of unbounded caregiving demands. Many caregivers measure their mastery of the situation by the routines they have established for getting the job done.

It is curious, however, that caregivers often speak of these routines in other terms. Rather than stop with talk of efficiency or expediency, many go on to speak of the *rightness* or even special *efficacy* of doing the task just this way. They may feel that the care routines actually have a medical effect or restorative power. They adhere to the routine even when the parent's condition has changed significantly and thereby made the routine inefficient, a sign that the routine has a meaning *apart* from its function in getting the job done. When these conditions remain, routine gives way to *ceremony* or *ritual*. The routine becomes a symbol of something else and begins to carry its own set of meanings.

Why routines, which have a clear value in limiting the disruptiveness of caregiving, should shade into ceremonies that may not do so is an interesting question. One respondent, a son caring for his mother, is worth quoting at length on this issue because his case illustrates how these routines shade into rituals in ways that are not always conscious to caregivers. He speaks of his routines as "shortcuts," or efficiency techniques, that benefit both his mother and himself, the former because such care prevents skin breakdown and additional illness, the latter because the routines allow him to concentrate his energies and complete the task efficiently.

> As time went on, and my mother became more physically deteriorated and less conscious about me and her as far as her dignity was concerned, it became more a matter of fact, or routine, for me to do things: A, B, C, D, or 1, 2, 3, 4, everyday. It's probably more boring because of the routine. You get up an hour and half earlier in the morning, make the breakfast, wash her, change her, diaper her . . . It was just my response of what I had to do. I had to attend to her with tunnel-vision precision. The more I would do, and the more consistently I would stick to my routine, the greater it was not just to my mother's benefit, but to mine too.

While this attitude toward the scheduling of care tasks may not sound like ritual, it is only a small step from such a routine to notions of magical causation and symbolic efficacy. For example, this caregiver goes on to describe a bathing-exercise ritual that he felt made his mother look younger and which rejuvenated her skin.

> I would pull her forward, massage her back; then I would take each arm separately, or both together, and exercise them . . . I would take my jacket off, roll up my sleeves, and I would start to perspire. The sweat would run down my forehead. I would massage her legs with the washcloth, then her feet, and I would go through each individual toe.

It does not seem wrong to describe this last routine as ritual, first because it increased the amount of time required for caregiving and second because the caregiver ascribed great, possibly magical, regenerative power to it. We might also add that he performed it *after* his mother was admitted to a nursing home and when she was already almost completely comatose.

The transformation of routine into ritual is prominent as well in the power caregivers ascribe to "going through the motions" of normalcy in the care of an Alzheimer's patient. Caregivers are counseled to find meaningful activity for the Alzheimer's victim or to surround him with objects (e.g., photographs) that anchor him to his former identity. Some caregivers recognize that such advice is largely wishful thinking for the advanced Alzheimer's patient, but others persist in the routine long after it could plausibly have such an effect. Some caregivers go further and feel that a *pretense* of autonomy for an impaired parent may have this effect. To foster such normalcy, caregivers devise systems for reminding the impaired parent where he or she is and what he or she is supposed to do. This may take the form of notes in large print placed at strategic points in the house. Caregivers may also purposely keep leases or accounts in the parent's name to encourage such autonomy, as the following quotation indicates:

> I had tricks. I always wanted things in Mom's name, to give her control. But I had to coach her on the phone. Later, I used paper plates [for] notes to my Mom, in big black magic-marker letters. It would say, "Stay inside. Do not leave." I'd put them in several places . . . Everybody in my neighborhood knew that my mother was impaired, but for the longest time I wanted to hide it. I coached her. The utilities and lease are in her name. I believe in the theory, "if you don't use it, you lose it." If you teach them and have them go through all the motions, you can keep them going through the lapses. It comes back.

Thus while caregivers clearly understand the benefits of routinizing caregiving tasks as an adaptive strategy, there is a tendency for these routines to take on a life of their own in the form of ceremonies that may rival the caregiving tasks in their disruptiveness.

Even routines that do not take on a ceremonial quality can become a problem. The routines may still gain a life of their own, which again interferes with caregiving. In such cases, the caregiving routine becomes more important than the object of such care, namely the elder whose needs mandate such care. For example, one caregiver actually spoke positively of the gastrectomy her mother had to undergo and the introduction of parenteral feeding for her. "The feeding tube makes care for Mother easy, a real breeze." On the one hand, the gastrectomy did in fact make caregiving easier. This caregiver's experience reminds us that when the impaired parent is *less* incapacitated, caregiving may actually be harder. An impaired parent who can walk may require more observation, emotional support, and cognitive guidance; an impaired parent able to swallow may require more time and effort to ensure proper food intake. On the other hand, in this caregiver's case, a caregiving routine seems to have displaced the goal of securing maximum health and independence for the impaired elder. Is such a caregiving routine adaptive when it distorts the reasons for rendering such care in the first place? We take up this point below.

## Caregiving and the Redefinition of Roles Within the Household

Caregivers render care for parents who are no longer capable of fulfilling the parental role and who may, in fact, appear to be reverting to earlier stages in the life-course; in such instances, the adult children begin to make decisions for them and, in extreme cases, may even diaper an incontinent parent. Consequently, caregivers often speak of their parents as "regressing" to childhood. The situation is further complicated by cognitive impairments, such as Alzheimer's disease, which may lead some parents to address their own children as a parent or spouse. This is especially unsettling to caregivers. Some caregivers to parents with Alzheimer's disease have taken the idea of regression a step further and claim that the final stage of the disease results in a parent assuming the fetal position once again, completing the imputed regression to childhood in an extremely vivid form.

It is not surprising, then, that a second set of adaptive strategies has emerged within caregiver households that revolve around the redefinition of roles within the family. Daily acts of personal care, such as bathing, diapering, grooming, and feeding, seem to be the most charged in this respect, since they force an adult child to assume a relation of parental intimacy with his or her own parent. Exposure to a parent's nudity is perhaps the greatest challenge to cross-sex caregiving, as when a daughter must diaper her father, or a son his mother. In such cases, the spouses of a patient may feel that this parent-child intimacy violates their own spousal intimacy. While daughters who are on very intimate terms with their mothers do not seem to chafe at the confusion of roles implied in such caregiving, other caregivers find that they need to redefine the role of parent and child in such situations.

One response to this home care situation is the *infantilization* of the parent (that is, speaking of the parent as a child) and the associated idea that this stage of life is characterized by "role reversal," in which children become "parents" to their own parents. A second strategy is to reconceive the parent as a *patient* and the caregiver as a nurse or doctor. A third strategy common among our sample of caregivers is simply to reconceive the parent as *someone else*, a stranger, someone who "used to be" Mother or Father.

### Infantilization: The Impaired Parent as a Child

If the parent is no longer a parent but is instead a "child" or "infant," then the threat to prior adult–child relations bound up with caregiving is circumvented. One caregiver's comments will speak for many:

> You know their whole physical make-up. You get real intimate. It's like taking care of a baby. You have to clean them up, dress them, remind them of things they have to do . . . We needed to reassure her, give her compliments. It's like with a child. You reverse roles. She even called me Mom when she first got sick.

This redefinition of roles obviously builds upon strong similarities between care for the impaired, incontinent parent and care for a child. It is notable, however, that caregivers who make such statements are clearly aware of the ways caring for such a parent is *not* like caring for a child. They selectively emphasize certain elements, choosing to ignore, for example, the different contexts for such incontinence and the different outcomes for the dependency of child and impaired parent. This selective emphasis points to the importance of the quality of the relationship between the parent and child in determining the caregiver's recourse to this strategy. Infantilization as an adaptive strategy appears to be linked to issues of control on the one hand, and to the attempt to recapture (or perhaps create for the first time) an intimacy associated with the caregiver's own childhood on the other. Thus many daughters report that they enjoy being with a mother more *after* they become caregivers. Many report a return of an idyllic childhood warmth to their household.

### The Elderly Parent as a Patient

The conversion of a parent to a patient is an alternate strategy in redefining the role of parent and child. While not incompatible with the infantilization of the parent, this strategy emphasizes the *illness* of the parent rather than functional limitations, as the following excerpt shows:

> As time went on and my mother's situation got worse, little by little I adjusted [the bathing routine]. I would have to be there all the time. I was afraid she would drown. My feeling changed. At the very beginning, I still mentally maintained a strong mother–son identity, when it would come to the feeling of dignity. As my mother's physical and mental state deteriorated, my mother almost became a patient, and I became a doctor or nurse . . . I was very much aware of this psychologically. I [now] saw her as a person who had an illness and needed care. That became more so as her situation deteriorated.

By emphasizing the sickness of the parent, the parent is redefined as a patient. In this way, the disruption of parent–child relations is again circumvented as roles are redefined. The use of this adaptive strategy appears to be linked to the caregiver's prior exposure to nursing and medical experience. For example, the caregiver quoted above served as a paramedic in Vietnam and explicitly drew on this experience in thinking about the care for his mother.

### The Impaired Parent as a Stranger

The final adaptive strategy related to redefinition of parent–child roles involves the conversion of the parent into some other, perhaps only distantly known, person. Here caregivers admit that they "pretend" the impaired parent is someone else, "a person," as one caregiver put it, "who I visit a few times a day." They may say they are unsure if their mother or father is still the same person.

One case in our sample is particularly striking as an illustration of this strategy because here household caregivers were able to view a parent as two different people: one who was still the parent and another who was someone else. The impaired mother fluctuated between two conditions, a relatively docile state, "the old Maggie," and a more frightening, irrational state, "the other Maggie." The caregivers even mention the analogy to Dr. Jekyll and Mr. Hyde, though they invert it.

> She turned into Mrs. Jekyll. She wouldn't go to bed. She started to holler and really carry on. We would say she turned into the other Maggie. When she was the old Maggie, she was quiet. When you talked to her, she answered . . . But when she went into the other Maggie, she would get very agitated. Her fingers would go like this. Her eyes would be going back and forth. And she would start talking. It would all be in the past. She would imagine there were people downstairs. She would call out for dead relatives. It would go on all day and into the night. Then she would sleep a day. And then she would be the other Maggie, say, for so many weeks. Then she would change again.

In the one condition, she is the mother; in the other, she is not. Denial that this second "Maggie" is the parent is evident in a distinct name given to her. This division of the mother into two people according to the fluctuations in her condition is an extremely important illustration of the caregiver's ability to view a parent as someone who is both a parent and a stranger to them. In more extreme cases, caregivers are driven to deny that "the person upstairs," as one spoke of her father, really is a parent.

## Conclusion: Adaptation Strategies and Interventions for Caregivers

In this chapter, we have briefly reviewed the ways households reorganize to meet the caregiving needs of an impaired parent. We saw that even before the relocation of parent and caregiver to a common household, households "preadapt" to caregiving demands. Quasi-households emerge as caregivers prepare for the eventual move of the parent. Equally important, adult children who will assume the major caregiving responsibility select themselves to the role. If they do not actually exclude rival sibling caregivers, they give their siblings opportunities for not taking the initiative in caregiving. The pre- or self-selected primary caregiver often feels a need to provide the impaired parent with a family, as well as with the care that only a family can provide.

Given this concern for the parent's well-being, the major problem for caregivers is to set limits in the obligation to render care, for caregiving demands can easily overwhelm a household. Since care *for* a parent quickly comes to be seen as a measure of how much one cares *about* a parent, setting limits is not easy. Even caregivers who have undertaken heroic self-sacrifices for an impaired parent still wonder if they have done enough. For some, only the death of the parent at home offers a guilt-free release from the obligation to render care. Thus drawing a boundary between caregiving tasks and other obligations, wants, and needs becomes an overriding necessity.

Caregiver households erect such boundaries through adaptation strategies. Two such strategies discussed here are the use of routines for caregiving tasks and the redefinition of parent-child roles. Routines for personal and nursing care make caregiving tasks more discrete. The tasks become a distinct part of the day, which can be marked off and considered complete. Other parts of the day are thereby defined as noncaregiving time. Likewise, routines for care establish a division of space within the home. Care demands are performed in a certain place, at a specific time, and in a certain way; these define the tasks as separate from other household and personal activities. Redefinition of roles sets limits to caregiving obligations in another way. The parent is redefined as a child, patient, or stranger. These redefinitions all have the same effect: If the parent is no longer viewed as a parent, one's obligation to render care is attenuated. Redefining the role of the parent also allows caregivers to perform tasks that would normally be seen as inappropriate, such as bathing, diapering, or simply taking control of decisions regarding the parent.

These adaptation strategies evolve within households in an unplanned fashion. They emerge in response to concrete caregiving demands and through a great deal of trial and error. For example, while it is unclear how long it takes a household to establish routines for completing caregiving tasks, our research shows that some households achieve such routinization early on and quickly master caregiving challenges. Other households go through a period of false starts and continual recalibration of tasks and routines until they reach an adequate arrangement. Still other households never seem to reach a level of routinization for care tasks and find themselves in a situation of unending "crisis management." One focus for intervention, then, would be programs to teach caregivers how to establish routines for caregiving tasks. It should be noted that an informal network for sharing ideas on caregiving routines is already in effect by caregiver support groups, which disseminate information on successful management of caregiving tasks. This model should be extended more generally as an adjunct to hospital and adult day care programs.

Based on our research on the routinization of caregiving tasks, an intervention geared to the promotion of such routines should have two goals. First, successful routines for caregiving should be disseminated. Caregivers who have had success with routinization of caregiving tasks should be encouraged to share their experience. One case resulting in the successful dissemination of such a routine is worth mentioning here. One caregiver was at a loss in regard to her mother's continual bouts of severe constipation, which required enemas and suppositories, and made relations with her bedridden mother more difficult. In a Children of Aging Parents (CAPS) support group in Levittown, Pennsylvania, she learned that a daily breakfast involving a mixture of unprocessed bran, applesauce, and prune juice spread on bread was a great help in promoting regularity. The caregiver incorporated this routine into her overall morning caregiving regime. This sort of practical information on ordering caregiving tasks would go a long way toward reducing a caregiver's burden.

The second goal of such an intervention is more difficult. As mentioned above, caregiving routines often take on a ceremonial or ritual sphere, and this ritual component may interfere with the goal of such routinization. Caregiving rituals may make the caregiving tasks more burdensome rather than less, and they may even displace the overall goal of such caregiving. In the latter case, performing the ritualized routine may become more important than actually caring for the impaired parent. The case of the caregiver who welcomed her mother's gastrectomy and parenteral feeding is a case in point. Thus a second goal of such an intervention would be to make caregivers aware of the tendency for such routines to become ritualized. Caregivers may need an outside perspective to tell them when the routine has become an oppressive or inadequate ceremonial. This may be more problematic, as the case material cited above illustrates. If a caregiver feels his routine of washing rejuvenates his mother and he is willing to spend the extra time this ritual requires, should he be dissuaded from doing so? While the goal of the intervention is to make caregiving easier, we must be careful not to upset stronger, more profound beliefs that allow caregivers to take on so fundamental a commitment.

The role redefinition strategy could also be taught to caregivers, perhaps in a similar support group environment. While this recasting of roles seems to come naturally to caregivers, at the very least caregivers could be counseled not to feel guilty about their inability to see the demented parent as a parent. More radically, caregivers could be encouraged to regard the impaired parent more as a patient than a child or stranger. This redefinition may be most appropriate in later stages of impairment, since it avoids the enmeshment characteristic of parentchild role reversal and the guilt associated with viewing the parent as a stranger.

## Acknowledgment

The research reported here was supported by an NIMH program project grant (MH43371) to the Philadelphia Geriatric Center, "Family caregiving and the dependent elderly," M. Powell Lawton, E. Brody, and R. Pruchno, principal investigators. I thank Elaine Brody and Robert Rubinstein for allowing me to use transcript materials from earlier pilot interviews with caregivers, and Jay Gubrium and Andrea Sankar for comments on an earlier draft of the paper.

## References

Albert, S. M. (1990). Caregiving as a cultural system: Conceptions of filial obligations and parental dependency in urban America. *American Anthropologist*, 92(2).

Brody, E. (1985). Parent care as a normative family stress. *The Gerontologist*, 25(1), 19–29.

Doty, P. (1986). Family care of the elderly: The role of public policy. *The Milbank Memorial Quarterly*, 64(1), 34–75.

Ikels, C. (1983). The process of caregiver selection. *Research on Aging*, 5, 491–509.

Pelto, G., and Pelto, P. (1984). Anthropological methodologies for assessing household organization and structure. In D. E. Sahn, R. Lockwood, and N. S. Scrimshaw (eds.) *Methods for the evaluation of the impact of food and nutrition programs* (pp. 204–25). Tokyo: The United Nations University.

Simmons, R. G., Klein, S. D., and Thorton, K. (1973). Family decision-making and the selection of a kidney transplant donor. *Journal of Comparative Family Studies*, 4, 88–115.

# 26 The Unencumbered Child: Family Reputations and Responsibilities in the Care of Relatives with Alzheimer's Disease

## Judith Globerman

Many family caregiving issues related to caring for a relative with Alzheimer's disease have been explored in depth (Boss, Caron, Horbal, and Mortimer, 1990; Chenoweth & Spencer, 1986; Semple, 1992; Skaff and Pearlin, 1992; Zarit, Todd, and Zarit, 1986). Alzheimer's disease research has tended to examine family patterns, experiences, and interventions for families by studying one family member, the primary caregiver (Horowitz, Silverstone, and Reinhardt, 1991; Quayhagen and Quayhagen, 1989). Researchers have begun to explore why some members choose to do caregiving, are designated as caregivers, or end up caregiving for relatives in need. Dwyer, Henretta, Coward, and Barton's (1992) longitudinal study of adult children's participation in care of their impaired elderly parents found that siblings' caregiving roles shift. Substantial numbers of adult children became caregivers over time, while other siblings relinquished involvement. Gender, proximity, employment, and marital status of adult children, as well as gender and marital status of the impaired parent, affected involvement over time. Although a complicated process of negotiation was suggested by Dwyer et al.'s findings, we still know little about the way caregiving decisions are made in families.

Gubrium's (1988) exploratory study of family caregivers found that past patterns, habits, and expectations influenced decision making and the apportioning of caring responsibilities in families. Gubrium found that kinship priority was not static or automatic. He found that family members' competing responsibilities and allegiances influenced their decisions. Finch and Mason's (1993) data also strongly support the fluidity of patterns of caring. They found that notions of obligation and responsibility do not structure family patterns but, instead, that "responsibilities build up incrementally over time through quite complex processes in exchange relationships" (p. 79).

In research on families with relatives with Alzheimer's disease, it has been noted that caregivers have numerous competing responsibilities, obligations, allegiances, and roles. Gubrium's (1988) findings beg the question of who does what and why, when all are stretched in multiple ways, and he began to explore this by identifying

Original publication: Globerman, Judith, "The Unencumbered Child: Family Reputations and Responsibilities in the Care of Relatives with Alzheimer's Disease," *Family Process* 34 (1995), pp. 87–99.

different "family types." Matthews and Rosner (1988) also began to address this question in their research on pairs of sisters. Identifying five participation styles and several factors that affected which style one adopted, they raise the issue of historical family relationships and personality types.

Finch and Mason (1993) examined this question exploring notions of filial obligation and moral codes of responsibility, and the concomitant apportioning of care. They found that norms and rules do seem to operate as guidelines, and that obligations have limits. They also found that roles vary according to competing commitments that then have to be negotiated. Finch and Mason's research moves us closer to an understanding of family decision making. The way in which negotiations are shaped in family life sheds new light on family members' commitments.

Bedford's (1992) research highlights the importance and significance of the relationship between early parent-child ties and later life relationships. Finch and Mason (1993) also explore how family history influences family members' negotiations over care, and they found that these negotiations are influenced by family reputations.

In an exploratory, long-interview study of relatives with Alzheimer's disease (AD), Globerman (1994) found that family members described returning to the family of origin carrying the reputations they had as children: they took responsibility for caregiving according to their self-perceptions and in the ways their kin expected of them, based on what they were like in the family of origin. Three subgroups of family members were identified in the preliminary study: (1) primary caregivers; (2) other somewhat or very involved relatives who were not designated as primary caregivers; and (3) unencumbered relatives who were marginally involved or uninvolved in caregiving.

These findings raised important questions regarding family decision-making processes, family negotiations, family organization, and the ways families apportion care, areas that had not been studied previously. This led to the development of qualitative, in-depth interviews to explore relationships, roles, and decision making in families with multiple kin (primary caregivers, involved but not primary caregiving relatives, and unencumbered family members).

## Methods

A qualitative long-interview method (McCracken, 1988) was first used to explore family patterns, decision making, and the apportioning of care. Knowing little about unencumbered and uninvolved adult children, an exploratory methodology was most appropriate. The research goal was to examine how families decide who does what, and why do they make these decisions. Based on the previous, preliminary finding (Globerman, 1994) that one child appears to be exempt, unencumbered, and even entitled to some different stance, participants would be asked to describe and reflect on their roles and those of their siblings in their families of origin.

### Sample

To control for cultural influence on family involvement, decisions, roles, and negotiations around care, a multiservice site for the Jewish elderly was selected to allow for an ethnically homogeneous sample. A nonprobability sample included all available kin of individuals with senile dementia of the Alzheimer's type, diagnosed within the last year at the geriatric psychiatry clinic. Sixty families were mailed letters indicating that we were interested in interviewing multiple members of families who had relatives with AD, both those members involved in caregiving and those not involved. Thirty-eight families (97 individuals) participated in interviews. This article reports on the qualitative interview data from 18 families, 54 individuals (3 spouses of persons with AD, 36 adult children and 11 of their spouses, and 4 grandchildren). Data analysis was terminated when categories were saturated and no new themes and patterns related to unencumbered children emerged. Our method of theoretical sampling for analysis is consistent with the grounded theory methodology (Strauss and Corbin, 1991). Interviewees were individuals who considered themselves primary caregivers, others who had some caregiving responsibilities, and uninvolved family members.

### Procedure

The interview guide, with open-ended questions about the respondents' experience, the involvement of others, the impact of AD on their lives, and family patterns, was developed on the basis of findings from the preliminary study (Globerman, 1994). Family members were interviewed individually in a location of their choice, usually their own homes. Interviews ranged from 1½ to 3 hours and were audiotaped and transcribed. Five social workers trained in qualitative interviewing conducted the interviews.

### Data analysis

Data were analyzed according to McCracken's Long-Interview method (1988). The transcripts of different family members describing the same events were examined to "gain access to the cultural categories and assumptions" the participants used to describe their experiences (McCracken, 1988, p. 17). McCracken's data analysis method uses an editing approach to text analysis whereby the researcher explicitly and systematically reduces and reassembles the data (Crabtree and Miller, 1991). The McCracken method of analysis has five stages (pp. 44–6). Stage one begins with an examination of printed transcripts for "utterances" that are treated independently of each other and constitute observations. In stage two, these observations are examined independently as the researcher attempts to determine their meanings, according to the literature, the researcher's cultural review (the systematic process of unearthing the researcher's knowledge, values, and assumptions about the respondents), and other evidence in the transcript. The third stage examines observations in relation to each other, looking for themes, patterns, and interconnections. This stage of analysis takes the observations and begins to link them to each other and to what is known in the literature. The fourth stage continues to look for themes and patterns of "intertheme consistency and contradiction" (McCracken, 1988, p. 42). Stage five compares themes between interviews, within kin-groups and across kin-groups.

Two interviewers and I (as Principal Investigator) independently examined the transcripts, discussed the emergent themes, and developed codes. The codes were then independently applied to five clean, unmarked interview transcripts in order to check interrater reliability. Only codes and accompanying thick description that yielded 100 percent agreement between the three raters were used. This method of establishing "confirmability" involved the three raters in careful examination of the transcripts to determine the "trustworthiness" of the category codes (Lincoln and Guba, 1985). When we were satisfied that the codes were both valid and reliable through full agreement between raters, the data were then managed using the qualitative software computer program "Ethnograph" (Seidel and Clark, 1984). Quotations supporting the category codes were organized using Ethnograph and again subjected to review for content validity by the three raters.

## Results

Respondents described their caregiving roles in terms of the jobs people did for their relatives, and the extent of involvement of different family members. Sometimes members of the same family shared caregiving, sometimes they competed. However, in many families, members described one sibling, a son or daughter, as separate and unencumbered with caregiving responsibilities. This separate adult child also identified this difference. These adult children were not identifiable by gender or birth order. We called them "the unencumbered" children. Although not a representative, random sample, there were nine daughters and nine sons who were "unencumbered" in the 18 families. Similarly, they were evenly distributed by birth order, and in families without daughters or without sons. Five broad patterns relating to the unencumbered children emerged in all 18 families: 1) their characterization; 2) their focus compared to that of their siblings; 3) the different nature of their suffering; 4) their sense of responsibility; and 5) their protection and entitlement.

### Characterization

The exempt or unencumbered children were characterized by themselves and their relatives with descriptions such as "absent-minded," "not all that dependable," "a loose cannon, very emotional," "selfish," "spoiled," "high-strung," and/or "pampered." The common characteristic was that these children stood out, were described differently, or somehow identified separately in some way by relatives. In one family the unencumbered daughter was the "family brain." She described herself and her sister:

> I was the bright one and she was the dumb one. That was the way we were seen by our parents, and we saw ourselves as different from each other.

Her sister's description was similar and served as an explanation for why the unencumbered one was exempt from caregiving responsibilities:

> My sister was always classified to be the intellectual. I was classified to be the business person.

In one family, the unencumbered child was the "black sheep" who was exempt because of his difference:

> I was the trouble maker and my brother the goody-goody . . . I always needed more caring.

The above descriptions were used by families to explain why a particular member was unencumbered with caregiving responsibilities. These characterizations were also described as longstanding:

> Even growing up, I could see her getting out of things around the house, like in household things.

The unencumbered child also identified his or her distinction in the family and the history of this pattern:

> I was the kind of kid who would let something go . . . and eventually mom would [look after it].

The sister of the "intellectual" describes the history of the pattern in her family:

> It was always like that, always like that. Even as teenagers. I remember my mother had given me chores or something, and my sister always liked to read. I tend to do more of the hands-on things, whereas my sister tends to do a lot of reading and things like that.

The uninvolved adult children, although sometimes described by their siblings as unstable, did not describe themselves as unwell or as suffering from psychopathology. They described and presented themselves in interviews as very successful and competent parents, business people, and professionals, but they were characterized as incompetent by themselves and by siblings in relation to caregiving responsibilities in the family of origin. A high school teacher was described by a sibling as "not dealing from a full deck," and by another sibling: "We wouldn't leave that to her because she's not a detail person and could never handle it." A very successful businessman, who was the unencumbered child, was described by his siblings as "highstrung" and, although competent in business, not competent in caregiving:

> He's phenomenal in business, but dealing with those kinds of things [Alzheimer's disease and caregiving demands], it's very traumatic for him, and therefore he shies away.

These unencumbered children stood out in the family and also saw themselves this way. A daughter described her siblings' feelings about her: "Nobody trusts me and people are scared of me or feeling I'm a weirdo . . . I was a flaky kid, and I'm a flaky adult." An unencumbered daughter described herself:

> I'm ten years older than one sister and seven years older than the other, but in reality of life, I'm the youngest of the three because my life has been a little more sheltered, pampered, more taken care of . . . I may be the eldest of my two sisters, but in essence they are stronger than I am.

In this study, the families emphasized not only a clear descriptive characterization of the unencumbered individual, but also a complex characterization that included the way these individuals and their families viewed the world, took responsibility, and suffered. Unencumbered children as well as their relatives all identified the differences between those who were uninvolved and those who were involved in caregiving.

*Focus*

The focus of all the unencumbered children's descriptions of their experiences with an AD relative and with their families differed from other family members. Both caregivers and noncaregiving but involved relatives focused on the burdens of caregiving, their developmental tasks, their responsibilities, and the need to balance activities. They spoke about the burden:

> I really don't know where I get all the time, or where I get the ability to handle it; and now I'm feeling the stress and the strain of it all.

About the suspension of their own lives:

> There used to be social activities . . . I used to be more involved. I was tied up that way [when kids were smaller], but I still went out; but now I have my father and my kids, and my family, and the business.

About their sense of responsibility:

> There's only so much you can do. So, I try to be as supportive as I can of everybody and everything. And there are moments when I break down a little bit, but I'm generally able to come up and say, "Well, I have to do this; this has to be done."

And about the difficulties of balancing their lives:

> I'm working full-time now. I have my own family to take care of, a house to take care of, and all of a sudden you have these doctors' appointments. It's hard to get time off work. I have my own personal doctors' appointments, and sometimes for my children. I kind of have to weigh which ones are important to go to.

Unlike these other children, the unencumbered children did not speak about their experiences of burden or their responsibilities. Their focus tended to be more self-centered: they appeared to process their worlds in terms of themselves. They spoke of personal losses, often with a sense of unreality. This took several forms: a focus on the effect of their relative's Alzheimer's disease on the loss of their own identity; a focus on the loss of a special relationship with the AD relative; and unrealistic notions about the disease. In terms of loss of their own identity, they focused on the relationship with their parents and the need for acknowledgment, even though this was often quite unrealistic. This feature was not evident in transcripts of the other children. An unencumbered daughter described her pain and her need for recognition from her parents:

I'm peeling an orange for my daughter, so I peel one for mom and dad . . . I didn't get a thank you, and I wouldn't expect it from mom because [she's] like a child . . . Then my sister and I talked about it and she said, "Well, when did dad say thank you about anything." So those are the gaps I have. I'd like to see dad saying "Yah, you're okay."

A second aspect of this focus on self related to their focus on the loss of a special relationship with the AD relative – again, a focus that did not emerge in the transcripts of the other children. An unencumbered daughter spoke at length about her feelings of loss:

I spent so much time crying. I wept thinking that this could happen to this wonderful mother of mine, and I could not accept it, whereas my sisters always said, "This is her illness and this is what Alzheimer's does to a person." And they were realistic and I'm not realistic. . . . They would say, "Well, one day ma has to die," and I said, "I don't want to talk about it, and I don't want to hear you ever say that." It's something I couldn't accept within myself. If there would ever come a day when I wouldn't be able to hug her and kiss her and tell her how much I loved her . . .

Whereas the other relatives focused on the horrible effects of the disease on their relative, the unencumbered child focused on the effects on themselves and the loss of a special, beautiful, perhaps unresolved relationship with their AD relative. According to the other relatives, the relationships that were mourned were not beautiful and close-knit. What the others saw was that the unencumbered child had constructed a fantasy about the relationship or had always been unrealistic about the relationship with the AD relative. An unencumbered adult daughter described her view of the world:

My husband often says, "You live in a world of rose-colored glasses," and I say, "What's wrong with that? It's a beautiful world." . . . I'm a positive thinker. To me the world is bright and people are beautiful. I love life. I love what I do . . . I'm a cheer-up lady and a ray of sunshine.

Her sister described her in a similar fashion:

When she speaks of her family, she tells everyone that it's the most marvellous, close-knit family that ever was. We're a normal family, where each one of us has a different nature. But she sees things through rose-colored glasses, the way she wants to see them – wonderful for her. I'm a bit more realistic.

A third focus related to the unrealistic quality of the unencumbered child's view of the disease. They looked for a magic pill, did not want to use the words "Alzheimer's disease," did not want to focus on the future, or face the disease. An unencumbered daughter in her mid-forties spoke about how her mother's dementia was a normal aging process and how she herself was also experiencing forgetfulness. A sister of an unencumbered adult daughter described her unencumbered sister's experience of mother's disease:

If she called me, she was usually in tears – "I went to the home today and ma was like this and ma was like that. Oh, today she was dancing, today she was singing." I said,

"Gee, you are very lucky, when I'm there, she's not dancing with me." She would always make it like she's better. She wouldn't accept the fact of how ill my mother was. Good for her that she could see her like that. I couldn't. I saw my mother . . . I could see what was happening.

Other relatives worried about their unencumbered sibling's ability to cope because of this lack of reality testing: "She's very emotional, and I hope she'll be able to cope with my parents, going down, because that's where they are going."

Whereas other relatives were sometimes fatalistic about the future and disease, the unencumbered child avoided it:

I've buried myself in a lot of external activities for a long time and I'm very busy right now, but I've also had other times when I've been busy. I think the busy-ness has increased in time. To what extent that the relationship between how busy I am and trying to block or run away from my parents' situation and my husband's situation, there is probably a connectedness there.

In contrast, caregiving children were realistic about the future:

I would imagine as the disease onsets more so, and if she gets to a worse condition, it will be harder to deal with, both frustration, impatience, embarrassment. And then again, what do you do? . . . If I'm honest with myself, I don't really want her living with me.

The unencumbered child's avoidance appeared unrelated to caregiving in the future. Their avoidance encompassed an avoidance of awareness of what care was needed, a lack of interest, a fear, an avoidance of the disease, or an avoidance of education and information. An unencumbered daughter described herself:

It didn't have a major effect on me, or I blocked it out at the beginning. Now that it's getting worse, I block it out as well, very much. I don't see much of my parents, which is a form of protection for myself. I get irritated. I get frustrated. I don't know much about it . . . I've always blocked, so it's nothing. This is just something more that I block . . . I'm not looking to the future at all. My sister keeps on telling me to look into the future because this is what's going to happen, but it hasn't had an effect on me as of yet . . . I have a superficial understanding because I don't want to understand.

Unencumbered children participated less in support and educational groups, as exemplified by one unencumbered daughter:

I did not attend meetings because I have no patience for meetings, and I didn't think meetings would do anything for me. I did what my heart dictated me to do, and I didn't want to go to any meetings.

A focus that centered on one's own pain and one's self identified the difference between the unencumbered child and other children. Denial, lack of acceptance, fear, avoidance, and having unrealistic ideations were common in the unencumbered children, and can be explained in various ways. These reactions, at different stages, are considered functional and healthy by some analysts of human behavior, and dysfunctional by others (Friedman, 1991; Keizer and Feins, 1991; Lawrence, 1992). What is distinct is that the data identify a recurrent theme in families of how family legacies play an important part in negotiations and apportioning of care and responsibilities.

### Nature of suffering

Although not involved, or only minimally involved in caregiving tasks, the unencumbered children were very wrapped up and involved in the disease in their own ways. All of the unencumbered children did express suffering, even though they did not experience burden in the same way as their relatives. However, it is likely that their suffering would not show up in an assessment of burden or depression. It was not about role strain, role conflict, difficulties in negotiating with others, exhaustion, and pulls that the others experience. Involved children described their suffering:

> That's the frustration. We can't do anything. It could be very long-lasting. If you get a disease that is terminal, you cry. You know it's going to end at a point in time and it's over. She could live for another fifteen years, and this gets progressively worse, and I probably will get progressively more impatient.

The unencumbered children's suffering focused on an internal tearing-apart. It seemed to include a panic about self-identity. An unencumbered daughter talked about her fear of relating to her sister after her mother's death because of the similarities between them:

> I will either fall totally apart and that will be it, or I will be strong in front of them and behind the scenes will fall apart. So, if behind the scenes you fall apart, I most probably will have a hard time relating to my sister who is so much like my mother; that would be painful for me.

An unencumbered daughter described her experience of dealing with her mother's Alzheimer disease in terms of her own losses:

> I guess that I arrived at the feeling that she did the best she could, and she didn't set out to hurt me. And I just feel again, the sense of, gee, I wish it had been different. I wish that I had felt a lot more warmth and caring. There was caring, but not in a way that someone as sensitive as me would feel it . . . I remember once asking a doctor, "Is it normal to feel such love for *my* daughter?" I just felt like it was almost a surge of love. He said, "It is, yes it is," and it was almost like I felt he was saying, "You poor kid, you should have to ask a question like that?"

This focus on the self and the sense of loss of one's identity with the loss of the relative with Alzheimer's disease, sets the unencumbered children apart from others in the family. In keeping with this, their sense of responsibility differed from that of their relatives.

### Different sense of responsibility

The involved siblings apportioned care and divided responsibilities in accordance with how they viewed themselves and were viewed by others in the family of origin.

Although others sometimes shared responsibility for caregiving, took on different kinds of jobs, negotiated different responsibilities, and had variable amounts of responsibility, they took ownership and responsibility for the way things were and how they were or were not changing. They attributed problems in apportioning care to real events, to the disease, and to family issues, and described setting limits, feeling guilty, and making decisions and choices.

In contrast, all of the unencumbered children had different notions of responsibility. They did not talk about it in the same way. They saw involvement as others' responsibility. An unencumbered child spoke about being sheltered and not managing money:

> My sisters have power of attorney . . . That was all right with me because I didn't want to know anything about it. Here we go again – away from reality . . . I don't want to know about it, and I don't say that's smart or intelligent, but that's the way it is . . . My sisters can do everything. They are independent. They can do everything on their own and I need my husband . . . That's what I mean by sheltered and protected and looked after.

A caregiving daughter-in-law spoke of the unencumbered daughter's sense of responsibility:

> She likes to do what she wants to do, and I think it was almost a relief for her when it was decided that her mother would come here, because it wasn't going to be in her hair . . . She doesn't work outside the home, hasn't ever, is a bit pampered . . . She's accustomed to doing what she wants, whenever she wants . . . and she doesn't want anything to interfere with her lifestyle . . . She doesn't put herself out.

A son spoke of his unencumbered brother's sense of responsibility and the difference in their involvement:

> My brother is more selfish than I am. His problems are of utmost importance to him, and everybody else's problems and all other problems are secondary . . . That's the way he views life, and maybe that's important and he needs that. I am more aware of all the problems and how they will ultimately impact on me, and maybe I'm more defensive about it and therefore I get more involved.

Responsibility meant something very different for caregiving children and their involved siblings than it did for the unencumbered child. These data point to the pattern whereby unencumbered children did not believe they had responsibility or should take responsibility for caring for their relative. They saw themselves as justifiably unencumbered, and they felt confused when confronted with messages from their siblings suggesting that they should do more.

### Protection and entitlement

The caregiving children and noncaregiving involved others struggled with apportioning care. They returned to family-of-origin reputations and, because of the crisis nature of the disease, they found it difficult to negotiate new ways of being with their relatives. They evaluated and criticized each other for what they each did, and monitored each other's responsibilities. What was interesting in this process is that there was a tendency to excuse or protect the unencumbered children more than the others. Even though they evaluated both other relatives' and the unencumbered child's jobs, obligations, and responsibilities, at the same time they exempted or excused the unencumbered one from caregiving responsibilities. A brother entitled his unencumbered sister to be excused from responsibility:

> It might be a little different if she had a husband. She goes around in her social activities, so her activities take care of her . . . There's only so much time in the day, and you've got to attend to your own personal things as well.

His other sister was not excused from caring for their parent even though she had her own family to look after. Her family members were not seen as competing obligations, but as people to help her out: "My older sister has a husband. She has her family, and certain of those people look after certain things."

Although family obligations are strong in Jewish families (Goldscheider, 1986; Silberman, 1985), in the themes and patterns that emerged in this study, the obligations of Jewish women for family caregiving were not consistent. According to Jewish cultural patterns, one would expect to see few unencumbered daughters, and family caregiving should emerge as a priority over personal life tasks. In this nonrepresentative sample, birth order and gender were not explanations for unencumbered status or protection from responsibility. The first-born male child was as frequently unencumbered as the first-born female child. Unencumbered children were almost all married, except for one divorced daughter, one divorced and one single son. There were no patterns evident in these data to suggest that the unencumbered children were those who were at any particular life-cycle stage; unencumbered children were excused because they were married as readily as they were excused because they were single.

Matthews and Rosner (1988) identified a pattern of participation – "dissociation" – that is similar to that found in unencumbered children. However, the unencumbered children in our study were often involved as backups or in circumscribed ways. Matthews and Rosner's finding of a gender difference in this category is interesting. They found that when a sister dissociates, the others provided "an elaborate explanation for her nonparticipation" (p. 190), whereas they excused the brothers without explanation. In our data, descriptions of *both* brothers and sisters who were the unencumbered children were accompanied by explanations that served to protect, pardon, and exempt these children from the burden of responsibility. Although our sample was not representative, our finding of no gender differences is not inconsistent with Miller and Cafasso's (1992) meta-analysis of studies on gender differences in caregiving, which found very small differences in the assignments of *meanings* to caregiving behaviors. Finley, Roberts, and Banahan (1988) also found no gender differences in filial *attitudes* in their research on adult children of aging parents. Our exploratory findings suggest additional complexity to the ways male and female adult children experience caregiving. Brothers as well as sisters in our research were unencumbered with caregiving responsibilities and excused. A sister was excused because she was perceived as incapable:

She'd never be able to do it, even though she's a high school teacher. She couldn't do this kind of thing, the organizing. So that's okay. It's okay because she's incapable of doing it and doesn't want to do it.

Another sister was excused because of "emotional problems":

My sister has some emotional problems, and so we have to sort of overlook that. She's had her problems over the years, and, you know, she does what she can . . . My sister is not emotionally equipped to deal with the situation.

An unencumbered brother was excused because his marriage was in difficulty: ". . . a trying time now at home. I don't know if there's going to be a divorce or not, so things aren't quite steady there for him." A sister described "excusing" her unencumbered sister:

She always had something that she was busy doing which was more important. I resigned myself, don't ask her because she's just going to give you the same reply all the time. You can't depend on her for relief, don't count on her . . . She just needs to be in control. She's very charming. She needs to be told how wonderful she is. She just needs all these things, so I just felt there's no point in fighting . . . This is the way she is. She's not going to change. She has to go out. She has to do her dance things. That was good for her . . . She's not capable, and I just accepted that.

When her husband objected, she responded, "What is there to say? This is the way she is. I don't expect her to do anything."

## Discussion

These exploratory findings suggest that decisions about apportioning care are related to family legacies and not exclusively related to caregiving demands, proximity, or gender. This research was based on a purposive, convenience sample taken from a multiservice site for Jewish elderly; the objective was not to generalize to the population, but to explore and understand a pattern that emerged in these families. These data, illuminating the "unencumbered child," further reflect the movement of relatives back to the family of origin and the role of family history in the apportioning of care (Globerman, 1994).

Why do the families protect, reinforce, allow, or entitle a family member to opt out or be unencumbered? The answers likely lie in our understanding of theories of family life. Finch and Mason's (1993) symbolic interactionist work suggests that individuals are not role-playing automatons but, rather, actively construct themselves within their families, taking on "roles" and shedding "roles" through negotiation. Their analysis stimulates questions about why individuals' reputations, which "are both a product of past negotiations with kin and a component of future negotiations" (p. 149), exist as they do, and are so powerful for some and less constricting for others.

The work of Boss (1991) and Boss et al. (1990) on boundary ambiguity and ambiguous loss is also built on the symbolic interactionist tradition. Their finding that families construct their family life so as to tolerate the ambiguity of a present-but-psychologically-absent member fits with the experience of the family members in our study. That unencumbered children suffer the loss of the psychologically absent AD relative differently than the other children may represent a different perception and experience of boundary ambiguity. The unencumbered may be less able to move toward closure, may be experiencing more denial, or may be less able to develop a tolerance for the ambiguity than the other children who are, day to day, interacting with and seeing the AD relative.

The unencumbered's suffering, which appears in these data to reflect a self-focus and a sense of loss of self, may be explained in a number of ways (Baker and Baker, 1987; Bowlby, 1980; Donley, 1993). That these patterns from family legacies haunt adults – patterns they feel distant from in their outside-the-family-of-origin lives – suggests the need for theoretical examinations of family life. Understanding how family reputations develop, are maintained, and returned to, in terms of current family theory, can inform relevant family practice.

Models of intervention with families with relatives with Alzheimer's disease have tended to take a systems perspective, which begins with and focuses primarily on the identified primary caregiver, encouraging families to talk together and negotiate different responsibilities (Knight, Lutzky, and Macofsky-Urban, 1993). However, if one recognizes the differentiation of the self, as demonstrated by the unencumbered child, one may see that "the basic problem in families may not be to maintain relationships but to maintain the self that permits nondisintegrative relationships" (Friedman, 1991, p. 156; original emphasis omitted). Thus, family support groups – a common treatment model for families coping with AD – that focus on helping caregivers to ask for needed help from relatives, and teaching them how to set limits, may be unsuccessful due to the deep-rooted patterns the family has developed over time. Interventions that focus on differentiation of individuals in families – "where they end and others in their life begin" – may be more appropriate (Friedman, 1991, p. 156) than those that focus on equilibrium. These findings also emphasize the importance of exploring family interventions that include uninvolved members as well as involved relatives.

These exploratory findings suggest several researchable hypotheses related to family life with a relative with Alzheimer's disease. In relation to the family's distribution of responsibilities, one hypothesis the data suggest is that family legacy influences who is the primary caregiver, and could help explain why gender, proximity, employment, and marital status are key variables. In keeping with this, it would be important to examine the ways in which family legacy explains why one child is called upon, chooses, is chosen, or ends up as the designated primary caregiver or the unencumbered child, while others of the same gender, proximity, birth order, or employment status are not in these positions. Future research examining family history and patterns may be predictive of future caregiving involvement of the family and would be most helpful in planning effective intervention programs and policies. The study findings also suggest the need for research on interventions, particularly, whether selected interventions based on a family's legacy are more successful than those that group together families with AD relatives. Practice-based research comparing the effectiveness of different theoretically based interventions for individuals with similar and different family patterns is also critical to effective practice.

The nature of the Alzheimer's disease crisis and the inability of family members to negotiate with each other, the unpredictability of the disease, the assault on mental functioning, and the hereditary aspects all contribute to the emergence of family-of-origin patterns. The wealth of theory and research on family functioning has not been applied to this population; research on families with AD relatives has neglected to examine families – particularly the uninvolved, "unencumbered" children. These data suggest that we should view family caregiving for relatives with Alzheimer's disease as a complex process that demands complex analysis and theoretically based approaches.

## Acknowledgments

I gratefully acknowledge Health and Welfare Canada for its continuing support of this research through a National Health Research and Development Program grant. I also thank D. McPhee, S. Urman, L. Gallagher, D. Levine, W. Gage, and the reviewers for their helpful comments.

## References

Baker, H. S., and Baker, M. N. (1987). Heinz Kohut's self psychology: An overview. *American Journal of Psychiatry* 144: 1–9.

Bedford, V. H. (1992). Memories of parental favoritism and the quality of parent–child ties in adulthood. *Journal of Gerontology: Social Sciences* 47(4S): 149–55.

Boss, P. (1991). Ambiguous loss (pp. 164–75). In F. Walsh and M. McGoldrick (eds.), *Living beyond loss: Death in the family*. New York: W. W. Norton.

Boss, P., Caron, W., Horbal, J., and Mortimer, T. 1990. Predictors of depression in caregivers of dementia patients: Boundary ambiguity and mastery. *Family Process* 29: 245–54.

Bowlby, J. (1980). *Attachment and Loss. Vol. III: Loss: Sadness and depression*. New York: Basic Books.

Chenoweth, B., and Spencer, B. (1986). Dementia: The experience of family caregivers. *The Gerontologist* 26: 267–72.

Crabtree, B. F., and Miller, W. L. (1991). A qualitative approach to primary care research: The long interview. *Family Medicine* 23: 145–51.

Donley, M. G. (1993). Attachment and the emotional unit. *Family Process* 32: 3–20.

Dwyer, J. W., Henretta, J. C., Coward, R. T., and Barton, A. J. (1992). Changes in the helping behaviors of adult children as caregivers. *Research on Aging* 14: 351–75.

Finch, J., and Mason, J. (1993). *Negotiating family responsibilities*. London: Tavistock/Routledge.

Finley, N. J., Roberts, D. M., and Banahan, B. (1988). Motivators and inhibitors of attitudes of filial obligation toward aging parents. *The Geronotologist* 28: 73–8.

Friedman, E. H. (1991). Bowen theory and therapy (pp. 134–70). In A. S. Gurman and D. P. Kniskern (eds.), *Handbook of family therapy (Vol. II)*. New York: Brunner/Mazel.

Globerman, J. G. (1994). Balancing tensions in families with Alzheimer's disease: The self and the family. *Journal of Aging Studies* 8: 211–32.

Goldscheider, C. (1986). *Jewish continuity and change*. Bloomington: Indiana University Press.

Gubrium, J. F. (1988). Family responsibility and caregiving in the qualitative analysis of the Alzheimer's disease experience. *Journal of Marriage and the Family* 50: 197–207.

Horowitz, A., Silverstone, B. M., and Reinhardt, J. P. (1991). A conceptual and empirical exploration of personal autonomy issues within family caregiving relationships. *The Gerontologist* 31: 23–31.

Keizer, J., and Feins, L. C. (1991). Intervention strategies to use in counseling families of demented patients. *Journal of Gerontological Social Work* 17 (1/2): 201–16.

Knight, B. G., Lutzky, S. M., and Macofsky-Urban, F. (1993). A meta-analytic review of interventions for caregiver distress: Recommendations for future research. *The Gerontologist* 33: 240–8.

Lawrence, L. (1992). Till death do us part: The application of object relations theory to facilitate mourning in a young widows' group. *Social Work in Health Care* 16(3): 67–81.

Lincoln, S., and Guba, E. G. (1985). *Naturalistic enquiry*. Beverley Hills CA: Sage Publications.

Matthews, S. H., and Rosner, T. T. (1988). Shared filial responsibility: The family as the primary caregiver. *Journal of Marriage and the Family* 50: 185–95.

McCracken, G. (1988). *The long interview*. Newbury Park, CA: Sage Publications.

Miller, B., and Cafasso, L. (1992). Gender differences in caregiving: Fact or artifact? *The Gerontologist* 32: 498–507.

Quayhagen, M. P., and Quayhagen, M. (1989). Differential effects of family-based strategies on Alzheimer's disease. *The Gerontologist* 29: 150–5.

Seidel, J. V., and Clark, J. A. (1984). The Ethnograph: A computer program for the analysis of qualitative data. *Qualitative Sociology* 7 (1/2): 110–25.

Semple, S. J. (1992). Conflict in Alzheimer's caregiving families: Its dimensions and consequences. *The Gerontologist* 32: 648–55.

Silberman, C. (1985). *A certain people: American Jews and their lives today*. New York: Summit Books.

Skaff, M. M., and Pearlin, L. I. (1992). Caregiving: Role engulfment and the loss of self. *The Gerontologist* 32: 656–64.

Strauss, A., and Corbin, J. (1991). *Basics of qualitative research*. Newbury Park, CA: Sage Publications.

Zarit, S., Todd, P., and Zarit, J. (1986). Subjective burden of husbands and wives as caregivers: A longitudinal study. *The Gerontologist* 26: 260–6.

# 27 Nursing Homes as Trouble

## Timothy Diamond

This chapter concerns certain contradictions between the organizational principles of nursing homes and the health and well-being of residents within them. I have encountered these principles in the course of a participant observation project during which I trained as a nursing assistant and worked in two nursing homes in a large metropolitan area.

The principles that I discuss fall under one general theme: the dominance of a medical model in the organization of nursing homes. I have found, as others have discussed (e.g., Bowker 1982; Estes and Harrington 1981; Gubrium 1978), that presuppositions of sickness and medical management are built into the everyday life of nursing homes in ways that can be counterproductive to residents' health. I take up this theme of medical dominance by illustrating four contemporary components of it that had significant influence on my work experiences. These are the increasing formalization of nursing assistant work within a medical hierarchy, the predominance of medical tasks over other facets of this work, the development of inspection systems based on the records of these tasks, and the overarching assumptions of illness, particularly mental illness, that pervade nursing home culture. Each of these components constitutes a section of the chapter. In the conclusion, I speculate about how each one of these reinforces the others as part of the emerging organizational structure of nursing homes and how they influence everyday life in ways that are very different for residents, staff, and administrators. In the process, they create a climate of trouble for some.

This research has been guided by the sociology of mental illness literature, especially Foucault (1965), Goffman (1961), Rosenhan (1973), Scheff (1975), Smith (1978), and Szasz (1961). Because the vast majority of nursing home residents are diagnosed as having some form of mental impairment (Butler 1982; Moss and Halamandaris 1977), this literature is relevant for considering how nursing homes create, as well as care for, mentally impaired people. This chapter also draws on a body of ethnographic studies of nursing homes, most notably Bowker (1982), Fontana 1977), Glasscote et al. (1976), Gubrium (1975, 1978), Smithers (1977), and Standard (1973). The approach taken here differs somewhat from this material by relating the everyday world of nursing homes to certain macropolitical forces that shape them. This is a perspective advocated, for example, by Burawoy (1979), Emerson and Messinger (1977), and Smith (1981). Following Emerson and Messinger, the chapter is an attempt to link the micropolitics of trouble in a social control institution with

Original publication: Diamond, Timothy, "Nursing Homes as Trouble," from (ed. Emily K. Abel and Margaret Nelson) *Circles of Care: Work and Identity in Women's Lives* (State University of New York Press, 1990), pp. 173–87.

macropolitical forces. The macropolitical force at issue is capitalist medicine as a defining principle of organization in nursing home culture.

One feature of the two homes where I worked, not unlike the situation throughout the United States, is that they are specifically gendered organizations: the vast majority of residents and nursing staff are women. Most of the following data, therefore, are provided by women. Another feature of the two homes is that the residents are impoverished people. Most are supported solely by Medicaid funds. Therefore the settings from which these observations are drawn do not exemplify all nursing homes. The objective, however, is to portray situations that can arise out of principles that guide nursing home organization in the United States in general. Each section describes one situation in which the context of capitalist medicine is linked intrinsically to the everyday world of nursing homes in ways that create trouble for nursing assistants and residents.

### Nursing Assistants in the Health Care "Team" (or, "How do they Expect Us to Live on $209?")

While the job of nurses aide has existed almost since the beginning of the modern hospital (Reverby 1979), the position is becoming more formalized as a certified part of the health care hierarchy. This formalization is coemergent with the growth of nursing homes, which already account for the majority of jobs in this rapidly growing field. Currently, nearly 1.25 million nursing assistants work in the United States, and the Occupational Outlook Handbook (1980–1) predicts 94,000 annual openings at least through the next decade, almost all of which will be in nursing homes.

One trend in this development is the requirement for certification prior to work. Beginning this project, I anticipated that I could enter directly into a nursing home for on-the-job training, but historically I was too late. Now, in order to do this work, one must first be certified through a state-approved training program as a certified nursing assistant (a title that now replaces nurses aide). In classified newspaper columns throughout the country, there are advertisements for vocational schools that offer such training. The schools get many applicants, mostly poor women, who are attracted to the relatively good prospects for employment, the caring-oriented duties of the job, and the possibility – however remote – of moving up in the ranks of the nursing profession. Unless one is formally trained in nursing (many foreign-trained nurses work as nurses aides), this certification procedure is required. Training in the school I attended lasted six months, with classes twice a week and one full day per week of clinical training in a skilled nursing facility. The cost, including tuition, uniforms, and textbooks, was just under $1,000.

School officials and textbooks (e.g., Schneidman et al. 1982) describe this training as a privilege because it gives the worker professional status on the health care "team." When the owner of our school started his first pep talk with a mix of medical and military imagery, we might have taken it as a warning as well as a welcome. "Welcome to the firing line of health care!" he said. Once out in that firing line, our place on the team was made clear in many ways. Surely one of the ways – the most talked-about by nursing assistants – is the low wage. I remember my coworker, Deborah Moffi[1] gasping at the sight of our first paychecks – take-home pay of $209 for two weeks of work, including a weekend: "Two-hundred nine dollars?" she shrieked, "How do they expect us to live on $209?" Deborah's complaint was no idle grumbling over low pay. She was experiencing a contradiction present in certain emerging forms of wage labor. As British sociologist Veronica Beechey (1978) points out, in the service sectors occupied overwhelmingly by women, pay rates fall below the actual cost of subsistence. This appeared to be the case for many nursing assistants with whom I worked. Many, if not most, were sole supporters for a family. At $104.50 per week – which is $3.50 per hour minus deductions – they often complained about not having enough money for food, rent, utilities, and transportation. In short, the wage creates poverty. The newly "professionalized" health care workers become impoverished, even with full-time jobs. For the women (and the small number of men) who work in this new profession, the wage structure creates considerable difficulty in their personal lives and, in turn, a context of constant strain in their work lives. Because nursing assistants are by far the largest category of workers in nursing homes (Occupational Outlook Handbook 1980–81), the wage structure is a significant factor in making nursing homes troublesome environments.

### Medical Dominance of Nursing Assistant Work (or, "Get Back to Work, You've got Sixteen Vitals to Do.")

In nursing homes, the work routine is defined in terms of medical tasks. This is seen most clearly in the chart, a record of each resident's care. This is the instrument through which the work process is transformed into administrative discourse, or *documentary reality*, to use Smith's (1974) phrase. The job description manual at one of the homes where I worked indicates unequivocally the central place of charting in the work process of nursing homes: "Remember," it reads, "if it is not charted, it didn't happen."

Apart from the more abstract questions raised by such a mandate (for example, "if it didn't happen, but it is charted, did it happen?"), this instruction frames what is and is not legitimate work. The chart becomes a record not only of the resident but also of the work of the nursing staff and of the formal relationship between residents and staff. And this formal relationship is dominated by medical tasks. As the director of nursing told us repeatedly, "The most important task you have is to get them up and get them to take their meds." The second most important task is the monitoring of what are called "vitals" in medical discourse – blood pressures, temperatures, pulses, and respirations. Vitals have to be taken on every shift for every resident, although some residents are quite healthy and show unvarying vitals for all the years they have lived at a home. After this our job entails, according to our training manual, regimens of bathing and feeding residents, bedmaking and cleaning, conducting an exercise class (called Activities of Daily Living), bedchecks twice a shift, and participation, at the beginning and end of every shift, in the nurse's report on troubles of the day. These are the tasks that were charted on one of the twelve forms I filled out each day. Nursing assistants are quite busy in this medically framed round of activity, frequently under pressure to complete these tasks and document them properly in the charts.

In the course of the work, much that nursing assistants do is not charted or chartable. Not the least of this is the constant social, emotional work of caring for residents who, in the midst of loneliness and confusion, are often in great need of human contact. Yet in the charts, job descriptions, textbooks, and training, caring work remains invisible and unnamed. It is not officially recorded or rewarded; whether and how it is to be done is passed on only in an oral tradition. Sometimes doing it is even cause for reprimand. Under present organizational principles, medical tasks can dominate – or even cancel – caring work. One expressive moment of this for me was when I stopped to sit with Mary Karney, a seventy-seven-year-old resident, who was crying on her bed. Before I could find out why she was crying, I was interrupted by my supervisor who scolded me for sitting down with Mary, reminding me that I had sixteen more vitals to do before bedcheck. My job priorities did not include sitting with Mary Karney.

This kind of incident can be recounted by nurses everywhere. In this instance, the routine taking and recording of blood pressures not only took precedence over, but in effect precluded, tending to Mary's sadness. The point of relating this experience is not to assert that this is how nursing homes are, but rather to ask under what social and organizational conditions can a nursing assistant tending to a crying resident be considered not doing the job? Clearly this "logic" of the work process did not arise from Mary Karney's standpoint, or from mine as I sat there, or even between myself and the supervisor. It descends from an administrative logic that is far removed from that moment. It seems that in this logic the purpose of the work is maintenance and, equally important, the recording of this "maintenance in codifiable and quantifiable terms. Marie Campbell (1982), following Dorothy Smith (1974, 1981), discusses nursing in the context of capitalist medicine as being transformed into an "administrative reality" of categories and documents; in the documentary discourse, nursing becomes defined in terms of tasks and abstract management technologies. These, in turn, create nursing as a commensurable and cost-accountable work process.[2]

To return to Mary Karney, it should not be surprising that her blood pressure was high that day – she was upset. There was a place to record her high numbers, but not her crying. Just to sit with Mary Karney to offer her social contact is not a formal part of the work. It is not a quantifiable, cost-accountable component of capitalist medicine, not a gesture that conforms to capitalist administrative logic. In the official view, this presumably "natural" work remains implicit, taken-for-granted, or even, as in that moment with Mary, cancelled altogether. In that troublesome incident an administrative logic, centered on the presumed preeminance of medical tasks, was superimposed on everyday life. To walk away from her at that moment was consistent with the logic of capitalist medicine, but it completely contradicted my sense of health care – and Mary's.

## Nursing Homes as Capitalist Industry (or, "Hey, that's No Bag Lady, That's One of My Residents!")

Nursing homes represent a major growth industry at this time (Dunlop 1980). One financial journal describes an investment in nursing homes as "Gray Gold" – a stock of increasingly high value (Blyskal 1981). Growth of this sphere as a capitalist industry provides an example of the transference of social services from state and federal operation to that of private corporations (see Estes and Harrington 1981; Scull 1977, 1981; Warren 1981). One can see the logic of profit entering directly into the everyday life of residency in a nursing home and creating trouble therein. To illustrate this, I consider three incidents from my work experience. One relates to inspection of the wards, the second to the money that is transferred from nursing home administration to residents, and the third to nursing homes' vested interest in bed occupancy.

One day at the intermediate-care facility there was an inspection – a state requirement in nursing homes that receive Medicaid payments. Our inspection was conducted by a multinational medical management corporation, which would then report back to the state. I arrived for the 3:00–11:30 p.m. shift, anxious to find out if we had passed that morning's inspection. We had passed, but the nursing assistants and residents did not seem to care or even notice. After pursuing the issue, I realized that no member of the inspection team had ever entered the wards or spoken with residents or nursing staff. Life went on as normal, which, in this home, included many things that would not legally pass an on-site inspection. Inspection turned out to be purely an administrative process that transpired in the business office. The inspection practices related exclusively to the documentary reality (Smith 1974, 1981) generated within the office in the forms of numbers and costs and information from the medical charts. The documents, not the residents, provided the basis of the inspection. Little wonder that no one noticed; even as the inspection was in process, the wards were hidden from public view. This is not to suggest that wards of total institutions ever have been open to public view; the current procedures signify the current version of a continuing problem of hiding the life of people in total institutions.[3] Now the information that forms the criteria of inspection begins and ends in a computer through various boxes checked by personnel along the way. The state reimburses the nursing home on a cost-per-unit basis, units defined in a computer-adaptable language. Under these conditions, *inspection* – a word derived from the latin word meaning *to look at* – completely circumvents looking at human beings and their actual living conditions.

In the two homes in which I have worked, almost all the residents are on Medicaid. I use *on* Medicaid because *receive* does not capture the exchange. The state pays the nursing home, not the resident. Currently, this is approximately $1,000 per month per resident. In both homes, residents received a cash allowance of $25 per month. From this they had to buy all personal items (toiletries, stamps, phone, coffee, cigarettes). The money vanished rapidly. If a resident smoked (and nursing homes can be smoking cultures), the entire fund was less than the cost of smoking. A few days after "payday" residents were penniless.

One dramatic consequence of such a structure can be seen on the streets of any urban ghetto. Some nursing home residents are quite ambulatory and are "free" to leave the home at certain times. Yet, what kind of freedom results from such pennilessness? While walking to work one day, off in the distance I saw a woman rummaging through the trash. In my mind, I dismissed her with the typical slur, "Oh, another bag lady." But when I walked closer I realized, "Hey, that's no bag lady, that's June, one of my residents." After a short conversation with her, it became clear why she was exploring the trash: It was only the middle of the month, but her $25 was exhausted. She was looking for something she might trade or sell. Although $1,000 had passed from the state to the nursing home in her name, she was on the streets to barter.

Where I worked, residents were frequently in trouble with police for indigent-type transgressions, such as loitering, shoplifting, or begging. At one point, all residents were barred from a local church because too many took money from the collection plate. All of this occurs while $12,000 per year is passing somewhere over each resident's head. Ralph Sagrello, a resident for nine years, summarized his situation sardonically in a conversation during which I had asked him if he were on public aid. "Public aid?" he responded, "I'd rather call it poverty aid!" In this he expresses another contradiction that is possible under contemporary organizational principles of nursing homes. Left to the "entrepreneurial tendencies" (Emerson, Rochford and Shaw 1981) of privately owned social control institutions, residents can become beggars.

These incidents lead into a third issue, the vested interest in institutionalization that is intrinsic to private social control institutions. It has been well documented that policies of deinstitutionalization (which existed at least nominally in the 1970s) have virtually dissolved (Bassuk and Gerson 1978; Habenstein and Kultgen 1981; Lerman 1982; Rose 1979; Scull 1977, 1981; Warren 1981). The actual history of the closing of state hospitals is better understood as "transinstitutionalization," which is, according to Warren's analysis, "the transfer of responsibility for 'social junk' [Scull's term] from state budgets to various combined welfare-private profit systems that cost the state less and provide numerous entrepreneurial opportunities" (1981: 726). The people who were formerly inmates in state mental hospitals now reside in nursing homes, where they and older people who have no other place to go have become "lucrative commodities" (Scull 1981: 747). It appears, in fact, that once they enter, people do not leave nursing homes except to go to another or to die. In the two years, 1980 and 1981, only three people left my four-hundred-bed facility for a more independent living situation. In this home, we were even instructed to avoid applying the term *independence* to residents. As the activities director once put it, "We try to avoid using the word independence in this place. Otherwise, we have no purpose here."

These three illustrations identify the residents in the homes where I worked as penniless beggars and as commodities. My intent is not to expose "bad" or "unscrupulous" administrators, or to provide yet another report documenting administrators' abuses in this basically natural and inevitable institution. It is, rather, to question the basic capitalist principles underlying such institutions. Their project, in their own terms, is to provide the most cost-effective health care. For the most part, their administrators do not intend to produce beggars. To argue this would be crude psychologism, not sociological analysis of capitalism in process. Something deeper in the fabric of nursing homes is operating that allows administrative logic to proceed with no recognition of the depraved conditions under which the human products of this industry can come to live. Something mediates and obscures a vision of this impoverishment.

One key to what obscures this vision is implicit in comments offered by my intermediate facility's social service coordinator. Despite the fact that some residents are physically and mentally quite agile, the coordinator frequently described them as patients who will never improve. "Keep in mind," she said, "the more you get to know these patients, the more you know there's always something for them to improve upon." The concept of the resident as perpetual patient reinforces the principle of vested interest in institutionalization and is consistent with the other themes discussed so far – the medical hierarchy, the task-centeredness of the institution, and the medicalized accounting system. But this ideology is more directly an expression of still another principle that pervades nursing home culture. This is the overriding assumption that residents, because they are old or just because they are there, are mentally ill.

### The Documentary Reality of Mental Illness (or, "You Know, Rose, This Place Drives Me up the Wall.")

Guiding the everyday treatment of nursing home residents is the presupposition that mental impairment is at least part of a resident's diagnosis. The most prevalent diagnostic categories that describe residents' conditions are senile dementia, Alzheimer's disease, organic brain syndrome, and undifferentiated chronic schizophrenia. The first two comprise 50 percent of all nursing home diagnoses (Butler 1982; Moss and Halamandaris 1977).

In a meeting, the director of nursing once announced the prevalence of mental illness with the claim that "70 percent of our residents come from the state hospital." Such a statistic, I later estimated, was nowhere near the reality. Roughly 35 percent had at one time been state hospital inmates, and most of these had been in halfway houses during the 1970s. In the same presentation, we were reminded that the older one gets, the more one becomes like a little child (an assumption that I soon discovered can be very insulting to some residents). These descriptions were followed with a warning about what kind of behavior to expect: "We expect trouble from these residents; that's why they're here." In this way, the residents become defined not as *in* trouble but *as* trouble. Emerson and Messinger, in discussing the micropolitics of trouble, suggest that "a deviant should be understood not only as one who is morally condemned, but also one who is sided against" (1977: 131). In this meeting, the residents were recreated as troublemakers and the staff was encouraged to side against them.

The point of this is not to indict the director who was, in many ways, a very good nurse. It is to highlight the power of the mental illness model in these settings. The director probably was not intentionally deceiving us any more than the administrators are intentionally creating beggars, but rather was reflecting an overarching ideology in which the notion of "70 percent from state hospitals" seems to make sense within the context of the current operation. As this ideology is perpetuated, mental illness becomes an organizing principle of nursing home culture.

As nursing assistants, we were encouraged to read the charts frequently so we could "get to know the residents better." Each chart has seven sections,[4] all of which spin off the first – the admitting diagnosis. Following this are the psychiatric report, medical consultants' reports, laboratory report, drug regimen, social and medical history, and activities program. The charts define residents in terms of their medical and psychiatric troubles. To read the charts, then, is to get to know the residents better through their sicknesses. With the chart providing the basic documentary reality, the director's warning that we should expect trouble is brought to a full ideological circle: if we want to know why a resident is causing trouble, we need only to look in the chart to find the cause.

Furthermore, after reading a resident's chart one learns almost nothing about these women's and men's lives – the 60 to 70 years that they lived prior to admission. As with caring work, there is no documentary space for residents' personal or social histories. It, too, is passed on only in an oral tradition in informal conversation. Social history is not a part of the formal principles or documents that record the staff-resident relation, and it is not a part of the way nursing assistants are instructed to get to know the residents better.

One could imagine alternative entrees into residents' existence. Suppose, for example, nursing assistants were introduced to residents through a sociological rather than a medical or psychiatric account of their lives. Then Mary Karney would not have been presented to us as having senile dementia but as a mother of three, whose husband died and children moved away, and who lived alone for fifteen years. Then, the little money she had she spent in other nursing homes. The Medicaid home where I met her was, for her as it was for many, the end of a series of homes, after private funds and Medicare had run out. Rosemary Phillips, age sixty-one, would not be a "chronic undifferentiated schizophrenic," but a mother of two, whose husband beat her and took off with the kids. Left emotionally broken and without resources, she struggled along with part-time work and community mental health services. Neither is available any more. Viola Steward, age seventy-seven, has an admitting diagnosis of "mild cataract, mild dementia." She quit her job forty years ago to take care of her parents; thirty years later, both of them had died. Viola, two years later and then penniless, broke her hip. She was in her third nursing home when I met her.

As with these three, each resident has a personal history that can be traced backward from admission to specific relations in a social history. Doing so reveals certain commonalities obscured by presentation in terms of psychiatric disorders. For example, most of the women entered the nursing homes where I worked quite poor, and their existence there is a continuing process of impoverishment. These are people for whom the bottom fell out. Mothers, wives, and daughters whose familes disintegrated over time. Women – and men – who lost both family and jobs. Now they are completely without resources or means of obtaining them.

These are sociological sketches. Whatever their limitations, they provide some kind of explanatory link between admission and former life. By contrast, the psychiatric explanation as embodied in the chart obscures and actually destroys this link. The basic social institutions that formed the contours of these residents' lives – family, parenthood, religion, work – if present at all in the charts are there as boxes to be checked. The resident becomes identified as a patient by the staff, while the psychiatric diagnosis separates the resident as a patient from the staff. There seems, in short, to be a radical gap, a rupture in meaning generated by the medical discourse that subsumes residents' lives upon admission. It separates their identities both from staff and from their own social histories. No sociological linkage is offered in staff discourse as to how the defining characteristics of Mary Karney's life got changed from motherhood, to poverty, to senile dementia. Without this, residents are introduced in the nursing home only as the end point of this progression, only as sick.

To close this section, I want to call attention to the basic technology of this mental illness model – drugs. In my nursing homes, sedatives were used heavily, with profound impact on residents' behavior. I came to realize that the director of nursing was quite serious in telling us that "the most important job you have is to get them up and get them to take their meds." According to the house rules, residents must take the medications that are assigned to them. They can refuse just about everything, including eating, but they cannot refuse medications. Sedatives are prescribed as a matter of course for the diagnoses of most nursing home residents. One result was a culture of sleep. Residents slept so much in the homes where I worked that my conceptions of sleeping and waking were jolted. I had tended to dichotomize the two, thinking of them as distinct states of consciousness. But life as a nursing home resident is, for many, somewhere between the two. It is not uncommon for a resident to fall asleep in the middle of a conversation. Some wake up only for meals and medication.

Once again it was Mary Karney who captured the personal trouble that this environment fosters. Mary is a bright woman, and we had many jovial, animated conversations. Still, she is heavily sedated although she struggles against it. One evening, when she was leaning up against the wall in line for the 8:00 p.m. meds, I overheard her make a comment to another resident. Stupefied and about to become more so, she turned to Rose standing behind her and whispered in the slow voice of a person trying to wake up, "You know, Rose, this place drives me up the wall." In this chilling metaphor of entrapment, she was not only complaining about the troubles of her life, she was attributing active agency to the nursing home in the creation of those troubles. For her, the relevant context in which to understand her feelings of entrapment is the institution, not the senile dementia. In this she disagrees with the authorities and the discourse of the entire organization in which she resides.

Yet Mary's continually imposed state of stupor is not an isolated cause of personal trouble for her; it is part of a climate. The issue is overly simplified if psychiatry and sedatives are isolated as the villains. As a primary mode of therapy, intervention, and control, sedatives provide a mechanism that follows not just from a logic of psychiatry but from all of various organizational principles so far discussed. Drugs are cost-accountable, profitable, and medical; they are easily coded while being quite mysterious to residents and nursing assistants. They are easily inspected, quantified, increased, decreased. It is not adequate to give drugs independent causality, as in the belief that "the trouble with nursing homes is they give too many drugs." Drugs reflect the culture, they do not create it. They are the basic technology of a larger process.

## Conclusion

In this chapter, I have examined the domination of medical ideology in the culture of nursing homes as expressed through four themes: the increasing formalization of nursing assistant work, emphasis on medical tasks in that work, the development of accounting systems based on these tasks, and the overarching presumption of illness, specifically mental illness. As each one of these becomes more taken-for-granted in the culture, they serve to conceal as well as to reveal. The notion of professionalization of nursing assistants conceals the impoverishing wage structure in which they work. The task-centeredness can hide and prevent the emotional work of caring for human beings. The accounting systems can make wards completely hidden from view even while "inspections" go on regularly. They can also foster a resident population that is begging in the streets by mid-month. They can, in the interest of bed-occupancy, obliterate any chances of a resident's independence. The foundation of all of this is the presupposition of mental illness. Although the concept of mental illness has changed – taking on new syndromes specifically for older people – the label retains its power to reduce a person's public identity to a psychiatric disorder.

To the extent that each of these forces is present in any nursing home, it generates conditions counterproductive to health care. While these have been discussed as somewhat discrete elements, it may be better to see them as parts of a general process. In the two homes where I worked, it was easy to see how they all reinforced one another. Mary Karney shows up so frequently in these incidents not only because I got to know her so well, but because she embodies simultaneously so much of what these troublesome incidents portray. To be with Mary on a daily basis is to come to see her crying, invisibility, poverty, dependence, and drug stupor as indistinguishable. They all appear in terms of each other and reinforce one another.

Similarly, nursing assistants must absorb these troubles as a whole interrelated process. Their subordination in a medical hierarchy reinforces the invisibility of their labor, which reinforces their impoverishing wage. In turn, the cultivation of caring work is suppressed, both by the task-centeredness of the work and the daily strains of poverty.

These processes simultaneously reinforce each other at the administrative level as well. At this level, however, they do not appear as trouble but as a rational model of organization. The medical tasks are carefully monitored by the accounting systems; profit is increased if wages can be kept low and if residents' allowances can be kept to a minimum; inspection is streamlined if it is conducted totally as an analysis of quantifiable data. Permeating these dynamics is the presumption of residency based on sickness and a profitable technology based on drugs.

For residents, staff, and administration, then, these processes are present together, although in different ways, as part of the ongoing culture of nursing homes. It may be that these coalesce only in the kinds of homes where I worked, where people are without resources. Surely they appear in particularly glaring ways in such settings. Yet the very depravity of these settings may reveal not so much their uniqueness as the principles and forces underlying the emerging organization of nursing homes. Perhaps these problems are merely muted as we look at homes where residents can afford to mitigate these forces. To the extent that this is true, the sociological and political issue changes from troubles in nursing homes to nursing homes as trouble.

## Notes

1   All names are pseudonyms.
2   For a discussion of similar processes in other organizations, see Altheide and Johnson 1980.
3   For a discussion of nursing homes as total institutions, see Johnson and Williamson 1980.
4   The chart is a document that is carried over into nursing homes from the classical model of the cause- and cure, acute-disease hospital. In this latter setting the presumption is that the chart signifies only a transitory part of patients' lives, their illness. But in nursing homes, because people are there for the rest of their lives, their medical records becomes their life records and their sick role statuses become permanent ones.

## References

Altheide, D., and J. M. Johnson (1980) *Bureaucratic Phenomena* (Boston: Allyn and Bacon).

Bassuk, E., and S. Gerson (1978) "Deinstitutionalization and Mental Health Services," *Scientific American* 238(2): 46–53.

Beechey, V. (1978) "Women and Production: A Critical Analysis of Some Sociological Theories of Women's Work," in *Feminism and Materialism*, eds. A. Kuhn and A. Wolpe (Boston: Routledge and Kegan Paul), pp. 155–97.

Blyskal, J. (1981) "Gray Gold," *Forbes* 128 (November 23), pp. 80, 84.

Bowker, L. H. (1982) *Humanizing Institutions for the Aged* (Lexington, MA.: Lexington Books).

Burawoy, M. (1979) *Manufacturing Consent* (Chicago: University of Chicago Press).

Butler, R. (1982) "Care for the Aged in the United States." Paper presented at the Centre d'Etude des Mouvements Sociaux, Paris, April 14.

Campbell, M. (1982) "Social Organization of Knowledge Research on Nursing," in *Research – A Base for the Future?* (conference proceedings). Nursing Research Unit, University of Edinburgh, Scotland.

Dunlop, B. D. (1980) *The Growth of Nursing Home Care* (Lexington, MA: Lexington Books).

Emerson, R. M., and S. L. Messinger (1977) "The Micro-Politics of Trouble," *Social Problems* 25(2): 121–34.

Emerson, R. M., Rochford, E. B., and L. S. Shaw (1981) "Economics and Enterprise in Board and Care Homes for the Mentally Ill," *American Behavioral Scientist* 24(6): 771–85.

Estes, C. L., and C. A. Harrington (1981) "Fiscal Crisis, Deinstitutionalization and the Elderly," *American Behavioral Scientist* 24(6): 811–26.

Fontana, A. (1977) *The Last Frontier* (Beverly Hills: Sage Publications).

Foucault, M. (1965) *Madness and Civilization* (New York: Random House).

Glasscote, R., et al. (1976) *Old Folks at Homes* (Washington, D.C.: Joint Information Service of the American Psychiatric Association and the National Association for Mental Health).

Goffman, E. (1961) *Asylums* (Garden City, N.Y.: Doubleday).

Gubrium, J. F. (1975) *Living and Dying at Murray Manor* (New York: St. Martin's Press).

Gubrium, J. F. (1978) "Notes on the Social Organization of Senility," *Urban Life* 7(1): 23–44.

Habenstein, R. W., and P. B. Kultgen (1981) *Power, Pelf and Patients* (Columbia, Mo.: Missouri Gerontology Institute).

Johnson, E. F., and J. B. Williamson (1980) *Growing Old* (New York: Holt, Rinehart and Winston).

Lerman, P. (1982) *Deinstitutionalization and the Welfare State* (New Brunswick, N. J.: Rutgers University Press).

Moss, F. E., and V. J. Halamandaris (1977) *Too Old, Too Sick, Too Bad* (Germantown, Md.: Aspen Systems).

Occupational Outlook Handbook (1980–81) *Bulletin 2075* (Washington, D.C.: U.S. Department of Labor).

Perruci, P. (1974) *Circle of Madness* (Englewood Cliffs, N.J.: Prentice-Hall).

Reverby, S. (1979) "The Search for the Hospital Yardstick: Nursing and the Rationalization of Hospital Work," in *Health Care in America: Essays in Social History*, eds. S. Reverby and D. Rosner (Philadelphia: Temple University Press), pp. 206–25.

Rose, S. M. (1979) "Deciphering Deinstitutionalization: Complexities in Policy and Program Analysis," *Milbank Memorial Fund Quarterly* 57(4): 429–60.

Rosenhan, D. L. (1973) "On Being Sane in Insane Places," *Science* 179(4070): 250–8.

Scheff, T. (1975) *Labeling Madness* (Englewood Cliffs, N.J.: Prentice-Hall).

Schneidman, R., S. Lambert and B. Wander (1982) *Being a Nursing Assistant* (Bowie, Md.: Robert J. Brady).

Scull, A. (1977) *Decarceration: Community Treatment and the Deviant* (Englewood Cliffs, N.J.: Prentice-Hall).

Scull, A. (1981) "A New Trade in Lunacy," *American Behavioral Scientist* 24(6): 741–54.

Smith, D. E. (1974) "The Social Construction of Documentary Reality," *Sociological Inquiry* 44(4): 257–68.

Smith, D. E. (1978) "K is Mentally Ill: The Anatomy of a Factual Account," *Sociology* 12(1): 23–53.

Smith, D. E. (1981) "The Experienced World as Problematic: a Feminist Method." The Twelfth Annual Sorokin Lecture, University of Saskatchewan, Saskatoon, January.

Smithers, J. A. (1977) "Institutional Dimensions of Senility," *Urban Life* 6(3): 251–76.

Stannard, C. (1973) "Old Folks and Dirty Work: The Social Conditions for Patient Abuse in Nursing Homes," *Social Problems* 20(3): 329–42.

Szasz, T. (1961) *The Myth of Mental Illness* (New York: Harper and Row).

Warren, C. A. B. (1981) "New Forms of Social Control," *American Behavioral Scientist* 24(6): 724–40.

## Further Reading to Part VIII

Abel, Emily K. and Margaret K. Nelson (eds). 1990. *Circles of Care: Work and Identity in Women's Lives*. Albany, NY: SUNY Press.

Abel, Emily K. 1991. *Who Cares for the Elderly? Public Policy and the Experiences of Adult Daughters*. Philadelphia: Temple University Press.

Burnley, Cynthia S. 1987. "Caregiving: The Impact on Emotional Support for Single Women," *Journal of Aging Studies* 1: 253–64.

Diamond, Timothy. 1992. *Making Gray Gold: Narratives of Nursing Home Care*. Chicago: University of Chicago Press.

Foner, Nancy. 1994. *The Caregiving Dilemma: Work in an American Nursing Home*. Berkeley: University of California Press.

Gubrium, Jaber F. 1993. *Speaking of Life: Horizons of Meaning for Nursing Home Residents*. Hawthorne, NY: Aldine de Gruyter.

Henderson, J. Neil and Maria D. Vesperi (eds). 1995. *The Culture of Long-Term Care: Nursing Home Ethnography*. Westport, CT: Bergin & Garvey.

Lewis, Jane and Barbara Meredith. 1988. "Daughters Caring for Mothers," *Ageing and Society* 8: 1–22.

Motenko, Aluma K. 1988. Chapter 6, "Respite Care and Pride in Caregiving: The Experience of Six Older Men caring for their Disabled Wives." Pp. 104–27 in *Qualitative Gerontology*, edited by Shulamit Reinharz and Graham D. Rowles. New York: Springer.

# Part IX

## Death and Bereavement

# 28 A Death in Due Time: Conviction, Order, and Continuity in Ritual Drama

## Barbara Myerhoff

When the fig is plucked in due time it is good for the fig and good for the tree.

Mankind has ever chafed over its powerlessness in facing the end of life. Lacking assurance of immortality and insulted by the final triumph of nature over culture, humans develop religious concepts which explain that if not they, someone or something has power and a plan. Then death is not an obscene blow of blind chance. No religion fails to take up the problem, sometimes affirming human impotence thunderously:

> Know that everything is according to the reckoning and let not thy imagination betray thee into the hope that the grave will be a place of refuge for thee. For without thy consent wast thou created and born into the world, without any choice; thou art now living without volition, and will have to die without thy approval; so likewise without thy consent wilt thou have to render account before the supreme King, the Holy One, praised be He. (Goldin 1939: 220)

Nevertheless, people yearn for a good death, timely and appropriate, suggesting some measure of participation, if not consent. Occasionally, a subtle collusion occurs where human and natural plans seem to coincide, revealing a mysterious agreement between mankind, nature, and the gods, and providing a sense of profound rightness and order that is the final objective of religion, indeed of all cultural designs. Belief and reality are merged at such times and death is more partner than foe. The questions of supremacy and power are rendered irrelevant and an experience of unity and harmony prevails.

This paper presents such an event, tracing its origins and following its consequences, over a period of several months.[1] The entire sequence is analyzed as a single event, a drama of several acts. It is a social drama in Victor Turner's (1974) sense, but it is more strikingly a cultural drama, illustrating how a group draws upon its rituals and symbols to face a crisis and find a resolution; it handles conflicts, not of opposing

Original publication: Myerhoff, Barbara, "A Death in Due Time: Conviction, Order, and Continuity in Ritual Drama," from (ed. Marc Kaminsky) *Remembered Lives: The Work of Ritual Storytelling and Growing Older* (University of Michigan Press, 1992), pp. 159–90.

social relationships, but between uncertainty and predictability, powerlessness and choice. A final reconciliation is achieved when the community has selected among and modified its prevailing conceptualizations, using some traditional materials, improvising and innovating others, until it has made a myth of a historical episode and found messages of continuity, human potency and freedom amidst threats of individual and social obliteration.[2]

The case is an especially useful one for the light it throws on some of the general characteristics and functions of ritual. Ritual has been defined variously, but there is a core of agreement as to its form and uses. It is prominent in all areas of uncertainty, anxiety, impotence and disorder. Ritual dramas are elaborately staged and use presentational more than discursive symbols, so that our senses are aroused and flood us with phenomenological proof of the symbolic reality which the ritual is portraying. By dramatizing abstract, invisible conceptions, it makes vivid and palpable our ideas and wishes, and as Geertz (1973: 112) has observed, the lived-in order merges with the dreamed-of order. Through their insistence on precise, authentic and accurate forms, rituals suggest that their contents are beyond question – authoritative and axiomatic.

Ritual inevitably carries a basic message of continuity and predictability. Even when dealing with change, new events are connected to preceding ones, incorporated into a stream of precedents so that they are recognized as growing out of tradition and experience. Ritual states enduring and underlying patterns, thus connects past, present and future, abrogating history and time. Ritual always links fellow participants but often goes beyond this to connect a group of celebrants to wider collectivities, even the ancestors and those yet unborn. Religious rituals go farther, connecting mankind to the forces of nature and purposes of the deities, reading the forms of macrocosm in the microcosm. And when rituals employ sacred symbols, they may link the celebrant to his/her very self through various stages of the life cycle, making individual history into a single phenomenological reality.

Ritual appears in dangerous circumstances and at the same time is itself a dangerous enterprise. It is a conspicuously artificial affair, by definition not of mundane life. Rituals always contain the possibility of failure. If they fail, we may glimpse their basic artifice, and from this apprehend the fiction and invention underlying all culture.

> Underlying all rituals is an ultimate danger, lurking beneath the smallest and largest of them, the more banal and the most ambitious – the possibility that we will encounter ourselves making up our conceptions of the world, society, our very selves. We may slip into that fatal perspective of recognizing culture as our construct, arbitrary, conventional, invented by mortals. (Moore and Myerhoff 1977: 22)

Rituals then are seen as reflections not of the underlying, unchanging nature of the world but the products of our imagination. When we catch ourselves making up rituals, we may see all our most precious, basic understandings, the precepts we live by, as mere desperate wishes and dreams.

With ritual providing the safeguards of predictability, we dare ultimate enterprises. Because we know the outcome of a ritual beforehand, we find the courage within it to enact our symbols and what would otherwise be preposterous. In ritual, we incorporate the gods into our bodies, return to Paradise, and with high righteousness destroy our fellows.

What happens when a ritual is interrupted by an unplanned development, when it is not predictable, when accident rudely takes over and chaos menaces its orderly proceedings? What do we do if death appears out of order, in the middle of a ritual celebrating life? Such an occurrence may be read as the result of a mistake in ritual procedure, as a warning and message from the deities, or as a devastating sign of human impotence. But there is another possibility. The unexpected may be understood as a fulfillment of a different, loftier purpose, and a new, higher order may be found beneath the appearance of the original disruption. A ritual may be transformed in midstream to take account of reality and thereby fulfill its purposes. Then a new meaning and a new ritual emerge, made from older, extant symbols and rites. This occurred in the case to be described, where it might be said that culture had the last word after all.


## Ethnographic Background

The death in question was unusually dramatic. Jacob Kovitz died in the middle of the public celebration of his ninety-fifth birthday. The ceremony was being held at a senior citizens' community center, the focal life of a small, stable, socially and culturally homogeneous group of elderly Jewish immigrants who originated in the shtetls of Eastern Europe. Now, alone and old, the earlier pressures to be assimilated Americans had abated. They were free to revive and elaborate a way of life which combined elements from their childhood beliefs and practices with modern, American features, suited to the needs of their present circumstances. These were harsh. Family members were distant or dead. Most of the group were poor, very old and frail, suffering from social and communal neglect, extreme loneliness, and isolation. As a people, they were marginal to the concerns of the larger society around them. Their social, political, physical and economic impotence were pronounced and except on a very local level, they were nearly invisible.

Added to these afflictions was their realization that the culture of their childhood would die with them. The Holocaust wiped out the shtetls and all their inhabitants. They clearly apprehended the impending complete extinction of themselves as persons and as carriers of a way of life. The group was entirely age-homogeneous, and except for ceremonial occasions, no real intergenerational continuity existed. Their own membership was being depleted constantly, and there was no one to replace them. Death and impotence were as real as the weather and as persistent.

Moreover, the social solidarity of the group was weakened by the people's ambivalence toward one another, due in part to enforced association and perhaps, too, to displaced anger. Their cultural traditions inclined them to a certain degree of distrust of non-kin, and despite the stability, homogeneity and distinctiveness of past experiences, circumstances and extensive time spent together, they had less than entirely amiable feelings for each other. Factions, disagreements, and long-standing grudges marred their assemblies, most of which took place in secular and sacred rituals within the Center and on benches outside it.

Ideologically, they were united by their common past above all. This was expressed as Yiddishkeit, referring to the local customs, language and beliefs that characterized their parental homes and early life in the shtetl. Very few were orthodox in religious practices. They had broken with strict religious Judaism before leaving the Old Country. A great many were agnostic, even atheistic and anti-religious. But all were passionately Jewish, venerating the historical, ethnic and cultural aspects of their heritage. Most had liberal and socialist political beliefs and had been active at one time or another in the Russian Revolution, various workers' movements, labor unions and similar activities. Since the Holocaust, all were Zionists, despite some ideological reservations concerning nationalism. For them Israel had become an extension of their family, and its perpetuation and welfare were identified as their own. This constellation of beliefs and experiences – the childhood history of the shtetl, Yiddish language and culture, secular and ethnic Judaism, and Zionism – were the sacred elements that united them.[3]

For a dozen years, birthdays had been celebrated by the members in their small dilapidated Center. These were collective occasions, grouping together all those born within the month – modest, simple affairs. Only Jacob Kovitz had regular birthday parties for him alone, and these parties were great fêtes. This reflected his unusual standing in the group. He was a kind of patriarch, a formal and informal leader of the group. He had served as its president for several years, and even after leaving the community to live in a rest home, he returned frequently and had been named president emeritus. He was the oldest person in the group and the most generally venerated. No one else had managed to provide leadership without becoming entangled in factional disputes. He regarded himself and was generally regarded by others as an exemplar, for he had fulfilled the deepest wishes of most people and he embodied their loftiest ideals.

Jacob Kovitz enjoyed the devotion of his children, four successful, educated sons, who demonstrated their affection by frequently visiting the Center and participating in many celebrations there. At these times they treated the members with respect and kindness, and always they were generous, providing meals, entertainment, buses for trips and other unusual gratuities. Moreover, when the sons came they brought their wives, children and grandchildren, many of whom showed an interest in Judaism and Yiddishkeit. Family was one of the highest values among all the old people, and here was a family that all could wish for.

Jacob himself had been a worker. He had made and lost money but never lost his ideals and concerns for charity and his fellows. Without a formal education, he had become a poet and was considered a Yiddishist and a philosopher. He was not religious but he had religious knowledge and practiced the life of an ethical and traditional Jew. Jacob was a courageous and energetic man. After retirement he had become active in organizing senior citizens' centers and he drew the attention of the outside world for what his people regarded as the right reasons. All this he managed with an air of dignity and gentleness. Without dignity, no one was considered worthy of esteem by them. Without gentleness and generosity, he would have aroused sufficient envy to render him an ineffective leader. He was accepted by everyone in the group, a symbol and focus of its fragile solidarity.

Jacob also symbolized and modeled a good old age. He advised his followers on how to cope with their difficulties, and he demonstrated the possibility that old age was not necessarily a threat to decorum, pleasure, autonomy, and clarity of mind.

Following the usage suggested by Moore and Myerhoff (1977), the ritual of Jacob's party-memorial is described in three stages: (1) its creation, (2) its performance and (3) its outcome, sociologically and in terms of its efficacy.

## The Creation of the Ceremony: Format, Ritual Elements, Symbols

The explicit plan in the design of the ceremony specified a format with several ritual elements that had characterized Jacob's five preceding birthday parties. These were (1) a *brocha*, here a traditional Hebrew blessing of the wine; (2) a welcome and introduction of important people, including the entire extended Kovitz family, present and absent; (3) a festive meal of kosher foods served on tables with tablecloths and flowers and wine, paid for mostly by the family but requiring some donation by members to avoid the impression of charity; (4) speeches by representatives from the Center, sponsoring Jewish organizations under which the Center operates, and local and city groups, and by each of the Kovitz sons; (5) entertainment, usually Yiddish folk songs played by a member of the family; (6) a speech by Jacob; (7) a donation of a substantial sum to the Center for its programs and for Israel by the family; (8) an invitation to those present to make donations to Israel in honor of the occasion; and (9) a birthday cake, songs, and candles.

The format had a feature often found in secular ritual dramas. Within it fixed, sacred elements alternated with more open, secular aspects, as if to lend authenticity, certainty, and propriety to the open, more optional sections. In the open sections, modifications, particularizations, and innovations occur, tying the fixed sections more firmly to the situational details at hand, together providing a progression that seems both apt and traditional. In this case, for example, the *brocha* is followed by the meal, the meal by a toast, the toast by a speech, the speech by a song, then the song by another speech, and so on. The *brocha*, songs, donations, and toasts are predictable; they are unvarying, ritual elements and symbolic acts. The personnel, as representatives, are also symbolic, signifying the boundaries of the relevant collectivities and the social matrix within which the event occurs, but the specific contents of their speeches are less predictable, although they inevitably repeat certain themes.

In this case the repeated themes of the speeches touched on the character, accomplishments, and personal history of Jacob; the honor he brought to his community and family; the honor the family brought to their father and their culture; the importance and worth of the attending Center members; the beauty of Yiddish life; the commonality of all those individuals, organizations, and collectivities in attendance; the perpetuity of the group and its way of life.

The style of the ceremony was another ritual element, familiar to all those who had attended previous parties, and familiar because it was drawn from a wider, general experience – that of many public festivities among strangers and mass media entertainment. It reached for a tone that was jovial, bland, mildly disrespectful, altogether familiar, and familial. It was set by a master-of-ceremonies (a son, Sam) who directed the incidents and the participants, cuing them as to the desired responses during the event, and telling them what was happening as the afternoon unfolded. Despite a seemingly innocuous and casual manner, the style was a precise one, reaching for a particular mood – enjoyment in moderation, and cooperation, unflagging within the regulated time frame. Things must always be kept moving along in ritual; if a lapse occurs, self-consciousness may enter, and the mood may be lost. This is especially important in secular rituals, which are attended by strangers or people from different traditions, to whom the symbols used may not be comprehensible. Ritual is a collusive drama, and all present must be in on it.

In this case specific direction was unusually important. The old people are notoriously difficult to direct. They enter reluctantly into someone else's plans for them; for cultural and psychological reasons, they resist authority and reassert their autonomy. For biological reasons they find it hard to be attentive for extended periods of time and cannot long delay gratification. Programs must be short, emotionally certain and specific, skillfully interspersing food and symbols. The people can be engaged by the calling of their names, by praise, and by identifying them with the guest of honor. But their importance must not be inflated overmuch, for they are quick to perceive this as deception and insult. Furthermore, the old people must not be too greatly aroused, for many have serious heart conditions. Perhaps it was the intense familiarity with their limits as an audience or perhaps it was the uncertainty that underlies all secular ceremonies that caused the designers to select as the master of ceremonies a directive leader, who frequently told the audience what was occurring, what would come next, and reminded them of what had occurred, reiterating the sequences, as if restatement in itself would augment the sense of tradition and timelessness that is sought in ritual.

The affair was called a birthday party, but in fact this was a metaphor. The son Sam said in his speech, "You know, Pa doesn't think a birthday is worth celebrating without raising money for a worthy Jewish cause." The event had a more ambitious purpose than merely celebrating a mark in an individual life. The birthday party metaphor was used because it symbolized the people's membership in a secular, modern society. But as only a birthday, it had little significance to them. None of them had ever celebrated their birthdays in this fashion. Indeed, it was the custom to remember the day of their birth by reckoning it on the closest Jewish holiday, submerging private within collective celebrations. More importantly, the event was a *simcha*, a *yontif*, a *mitzvah* – a blessing, a holiday, a good deed, an occasion for cultural celebration and an opportunity to perform good works in a form that expressed the members' identity with the widest reaches of community, Israel and needy Jews everywhere.

Its most important message was that of perpetuation of the group beyond the life of individual members. This was signified in two ways, both of which were innovations and departures from Kovitz's usual birthdays. First, temporal continuity was signified by the presence of a group of college students, brought into the Center during the year by a young rabbi who sought to promote intergenerational ties. It was decided that the young people would serve the birthday meal to the elders as a gesture of respect. That a rabbi was there with them was incidental and unplanned, but turned out to be important. Second was Jacob's announcement that he was donating funds for his birthday parties to be held at the Center for the next five years, whether he was alive or not. Occasions were thus provided for people to assemble for what would probably be the rest of their lives, giving them some assurance that as individuals they would not outlive their culture and community.

Another of the repeated ritual elements was the personnel involved. Most of these have been identified, and reference here need be made only to two more. These were the director of the Center and its president. The director, Abe, was a second-generation assimilated American of Russian-Jewish parentage. A social worker, he had been with this group a dozen years and knew the people intimately, usually functioning as their guardian, protector, interpreter, and mediator. He, along with Jacob and his sons, developed the format for the ceremony and helped conduct it. The president, Moshe, was a man of eighty-two, with an Hasidic background.[4] He was a religious man with a considerable religious education, and a Yiddishist. It was to him that questions about Judaism and its customs were likely to be referred. After Jacob he was the most respected man in the group, and one of Jacob's closest friends.

Symbols carry implicit messages, distinguishable from the overt ingredients intended by the designers of a ritual; they are part of its creation but not clearly planned or controlled. When they are well chosen and understood, they do their work unnoticed. The following are the symbols within the planned ceremony. Others were spontaneously brought in when the ceremony was interrupted and they will be taken up later.

Many of the symbols employed have been mentioned. Every Yiddish word is a symbol, evoking a deep response. The man Jacob and his entire family were significant symbols, standing for success, fulfillment of Judaic ideals, and filial devotion. The dignitaries and the publics they represented, too, were among the symbols used. The birthday metaphor with cake, candles, and gifts was a symbol complex along with "M.C.," "Guest of Honor," and the tone of the program, which incorporated American, contemporary secular life. Also present were symbols for the widest extension of Judaic culture and its adherents, in the form of references to Israel and *mitzvas* or charity and good works. The attendance of small children and young people symbolized the continuity and perpetuity of Judaism. The traditional foods symbolized and evoked the members' childhood experiences as Jews; they were the least ideological and possibly most powerfully emotional of all the symbolic elements that appeared in the ritual.

### Antecedents of the Ritual

Everyone at the Center knew that Jacob had been sick. For three months he had been hospitalized, in intensive care, and at his request had been removed by his son Sam to his home so that he could be "properly taken care of out of the unhealthy atmosphere of a hospital." Before, Jacob had always resisted living with his children, and people interpreted this change in attitude as indicative of his determination to come to his birthday party. The old people were aware that Jacob had resolved to have the party take place whether he was able to attend or not. People were impressed, first, because Jacob had the autonomy and courage to assert his opinions over the recommendations of his doctors – evidently he was still in charge of himself and his destiny – and second, because Jacob's children were so devoted as to take him in and care for him. But most of all they were struck by his determination to celebrate his birthday among them. They were honored and awed by this and closely followed the daily developments that preceded the celebration: details concerning Jacob's health, the menu for the party, the entertainment – all were known and discussed at length beforehand.

As the day grew close, much talk concerned the significance of the specific date. It was noted that the celebration was being held on Jacob's actual birthday. The party was always held on a Sunday, and as the date and day coincided only every seven years, surely that they did so on this particular year was no accident. Again, they noticed that the month of March was intrinsically important in the Hebrew calendar, a month of three major holidays. And someone claimed that it was the month in which Moses was born and died. He died on his birthday, they noted.[5]

A week before the event, it was reported that Jacob had died. Many who were in touch with him denied it, but the rumor persisted. Two days before the party, a young woman social worker, a close friend of Jacob's, told the college group that she had dreamed Jacob died immediately after giving his speech. And she told the people that Jacob's sons were advising him against coming to the party but that he would not be dissuaded. Nothing would keep him away.

The atmosphere was charged and excited before the party had even begun. Abe, the director, was worried about the old people's health and the effects on them of too much excitement. There were those who insisted that on the birthday they would be told Jacob had died. Jacob's friend Manya said, "He'll come all right, but he is coming to his own funeral."

And what were Jacob's thoughts and designs at this point? It is possible to glimpse his intentions from his taped interviews with a son and a granddaughter. In these, common elements emerge: he is not afraid of death but he is tormented by confusion and disorientation when "things seem upside ways," and "not the way you think is real." Terrible thoughts and daydreams beset him, but he explains that he fights them off with his characteristic strength, remarking, "I have always been a fighter. That's how I lived, even as a youngster. I'd ask your opinion and yours, then go home and think things over and come to my own decision." He describes his battles against senility and his determination to maintain coherence by writing, talking, and thinking. He concludes,

> I was very depressed in the hospital. Then I wrote a poem. Did you see it? A nice poem. So I'm still living and I have something to do. I got more clearheaded. I controlled myself.

Jacob had always controlled himself and shaped his life, and he was not about to give that up. Evidently he hoped he might die the same way. "I'll never change" were his last words on the tape.

It was difficult for Jacob to hold on until the party and to write his speech, which seemed to be the focus of his desire to attend. Its contents were noteworthy in two respects: first, his donation and provision for five more parties; and second, his statement that whereas on all his previous birthdays he had important messages to deliver, on this one he had nothing significant to say. Why, then, the desperate struggle to make this statement? The message, it seems, was that he could and would deliver it himself, that he was still designing his life and would do so to the end. The preparations for and the manner of the speech's delivery conveyed and paralleled its message.

## The Performance of the Ritual

The day of the party was fair and celebrants came streaming toward the Center out of their rented rooms and boardinghouses down the small streets and alleys, several hours too early. That the day was set apart was clear from their appearance. The women came with white gloves, carrying perfectly preserved purses from other decades, and wearing jewelry, unmistakable gifts from their children – golden medallions bearing grandchildren's names, "Tree of Life" necklaces studded with real pearls; Stars of David; gold pendants in the form of the word *Chai*, Hebrew for life and luck. All were announcements of connections and remembrance. Glowing halos from umbrellas and bright hats colored the ladies' expectant faces. Men wore tidy suits polished with use over well-starched collar-frayed shirts.

The Center halls, too, were festively decorated and people were formally seated. At the head table was the Kovitz family and around it the dignitaries. Jacob, it was learned, was behind the curtain of the little stage, receiving oxygen, and so the ceremony was delayed for about half an hour. At last he came out to applause and took his seat. Music called the assembly to order and people were greeted with *shalom*, Hebrew for peace. The guest of honor was presented, then introductions followed, with references to the Kovitz family as *mishpoche* ("kin"), the term finally being used for the entire assembly. By implication, all present were an extended family. Each member of the Kovitz family was named, even those who were absent, including titles and degrees, generation by generation. The assembly was greeted on behalf of "Pa, his children, his children's children, and even from their children." The religious *brocha* in Hebrew was followed by the traditional secular Jewish toast *Le' Chayim*. Sam set out the order of events in detail, including a specification of when Jacob's gift would be made, when dessert would be served (with speeches), when the cake would be eaten (after speeches), and so forth. The announcement of procedures was intended to achieve coordination and invite participation. The audience was appreciative and active. People applauded for the degrees and regrets from family members unable to attend, and recognized the implicit messages of continuity of tradition, respect from younger generations, and family devotion that had been conveyed in the first few moments.

The meal went smoothly and without any public events, though privately Jacob told the president, Moshe, that he wished people would hurry and eat because "*Malakh-hamoves* [the Angel of Death, God's messenger] is near and hasn't given me much time."

As dessert was about to be served, Sam, acting as master of ceremonies, took the microphone and began his speech, in which he recounted some biographical details of Jacob's life and certain cherished characteristics. He emphasized his father's idealism and social activism in the Old Country and in America, and spoke at some length about the courtship and marriage of his parents. Though his mother had died twenty-four years ago, she remained a strong influence in keeping the family together, he said.

During Sam's speech, Jacob was taken backstage to receive oxygen. People were restive and worried, but Sam assured them that Jacob would soon return and the program continue. Eventually Jacob took his seat, leaning over to tell one of the young people in English, and Moshe in Yiddish, that he had little time and wished they would hurry to his part of the program, for now, he said, "*Ikh reingle sikh mitn Malakh-hamoves.*" "I am wrestling the Angel of Death."

The program was interrupted briefly when all those in charge recognized Jacob's difficulty in breathing and gave him oxygen at his seat. A pause of about ten minutes ensued. The thread of the ritual lapsed entirely while people watched Jacob being given oxygen. Moshe and Abe were worried about the impact of this sight on the old people. The previous year someone had died among them and they had been panic-stricken. But now all were rather quiet. They talked to each other softly in Yiddish. At last Sam took the microphone again and spoke extempore about his father's recent life, filling the time and maintaining the ritual mood until it became clear that Jacob was recovering. Sam told the group that maybe his wife's chicken soup – proper chicken soup prepared from scratch with the love of a *yiddishe mame* – had helped sustain Jacob. This was received with enthusiastic applause. Most of those in the audience were women and their identity was much bound up with the role of the nurturant, uniquely devoted Jewish mother. In fact, the earlier mention of the importance and remembrance of the Kovitz mother had been received by many women as a personal tribute. They also appreciated the appropriateness of a daughter-in-law showing this care for a parent, something none of them had experienced. Sam went on to explain that since leaving the hospital Jacob had "embarked on a new career, despite his age." He was teaching his son Yiddish and had agreed to stay around until Sam had mastered it completely. "Since I am a slow learner, I think he'll be with us for quite a while." This too was full of symbolic significance. The suggestion of new projects being available to the old and of the passing on of the knowledge of Yiddish to children were important messages.

Sam went on, extending his time at the microphone as he waited for a sign that Jacob was able to give his speech. By now Sam was improvising on the original format for the ritual. He made his announcement of the gift of money, half to the Center for cultural programs, half to Israel, reminding the audience that Jacob did not believe a birthday party was worth celebrating unless it involved raising funds for deserving Jewish causes.

Still Jacob was not ready, so the microphone was turned over to Abe, who improvised on some of the same themes, again and again, touching important symbolic chords. He, like Sam, referred to Jacob as a stubborn man and to Jews as a stiff-necked people, tenacious and determined. He reassured the assembly that they were important people and would be remembered, that outsiders came to their Center to share their *simcha* and appreciate their unique way of life. They, he said, like Jacob, would be studied by scientists one day, for a better understanding of the indivisibility of mental and physical health, to see how people could live to be very old by using their traditions as a basis for a good and useful life. He finished by emphasizing Jacob's most revered qualities: his devotion to his people, his learning and literacy, and his courage and dignity. He was an example to them all. "And," he went on, "you, too, you are all examples."

At last the sign was given that Jacob was ready. Abe announced the revised sequence of events: Jacob's speech in Yiddish, then in English, then the dignitaries' speeches, then the cake. Jacob remained seated but began his speech vigorously, in good, clear Yiddish.[6] After a few sentences he faltered, slowed, and finished word by word. Here are selections from his speech in translation:

Dear friends: Every other year I have had something significant to say, some meaningful message when we came together for this *yontif*. But this year I don't have an important message. I don't have the strength . . . It is very hard for me to accept the idea that I am played out . . . Nature has a good way of expressing herself when bringing humanity to the end of its years, but when it touches you personally it is hard to comprehend . . . I do have a wish for today . . . It is that my last five years, until I am 100, my birthday will be celebrated here with you . . . whether I am here or not. It will be an opportunity for the members of my beloved Center to be together for a *simcha* and at the same time raise money for our beleaguered Israel.

The message was powerful in its stated and unstated concepts, made even more so by the dramatic circumstances in which it was delivered. Jacob's passion to be heard and to complete his purpose was perhaps the strongest communication. He was demonstrating what he had said in the earlier interviews, namely, that he sustained himself as an autonomous, lucid person, using thinking, speaking, and writing as his shields against self-dissolution and senility.

Jacob finished and sat down amid great applause. His and the audience's relief were apparent. He sat quietly in his place at the table, folded his hands, and rested his chin on his chest. A moment after Sam began to read his father's speech in English, Jacob's head fell back, wordlessly, and his mouth fell open. Oxygen was administered within the surrounding circle of his sons as Abe took the microphone and asked for calm and quiet. After a few moments, his sons lifted Jacob, still seated in his chair, and carried him behind the curtain, accompanied by Moshe, Abe, and the rabbi.

Soon Abe returned and reassured the hushed assembly that a rescue unit had been called, that everything possible was being done, and that Jacob wanted people to finish their dessert:

Be assured that he knew the peril of coming today. All we can do is pray. He's in the hands of God. His sons are with him. He most of all wanted to be here. Remember his dignity and yours and let him be an example. You must eat your dessert. You must, we must all, continue. We go on living. Now your dessert will be served.

People complied and ate quietly. Regularly Abe came to the front to reassure them, with special firmness when the fire department siren was heard outside. He explained at length all the steps that were being taken to save Jacob, and concluded.

He's very delicate. Your cooperation is very beautiful. Jacob wants us to continue. You heard his speech. We all have a date to keep. Out of love and respect for Jacob we will be meeting here for the next five years on his birthday. We will be here, you will be here, whether to celebrate with him or commemorate him. They are taking Jacob away now. The hospital will telephone us and we will tell you how he is doing.

People complied and continued eating. There were many who quietly spoke their certainty that Jacob was dead and had died in their midst. The conviction was strongest among those few who noticed that when the rabbi and Moshe left Jacob behind the curtain, they went to the bathroom before returning to their seats. Perhaps it was only hygiene, they said, but it was also known that religious Jews are enjoined to wash their hands after contact with the dead. Hence the gesture was read as portentous. One of the religious men moved his lips quietly, not praying but uttering, "*Ehad,*

*ehad, ehad*," Hebrew for "one". This is to be the last word heard or, if possible, said at the exact moment of death.[7]

The room was alive with hushed remarks:

> He's gone. That was how he wanted it. He said what he had to say and finished.
> It was a beautiful life, a beautiful death.
> There's a saying, when the fig is plucked in due time it's good for the fig and good for the tree.
> Did you see how they carried him out? Like Elijah, he died in his chair. Like a bride groom.
> He died like a *tzaddik*.[8]
> Moses also died on his birthday, in the month of Nisan.[9]

Order was restored as the dignitaries were introduced. Again the ritual themes reappeared in the speeches: Jacob's work among senior citizens, the honor of his family, his exemplary character, and so forth. A letter to Jacob from the mayor was read and a plaque honoring him preferred by a councilman. Then a plant was given to his family on behalf of an organization, and this seemed to be a signal that gifts were possible and appropriate. One of the assembled elderly, an artist, took one of his pictures off the wall and presented it to the family. A woman gave the family a poem she had written honoring Jacob, and another brought up the flowers from her table. The momentum of the ritual lapsed completely in the face of these spontaneous gestures. People were repeatedly urged by Abe to take their seats. The artist, Heschel, asked what would be done about the birthday cake now that Jacob was gone, and was rebuked for being gluttonous. With great difficulty Abe regained control of the people, reminding them sternly that the ceremony had not been concluded. There remained one dignitary who had not yet spoken, Abe pointed out, and this was insulting to the group he represented.

Abe was improvising here, no longer able to utilize the guidelines of the birthday metaphor. The ceremony threatened to break apart. In actuality, Abe was worried about letting people go home without knowing Jacob's fate. It would be difficult for him to handle their anxieties in the next few days if they were left in suspense. No one wanted to leave. The circumstances clearly called for some closure, some provision of order. The last dignitary began to talk and Abe wondered what to do next. Then the phone rang and everyone was still. The speaker persisted, but no one listened. Abe came forward and announced what everyone already knew.

> God in his wisdom has taken Jacob away from us, in His mystery He has taken him. So you must understand that God permitted Jacob to live ninety-five years and to have one of his most beautiful moments here this afternoon. You heard his last words. We will charter a bus and go together to his funeral. He gave you his last breath. I will ask the rabbi to lead us in a prayer as we stand in solemn tribute to Jacob.

People stood. About a dozen men drew *yarmulkes* out of their pockets and covered their heads. The rabbi spoke:

> We have had the honor of watching a circle come to its fullness and close as we rejoiced together. We have shared Jacob's wisdom and warmth, and though the ways of God are

mysterious, there is meaning in what happened today. I was with Jacob backstage and tried to administer external heart massage. In those few moments with him behind the curtain, I felt his strength. There was an electricity about him but it was peaceful and I was filled with awe. When the firemen burst in, it felt wrong because they were big and forceful and Jacob was gentle and resolute. He was still directing his life, and he directed his death. He shared his wisdom, his life with us and now it is our privilege to pay him homage. Send your prayers with Jacob on his final journey. Send his sparks up and help open the gates for him with your thoughts. We will say Kaddish. "*Yitgadal veyitakadash shmeh rabba* . . . [Sanctified and magnificent be Thy Great Name]."[10]

The ritual was now unmistakably over but no one left the hall. People shuffled forward toward the stage, talking quietly in Yiddish. Many crossed the room to embrace friends, and strangers and enemies embraced as well. Among these old people physical contact is usually very restrained, yet now they eagerly sought each other's arms. Several wept softly. As is dictated by Jewish custom, no one approached the family, but only nodded to them as they left.

There were many such spontaneous expressions of traditional Jewish mourning customs, performed individually, with the collective effect of transforming the celebration into a commemoration. Batya reached down and pulled out the hem of her dress, honoring the custom of rending one's garments on news of a death. Someone had draped her scarf over the mirror in the ladies' room, as tradition requires. Heschel poured his glass of tea into a saucer. Then Abe took the birthday cake to the kitchen, and said, "We will freeze it. We will serve it at Jacob's memorial when we read from his book. He wouldn't want us to throw it away. He will be with us still. You see, people, Jacob holds us together even after his death."

Finally, the Center had emptied. People clustered together on the benches outside to continue talking and reviewing the events of the afternoon. Before long, all were in agreement that Jacob had certainly died among them. The call to the rescue squad had been a formality, they agreed. Said Moshe,

> You see, it is the Jewish way to die in your community. In the old days, it was an honor to wash the body of the dead. No one went away and died with strangers in a hospital. The finest people dressed the corpse and no one left him alone for a minute. So Jacob died like a good Yid. Not everybody is so lucky.

Over and over, people discussed the goodness of Jacob's death and its appropriateness. Many insisted that they had known beforehand he would die that day. "So why else do you think I had my *yarmulke* with me at a birthday party?" asked Beryl. Sam commented, "After a scholarly meeting it is customary to thank the man. Jacob was a scholar and we thanked him by accompanying him to Heaven. It's good to have many people around at such a time. It shows them on the other side that a man is respected where he came from." Bessie's words were "He left us a lot. Now the final chapter is written. Nu? What more is there to say. The book is closed. When a good man dies, his soul becomes a word in God's book." It was a good death, it was agreed. Jacob was a lucky man. "*Zu mir gezugt* – it should happen to me" was heard from the lips of many as they left.

## Outcome: Sociological Consequences

Two formal rituals followed. The funeral was attended by most of the group (which, as promised, went in a chartered bus), and a *shloshim* or thirty-day memorial was held at the Center, when the birthday cake was indeed served, but without candles.

At the funeral, the young rabbi reiterated his earlier statement concerning the electricity he had felt emitting from Jacob just before he died, described how Jacob used his remaining strength to make a final affirmation of all he stood for, and revealed that, at the last moment of his life, Jacob – surrounded by all the people he loved – believed in God.[11] In his eulogy, Jacob's son Sam said, "In our traditions there are three crowns – the crown of royalty, the crown of priesthood, and the crown of learning. But a fourth, the crown of a good name, exceeds them all." Spontaneously, at the graveside, without benefit of direction from funeral officials, many old men and women came forward to throw a shovel of earth on the grave, sometimes themselves tottering from the effort. Each one carefully laid down the shovel after finishing, according to the old custom. Then they backed away, forming two rows, to allow the Angel of Death to pass through. They knew from old usage what was appropriate, what movements and gestures suited the occasion, with a certainty that is rarely seen now in their lives. Moshe, one of the last to leave, pulled up some grass and tossed it over his shoulder. This is done, he explained later, to show that we remember we are dust, but also that we may be reborn, for it is written: "May they blossom out of the city like the grass of the earth."

A month later, the *shloshim* was held. In it a final and official interpretation of Jacob's death was forged and shared. He was a saint by then. He must be honored, and several disputes were avoided that day by people reminding one another of Jacob's spirit of appreciation and acceptance of all of them and his wish for peace within the Center. The cake was eaten with gusto as people told and retold the story of Jacob's death.

Funeral and *shloshim* were the formal and public dimension of the outcome of Jacob's death. Informal, private opinions and interpretations are also part of the outcome. These were revealed in subsequent individual discussions, informal interviews, casual group conversations, and a formalized group discussion on the subject. On these private, casual occasions people said things they had not, and probably would not, express in public, particularly about matters that they knew might be regarded as old-fashioned, un-American, or superstitious. In confidence, several people expressed wonder at and some satisfaction in what they regarded as the divine participation in the event. One lady said with a chuckle, "You know, if the Lord God, Himself, would bother about us and would come around to one of our affairs, well, it makes you feel maybe you are somebody after all." Said Bessie,

> You know, I wouldn't of believed if I didn't see with mine eyes. Myself, I don't really believe in God. I don't think Jacob did neither. If a man talks about the Angel of Death when he's dying that don't necessarily mean anything. Everybody talks about the Angel of Death. It's like a saying, you know what I mean? But you gotta admit that it was not a regular day. So about what really went on, I'm not saying it was God working there, but who can tell? You could never be sure.

Publicly the subject was discussed at great length. A debate is a cherished, traditional form of sociability among these people. And this was certainly a proper topic for a *pilpul*.[12] A kind of *pilpul* was held with a group in the Center that had been participating in regular discussions. One theme considered by them in detail was the young social worker's dream, in which she anticipated the time and manner of Jacob's death.[13] Dreams, they agreed, must be carefully evaluated, for they may be sent by God or the demons, and as such are not to be taken as prophecy on face value. After much discussion one of the learned men in the group said that perhaps the young woman should have fasted on the day after the dream. This assures that the previous night's dreams will not come true. Sam quoted Psalm 39, in which King David prayed to God to know the measure of his days. The request was denied because God decreed that no man shall know the hour of his death. Could it be that God granted Jacob what he had denied Kind David? Why had the girl had the dream? She knew nothing of these matters. Why had it not come to one of them, who understood the significance of dreams? After an hour or so of disagreement only two points were clear. First, that the news of the dream had received widespread circulation before the birthday party; and second, that it added to people's readiness to participate in a commemoration instead of a party. It made what happened more mysterious and more acceptable at the same time. Did it convince anyone that God had had a hand in things? Some said yes and some no. Perhaps the most general view was that expressed by Moshe, who on leaving said, "Well, I wouldn't say yes but on the other hand I wouldn't say no."

Another aspect of the ritual's outcome was the impact of the day on various outsiders. The attending dignitaries were included in the moment of *communitas* that followed Jacob's death, and were duly impressed. Before leaving, one of the Gentile politicians told the people around her, "I have always heard a lot about Jewish life and family closeness. What I have seen here today makes me understand why the Jews have survived as a people." This praise from an official, a stranger and a Christian, to a group that has always regarded Christians with distrust and often deep fear, was a source of great satisfaction, a small triumph over a historical enemy, and an unplanned but not unimportant consequence of the ritual.

The events of the day were reported widely, in local newspapers and soon in papers all over the country. Members of the audience were given opportunities to tell their version of what happened when children and friends called or wrote to ask them, "Were you there that day . . . ?" The impact on the Center members of the dispersion of the news to an outside world, ordinarily far beyond their reach, was to give them a temporary visibility and authority that increased their importance, expanded their social horizons, and accelerated their communication with the world around them. These, along with their heightened sense of significance, were the apparent sociological consequences of the ritual.

## Outcome: The Efficacy of the Ritual

How shall the success of a ritual be estimated? How is one to decide if it has done its work? These are among the most complex and troublesome questions to be faced in dealing with this topic. It is not impossible to examine efficacy in terms of the explicit intentions of the performers. But it is necessary to go beyond this and inquire, too, about its unintended effects and the implicit, unconscious messages it carries. Then, one may ask, for whom did it work? For there may be many publics involved. In religious rituals even the deities and the unseen forces are addressed and, it is hoped, moved by the performance. The official plan for a ritual does not tell us about this. Many levels of response may be specified, for this is not given by the formal organization of a ritual. Sometimes audiences or witnesses are more engaged by watching a ritual than are its central subjects and participants. When we inquire about conviction, it is necessary to ask also about the degree and kind of conviction involved, since a range of belief is possible, from objection and anger if the ritual is incorrectly performed, through indifference and boredom, to approval and enjoyment, and finally total and ecstatic conviction. The long-range as well as immediate effects of the event must be taken into account, since rituals have consequences that reach past the moment when they occur; their outcome is usually to be known only in due time. It is impossible to take up all these questions. The fieldworker never has such complete information. And the symbols dealt with in ritual are by definition inexhaustible in their final range of referents. Subjects cannot verbalize the totality of their apprehensions in these areas because so much of their response is unconscious. Inevitably there are blanks in our inquiry, and ultimately the fieldworker interested in such questions takes responsibility for inference in explanation, going beyond the observed behavior and "hard" data; to do otherwise would mean losing all hope of understanding the issues that make ritual interesting in the first place. In discussing ritual, an analysis of outcome is always an interpretation and an incomplete one.

All rituals are efficacious to some degree merely by their taking place. They are not purposive and instrumental, but expressive, communicative, and rhetorical acts. Their stated purpose must be regarded not as an illustration of a piece of life but as an analogy. No primitive society is so unempirical as to expect to cause rain by dancing a rain dance. Not even Suzanne Langer's cat is that naive. A rain dance is, in Burke's felicitous phrase, a dance with the rain, the dancing of an attitude. The attitude is the one described earlier – collectively attending, dramatizing, making palpable unseen forces, setting apart the flow of everyday life by framing a segment of it, stopping time and change by presenting a permanent truth or pattern. If the spirits hear and it rains, so much the better, but the success of the ritual does not depend on the rain. If a patient at a curing ceremony recovers, good, but he or she need not do so for the ritual to have successfully done its work. A ritual fails when it is seen through, not properly attended, or experienced as arbitrary invention. Then people may be indifferent enough not to hide their lack of conviction; their failure or refusal to appear to suspend disbelief is apparent and the ritual is not even efficacious as a communication.

In the case of Jacob's death, matters are complicated because two rituals must be considered: the intended birthday party, a designed, directed secular affair with nonreligious sacred nuances, transformed spontaneously by a collectivity into a nonplanned, fully sacred religious memorial.

The birthday party, as far as it went, was a success. It is hard to imagine how it could have failed to make its point and achieve its purposes, which were entirely social. It was convincing to all concerned and received by the audience with appreciation and cooperation. It demonstrated social connections and implied perpetuity of a collectivity beyond the limited life span of its central figure. It honored the man Jacob and his friends, values, and traditions. It reached beyond its immediate audience to include and allow for identification with a wider, invisible Jewish community. The goals of the birthday party were relatively modest and not unusual for secular ceremonies of this sort. The turning point occurred when Jacob died; the message and impact of the day's ceremonies took on a new dimension, and the sacred ritual replaced the social, more secular one.

In dying when he did, Jacob was giving his last breath to his group, and this was understood as a demonstration of his regard for them. His apparent ability to choose to do what is ordinarily beyond human control hinted at some divine collaboration. The collective and spontaneous reversion to traditional religious death rituals was hardly surprising. Death customs are always elaborate and usually constitute one of the most tenacious and familiar areas of religious knowledge. According to some authorities, saying Kaddish makes one still a Jew no matter what else of the heritage one has relinquished.[14] The saying of Kaddish makes palpable the community of Jews. According to the rabbi at the party-memorial, the Kaddish always includes not only the particular death at hand but all a person's dead beloved and all the Jews who have ever lived and died.[15] Mourners coalesce into an *edah*, a community, connected beyond time and space to an invisible group, stretching to the outermost reaches of being a people, *Kol Isroel* – the ancestors, those unborn – and most powerfully, one's own direct, personal experiences of loss and death.

For religious and nonreligious alike that day the Kaddish enlarged and generalized the significance of Jacob's death. At the same time, the Kaddish particularized his death by equating it with each person's historical, subjective private griefs, thus completing the exchange between the collective and the private poles of experience to which axiomatic symbols refer. When this exchange occurs, symbols are not mere pointers or referents to things beyond themselves. A transformation takes place: "Symbols and object seem to fuse and are experienced as a perfectly undifferentiated whole."[16] Such transformations cannot be planned or achieved by will, because emotions and imagination, as D. G. James observes, operate more like fountains than machines.[17] Transformation carries participants beyond words and word-bound thought, calling into play imagination, emotion, and insight and, as Suzanne Langer says, "altering our conceptions at a single stroke." Then participants conceive the invisible referents of their symbols and may glimpse the underlying, unchanging patterns of human and cosmic life, in a triumph of understanding and belief. Few rituals reach such heights of intensity and conviction. When this occurs, all those involved are momentarily drawn together in a basically religious, sometimes near ecstatic mood of gratitude and wonder. That Jacob's death was a genuine transformational moment was attested to by a profound sense of *communitas* and fulfillment that people appeared to have experienced with the recitation of the Kaddish.

We are interested in the unintended, implicit messages conveyed by ritual as well as the planned ones. Therefore, in this case it must be asked, What were the consequences of the set of items that suggested uncanny, inexplicable factors – Jacob's references to the presence of the Angel of Death, his seeming ability to choose the moment of his death, and the prophecy of his death in the form of a dream? The questions are particularly important because ritual is supposed to deliver a message about predictability and order, and here were intrusions beyond human control and therefore disorderly and unpredictable.

Paradoxically, these very elements of the uncanny, mysterious, and unpredictable made the ritual more persuasive and more convincing rather than less so. All these surprises were clothed in a traditional idiom, and while perplexing were not unfamiliar. There were well-used accounts for such matters; there were precedents for prophetic dreams, the presence of the Angel of Death, the deaths of the *tzaddikim*, and of Moses. Conceptions existed for handling them, and if most people involved did not deeply believe in the dogma, they were not unwilling to consider the possibility that explanations previously offered, though long unused, might have some validity after all.

Renewed belief in God at the end of life is hardly rare, and indeed it might even be that people were more reassured than frightened at the turn of events of the day. When a man dies, as Evans-Pritchard reminds us, a moral question is always posed: not merely, Why does man die? But why this man and why now? In our secular society, we are often left without an answer, and these celebrants, like most whose religion has decayed or been jettisoned, were ordinarily alone with these questions, dealing with ultimate concerns, feebly and individually. The result of Jacob's death, however, was the revival of the idea, or at least the hope and suspicion, that sometimes people die meaningfully; occasionally purpose and propriety are evident. Death in most cases may be the ultimate manifestation of disorder and accident but here it seemed apt and fulfilling. More often than not death flies in the face of human conception, reminding us of our helplessness and ignorance. It finds the wrong people at the wrong time. It mocks our sense of justice. But here it did the opposite and made such obvious sense that it came as a manifestation of order. It helped fulfill the purposes of ritual, establishing and stating form drawn forth from flux and confusion.

Remarkably enough, in this ritual the distinction between artifice and nature was also overcome. The ritual, though unplanned, was not susceptible to the danger of being recognized as human invention. Ironically, because no one was clearly entirely in control – neither Jacob nor the designers and directors – and because it unfolded naturally, the ritual was received as a revelation rather than as a construction. It did not suffer the usual risks of ritual, displaying the conventional and attributed rather than intrinsic nature of our conceptions. Had there been no intimations of the supernatural, the death would probably have been frightening, because it would have exaggerated mortal powers beyond the credibility of the people participating. The hints of mystery suggested powers beyond Jacob's control, making a religious experience of one that otherwise might have been simply bizarre. Despite the interruption of the party and the resultant radical change of course, the celebration that occurred had that very sense of inevitability and predictability of outcome which is the goal of all human efforts in designing and staging a ritual.

### Ritual and Time

Any discussion of ritual is ultimately a discussion of time. In the case of a ritual dealing with death and birth, the theme of time is thrown into high relief. Ritual alters ordinary time, emphasizing regularity, order, predictability and continuity. Ironically, it uses repetition to deny the empty, diffuse, trivial, endless, repetitiveness of human and social experience. It finds hints of eternity in recurrences, presented in rituals as re-enactments of timeless patterns, proper and inevitable. Chance is not necessarily denied in ritual, but may be incorporated into a larger framework, where its mutability is reduced in scale and contained within a grander, tidier totality. By inserting traditional elements into the present, the past is read as prefiguring the present, and by implication, the present foreshadows the future. Religious rituals are more sweeping than secular ones in this elongation of time, since sacred rituals aspire to be eternally true, where secular rituals usually refer only to remembered human history. When religious rituals are completely successful, history is transformed into myth, *illud tempus* of no time, no beginnings and no endings.

Ritual disrupts several distinct kinds of time. First, it interferes with the ordinary public broken-up sense of time, where hard, precise and measurable units are used to coordinate collective life. Here, time marches along with great regularity, regardless of human response, stimulation, emotion and mood. Public, quantitative time is quite unsuitable to the mood sought in ritual, which attempts precisely to sweep us away from this objective and rational, evaluative frame of mind. Ritual, like art, may disrupt this kind of time merely by interesting us sufficiently.

A second time sense pertinent to ritual is the subjective, individual perception of events. This is Bergson's duration, intuited flowing, paced according to personal significance. This time is quite irregular, both internally and among assembled individuals. Rituals reach for this time sense, appropriate to a mood of conviction. But then, it is necessary in ritual to coordinate the participants so that their private temporal experiences are shared without being too tightly regulated. Synchronization of some sort is necessary, and when it is achieved its collective force is considerable. It is in part this simultaneity of individual time that gives such power to *communitas* states. When the integration of individual moments and responses occurs within the ritual context, a temporary collectivity is made of the participants.

Another kind of temporal interruption may occur in ritual, especially in rites of passage. This is the integration of the individual across the time span of the life cycle, so that a retrieval of a sense of personal integration is achieved. Fragments of experience associated with different phases of personal history are brought to life in ritual, bringing with them their original social and emotional contexts. These assembled fragments allow one to re-experience oneself as a child or youth, to feel again that earlier person as comprehensible, familiar, still present within. Coherence of the "I" is not inevitable, as Fernandez (1974) points out, and the chaos of individual experience, especially when the experience covers great periods of time and sharp disruptions in culture or society, can be acute. How can one identify with the feelings and perceptions of the child one was so long ago? How can one retrieve and recognize all the creatures one has ever been?

Because ritual works through the senses and largely without interference by the conscious mind, it has a singular capacity for bringing back earlier emotions, and allowing one to return to earlier states of being. The past returns with the ritual movements, gestures and recapitulations that link the individual to numinous, unaltered fragments of previous times. Perhaps more than any other thinker, Proust was fascinated with this process. He felt that the past could sometimes be recaptured in its original purity, without the modification of intervening events and without passing through the crucible of the conscious mind. When such re-experiences of past time come back, usually evoked through the senses, unaltered by the chemistry of thought, untouched by time, they carry with them their original, pristine associations and feelings. Mendilow (1952) refers to this experience of timelessness as

> hermetical magic, sealed outside of time, suspending the sense of duration, allowing all of life to be experienced in a single moment. . . . These are pin-points of great intensity, concentrations of universal awareness, antithetical to the diffuseness of life. (1952: 137)

Such moments are beyond the experience of duration and flow. In them one may experience the essence of life, eternally valid, very close to the sacred *illud tempus* where history becomes myth.

The rituals that are the most resonant and basic are those associated with the earliest social experiences, inevitably experiences of nurturance and dependence – familial, domestic, often non-verbal, profoundly physiological. In our own world of plural cultures, we often speak of the first, familial experiences as one's ethnic origins, a label for the events associated with first foods, care, language, songs, tales and the like, carried forever by rituals and symbols. Ethnic materials are redolent with early, fundamental associations, and thus contain the possibility of carrying one back to earlier selves, overcoming time and change. Consider the statement made by one of the old men present that day at Jacob's birth-death ritual.

> Whenever I say Kaddish, I chant and sway, and it comes back to me like always. I remember how it was when my father, may he rest in peace, would wrap me around in his big prayer shawl. All that warmth comes back to me like I was back in that shawl where nothing, nothing bad could happen.

The Kaddish prayer was probably the most important single ritual that occurred on the day of Jacob's death. It was the most potent emotionally, the most frequently and deeply experienced ritual event, the most ethnically rooted moment, sweeping together all the individuals present, connecting them with earlier parts of self, with Jacob the man, each other, with Jews who had lived and died before, and finally with the great heroes and holy figures of Jewish myth and history. The life of the single man, Jacob, was made into an archetypal event, a myth enacted by mortals whose mundane affairs were enlarged to become full of light and portent. Here is ritual achieving its final purpose, of altering our everyday understandings. Ultimately we are interested in ritual because it tells us something about the mythic condition, the human condition and our private selves at the same time. It may portray an archaic event, but it must be an event that we experience, and the characters, though different from us, must shed light on our own condition. Jacob is a symbol by the end of the day, and as such the pinpoint from which radiated the enlarged meanings of his life and death as well as the immediate ones, the grand and the minute, the remote and the particular – all simultaneously presented, and implying each other.

It might be said that the rituals surrounding Jacob's death altered time in still one more way – by giving the people present more time. Contained in the intimations of the immortal, which most people felt were so present all the day, is the possibility of immortality – perhaps oblivion after death was not a certainty after all.

The old people's long lives stretch far behind them and there is little time ahead. The time they have remaining is heavy and hard to fill. They are not known outside their own small, dying circle. They have no reason to expect their children to remember them more after death than they do in life. They bear besides the enormous burden of individual extinction the knowledge that their way of life is passing out of existence with them. Said one of Jacob's friends:

> It's hard enough to die. All right, we all have to die. But when I think about the streets of my little town, no one will come down the streets anymore. There is nothing left. Maybe even there aren't my parents' gravestones left. That good life, our good Yiddish life, our beautiful language, nobody to talk it any more. Whether there's a god or not, I don't know. What I do know is if there is a god, he's playing marbles with us.

Jacob's death couldn't change the hard realities. But if people lived only by realities there would be no rituals, no symbols, no myths. The power of rituals, myths and symbols is such that they can change the experience we have of the world and its worth. Jacob's death rites may be considered an extraordinarily successful example of ritual, changing the world at a single stroke, opening the experience of more connections, more perpetuation, making a little less certain the oblivion of a culture and collectivity than anyone had thought possible before the day began.

## Notes

1    Methods used as the basis for this paper were the conventional anthropological techniques of participation-observation, interviews, tape recordings, group discussions, film and photographs. I was fortunate in that there were many records of the events of the day described. The entire sequence was filmed, and I photographed and taped it. Those present at the ceremony numbered about 200. My interpretation is based on protracted discussions before and after the event with about 50 of the people present.

2    In a later version of this essay, titled "A Death in Due Time: Construction of Self and Culture in Ritual Drama" (1984), Myerhoff here inserted the following discussion under the heading of "Death as a Cultural Drama":

> Jacob Kovitz [Koved in *Number Our Days*] died in the middle of his ninety-fifth birthday . . .

>> The case is remarkable for several reasons: it illustrates the use of ritual to present a collective interpretation of "reality," and it demonstrates the capacity of ritual to take account of unplanned developments and alter itself in midstream into a different event. Further, it illuminates how one man can make himself into a commentary upon his life, his history, and his community, mirroring his social world to itself and to himself at the same time. The case is an example of the transformation of a natural, biological event – death – into a cultural drama, shaped to human purpose until it becomes an affirmation rather than a negation of life.
>>     Though quite rare in our times, such deaths are not unprecedented. The French social historian. Philippe Ariès refers to ritualized, ceremonial deaths as "tamed," and points out that in the Middle Ages, knights of the *chanson de geste* also tamed their deaths. Forewarned by spontaneous realization of imminent departure, the dying person prepared himself and his surroundings, often by organizing a ritual and presiding over it to the last. Death was a public presentation, often simple, including parents, children, friends, and neighbors. Tamed deaths were not necessarily emotional. Death was both familiar and near, evoking no great fear or awe. Solzhenitsyn, too, as Ariès notes, talks about such deaths among peasants. "They didn't puff themselves up or fight against it and brag that they weren't going to die – they took death calmly . . . And they departed easily, as if they were just moving into a new house." Death was not romanticized or banished. It remained within the household and domestic circle, the dy-

ing person at the center of events, "determining the ritual as he saw fit."

Later, as the concept of the individual emerges, distinct from the social and communal context, the moment of death came to be regarded as an opportunity in which one was most able to reach – and publicly present – a full awareness of self. Until the fifteenth-century, the death ceremony was at least as important as the funeral in Western Europe. . . .

All the elements of a tamed death are present also in the case of Jacob's birthday party: his foreknowledge of death, its occurrence in a public ceremony, which he directed, his attitude of calm acceptance, his use of the occasion to express the meaning of his life, and the presence and participation of those with whom he was intimate.

Unlike the Eskimo or the medieval knight, Jacob constructed his death alone, without support of established ritual and without expectation of cooperation from his community. This was his own invention, and his only partner was *Malakh-hamoves*, the Angel of Death, who cooperated with him to produce a triumphant celebration that defied time, change, mortality, and existential isolation. Through this ritual, Jacob asserted that his community would continue, that his way of life would be preserved, that he was a coherent, integrated person throughout his personal history, and that something of him would remain alive after his physical end. – Ed.

3   Here I am distinguishing between "religious" and "sacred" and treating them as categories that may exist independently or be joined. Where ideas, objects, or practices are considered axiomatic, unquestionable, literally sacrosanct, they are "sacred," with or without the inclusion of the concept of the supernatural. Their sacredness derives from a profound and affective consensus as to their rightness; their authority comes from their embeddedness in many realms of tradition. Over against the sacred is the mundane, which is malleable and negotiable. When sacredness is attached to the supernatural, it is religious *and* sacred. When sacredness is detached from the religious, it refers to unquestionably good and right traditions, sanctified by usage and consensus.

4   Hasids (Hasidim) were, and are, a deeply religious, semi-mystical group practicing a vitalized, fervent form of folk Judaism originating in Eastern Europe during the mid-eighteenth century.

5   In fact, Moses died on the seventh of Adar. He did, however, die on his birthday.

6   All these people are completely multilingual and use different languages for different purposes, with some consistency. For example, political and secular matters are often discussed in English; Hebrew is used to make learned, final points in settling debates; Russian and Polish appear in songs, poems, reminiscences, in arguments and bargaining. Yiddish, the *mame loshen*, punctuates all the areas, but appears most regularly in times of intense emotion. It is also used most in conversations about food, children, cursing, and gossiping. For some, Yiddish has connotations of inferiority since it was associated with female activities, domestic and familial matters (in the shtetl, few were educated in Hebrew and so Yiddish dominated the household). It was the language of exiles living in oppression and, later, of greenhorns. For others, the Yiddishists in particular, it is a bona fide language to be treated with respect and used publicly. Careful pronunciation, proper syntax, and avoidance of Anglicized words are considered signs of respect for Yiddishkeit. On the whole, Jacob was always careful in his Yiddish, and this was seen as an indication of his pride in his heritage.

7   *Ehad* is the final word of the phrase, "The Lord is One," which according to some authorities signifies that the soul unites with Deity as the word "one" is said (Goldin 1939: 109).

8   A *tzaddik* in Hasidic tradition is a saintly man of great devotion, often possessing mystical powers. It is noted that important Hasids sometimes died in their chairs, and it is said that they often anticipated the dates of their death. There is also a suggestive body of custom surrounding the symbolism of the chair, which figures importantly in at least two Jewish male rites of passage. In Hasidic weddings it is customary for the bridegroom to be car-

ried aloft in his chair. And an empty chair is reserved for the prophet Elijah at circumcisions; this is to signify that any Jewish boy may turn out to be the Messiah, since Elijah must be present at the Messiah's birth.

9   As noted above, Moses died on the seventh of Adar, on his birthday; he was allowed to "complete the years of the righteous exactly from day to day and month to month, as it is said, the number of thy days I will fulfill" (Talmud Bavli Kaddushin 38A). Hence the tradition in folklore that the righteous are born and die on the same day. Elijah did not die in his chair, however. He is believed to have "been taken up by a whirlwind into Heaven," passing out of this world without dying. His "passage" was not a normal death in any event, and this is probably why his death was brought up in this discussion. These points were clarified in personal communication by Rabbi Chaim Seidler-Feller of Los Angeles.

10  In Jewish mysticism, represented in the Kabbalah, a person's soul or spirit is transformed into sparks after death. "Kaddish" is a prayer sanctifying God's name, recited many times in Jewish liturgy; it is known also as the Mourner's Prayer and recited at the side of a grave.

11  Others disagreed with this and were certain that Jacob died an agnostic. They did not confront the rabbi on the matter, however; said Heschel, "If it makes the rabbi happy, let him believe it."

12  Literally, *pilpul* means "pepper" and refers to the custom of lively scholarly argument about religious texts.

13  Dreams were very significant among shtetl folk, being elaborately discussed and much used in pursuit of symbolic meanings and ritual usage. Indeed, four members of the group owned and used dream books, which they had brought with them from the Old Country.

14  Joseph Zoshin, "The Fraternity of Mourners," in J. Riemer, ed., *Jewish Reflections on Death* (New York, 1974).

15  The rabbi was in attendance fortuitously that day, in his capacity as leader of the young people. Without him the Kaddish would not have been said. His unplanned presence was subsequently interpreted by many as another sign that the memorial was meant to take place when it did.

16  Suzanne K. Langer, *Philosophy in a New Key* (Cambridge, Massachusetts, 1957).

17  D. G. James, *Scepticism and Poetry* (London, 1937).


## References

Fernandez, James W. 1974. "The Mission of the Metaphor in Expressive Culture," *Current Anthropology* 15: 119–33.

Geertz, Clifford. 1973. *The Interpretation of Cultures*. New York: Basic.

Goldin, Hyman E. 1939. *Hamadrikh, The Rabbi's Guide: A Manual of Jewish Religious Rituals, Ceremonials and Customs*. New York: Hebrew Publishing Co.

Mendilow, Adam A. 1952. *Time and Experience*. London: Peter Nevill.

Moore, Sally F. and Barbara Myerhoff (eds.). 1977. *Secular Ritual: Forms and Meanings*. Assen, Holland: Royal Van Gorcum Press.

Myerhoff, Barbara. 1984. "Rites and Signs of Ripening: The Intertwining of Ritual, Time, and Growing Older. In *Age and Anthropological Theory*, edited by David Kerzer and Jennie Keith-Ross. Ithaca, NY: Cornell.

Turner, Victor. 1974. *Wampeters, Foma and Granfalloons*. New York: Delta.

# 29 Death in Very Old Age: A Personal Journey of Caregiving

## Betty Risteen Hasselkus

Death in old age is referred to as normative death (Kastenbaum, 1985; Moss and Moss, 1989); it is an expected event. More than two thirds of all deaths in the United States are of persons 65 years old or over (Brody, 1984). Caregiving for someone who is old and dying is, it appears, also a normative event (Brody, 1985). As Lynn stated, "Almost all of us will die of a chronic illness, with a time sequence that will give substantial warning" (1991, p. 69). That period of "substantial warning" is usually a time when help and care are required from another person.

Approximately one-third of all deaths occur in people who are 80 years of age or older (Brody, 1984). Occupational therapists who work in geriatrics are likely to find themselves involved in the care of very old dying persons. Although dying patients are no longer routinely ignored by the health care system, professionals, patients and families continue to flounder "for lack of a clear set of goals and aspirations for the final phase of life" (Lynn, 1991, p. 70). The death of a patient may be viewed only as a negative and unsatisfying professional experience. Professionals may be hesitant to support the dying process, recognizing only their roles of continued support for life while it lasts.

This paper describes a personal journey of caregiving for a very old dying person. My mother died at age 91 on October 10, 1991. I entered that caregiving journey as a novice, with little knowledge or firsthand experience in caring for a dying person. I found myself transformed by the experience – as a private person and as a professional. It was my mother's final legacy to me that I was able to share her last days so intensely and to be alone with her at that most intimate and sacred moment – the moment of death. The gift of that shared experience has enlarged my awareness of the many dimensions of caregiving for a dying person and helped me to define the potential role of the health professional during the dying process.

## The Story

### The prelude to dying

When a person lives for 91 years, it is likely that he or she will experience a lengthy period of chronic illness before death. My mother, from about age 82 years onward,

Original publication: Hasselkus, Betty Risteen, "Death in Very Old Age: A Personal Journey of Caregiving," *American Journal of Occupational Therapy* 47 (1993), pp. 717–23.

had lived with diminishing vision, increasingly impaired hearing, and severe degenerative joint disease. Despite progressive frailty and widowhood, she could not bring herself to seriously consider moving out of the house that she and my father had built, and instead gradually instituted a succession of mini-modifications over the years to accommodate her changing needs.

I was a caregiver from a distance during most of those years, occasionally offering suggestions derived from my occupational therapy training, but more often watching with some amazement as, time after time, she adapted her home and her daily activities to accommodate her changing physical capabilities. She arranged to have her clotheslines lowered, purchased a bath bench, and installed a shower hose in the bathtub and railings by the outside steps. She put an extra cushion on the living room chair, purchased magnifiers and a large-numbered telephone dial, sold her car, and hired people to help with the yard and the cleaning and transportation. She no longer put daily dishes away in the cupboard between meals but, instead, kept them conveniently in the dish rack in the sink. She asked us to help move her bedroom furniture down to the small sewing room on the first floor, and her visits upstairs became less and less frequent.

About a year and a half before she died, the first ominous signs of lymphoma appeared. My mother referred to the diagnosis warily as "this leukemia business" and we all avoided use of the word "cancer," but she began to engage in activities that represented putting her life in order. She reminded me that I was executrix of her will. She prepared for my increasingly frequent visits (I lived an hour away) with lists of items to review – the whereabouts of her bank statements, checkbook, and key to the lockbox at the bank; the envelope in the dining room cupboard that contained the obituary she had written for herself; the small notebook in the desk in which she had enumerated household items specifically designated for me or my sister or my brother; the linens in the upstairs dresser with the lovely embroidery and tatting done by her mother; the satin and net dress she had worn when she gave her salutatorian address at her high school graduation. She told me, "I want you to know where these are; I want someone to know *what* these are."

The summer of that final year was precarious. My mother and I began to talk on the telephone every day, and I or another family member went home almost every weekend. Twice my mother fell in her downstairs bedroom and had to call a neighbor for help in getting up. Her visual impairment had progressed to the point where she could no longer take care of her financial records or other correspondence. My mother's appetite and interest in cooking decreased, leading to weight loss and worry by the family about nutrition. Eventually she arranged for a helper to come in twice a week and for mobile meals to be delivered daily.

By late summer, the lymphoma seemed to be increasingly active; my mother was experiencing recurrent fluid around the lungs and edema in her lower legs. The benefits from repeated thoracenteses and medications to combat the fluid retention were short-lived. The neighbors became increasingly alarmed, telephoning my sister and me to express their concern about my mother's ability to continue to live by herself. Finally, on Friday, September 6, 1991, on arriving at her home to find her extremely short of breath, I offered to help contact her doctor. She concurred, and later that day, she was hospitalized with congestive heart failure. We did not know it yet, but her work of dying had begun.

## The work of dying

During the next 4 weeks, my mother experienced continued shortness of breath with any activity and came to rely on supplemental oxygen 24 hours a day. My brother and visited local nursing home facilities and gathered information, and, after 2 weeks in the hospital, I transported her to a health care center in my city. The doctor expressed hope that she would show improvement with some rehabilitative therapy and close monitoring of medications. She was eating less and less, however, and her activity became limited to taking care of her basic needs and long periods of sitting quietly in her chair.

On October 3, my mother was conveyed to our large university research hospital and admitted to the hematology floor. I met the ambulance at the door, feeling relief to have her there and (in hindsight) an unrealistic hope that we would now find out what was causing this decline and be able to do something about it.

Upon the move to this hospital, my mother voiced the request that she not have visitors. For my mother, a social and talkative being all her life, the withdrawal was remarkable. We both must have felt the need to stay focused, my mother on the work of being very ill and I on the work of caregiving.

In those last days of her life, I learned the importance of sitting quietly and letting topics come up. Mother began to gradually ease me into her reality of dying. On the afternoon of the third day of her hospital stay, she reminded me again of the envelope in the dining room cupboard with information about her life. Then unexpectedly she said, "We never did have any solos." I was not sure I understood what she said or meant, but then I realized she had shifted to talking about her funeral service. "We never had any visitation either, but you do what you want – I'd just as soon people would remember me the way I was. Some people have everyone sing a hymn, but that's kind of hard." Now *my* work had to begin: my mother was facing her dying and I needed to as well. And so I steadied myself and joined the conversation. I asked her, "Is there anything from the Bible you especially like?" She answered, "Oh, the 23rd Psalm, I always liked that."

I talked to my brother shortly thereafter, making him aware of my mother's state of mind and the wishes she was expressing. He mentioned the conversation to my mother's primary hospital physician, and we were both somewhat taken aback by the doctor's reaction. He viewed her comments as "worrisome" and as a sign of "discouragement" on her part. My brother and I were becoming a part of our mother's reality of dying, but it seemed that her physician was not yet ready to do so. We were witnessing the classic inner struggle of professional healers – the competing claims about the patient "being 'in the process' of living versus being 'in the process' of dying" (Marshall, 1992, p. 61).

During her last days, my mother continued to take care of other final matters. She expressed concern about her sterling silver flatware. She was emphatic about not wanting to be buried with her rings on. She hoped we would not argue over who would get these items. She mentioned an unfulfilled promise of giving a memento from her teacup collection to a friend, and discussed with me which cup she wanted me to give her. She talked more about the funeral service, wanting our childhood piano teacher and longtime friend to play the organ. She did not talk about what she wanted to wear for her burial, but she did express the wish that her usual hairdresser would do her hair. My mother talked of these concerns very calmly, and it was I who struggled with the almost overwhelming emotionality of the discussions.

At the same time that these new concerns evolved for my mother and for me, other lifelong interests continued. The leaves on the trees in Wisconsin turn spectacular colors in the fall. My mother's hospital room afforded her a panoramic view over the University of Wisconsin campus and the nearby lake shore. Even with her diminished vision, she could enjoy the changing colors outside her window. I remembered the time when I was a college student and a letter from home contained not only a note but also two brilliantly colored maple leaves from the tree in our backyard – my mother's way of sharing her appreciation of the beauty in nature with her daughter.

I strived to think of ways to fill the days with some meaningful activity. We did word puzzles together from the daily newspaper – a routine activity she had practiced for years. I combed her hair and understood the sense of caring that is experienced from just such ordinary acts. I read and reread her correspondence and cards to her. I took small sewing projects along to work on while we were together. Of course, I kept my briefcase at hand with paperwork to do while she slept – trying to fulfill my other expected responsibilities during this time, difficult though that was.

My mother continued to take charge of certain aspects of her daily life. Her appetite was minimal and breathing difficulties made eating extremely exhausting. Ignoring her discomfort, the dietitian consistently came during the noon meal to talk about menu choices for the next day. It was the worst possible timing for a discussion that my mother had no interest in pursuing anyway. The dietitian proved to be a source of extreme irritation and my mother eventually told her so directly. Mother's generalized anxiety about the meal trays continued, however, and on the day before she died, she asked me not to allow "them" to bring any more meals in to her room.

### The moment of death

The telephone rang during breakfast on the morning of October 9. It was a nurse at the hospital, calling to tell me that my mother's condition had changed; she had experienced what appeared to be a myocardial infarction that morning and had been unresponsive for a few minutes. Though she was responsive again at the time of the telephone call, the nurse advised me to come to the hospital. That nurse became my ally and anchor during the next day and a half.

The doctors were conferring when I arrived. During the previous days of hospitalization, it seemed to me that the physicians had projected an attitude of optimism about finding an effective treatment approach to counteract my mother's problems. My brother, sister, and I had all expressed gratitude for their diligence, but we had all also tempered the discussions with our own beliefs and those of our mother about not taking any extraordinary measures and accepting death. The nurse became the key figure at this new turning point in my mother's health care. She told me later that as the physicians grappled with the question of what to try next, she turned to them and said, "You don't *have* to do anything."

Shortly thereafter three physicians came down the hall and took me aside. They reviewed my mother's history to date – the litany of symptoms and treatment trials. They outlined what they would be willing to continue to try but indicated little hope that any such attempts would make a meaningful difference in her condition. None of the three actually said the word "dying," so I finally asked them if our discussion meant that she was dying. The answer to my question was "Yes," and they also said "We will turn our attention to supporting her while she is dying and she may remain here until she dies." Just as I was grateful to have my husband with me during that conversation, so, too, did they seem to need the support of each other. The nurse said afterwards, "That was very difficult for them to do."

And so the vigil began. For the remainder of that day my mother and I stayed together, I holding her hand and she mostly resting. Once she pointed toward the ceiling in one corner of the room, turned to me with a lovely smile on her face, and told me she saw a "little girl crossing the street." She fretted a bit about my having to miss work. She remarked that it was "hard to breathe." She commented that she thought she had had a wonderful life and had always been proud of her family. Otherwise we were mostly silent.

My brother arrived late in the afternoon and I took the opportunity to go outside for a walk along the lake. Later by her bedside, I pulled out a box of candy brought by a friend and offered it to my brother. My mother, ever mindful of my brother's tendency to be overweight, perked up enough to admonish him, "Only one." We both smiled at this nearly final expression of her many years of mothering.

My brother and sister-in-law stayed at the hospital throughout the night. When I returned the next morning, Mother was no longer fully conscious and her breathing was very labored. My brother and his wife went to my home to get some rest, and I was again alone with my mother. And then the nurse came into the room and did a beautiful and wonderful thing. Very tenderly, she washed my mother, combed her hair, gently rubbed lotion onto her thin body, and then dressed her in clean pajamas. To me it was like a ritual of anointment, a last rite in preparation for the imminent final moment. I thought that at some inner core of my mother's consciousness, the cleansing must have felt like a final act of readiness for death.

The doctors came in once more – all three of them. All agreed that "it" wouldn't be much longer. They offered comforting words to me, and then they all left.

I sat next to the bed again, holding my mother's hand. I counted her respirations and they were 13 per minute, with long pauses between. I told her that I loved her. I counted her respirations again and this time they were 9 per minute. I turned to gaze out the window at the beautiful autumn colors. And when I looked back, the respirations had stopped.

How is it possible to describe such a moment? Never before had I been present at the moment of death. Bertman said, "No matter how prepared for the event one thinks one is, how anxious for it to happen, the moment of death is unprecedented, possessing a strange majesty of its own" (1980, p. 344). I had anticipated the event with fear, and yet when it came, I felt only a powerful sense of communion with what was happening. After a few minutes, I pushed the call button and Mother's nurse was with me once again; she hugged me and comforted me, and then proceeded with the after-death work of a hospital nurse.

## Reflections About the Story

What is the meaning of the experience of caregiving for a dying person? To care for someone who is dying is inherently paradoxical, because the caregiver must both actively engage in the helping process and actively disengage in preparation for the impending death. Professional and family caregivers must live with the contradictions of providing comfort and enhancing life while also recognizing and supporting the approaching death. Sankar, in her study of dying at home, stated that "perhaps the most vexing and difficult aspect of the care is that no matter what the caregiver does, the dying person's health, with the possibility of a few brief remissions, will continue to decline" (1991, p. 77). Yet paradoxically, Sankar's subjects overwhelmingly found caring for the dying person to be "one of the most significant accomplishments in their lives" (1991, p. 154). Such a finding is surely strong testimony to the potential for fulfillment in the process of caregiving for the dying, even in the face of the inescapable outcome.

### The caregiver–care receiver relationship

Vezeau and Schroeder (1991) have stated that caregiving may be approached as a means to an end or as an end in itself. They wrote that "when outcome is primary, the nature of the relationship is directed toward that goal, whatever it may be; caring becomes an instrument. When caring exists unrelated to outcome, the value is the relationship itself" (p. 14). Although it does not make sense to claim that caregiving for dying persons is unrelated to outcome – surely an approaching death wields a powerful influence on caregiving during the living-dying interval – nevertheless, caring for a dying person can serve primarily as a means to enter, understand, and share the dying experience. The fulfillment found in the caregiving–care receiving relationship itself can become the ultimate good in the experience, for both the dying person and for the person giving care.

A relationship with a dying person has dimensions of meaning that do not exist in any other relational situation. For the professional and family caregiver, the sense of doing something and helping as key components of the caregiver – care receiver relationship must be redefined. Levine contrasted the work of caring for dying persons to the traditional helping model, suggesting that the caregiver's primary goal should be to "work to dissolve the separateness . . . Become one with the other. No help, just being" (1982, p. 157). Benner (1984) spoke of this goal as *presencing*. Presencing is a "person-to-person kind of thing, just being *with* somebody, *really* communicating with people" (p. 57).

Is it possible for professional or lay caregivers to dissolve the separateness between themselves and the dying person? Dying is a life experience that resonates with isolation in the existential sense, that is, isolation of persons from one another in an "ultimate unbridgeable separateness" (Levine et al., 1984, p. 218). Being a caregiver for a dying person hurls one into a deeply felt confrontation with the experience of separateness from others. Yalom used the term "boundary situation" to describe such a confrontation (1980, p. 159). The shared experience of approaching death starkly reveals the unbridgeable and ever-increasing separateness between the dying person and surrounding caregivers. Coincidentally, the same experience may unite the dying person and the caregiver by a powerful bond of being. Therein lies both the paradox and the fulfillment. Benner (1984) and Levine et al. (1984) urged caregivers, first and foremost, to work to dissolve that separateness by being wholly present in the dying experience.

As a daughter–caregiver for my dying mother, I entered this boundary situation with a long history of established intimacy. The encroaching sense of separateness between my mother and me that gradually but relentlessly threatened this last shared experience was counteracted by the equally powerful emotional bond already in place. The final moment of death was a moment of communion, not separateness.

A health professional does not have this history of intimacy to bring to the caregiving experience. In fact, because we professionals view our roles so strongly as helpers, we must work harder at overcoming the separateness that threatens the relationship. Levine (1982) has called being a helper "a trap" that promotes separatism. The trap leads to the "separatism which sometimes comes when you use another to reinforce your self-image, to make yourself feel that you are living up to who you are supposed to be" (1982, p. 168). As occupational therapists, we may feel that we must be helpers and so the differentiation between "I" and the "other" is unwittingly accentuated, thereby reinforcing an existential separatism.

How can we as professionals be more wholly present to another in the dying experience? Clayton, Murray, Horner, and Greene (1991) discussed the phenomenon of *connecting* as a catalyst for professional caregiving. Strategies for connecting include the creation of meaningful experiences shared by the patient and professional; sensitive responses by the professional to the needs and wishes of the patient; facilitation of continued community linkages; the enabling and acceptance of the patient's need for reciprocity; the showing of honest affection; and the inclusion of family, friends, and other important persons in the circle of care. Often, the family member already has all of these means of connecting. The professional, however, does not, and so he or she must create strategies to help bridge the separateness and to be present in the dying.

### Stages of professional growth

Harper (1977) conceptualized the development of the health professional's learning to work in dying and death as a five-stage process. Stage I in Harper's schema is Intellectualization. In this stage, the worker obtains "a professional grasp and understanding of the diagnosis, illness, treatment, and prognosis" (p. 102). Occupational therapists in Stage I wrap themselves in their professionalism and helper roles and are ruled by the traditional treatment model of assessment, goal setting, treatment, and outcome evaluation. During Intellectualization, the professional's need to provide tangible services prevails.

Harper's Stages II and III, Emotional Survival and Depression, reflect difficult growth periods for the helper. In Stage II, the professional begins to understand the magnitude of the dying experience, becomes increasingly uncomfortable with the dying process, and experiences sadness and guilt. This initial emotional involvement expands into Stage III, during which grieving, depression, and exploration of feelings about the professional's own death occur. Stage III is a critical period in which the professional may either "grow or go" (p. 57). If no sense of satisfaction for the professional accompanies the pain and grieving, then the worker is likely to retreat from practice with dying patients, that is, to go.

If the professional can continue to grow, then Stage IV, Emotional Arrival, offers a sense of freedom – not from the pain but from its incapacitating effects. Stage IV is characterized by increasing comfort with the dying and an ability to cope with the approaching loss of the relationship. Finally, in Stage V, the professional reaches Deep Compassion, and is able to comfortably participate in "death talk" (funeral arrangements, wills, unfinished business) (p. 103). During Deep Compassion, the helper no longer views the death as a personal failure, but experiences a sense of self-fulfillment and satisfaction in the shared dying experience.

The professional caregivers for my mother illustrated the full continuum of Harper's stages of growth and development. The physician's use of the term "worrisome" to describe my mother's discussion of her funeral service seems to suggest his position in Stage I. He viewed my mother's death talk as problematic. He was in his professional role of diagnostician and healer, seeking to provide tangible services. Not until the day before my mother died did the physicians engage in death talk. I appreciate now more than ever the personal passage that occurred within each physician during those few days, as each gradually yielded to the dying experience, to sharing it and being present in it. The yielding was seen as concern about keeping my mother pain free, about offering solace to me and my brother, and about making decisions that would enable my mother to die in relative comfort.

I think my mother's nurse helped the physicians to complete their journeys. She seemed comfortable with the dying much earlier, she talked openly about death and, in effect, suggested to the physicians that they relinquish their professional roles ("you don't *have* to try anything"). This nurse exemplified the full dimensions of the Deep Compassion stage. She shared in and also created important aspects of the unfolding experience. Together we created a repertoire of experiences and meanings. We shared and showed honest affection for each other and for my mother. We *connected* with each other and with my mother, and as a result, we achieved a sense of fulfillment and satisfaction from the experience.

## Contradictions in occupational therapy

The hospice literature of occupational therapy suggests an ambivalence about the professional's role with a dying patient. The paradox of the patient's dual state of being, both living and dying, is revealed in the contradictory statements of the purposes of occupational therapy in terminal care. For example, the American Occupational Therapy Association position paper titled "Occupational Therapy and Hospice" (AOTA, 1986) strongly emphasized a treatment philosophy of "helping people with life-threatening diseases adapt to changing life situations in order to live as fully and comfortably as possible" (p. 839). The focus in this approach is on continued participation in life, maximizing remaining abilities, and maintaining involvement in daily tasks and roles (AOTA, 1986; Fernstrom, 1990; Lloyd, 1989; Picard and Magno, 1982; Pizzi, 1984). Flanigan (1982) and Gammage, McMahon, and Shanahan (1976) tempered their focus; they advocated helping dying persons to live each day with a concurrent goal of "helping a person prepare for death" (Flanigan, 1982, p. 275). As the terminal illness progresses, the dying person must be helped to "downgrade" activities to match waning energies and capabilities (Flanigan, 1982, p. 275). Gammage et al. (1976) proposed a unique occupational therapy role for "assisting a dying client to relinquish his [sic] occupational roles" (p. 294). Within this context, the therapist and dying client work together to continually reevaluate the status of occupational roles so that expectations for occupational participation remain appropriate to the client's functional capacity.

Thus we see in the occupational therapy literature on care of the dying the same paradoxical dictum to provide comfort and quality of life while also recognizing and supporting approaching death. The ability to be comfortable with the latter role is most likely the distinguishing characteristic of the health professional who is fully competent to work with patients who are dying.

### Presencing in occupational therapy

Occupational therapists, because of a focus on the everyday meanings of life, have powerful avenues available for connecting with clients. Pizzi (1984) described a case study that exemplified many of the components of connecting. The patient, a 78-year-old former chef and restaurant owner, was dying. He and the occupational therapist engaged openly in death talk and in discussions about activities of special interest for his remaining days. The patient's list of desired activities included playing cards, wearing street clothes, and preparing an Italian dinner. All three activities were realized during his final days, through the help of the therapist, but it was the Italian dinner that best exemplified a deep sense of presencing. The patient had weakened unexpectedly and precipitously on the day of the meal. Pizzi wrote, "After minimal discussion with [the patient] and his wife, it was decided that the meal would go as planned" (p. 256). The patient, his wife, and the therapist rethought the process and worked together to cook the spaghetti sauce and pasta, and to serve and eat it. Two days later, the patient died. At his funeral, his wife described the Italian meal that he had helped prepare and talked about how meaningful it had been to him.

Many components of connecting – the shared experiences, the response to idiosyncratic needs, the patient's need for reciprocity, the circle of care – were part of this everyday cooking activity. The occupational therapist connected as he entered and shared the dying experience with the patient and family through the use of occupation. Participation in meaningful occupation promoted a sense of communion, not a sense of an "I" helping an "other." A therapist can be truly present in the dying process by using his or her unique knowledge and understanding of occupation to promote connecting.

Being truly present in the dying experience means also being truly present in the experience of loss and grieving after the death. Moss and Moss (1989) explored the effect of death on the family caregiver and the deep sense of emptiness left by the sudden cessation of caregiving concerns and responsibilities. After my mother's death, I keenly felt the loss of my sense of self as daughter and caregiver. For weeks, I found myself still expecting the telephone to ring each evening near dinnertime. And for weeks, I found myself still wanting to call my mother to see how she was and to share happenings in my life. I could not stop visualizing my mother in the home she loved – watering her violets, puttering in the kitchen, or knitting in her chair in the living room. She was interested in everything I was doing. When I was away from home, she missed me as no one else has ever missed me. She was unabashedly proud of whatever I accomplished. In short, she cared about me in a way that only she, as my mother, could care.

Davidson (1985) characterized the caregiver's period of mourning as a process of adaptation to change. "The patient's presence, the responsibilities of caring, the worries and conflicts – all of which were orienting cues to the way life was to be lived before death – are now gone" (p. 132). Further, because in death the central figure is absent, surviving caregivers replay the final act of relating to the dying person over and over again until "finally we are able to grasp at the conscious and also the unconscious levels the extent of loss. Only after this has been realized can we relate in new ways to our world" (Davidson, 1985, p. 131). And so it was for me.

For health professionals, as well as for family caregivers, the death of a patient may be experienced as a profound loss. Perhaps ironically, the more connected and present the professional is in the dying experience, the more intense may be the grief response. Vachon (1985) discussed staff stress in hospice care, citing deaths that were difficult or that did not go as planned as especially stressful to staff members. According to Vachon, the death of a patient who had a special meaning to the staff person may lead to the need to temporarily withdraw from other patient contact "to escape the further loss of psychic energy" (1985, p. 119). Harper (1977) and Wetle (1990) suggested the need for structured opportunities for debriefings and support for staff members when patients die. "After a death occurs, debriefing provides opportunity for sharing feelings and concerns, expressions of sadness or relief, and a sense of closure" (Wetle, 1990, p. 220).

Thus, the professional, too, struggles to reorganize his or her life space before gaining a sense of release and freedom from the loss. Davidson (1985) asserted that, in this struggle, the professional engages in the normal and universal grieving process of remembering and caring, ultimately discovering renewed energy and new life with which to continue caregiving for others. Davidson urged the health care community to recognize and support grieving as a health-promoting and adaptive response to the death of a patient.

## Conclusions

Caregiving for my dying mother helped me to grow professionally in my understanding of the dying experience. My mother's gradual physical decline over a 10-year period was typical of the chronic nature of illness in old age. Uncertainty about the life-threatening aspects of these illnesses, together with my own inexperience in the care of people who are dying, probably delayed my presencing with my mother until those final days. Those of us involved in that caring time – the nurse, my mother, the physicians, my brother and sister, and I – helped each other be present for the dying. Together, we worked to shape the care being given and the care being received. With the sense of mutual sustenance, we were ultimately able to comfortably support the approaching death.

Lynn, a hospice physician, stated, "More than any other criterion, what 'dying well' requires is that the life being lived as death comes near be one that is 'befitting' to the life that was being lived before serious terminal illness" (1991, p. 70). Only through connecting can we know what is befitting to "the life that was being lived before." As occupational therapists, let us learn how to use occupation to dissolve the separateness and to reach a sense of communion in that final moment of death.

## References

American Occupational Therapy Association (AOTA) (1986). Occupational therapy and hospice (Position paper). *American Journal of Occupational Therapy*, 40, 839–40.

Benner, P. (1984). *From novice to expert. Excellence and power in clinical nursing practice.* Menlo Park. CA: Addison-Wesley.

Bertman, S. L. (1980). Lingering terminal illness and the family: Insights from literature. *Family Process* 19, 341–8.

Brody, J. A. (1984). Facts, projections, and gaps concerning data on aging. *Public Health Reports*, 99, 468–75.

Brody, E. M. (1985). Parent care as a normative family stress. *Gerontologist*, 25, 19–29.

Clayton, G. M., Murray, J. P., Horner, S. D., and Greene, P. F. (1991). Connecting: A catalyst for caring. In P. Chinn (ed.), *Anthology of caring* (pp. 155–68). New York: National League of Nursing.

Davidson, G. W. (1985). An emotional support system for mourners. In G. W. Davidson (ed.), *The hospice: Development and administration* (2nd edn., pp. 128–44). Washington. DC: Hemisphere.

Fernstrom, C. T. (1990). Occupational therapy in hospice home care. *Physical Disabilities Special Interest Section Newsletter.* 13(2), 3–4.

Flanigan, K. (1982). Occupational therapy in terminal care. *British Journal of Occupational Therapy*, 45, 274–6.

Gammage, S. L., McMahon, P. S., and Shanahan, P. M. (1976). The occupational therapist and terminal illness: Learning to cope with death. *American Journal of Occupational Therapy*, 30, 294–9.

Harper, B. C. (1977). *Death: The coping mechanism of the health professional.* Greenville, SC: Southeastern University Press.

Kastenbaum, R. (1985). Dying and death: A life-span approach. In J. E. Birren and K. W. Schaie (eds.), *Handbook of the psychology of aging* (2nd edn., pp. 619–43). New York: Van Nostrand Reinhold.

Levine, S. (1982). *Who dies? An investigation of conscious living and conscious dying.* Garden City, NY: Anchor.

Levine, N. B., Gendron, C. E., Dastoor, D. P., Poitras, L. R., Sirota, S. E., Barza, S. L., and Davis, J. C. (1984). Existential issues in the management of the demented elderly patient. *American Journal of Psychotherapy*, 38, 215–23.

Lloyd, C. (1989). Maximizing occupational role performance with the terminally ill patient. *British Journal of Occupational Therapy*, 52, 227–30.

Lynn, J. (1991). Dying well. *Generations*, Winter, 69–72.

Marshall, P. A. (1992). Anthropology and bioethics. *Medical Anthropology Quarterly (New Series)*, 6(1), 49–73.

Moss, M. S., and Moss, S. Z. (1989). Death of the very old. In K. J. Doka (ed.), *Disenfranchised grief: Recognizing hidden sorrow* (pp. 213–27). Lexington, MA: D. C. Heath.

Picard, H. B. and Magno, J. B. (1982). The role of occupational therapy in hospice care. *American Journal of Occupational Therapy*, 36, 597–8.

Pizzi, M. A. (1984). Occupational therapy in hospice care. *American Journal of Occupational Therapy*, 38, 252–7.

Sankar, A. (1991). *Dying at home: A family guide for caregiving*. Baltimore: Johns Hopkins University Press.

Vachon, M. L. S. (1985). Staff stress in hospice care. In G. W. Davidson (ed.), *The hospice: Development and administration* (2nd edn., pp. 111–27). Washington, DC: Hemisphere.

Vezeau, T. M., and Schroeder, C. (1991). Caring approaches: A critical examination of origin, balance of power, embodiment, time and space, and intended outcome. In P. Chinn (ed.), *Anthology of caring* (pp. 1–16). New York: National League of Nursing.

Wetle, T. (1990). Death of a resident. In R. Kane and A. Caplan (eds.), *Everyday ethics: Resolving dilemmas in nursing home life* (pp. 209–22). New York: Springer.

Yalom, I. D. (1980). *Existential psychotherapy*. New York: Basic.

# 30 The Social Context of Grief Among Adult Daughters Who Have Lost a Parent

*Jennifer Klapper, Sidney Moss, Miriam Moss, and Robert L. Rubinstein*

In this article we examine the interface between grief, an intrapsychic and behavioral response to bereavement, and mourning, a process involving the social and cultural prescriptions for the expression of grief (Doka 1989).

That culture influences the way loss is perceived and experienced is well documented (Charmaz 1980; Eisenbruch 1984a, 1984b; Fox 1981; Gorer 1967; Rosenblatt 1975). Osterweiss, Solomon and Green (1984) note:

> Culture authorizes categories and norms for labeling the consequences of loss, priorities for ranking loss among other stressful life events, expectations about social support and coping styles, sanctioned idioms for articulating personal and family distress, and shared ways of regarding and responding to a death. The meaning of bereavement or other stressful life events may vary across groups with respect to who died and who is grieving.

Grief and mourning influence one another. There have, however, been few efforts to examine the dialogue between the cultural context of mourning and how individuals cope with the loss of a loved one (cf. Kalish and Reynolds 1976). We provide evidence, from a series of research interviews with married middle aged women who have lost their widowed elderly mother within the last six months, suggesting that survivors struggle both with intrapsychic and socially evaluative aspects of their experiences. In distinction to viewing culture as a unidirectional force that influences individual thought, emotion, and behavior, we examine ways in which the two domains, the intrapsychic and the culturally evaluative, affect each other in an interactive process.

In contrast to our approach, the clinical or medical model of grief is based on a weak folk model that suggests the intrapsychic experience of grief follows its own course and its own motivations, largely unaffected by the social world ("the stages of

Original publication: Klapper, Jennifer, Sidney Moss, Miriam Moss and Robert L. Rubinstein, "The Social Context of Grief Among Adult Daughters Who Have Lost a Parent," *Journal of Aging Studies*, 8 (1994) pp. 29–43.

bereavement"). There also appear to be a widely held, diffuse set of beliefs about the appropriate expression of grief. We argue here that the intrapsychic experience of grief can be understood by viewing not only culturally based ideals about coping with loss, but also the bereaved's perception of these expectations as enacted in her reactions as well.

In this article, we examine some intrapsychic aspects of loss and some key aspects of how sociocultural settings and demands interact with them. After describing our research project, we introduce case material illustrating how our research subjects perceived their inner experiences through a cognitively based veil of sociocultural norms, desires and expectations. Conceptually, we explore the control or management of grief, the experience of anticipatory grief, and what we here label "selfish grief."

## Intrapsychic Dimensions of Grief

Grief is the response by an individual to the loss of a significant other. This reaction occurs over time and may involve current or past losses that have occurred as well as the threat of loss in the future. Yet the loss of a person does not signify the loss of a relationship; the tie to the deceased endures, even when the relationship has been stressful or hostile. Memories, associations, possessions, visits to the grave, memorials, the legacy of the deceased and thoughts of reunion may persist. A normative experience, grief is a natural part of life. It is not a disease and rarely needs to be diagnosed, treated or cured. Although it has been addressed in the psychiatric literature (Horowitz, Krupnick, Kaltreider, Wilner, Leong, and Marmar 1981) it is rarely pathological (Gallagher, Dessonville, Brackenridge, Thompson, and Amaral 1981). It is a dynamic process, not an event.

As our case material below suggests, grieving is generally an active process, involving the survivor in making meaningful choices and engaging in purposeful activity. The process is not primarily a passive one in which the bereaved person goes through set stages, whether or not in some predetermined order. Responses to bereavement are variable in form and content and expressions of grief are also wide-ranging (Wortman and Silver 1989). Grief may include a range of expected responses such as intense emotional pain, sadness, denial, relief, guilt, fear, anger as well as somatic distress. Failure to experience or express any or some of these responses need not be associated with problematic grief (Deutsch 1937; Wortman and Silver 1989). The loss of a loved one may in fact not lead to pervasive sadness or depression. It may also involve conflicting feelings: awareness of mystery on the one hand and wish for control and order on the other hand. It occurs in a family context and often has multigenerational implications.

Grief involves a process of intrapsychic and social transition with both change of self and family. The survivor may experience a transformation of self as she takes on new generational roles, shifts her perception of her own finitude, and acknowledges pain and affirms the strengths that she has evidenced in the grief process. In our view, grief may lead to change and transformation rather than to "recovery" – as in a medical model of self.

## Grief as a Social and Cultural Phenomenon

The cognitive and affective components of grief are expressed not only within the context of personal emotion and experience but also interpersonally in culturally meaningful social settings. Further, there is interplay between the emotional response to loss and its socially informed cognitive appraisal (Beck 1979; Labouvie-Vief and Hakim-Larson 1989). Hochschild notes, "In a sense, society induces the self to induce and control feeling such that one continually socializes his or her feelings" (1975, p. 290). Here, we particularly focus on our informants' efforts to monitor, evaluate and control both the feelings and expression of grief. We explore ways in which the social context of the mother's death plays a role in both the management of internal feelings and external expression of grief.

As part of the larger socio-cultural milieu, there are important domains of ideas that individuals may use to shape and influence their experiences of grief. These include both spiritual beliefs and general ideas in popular culture about grief, bereavement and loss, many of which are grounded in the Puritan ethic emphasizing stoicism, activism, and individualism (Charmaz 1980). Thus, for some individuals there are dictates of spirituality that promise heavenly rewards and reunions. For others, there are the more wide-spread beliefs that exist in society dictating or suggesting the form and content of grief. There are said to be proper times and durations for grieving; proper expressions of grief; and popular notions about appropriate and inappropriate feelings and acts (Kalish and Reynolds 1976).

Although for some bereaved persons, religious beliefs provide an anchor and structure for responding to the loss of a loved one, for many bereaved persons the cultural diversity and diffuse secularity of modern life may result in no clear or systematized rules about how to respond to loss. There are, however, some types of losses for which the open expression of grief seems more or less socially acceptable. In losses that are unexpected and off-time, certainly, the elements of surprise and unnaturalness may make the intense display of grief more acceptable. However, some deaths that are disenfranchised (Doka 1989), anticipated or on-time may contain a social expectation of less grief. Each may be problematic if the personal experience of loss differs radically from cultural ideas about how one should grieve.

Further, with parental loss, there is a salient theme of *anticipatory orphanhood* (Moss and Moss 1989), defined as an expectation that a time will come when one will no longer have living parents. Although children imagine their mother will never die, they learn that old people die before younger people, eventually sensing that in some "legendary time" (De Beauvoir 1973) their parent will die before they do. As years pass and one's mother ages, a child may have experienced the death of her father (as in our study) as well as the deaths of other persons in her parent's cohort. Thus, death of an elderly parent may be seen as a normative, on-time occurrence (Neugarten and Datan 1973).

In addition, there may be culturally conditioned gender patterns affecting reactions to loss. Both men and women struggle to balance their concern for self and their concern for others. According to Gilligan, for women, "the problem of care and responsibility in relationships" constitutes an essential moral dilemma (1982, p. 73). Our informants have been influenced by a traditional definition of feminine goodness exemplified by self-sacrifice for the good of others (Gilligan 1982). Some women may see failure to react appropriately to the issue of self-sacrifice as a fundamental failure in feminine self-definition. As we will show below, this process may constrict or limit the expression of grief.

## Research Methods

The data on which this article is based were collected in 1990 in a project funded by NIA entitled the Middle Aged Child's Experience of Parental Death. This longitudinal, qualitative study is the first of its kind to systematically examine the meaning of the death of a parent. We interviewed 107 married daughters, age 40–68, whose widowed mothers, all over age 65, died three to six months prior to the interview. Thus, the mother's death represented the loss of the last parent. Participants were recruited primarily though newspaper and other mass media as well as social and health agencies and other personal and professional networking. The respondents were predominantly white, were Catholic (39%), Protestant (30%), Jewish (25%) (Other or No Response, 5%). All but one were high school graduates and 42 percent completed four years of college. They had a median family income between $50 and $60 thousand dollars. The mean age of the daughters was 52; 63 percent were employed. The average age of the mothers was 81.

Interviews usually lasted from 3 to 6 hours and were audiotaped. Ethnographically-based and conversational in tone, interviews covered topics that included the event of the mother's death; the funeral; the informant's anticipation of the death and personal reaction to the loss; change in daily routine with the death; reactions to other significant deaths; quality of the informant's relationship with her mother; caregiving for the parent; personal identity, generational succession and attitude to the death; and the personal meaning of the loss. Each informant completed a battery of standard measures of grief, depression and well-being. In addition, each interviewer completed a one to three page summary of highlights upon completion of the interview.

For analysis, the overall topic of this article was identified through team discussion and gross level, by case oral exegesis. Interview summaries were used to locate and document bereavement material. Transcripts were also examined for the presence of bereavement materials once key issues and cases had been identified. Continued discussion by the authors refined questions and issues. Another round of analytic readings and codings was undertaken to isolate and refine the material presented here. Each informant will again be interviewed after another year has passed.

## Internal Debates About the Expression of Grief

### The control of grief

Many adult daughters described aspects of a process of selectively controlling or managing their feelings of grief. Although there was individual variation in this process, here we will describe the general features of this overall process. This involved internal feelings about the loss and the externally motivated expression of feelings in a socio-cultural text. It is important to note that, while control could lead to denying or curtailing feelings (and it no doubt did for some), it also served, we believe, to *modify the feelings themselves* in a loss largely viewed as on-time, normative and worthy of moderate, but not extreme, grief so that feelings are more in line with social expectations.

Because the control of the expression of grief is determined by both individual motivations as well as culturally based ones, grief can be managed with reference to both the self and others. The individual may wish to adopt a number of management strategies. Some daughters in our sample sought to retain a sense of personal mastery despite the loss; some also sought to avoid personal vulnerability, a sense of orphanhood, or the threat of finitude and their own mortality in the face of the loss.

The social-cultural basis of management also has a broad range. We found some bereaved daughters wished to appear "strong" to their family and friends, maintaining the integrity of their social world. For example, one upper middle-class woman of Italian descent made clear that she would not allow herself to respond to the death in a volatile way, with wailing and hysterics like "some inner-city Italians" would do. Other daughters spoke of the expectations – both proscriptions and prescriptions – of their deceased mother as playing an important role in determining feelings and behavior. A few even patterned themselves on their recall of their mother's brief, muted, often unshared experience around the loss of the mother's mother. Daughters often spoke of protecting themselves, and others, by controlling their expression of grief, for example, protecting their own children from the burden of seeing the pain of grief, and possibly empathically experiencing it. A few daughters, too, said that they wanted to avoid an intense expression of grief for fear of evoking sibling jealousy that they were more loved and loving vis a vis their mother.

Motivations for control, both personal and social, occur within a social context which offers confusing and contradictory expectations about the appropriateness of one's feelings and the expression of them. Thus, emotions that well-up upon loss may be modified, contained, or denied in response to both personal and social demands.

Some adult daughters we interviewed sought to determine what was an appropriate amount and duration of the expressions of grief. Here, for instance, the idea that on- and off-time losses may be expected to evoke different types of socially acceptable responses is discussed by Mrs. James, a 53-year-old woman whose mother died at the age of 86, five months before our interviews.

Mrs. James compared the impact of different losses. As her mother was dying, her sister-in-law was losing her husband. She noted,

> My sister-in-law was carrying on [acting badly] pretty good, you know. And just going crazy . . . And I guess it could happen to me, it could happen to anyone of us, we could all, and my own personal feeling in this is: How would I personally react under the same circumstances? The overwhelming loss of a mate. My mother had lived. And how much life expectancy was there? She was 86 years old. . . . I mean I'm an independent business lady, right. I feel like I can go from here to all over the area by myself and do my own business and yet. I don't think I could exist for a day without my husband. And it's like this whole overwhelming thing when you suffer a loss, you really have to conjure up more strength than you ever thought you needed. And I get annoyed, I guess, with myself for not having built up my strength better and annoyed at other people secretly. You know, not outwardly. I never have shown it, but inwardly I get annoyed with people who lose a mate or a loved one and are morose or unsocial and miserable to be with.

In her view of bereavement, the type of loss suggests innate limitations or guidelines for the appropriateness of the display of grief: more for a spouse than for an 86 year old parent, but in both cases it should be outwardly circumscribed. This reflects what may be a widespread cultural sense of hierarchy in the permitted severity of grief: loss of a child (at any age) at the nadir, followed by loss of spouse, and finally the on-time loss of an elderly parent (Kalish and Reynolds 1976; Sanders 1980; Osterweis, Solomon, and Green 1984). There is a drive here to conform the inner aspects to the outward nature of the loss and the requirements of display.

Mothers of some of the women in our sample have told their daughters not to grieve for them. This may come from a parent's sense of having lived a full life, with some degree of ego-integrity (Erikson 1963) and recognizing that their own death is a normal event in the process of generational succession; it may reflect the mother's support for the daughter to move on with her life; or a wish that the daughter not suffer the same miseries as she had at her own mother's death. The admonition not to grieve may pose a real dilemma for the daughter because grief does in fact both express love and a wish to affirm the tie with a parent. For some women, curtailing grief may be seen as unloving and betraying the tie.

Vulnerability may be intensified if, in expressing grief, one faces disapproval by family or others. Mrs. James, noting the conflict between the socially evaluative and the emotional realms, spoke clearly of rejection of others' grief which implicated her own fear of similar rejection by others.

*Mrs. James*: You know [concerning] this outward [display], I mean I guess you should tear your clothes like they say, but you know . . . what I think is that it is therapy to mourn. I suppose it's good to scream and holler and carry on. But it's very self-centered. And it's like, I just think it's self-centered. I think that people who mourn constantly [it isn't a good thing]. I mean a certain amount you gotta cry, I mean and I certainly did a lot of it. I cried for about four months in a row.
*Interviewer*: Was it during this whole ordeal or was it *after* her death that you did most of your crying?
*Mrs. James*: Before.

Implicit in Mrs. James' description is a dichotomy between two sets of emotions: one is the empathic response to her mother's suffering and terminal illness, and the other is the daughter's anticipation of the loss of her mother. Overdisplay of emotion was not deemed appropriate in anticipation of her mother's death – after all she was 86 – and feelings should therefore be controlled. Her mother's suffering, as with the suffering by any intimate however, was more than worthy of a fuller expression of emotion some of which took place prior to the death.

Mrs. James also contrasted the experiences of her sister-in-law who "let herself go," emotionally with that of a niece whose husband had had an untimely death at the age of 30:

> But the irony is that here's my niece, with all these horrible things, and we're still able to sit and talk and laugh and carry on normally. And I believe that she thinks more than just thinking about herself. She thinks about other people.

In this view, the bereaved should not burden others and therefore feeling must be controlled.

Control of grief prior to loss may also play a role in the interactions between the daughter and her mother. Significantly, some daughters did not show their own deep feelings of sadness to their mothers during the last part of life, whether or not their mother was cognitively alert. This is a striking instance of the need to control grief in a specific social context. We found that many daughters controlled the expression of grief when with their mothers, but only did so with some difficulty. In future interviews we plan to look more closely at how this process of control develops and some of the ways in which it is perceived by the daughters.

### Anticipatory grief

As in the case of Mrs. James, above, women often told us that they grieved for their mother before she died. These anticipatory feelings were responsive both to the context of the middle aged daughters' social worlds and the specific characteristics of the parent. All daughters in this study had already had grandparents and fathers die. They live in a society in which being old carries some expectation of death. They recognize that at mid-life it is a normal and timely experience to have a mother die. More than 90 percent of the daughters indicated they had thoughts about the mother's death before she died. In our society, a normal and expected death is often seen as acceptable and as less a cause for strong grief reactions (Moss and Moss 1989) as well as in other cultures (Rosenblatt, Walsh, and Jackson 1976). Daughters not infrequently cited their mother's age as one means of legitimizing her death. Thus the social contexts of the loss play a role not only after the death but also in anticipation of it.

The process of dying in old age has become more prolonged over recent decades, as medicine and technology have enabled persons to continue living in spite of chronic illness. As more people live out a full lifespan, there is a pervasive anticipation of death and as Pollak (1980) suggests a process of dying in installments. Well before the death occurs, it is not unusual for family members to be told that "nothing more can be done" for a parent; learning of a terminal diagnosis marks the beginning of the living-dying interval (Pattison 1977).

As discussed here, anticipatory grief covers both partial grief (Berezin 1977) that is evoked by the parent's incremental deficits and impairments as well as the grief that occurs in anticipation of the parent's death (Kowalski 1986; Rando 1986).

In partial grief, the child mourns the loss of the mother's competence and sees each decrement and episode of suffering as an additional source of sadness for both the parent and herself. As the mother is less able to function independently, she has a decreased quality of life and may lose interest in her social world and in her future. With some impairments, she may be unable to communicate in her usual way and may not even recognize the daughter. The daughter's grief may be intensified as incremental losses are experienced.

Children of parents with dementia experience a profound loss, often for years prior to death. The child is faced with the ambiguous identity of her mother: as the person she was and as the person she has become. Boss, Caron, Horbal and Mortimer (1990) describe for example the sense of powerlessness of a daughter when the elder is physically present but psychologically absent.

In our study many respondents combined feelings of sadness for the mother's decline with the sadness they felt in anticipating the loss. Although the sources of these sadnesses differ conceptually, respondents often merged them into one feeling. Over 70 percent of our sample reported that they actually grieved for their mother before she died. Daughters were also able to distinguish the sadnesses that occurred before and after the death (Robbins 1990).

Mrs. Stein is a 68-year-old middle-class woman of Jewish background. Her mother died in a nearby nursing home of Alzheimer's Disease at age 90. For the final five years Mrs. Stein had visited her mother almost daily. Of that time, she noted:

> the illness set in and she was losing her own personality. My mother started to die five years ago, and I did my grieving starting [then]. I was torn so badly. I had to put Mom in that home and that was part of the mourning that I had at that time, which I didn't feel when she died. I mourned when she lived. It was a long, long funeral, I mean a long, long 5 years when she was in the nursing home.

Mrs. Stein had to cope with the painful reality of the person her mother had become while thinking of and yearning for the person she was. She was faced with the irreconcilable dual images of her mother – past and present. Reflecting this, anticipatory grief must be seen as a psychosocial process that reflects the dialectic of the daughter's wish to hold on to the mother as she was, while at the same time recognizing the reality of her pending death.

The last months or years of life are often characterized by medical remissions, relapses and partial recoveries, which serve to complicate both partial grief and anticipatory loss. Each time the mother survives a life-threatening situation for example she may take on an aura of strength and invincibility, giving an illusion that she will survive future onslaughts. The daughter may both welcome the recovery and dread the uncertainty it brings.

The process of anticipatory grief is set within the context of the mother's terminal care. Daughters commonly struggled with ethical and social issues when participating in decision making about reducing suffering or prolonging the mother's life. Thus, a daughter may indeed have some control over the final quality of life and the time of death of her mother.

Partial grief and anticipatory loss are often connected, as they were for Mrs. Stein. There was tension within her between the feeling of detachment that occurred as a result of partial grief and the feeling of closeness and caring that is often the response to the potential loss. In spite of these tensions, Mrs. Stein (nearly all of the daughters with whom we spoke), remained close to their mother offering support to the end.

Two years before her mother's death, Mrs. Stein was told that her mother did not have long to live. She noted,

> It's then that I wrote the poem, "Close Your Eyes, Mom." I came home and wrote it down and cried and cried. Yeah, I mourned deeply, deeply then too. I cried for years. I don't know when it started or when it ended.

The poem demonstrates her letting go while still holding close:

Close your eyes Mom,
Dad has waited so long.
With your mother, your father,
Your three little sisters,
All heard the same angel song.
Close your eyes, Mom,
Go meet with them, and then
It will seem as a flicker of an eye,
I'll be holding your hand again.

Anticipatory grief did not appear to occur for some daughters; this was especially so when the elderly parent had not been ill for long and was cognitively intact. In sudden deaths of highly functioning older persons, there may be little reason or no time to anticipate the loss. Daughters in these cases may have recognized that the mother was getting older and within the range of a socially acceptable and timely death. Anticipatory grief may also be reduced if, in spite of the parent's profound deficits, the child holds on to every shred of the parent's normal behavior and denies feelings of potential loss. Further within those social contexts in which the child sees the death as only a temporary separation before a permanent reunion in heaven, the grief in anticipation of death may be attenuated (Marris 1982).

### Selfish grief

Some daughters have described a phenomenon we label "selfish grief" which clearly involves the management or control of grief. A daughter may wish her mother were still alive and yearn for her after her death. She may, however, perceive her own desire for her mother's continued presence as a *selfish* wish on her part that could act to extend her mother's suffering if she were still alive. The expression of grief, which involves yearning for the continued presence of the mother, must then be suppressed and controlled. Concern for the mother's continued well-being, that she not suffer through extended illness, frailty or dependence, persists for some even after the mother's death.

In our interviews, two types of situations led to the development of selfish grief. The first draws on the history of the mother's illness and her pain or suffering. Debilitating effects of an infirm or aging body may have been both frustrating and difficult for the mother and daughter to manage. In some cases a daughter simply sees her own grief and longing for her mother's presence as demonstrating less concern for her mother's well-being than for her own wish to hold on to her frail and suffering mother.

The second situation involves the daughter's cultural expectations about the course of aging. For some, it includes utilizing a cultural image that equates advancing age with ever-increasing pain, suffering, and dependency. In this view, that a mother dies while still independent, cognitively alert, and experiencing a good life saves her from inevitable suffering from age or decline in the future. In contrast, the desire to keep one's mother around longer, selfishly, may relegate a mother to a course of progressive deterioration and certain suffering. Thus, in fact a mother's actual state of health prior to her death may not be a factor in a daughter's conclusion that she is selfish in her grief.

The theme of selfishness influences how the daughter grieves in several ways; three paths in reaction to the loss have been identified in our interviews.

One path leads to an acknowledged grief which is felt, but continually undermined, in fear of being selfish. For example, Mrs. Allen's reaction to the loss of her mother focused principally on relief that her mother would not suffer anymore. Her conflicting emotions were illustrated at the time of the funeral, however, when she said she could see her mother "lying there so peacefully that I knew she was at peace. And yet, you know . . . it all comes back to the same thing: you'll never see her again." Although Mrs. Allen never denied feeling the loss, as the interview progressed she consistently overrode expressions of her own sadness with a statement immediately following that, most importantly, her mother's suffering was now over. Thus in controlling her expressions of selfish grief, her concern for her mother's well-being prevailed at the expense of her own grief.

She noted:

It's so final. But at least I try to comfort myself, I say, "Well, her suffering is done". You always hope when you see something like that, that wherever they go after death, that they find a better place.

However, when asked if thinking about her mother in any way provided comfort to her, she responded:

*Mrs Allen*: Comfort that I know she's at peace. But then selfishness creeps in there too . . . that, I don't know. I wish I had a little more time with her.

*Interviewer*: And you see that as being selfish? Why is that?

*Mrs. Allen*: I guess because we have no control over our destiny . . . You're making a demand that you have no control over. I guess if I had control over it, I would have made her well. I would have made her whole. I put that in the selfish bracket [I label it as selfish]. Well, and then you figure that you have no right to say that.

Mrs. Allen felt the loss of her mother but tended to negate her own feelings and wishes for her own happiness in deference to her mother's welfare.

A second path for selfish grief eventuates in a daughter controlling her own expression of grief in order to respond to the needs of family members. Here a daughter sees herself as selfish regarding both her mother and her immediate family. Family members may plead that they are being neglected as a result of the daughter's grief and perceived self absorption. Her husband and children may see the daughter's grief for her own mother as a display of familial disloyalty. As a result, the daughter may need to control the expression of her grief.

Mrs. Bernstein, a teacher, was told by a friend that in observing strict religious guidelines in Judaism for mourning behavior she was being selfish and uncaring toward both her mother and her husband. Four months after her mother's death, Mrs. Bernstein, dressed in black, did not listen to the radio, watch television, or go out for enjoyment. She cried repeatedly through much of our interview. A friend, she noted, commented that since Mrs. Bernstein was staying in, her husband was also forced to stay in, missing dinner parties, dancing, and movies. Mrs Bernstein countered that she was mourning out of respect for her mother and for her own needs. Yet, as she continued to receive messages from friends and family criticizing her consistent behavior as selfish and foolish, she began to question both her outward expression of grief and her own intense inner feelings. When asked about her initial reaction to her mother's death, she responded,

> *Mrs Bernstein*: I was shaking all over, my legs. . . . I couldn't stand up on my feet, I had to sit down right away. My legs, my knees became numb. I couldn't think. I couldn't talk . . . But in a way I think it was selfish of me to want her, you know, because maybe it was a blessing that she didn't suffer anymore.
> *Interviewer*: You said you felt selfish in some way?
> *Mrs. Bernstein*: Well, no. Now, it's now [when] I'm trying to reason with myself that it was selfish of me to feel so bad when she passed away. Because maybe . . . it was a blessing for her.

The grieving she did for herself, labeled as selfish by others, was therefore under the process of internal control, while at the same time she was able to give increasing attention to her husband and family.

A third path a daughter may take as she copes with selfish grief may control and possibly negate grief. Here a daughter may feel that grief is inappropriate if it focuses on the feelings of those still living, while the true focus belongs on feelings of the deceased. Therefore grief itself becomes selfish and inappropriate.

Mrs. Rogers, whose mother died at the age of 82, said, "When you love somebody, you want them to have peace and comfort, and not for your own sake to be around in a terrible state." Indeed, she felt it was not only selfish, but also an "abomination" to the deceased to grieve, to react any way other than the way one "should," if the deceased was elderly. "Should" meant not becoming emotional in public or suffering from sadness or depression in private. "One should be happy that the parent did not need to suffer anymore."

These expectations for grief hinge critically on the age of the loved one who dies. Four years ago, Mrs. Rogers' granddaughter died at the age of one and a half. She communicated, at first non-verbally, the intensity and depth of her grief over this loss, finally forcing out the words:

> I was endless getting over it. You never do. A parent, it seems a progression of time and age. But a little child, it's just a shame. She was dearly loved. So, that's the one that devastated me.

Mrs. Rogers seemed to be saying that grief over a child's death is rational, necessary and sanctioned, while grieving for an elderly person is inappropriate. She expressed no conflicting emotions regarding her mother's death. Her concern for her mother's welfare led to her control of grief.

Why is grief over an elderly parent's death cast as selfish? Gilligan's work provides insight into a process that may operate in this situation. Although challenged on some dimensions (related to sampling bias and data analysis problems), Gilligan's work cannot be dismissed and at worst provides a challenging perspective from which to explore as we do here.

Selfishness is a key concept in Gilligan's perspective; in our study some respondents identified selfishness as a critical motivator for the control of behavior and affect after the death of a parent.

Selfishness implies a regard primarily for oneself with little attention or responsibility to others. For women, responsibility may truly be defined by what Gilligan calls "responsiveness," an interactive process implicating the moral self in gaining awareness of and responding to perceived needs in relationships (Gilligan 1986, p. 7). Such responsiveness can be distinguished from more traditional definitions of responsibility that involve such characteristics as reliability in fulfilling previously agreed obligations. When a loved one dies, the quality of the accustomed "responsive" or interactive mode of the relationship is necessarily changed. For some daughters, the responsive mode continues actively and in continued concern for the mother's well-being even after her death. Imagining the suffering the mother might have endured had she lived, grief in this context then may be seen as indulgent in the face of a continuing sense of responsibility for the mother's well-being. This too precludes a fuller concern for oneself as would be demonstrated by a more complete venting of grief. Of note here is that the daughter's focus of concern is sometimes seen as a mutually exclusive choice: she feels she must choose between attention to herself and the relief of her mother's suffering. Hence, the daughter fully experiencing her own sadness may become morally problematic.

There were women in our study who saw no conflict such as that described above, maintaining simultaneously both a deep concern for their mother (relief that she is no longer suffering) and a deep concern for themselves (honoring their own feelings) as they grieved over the loss. Gilligan's understanding of women's morality depicts the process of a woman developing a concern for the well-being not only of others, but of herself as well, in struggles over care and responsibility in relationships. In this task a woman must transcend the traditional moral imperative in which she places other before self, reaching an "inclusive solution" (Gilligan 1982, p. 14) which does not negate the self in relationships, but includes it. A primary task for the bereaved individuals is to find a new place for the loved one inside themselves, so internalizing aspects of the deceased. Different views of the self and of responsibilities in relation to others may be important in this reformative stage after a loss.

## Discussion

The interplay between the intrapsychic and the sociocultural is complex and has been underdeveloped in the loss literature. Because of the continuing psychological bias in the study of loss and bereavement, social aspects of this experience have been minimized. Indeed, the dominant psychoanalytic perspective of bereavement has conceptualized grief as an intrapsychic phenomenon with its expression governed through mechanisms such as denial or repression. Further, medical or clinical models of the stages of bereavement have emphasized both the mechanical and the abnormal in bereavement. In contrast we argue here for a more socially informed approach to bereavement.

Evidence from middle aged daughters suggests that they struggle to construct a social reality out of the difficult nexus of feelings, interpretations and actions. In response to their social contexts, they have developed a variety of mechanisms that control and shape aspects of their grief. They struggle with understanding the social requirements and dictates of a loss, whether on-time or off-time. What is of central importance is that social issues shape the inner experiences of bereavement.

Although we have stressed here the effects of the social context of the loss, we recognize that our pluralistic society does not have strict rules for how a daughter should respond, but rather a variety of diffuse sets of rules and notions. The daughters with whom we spoke operated with such diffuse sets of ideas. There are few clear guidelines about appropriateness of feelings and behaviors. Few were part of a specific community that clearly outlined aspects of mourning, gave guidance in carrying this out, or gave support in the context of community values.

Certainly and perhaps ironically, efforts to control grief can help maintain an enduring tie to the deceased by not permitting a fuller expression of feelings at the time of the death and forcing their gradual and managed expression over time. The desire to reduce the parent's suffering, or potential for suffering had she not died, may also serve to emphasize the maintenance of a bond in a similar way. Through a variety of processes, the demands of control may indeed shape the survivor's inner feelings, changing and deflecting them. How these controlled feelings emerge later, or in other contexts or ways, is beyond the scope of this article.

We suggest that control of the expression of grief may occur in many losses, although this may especially be a part of on-time parental loss. The control results from the interaction between, on the one hand, social cues and cultural demands and, on the other hand, the internal struggle of the bereaved person to acknowledge the loss. There is a range of typical and expected responses to the loss, based in part on the cultural ranking of the loss.

We suggest too that the themes presented here are relevant to the grief of persons experiencing other types of losses and deserve further attention in research and clinical work in the mainstream area of death and dying: spousal bereavement.

## Acknowledgment

Supported by National Institute on Aging Grant #R01 AG08481, The Middle Aged Child's Experiences of Parental Loss.

## References

Beck, A. T. 1979. *Cognitive Therapy and Emotional Disorders*. New York: New American Library.

Berezin, M. 1977. "Partial Grief for the Aged and Their Families." In *The Experience of Dying*, edited by E. M. Pattison. Englewood Cliffs, NJ: Prentice-Hall.

Boss, P., W. Caron, J. Horbal, and J. Mortimer. 1990. "Predictors of Depression in Caregivers of Dementia Patients: Boundary Ambiguity and Mastery." *Family Process* 29: 245–54.

Charmaz, K. 1980. *The Social Reality of Death*. Reading, MA: Addison-Wesley.

De Beauvoir, S. 1973. *A Very Easy Death*. New York: Warner Books.

Deutsch, H. 1937. "Absence of Grief." *Psychoanalytic Quarterly* 6: 12–22.

Doka, K. 1989. *Disenfranchised Grief*. Lexington, MA: Lexington Books.

Eisenbruch, M. 1984a. "Cross-Cultural Aspects of Bereavement, I: A Conceptual Framework for Comparative Analysis." *Culture, Medicine and Psychiatry* 8: 283–309.

Eisenbruch, M. 1984b. "Cross-Cultural Aspects of Bereavement, II: Ethnic and Cultural Variations in the Development of Bereavement Practices." *Culture, Medicine, and Psychiatry* 8: 315–47.

Erikson, E. 1963. *Childhood and Society*. New York: Norton.

Fox, R. 1981. "The Sting of Death." *Social Service Review* 55: 42–59.

Gallagher, D., C. Dessonville, J. Brackenridge, L. Thompson, and P. Amaral. 1981. "Similarities and Differences between Normal Grief and Depression in Older Adults." *Essence* 5: 127–40.

Gilligan, C. 1982. *In A Different Voice: Psychological Theory and Women's Development*. Cambridge, MA: Harvard University Press.

Gilligan, C. 1986. "On *In a Different Voice*: An Interdisciplinary Forum." *Signs* 11(2): 304–33.

Gorer, G. 1967. *Death, Grief, and Mourning*. Garden City, NY: Doubleday.

Hochschild, A. R. 1975. "The Sociology of Feeling and Emotion: Selected Possibilities." Pp. 280–307 in *Another Voice*, edited by M. Millman and R. M. Kanter. Anchor Books/ Doubleday.

Horowitz, M., J. Krupnick, N. Kaltreider, N. Wilner, A. Leong, and C. Marmar. 1981. "Initial Psychological Response to Parental Death." *Archives of General Psychiatry* 38: 316–23.

Kalish, R. A. and D. K. Reynolds. 1976. *Death and Ethnicity: A Psychocultural Study*. Los Angeles, CA: University of Southern California Press.

Kowalski, N. C. 1986. "Anticipating the Death of an Elderly Parent." In *Loss and Anticipatory Grief*, edited by T. Rando. Lexington, MA: Lexington Books.

Labouvie-Vief, G. and J. Hakim-Larson. 1989. In *Midlife Myths*, edited by S. Hunter and M. Sundel. Newbury Park, CA: Sage.

Marris, P. 1982. "Attachment and Society." In *The Place of Attachment in Human Behavior*, edited by C. M. Parkes and J. S. Hinde. New York: Basic Books.

Moss, M. S. and S. Z. Moss. 1989. "The Death of a Parent." In *Midlife Loss*, edited by R. A., Kalish. Newbury Park, CA: Sage Publications.

Neugarten, B. L. and N. Datan. 1973. "Sociological Perspectives on the Life Cycle." In *Life-Span Developmental Psychology*, edited by P. Baltes and K. W. Schaie. New York: Academic Press.

Osterweis, M., F. Solomon and M. Green. 1984. *Bereavement: Reactions, Consequences, and Care*. Washington, DC: National Academy Press.

Pattison, E. M. 1977. *The Experience of Dying*. Englewood Cliffs, NJ: Prentice-Hall.

Pollak, O. 1980. "The Shadow of Death Over Aging." *Annals of the American Academy of Political and Social Science* 117: 75–6.

Rando, T. 1986. *Loss and Anticipatory Grief*. Lexington, MA: Lexington Books.

Robbins, M. 1990. *Midlife Women and Death of Mother*. New York: Peter Lang.

Rosenblatt, P. C. 1975. "Uses of Ethnography in Understanding Grief and Mourning." Pp. 41–9 in *Bereavement: Its Psychosocial Aspects*, edited by B. Schoenberg, et al. New York: Columbia University Press.

Rosenblatt, P. C., R. P. Walsh, and D. A. Jackson. 1976. *Grief and Mourning in Cross-Cultural Perspective*. New Haven, CT: HRAF Press.

Sanders, C. M. 1980. "A Comparison of Adult Bereavement in the Death of a Spouse, Child and Parent." *Omega* 10: 303–22.

Wortman, C. and R. Silver. 1989. "The Myths of Coping with Loss." *Journal of Consulting and Clinical Psychology* 57: 349–57.

## Further Reading to Part IX

Charmaz, Kathy. 1980. *The Social Reality of Death*. Reading, MA: Addison-Wesley.

Glick, Ira O., Robert S. Weiss, and C. Murray Parkes. 1974. *The First Year of Bereavement*. New York: Wiley.

Kaufman, Sharon R. 1998. "Intensive Care, Old Age, and the Problem of Death in America," *The Gerontologist* 38: 715–25.

Lopata, Helena Znaniecka. 1973. *Widowhood in an American City*. Cambridge, MA: Schenkman.

Pickard, Susan. 1994. "Life After a Death: The Experience of Bereavement in South Wales," *Ageing and Society* 14: 191–217.

Sankar, Andrea. 1991. *Dying at Home*. Baltimore: Johns Hopkins University Press.

Sudnow, David. 1967. *Passing On: The Social Organization of Dying*. Englewood Cliffs, NJ: Prentice-Hall.

# Index

THE NORTHERN COLLEGE
LIBRARY
72531    BARNSLEY